FAR EAST

WENSCHOW RELIEF MAP

Drawn and Printed by Karl Wenschow GmbH.
Munich. Western Germany

U.S. Copyright by Denoyer-Geppert Company
Chicago

160   70° E.o.Gr.

THE FAR EAST
IN THE
MODERN WORLD

THE FAR EAST

IN THE

MODERN WORLD

HOLT, RINEHART AND WINSTON

FRANZ H. MICHAEL

University of Washington

GEORGE E. TAYLOR

University of Washington

NEW YORK

Preface

THIS BOOK is intended to introduce the general reader to the Far East and to lay a foundation for those who wish to proceed to the study of more specialized fields of interest. An effort has been made to describe the general character of Far Eastern societies and the ways in which they have responded to the impact of Europe, America, and Russia. A considerable amount of attention has been paid to American policy in the Far East and to the impact of world communism.

The transformation which has taken place in the Far East in modern times has been the result of an external impact as well as of forces within Far Eastern societies themselves. The great changes which took place in Europe, America, and Russia and the inclusion of the Far East in the world political system have been extensively studied. Not until the last few decades, however, has any concentrated effort been made to analyze the societies of the Far East. More and more American scholars have studied the languages of China and of Japan and concerned themselves with the history, government, politics, and literature of those countries. The new scholarship has considerably revised our concepts of all Far Eastern countries and has made it possible to re-evaluate every aspect of their development.

Today the Far East as a regional story has come to an end. It no longer has the unity and character formerly given it by the dominating and independent civilization of China. Other civilizations have come in to compete, and all Far Eastern countries have followed their own courses. The Far Eastern world has become part of a more complex story, and China, the heart of the traditional Far East, is now part of the Eurasian Communist orbit. In this book we have tried to indicate some of the factors which have brought about this great transformation. We believe that the better we under-

stand the reasons for this transformation, the better we may estimate the
nature of the problems we face today.

If this book were to be dedicated to anyone, it would be to our long-
suffering colleagues in the Far Eastern and Russian Institute of the University of Washington. For their inspiration and personal assistance we are
deeply indebted. All have helped and some have read portions of the manuscript with critical care. The Assistant Editor of the Institute, Miss Gladys
Greenwood, has worked with us through all the writing and revising of the
manuscript, and we have relied heavily on her unerring judgment in matters of substance as well as of form. We are most grateful. For the errors which
we have committed in spite of the aid of our colleagues and friends we are
alone responsible and would appreciate any corrections brought to our attention. We regret that owing to the character of the book we were unable
to give credit in footnotes to the many authorities upon whose published
work we have drawn so heavily for facts and ideas.

March 15, 1956   F. H. M.
Seattle, Wash.   G. E. T.

Contents

THE FAR EAST
IN THE
MODERN WORLD

The Far East in World History

THE Far East has been one of the great centers of human culture throughout the whole of recorded history. Like Ancient Egypt, Greece, and Rome, and like India, the Far East has been one of the main areas of cultural development, an independent source of ideas and institutions. The center of the Far Eastern world was China, whose cultural influence dominated and pervaded the whole area which has come to be known as the Far East.

At the time when the term came into use the Far East was the most distant frontier of exploration, commerce, and adventure on that long eastward route that took European and American seafarers around the Cape of Good Hope, across the Indian Ocean and through the Straits of Malacca to the China Seas. In the age of sail the Far East embraced all the countries which lay beyond India, the countries which came within the world of China, and today we still use the term to include all those lands which have felt, in some measure, the influence of Chinese civilization, even though some of them have also been strongly affected by competing influences from India. The border lands of Inner Asia, Tibet, Turkestan, Mongolia, and Manchuria; the Russian Far East, Korea, the islands of Japan; the countries of Southeast Asia, Vietnam, Laos, Cambodia, Thailand, Burma, and the Malay Peninsula; the island groups of Indonesia and the Philippines—all these have come, at one time or another, within the confines of the Chinese world.

The Far East maintained its cultural identity until modern times, but

I

not because it developed in isolation. There were many contacts with other centers of civilization. Buddhism became a formative influence in the countries of Inner Asia, China, Korea, Japan, and Southeast Asia, even though it disappeared in India, the land of its birth. While one stream of Islam spread through India to Malaya and Indonesia, another moved through Inner Asia into China itself. Other religions, including early Christianity and Judaism, also reached China. Nor was there any lack of commercial relationships between the Far East and other parts of Asia and Europe. Caravan routes through Central Asia and sea routes to the Middle and Near East linked the Far East to the rest of the known world. Roman coins have been found in China, and Chinese silks are known to have been worn by women in Rome. Commerce continued to flow along the same routes at various times during the Middle Ages. In the thirteenth century Marco Polo, an Italian merchant, was for many years an official serving the Mongol dynasty in China. A more direct contact between Europe and the Far East was established in the sixteenth century when the Portuguese rounded the Cape of Good Hope and the Spanish crossed the Pacific from the Americas. By the sea routes came soldiers, missionaries, and traders to all parts of the Far East. At this time the Spanish and the Dutch established their colonial empires in the Philippines and the East Indies. But while some of the weaker countries of the Far East were taken over by European powers as colonies, China, the center of this world, remained intact. Part One of this book describes the societies, the political institutions, and beliefs of the traditional Far Eastern world.

By the beginning of the nineteenth century inroads had been made by the Spanish and Dutch colonizers, but there was still an independent traditional Far Eastern civilization, accepted and respected by the West. Certainly China and Japan were strong enough to deal with other countries on their own terms and on the basis of their own view of the world.

The whole basis of the relationship between the Far Eastern and the Western worlds was destroyed by revolutionary changes in the West. The development of the modern West took place over a period of three centuries during which time the Renaissance and the Reformation, the American and French revolutions, and the Industrial Revolution changed the whole character of Western society. These changes brought about a modern Western civilization which became worldwide in its influence, submerging older cultures in its path or compelling them to adjust to Western patterns. When the Western powers, in the nineteenth century, forced the civilization of the Far East into their world system, they brought to an end the long period of independent growth and tradition.

The expansion of Europe in the nineteenth century was a new phenomenon, different in character from the mercantilist expansion of the preceding centuries. It was also under the new leadership of the Anglo-Saxon powers, Great Britain and the United States. Of these the United States was by far the more aggressive and revolutionary in its political and economic ideas. The new American Republic found itself engaged in a worldwide fight for political and economic survival in the teeth of the prevalent mercantile system, which preserved colonial trade for the mother countries and, wherever possible, maintained monopolistic practices in the noncolonial areas. The Americans used the weapons they had at hand to break down the monopolistic trade practices not only of other European powers but also of the British. These weapons, which sound so conventional today, were revolutionary in their time. They were the doctrines of the freedom of the seas, of private enterprise in international trade, of equality of commercial opportunity, and of the right of neutrals to trade with belligerents. These weapons challenged the assumptions and practices of most of the European powers. They were more than the devices of a weak and desperate power playing for stakes; they were the very stuff of the American Revolution. Wherever Americans went, they took with them, in a world largely ruled by monarchies, the hated doctrine of republicanism. In a world economy dominated by monopolistic trade practices they operated as independent merchants backed by a nation demanding freedom to trade and reciprocal commercial opportunities. In an age of privateering and piracy, of convoys and blockades, they fought for freedom of the seas. In the early days of the Republic Americans took with them, wherever they went, the ideological dynamite of the American Revolution.

It is in this sense that the American Revolution begins the story of the modern Far East. The mercantile system of the Western world, with its monopolistic trade practices and its great monopoly trading companies, was well suited to dealing with China, Japan, and other countries of the Far East, which had their own type of state trading monopolies. It was the impact of American ideas and actions on the British commercial system and on the Chinese empire that marked the beginning of the great changes which distinguish the second half of the nineteenth century. It was America that set the pace, that challenged the long established patterns of trade and international politics, that helped to put the East in motion. American ideas, it is true, would not have been so effective had they not found support among America's strongest rivals, more especially the British. Just as there were powerful political forces in England that supported the American Revolution, so there were strong commercial interests which shared with the Americans the ambition to destroy the East India Company trading monopoly. The monopoly was abolished in 1834 and the British then became the champions of free trade and private enterprise. The forces of the Industrial Revolution, which had started in England, were now combined with the political and social ideas of the American and French revolutions to bring about a revolution of such a nature that no civilization could remain outside its orbit.

The Western powers extended their influence over the whole Far East during the second half of the nineteenth century. Some countries were taken over as colonies, while others adopted Western forms of organization and maintained their independence. China, the heart of the Confucian world, resisted the longest and suffered the most; the pressure from the West coincided with a deep cultural and political crisis within. The age-old moral and political Confucian system, under attack from all sides, slowly disintegrated. The once dominant empire of China became a political and ideological battleground. Where there had been strength, there was now weakness; where there had been a system of moral and political philosophy, there was now confusion and doubt. All efforts to adjust the Confucian world view to modern conditions were defeated by the advocates of Western rationalism and pragmatism which did not themselves provide any adequate substitute. The end of the empire in 1911 was marked by a decline in Chinese political thought, a decline which accounts for much of the inner weakness of the Chinese republic. The collapse of Confucianism in China, Korea, and Vietnam, the inner Chinese world, stands out in contrast to the endurance of corresponding systems of belief, such as Buddhism, Hinduism, Islam, Shintoism, and Christianity, in surrounding countries.

The adjustments of Far Eastern societies to the world system of international and economic relations which the West imposed were complicated by a struggle between the imperial powers in which the Far Eastern countries participated. Japan, in particular, played an independent role as an imperial power in her own right. The whole Far East was eventually drawn into the European struggle of World War I. Part Two of this book describes what happened to the societies of the Far East during the century in which the Western powers forced them into a world system.

Part Three of this book deals with the countries of the Far East since the Bolshevik Revolution of 1917, which marked the beginning of a fateful cleavage in the Western world itself. The doctrines of Marx, Engels, and Lenin came out of Western philosophy and the European socialist movement. After the establishment of state power in Russia the Communists concentrated a great deal of their energy on the conquest of the countries of the Far East. The international Communist movement, directed from Moscow, seized every opportunity to establish Communist parties in that part of the world and to exploit Asiatic nationalism for its own ends. In the period between the two world wars Communist penetration in the Far East advanced and retreated within a complex of many conflicting forces such as imperialism, nationalism, and the continuing process of westernization.

After World War II the Communist position was immensely strengthened by the conquest of China and further expansion into Korea and Vietnam. These gains, added to those already secured in Eastern Europe, made the Soviet orbit a power bloc of enormous strength and prestige which posed for the rest of the world the continuing threat of further subversion and aggression. It was this development which forced upon the world a division into two camps, distinguished from each other by fundamentally different beliefs and institutions.

The countries of the Far East became a battleground between the Communist and Free worlds but the struggle there was different from that in Europe. For the countries of the Far East it was not a problem of defending an established democratic and industrial order as it was in Western Europe. The societies of the Far East, however advanced, were still in a state of transformation. In their reaction to the two sides in the worldwide struggle they had another point of reference, their own non-Western past. Part of their problem lay in the fact that traditional beliefs were often in conflict with Western ideals and this conflict had not yet been resolved. One alternative was to abandon the old values together with the partly absorbed Western ideals and fully accept the materialistic philosophy of Communist doctrine. The other alternative, for those who were free to choose, was to draw spiritual strength from their own traditions and adjust themselves to the ideals of the Free World.

The Bolshevik Revolution led to the founding of a totalitarian dictatorship whose materialist philosophy denied the idealist and humanist tradition of the West. Because this conflict concerned more than power politics, because it involved the fundamental values of individuals as well as of societies, it slowly led to a new regrouping of the peoples and the states of the world. During this period the conflict that went on in the minds of men was not always expressed in open action. The front of the stage was occupied by the Japanese scheme for empire and the cataclysm of World War II. But after the war the results of thirty years of intellectual and social conflict, of organized subversion and international maneuvering, became apparent. The peoples of the Far East were to play a major role in this conflict.

Those who do not respect the experience of man, which is history, find it difficult to comprehend the attitudes, values, or institutions of other peoples. This is because the past is always living in the present. In no part of the world is this more evident than in the Far East. The most instructive approach to the contemporary problems of the Far East is still by way of the great tradition of Chinese civilization.

PART ONE

The Civilization of
the Far East

CHAPTER I

Imperial China

CHINA—A GREAT POWER

THE Chinese empire, at the time of the American Revolution, was one of the great powers of the world. Its population of over three hundred million people was by far the largest of any state in the world. Its territorial extent of over four and a half million square miles was exceeded only by that of Tsarist Russia. This empire included dependencies in Inner Asia, where Chinese administrators and soldiers ruled in the name of the emperor, and tributary states, such as Korea, Annam, and Burma, which sent tribute missions to Peking in recognition of Chinese superiority. The wealth and splendor of the Chinese court and empire were known all over the world. European visitors admired the great cities of China, with their magnificent architecture and orderly life, and were impressed by China's engineering achievements and handicraft industries. There were many Europeans of the eighteenth century who were intrigued by the "wisdom of the East" and wanted to emulate the principles of government as they were thought to exist in China. China was thought of as an impressive example of the realization of their ideal of a benevolent monarchy in which government was carried on by enlightened scholar officials. Voltaire, Leibnitz, and Montesquieu, among others, used their impressions of China in the formulation of their philosophical and political ideas. A French school of economists, the physiocrats, saw in the control of the Chinese government over the economy a justification of their own theories. The arts of China were greatly admired and left their imprint on the style and taste of the time. The prestige of China was at its height in Europe as well as in Asia.

The attraction which China held for eighteenth-century Europe was all the stronger because of the very difference of Chinese civilization from that of Europe. Nothing in Europe since the Roman Empire could be com-

9

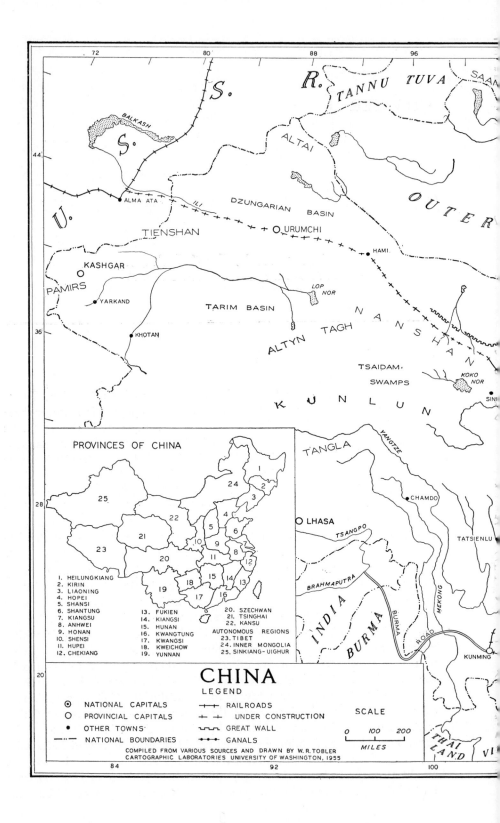

72 80 88 96

R. TANNU TUVA SAA

S. ALTAI OUTER

BALKASH

S.

44

U. ALMA ATA ILI DZUNGARIAN BASIN

TIENSHAN ○ URUMCHI

HAMI

KASHGAR ○ NAN SHAN

PAMIRS ● YARKAND LOP NOR

TARIM BASIN KOKO NOR

36 ● KHOTAN ALTYN TAGH SINI

TSAIDAM.

SWAMPS

K U N L U N

PROVINCES OF CHINA T'ANGLA YANGTZE

1 ● CHAMDO

28 25 24 2 3 ○ LHASA TSANGPO TATSIENLU

22 4

21 5 6 BRAHMAPUTRA MEKONG

23 20 10 9 8 7 INDIA BURMA BURMA ROAD

11 12 KUNMING

19 18 15 14 13

1. HEILUNGKIANG 17 16

2. KIRIN

3. LIAONING 20. SZECHWAN

4. HOPEI 13. FUKIEN 21. TSINGHAI

5. SHANSI 14. KIANGSI 22. KANSU

6. SHANTUNG 15. HUNAN AUTONOMOUS REGIONS

7. KIANGSU 16. KWANGTUNG 23. TIBET

8. ANHWEI 17. KWANGSI 24. INNER MONGOLIA

9. HONAN 18. KWEICHOW 25. SINKIANG-UIGHUR

10. SHENSI 19. YUNNAN

11. HUPEI

12. CHEKIANG

20

CHINA
LEGEND

⊙ NATIONAL CAPITALS ┿┿ RAILROADS SCALE

○ PROVINCIAL CAPITALS ┿ ┿ UNDER CONSTRUCTION

● OTHER TOWNS· ┗┛┗┛ GREAT WALL 0 100 200

——— NATIONAL BOUNDARIES ●┿● CANALS MILES

COMPILED FROM VARIOUS SOURCES AND DRAWN BY W.R.TOBLER
CARTOGRAPHIC LABORATORIES UNIVERSITY OF WASHINGTON, 1955

THAI LAND VI

84 92 100

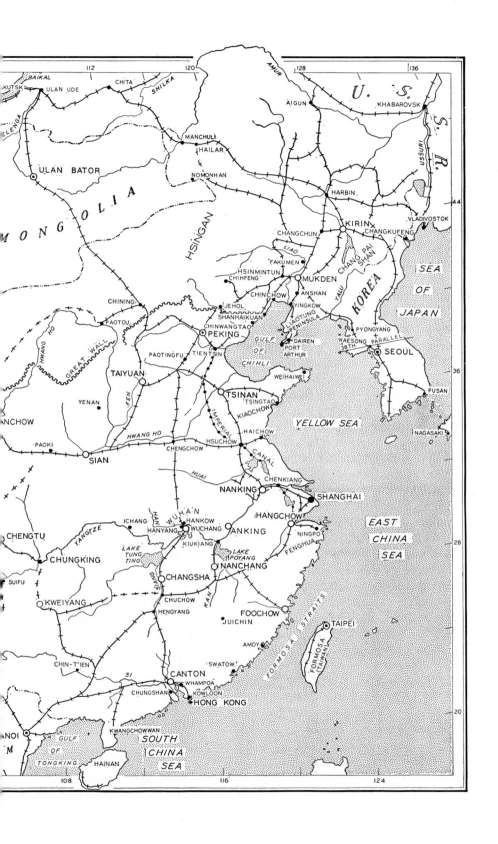

BAIKAL
IKUTSK
ULAN UDE
ENA
CHITA
SHILKA
AMUR
U. S.
AIGUN
KHABAROVSK
S. R.
MANCHULI
HAILAR
ULAN BATOR
NOMONHAN
HARBIN
M O N G O L I A
HSINGAN
VLADIVOSTOK
CHANGCHUN
KIRIN
CHANGKUFENG
44
LIAO
CHINING
FAKUMEN
HSINMINTUN
CHANG PAI SHAN
CHIHFENG
MUKDEN
KOREA
SEA
PAOTOU
CHINCHOW
ANSHAN
OF
JEHOL
YINGKOW
JAPAN
HWANG HO
SHANHAIKUAN
LIAOTUNG
GREAT WALL
CHINWANGTAO
PENINSULA
PYONGYANG
PEKING
DAIREN
KAESONG
18TH
PAOTINGFU
TIENTSIN
GULF
PORT
PARALLEL
TAIYUAN
OF
ARTHUR
SEOUL
CHIHLI
36
YENAN
FEN
WEIHAIWEI
PUSAN
NCHOW
TSINAN
IMPERIAL
TSINGTAO
PAOKI
HWANG HO
KIAOCHOW
YELLOW SEA
NAGASAKI
SIAN
CHENGCHOW
HSUCHOW
HAICHOW
CANAL
HUAI
CHENKIANG
NANKING
SHANGHAI
WUHA'N
HAN
ICHANG
HANKOW
HANGCHOW
EAST
CHENGTU
HANYANG
WUCHANG
ANKING
NINGPO
CHINA
YANGTZE
KIUKIANG
LAKE
SEA
LAKE
POYANG
FENGHUA
28
CHUNGKING
TUNG
TING
NANCHANG
SUIFU
CHANGSHA
KAN
KWEIYANG
CHUCHOW
HENGYANG
FOOCHOW
JUICHIN
FORMOSA STRAITS
CHIN-T'IEN
SI
AMOY
TAIPEI
CANTON
SWATOW
FORMOSA
(TAIWAN)
20
WHAMPOA
CHUNGSHAN
KOWLOON
HONG KONG
NOI
KWANGCHOWWAN
SOUTH
M
GULF
CHINA
OF
SEA
TONGKING
HAINAN
108
116
124
112
120
128
136

pared with the great cultural and political unity of China. The massive
homogeneity of Chinese civilization stood out in sharp contrast with the
political, ethnic, and religious divisions within the European peninsula. The
Chinese way of life differed from that of Europe in practically every respect.
It had followed an entirely different line of development. The main characteristics of this Chinese civilization can best be understood in historical
perspective, a perspective which includes the development of Chinese society,
government, and ideas. This development was closely related to the geographical setting in which it took place.

1. Geographic and Economic Foundations

Influence of Geography on Chinese Civilization

The geographical area within which Chinese civilization
took shape is known as "China proper." This is the area of the great plains
and mountain valleys which lie between the China Sea and the high mountains and steppes of Inner Asia. It is separated from Southeast Asia by river
gorges and jungle-covered mountains. This agricultural base of China,
sloping down towards the sea from the high plateaus of Inner Asia and
watered by great rivers such as the Yangtze and Huangho, forms a large
unit of the Asiatic continent. It is about one and a half million square miles
in area. Geographically and historically it can be divided into northern and
southern halves, which are separated by the Tsingling mountain range, a
continuation of the Central Asiatic Kunlun range, and by other mountain
ranges which stretch eastward to the foothills near the city of Nanking.

Chinese civilization first developed to the north of this dividing line,
in the valleys of the tributaries of the upper Huangho. The people who
established Chinese civilization in this North China area were very likely a
mixture of various ethnic stocks. To what degree native elements were
mingled with peoples from Central Asia or from the north in the first period
of Chinese cultural development is an open question. In later historical
times there has been a constant influx of Turks, Mongols, Tungus, and other
tribal groups from the north and northwest, who intermingled with the
Chinese. The Chinese are therefore an ethnic mixture.

The North China area, where Chinese civilization first took shape, has
a special soil called loess, a type of soil found in only a few other places on
the globe. Loess soil is air-borne by the strong seasonal winds which blow
between the high plateaus of Central Asia and the Pacific Ocean. Inner
Asia is extremely cold in winter and hot in summer, but the temperature of
the ocean area is less variable. In the fall the low pressure area of Inner Asia
draws winds from the sea, while in the spring dry winds blow from the high
pressure areas of Central Asia toward the sea. When these dry winds speed
over the Gobi Desert and the steppe lands of the northwest, they gather dust
which they later shower over the northwestern mountains and plains of
North China. This process, which has gone on for tens of thousands of years,
has built up a loose soil which in some places is hundreds of feet deep.

It has covered successive layers of grass and has retained their minerals. It has a sponge-like quality, is easily worked, and is quite fertile where water is available.

In this loess territory the proto-Chinese people made the decisive step from a primitive life of hunting and food-collecting to organized, settled agriculture. They overcame the problem of insufficient rainfall by constructing canals and ditches to bring water to their fields. The many separate agricultural settlements were each under military leadership, which organized defense against the raids of other settlements and of the more primitive tribal peoples. This period was the feudal age in Chinese history, a period lasting from the second millennium to the last centuries before the Christian era. During this time the settled agrarian settlements grew in number and size throughout North and Central China.

With the growth of the feudal states the warfare between them became more and more destructive. The feudal states grew fewer in number and larger in size, until a single centralized authority was set up in 221 B.C. by the Ch'in dynasty. By this time the whole North China plain was settled and a problem had arisen which could be solved only by a much stronger and more unified authority than that of the feudal states. This was the problem of controlling the Yellow River.

The Huangho or Yellow River has posed one of the greatest engineering problems of all times. Its name is derived from its muddy color, due to an extraordinarily high sediment content, by far the highest of any large river. The sediment, picked up in the loess territory of its upper course, is carried along as the river moves swiftly through mountain territory; but when the current slows down in the plains, the sediment settles and gradually fills the river's bed. All along its lower course, the river had to be diked. The sediment deposited in the river bed forced the water level higher and higher and the dikes had to be built up accordingly. Eventually the river flowed above the level of the surrounding countryside. At this stage any neglect of the dike system would lead to catastrophe. Sometimes, when the central government had become weak, dikes were damaged by warring local factions intent on flooding each other's territory. When the river broke through the dikes and sought new ways to the coast, disastrous floods resulted. Such floods cost millions of lives and gave the river its name of "China's Sorrow." The river has changed its course many times during the course of history and has flowed into the Yellow Sea at various places between the modern city of Tientsin and the mouth of the Huai River, close to the Yangtze. Control of this river could be undertaken only by a centralized administration which was able to organize large labor forces. Such an administration was first established in North China.

Chinese agriculture could not expand from North China to the high plateaus and steppes of the northwest where the arid climate set a natural limit. The line between agriculture and nomadism followed the climatic border. It was along this line that the Ch'in dynasty completed the Great Wall. The moving frontier of Chinese culture and government, therefore, expanded towards the south. From the river valleys of the northwestern plateau and the great North China Plain, Chinese civilization moved into the large valley of the Yangtze River and the "Red Basin" of Szechwan. It moved up the valleys of the southern Yangtze tributaries and into the coastal areas of Fukien and the river systems of the modern southern provinces of Kwangtung and Kwangsi. Finally it penetrated the high southwestern plateau of the modern province of Yunnan. Wherever the terrain would permit, Chinese peasants cultivated the valleys and the mountain slopes.

In this move the Chinese destroyed or assimilated more primitive groups. Only in the more remote mountain areas did primitive tribal groups, such as the Miao and the Yao in Kweichow and Yunnan, and the Lolos and the Mosos of the Tibetan border areas, survive by clinging to their own way of life. These remnants of proto-Chinese groups accepted some forms of Chinese agriculture but retained some of their own social structure, linguistic and ethnic characteristics, and their forms of autonomous rule under tribal chieftains. With these exceptions Chinese culture became predominant.

The experience with dikes and irrigation systems gained in the north was systematically applied in this growing Chinese realm. Vast areas, such as western Szechwan, were made fertile through ingeniously devised irrigation systems. The whole river system, the very basis of Chinese agricultural expansion, was developed for irrigation, flood control, and communication.

The largest of these rivers, the Yangtze, originates in the foothills of the Kunlun Range at a point not far from the source of the Yellow River. Its length is 3,200 miles, a little more than that of the Yellow River. It first turns southward through the southwestern and western provinces of Yunnan and Szechwan and then takes its course through central China eastward toward the sea. While no major Chinese city is located on the Huangho because of the danger of flood, the Yangtze with its tributaries has served as a main center of economic life and an artery of communication for ten of the eighteen provinces of imperial China. On its banks are located the principal cities of old and new China, such as Chungking, Hankow, Kiukiang, Anking, and Nanking, and near its mouth is the modern metropolis of Shanghai.

The Yangtze, too, has had its flood problems, though they are somewhat different in nature from those of the Huangho. When Chinese agriculture spread into central and south China, it denuded the mountains of forests, except in remote areas. This destruction of the protective forest belts caused floods since there was nothing to retain the water on the mountain slopes. Whenever heavy rains occurred at the same time at the headwaters of the Yangtze and its tributaries, the places of conflux became the main zones of flood danger. A look at the map shows great lakes, the Tungting and the Poyang, at points where the Yangtze is met by tributaries from the south. These lakes were natural reservoirs for the overflow and modified, but did not prevent, the floods in these regions. Other critical areas were at Wuhan, where the Han River joins the Yangtze from the north, and the lower Yangtze area around Nanking.

Besides these two great rivers, the Yellow River and the Yangtze, a number of other rivers have played an important part in Chinese development. The Pei-ho which flows into the Gulf of Chihli at the city of Tientsin has been used for irrigation and communication. The Huai River in the North China Plain, between the Yellow River and the Yangtze, always posed major problems of flood control because of the uncertainty of its outlet into the Yellow Sea. The flood problems of the Huai area were aggravated by the occasional shifts of the Yellow River southward into the drainage system of the Huai River. The river system of South China has dominated the economic life of the two provinces of Kwangtung and Kwangsi. Three rivers, the Tung-kiang or East River, the Pei-kiang or North River, and the Si-kiang or West River merge at the city of Canton where they form the Pearl River delta. The West River is the main communication link between the provinces of Kwangtung and Kwangsi. The three rivers provide an inland network of communications for the port of Canton which has long been a trading center between China and Southeast Asia, the Middle East, and more recently Europe.

After central China was developed, one of the main problems of administration was to link this rich agricultural area with the main center of government, which was first located in the upper Yellow River valley and later at Peking. The northern rivers, because of heavy sedimentation, were not as useful for navigation as were the Yangtze, its tributaries, and the other rivers of the south. The main communication system in the north was overland transport on two-wheeled carts. For the grain tribute to the capital this was impractical, as man and mule would eat more than they could carry over the long distance. The stormy sea routes from the mouth of the Yangtze to the Pei-ho were risky and infested with pirates. In the thirteenth century, after centuries of experience with canal building, imperial China constructed the Grand or Imperial Canal to connect the city of Hangchow, south of the Yangtze, with the capital city of Peking in the north. The building of this great canal, in which the Chinese had to overcome the complicated engineering problems of intersecting the Yangtze River and the Yellow River, was a tremendous achievement. The maintenance of the canal and the organization of the grain transport were the responsibility of special administrative agencies.

The high productivity of Chinese agriculture was due to intensive methods of farming in which the use and control of water were of decisive importance. The construction and maintenance of the dikes, canals, and irrigation systems which were necessary for this purpose required the large-scale organization of mass labor. The mass labor was organized by scholar-officials under the control of an absolute monarchy.

Regions of China

The vastness of the territory of China proper and the great contrasts in climate and terrain provided the conditions for many regional differences. With the expansion of Chinese civilization into region after region there was imposed on the whole country the same political and social system. The distinct geographical regions which were linked by this uniform system continued, however, to be important. They provided bases for local patriotism, for specialized economic development, and for the subdivisions of the central administrative system. They were occasionally bases for political opposition to the imperial government.

The North China Plain, dominated by the Yellow River, is the largest area of continuous level land. It stretches from the Great Wall in the north to the Yangtze Valley in the south; it is bounded by mountains in the west, and by the sea and the Shantung promontory in the east. This area became the center of early imperial China. It was here that the Chinese had to solve the problem of controlling the Yellow River. The fertile soil of this great plain has supported a dense population. Close to its northern border is the capital city of Peking, famous for the beauty of its imperial palaces and temples.

To the east of the North China Plain lies the Shantung peninsula, which juts out into the Yellow Sea and provides the few natural harbors in the otherwise sandy north Chinese coastline. It is a mountainous area surrounded and intersected by lowlands, which are in reality a continuation of the North China Plain. It was in this region that Confucius was born and that the sacred mountain of Taishan is situated.

To the west of the North China Plain are the loess lands of the northwest, the mountain ranges and the valleys of the upper Yellow River and its tributaries. It was this area between the plain and the high plateaus of Central Asia that was the cradle of Chinese civilization. Its mountain fastnesses have provided a natural defense for more or less autonomous administrations during periods of weak central control. Along the border of Inner Mongolia and in the Kansu corridor to Turkestan a substantial Moslem minority has asserted, at various times, a regional autonomy. By the eighteenth century the northwest was no longer as rich agriculturally as other areas of China, partly because of the government's neglect of irrigation over a period of several centuries.

The region of the Yangtze Valley, from Ichang to the sea, is the richest agricultural area in China. It provided the highest tax returns for the imperial government. It was to bring the produce of this region to Peking that the Grand Canal was built. This is a region of green rice fields and thousands of miles of canals and waterways. Three main tributaries, the Han, the Siang, and the Kan rivers, with their agricultural plains and canal systems, are included in the Yangtze region.

To the west, the upper part of the Yangtze forms, with its tributaries, the "Red Basin" of Szechwan province. The word Szechwan means four streams, and the term Red Basin is derived from the red color of the soft shales and sandstones of the region. This is an area of hills and low mountains, extremely fertile and highly irrigated, and covered with terraced fields. Secluded from the rest of China by high mountain ranges, Szechwan has often served as a military base and has frequently been an area of autonomous regimes.

The coastal region to the south of the Yangtze is made up of the provinces of Chekiang and Fukien. It is separated from the inland areas of the Yangtze tributaries by mountain ranges which extend in a general northeastern-southwestern direction. This coastal region has excellent harbors, but the mountains and the short rivers limit access to the interior. In addition to agriculture, which includes tea and silk production, there are trade and fishing and a considerable amount of small-scale coastal navigation. As each of the coastal towns has only a small isolated hinterland, a multiplicity of local dialects prevails. This area has tended to look more towards the sea than inland, and it is from here that many Chinese emigrated to the South Seas. Opposite the Fukien coast lies the island of Formosa, a province which has had many ties with Fukien and Kwangtung, from which its Chinese population came. In agriculture it closely resembles the coastal provinces. In the mountainous areas of Formosa, where the Chinese did not penetrate, primitive tribal groups remained.

The two provinces of Kwangtung and Kwangsi form an economic region which is built around the Sikiang river system. Kwangtung is by far the more heavily populated. The tropical climate, with its high humidity and temperatures, permits the growing of two to three crops a year. The city of Canton, at the delta of the river system, was the main overseas trading city of imperial times. Hundreds of thousands of "boat people," who live on local trade, have congregated in the many waterways of the city of Canton and the surrounding delta.

The southwest region, which includes the provinces of Yunnan and Kweichow, is a series of high plateaus. They are dissected by the upper courses of the main rivers of Southeast Asia and southern China. The high altitude produces a moderate climate, but only a small proportion of the land can be cultivated. The Chinese hold the good land, leaving the less accessible mountain areas for tribal groups, who make up half the population. Mainly in Yunnan, but also in Kweichow, there is a strong Moslem minority. There have been several occasions in Chinese history when the southwest region was a base for autonomous regimes.

The geographical regions of China, with all their differences, can be divided into two groups—North China on the one hand, and South and Central China on the other. The dividing line is the Tsingling range. The north, which is largely a loess area, has uncertain and limited rainfall, a dry climate of extreme cold and heat, and strong seasonal winds. It is also the land of the Yellow River and its floods. The staple crops in this part of China are wheat, millet, kaoliang, sweet potatoes, peanuts, and many kinds of beans. The growing season is from four to six months, so that the land produces one, or at the most two, crops a year. The average family farm of two to three acres is slightly larger than that in South China. As the rivers are more dangerous than helpful, communication in imperial China was mostly overland, except for the Imperial Canal. Two-wheeled carts drawn by horses or mules cut deep tracks through the soft soil. Villages are mostly made up of one-story houses and are not so crowded as in the south. The northern coastline, with the exception of the Shantung peninsula, has no major inlets and there is little coastal navigation or interest in maritime ventures. The north is the region in which Chinese civilization developed and from which imperial control was extended. It was also that part of China most overrun by Central Asiatic peoples. The language of the north is more uniform than that of the south and is more or less related to the official language spoken by the imperial bureaucracy all over the country.

The south, whose mountains prevent the development of strong seasonal winds, has a more temperate climate and a much greater humidity. Rice is the staple crop. Tea and silk provide extra sources of income. The growing season is almost double that of the north, and the land produces at least two and sometimes three to four crops per year. Because of the mountain areas, the total cultivated land is relatively less than that in the north, but in the cultivated river plains and valleys the density of population is much greater, and the average acreage of land per family unit is smaller than in the north. The rivers serve for irrigation and for communication and are dotted with sailing junks and small boats. The seacoast has many inlets and harbors which permit fishing and coastal navigation, but in most places the mountains prevent good hinterland communication. Every inch of cultivable soil is planted; no room is left for roads, and traffic has to zigzag along the slippery paths between the rice fields. Loads are carried in baskets, balanced on bamboo poles on the shoulders of peasants or coolies, or in wheelbarrows. The nature of the coastline, the characteristics of the people, and the economic conditions are some of the factors that for several centuries have made southern China the almost exclusive source of Chinese emigration overseas.

In spite of the great variations in the landscape—the yellow dryness of the North China Plain, the barren mountains of the northwest, the rivers, canals, and lakes of central China, and the terraced rice paddies in the valleys and on the slopes of the south and west—there has been the concept of a united China. Once the imperial state had been established and the Chinese people had filled the territory of China proper, the economic and social patterns which had been worked out on China's geographic foundations had such strength that they persisted even through times of internal crisis and foreign conquest.

The concept of one China owes much to the language. The spoken languages of the north and the west do not differ too widely; it is mainly in the mountainous coastal and southeastern provinces, which are separated from the hinterland, that there are many dialects which differ widely from each other. In imperial times this problem was overcome by the use of an official spoken language, the so-called Mandarin, by the court and the ruling class. Even more important, the written language, which consisted of ideographs, was the same for all. Geographical divisions proved no obstacle to literary unity.

Of still greater significance for the unity of China was the fact that the economic resources of the Chinese empire were sufficient to fill practically all of its needs. China produced within its borders all that it needed of food, clothing, housing and of the products of handicraft. When the British diplomatic mission of 1793 demanded that the Chinese empire be opened up to extensive Western trade, the Emperor Ch'ien-lung could refuse this demand in a letter to King George III in the words, "Our Celestial Empire possesses all things in prolific abundance and lacks no product within its own borders. There is therefore no need to import the manufactures of outside barbarians." He was speaking no less than the truth for the China of his time.

Population and Resources

At the time of the Emperor Ch'ien-lung, however, a development was already taking place which later endangered this economic self-sufficiency. This development was the phenomenal growth of population which had been going on since the seventeenth century. The Chinese population grew from an estimated 100,000,000 people at the beginning of the Manchu dynasty in 1644 to an estimated 360,000,000 by the first decade of the nineteenth century. This growth has continued. In 1954 the Chinese Communists estimated the population at 580,000,000 for the mainland.

The problem of population is closely related to that of the methods of agricultural production. Chinese agriculture has always been fundamentally different from that of the Western world. In the West population density came only with modern industry. Before this time Western agriculture was extensive; it depended on rainfall and on a system of rotation of crops in which the land was allowed to lie fallow one year out of three, or was planted with light crops in order to recover from previous use. As no great public works were necessary for this type of agriculture, it was not necessary for the state to organize labor on a large scale. Extensive agriculture required fewer men in the fields, and its low yields could not support a dense population. Chinese agriculture, on the other hand, has always been marked by an intensive use of labor on the individual plots of land and a great need for mass labor for dike building and other public works. The Chinese therefore tended to live crowded together in any region which they brought under cultivation. The intensive methods of agriculture, with their comparatively high yields, provided sufficient food to feed a dense population. It is for this reason that the movement of Chinese into new territories was not undertaken by individual pioneers but by communities which were organized by officials. By the time of the Manchu dynasty there was very little land left uncultivated and the rate of population increase seems to have been much higher than at any previous time. The density of the population in relation to cultivated land increased considerably. There are no exact figures for imperial times, but there are rough estimates for the period just before World War II which put the population density in North China at 647 persons per square mile of cultivated land. In the rice-growing area of the lower Yangtze River it was over 1,500 persons per square mile. In some of the agricultural areas of the south and southwest the density reached well over 2,000 persons per square mile of cultivated land. The pressure of population contributed to the political disturbances which followed shortly after the Ch'ien-lung period, and led eventually to the fall of the Manchu dynasty. But the political changes which followed the fall of the dynasty brought no answer to the problem of population.

The development of a modern economy in China raises problems with which the old Chinese empire was not concerned. In China the resources for modern industrial development are limited. China has sufficient coal and potential water power for industrialization. She also has considerable reserves of copper and tin and produces more antimony and tungsten than any other country. Her known resources of iron, however, are limited. Oil has been found in the northwest and has been manufactured from shale in Manchuria. But the known resources of oil will not go very far and are certainly not sufficient for the needs of a first-rate industrial power. The geographical foundations which made possible the power of imperial China are not adequate in themselves to give to contemporary China a similar position in the modern world.

2. CHINESE SOCIETY

What kind of society?

The question of the nature of Chinese society has fascinated Europeans ever since there was sufficient contact with China to provide a body of knowledge about her institutions. Europe of the eighteenth century, the Age of Reason, was particularly impressed by the image of a society dominated by the gentlemen-scholars, the literati. On the basis of their fragmentary knowledge of China some of the leading European thinkers formed an idealized picture of a rational social order free from superstition, from which the Europe of the time could draw inspiration. The classical economists of England recognized in China an economic system very different from anything they knew in Europe. In the early days of the American Republic, when commerce was a vital activity, John Quincy Adams declared that China was a non-commercial empire. These earlier impressions were later systematized by such sociologists as E. T. C. Werner, a Spencerian, who made a descriptive study of Chinese society in which he stressed the role of the scholars as the leading group. The German sociologist, Max Weber, who was interested in the relationship of ideology to society, brought out the importance of humanistic education in the training of a bureaucracy in China. Karl Marx, who believed in a classification of societies according to the ownership of the means of production, ascribed to China and other Oriental countries such as India, a mode of production different from that of Europe. He referred to what he called an Asiatic mode of production, a concept which he did not develop and which his Communist successors tried to explain away. In fact, the question of the nature of Chinese society became a matter of doctrinal conflict among Marxists. (See pp. 334–35.) The whole Marxist discussion of Chinese society has tended to obscure the insights of independent scholars such as Max Weber and to make of a scientific problem a political issue.

American social scientists do not agree upon any generally accepted system of classifying societies. It is not possible, therefore, to fit China into an accepted classification of societies. The special nature of Chinese society and its differences from others can best be indicated, perhaps, by identifying the group which had dominating status and power and by analyzing the way in which it exercised control.

Chinese society was dominated by institutionalized public function-aries—bureaucrats—who were set apart from the population by education, prestige, and position. These were the scholar-gentry. All important affairs, whether formally a part of government administration or not, were handled by this group either as officials in government service or as gentry in their districts and provinces. When in official position, these men carried out imperial edicts and applied the laws of the dynasty. But as gentry of the districts and the provinces they managed public affairs in a uniform pattern according to traditional rules. The larger tasks they handled as an organized group. There was no other group that could challenge their leadership. Because all the political and social institutions of China were bureaucrat-ically managed, Chinese society can be usefully designated as a bureaucratic society. For this kind of society there was no parallel in the history of western Europe. China had no feudal lords or feudal relationships, no military aristocracy, orders of chivalry, no serfs bound to the soil, no fiefs, no entailed estates, and no hereditary status groups. Nor was there anything in China to parallel the institutions of early commercial capitalism in the West. There were no free cities, no independent merchant class, no free competition, and no popular participation in government. The states of Europe had their officials but their functions were limited. In no way can their role be com-pared with that of the bureaucracy of China which managed the govern-ment, the army, and the economy, which upheld the ideology, and which dominated both state and society.

The Chinese bureaucracy was a non-hereditary group of trained men who monopolized all positions of authority. Their authority extended from the management of the highest affairs of state to the settlement of the petty quarrels of a village. This authority reached into every field of human affairs, political, economic, military, and ideological. No other group was ever permitted to have independence of action, in any sphere, outside of bureau-cratic control. No merchant class, no independent military class, no group of powerful landowners, for example, were ever allowed to challenge the political and social monopoly of the bureaucracy.

The bureaucratic state took shape over a long period of time. Chinese feudalism came to an end during the last centuries of the pre-Christian era, giving place to a unified imperial state. It was at this time that China proper was unified by military force and a centralized government was first estab-lished. The institutions of unified government came to be built on a society in which centrally directed authority eventually penetrated into every aspect of life and thought. The state undertook tasks of a magnitude far beyond anything undertaken or contemplated by any European government before the modern period. To control effectively a geographical area of such vastness and variety was in itself a tremendous task. For one thing it could not be held together as a loose military confederation. The old feudal armies disappeared. The Chinese imperial army was a mass army, organized along rational lines, fed and paid by the state and directed by appointed government officials. Its leaders were part of the bureaucracy.

For another thing, the state had to establish a uniform administrative system in order to keep this vast area together. Such a system could be run only by a bureaucracy composed of men who shared the same loyalties and ideas and who were adequately trained for the task. Chinese society was distinguished most, perhaps, by its monolithic ideological system, based on Confucianism. This system provided the moral justification for authority in society. It was developed and propagated by a group of educated men who not only provided leadership in society but also supplied the officials who ran the government. This educated elite monopolized the body of knowledge of human relations and of the moral order on which Chinese society rested.

The educated bureaucracy made it possible for the state to undertake tasks which were vital to the development of the political and economic structure of China. These were the public works. The control of water was of first importance for the protection of human life and for the fullest development of the Chinese type of intensive agriculture. The intensive agricultural methods that went with the spread of Chinese civilization required a complex system of waterworks for irrigation, drainage, and flood control. First in order of magnitude was the control of the Yellow River whose devastating floods were beyond the capacity of individuals, villages, or even smaller states, to handle. The unification of China provided the central authority and direction which were mandatory for the planning and maintenance of an extended dike system. The experience gained in the struggle with the Yellow River was applied to other problems of water control. In order to improve communications and to consolidate its power the government constructed canals, of which the most outstanding was the Grand Canal, an elaborate bureaucratic enterprise.

Public works were not limited to water control. They included the building of roads and the construction of the Great Wall. This huge defense work along the northwest frontier, from the deserts of Inner Asia to the Gulf of Pechili, was built to keep out the mobile forces of the nomadic peoples on China's inner Asiatic borders. The wall literally grew with China's administrative system. The first sections were built by individual states to defend themselves against the peoples of the steppes. When these states were merged by conquest into the Chinese empire in the third century B.C., the small defense works were built into the Great Wall.

Public works required public labor, and public labor required public management. The construction and maintenance of all these public works required skilled management not only for their planning but also for the recruiting, organizing, and feeding of large peasant labor forces. Control of public labor by a bureaucracy became a distinguishing characteristic of China's economic and social system. It was facilitated by a periodic census to keep count of the labor force. The government also kept records of agricultural land, important for the uniform land tax imposed to support the armies, the administration, and the public works.

Once established, the bureaucratic pattern of Chinese society could not be easily changed. The bureaucratic spirit penetrated into all the critical areas of Chinese life and infused all Chinese social and economic institutions. Within the framework of this bureaucratic system no alternative principles of political organization and no competing political theories could establish themselves. Many dynasties followed each other in China, some established by foreign conquerors, but under each rule, the Chinese bureaucratic institutions always reasserted themselves.

The Scholar-Gentry

Chinese society in imperial times was dominated by an upper class of educated men, the scholar-gentry, the so-called *shen-shih*. They were set apart from the large mass of the population, the commoners—the innumerable peasants of the villages and the artisans and merchants of the towns. The scholar-gentry were distinguished from the commoners, not by virtue of hereditary status or of wealth but by virtue of their educational qualifications. They are also called the literati, because they were the bearers of China's humanist tradition. The members of the scholar-gentry held a monopoly of official positions; no one outside of this group could be appointed. Office-holding was a source of authority and wealth, but at any one time only a small proportion of the scholar-gentry was in office. The bulk of the gentry carried out, on a quasi-official basis, the management of local affairs. The members of the scholar-gentry, whether in office or out of office, controlled and directed all important aspects of public affairs. It was this role that gave them their elevated position in society.

Membership in the scholar-gentry depended on educational qualifications. Knowledge, ability, and moral qualities were the prerequisites for the management of public affairs. During the last centuries of imperial China the government established an examination system by which it set up formal standards for educational achievement. Successful candidates in the examinations were granted academic degrees which entitled them to the privileges of membership in the scholar-gentry. The scholar-gentry were thus a certified educated group.

The examination system was an elaborate institution. The examinations began with local selective tests in the districts, the successful candidates being admitted to the lower examinations which were held twice every three years in the prefectures. The number of those who could pass the examination was fixed by quota, and the number of candidates was usually very much greater than the quota. Those who passed received degrees, and in some cases stipends, and were regarded as members of the privileged scholar-gentry group. They could improve their status within the group by taking higher examinations in the provincial capitals, thus securing further advancement through higher degrees. A small number of the most successful scholars passed the highest examination held at the imperial capital.

Descriptions of the Chinese examination system have often put considerable emphasis on the fact that any intelligent farm boy could be admitted to the examinations and therefore had a chance to rise to the highest position in the land. In practice the selection was limited because success in the examinations depended on an expensive and lengthy education to which the candidate had to dedicate all his time from early youth. While examinations were public, education was private, and only those with means could provide teachers and books for their sons. The student had to be supported by his family or a group of families and friends. He had no time to labor in the fields, but led a life apart in which manual labor was regarded as undignified. A scholar showed by his physique that he did not belong to the common people; scholarly frailty, a pale complexion, and long fingernails indicated his gentle qualities and professional dignity. Because of the difficulty and expense of preparing for the examinations the majority, but not all, of the candidates came from the families of the scholar-gentry class itself. Yet there was in practice considerable social mobility. Because success in the examinations depended on individual ability, there were always a number of men from commoner families who achieved gentry status. At times about one-third of the gentry families came from commoner status and an equal number of families slid down into the mass of commoners.

Examination, though in theory a necessary proof of the intellectual and moral qualities of leadership, was in practice not always the sole way of entrance into the ruling class. There were times in which the government sold academic titles which admitted the buyer to the scholar-gentry group. Many titles were sold during the last dynasty (the Ch'ing or Manchu dynasty, 1644–1911). Though literacy was always required of the buyer, this form of entrance made it possible for those who had the means to avoid the long hard path of preparation for the examinations. The buyers of such titles, however, never achieved the prestige of the regular members of the gentry group even though they were able to obtain lucrative official positions through appointment or further purchase.

Education in imperial China was education for rule, not for the advancement of knowledge. By means of the educational system the scholar-gentry gained the skills needed for the management of people and affairs: skill in the writing of the official language, knowledge of the history and practice of government, and proficiency in the handling of affairs within the existing social order. But the most important part of the education was inculcation in the ethical precepts of Confucianism which were the heart of the Chinese cultural tradition. In these precepts there was expressed the Chinese ideal of the moral individual in a moral society. It was the Confucian view that education was a process of learning and self-discipline through which the educated man acquired the moral qualities and the strength of character that would enable him to fulfill his responsibilities in society. He was expected to have a high sense of public duty and, as an official, to be loyal to the emperor. The good and loyal official was even expected to commit suicide and perish with his ruler if the dynasty were defeated. While many officials managed to switch their loyalties in sufficient time, many chose to die. For the gentry the ideal was "to be first in worrying about the world's troubles and last in the enjoyment of its pleasures." This ideal of selfless service was not always practiced, but it was believed in as the standard of gentry behavior.

Training in the Confucian classics was designed to develop a common outlook, a common sense of values, not to provide the technical knowledge which the gentry needed in their day-to-day work. Practical knowledge of affairs was acquired through reading and experience. China had a vast literature on geography, irrigation, engineering, and administration, on economics, mathematics, and the military arts. Treatises were available on agriculture and all its branches such as sericulture and tea and rice production. There were gazetteers for every administrative district, prefecture, and province, compiled by commissions composed of gentry. These contained information on the history, geographical features, population statistics, land area and utilization, public works, military organization, and biographies of members of leading families, and other matters of interest in the particular area. These handbooks, which were printed and illustrated, were used by officials and gentry for their guidance. Such material did not enter into the content of the examinations. Through their education in the classics the scholar-gentry were expected to have acquired the mental training to enable them to handle this material and to master their many and various assignments.

The scholar-gentry, at the beginning of the nineteenth century, numbered about 1,100,000 persons. Together with their immediate families, who shared their privileged position, they comprised about five and a half million people or roughly one and a half per cent of the population. A very small minority of this number was sufficient to fill the forty thousand official positions which the dynasty had established. This meant that even with a comparatively high turnover the large majority of the gentry never came to hold public office; they stayed at home in their own districts. Gentry serving as officials always served away from home. Those who never held office or who were temporarily out of office were by no means excluded from public affairs. On their own responsibility, or in cooperation with the officials, they dealt with the many affairs in their districts or provinces which were not undertaken by the government.

The functions of the gentry were many and varied. The government, whose officials were few in relation to the area and the number of people they had to administer, reserved to itself control over such decisive administrative matters as the armed forces, taxation, appointment and supervision of officials, justice, and the examination system, but there was much it could not and did not do by itself. The gentry were expected to handle by themselves those affairs which the officials did not undertake and to cooperate with the officials in certain large-scale undertakings. There was no strict dividing line between the activities of the gentry and of the officials in many of these fields. But there were certain traditional gentry responsibilities. One of these was the arbitration of disputes among individuals and communities. In practice the gentry handled most of the civil disputes since it was to everyone's interest to avoid the court of the magistrate. The magistrate, who was responsible for peace and order in his district, applied to all cases the Penal Code, the only body of law in existence. The gentry also sponsored and organized most of the local charity and welfare activities such as setting up rice kitchens and distributing grain to the poor. They attended to the upkeep of temples and saw to such matters as the erection of memorial arches. The gentry were the teachers who prepared candidates for the examinations and instructed the people in the moral principles of Confucianism. They participated in local sacrifices and in the village lectures in which themes from Confucian doctrine were expounded.

The most important function of the gentry, however, was the management of public works in cooperation with the officials. On the carrying out of these great public tasks of flood prevention, irrigation, and canalization the economic life of China depended. The large-scale projects, such as the Yellow River dikes and the drainage system of the Huai River, required highly organized and centralized direction. These large projects were part of the official responsibility of the government, and in some cases separate agencies were set up to deal with them. But in most cases the building of dams, dikes, and canals, and of roads and bridges, was planned, organized, and supervised by the gentry. Local irrigation systems were frequently managed by the gentry alone. Often such activity required the approval of officials. Sometimes it led to joint official-gentry direction and financing of the work; sometimes an officially initiated program was carried out under the guidance and control of local gentry. Indeed there were probably few public works, large or small, in which the gentry did not have some of the responsibility.

In all the public works the task of organizing, feeding, and directing vast masses of human labor was the major concern. The masses of the people accepted the leadership of the gentry in this as in all other matters. They regarded the gentry as men of learning, authority, and prestige whom it was customary to respect and dangerous to disobey.

In times of crisis, when government authority was weakened, the gentry frequently usurped government prerogatives. When the government troops were unable to give protection, the gentry organized and led local military corps to defend their home districts and provinces. Unable to assert its own authority the government had no choice but to tolerate the taking over of military authority by the gentry. Such a usurpation of the functions of the state could be tolerated on a small scale, but when it became widespread the government could not long survive.

The gentry were the better able to carry out their functions because of the privileged position and recognized status which they had acquired. They had social and political as well as legal privileges. They had a special status before the law and were immune from certain humiliating punishments. Special kinds of clothing and special insignia—buttons of silver or gold denoting their gentry rank—marked them off from the crowd. If they were officials, their servants and attendants cleared the way for them as they passed through the streets. The gentry, in some cases, received subsidies from the government. More important, they were exempted from labor conscription and certain types of taxes; they could use their position to escape the onerous surtaxes and lighten their general tax burden. Whereas the large mass of the commoners stayed away from the magistrates, whom they feared and to whom they had to kowtow, the gentry could approach all officials directly as colleagues and social equals. All this characterized them as a privileged upper class and gave them the necessary prestige for their position of dominance and leadership in society. Membership in this upper group, with its prestige, wealth, and possibility of high office, was the most enviable position which could be gained in Chinese society.

The path to gentry position was through the examination system. The degrees which they acquired certified their knowledge of human relations and affairs and of the ethical principles which were believed to underlie them. It was knowledge of these matters which qualified the gentry for their position. This interpretation runs counter to the view that the Chinese gentry got their wealth from land and that this wealth made them politically powerful. Such a view is erroneous. The gentry did not derive most of their income from land, and landed estates could not easily be held together. They derived their main income from services. According to a recent study the gentry, which made up about one and a half per cent of the population, received about one fifth of the national income. Of this, about half came from services, a little less than a third came from land, and the remainder from entrepreneurial or business activities of one kind or another. For the purpose of this analysis there are included under services salaries and stipends received from the government and also the many legitimate or irregular payments received for public services and the fees from teaching. These figures apply to the gentry as a whole. Most of the gentry actually depended for much more than 50 per cent of their incomes on services. A small number of gentry families monopolized a large part of the income from land, but in most of these cases the large landholdings were acquired with the wealth first secured from high office. Even this income depended, in large measure, on continuing gentry status. Because of their privileged position the gentry's income from land was higher, more secure, and less burdened with public obligations than was the commoner's income from land. But gentry status could not be assured by the possession of large landed estates. Nor could large landed estates, the exception rather than the rule in China, be easily held together for any length of time because there was no rule of primogeniture. The division of property among the male heirs on the death of the head of the family led to a continual parceling out and redistribution of lands. The gentry, it is clear, had neither a large income from land nor a permanent hold on large landed estates. Under these conditions land could not be the basis of political power.

It must be emphasized that each member of the gentry was attached to his district and province. This was the administrative area in which he passed the examinations and was listed on the government rolls. It was in this area, and in none other, that he was expected to carry out his functions. In this way the government made sure that there would be trained and responsible leaders within each administrative area. But to keep this group small and manageable the government limited the number of gentry for each district and province through the examination quotas.

The degrees and privileges granted by the government bolstered the gentry's status but did not provide the substance of their authority. This authority, derived from their training, education, and knowledge, set them apart from the common people. The scholar-gentry represented the cultural tradition of China. From the scholar-gentry came the philosophers, the historians, the poets, the painters, and the men of affairs. The greatness of Chinese civilization, its thought, its art, its moral and ethical principles, were cultivated, preserved, and developed by this group.

A great barrier of education and of political, social, and economic privilege divided the gentry from the common people of China. There was, however, a marginal group of would-be gentry composed of aspiring scholars and of candidates for the examinations. This group of non-certified scholars shared some of the functions—such as teaching—and even some of the prestige of the scholar-gentry. But they shone only in reflected glory; they spent their lives in the scramble for degrees because it was only by acquiring the degrees that they could enjoy the full status and great advantages of the scholar-gentry. This marginal group was actually larger in numbers than the gentry but it still made up only a very small section of the large mass of the common people of China.

Commoners

PEASANTS. About 80 per cent of the common people were peasants. The peasant class, or Chinese *nung*, was considered second in the social scale which the scholar-gentry themselves had set up. In this scale the scholar-gentry counted themselves first and then listed the peasants, the artisans, and the merchants. The classes were listed in this order to indicate the functional importance of each group in Chinese society. A distinction between these four groups is still useful today, if it is understood that there was a very wide gap between the gentry and the three other groups, who were all commoners.

The peasants were listed first among the commoners because the predominance of agriculture made them the most important group for production. They also made up the large reservoir of manpower which provided the labor for public works and the conscripts for increased military forces in times of expanded military activities. The average income of the peasants was lower than that of the merchants and artisans who, however, were less important in the eyes of the agrarian-minded ruling group.

The social status of the Chinese peasant was much higher than that of the peasant of feudal Europe. China had a free peasantry. The peasant was free to move, to buy and sell property, and to rise to scholar-gentry status by taking the examinations. He paid his taxes and gave his labor and military service to the government, not to a feudal lord. Nor was the tenant any less free than the owner of land; he was not bound to the soil, and had to render no personal services to his landlord. Although most of the peasants lived close to the minimum subsistence level and were economically exploited, they were not brutalized as were the peasants of medieval Europe or Russia. They had an honorable position in society, and their well-being was traditionally a concern of the government.

The life of the peasant was based on his relationship to the land, the conditions of its use and ownership. China's system of intensive agriculture and the laws of inheritance both combined to keep the unit of cultivation very small. A great amount of careful labor went into every plot of ground in order to bring the highest possible return; nothing was ever wasted. The fertility of the soil was carefully maintained. The peasant carried the silt from irrigation ditches to spread over his land. In every part of China human fertilizer was carefully preserved and used. As all of his land was used for crops and there was no pasture for grazing animals, the peasant had little animal fertilizer to add to these resources.

This system of agriculture, in which the soil was cultivated so intensively, did not permit the cultivation of large areas by individual families. It was this fact, combined with the laws of inheritance, which kept the individual plots so small. The problem was aggravated by the population pressure that developed under the Manchu dynasty. As the growth of population was not matched by any corresponding increase in the amount of land brought under cultivation, the average plot became too small to feed a family properly. According to modern statistics the average farm consisted of about three acres in North China, where the staple crops were millet and wheat, and about one and a half acres in South China, where the staple crop was rice. With such a small unit of production the peasant lived always on the edge of catastrophe, and at times of natural calamities or political disturbance millions perished through starvation. Yet it was the peasants who had to provide the food for the court, the officials, the armies, the gentry, and the urban population of artisans and merchants. The peasants paid heavy taxes to the officials or high rents to the landlords; they also supplied the labor for the public works. In North and Central China the corvée labor was an even heavier burden on the peasantry than was the tax or rent.

In the Manchu dynasty, as in many other periods of imperial history, the majority of the peasants owned their land. But not all of the peasants were landowners; a substantial number of them rented all or a part of the land they worked from landlords, who were mostly gentry, or else merchants or well-to-do artisans, or occasionally rich peasants. At times of dynastic decline the number of tenants usually increased, as it did during the last century of the Manchu dynasty. But the economic condition of the peasant was not necessarily better if he were an owner-cultivator instead of a tenant. It was the conditions of landownership and tenancy, the amounts that had to be paid in taxes or rents, that affected the life of the peasants.

The peasant owner had to pay the land taxes and all the surtaxes which officials might impose. The tenant paid rent to the landlord who was himself responsible for the land tax. The rent usually consisted of anything from 40 to 70 per cent of the main crop. Which was more oppressive, tax or rent, depended on time and circumstances. In times when the government was weak, corrupt officials increased the surtaxes on the small owners and the landlords extorted exorbitant rents from the tenants. It was in such periods that the peasants sought to escape from these unbearable burdens through banditry and eventually through open rebellion.

The peasant worked hard to make his small plot of land produce enough to feed himself and his family and to meet all his obligations to the official, the landlord, or the moneylender. After the deduction of tax or rent, hardly enough was left from what he produced to feed his family. When crops were poor, the peasant would fall into debt, and once in debt would rarely be able to work himself out of the hands of the usurers, who demanded exorbitant rates of interest. The peasant's life was therefore a constant struggle. His diet was millet and wheat or rice and vegetables. Only rarely could he afford pork, poultry, or fish. At village or family feasts good eating was an important source of social enjoyment. Peasants lived in very simple houses built of sun-dried bricks and covered with roofs of straw. There was very little furniture. The houses in the north usually had a bed, or k'ang, of brick and pounded earth, under which a fire could be built. In the south the peasants slept on beds made of wooden planks or bamboo wicker. Families who could afford it had tables and chairs. Fuel was a luxury and was used mostly for cooking. In the cold winters of the north the peasant kept himself warm by wearing all the padded gowns he possessed.

The peasants lived in villages rather than on separate homesteads. The villages varied in size from small hamlets to large communities of several thousand families. They were often surrounded by walls of pounded earth for defense against bandits. The village was not only a working community but also a social unit. The village temple was the main center of community gatherings where sometimes opera performances were presented. Weddings, funerals, and general festivals tended to be village affairs. Much has been made of the so-called democratic government of the autonomous village, but the village government was neither democratic nor autonomous. The important affairs of the village, such as tax collection and local security, were handled by the heads of subadministrative organizations appointed by the officials. These organizations were the so-called pao-chia and li-chia systems which were superimposed on the villages by the government in order to keep close control of the behavior of the people. The *li-chia* system was originally used for tax collection and the *pao-chia* for police supervision, but the distinction was not often maintained. Both systems were based on the principle of collective responsibility for units of ten, one hundred, or more families, the head of each unit being appointed by government officials. The heads of these units or of similar organizations were sometimes called village elders or headmen. A great number of local affairs were also handled by the scholar-gentry. The life of the peasants and the organization of their villages was in no way democratic.

ARTISANS AND MERCHANTS. In imperial China the economic and political center of rural society was the town, the seat of administration and the location of handicraft and of trade. The town was also a center of defense, protected by walls and moats. The city gates, with their curved roofs, rose high above the walls and could be seen from far away. The town and the surrounding countryside formed an economic unit, and in the markets of the town the peasant sold his small surplus to buy the products of the artisan.

The artisans, or *kung*, made tools, instruments, and luxury products. As in medieval Europe, there were many kinds of artisans, such as coppersmiths, tinsmiths, silversmiths, carpenters, and weavers. There was no strict division between employers and employees, the shops being a kind of famiiy organization, with masters and apprentices working together. Over a period of years the apprentice learned his trade in exchange for maintenance. Each branch of work had its own standards which were upheld by guild organizations. The guild regulated standards, prices, and quality of goods, working conditions of apprentices, and the like, and was also a mutual self-help organization of the members of the trade. As such, it represented their interests vis-à-vis the all-powerful officialdom, and to some extent helped them to resist heavy burdens in taxes and other exactions which the officials might impose. The guild usually elected officers and employed a secretary, who was generally a member of the scholar-gentry and therefore able to negotiate with the officials on an equal basis. The guilds served also as social organizations for their members, with wealthier groups having their own guild halls and entertainment. They also fulfilled functions of arbitration within the membership itself and with the members of other guilds or groups. In the towns the artisans were usually located by trade, each in his own street, which was named accordingly. Work and sale were carried on in the same place of business, and while buying over the counter the customer could see the artisans at work.

The towns were also the home of the merchants or *shang*. In China there were many differing forms of trading activities. Colorful figures in Chinese towns were the street vendors who identified their various goods through special chants, calls, and sounds when they made their rounds at regular hours. The larger and more important trade was carried on by well-to-do merchants who used considerable capital in their business. These merchants handled the distribution, throughout the whole of China, of goods such as silk or tea which were produced only in certain parts of the country. As some of these enterprises required capital for long-range operations a pre-modern banking system developed in certain provinces.

The merchants were generally wealthier than the artisans, but in the existing Chinese system, they were in no way independent. There was no freedom of enterprise and no system of commercial laws to protect the merchant from official interference. His situation was always uncertain, his temporary security depending on the good graces of the officials who could exact contributions from him. Various fields of economic activity, such as salt mining and distribution and other mining activities, were official monopolies, sometimes licensed to private merchants. The merchant was thus under the control of the bureaucrat. It was for this reason that a merchant would try to place his sons in the all-powerful upper class of scholar-gentry either through examinations or the buying of titles. In other cases the merchants themselves purchased their way into the gentry. Others who were already gentry used their position and connections for profit-making in commercial ventures. But as the traditional outlook regarded private profit-seeking as an activity not worthy of a gentleman and scholar who handled public affairs, members of the gentry often carried on such commercial activities under different names. Trade was a non-gentry activity, and merchants were commoners who were always under the control of the officials and the gentry.

The merchants, like the artisans, were organized into guilds. The guilds, which were usually limited to one trade, were composed of merchants from the same province or prefecture. They eliminated competition among the members of a trade in the same administrative area but strengthened them in their competition with guilds from other areas. For their members they set prices and rules for business practice, arbitrated disputes, provided aid in case of need, and maintained clubs for the use of their members when doing business in other provinces. They also handled relations with the officials, negotiating the payment of fees and contributions and seeking to protect their members from exorbitant demands. Some of the merchant guilds were quite wealthy and had considerable funds for guild halls, entertainment, and mutual support. In times of unrest and insecurity, the guilds occasionally organized their own local military corps to protect their members.

SOLDIERS. The Chinese have occasionally listed soldiers, or *ping*, in addition to the traditional four social classes, as the fifth and lowest of all. This custom has given rise to the myth that by placing the soldiers at the bottom of the social scale the Chinese were indicating their pacifism and their contempt for military affairs. The Chinese were neither pacifist nor unmilitary, and there was no special military class. The officers of the army were officials who had passed examinations and were members of the gentry. There was no strict line drawn between civil and military responsibilities. In addition to the military officers many of the regular officials had military responsibilities for the defense of their administrative areas. The element of disregard was intended only for the common soldiers, not for the military leaders and officials. The common soldiers of the regular armies were miserably paid and badly treated. They were either forcibly conscripted or were men who had fallen upon evil times and had no other choice.

"*Mean People*"

The lowest social class of all was the so-called "mean people," a social stratum below that of the commoners. They were few in numbers and were made up of actors, barbers, members of other lowly professions, prostitutes, and domestic slaves. Such people were regarded as being greatly inferior to all others and were excluded from the examinations and therefore from any opportunity to rise in the social scale.

The Family

The hierarchy of status and position found in society as a whole parallels a similar hierarchy of authority within the smaller social unit of the family. The father, as head of the family, had complete authority over its members, within the framework of the moral code of Confucianism. The same code sanctioned the authority of the male over the female and of age over youth. The authority of the father was fully backed by the law; it was a very serious offense for a son to strike his father. The father owned all the family property and decided all issues. He had wide powers to punish and full authority over the personal lives of other members of the family, including the selection of wives and husbands for his children. He could even sell members of his family into slavery, although such action was not socially approved. From early youth children were trained in filial piety and the appropriate obediences. Obedience to the father was the living expression of respect for the family line of which the living generations were only part. The family carried out services to its ancestors. It was the duty of the sons to produce sons so that the patrilineal line could be continued. Within the same generation the older member had authority over the younger and was responsible for him.

Women had to obey their husbands and had no property rights. In the family as in society they were inferior to men. When they married, they went to live with the family of the husband and came under the authority of the mother-in-law. While the husband could take a second wife or concubine, the wife was not supposed to remarry when widowed. Upper-class women were also subjected to the long and painful process of footbinding in order to acquire the much prized "lily feet." In the relationship of men to women, as well as in the relation of father to son, and of older to younger brother, authority was matched by responsibility. The linking of authority and responsibility in these paternalistic relationships assured the weaker party the status and protection sanctioned by the moral code.

Imperial China is usually thought of as a land of large families, with many generations living under the same roof. Such families were the exception rather than the rule. It was only the upper gentry and the rich who could afford to keep together many generations of a large family in one household, and to have many concubines to provide many children. The average family was small; it consisted of about five members. In spite of a high birth rate, the number was kept down by disease, infanticide, and the smallness of the landholdings. The poorer the family the less the incentive to stay together. On the other hand the relatives of rich gentry families preferred to live under the same roof for reasons of prestige and protection.

The importance of kinship relationships, both patrilineal and matrilineal, is reflected in the language, which has a great variety of terms to indicate all the different degrees of relationship. Within this kinship group, even if it did not live together, the traditional obligations of respect and responsibility were maintained. A great deal of pressure was brought to bear on any member of the kinship group who had prospered to carry out his obligations towards his relatives. In some cases, especially in South China, the kinship group made up a whole village. These were the so-called clan villages. In other cases two or more such clans composed a village. As a rule, however, the clans were not so cohesive, and villages usually consisted of many unrelated families. But in these cases also responsibility to the kinship group tended to come before neighborhood obligations. In this system of family relationships the individual had to accept his standing and obligations and could express his personality only as a member of the group. The family rather than the individual was the basic unit of society.

3. THE GOVERNMENT

The institutions of government, like those of society, had become firmly established in China during the last centuries of imperial rule. Dynasty followed dynasty but the general pattern of government and society did not change. From 1644 to 1911 the government of China rested with a dynasty of foreign conquerors, the Manchus, who called themselves the Ch'ing. The Manchus made no significant changes in the organization of government; in fact they ran it as they found it, except for the obvious measures they took to maintain their military control. New dynasties were always established by military conquest, but whether the new rulers came from within China or from without, the traditional Chinese pattern of government always reasserted itself.

However different were the historical circumstances, a certain sequence of events appears to have recurred. Emerging in a time of crisis and coming to power by military conquest, a new dynasty would unify the country and centralize authority; its rule would then lead to a period of high development and strength; and from there to decline and break-up, a period of chaos and confusion, and a new crisis from which eventually a new dynasty would emerge. The contrast between the changes in the dynasties and the tenacity of the institutional patterns indicates that the reasons for the rise and fall of dynasties must be looked for in the system of government itself.

The Central Government

The head of the Chinese government was the emperor. In the name of the emperor and under his personal control, government was carried on by a highly developed administrative organization. The direction of government under the emperor was at times in the hands of a prime minister, at other times divided between several agencies or managed by a government council.

During the latter part of the Ch'ing dynasty, the highest government agency was the Grand Council, established in 1730, which met with the emperor every morning to discuss and decide matters of high policy. The execution of policy was in the hands of six boards or ministries. The Board of Civil Office dealt primarily with appointments and dismissals of the administrative staff; the Board of Revenue dealt with the collection and allotment of the revenue that came in from the provinces; the Board of Rites dealt with the examinations and the highly developed ceremonial of government; the Board of War dealt with military organization and central direction of military affairs; the Board of Justice handled legal cases on the highest level; and the Board of Works dealt with the supervision and direction of public works undertaken by the central government. In addition to these boards, there were some other organs of central government, such as the so-called Censorate, consisting of a group of central government officials entrusted with the supervision of all government activities and with the duty of reporting all improprieties and violations of the moral and legal principles of the imperial government. A Court of Dependency Affairs handled the relationship of the central government with the Inner Asian dependencies.

Provincial Administration

The imperial administration at the capital of Peking was superimposed upon the eighteen provinces of China proper. Most of these provinces were natural geographical units such as river valleys or high plateaus. For administrative purposes several of the provinces were paired together because they composed a larger geographical and economic unit. The provincial divisions of the last dynasty continued with little change under the Republic and the Chinese Communist regime. The province in which Peking was located, now called Hopei, was formerly known as Chihli, which means direct administration. To the east lies the province of Shantung, a mountain range and a peninsula, the birthplace of Confucius. To the west the province of Shansi, which encloses the valley of the Fen River, is separated by mountain ranges from the North China Plain, and by the Yellow River from the neighboring province of Shensi. The two northwestern provinces of Shensi and Kansu are on the old caravan route to Central Asia. The province of Honan, south of the Yellow River, is a part of the great plain. The provinces of Kiangsu, Anhwei, and Kiangsi lie in the rich lower valley of the Yangtze River and its tributary, the Kan River. Hupei and Hunan, the rice bowl of central China, are in the central part of the Yangtze River system. The large and rich province of Szechwan, above the Yangtze River gorges, takes in the upper Yangtze and its tributaries. On the eastern coast, south of the Yangtze River, are the provinces of Chekiang and Fukien. The southern provinces of Kwangtung and Kwangsi enclose the southern river system within their borders. On the high inland plateaus of the southwest are the provinces of Yunnan and Kweichow.

Each of these provinces had its governor who had general responsibility for provincial affairs. Because of their special importance or size the provinces of Chihli and Szechwan each had a governor-general. With the exception of the three provinces of Shantung, Honan, and Shansi, which are located around the capital, all other provinces were grouped under governors-general according to the geographical combinations which have just been listed. The governors-general had over-all authority over the provincial governors and the provinces under their jurisdiction and in addition had direct military command over a unit of the central army garrisoned at their headquarters.

There were also a number of other provincial officers who were entrusted with special functions for which they were directly responsible to the court. A financial commissioner handled the provincial tax collection and payments to the central treasury. A judicial commissioner decided judicial cases on the provincial level. A provincial director of studies arranged the lower examinations in the prefectual cities and supervised the lower gentry. In some provinces salt intendants dealt with the administration and income of the government salt monopoly, and grain intendants handled the grain tribute. In military affairs, a provincial commander-in-chief was in charge of the central military units of the province. These officials were lower in rank than the governors-general and governors and therefore under their authority. But they were directly appointed by the central government and reported to it.

Local Administration

Under this provincial administration there were the intermediate administrative units of the circuits and prefectures, and below these, the main units of local Chinese administration, the districts, or in Chinese, *hsien*. China proper was divided into over fifteen hundred districts. The district magistrate, combining in his person all government authority for his area, was the official who dealt directly with the people. He was responsible for the local collection of taxes, maintained peace and order, directed public works in his district, was the local judge and the arbiter in all things with which the government concerned itself. For the population at large, he was the representative of government authority, "the father and mother of the people." As the average district had a population of about two hundred thousand people, the magistrate could not carry out all the tasks of administration himself. Besides his personal staff, the district magistrate had the help of the heads of smaller administrative units, such as the *pao-chia* and *li-chia*, to carry on police work and tax collection. Even so, his task of maintaining order and carrying out government policy would have been difficult without the cooperation of the scholar-gentry of his district.

Central Control

The functioning of the government depended on firm control by a directing central authority, the emperor. According to legendary history, the institution of the Chinese emperor existed even in prehistoric times. In the feudal age of the second and first millennium before Christ, there was a loose hierarchy of feudal lords and rulers under the overlordship of a king. When the state of Ch'in unified China, its ruler, Ch'in Shih Huang Ti, became the first emperor, the head of the new bureaucratic administration. The position of emperor was hereditary within the ruling family of each dynasty. The emperor's right to rule was based on the so-called "mandate of Heaven," which invested him with the sole authority for all government.

The emperor was all powerful in theory, but in practice he had to rule through his administrative organization. His real power depended on the degree of control he exercised over the bureaucracy and over the scholar-gentry, the ruling social group. To have these men within his "grasp" or "sway" was the main objective of the emperor in every dynasty. The danger that members of this group would become independent of the central authority and gain their own political power and influence was ever present. Under the imperial administrative system, as it developed over the centuries, innumerable highly sophisticated measures were devised to build up and strengthen central control.

The introduction of the examination system made it possible for the imperial government to determine membership in the privileged group of scholar-gentry. The government controlled the examinations. It set quotas for the number of candidates permitted to pass, thus controlling admission to the gentry and limiting their number. But even after admission through the first examination, the members of the gentry were required to take minor examinations at regular intervals to keep their standing. Further efforts were necessary if they wished to raise their standing by passing the higher examinations.

The government thus kept the gentry busy in an "examination life" in which they had to overcome one hurdle after another to retain their status and advance themselves. The government also determined the content of the examinations, using them to instill in the intellectual elite the fullest loyalty to the dynasty. The minds and energies of the scholar-gentry were thus captured for the purposes of the government.

The officials were controlled by an intricate system of administrative checks and balances. The system developed during the whole period of Chinese imperial history and reached its greatest refinement under the Ch'ing dynasty. To prevent officials from establishing independent sources of power, no official was permitted to hold office in his home district or province. Frequent rotations brought new men into positions and created lengthy intervals between times of office-holding. The period of office in any one place was limited to a maximum of about three years but was in practice often shorter. Another means of checking the power of officials was a division of responsibility; each official had only limited authority and was directly responsible to the central government for his work. Often this authority would overlap or conflict, thus giving the court the power to manipulate officials and to play them off against each other.

Provincial administration was a typical example of the system of divided authority. The commissioners of finance and justice and the salt and grain intendants handled very important aspects of provincial administration and had the right to memorialize directly to the throne. The provincial director of studies had the special responsibility of supervising the lower gentry of his province and reported directly to the central government. This division of authority constituted an important check on the power of the governors and governors-general who were in theory responsible for all provincial affairs and were superior in rank to these other officials.

Most important of all, there was a similar division of authority between the general administrators and the military officers, and also among the military officers themselves. The governor-general had over-all military authority within his area and direct command of a military unit. Yet his provincial commanders-in-chief, who commanded all military units, were also directly responsible to the central government for the military safety of the province. There was a military chain of command between the provincial commander-in-chief and his lower officers, but at the same time military officers were under the authority of the local officials. The government also required some of the officials on the provincial level to give secret reports on each other. The elaborate system of recommendation and reporting made the officials dependent on one another without giving anyone exclusive authority within his area. This division of authority and the resulting inner rivalries of the service did not contribute to the efficiency of the administration. Nor were they meant to do so. They were meant to secure central control over the administrative organization and to prevent the emergence of autonomous or independent local leaders.

The dynasty also possessed a special corps of loyal and reliable servants. Among the officials at the capital there was an inner group of loyal men who spent their whole careers in the central agencies. These high officials staffed the six ministries, the special agencies, and the state council. They made the policy and directed affairs. The men who accepted posts in the provinces—the district magistrates, the prefects, the provincial commissioners, the governors and governors-general—rarely returned to the capital to join this inner group. This was true even of the highest provincial officials, from the prefects up, who had usually started their careers at the capital. In addition to this inner core of officials upon which the dynasty could rely there were special officials to supervise and control the whole administration. The so-called censors were a group of officials who were sent out to investigate complaints or problems and to check all irregularities. Their loyalty was to the state and the dynasty rather than to the person of the emperor himself. Even the emperor was subject to their criticism.

The emperor's closest assistants were the eunuchs. The evils of this institution have been described more often than its political significance. From among the eunuchs, who were employed as guardians of the imperial harem, the emperor often chose political confidants and advisers. Having no families and coming from poor commoner families or from the "mean people," the eunuchs were entirely dependent on the throne. There was no possibility for them to build local power or to establish family cliques. Their low social standing made them natural antagonists of the gentry. The emperor could therefore use them to offset the power of the high officials. Under previous dynasties, though not under the Ch'ing, eunuchs were sometimes appointed to positions of high authority. Some were even in charge of military campaigns. Such positions of power carried no corresponding social prestige but gave ample opportunity for large-scale graft. The vast corruption at the court towards the end of the Ch'ing dynasty was in part due to the eunuchs and their close relationship with the throne.

The ultimate source of imperial power was the army. All Chinese dynasties, whether of Chinese origin or established by foreign invasion, came to power by military conquest; none could last without reliable military forces. The central control of the army was as much a problem for the emperor as was the central control of the whole administration. An ambitious army commander combining political power with his military authority could threaten the safety of the dynasty. Administrative officials who gained independent control of military forces might free themselves from central control and rise in rebellion.

Military officers were controlled by much the same methods as were administrative officials. In the first place, army officers were members of the gentry and were subject to the same discipline as were other members of the gentry. Army leaders were appointed for a limited period of time, and were frequently removed and shifted to other units. Their functions and authority overlapped those of the civil administrators, a further example of the system of checks and balances of the Chinese administration. The administration of the army was concentrated in the Board of Military Affairs; there was no chief of staff. A commanding officer was appointed for each campaign. The main armies were stationed close to the capital for protection and to be available for major campaigns, but garrisons were distributed in important locations over the provinces to deal with local trouble.

To this administrative and military system the Ch'ing rulers added special features in order to bolster their power. They brought in their own army and devised additional administrative controls. The tribal group which set up the Ch'ing dynasty originated in Manchuria near the Korean border. Before they conquered China proper, the Manchus had conquered the whole of Manchuria. There they established a military organization, known as the banners, which was composed of the people living in Manchuria—the Manchus, the Mongols, and the Chinese. It was with the banner forces that the Manchus invaded China. After the conquest of China they kept their Manchurian banner forces intact, using them to garrison the capital and key locations in the provinces. These garrisons of loyal forces were strategically disposed in such a way as to control the more numerous Chinese military units which were scattered in smaller garrisons.

The Manchus, like other conquerors before them, did not possess the trained elite with which to staff a large administration in China. They had to rely on the Chinese to do the governing. They had enough trained men to intermix with the Chinese officials in the top positions of the central government and of the provincial administration, but few of them were of the caliber of the educated Chinese. Manchus were often appointed, however, as governors-general and less frequently, as governors of provinces. The Manchus also placed a Manchu official at the side of the Chinese in the most important agencies of the central government in order to keep a direct check on administration. These additional safeguards were especially useful at the beginning of the dynasty, but once the dynasty was established the Manchus had little to fear for themselves and on the whole could count on the loyalty of the Chinese bureaucracy. What they had to fear was what all previous dynasties had feared—the exhaustion of the "mandate of Heaven." No dynasty could remain indifferent to the popularly-held belief that dynasties rose and fell according to the "will of Heaven." According to this belief the heavenly mandate lasted only as long as the dynasty retained its moral qualification to rule. Inner decay and weakness were taken as signs that the heavenly mandate was exhausted and that the people could exercise their traditional right of rebellion. This popular belief was of real political importance and could become a powerful weapon in the hands of any rebellious leader aspiring to set up a new dynasty. It was not, however, the full explanation of the rise and fall of dynasties; the explanation must be sought in the system of government itself.

Internal Crisis

During the whole course of Chinese imperial history there was an inherent conflict between the dynasty and the bureaucracy, between the state and the scholar-gentry. In its efforts to maintain a strong centralized administration the dynasty came in conflict with the self-interest of the gentry and officials who tended to build up their sources of local power. What occurred in times of crisis was a breakdown of the central control of the throne over the administration and the gentry. The system of divided authority, which served its purpose so long as the central direction was strong, contributed to the disintegration of the administration when central authority was weak.

The opportunity for members of the bureaucracy and scholar-gentry to exploit their dominant position for personal advantage existed at all times. A strong central government could check this trend and retain its controlling position. When the reins were slack, the opportunities for individual profit in this complicated system of administration were exceptional. The tax system was so loosely organized that opportunities for exploitation abounded. The land tax, the main source of government income, was fixed by the central government according to estimates of the amount and the yield of land under cultivation. Such estimates remained unchanged over long periods, even when the land or the yield increased. On the basis of these estimates each provincial administration was given a quota which it had to contribute to the central treasury. Each province in turn distributed this requested amount among the prefectures and districts. The government was thus concerned with the tax quotas to be handed in, rather than with the actual tax collected by the officials. As the quotas remained unchanged, increase of production would bring in a higher tax to the local official without an increase in payment to the central government. Furthermore, the quotas were maximum quotas, and reductions were granted when administrators could make credible claims for bad harvests due to natural catastrophes or other reasons. It was always presumed that at each level of administration some of the funds collected would be used for the payment of staff and other expenses since salaries were known to be inadequate. It was taken for granted that a discrepancy would exist between the taxes collected and those surrendered and that the difference would be used at the various levels of local administration.

Under this system the amount retained by the official was limited only by cursory central supervision and the sense of responsibility of the individual official. The weaker the central government, the less it could control the behavior of its officials and of the gentry. The more graft occurred, the harder it was for those with a higher moral sense to resist the temptation to follow the example of all the others. In such a situation, officials profited by withholding from the quota a growing proportion of the regular tax, and made it a regular practice to impose, under all sorts of pretexts, numerous surtaxes which increased the tax burden many times. A rapid increase in the amount of taxes extorted from the people, concurrent with a shrinking of the income flowing into the government coffers, was a typical sign of government decline. Extortionate taxes caused a growing agitation among the exploited peasant taxpayers, while financial stringencies weakened the government's ability to cope with such unrest.

The decline of financial control by the government had its counterpart in the financial activities of the scholar-gentry. Less government supervision resulted in greater possibilities for the gentry to profit by an expansion of activities and functions. The more corrupt the administration became, the more it neglected its ordinary responsibilities. As a result the gentry extended their activities in public works, arbitration, charity undertakings, and even in the field of protection and defense against local unrest. All this strengthened the position of the gentry leaders and incidentally increased their possibilities of income.

The scholar-gentry enjoyed exemption from the corvée as already indicated. They escaped, therefore, the additional tax burden imposed on the non-gentry landowners in lieu of labor service. The political strength of the scholar-gentry enabled them to manipulate these privileges and not only to escape all the surtaxes imposed by the officials but also to gain a reduction of, or complete exemption from, the regular land tax. The greater the amount of tax evaded by the scholar-gentry, the heavier the taxes imposed on the small landholder. More and more peasant owners were forced to sell their land to pay their debts. This land was bought by the gentry. With the increase of tax-favored land the tax burden on the remaining peasant owners became heavier still. As a result the position of all peasants deteriorated rapidly. The increasing number of tenants had to deal with even more powerful landlords who extorted from each peasant a rent which left him with only the barest minimum of subsistence. Those who still retained their own land faced a crushing tax burden. At last peasant discontent led to outbreaks. Peasants who had left their land organized into small bands which lived by looting. Small-scale and then large-scale "banditry" accompanied the decline of each dynasty. Peasant unrest and peasant rebellion were a typical phenomenon in Chinese history at times of dynastic decline. These uprisings could be used by newly emerging leadership to build up political power and challenge the dynasty.

While the burden of the tax-and-rent-paying small peasantry became less and less bearable, a larger share of tax income was diverted by the officials into their own pockets. Corruption flourished and the state became poor. Dikes and irrigation works fell into disrepair, and man-made catastrophes added to the distress of the large mass of the people.

The breakdown of the administration had its most fatal result in the decline of the central government's military forces. Together with the rest of the administrative machine with which it was so closely linked, the military organization was also affected by corruption and became increasingly useless. Indeed, it was the decline of the army which encouraged the disregard of central authority and the growth of local corruption and autonomy. When uprisings occurred, the army could no longer enforce order. Through their own exactions the troops had themselves become a source of disorder. As a result, a new type of military development occurred—the formation of local corps. Local communities, no longer protected by an efficient and tolerable administration and an effective military force, organized in various forms for their own defense against desperate peasants and bandits. This kind of self-help had to be tolerated, if not approved, by the officials. The local corps, however, sometimes attacked neighboring communities or even the local officials themselves. Small-scale warfare thus ensued in many parts of the country. The orderly members of each community and even the local officials closed their eyes to the ventures of their own military organization into neighboring territory so long as they themselves were protected. A twilight situation of confused local struggle evolved.

The leadership of these local corps fell naturally into the hands of people equipped for it by their personal qualifications as well as by their standing in the local communities. There were two main sources from which this leadership could come, the gentry and the secret societies. The logical people to organize the community defense, whenever the government ceased to function adequately, were the recognized leaders of the local communities, the scholar-gentry. They recruited men for local corps, collected contributions or assessments, administered such funds, and led the corps in fighting. Such gentry leaders thus came to move from their general position of social influence and prestige into the actual control of military forces, of financial resources, and of an administrative staff.

Sometimes, however, commoners succeeded in organizing such forces and gained through them a position of local importance. This was especially true when these commoners were local leaders of secret societies and through them could command a following. In the last centuries of imperial history most rebellions against the government originated with the secret societies.

Secret societies were organizations for mutual protection of their members against the oppression of officials as well as the hazards of social disorder. As no organized political opposition was permitted in the Chinese state such opposition had to be illegal and therefore secret and underground. The secret societies had secret membership and leadership, and their members communicated with each other by secret signs, symbols, and language and were bound together by blood oaths. They had various kinds of religious ceremonies and beliefs which were opposed to the official Confucian ideology.

The secret societies were of two main types. In the north there was more emphasis on religious rites, taken largely from Buddhism and popular beliefs. Most of the members came from the peasantry for whom the secret society was the only possible form of protective organization. In the north this type of religious society was tightly organized and disciplined. The White Lotus Society was one of the best known. In the south the secret societies put more emphasis on economic protection and profit and sometimes engaged in racketeering. In addition to peasants there were large numbers of petty merchants, porters, boat people and even occasional gentry members. The southern societies formed a loose federation of autonomous branches of the Triad society.

These secret societies were centuries old; they survived periods of strong government because of their ability to operate underground. But in times of political unrest both the northern and southern types of secret societies were well suited to provide the leadership for rebellion. They had the organization and the discipline, the leadership and the ideology, the funds and the system of communications, and the nucleus of a military force.

The secret societies competed with the gentry for the leadership of local forces and the control of local administration. With the collapse of the machinery of central government the very thing happened that the dynasty had used every measure to prevent—the rise of local power under local leadership.

Out of a struggle between these local forces there arose larger regional units of power. Stronger forces attracted or conquered weaker ones. The leaders of the larger armies set up regional administrations in the areas controlled by their military forces. These regional administrations replaced the imperial government over an ever increasing territory. Eventually one leader would bring all others under his control and establish a new dynasty. The cycle would thus have run its course.

It was this interplay between the growth of local and regional forces and the central administration that explains the cycles in Chinese dynastic history. Only a strong centralized government could guarantee peace and maintain the great public works. But the establishment of central authority required overwhelming organizational and military strength. Decades and sometimes centuries of decentralization and strife preceded the establishment of a new and strong dynasty. The leaders of rebellious local forces might come from the commoners, but they could succeed only if they established a new effective administrative machine. To do that they needed the support of a substantial number of the scholar-gentry, the only group which had been educated for government. While control of the government changed hands, the system remained the same. There was always a fundamental need for an educated elite which could command the obedience of the peasant masses and knew how to organize and manage them. But this elite, the scholar-gentry, could not function without the central direction provided by the imperial institution. The tradition of a strong bureaucratic system managed by an educated elite under central direction has remained a factor in modern China.

4. IDEOLOGY

Confucianism

The civilization of China was distinguished by one of the great ideological and ethical systems of world history, Confucianism. It was this system which informed the political and social institutions of China with the concepts of a moral order. The main tenets of Confucianism came from the Confucian school of philosophers and scholars, but as the system developed over the centuries it absorbed important contributions from other religious and philosophical sources, both from within China and from without.

The main source of the Chinese ideological and ethical system was the teachings of Confucius himself and of his early disciples. This was the Confucianism of the classical texts and of the early years of the empire. Confucius (551–479 B.C.) lived at the time of China's transformation from a feudal to a bureaucratic society. It was a time of continued internecine warfare in which all moral values of the past tended to break down. The skilled politicians and administrators of the new bureaucratic states were replacing the feudal warriors of the past. These new leaders, Machiavellian in outlook, were bound by no ethical code. In the chaotic battle of all against all, the great minds of the period searched for new values. This was the time of the classical philosophers, of the so-called "Hundred Schools" of thought which competed with each other in the creation of new philosophical systems.

One of these philosophers was Confucius, who gathered around himself a number of disciples to whom he taught his philosophy and who handed it on. The discussions were preserved as the sayings of Confucius in the *Analects*, one of the classical texts of Confucianism. Confucius also exerted his influence through the editing of historical records, collections of poetry, and rules of etiquette, to all of which he gave his own moral interpretation. By the choice of terms in his recording of events Confucius indicated his moral approval or disapproval. By this process, which he called the "rectification of names," Confucius set up moral standards which for his time were both new and revolutionary. They were not, however, immediately accepted. The most popular system of this period was the utilitarian philosophy of Mo Ti (5th–4th century B.C.), who emphasized the practical as opposed to the moral training of the new administrative class. Another school, which flourished in the third century B.C., was that of the Legalists, who stressed the need for laws which should be applied equally to all, thus abolishing the inequalities of the feudal structure. Neither of these schools, however, provided a satisfactory ethical system for the new society. Confucianism, on the other hand, provided a new system of values and established an ethical code for the new ruling group. Although the other schools at first predominated, Confucianism eventually came to be the official philosophy under the imperial bureaucratic regime.

The Confucian moral order begins with the concept of the moral personality. The moral qualities in man had to be developed through a cultivation of the personality. The fundamental assumption of all Confucianists, stemming from the teachers of the classical period, was that the human personality could be cultivated through learning. To this assumption was later added the concept of developing the moral personality through self-discipline, a concept which the Confucianists owed to Buddhism.

The Confucianists stressed two main qualities in the moral personality. One was *Jen*, or humaneness, the attitude displayed towards other human beings; the other was *I*, or sense of moral duty and obligation, the attitude that a man displayed towards himself. The emphasis on these two qualities indicate the humanistic aspect of Confucianism and its high sense of moral duty. These qualities were essential to the moral personality of the individual, and they also linked him to a moral social order. Their cultivation, indeed, was the means by which moral man would be brought into harmony with moral society, the real aim of Confucianism.

The Confucianists put particular stress on the concept of *Li*, the principle of social conduct which permeated the social order and was to be observed by the moral personality. Confucius himself laid down the principles of social behavior by listing a number of rules of etiquette and of ritual. By setting up formal rules for social behavior Confucius aimed at overcoming the disorder of his time and at shaming people into accepting his new standards. These rules were the formal expression of the ethical code which was meant to give inner cohesion to Chinese society, and they became a more important influence than any rules of law.

Confucius sought to base the social order on five human relationships. Three of these were taken from the family, the one institution whose loyalties survived the collapse of feudal relationships. These were the obligations of son to father, of wife to husband, and of younger brother to older brother. Confucius extended this pattern of relationships to those of friend to friend and of subject to ruler. These five basic relationships formed a system in which the pattern of obligation and authority in the family was projected into social and political relationships. A friend was to regard a friend as he would a younger or elder brother, and the ruler was spoken of as the father of his subjects, who were his "little children." It was also essential that the ruler himself should understand and practice the ethical principles which Confucius described because it was the ruler's example which the people would follow. He should possess what in Chinese was called *Te*, usually translated as "virtue," the quality of being in harmony with the ethical system.

The Confucian system placed man and his social and political life in relation to the universe. Man was between heaven and earth, and human life had to be in harmony with the universe. Heaven symbolized the directing force in the universe and all life had to follow "the will of Heaven." To bring humanity into harmony with the will of Heaven was the task of government. The emperor was thought of as an agent, an intermediary between Heaven and mankind. He was "the son of Heaven," not because of any divine descent or origin but because of his position of moral responsibility. He was entrusted with the so-called "mandate of Heaven" to bring about harmonious relations between the human sphere and the universe. His was a trust to be fulfilled through his virtuous actions, and he was responsible to Heaven for the results. The mandate of Heaven was conditional on his performance.

The concept of an ethical justification for government and of an ultimate moral sanction applied to the officials as well as to the emperor. Officials were to be selected from sage and wise men. Confucius describes in extended and detailed form his rules of behavior for this elite, the *chün-tzu*, or superior men, who by their character were set apart from the mass of "low" people whom they ruled through the influence of example. In his sayings he indicated what a *chün-tzu* should or should not do. The elite were to be distinguished from the mass of the people by moral character and understanding. In contrast to other schools which stressed practical and technical training for administrators, Confucius regarded the moral code as the essence of administrative knowledge.

Confucianism in its classical form was concerned with the moral order in human relationships. It did not contain a system of speculative metaphysics. Confucius himself was not intellectually concerned with the life after death, but he was not areligious. Though he did not claim to have knowledge of the world of the spirits, he had a deep reverence for tradition. Religious experience was for Confucius a matter on which he did not care to speak very often, but on those occasions when he did, he referred to it with a reverence which suggested that religious experience was sacred to him. He accepted and approved existing religious practices connected with ancestor worship, and "sacrificed to the [ancestral] spirits as if they were present." Confucius did more than accept existing ritual, he prescribed the rites for what came to be the cult of ancestor worship. The most important of the rites was a communal meal, shared with the dead. Great emphasis was also put on funerals, on the etiquette of mourning and other observances connected with the ancestral cult. Confucius, it is clear, did not question the religious beliefs of his time. He added to their ritual, used them as the religious sanction for his moral order, and left them stronger than he found them.

The disciples of Confucius formulated his teachings into a school of thought. The most outstanding of Confucius' followers, Mencius (372–289 B.C.), expanded the social and economic ideas of Confucius and stressed the well-being of the people as one of the main objectives of government. "The people," he said, "are the most precious and venerable thing. The spirits of the grain come second. The princes are of least importance." Mencius further developed the idea of the responsibility of the mandate of Heaven into the principle that bad rulers lost their right to rule. When the emperor no longer possessed virtue, the mandate of Heaven was withdrawn and the dynasty could be replaced. This interpretation of the emperor's responsibility gave the Confucian school, as developed by Mencius, its broad popular appeal. In the eyes of the peasant population of China the emperor's qualifications for his job could be easily judged from events themselves. Natural catastrophes, civil war, disorder, famine, and suffering, all these were indications of lack of virtue and Heaven's discontent; and celestial signs such as comets or earthquakes were heavenly warnings. When things went wrong and the heavenly mandate had expired, there existed the so-called right of rebellion. In practice, this right of rebellion, which permitted a new leader to destroy the dynasty and supplant it with his own, was a right proved only by success.

Taoism

The main stream of classical Confucianism was enriched by contributions from the two great religions of China, Taoism and Buddhism. These two religions, particularly Buddhism, provided Confucianism with a metaphysical system which put into a universal setting the concept of the moral order in human affairs. The importance of Taoism in Chinese thought was its speculation about the forces in the universe. Much of the Taoist system was antithetical to Confucianism to whose formalistic and overdisciplinary tendencies it provided a necessary contrast.

Taoism had its roots in beliefs in the magic forces of nature. Out of primitive ideas of the existence of spirits in nature which manifested their magic forces in many ways, there was formed the concept of *Tao* as the way in which the universe moved. Derived from observation of nature, of the path of the stars, of the cycle of the seasons, of the succession of growth and decay, *Tao* became an abstract principle expressing the stream of all existence.

From the same observation of nature was also derived the belief in two opposing forces, a negative and a positive one, which through their interplay determined the process of *Tao*. These forces, in Chinese *Yin* and *Yang*, could be night and day, dark and light, weak and strong, female and male, and every similar duality. These opposed and interrelated forces were believed to create through their interaction the course of all life, material and spiritual. The concepts of *Tao*, and of *Yin* and *Yang*, were the basic metaphysical beliefs of all Chinese philosophy, and were also accepted by Confucian scholars. Taoism as a philosophical school developed these general beliefs into a system which aimed at creating an intuitive harmony of man with *Tao*. As a philosophy, Taoism is attributed to Lao-tzu, a half-legendary philosopher of the sixth century B.C., and his disciples of the fourth century B.C. Of the flourishing philosophical schools of that time Taoism was the oldest. Taoist philosophy stressed the human achievement of harmony with nature to be accomplished through "non-action."

The oldest text of Taoism, the *Tao Te Ching*, has been ascribed to Lao-tzu himself. According to legend Lao-tzu retired from the world of affairs and, when crossing a mountain pass into unknown country, related his ideas to the pass official. These were then written down in this Taoist classic.

Tao is seen as the material source, as well as the spiritual content, of all things. It is the change as well as the thing which changes. According to Lao-tzu: "There is a thing chaotic and still complete that existed before heaven and earth, silent and without body. It exists by itself alone and without change. It reaches everywhere and finds no obstacle. It can be taken as the mother of all things. I do not know its name; therefore, I call it *Tao*." To be in haromony with *Tao* was possible not through action, which provokes conflict and reaction, but through a yielding to the forces of nature.

Harmony with nature was also a part of the Confucian concept of state and society. But the individual non-action of the Taoist was contrary to the planning and order of the Confucian social system. Taoism became, therefore, a philosophy in opposition to the existing system. A refuge for those who despaired in times of political chaos, Taoism flourished especially during the first centuries of the Christian era, a period during which it left its mark on Chinese thought. In the third century A.D., the famous Seven Sages of the Bamboo Grove "all revered and exalted the void and 'non-action' and disregarded the rites and law. They drank wine to excess and disdained the affairs of this world." To the true Taoist scholar the "affairs of the world seem like duckweed to a drunken man." This escapism found extreme expression in the attempt to affect the forces of nature through magic and alchemy. Taoists searched for gold, for medical drugs, and for the elixir of life. Such a philosophy could flourish only under the special conditions of the time. As a philosophy Taoism made its permanent contribution through its influence on Confucianism.

Taoism continued to have an influence on Chinese culture, however, as a popular religion. As a religion it provided a system of rewards and punishments both in this world and in the next. There was a pantheon of Taoist divinities and immortals derived from both legendary and historical persons and including guardian spirits, the Kitchen God, the God of the Dipper, and the Jade Emperor, who controlled this world of spirits with the aid of other mythological figures. Taoist priests used their magic to drive out evil spirits with charms and ceremonies. The acceptance by Taoism of a moral code for human action, on which it based a simple concept of reward and punishment for good and bad deeds, was in sharp contrast with the original philosophical tenets of Taoism and indicated a borrowing from Confucian moral philosophy. The original spirit of Taoism survived with the least change in another sphere of Chinese culture, that of art. Here its influence surpassed that of the sober social philosophy of Confucianism. The closeness of Taoism to nature and the search for the inner reality behind appearances found their expression in the works of China's great poets and painters.

Buddhism

Confucian thought was influenced more decisively by the other great religion of China, Buddhism, than it had been by Taoism. Buddhism first came to China from India in the second century B.C., and during the next centuries overshadowed Taoism to such an extent that the Taoists had to borrow heavily from Buddhist mythology and imagery in order to retain any popular appeal. In order to compete the Taoists also adopted the Buddhist methods of church organization. For the Confucianists Buddhism was a much greater challenge than Taoism had ever been. Taoism had been unconcerned with society and therefore did not compete with Confucianism in the field of social organization. Buddhism was the more dangerous not only because it rejected the Confucian concept of society altogether but also because it had its own organization and political influence. In the political struggle between the two the Confucianists eventually triumphed, but in order to gain the upper hand they had to imitate Buddhism by providing for a metaphysical system. In this process they borrowed heavily from Buddhist thought which they molded into their own system.

Buddhism served a religious need of the Chinese people which had not been satisfied by either Confucianism or Taoism. It was the Buddhist belief that all existence is suffering, that the continuation of existence (and therefore of suffering) arises from desires and their fulfillment, and that salvation lies in the cessation of personal existence which can be attained only through freedom from desire. According to the Buddhists no being was limited to a single existence closed by death; all beings were continually reincarnated. In order to escape suffering it was necessary to avoid reincarnation. It was believed that each being was formed of many parts, or *dharmas*. These dharmas were the components of all phenomena from the physical to the spiritual. A being made up of these elements could therefore be dissolved by breaking the chain of causality that held it together. Ultimate salvation thus lay in the elimination of the self, which was to be gained by an understanding of the causality of things, a condition known as Enlightenment, or the entering into Nirvana, a state which could not be described. Such were the teachings of Gautama Buddha who lived during the sixth century B.C. Buddhism almost disappeared in India, the land of its origin, but it spread to most of the countries of the Far East. Here it took two main forms, the Hinayana and the Mahayana.

The Hinayana (literally "small vehicle") school, which became established in Southeast Asia, was closer to the original Buddhist principle that one should lead a life of abstention and renunciation to break the chain of causation that led from earthly desires to the miseries of existence. In Mahayana ("big vehicle") Buddhism, which spread through Central Asia, China, Korea, and Japan, a greater emphasis was placed on more direct ways to salvation. Good works, the reciting of holy scriptures, and faith itself were believed to lead directly to salvation. Each being was believed to be able to reach the state of Buddhahood through many reincarnations.

The changes in Mahayana Buddhism were largely the result of Chinese influence. The principle of salvation by faith and charity, dominant in the Mahayana Buddhism of China, was developed through a number of Chinese Buddhist schools of thought. The belief in salvation and the possibility of abridging the sufferings of the beings in transmigration, led to the practice of giving masses for the dead, a practice which fitted well into the Confucian tradition of ancestor worship. Amida (or Amitofu) became a popular Buddha figure who would help those who appealed to him in faith or by acts of charity. The idea of Bodhisattvas, beings who had reached the final stage of perfection but remained in the world out of mercy to help others, spread for the same reason. The figure of Kuan Yin, a goddess of mercy to whom the faithful turned for help, was one such Bodhisattva. A vivid scene of hells and purgatories was added to the stages of existence, and eventual salvation from the suffering of all existence was found in a "western paradise."

The great spread of Buddhism in China came in the third century B.C., when the country was divided, the north being controlled by dynasties of invaders. Most of the trained administrators and scholars moved south with the Chinese political leaders. With the shortage of men of learning in the north, Buddhist scholars began to play a major part in politics. But the Confucian scholars in the south also became students of Buddhism. As a strong and proud elite they were particularly attracted by the Buddhist concern with the status and the intellectual and spiritual life of the individual. This aspect of Buddhism fortified them in their will to resist control by a powerful government. On the popular level, the political confusion and misery of the times made Buddhism, with its emphasis on the misery of existence, particularly attractive. By the fifth and sixth centuries A.D., Buddhism had spread throughout the length and breadth of China, and its temples and monasteries covered the landscape. When the country was reunited by Chinese dynasties, however, Confucianism reasserted itself and Buddhism went through periods of heavy political persecution. It ceased to be a part of the official ideology of the scholar officialdom but retained political influence on another level by providing an ideological basis for the secret societies. The secret societies made use of the idea of brotherhood, practiced by the Buddhist monks, and the absence of social distinctions, both of which were part of Buddhist belief. Through the secret societies Buddhism continued to be a political force but more important still was its role as the leading popular religion in China.

Neo-Confucianism

The Confucianism which reasserted itself as the dominant official cult in the eleventh century was much broader than the classical humanist doctrines of Confucius and Mencius. It has become known as neo-Confucianism. Confucianism had been greatly influenced by its struggle with Taoism and Buddhism. Under the influence of this struggle Confucianism developed a system of metaphysics which provided a new sanction for the old moral order. The Confucianists naturally attacked the Buddhists for their asocial attitudes and especially for their neglect of the family. The main battle however was in the realm of intellectual speculation. The Buddhist doctrine of the Void denied the reality of the phenomenal world, a position which was anathema to the Confucianists, who opposed the mystical Void with their concept of Reason. Reason was identical with what was called the Great Ultimate, which worked through the principles of *Yin* and *Yang*, the positive and negative forces of the Great Ultimate. The agency through which Reason or the Great Ultimate operates is the Vital Force which brings about, through the interaction of *Yin* and *Yang*, the world of reality. To the neo-Confucianists Reason and the phenomenal world—the One and the Many—were the same. The concept of the One and the Many as being indistinguishable is Buddhist, but the Confucianists added to it Reason, thus expanding the concept of a moral order in human affairs into the concept of a moral universe. It was the task of the Confucianist to understand this concept of Reason. To this task he had to bring intellectual discipline, "sincerity," and "seriousness," qualities which were taken from the examples of Buddhist meditation and learning.

Neo-Confucianism became the orthodoxy of imperial China. A state cult was developed for the state civil service and the scholar-gentry. There was a Confucian temple in every center of imperial administration. Here the officials carried out the rituals of worship and sacrifice at fixed times. The objects of worship included Confucius himself and many other historical figures and outstanding officials who had been selected posthumously for this high honor. At first images were placed in the Confucian temples, but these were destroyed in a reform movement in the sixteenth century, after which time only tablets inscribed with names and titles were permitted as objects of reverence and worship. The emperor himself carried on the state cult by offering sacrifices on the Altar of Heaven.

The emperor, the court, the officials, and the scholar-gentry were well aware of the moral duty imposed upon them by the ethical principles of Confucianism. Imperial edicts and writings continually enlarged upon the theme of moral responsibility. It was also in the minds of the scholar-gentry for whom "the rise and fall of the state was each man's responsibility" and whose moral obligation was to be "the first to accept the worries of the world and the last to enjoy its pleasures." Confucianism was the code of honor and morals for the court, the scholar-gentry, and bureaucracy.

The cult of Confucianism was not limited to the court, the officials, and the scholar-gentry. It had to be accepted by the whole population. It was the special task of the local officials and the scholar-gentry to inculcate upon the people, through example and teaching, the tenets of Confucianism. Respect for learning and for the scholar steeped in the classics became a characteristic of Chinese culture. On these attitudes depended the authority of the scholar-gentry over the people they managed.

The emperor used Confucianism to strengthen his control over the gentry and through them over the population as a whole. The more authoritarian aspects of Confucianism were stressed in the imperial edicts and rescripts and in the examinations. There was a tendency to place more emphasis on orthodoxy than on thought. This was especially true under the last dynasty, the Ch'ing. The Manchu conqueror had helped more to consolidate and entrench Confucian orthodoxy than to change it, for the Manchus brought with them no views of the world or of society that could challenge those of the Chinese. In fact the Manchus were more fearful of intellectual ferment and ideological change than were most of the Confucianists themselves. During the last centuries of the Ch'ing dynasty style and form were given undue importance in order to compensate for the strictness and inflexibility of the official doctrine. Examination candidates spent their time in the study of the correct form of the "eight-legged essay" to the disadvantage of a real study of Confucian principles.

In spite of orthodoxy there was always diversity to be found in the broad stream of Confucian thought. There was an important school of Confucian scholarship under the Ch'ing dynasty which rebelled against neo-Confucian doctrines. This school occupied itself with a re-examination of the classics with a view to applying their social and political teachings to the events of the time. The scholars of this school leaned towards an empirical approach. They used new methods of critical investigation, doubting the neo-Confucian interpretation of the classics and demanding historical and objective evidence. This school did not depart from the Confucian frame of reference, and its vitality indicated that the Confucian movement still retained a regenerative power to grow and change.

The neo-Confucianists, by linking the social and political order to the moral order of the universe, created a sort of closed intellectual system. Social and political reality, in this system, were so intimately bound up with the metaphysical order that the collapse of any part of this system was likely to lead to the collapse of the whole. The Confucian scholar studied phenomena as part of the moral order rather than for their own sake. The approach of modern science was foreign to him. Orthodox Confucianism resisted the modern West as long as possible because it was a closed system which could not easily compromise. With the triumph of the West over the economic and social order of Confucian China, imperial Confucianism itself collapsed and for a time all Confucian beliefs were discredited. It is still too early to know whether this great intellectual and moral tradition will ever again display its regenerative power.

CHAPTER II

The Chinese Dependencies—Inner Asia and Korea

1. CHINA AND HER DEPENDENCIES

IMPERIAL China was the center of the Far Eastern world. The sheer size of the country, the mass of her people, and the wealth of her agricultural production gave China a focal position among other Far Eastern countries. Culturally, institutionally, economically, and militarily, she dominated and influenced her neighbors.

Most of these countries were Chinese dependencies and their rulers vassals of the Chinese emperor. Their position as kings or khans, or whatever the title they held, had to be confirmed by the emperor, who bestowed upon them the seal of office which added to their prestige and gave them a justification for their rule. They were also given the Chinese calendar with its changing intercalary modifications as arranged by the Chinese astronomers.

The official relationship between the imperial court and the Inner Asian dependencies was handled by a special Chinese government agency, which under the Ch'ing dynasty was the *Li-fan-yüan*, or Court of Dependency Affairs. The Board of Rites dealt with all other dependency affairs. The importance of this relationship was stressed in complicated forms of etiquette. For instance, on documents exchanged between emperor and vassal, the emperor's name was always placed higher to indicate his superior position. In the family terms used in the Confucian political system, this relationship was compared to that of older and younger brothers.

In practical terms vassalage implied protection and support between

53

emperor and vassals. The emperor was to protect his vassal against outside attacks or internal uprisings, while the vassal was to provide the emperor with auxiliary forces when needed. Such military cooperation was, however, greatly modified and limited by distance and political conditions; and it remained more a principle of policy, occasionally exploited, than a rule which was regularly applied.

The vassal was also obligated to pay tribute to the emperor. Most of the dependencies sent yearly tribute missions to the Chinese capital bringing a fixed amount of products. Such tribute could vary from a nominal quantity of gifts to a real financial burden. In exchange for the tribute the mission received presents from the emperor to take home to their ruler. The value of the presents could vary according to the political importance of the respective vassal. The exchange of tribute and presents could mean anything from taxation of the vassal to subvention by the emperor; it could also be a kind of trade relationship between China and the dependent country. As the tribute bearers frequently carried along other goods besides those given to the emperor in tribute and exchanged them for goods to take home, the tribute missions were an opportunity for trade relations and profit. While at the capital the members of the missions were quartered in official buildings and were the guests of the emperor. Because the tribute missions were a privileged form of trade, exploited by the officials, the size of the missions and the time of their stay often had to be regulated by the court so that they would not become an excessive burden to the treasury. These tribute missions were both a mark of political dependency and a form of economic contact between the courts and officials of the ruling and the dependent country.

China's neighboring peoples had different modes of life; some had agricultural systems like that of China, some were nomads, some had mixed economies of nomadism and agriculture. The Koreans in the northeast and the Annamese and other groups in the south were agricultural people. Their mode of life was very similar to that of the Chinese, but their different ethnic identities were preserved because of their physical separation from China. They were not far enough from the Chinese empire to escape its political impact, and yet they were geographically too detached to be permanently incorporated into China's administration.

Their ideology and their social and political institutions followed in many ways the Chinese pattern. From China came Confucianism with its ancestor worship. As in China, Buddhism played a part not only in the religion but also in the political development of these agricultural countries. More significant still was the strong effect of the Chinese example on social and political institutions. The economy, like that of China, was managed by an upper stratum of appointed officials. These officials were educated in the Confucian classics and most of them acquired their social and political position through government examinations, modelled after the Chinese system. In these countries admission to the examinations was much more limited than in China and the ruling class tended to be self-perpetuating. The political structure, however, like that of China, was essentially bureaucratic.

The steppe people of Central Asia and the nomads of the northeastern forests had their own special types of economy, both based on animal husbandry. The possession of large numbers of horses gave them a mobility which made them dangerous to their settled agricultural neighbors.

The nomad economy and the Chinese economy were complementary. The nomads, especially such groups as the Mongols, who had no agriculture at all, depended on the Chinese for such vital commodities as grain and tea and products of handicraft, such as tools and vessels or luxury items of clothing and comfort. In exchange, they provided horses or other animals, and wool and leather for Chinese use. But between these contrasting societies there was always danger of conflict. The nomad raiders could sometimes seize by force from the settled Chinese all the goods and luxuries they needed; or the Chinese might impose their military control over the frontier nomads. The nomad tribes were linked to China by a system of vassalage, as were Annam and Korea, but unlike these two countries the nomads were a constant military threat to China. Every Chinese government was well aware of this nomad threat against which the Great Wall was not always a successful barrier. The nomads could be held in check only if Chinese authority extended beyond the wall. At times when the Chinese government was strong, Chinese commissioners with military garrisons were established in nomad territory. By a policy of divide and rule the Chinese tried to control nomad rulers and keep them from combining to attack Chinese territory by setting them against each other. But these and other measures could be successfully maintained only by a strong imperial government. In periods when the Chinese government was in decline, a weak China attracted nomad raids and invited invasion and conquest. Dynasties of nomad origin were actually established in China during various periods of her history.

The invasions and conquests of China did not, however, change the fundamental relationship between agricultural China and the peoples of the steppe. Even under foreign domination China was the political center of gravity because the nomad conquerors set up their government in China. From their new base in China they controlled the steppe. Mongolia could be ruled from China, but China could not be ruled from Mongolia. When the nomad rulers moved into China they changed not only the location but also the character of their government. Nomad conquests of China were more than military affairs. Each was a process of development and transformation in which the nomad acquired the ability and the organization to handle a Chinese bureaucratic administration. With each successive stage of his military conquest the invader grew in his understanding of Chinese administration. China could not be governed like a nomad tribe. The collection of taxes, the control and management of labor, the direction of public works, and all the manifold activities of the Chinese government could not be carried on without the bureaucracy. If the nomad was to accomplish more than a routine raid, if he was to stay, tax, and exploit the land, he had to accept the Chinese type of administrative organization. Conquest could not be accomplished in a quick campaign. The Mongol and Tungus cavalry forces

that broke through the Great Wall could not rule China simply by destroying the dynasty and its military forces. The advice given one of the earlier
conquerors was: "You can conquer China on horseback, but you have to
dismount to rule."

Nomad conquests of China therefore occurred by successive stages. The
would-be conqueror first took border areas in which he learned to organize
the Chinese type of administration. When he later moved into China proper
he knew how to govern it. While preserving much of his ethnic identity even
after the conquest, the conqueror adopted Chinese political institutions both
before and during the conquest itself. The conquest dynasty became as
bureaucratic and as Confucian as a dynasty of Chinese origin. Whichever
type of dynasty ruled, Chinese or "barbarian," the political relationship
between the Chinese imperial government and its dependent neighbors
changed but little. The political center of the Chinese empire always remained in China.

Chinese control over the Far Eastern world varied in extent as well as in
degree. Close neighbors, such as Korea and Annam (the latter to be discussed under Southeast Asia), were under Chinese control during a considerable part of their history. Chinese dominance over Chinese Turkestan and
the caravan routes of Central Asia dates back to the Han dynasty and was
always re-established after periodic lapses. Mongolia and Tibet, the areas
from which the Chinese government was threatened during various periods
of history, eventually came under Chinese colonial control. Manchuria,
whose southern part was Chinese in population and type of economy, was
more closely linked to China proper than any of the other areas.

Chinese influence and control were at times extended beyond the circle
of the most immediate dependencies. The countries of Southeast Asia—
Burma, Thailand, Laos, and Cambodia—were Chinese tributaries at one
time or another. Chinese military influence went beyond Tibet into small
countries like Nepal and Sikkim. Even some of the island states of East Asia,
like Sumatra and Sulu, found it politically advantageous to establish with
the Chinese imperial court a tributary relationship which gave them commercial profits, political prestige, and sometimes a semblance of protection.

2. Mongolia

Steppe Nomads

Among the peoples who had the most direct and fateful
relations with China, the first in importance were the nomad groups of
Central Asia. The economy of the steppe nomads was based on animal husbandry. The steppe country has a dry climate, and its limited rainfall and
water resources, while not sufficient for agriculture, provide enough plant
growth for animal husbandry. Steppe nomadism was an economy as specialized as agriculture, not a stage of economic growth preceding agriculture.

Steppe nomadism existed in many countries along the inner Asiatic border of China. In most of them nomadism existed side by side with agriculture in mutual dependence. The Tibetans, the Uighurs in Chinese Turkestan, the Tungus in Manchuria, practiced both nomadism and agriculture. But Mongolia was the nomad country par excellence; the Mongols never practiced agriculture even where conditions would have permitted them to do so. The Mongols, therefore, were peculiarly dependent on the Chinese for the products of agriculture.

The Mongols

The Great Wall formed the southeastern border of Mongol territory and divided it from the agricultural areas of northwest China. The Mongol territory included the Hsingan Range in the east, the upper reaches of the Shilka and the Selenga rivers, and the Saan Mountain Range in the north. The Altai Mountains formed the western and southwestern borders. Today about 4,000,000 Mongols live within this territory.

The Mongols are divided ethnically into two broad groups, the eastern and western Mongols. There are tribal subdivisions within each of these large groups. A third group, the Buriat Mongols, to the east of Lake Baikal, differ from the other Mongols in their ethnic composition, religion, and culture. The geographical separation of different Mongol groups has had an important influence on their political history. The Buriat Mongols came under Russian control when Russia expanded across Siberia and the Mongols in Turkestan were included under the Chinese administration of that area. Mongolia proper, the steppe land between the Altai Mountains and the Great Wall, is divided physically by the Gobi Desert into what has become known as Inner Mongolia, the strip of Mongol territory bordering China, and Outer Mongolia, which lies beyond the Gobi Desert. While Outer and Inner Mongolia were culturally very similar, the geographical division resulted in different political fates for the Mongols on either side of the Gobi Desert. Inner Mongolia was more directly under Chinese control than Outer Mongolia which eventually fell under Russian influence.

The economy of the Mongols is based on animal husbandry, the main animals being horses, camels, and sheep. Cattle are also raised in a few areas of richer pasture land, especially in the province of Jehol. Sheep provide meat, milk, skins, and wool and are the most important domestic animals. Horses and camels furnish transportation in the steppes and deserts. Camel's hair is used in clothing and is combined with wool to make felt for the yurts, the Mongol dwellings. Mare's milk is an important part of the Mongol diet. Fermented, it is used to make arakhi, a mild alcoholic beverage, which is also distilled into more potent forms. The horse is essential to the Mongol's life. To herd his animals, to hunt, to fight, to go anywhere from the longest to the shortest distance, the Mongol rides on horseback. The horse gave the Mongols the mobility necessary for a pastoral nomad life and also made possible the military cavalry units organized by these horsemen of the steppe. Wealth and power in Mongol society were estimated by the size of the animal herds, especially by the number of horses, which was much greater than economic or military use required.

Nomadism is by no means as mobile an economy as is sometimes believed. Each nomad group usually retained its pasturelands for a long period of time and moved between them at regular intervals. There were the short periodic movements between summer and winter pastures, but from time to time overgrazed pastureland had to be abandoned for several years. The defense of pasture lands against the encroachment of other groups and the defense of the herds themselves made a military type of organization necessary. Mongols were organized into clans, tribes, and confederations of tribes. In all these units leadership was in the hands of an hereditary aristocracy. This aristocracy ruled a larger group of free commoners, below whom there was a smaller group of so-called slaves, most of whom had been captured in raids. The leaders of the aristocratic nomad families had only a limited control over their followers. Discontented followers could leave one group and attach themselves to another, stronger unit. The strength of each group, therefore, depended on the leader's military ability and his success in providing for the well-being of the group. Secession from nomad groups involved not only a loss in manpower but also in animals; conversely, groups could grow through the attachment of new followers with their animals.

Nomad political structure was therefore fluid. An outstanding leader could rapidly accumulate power by building up his own group and then attracting other groups into his organization. Such sudden power concentrations within the lifetime of one leader were naturally a major threat not only to other weaker nomad tribes but also to neighboring sedentary people. The sudden outbursts of Mongol power at the time of Genghis Khan in the early thirteenth century A.D. can be explained only through the fluidity of the Mongol political organization. Genghis Khan rose during his lifetime from a young aristocratic leader, hunted by his enemies and supported only by a few loyal family followers, to the position of Great Khan. He became the overlord of all steppe people in Inner Asia and the founder of empires which his sons and grandsons extended from China throughout Asia to European Russia. This sudden accumulation of power had its counterpart in rapid disintegration and collapse, which occurred a little more than a century later, though parts of the Mongol power in Central Asia and Russia lingered on for centuries.

Since the Mongols needed the products of Chinese agriculture, the temptation was great for them to take what they wanted by force. Whether they were able to do so or not depended on the respective strength of the Mongols and the Chinese. In some periods China controlled the Mongolian steppes, and in others Mongol nomads invaded China. But neither side could absorb the other in the sense of converting it to its own way of life. Genghis Khan's grandson, Kublai, who established the Yüan dynasty in China, used the Chinese system of administration at his court in Peking. The Chinese commanders of cavalry armies that followed the defeated Mongols into the steppe could at best only exact tribute and maintain general control.

Lamaism

Mongol society was deeply affected by Lamaism which penetrated the Mongol world from Tibet and became firmly rooted during the sixteenth century. Lamaism as it had developed in Tibet was a form of Mahayana Buddhism, which laid great stress on monastic life. It held to a belief in saints or "living Buddhas," beings who had reached the stage of fulfillment and salvation but through reincarnation continued their earthly existence in order to bring about the salvation of others. These living Buddhas became founders and heads of lamaseries. The monasteries became powerful institutions which controlled territory and owned large herds. Each lamasery was headed by a "living Buddha," but actual administration was in the hands of an elected body of lama leaders. Because of their religious prestige, the lamaseries gained a dominant position among the surrounding tribal groups and became not only religious but also economic and political centers. Through the Lama Church commoners could become monks, or even "living Buddhas," and thus participate in the management not only of the religious but also of the secular affairs of the Mongols. While the heads of the tribes and clans were hereditary aristocrats, the heads of the lamaseries were commoners and their positions non-hereditary. Lamaism thus provided a group of celibate administrators who controlled the religious, political, and economic affairs of the territories of the lamaseries. The lamas, as a group, became even more powerful than the aristocracy. As the lamaseries offered an opportunity for commoners to rise to power and position, a large number of Mongols—estimates have been as large as almost half the male population—entered the monasteries as lamas. Each family supported one or more of its members in the monasteries, thus contributing to the upkeep of the lamaseries. Mongol society was deeply affected. It has been held that this trend led to a reduction in the population and modified the aggressive character of steppe nomadism.

Mongolia under the Ch'ing

The Manchus had established their control over the Mongols even before they began the conquest of China proper. They did this in the early seventeenth century by conquering some of the Mongol tribes and by forming political alliances with others. When they had established their dynasty in Peking, the Manchus followed the traditional Chinese methods of controlling the Mongols, particularly the policy of divide and rule. In order to prevent the concentration of power under great khans the Manchu dynasty grouped tribes together into leagues under Mongol leaders whom they nominated and controlled. The Manchus also supported the Lama Church as a stabilizing factor. They gave the church financial support and had a hand in the selection of the reincarnation of the "living Buddhas."

Tribute was an additional method of control. Most important was the occasional demand for a large tribute to be paid in horses, a demand which was designed to weaken the military strength of certain Mongol tribes. Because tribute was also a profitable exchange, carried on under the guise of political submission, it was attractive to the Mongols and therefore a particularly effective device for Chinese political control. These economic bonds were strengthened further by the marriage of Chinese princesses to nomad chieftains. The practice of sending Chinese princesses to nomad chieftains was of long standing. Indeed, Chinese poetry often laments the fate of these girls who, brought up in luxury, had to live with the primitive nomads and had to share the tent or yurt of the "smelly barbarian." But the political influence which these princesses and their attendants exerted was often considerable. Such marriage alliances with the Mongols were very frequent during the Manchu dynasty.

Under the Ch'ing dynasty, Outer and Inner Mongolia were firmly controlled. Manchu emissaries or *ambans* resided in Outer Mongolia. They commanded the banner garrisons which guaranteed Ch'ing control until the collapse of the Manchu dynasty and the Russian impact altered the power situation in Inner Asia.

3. Manchuria

Peoples of Manchuria

Manchuria is located to the north of China proper between Korea, the Russian Far East, and Mongolia. In Chinese the area was called the "Three Eastern Provinces." The name Manchuria was used only in international parlance after the area had become an object of international conflict. Manchuria was not a geographic, economic, or ethnic unit. It was an area in which there were many differing climatic and topographic conditions, ethnic groups, and economies.

The southern part of Manchuria had been a zone of Chinese agriculture and administration since prehistoric times. This Chinese "pale" of the lower Liao River Valley and the Liaotung Peninsula was linked with China proper only by a narrow agricultural corridor which lay between the sea and the mountains. The narrowest point of this corridor at Shanhaikuan was the place at which the Great Wall came down to the sea, leaving the Chinese in Manchuria outside its protection. Being cut off in this way from China proper, Chinese Manchuria was often overrun by invaders. As a result its population has been mingled with peoples of Tungus, Mongol, and Korean stock.

To the east and northwest of the Chinese part of Manchuria, there lived people of Tungus stock. Their territory extended to the Yalu River and across the Amur and its tributary, the Ussuri. The Tungus were forest nomads who lived largely by hunting and fishing and the raising of pigs, their main domesticated animals in addition to horses. They also had a scattered, extensive agriculture. Though not as numerous as the Mongols, the Tungus tribes also were dangerous as raiders and invaders of the Chinese territory in Manchuria and in China proper. Twice in history, a Tungus group succeeded not only in invading China but also in setting up a conquest dynasty there. The second of these dynasties was that set up in 1644 by the Manchus, a small Tungus group that came from the Long White Mountains at the border of Korea. Their leader called his followers Manchus, from which the international name, Manchuria, was later derived.

In the western and northwestern parts of Manchuria, across the Hsingan Range, there was steppe land peopled by Mongols. These Mongols, estimated to number about 2,000,000, were separated from the Mongols of Outer and Inner Mongolia only by political boundaries. Manchuria was never a "Manchu" country but a Chinese frontier area in which the Manchus, a small Tungus group, were one of the tribal groups that surrounded the Chinese pale.

Political Organization

In their relations with China the Tungus, like the Mongols, had a history of alternate conquest and control. Compared to the Mongols, the Tungus were few in numbers and their forest territory did not permit the same freedom of movement as did the steppe. It was therefore not so easy for the Tungus as for the Mongols to build up a large enough force for the conquest of China. On the other hand, Manchuria offered the invader a special advantage. The Chinese pale of Manchuria, isolated from the rest of China, was easier for a conqueror to take and hold than were other frontier areas within the perimeter of the defense line of the Great Wall. In Manchuria the conqueror could develop a Chinese type of administrative organization that would serve as a starting point for the administration of conquered territory within China proper.

It was in this way that the Manchus developed their political organization at the end of the sixteenth and the beginning of the seventeenth centuries. From their base in the Long White Mountains they increased their strength by raids into Chinese territory and the subjugation of neighboring Tungus clans. The more they penetrated into Manchurian Chinese territory, the more they learned of the administrative tradition from the Chinese officers and officials whom they captured or persuaded to join them. Before their conquest of China they set up in Mukden a central government with the six ministries of the Chinese system, staffed by Chinese and Manchu officials. They also adopted Confucian ideology.

The Manchus established, as part of their administration, a unique military and civil organization known as the banners which encompassed all the people of Manchuria. At first there were four of these banners; later the number was increased to eight. Each banner had its own flag from the color of which it took its name.

The banners represented a transformation of the previous clan-tribal structure of the Manchus into regular administrative units. People were assigned to each unit, and the officers had both military command and administrative authority over them. In setting up this organization the Manchus copied the administrative system of the military garrison areas set up by the Chinese Ming dynasty in Manchuria and other frontier areas. The Chinese themselves provided the administrative bridge over which the Manchus could move into the Chinese bureaucratic system.

The Manchu rulers also had to cope with the problem of establishing their authority within the ruling clan itself. The ruler himself secured direct control over three banners while the other five were distributed among other branches of the ruling clan. But the power of the families in charge of the banners was limited. The banners were assigned land, from which they derived their income. They had to provision themselves for the military campaigns and other services to the government. The land was assigned not in large blocks but in scattered units, a device which prevented the banners and their leaders from gaining independent local territorial power. In battle, units from different banners were combined into armies under commanders appointed for the occasion. In this way the ruler's authority was safely established over an integrated military bureaucracy.

The Manchus also used the banners to integrate the three population groups of Manchuria: the Chinese, the Mongols, and the Manchus. By the time the Manchus had conquered the whole of Manchuria, they had already become a minority, with the Chinese and the Mongols making up the larger part of the Manchurian population. The Manchus made use of these other peoples in their fighting force, including in each banner a Chinese and a Mongol section. But they insured their own control by seeing to it that the Manchu units outnumbered those in either the Chinese or Mongol sections, so that the largest part of the fighting force was Manchu. The total Manchu banner force that moved into China in 1644 has been estimated at about 169,000 men, consisting of about 83,490 Manchus, 49,500 Chinese, and 36,000 Mongols.

After the conquest of China, units of the banners were stationed in strategic places all over the country. But the home of the bannermen remained in Manchuria where they retained their land and their organization. In time a regular provincial, prefectural, and district administration spread over the agricultural regions of Manchuria and incorporated the banners. Manchuria was divided into three provinces, Shengking (later Fengtien), Kirin, and Heilungkiang. Each province was, however, under a Manchu general rather than under a governor, as were the provinces of China proper.

After the establishment of their dynasty in China, the Manchus tried to preserve Manchuria as a base of political power and strength and possibly as an area to which to withdraw if need be. A special administrative organization was maintained there. At Mukden the Manchus retained a separate government, with its six boards, even after they had established their central government at Peking. During the Manchu dynasty the Chinese population of Manchuria increased and agriculture expanded; but the Manchus regarded Manchuria as their special reserve and prohibited Chinese immigration in order not to be completely outnumbered in their homeland.

This policy was given up only at the very end of the dynasty when outside threats from Russia and Japan endangered not only Manchu but also Chinese control. With the development of railroads, the floodgates were opened for a growing Chinese immigration.

4. TIBET

Land and People

Tibet, like Mongolia and Manchuria, was a Chinese dependency. A country of high plateaus and mountains, Tibet stretches from the Pamir highlands in the west, to the rugged mountain border of the Chinese province of Szechwan in the east, and from the high ranges of the Himalaya in the south to the Kunlun, Altyn Tagh, and Nanshan ranges in the north. It covers an area of about 800,000 square miles. Large parts of this area are high mountain ranges, averaging over 17,000 feet in height and including the highest peaks on earth, such as Mt. Everest. The Tibetan plateaus have an average altitude of about 14,000 feet.

The geographical features of Tibet insured a natural isolation. However, from ancient times there have been trade routes between Tibet and China and between Tibet and India. The main routes from China led from Lanchou via Sining over the Kunlun and Tangla mountain ranges to Lhasa, and from Tatsienlu via Chamdo to Lhasa. From India the most important route led from Darjeeling through the border state of Sikkim to Chumbi and Lhasa. An alternate route led from Katmandu in Nepal to Shigatse.

The total population of Tibet has been estimated at about 2,000,000 people. The main bulk of the population is settled along the upper course of the Brahmaputra or Tsangpo River and its upper tributaries. The capital is the temple city of Lhasa, which has a population of about 60,000 people, almost half of whom are lamas. This part of Tibet is mainly agricultural. On the northern plateaus live Tibetan nomads and Mongol nomads are found in the Tsaidam area to the west of Kokonor. The Chinese-Tibetan border areas, known as Outer Tibet, are populated by both agricultural and nomad people. This is the area which the Chinese made into the provinces of Chinghai and Sikang in 1928. Sikang was incorporated into Szechwan province in 1955.

Tibet has both sedentary agriculture and steppe nomadism. The main crop is barley. The Tibetan nomad relies on the yak, a long-haired domesticated ox, native to the high Tibetan plateaus. Horses, camels, and—in some areas—sheep complete the nomad economy. The peasants live in fixed dwellings not dissimilar to those of China. They stand out in sharp contrast to the magnificent temples of Lhasa and the great monasteries. The Potala at Lhasa, the seat of the Dalai Lama, is one of the most famous temple buildings in Asia. The Tibetan nomad lives in tents made of wool which have given to the high plateaus the name of "the country of the black tents."

The majority of the Tibetans lived in the agricultural area where the center of political power was located. But the Tibetan nomads, like other steppe people, felt that their life was freer and more dignified and they looked down upon the sedentary life of the Tibetan peasant. The fact that Tibet had both agriculture and nomadism made it less dependent on China than was Mongolia.

Lamaism and the State

The Tibetan government was based on the agricultural areas from which it drew most of its taxes, but it could also depend on the military strength of the steppe nomads. Like the Mongols, the Tibetans had a group of hereditary aristocratic families set apart from the common people whom they ruled. But this system of aristocratic rule was submerged, even more than in Mongolia, by the bureaucratic influence of the Lama Church which shaped and controlled the Tibetan state.

Lamaism was established in Tibet in the twelfth century. In the sixteenth century it underwent a reform and the older so-called Red Sect was replaced by the Yellow Sect, which became the dominant, ruling church. Lamaism deeply affected the social and political structure of Tibet. It ended the monopoly of government by the aristocracy and provided Tibet with a new governing group, the lamas. The lamas were mostly of common origin, and even most of the "living Buddhas" were selected from commoner families. These monks filled the administrative positions of central and local government in the Tibetan state. A structure of central and local bureaucratic agencies was set up under the Dalai Lama as political ruler and head of the central Tibetan government. Next to the Dalai Lama were three chief counsellors of state, the heads of the three main monasteries in Lhasa. They were assisted by a Grand Council which handled the administrative orders of the Dalai Lama in consultation with the chief counsellors. In addition there was an assembly of all lay and ecclesiastical officials and of the abbots of the three leading monasteries in Lhasa which decided all the most important matters in the domestic and foreign affairs of Tibet. Tibet was also divided into local administrative units which were responsible to these central agencies at Lhasa.

In this administrative organization set up by the Lama Church, the aristocracy retained an important position. In central Tibet, members of aristocratic families were appointed to administrative offices in the bureaucracy. Although they lost their position as territorial rulers, their families were established permanently in the bureaucracy, in contrast to the monk officials of commoner origin who had to qualify individually for appointment. The aristocratic families had an income from tax-free land which was regarded as payment for their services. The aristocracy thus was integrated into the administration of central Tibet. In the northeastern border areas, however, aristocratic families often retained their hereditary positions of government over their own territory under the control of Lhasa. The bureaucratic government which had been established by the Lama Church went further in replacing aristocratic rule in Central Tibet than in the outlying territories. But the Lama Church dominated the scene, controlling not only the political administration but also most of the trade inside Tibet and with neighboring countries.

The Lama Church created a bureaucratic administration in Tibet and, to a lesser degree, in Mongolia—the main border countries of imperial China. Such an organizational development was of major interest to any Chinese dynasty which wanted to control these countries and restrict aggressive aristocratic leadership. Lamaism was therefore promoted and supported by the court at Peking. The Manchu dynasty, especially, gave assistance to the Lama Church and attempted to exert political control in Tibet through its influence over the lamaseries and the reincarnations. At times the representatives of the Chinese emperor interfered in the power conflicts within the church, sometimes managing the final selection of a child candidate for the reincarnation of a "living Buddha."

Chinese imperial control over Tibet was also exerted by a political representative in Lhasa who was supported by a Chinese garrison. The high point of Chinese military rule over Central Asia came during the Ch'ing dynasty when Chinese armies went across Tibet into the Indian borderlands of Nepal and Sikkim. Chinese control progressively weakened, however, and the Lama Church grew increasingly independent of Chinese influence.

The Chinese court attempted to retain its influence by exploiting an inner conflict among the church leaders. The secular ruler of all Tibet was the Dalai Lama at Lhasa, the highest "living Buddha" of the Yellow Sect. The nearest competitor for power was the Panchen Lama, the head of the Yellow Sect monastery of Ta-shi-lhun-po, close to the town of Shigatse. The Panchen Lama had a higher position in the spiritual hierarchy of the living Buddhas while the Dalai Lama had the highest secular power. The conflict in authority between these two highest living Buddhas and their respective supporters led occasionally to inner strife. It was this strife that the Chinese exploited in their effort to maintain control. In the nineteenth century, when Tibet was drawn into the struggle between the imperialist powers, British India backed the Dalai Lama, and the Panchen Lama remained an instrument of Chinese influence.

5. CHINESE TURKESTAN

The relationship of China to the central Asiatic region of Chinese Turkestan was of a different character. Sinkiang, as it is known today, has been the caravan link between China, Central Asia, the Near East, and Europe since pre-Christian times. Caravans have moved across this high road of world commerce since the time when the outer borders of the Roman empire and of imperial China almost met. It was the route which Marco Polo took in his travels to the China of the Mongol empire in the thirteenth century. The control of this strategic trade route has always been of great importance to China.

Chinese Turkestan consists of two Central Asiatic plateaus which lie between the Altai mountains in the north and the Kunlun Mountains in the south. They are divided by the Tienshan range. The Chinese have approached Turkestan through the Kansu corridor along the ancient caravan route whose branches continue through the northern and southern plateaus of Turkestan. The Altai mountain range constitutes the border of the northern half of Chinese Turkestan, the Dzungarian Basin, whose capital city is Tihua, or Urumchi. The southern part of Chinese Turkestan, the Tarim Basin, is bordered by the Pamirs, the Kunlun, and Altyn Tagh mountains which separate it from India and Tibet. To the east across the mountain ranges lies Russian Turkestan.

The Dzungarian and Tarim basins have been populated since ancient times by non-Chinese people. The Uighurs, who make up the large majority of the population, are a Turkish people. The total population numbers about 4,000,000 and besides the Uighurs includes other tribal groups and, in the cities, a small Chinese minority. The Uighurs have been Moslem since the fourteenth century.

Some of the Turkish people of this area are nomads of the steppes, but the majority of them live in towns with agricultural settlements strung along the caravan routes which follow the border areas of mountain and steppe. The rivers that come down from the high mountain ranges of the Pamirs, the Kunlun, the Tienshan, and their subordinate chains provide the water for intensive agriculture. These rivers dry up in the steppes and deserts of the Turkestan plains, but at the edge of the mountains they create agricultural oases that form a string of settlements along the outer rim of the Turkestan steppes. These settlements were way stations on the great caravan routes. They were also centers of local political power. As these isolated settlements were difficult to combine under a single government, it was possible for the Chinese to establish over-all control and to suppress occasional uprisings. Chinese control began in Han times, two thousand years ago, but the area was frequently independent and the periods of Chinese rule amount only to about five hundred years. In the Ch'ing dynasty the area was administered by Manchu banner generals supported by banner garrisons until, in 1878, a formal Chinese provincial administration was introduced. In 1955, under the Chinese Communist regime, Chinese Turkestan became the Sinkiang-Uighur Autonomous Region.

6. KOREA

Land and People

Korea was one of those agricultural countries on the periphery of China which were affected by Chinese culture. China gave Korea occasional military protection and maintained a limited tributary trade relation with her.

The Korean peninsula has an area of roughly 85,000 square miles. Its continental land borders are formed by two rivers, the Yalu and the Tumen, which separate it from Manchurian China and since 1860 from a twelve-mile length of Russian territory. The rest of the Korean border is the sea. Korea stretches out between the Sea of Japan and the Yellow Sea, to form a continental arm reaching towards the southern tip of the islands of Japan and separated from them by the Strait of Tsushima. Korea was the bridge between Japan and the Asiatic continent. Over it Chinese cultural influences were transmitted to Japan. And over it also passed invading armies on their way from the continent to Japan, and from Japan to the continent.

Korea is a mountainous country. Mountain range follows mountain range and no large plains exist. With the exception of the somewhat higher ranges on the Manchurian border, the mountains are not very high and are abrupt and scattered. The northern and eastern regions of Korea are especially mountainous and rugged, while the south and west are marked by hills, broad valleys, and small plains. Two-thirds of the modern population of over 23,000,000 live in this southern and western part which is best suited for agriculture. The north, with its mountains covered with forests of spruce, fir, larch, and pine, was little developed in the past, but it has natural resources such as coal, iron ore, gold, graphite, tungsten, zinc, and a great number of other minerals important for industrial development. Along the eastern coast, the mountains drop sharply to the sea and there are few natural harbors. The western coast has a more gentle slope and the main harbors are located there. There are no large rivers, but the short mountain streams provide great possibilities for hydro-electric development. Korea possesses the resources for considerable industrialization.

The staple crop of Korea is rice. In the north, millet, wheat and barley are grown. Beans are a major part of the diet. Fish from the coastal waters, some pork and fowl, supplement the Korean food supply.

The Koreans are a distinct ethnic group with their own language and cultural tradition. The tribes which inhabited Korea in prehistoric times were a mixture of Tungus and proto-Caucasian groups which penetrated Korea from Manchuria. These tribes were mixed with Chinese as a result of Chinese invasions of Korea.

Society

Korea was divided into several kingdoms, the northernmost of which occasionally extended its control over Manchuria. Korea was finally unified under one kingdom in the seventh century. The last ruling dynasty was the house of Yi (1392–1910). The Korean social structure was similar in many ways to the Chinese. The large majority of the Korean people were peasants who lived in numerous villages. They were governed by a small group of educated men who filled the official positions in the government. The education of the Korean upper group was largely patterned after the Chinese model. Education, which was private, was a preparation for government examinations through which successful candidates became eligible for official positions.

The beginning of the reign of the Yi dynasty in the fourteenth century was a flourishing period in art and literature. A phonetic alphabet was invented for the Korean language, but Chinese writing remained predominant because of the influence of Chinese philosophy and scholarship. Education of the learned began with the study of both Chinese and Korean writing as the basis of literacy, but higher education was based principally on the Chinese classics. Eventually Korean writing was mainly relegated to use by women who had no part in the official examination system and could not hold government positions. The educated Korean scholar used the classical Chinese language in government documents and in his political essays as well as in his private writing in prose and poetry. The Korean scholar differed from his Chinese counterpart, however, in his greater knowledge of languages, since he knew both Chinese and Korean and sometimes Mongol, Manchu, or Japanese.

Before the fifteenth century, Buddhism was a major influence among the educated as well as among the common people. Buddhist priests filled many of the highest official positions and were influential at court. Buddhist monasteries and temples were the schools for education, and Buddhist scholastic examinations led not only to religious but also to political prominence. In the fifteenth century, however, Buddhism was curbed; the property of many monasteries was confiscated, Buddhist examinations were abolished, and Buddhist tenets were replaced by Confucian principles and education. Though Buddhism retained some influence among the educated group, ancestor worship, filial piety, the Confucian principles of human relations and of harmony between the human world and the universe were as much accepted in the social and political system of Korea as they were in China.

The Koreans accepted the Confucian concept of the family, with the father as the autocratic head of the house and with older members having authority over the younger. Concubinage existed but, as in China, it was for the most part limited to the families of the upper group who could afford the expense. This upper group could also keep larger families together and provide for all members on the basis of the family wealth and income.

The Korean upper group differed from the Chinese gentry mainly in its greater hereditary continuity. The aristocratic families of Korea almost monopolized the educational system and the resulting access to privileges and official positions. With this greater monopoly of power went a strong factional rivalry between the various sections of this privileged upper group, those who were in power and those who were out. Intrigue and assassination were not uncommon, and the bitterness of this strife among cliques of the ruling scholar aristocracy helped to weaken the system as a whole.

The privileged upper group ruled the mass of the common people, most of whom were farmers. The farmers owned their land and could sell it or pass it on to their descendants. In theory the land belonged to the king, but his theoretical ownership was little more than the right to tax. The land was registered by the local official, who assigned the tax that the farmer was required to pay. The land was worked by the men and the women of the family with oxen and simple plows. The peasants had to provide for their own living and the tax exactions of the officials. Villages were organized under village elders who were responsible to the officials for collecting taxes and keeping order. As in China, units of five families were held mutually responsible for any infraction of the law committed by their members. Village life was simple and close to the existence minimum. Politically powerless, the Korean farmers could band together only in secret societies, which occasionally organized revolts when pressure and exploitation became unbearable.

The towns, which were primarily the seats of government were also the centers of trade and industry. Korea became famous for ceramics, porcelain, and lacquer ware, handicrafts which were introduced to Korea from China. As in China the artisans were organized in guilds, which regulated quality of work, price, and apprenticeship, and provided assistance to the members of the trade. In the towns lived the merchants, and they, too, were organized into guilds. An especially powerful group was the guild of peddlers and porters which controlled the transportation and the selling of products in the villages. This last guild was organized on a countrywide basis and had its headquarters at the capital.

Merchants and artisans were commoners and had no protection against official extortion except whatever their guild organizations could provide. For those who had no connections or protection, it was always wise not to reveal any wealth they might possess. In Korea the gap between the commoners and the ruling class was even wider than in imperial China.

Government

In its political structure Korea resembled the Chinese bureaucratic state. The king was an absolute monarch within his country. He maintained a large court and a harem, which was supervised by eunuchs. The successor to the throne was selected from among the king's sons.

The king, as the head of the central government, was assisted by three leading ministers: a prime minister, who was the highest official of the land, and two others. Under them the government was divided into the six departments of the Chinese system. The heads of these departments, together with the prime minister and his aides, formed a supreme council which was consulted by the king on general matters of policy. Under this central government, Korea was divided into eight provinces with governors appointed by the king and responsible to him. Under them were the local magistrates. Central control of this administrative system was maintained by the king's special envoys or commissioners, who were sent out into the provinces to supervise and report on the local administrators. A special group of so-called "night messengers" supervised these commissioners and reported also on the conditions in the provinces. They served as a check on any move towards autonomy by the local administrators.

The army was under the direct control of the central government. Three chief military officers formed the Board of War. The provinces had provincial commanders-in-chief who together with the Board of War formed the high command. These officials were appointed to their respective commands by the central government. Garrisons were distributed within the cities of the provinces, and each province had to maintain a provincial fleet. All were under the command of the king. The soldiers lived within their garrison communities and were given land to cover their expenses. The salaried officers were centrally appointed.

The Korean government, so strongly resembling the Chinese model, was, however, an autonomous unit related only loosely to the Chinese imperial government. The Chinese emperor was the suzerain or overlord of the Korean king and had the right to confirm the king's appointment and to give him the seal of office, so important in establishing the king's authority over his administration. China also provided Korea with its calendar, a most important symbol of government in an agricultural country. Finally China was responsible for the protection of its Korean vassal from foreign invasion.

In exchange for this protection Korea was bound to provide auxiliary forces if the empire needed them. Most important of all, the Korean court sent yearly tribute missions to Peking. The members of these tribute missions also took advantage of the opportunity to carry on a profitable trade on the side.

Korea became involved in the battle between the Ming dynasty and the Manchus. The Manchus, who invaded Korea before they conquered China, forced the Korean king to give up his loyalty to the Ming dynasty. Manchu overlordship continued until the end of the Sino-Japanese War in 1895.

CHAPTER **III**

Tokugawa Japan

---

1. JAPAN AND THE JAPANESE

JAPAN is a group of large islands which stretch in a thousand mile arc off the eastern shores of Asia. Placed along the Atlantic seaboard of America they would reach from Georgia to Maine; they cover an area of 147,611 square miles, about the size of California. The four main islands of this group are Hokkaido, Honshu, Shikoku, and Kyushu. Of these Honshu, the largest, contains half the population of contemporary Japan. Here is located the capital city of Tokyo. Kyushu, the southernmost island, is closest to China. Shikoku, lying to the southeast of Honshu, forms with it the so-called Inland Sea. Hokkaido, to the north, stretches to within a few miles of the island of Sakhalin and is the least developed of all the four main islands. Japan is situated close to the Asiatic continent. She has been close enough to assure constant contact but far enough away to absorb continental influences in relative seclusion.

The modern Japanese people are thought to be a compound of various strains which intermingled in very early times. It is thought that the Ainu, possibly an early Caucasian type, and now limited to the northern island of Hokkaido, originally inhabited the whole archipelago. They were driven to the north by migrations from two directions. The main group apparently came from the mainland by way of Korea or Sakhalin; others came from the south, possibly from the area of modern Indonesia and the Philippines. The most prevalent Japanese physical type is Mongoloid, with straight black hair, yellow skin, and the epicanthic fold of the eyelid. At the same time, there seem to be Negrito characteristics, possibly coming from southern peoples, and Caucasian characteristics, possibly coming from the Ainu. It is out of this mixture of many peoples that the Japanese have emerged as a distinct ethnic type.

7I

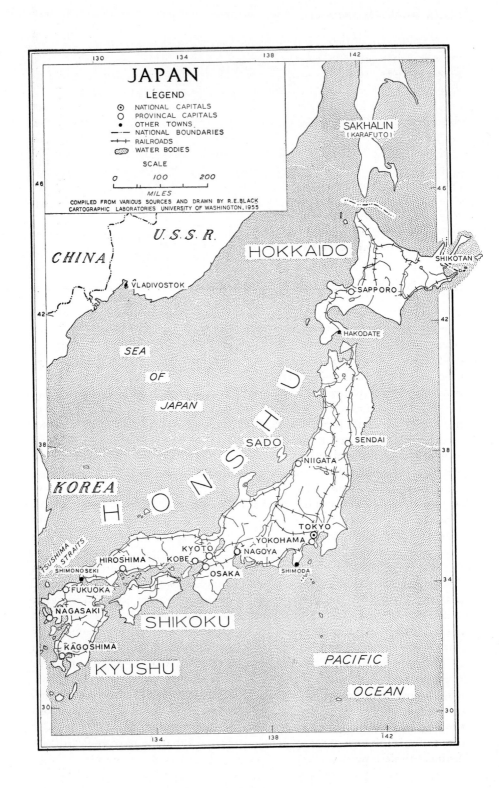

JAPAN

LEGEND
⊙ NATIONAL CAPITALS
○ PROVINCAL CAPITALS
• OTHER TOWNS
-·-·- NATIONAL BOUNDARIES
+++ RAILROADS
WATER BODIES

SCALE

0   100   200

MILES

COMPILED FROM VARIOUS SOURCES AND DRAWN BY R.E.BLACK
CARTOGRAPHIC LABORATORIES UNIVERSITY OF WASHINGTON,1955

130   134   138   142

46   46

CHINA

U.S.S.R.

HOKKAIDO

SAKHALIN
(KARAFUTO)

SHIKOTAN

VLADIVOSTOK

SAPPORO

42   42

HAKODATE

SEA

OF

JAPAN

H O N S H U

SADO

SENDAI

38   38

NIIGATA

KOREA

TOKYO

YOKOHAMA

KYOTO   NAGOYA

KOBE

HIROSHIMA

TSUSHIMA STRAITS

SHIMONOSEKI

OSAKA

SHIMODA

34   34

FUKUOKA

NAGASAKI

SHIKOKU

KAGOSHIMA

KYUSHU

PACIFIC

OCEAN

30   30

134   138   142

The climate of Japan is milder than would be expected in the latitudes between thirty and fifty degrees, largely because the Japan Current—the largest current in any ocean in the world—washes the southeastern shores of Japan and even sends its warm waters into the Japan Sea where it is known as the Tsushima Current. Although northern Honshu and the east coast of Hokkaido are influenced by the cold Okhotsk Current from the north and are colder than the rest of the country, there is no spectacular change in climatic conditions. The Japanese islands as a whole have a temperate climate and adequate humidity. The dry winds from Asia pick up moisture as they cross the Japan Sea and deposit it as snow during the winter months. In the summer the monsoon winds from the Pacific bring rain, humidity, and heat.

Japanese topography is marked by many mountainous areas and a small number of plains. Only 15 per cent of the land mass of Japan is level. The largest and most famous plain in Japan, the Kwanto Plain on which Tokyo is situated, has always been a potential source of economic and military power. Most of the level plains are much smaller and are crowded by the mountains. The greatest contrast of climate in Japan is caused by altitude rather than by latitude. Bamboo grows in northern Hokkaido and pines in southern Kyushu, depending upon the altitude. Slight differences in altitude result in sharp differences in land use. Because much of the mountainous area is too steep to terrace, half of Japan is still covered with forests, in marked contrast to China which is practically denuded of trees.

Japanese agriculture is based on wet farming. Rice is the main crop and can be grown in all parts of Japan. Irrigation is necessary but the short rivers of Japan require no large-scale flood control projects or irrigation works. The longest river is 292 miles long whereas the length of the Yangtze is 3,200 miles. While the Yangtze can be navigated some 1,630 miles inland from the sea, the rivers of Japan are almost useless for navigation. Under these conditions it was possible for the small political units of feudal Japan to handle their irrigation problems successfully on a local scale and to reach a comparatively high productive level of agricultural production.

Japanese population has always pressed heavily on the available means of subsistence. One of the reasons for this phenomenon arises from the system of intensive agriculture, which requires a great deal of human labor. There is therefore a strong economic drive towards a high birth rate. When the United States opened Japan to the modern world in the middle of the nineteenth century, Japan had a population of some 30,000,000 while the population of the whole United States was only 20,000,000 at that time.

The fact that Japan has many good harbors has made it possible for her people to supplement agriculture through fishing and maritime enterprise. Fish has long been a substantial part of the Japanese diet, and coastal fishing an essential part of economic life. The maritime skill of the Japanese was based upon fishing as a means of livelihood. Japan early developed a coastwise traffic, for the sea provided the natural highways that the rivers did not. From the twelfth century on, there has been considerable Japanese maritime enterprise beyond the shores of Japan. In the fifteenth century Japanese ships ranged as far as Siam and Malacca. Japanese pirates constantly infested the Chinese coast. Maritime ventures beyond home waters were prohibited from the seventeenth to the nineteenth centuries. But fishing and coastal navigation continued and the Japanese lost none of their maritime skill. The sea has remained one of the most important facts of Japanese geography.

What the land did not provide, the sea continued to supply. In modern times the Japanese built up a tremendous fishing industry which was estimated, before World War II, to have accounted for about half the world's entire catch. The Japanese diet continued to depend heavily on fish. With the advantage of good harbors and the stimulus of commercial fishing and foreign trade, Japan built a sizable merchant marine, the largest in Asia and exceeded by few others in the whole world. Like the English, the Japanese have had to sail the seas in order to live.

For modern Japanese industrial development the short rushing rivers have become a rich source of hydro-electric water power. But this is hardly adequate compensation for the lack of coking coal and other mineral resources essential for large-scale industry. Japanese production of zinc, salt, tin, lead, iron, and petroleum, before World War II, was only a fraction of what was needed for Japanese industry. Even copper, which is more plentiful, was imported, owing to the high cost of production from low grade ores. Japan has more than sufficient sulphur for her needs and is self-sufficient in iron pyrites. Japan has reasonably large quantities of coal, except for coking coal, and of gold and silver, but she has no nickel, aluminum, or magnesium. Most of the minerals necessary for industry therefore have to be imported. In order to become a highly industrialized country Japan built up her capital through the manufacture and export of textiles. For these textiles she produced her own silk supply but had to import cotton and wool. Japanese farming families provided cheap human labor, both male and female, for the textile mills. Industrial Japan supported a much larger population than did agricultural Japan, and by 1954 the population of the Japanese islands exceeded eighty million people. The steady growth of the Japanese population still poses one of the gravest problems for contemporary Japan.

2. Feudal Japan

Growth of Feudalism

The feudal society of Japan grew out of an earlier clan organization. Before the seventh century A.D. a number of patriarchal clans, of varying size and strength, cultivated the many small patches of agricultural land in which the highly dissected topography of Japan abounds. These clans did not always stay in one particular area. The Yamato clan, for example, moved from an earlier home in Kyushu to the eastern end of the Inland Sea and established itself on what later came to be known as the Yamato plain.

Here the Yamato clan established itself as the leading clan and exercised a loose authority over the other clans. At this time a clan was a group of family units which claimed common ancestry and worshipped a guardian god. Attached to the clan there were other families, organized according to their occupations, which eventually merged with the clan and accepted its mythology. The heads of the clans claimed authority by virtue of descent from mythological figures, or gods. The Yamato clan claimed a legendary origin from the Sun Goddess to whom all other clan deities came to be considered as subordinate. The Yamato clan became the imperial family in Japan and its legendary origin the imperial myth.

In the seventh century an attempt was made to impose a central government upon the many loosely associated clans. The new system, was based on the great model of the time, imperial China. Its introduction in 645 A.D. is known as the period of the Great Reform (Taikwa). The clans, which by this time had manors and serfs, were abolished and their functions were to be taken over by appointed officials and local dignitaries.

The attempt to control Japan through a bureaucratic system did not in the long run succeed, and in its stead there emerged a feudal order. The clans did not entirely disappear. The government's practice of paying its officials and of rewarding important families with the tax-free income from grants of rice land in time created a landed aristocracy. Landed estates grew in size through a process somewhat similar to that which took place in medieval Europe. Smaller landowners surrendered their land to powerful families in return for protection. In this way the area of privately owned land from which the imperial tax collector could get revenue eventually disappeared. The imperial court of the Yamato clan remained but had little revenue or power and the imperial officials had nothing but honary titles. Instead of a central government there were feudal families who administered and taxed their own territories. By the twelfth century A.D. the emperor was only a tool in the hands of a powerful feudal aristocracy.

During the following centuries, particularly the fourteenth and fifteenth centuries, there was internal confusion and continuous feudal warfare. The warfare led to the emergence of a large number of virtually independent domains and the warrior aristocracy lost its former unity. It divided into competing groups, each one of which limited its allegiance to a local feudal lord. These lords were called daimyo, the rulers of clan territories. Each daimyo had his retainers, or samurai, who were professional warriors. The most powerful of the daimyo became the shogun, or generalissimo, an office in which he was invested by the powerless emperor. Several clans fought their way to the position of shogun but were unable to retain control. It was not until 1603, when the Tokugawa clan established military control over the country, that the shogunate ceased to change hands and internal peace was established. The Tokugawa clan controlled the office of shogun until the end of the feudal system in the nineteenth century. The last two hundred and fifty years of pre-modern Japan is known as the period of the Tokugawa Shogunate.

The Feudal System

The Japanese under the Tokugawa created a highly original, complex, and in many ways advanced civilization. The nominal head of the state during this period was the emperor, who was always a member of the Yamato clan. In practice the emperor was merely a figurehead who who reigned but did not rule. The shogun tolerated the imperial family because it provided a symbol of ideological unity for the feudal order. The functions of the emperor were purely ceremonial. The imperial court resided in Kyoto, a city which became the center of court life and was known for the beautiful architecture of its palaces and temples. The financial resources of the imperial family were modest but under the Tokugawa it enjoyed more security than had come its way in earlier times. The emperor was surrounded by his court nobility, the Kuge, who held the high honorific positions and carried on the court ceremonies. But the real power was in the hands of the Tokugawa clan.

The Tokugawa clan had its capital at Yedo, the modern Tokyo, in the Kwanto plain, the largest single agricultural area in Japan. Here they built a great military fortress of enormous dimensions, planned to be impregnable. This seat of Tokugawa military power also became the political, economic, and cultural capital of feudal Japan.

The Tokugawa shogun left the daimyo of the other clans in full control of their respective territories. The daimyo had power of life and death over the people in their fiefs whom they ruled and taxed without outside interference. They were vassals, however, of the shogun, to whom they all owed allegiance.

The samurai of each clan were more than military retainers; they were the actual administrators of clan affairs. All of the daimyo, including the shogun himself, depended on the services of their samurai. The samurai owed unquestioning loyalty to his daimyo. In return for his loyalty and services the samurai received his support in fixed payments of rice. The samurai were a privileged hereditary group of warriors who alone had the right to bear arms and were not permitted to engage in trade or other pursuits which were considered to be below their dignity. The samurai carried two swords, the mark of his standing. These weapons were often the products of high craftsmanship and treasured family possessions. Among the samurai who held the important administrative positions were men of great culture and education.

The peasant ranked next below the samurai, but above the artisan and merchant. Peasants, artisans, and merchants, however, were all commoners; they could not bear arms and were treated with scant respect. If a samurai was offended by the behavior of a commoner he was permitted to cut him down and leave the body. Although the peasant was considered more important to society than the artisan and merchant, he was actually at the bottom of the economic scale because he was the main producer and carried the burden of supporting the other social classes. Every inch of land was surveyed for taxes, and a peasant had to deliver to his lord anything from 40 per cent to two-thirds or more of the crop. Peasant revolts against extortionate taxes were quite frequent, but they did not change the general situation. The peasants lived a life of utter simplicity, but except for those occasions on which they were driven to desperate action by ruthless oppression they lived peacefully.

During the period of Tokugawa rule there was a great development of town life in Japan. The cities and towns usually arose around the seats of the feudal lords. In these centers of feudal power were the samurai and the retinue of the lords and also the artisans and traders. In the long years of peace, trade and handicraft flourished and many of the merchants became rich by financing the court life of the feudal aristocracy. The largest city of all was Yedo which is believed to have exceeded the figure of one million people even before 1800. The merchants, with their guilds and their control over transportation and the rice market, dominated the economic life of the towns and also put their stamp on art and literature. Artisans and artists, who also lived in the towns, provided the ordinary tools for daily life as well as the luxury objects for the refined urban taste. Outstanding artists were highly respected.

Much of the artistic and literary life of Japan was centered in the geisha districts of the towns. The geisha were not prostitutes; they were well educated professional entertainers, versed in the arts of singing, dancing, and light conversation. In Japanese society the position of women was unequal and social life was normally limited to men. The geisha provided a type of social contact with women which the rigid social customs denied.

The growth of feudalism had a profound influence on the family as well as on the position of women. The decline of the paternalistic clan system led to the emergence of the family as a social unit. The long years of civil war strengthened the tendency towards primogeniture in the feudal families. Primogeniture was loosely applied. The successor was not necessarily the eldest son, and sometimes might be an adopted relative. In times of confusion and fighting it was important to have strong leadership in order to defend property. For the same reason the position of women, which had been high in previous times, declined under the feudal system. In all classes of society women held a subordinate position. The feudal lord really established a new form of clan composed of his own and other family units, not necessarily related to each other. It was to the interest of the daimyo to keep the clan together as a strong fighting force, but it was not to his interest to permit combinations of powerful families against him. The families of the vassals were kept under close surveillance and prevented from growing too powerful. The families of the commoners were limited in size and influence by their economic condition. Whatever the family, however, whether feudal or commoner, the role of the individual was subordinated to the family and all had to obey the head of the family. The system of loyalties within the family was very strong and was paralleled by the loyalties and obligations between lord and vassal.

Tokugawa Rule

The Tokugawa shoguns ruled Japan through a combination of military force and political strategy. The Tokugawa had come to power with the assistance of a group of trusted allies who came to be known as the Inner Lords. These were used in such a way as to make sure that the Tokugawa shogun had control of the whole Kwanto plain and other important strategic and economic areas in Japan. To the north and west of central Japan lay the fiefs of those daimyo who had accepted Tokugawa rule only after military defeat. The most powerful of these daimyo, known as the Outer Lords, were the western clans whose fiefs were located on the southern tip of Honshu, on Kyushu and Shikoku. The best known among these were the clans of Satsuma, Choshu, Hizen, and Tosa. As the Tokugawa were not strong enough to destroy these powerful clans, they had to take every possible precaution to keep them in subjection and to prevent them from combining their forces against the shogunate. The Tokugawa shogun rewarded his allies by granting them fiefs in strategic positions that commanded the domains of these former enemies. In this way the Tokugawa established a military superiority over the Outer Lords.

There were other strategies adopted by the Tokugawa to maintain their power. All daimyo were compelled to spend a part of the year in the shogun's capital at Yedo and to leave their families behind as hostages when they returned to their domains. In this way the shogun reaffirmed every year the allegiance of his vassals and also kept an eye on possible combinations of power against him. Severe restrictions were put on the building of fortifications and castles by unfriendly daimyo, and considerable sums of money were extracted from them for the building of public works to strengthen the power of the shogun. Only the Inner Lords and members of the Tokugawa family were allowed to hold office in the organs of government concerned with the country as a whole.

The Tokugawa set up their military dictatorship on the basis of more than military force and political strategems. They took steps to consolidate their rule on the basis of rigid social and political institutions. The feudal system was built on a pyramid of loyalties. The emperor expected loyalty and obedience from all the daimyo; the daimyo in their turn expected loyalty and obedience from their samurai; daimyo and samurai assumed loyalty and obedience from the commoners. The imperial clan was confirmed in its ruling position by the Tokugawa in order to strengthen the very concept of loyalty itself. The shogun did all things in the name of the emperor and acted on his behalf, deriving his authority from investiture by the emperor, a form on which the shoguns always insisted. On the basis of this authority they compelled the daimyo of all the fiefs, which numbered between 250 and 300, to sign written oaths of loyalty to the shogun in which they swore obedience and undertook not to assist enemies of the shogunate. The Tokugawa sought to intensify these loyalty relationships, originally based upon the concept of services and protection, by strictly defining the duties and responsibilities of every class in society. The shogun left the local daimyo to run his fief pretty much as he wished, so long as there was no challenge to his own authority. But the Tokugawa were particularly interested in establishing the prestige as well as the duties of the samurai throughout the country. For this reason they went out of their way to promulgate a harsh and ascetic code of ethics which, if followed to the letter, would maintain the samurai as a tough, loyal, and reliable class.

The shogunate accepted and supported the imperial family in its nominal position at the head of the state because the imperial institution provided the ideological unity for Japanese feudalism. The position of the imperial family at the head of the social order was based on the myth of its divine origin. This myth was derived from the religious system of Shintoism.

Shintoism

Shinto means literally the "Way of the Gods," and Shintoism is a popular belief in the presence of spirits in nature. These spirits are located in trees and rocks, mountains and rivers, and other objects of nature. Shrines were erected to these spirits and people went to the shrines for prayer and worship. Shintoism included the worship not only of the spirits in nature but also of the spirits of deceased persons. The idea of ancestor worship, which had received a stimulus from China, was linked with the general worship of spirits and applied specifically to the spirits of military heroes and of the ancestors of the imperial family. Ancestor worship had thus not only religious but also political importance; the imperial family derived its cultural function and its political position from the veneration of the imperial ancestors.

The political aspect of the emperor's part in Japanese life could, however, vary according to the emphasis placed upon the political content of Shintoism. This was not stressed by the Tokugawa, who in spirit and practice were a secular power group, but they thought it important to keep the emperor as a figurehead. If the shogun had attempted to destroy the imperial clan and to replace it by the Tokugawa clan he would have undermined the principle of legitimacy and have discredited the basis of authority for all clans.

Even the cultural function of the throne was at times carried out not by the emperor personally but by the crown prince. The Tokugawa period presents, indeed, an extreme application of the Japanese system of putting a nominal figure in the foreground while the actual functions of power are manipulated from behind the scenes. The same dualism can be noted occasionally in the actual management of many of the other clans where power often was not so much in the hands of the feudal lords, the daimyo, as in those of the feudal retainers, the samurai. Every shogun was theoretically appointed by the emperor, who also carried out the highest ceremonial services of the state. The shoguns addressed the emperor with all the formal respect due the head of the state. Yet the Tokugawa literally controlled the body of the emperor and no one could see him without going through their representatives, who were stationed at the court.

The Japanese emperor, unlike the Chinese emperor, was not thought of as having a mandate from Heaven which could be revoked. He ruled by divine right; by definition he could do no wrong. In China it was possible for a dynasty to be overthrown and for a new one to take its place and establish its legitimacy by the argument that the previous dynasty had exhausted the mandate. In Japan, however, the throne was inviolate. This meant that the advisers of the emperor could be changed if things went badly but not the imperial family itself.

Confucianism

The rule of the Tokugawa brought internal peace to Japan. With peace the tasks of government increased and it was necessary to have trained administrators. For these administrators the government and the daimyo turned to the samurai. The training of administrators required a philosophy of administration and an ethical code for the conduct of officials. For such things the most easily available source was the massive body of Confucian doctrine of which the Japanese had long been aware. There was much in Confucianism, indeed, to support the hierarchy of loyalties between people and between classes which the Japanese so strongly emphasized.

The Tokugawa soon set about the promotion of Confucian studies for the training of their officials. Taking from Confucianism only what suited their purposes they declared all the other studies to be heretical and pro-hibited them by edict. They were particularly interested in the Confucian philosophy of the school of Chu Hsi which emphasized the concept that good government depends upon the wisdom of the ruler and the obedience of the subjects. In the Confucian framework of loyalties, the shogun was expected to obey the emperor as he in turn expected obedience from those below him. The Tokugawa considered the philosophy of Chu Hsi to be sufficiently flexible, however, to cause them no embarrassment in view of the fact that their real power was in sharp contrast to their nominal position. So long as their power was too strong to be challenged, they had no problem; but when their real power declined, the principle of loyalty and obedience to the emperor rose up to haunt them.

Buddhism

The Tokugawa took the view that the state was responsible for setting up and enforcing standards of behavior for all classes of society. Political and moral philosophy were merged in one doctrine. There was not in Japanese, as there was in European feudalism, a deep conflict between the institutions of church and state for the reason that the Buddhist church, which alone could have become a rival for political power, was crushed by the shoguns shortly before the Tokugawa began their rule. The first of the

Tokugawa shoguns, Ieyasu, made certain, by his legislation, that the Buddhist church should not become powerful again.

The shoguns had good reason to be concerned about Buddhist influence. In contrast to the earliest Buddhist influence, which was limited mainly to the court, the Buddhism which came in with the beginning of feudalism in the twelfth and thirteenth centuries spread over the whole country where it was taken up by the rural aristocracy, the townspeople, and even the peasants. Buddhism in Japan, as in China from where the Japanese had taken it, stressed the doctrine of salvation through faith rather than through knowledge, and substituted for Nirvana the concept of a paradise in which life after death would be continued in a state of bliss. The True Pure Land School, which became the dominant Buddhist sect in Japan, propagated these beliefs which had a wide appeal. The Buddhist doctrine of equality for all was of great political importance. Some of the Buddhist congregations actually seized power from their feudal overlords, and temple castles arose from which Buddhist monks exercised territorial authority. These were the organizations which were crushed by the shoguns. As a popular religion, however, Buddhism continued to be the most important religion of Japan.

One of the sects which came in with the second wave of Buddhism in the twelfth and thirteenth centuries was Zen Buddhism. The word Zen means meditation. The Zen school emphasized intuition, gained through meditation, as the way to true enlightenment. It scorned the study of books and the appeal to reason, demanding instead a mental and physical discipline to prepare the mind for sudden revelation of the truth through intuition. This particular form of Buddhism appealed to the warrior class because it made a virtue of the hard, ascetic life. It went well together with the ethical code which the Tokugawa provided for the samurai.

Christianity and Seclusion

The Tokugawa might well have been satisfied with the measures they took to safeguard their domestic position if there had been no problems with outside powers. It was the fear that the threat from within might be combined with assistance from foreign countries that led the Tokugawa to take the decision, in 1637, to exclude all foreigners from the country, to prohibit Japanese from traveling abroad, and to limit foreign trade to one port.

The Tokugawa were in fear both of foreign arms and of foreign ideas. The first Tokugawa shogun, although watchfully aware of the development of Christianity in Japan where it was being vigorously promoted by the Jesuits, had not contemplated cutting Japan off from the rest of the world. Ieyasu was inclined to welcome foreign ideas, to encourage Portuguese and Spanish trade, and to promote Japanese maritime commercial expansion. He did not remove nor did he enforce existing anti-Christian edicts. The Christianization of Japan, which had begun with the arrival in that country of Francis Xavier in 1549, continued to make progress. As early as 1600, seventeen years before Ieyasu defeated his last enemies, it is estimated that there were 300,000 Japanese converts to the Catholic faith. Many, but not all, of the later converts were ordered into the Church by converted daimyo who were unfriendly to the Tokugawa. In fact, the adoption of Christianity was in many cases a mark of protest against the shogunate.

The Tokugawa could not dissociate Christianity from the military and political power of the states that sponsored it. Because Christianity taught allegiance to one God and undermined belief in the national deities, it seemed to the Tokugawa a challenge to the ideological basis of the state. The objections of the Tokugawa to Christianity therefore were based almost entirely upon political considerations. They came to feel that Christianity must be crushed because it represented a competing ideology and because its spread might lead to an alliance between domestic enemies and foreign powers. The Western powers themselves helped to confirm the Tokugawa in their fears that Christianity represented a serious political threat by accusing each other of aggressive designs on Japan. Nor were the missionaries overmodest in their estimates of Christian converts. The Jesuits claimed to have baptized more than half a million adults at the beginning of the Tokugawa period. The Tokugawa shoguns, therefore, took measures against Christianity even before they limited trade and foreign contact. Persecution reached its peak in 1625 by which time the government had broken the back of the Christian movement, and what remained could only continue underground. The Spanish occupation of the Philippines, which had done nothing to allay the fears of the Tokugawa, explains the fact that much of the venom of the Japanese rulers was directed against the Spanish, the first to be expelled from the country. The Portuguese and others were expelled somewhat later.

The Tokugawa were not averse to foreign contacts and foreign trade as such. It was the military strength of the European powers and the mutual rivalries of the Spanish, Portuguese, English, and Dutch that made them fear that the European powers had aggressive designs on their kingdom. Because of this military strength, the Tokugawa did not have open to them the alternative of driving the Western powers out of the Pacific. They had seen enough of the naval and military power of European nations to know that they could not successfully challenge the superiority of Western guns and ships. It has been suggested by Sir George Sansom that had not the Portuguese and other Europeans arrived upon the scene in the sixteenth century, the Japanese might well have established themselves in Formosa, the Philippines, and parts of Indonesia—as some of their rulers wished to do—and thus have begun a colonial empire in the Pacific. The superiority of Western guns and ships diverted the early imperialism of Japan and must be counted, therefore, as one factor leading to the policy of seclusion.

In 1637 the shogunate issued an exclusion edict which forbade the Japanese to travel overseas and limited all Western trade and contact to the non-Catholic Dutch who were permitted to maintain a trading establishment on the island of Deshima, opposite the port of Nagasaki. A limit was placed upon the size of ships that could be built in order to discourage ocean voyages. From this time on, the only Europeans allowed in Japan were the Dutch merchants. By these drastic measures the Tokugawa hoped to prevent foreign invasion and any possibility of outside assistance to their internal enemies, particularly to the western clans.

3. The Decline of Tokugawa Power

The Tokugawa shogunate lasted from 1603 to 1868. To maintain internal peace for this length of time was no small achievement. Japan, which had seen so little unity before this period, took unity for granted when the crises of the nineteenth century developed. During this period, however, new forces arose in Japanese society. The social and economic revolution that marked Japanese development under the Tokugawa came about, at least in part, as the result of some of the measures taken by the Tokugawa to keep themselves in power.

By requiring the feudal lords to visit the capital at Yedo every year and to leave members of their families there as hostages, the shogun laid the foundations for the development of court life. In Japan, as in Europe, court life proved a tremendous stimulus to the development of handicrafts, architecture, and the arts. The constant travel between Yedo and the furthest fiefs was undertaken not only by boat but also overland; it required therefore the building and maintenance of roads and the development of conveniences for traveling which could serve for these political journeys and for the transport of commodities and the movements of merchants. The physical basis for an extended exchange of goods was thus kept intact. At the same time new needs were created. The visits of the daimyo to Yedo and the residence of the members of their families in the capital city with its more expensive social life made it necessary for the daimyo to have currency to spend. Payment in kind and in services from the peasantry, which provided the necessities of life at home, had now to be transformed into money. As the need for funds increased, the warrior aristocracy had to obtain credit on the strength of its feudal income. The buying and selling of rice and the provision of credit to the feudal aristocracy brought wealth to rising merchant firms such as the House of Mitsui which played a part in Japanese life somewhat similar to that which the Fuggers had played in Europe. The same houses supported a clandestine trade with China mainly from the territories of the western clans.

The stratification of society, combined with the long period of internal peace, led to a disproportionate increase in the numbers of the non-productive warrior and administrative class whose members were expected to live on the surplus of a rice economy. For this and for other reasons, such as the occasional separation of daimyo from their fiefs, there developed an ever-increasing number of impoverished samurai. They had neither rice dues nor the opportunities to perform the functions to which they were legally restricted. Some went into scholarship, but many cluttered the cities and lost their class identity. Some took up foreign learning, to which they had access through the Dutch traders at the port of Nagasaki, an enterprise which involved considerable risk because it found no favor with the government. Some turned to writing and the arts, others mixed with the rising merchant class, but most lived in poverty. It is said that at times some farmers and most merchants were better off than the samurai. There is no social dynamite quite so powerful as that which can be generated by a social group which is accustomed to rule but has lost its opportunity to do so.

Japan under the Tokugawa saw the rise of a money economy which profited the socially despised class of merchants, encouraged the rise of great cities, and depressed the agricultural economy. The growing impoverishment of samurai and the enrichment of the merchants led to an increase in the number of intermarriages between commoners and aristocrats, all of which tended to break down the original simplicity and rigidity of the social order.

The efforts of the government to put back the clock were as frantic as they were unsuccessful. Nothing could stop the rise of cities and the merchant banking fraternity, and nothing could force the farmers back to the land from which they had fled because of oppressive taxation, famine, or other misfortunes. The Tokugawa continued to see the economic and social structure as they wished it to be rather than as it had come to be. Their approach to economics was limited to the idea of preserving rural society from the intrusions of commercial capitalism in the form of merchants and moneylenders. Such a concept excluded an understanding of the problems of money and credit. Hence the disastrous fiscal policies of the Tokugawa administration which continued to finance itself with borrowing, debasement of the currency, and heavy taxation.

When the extravagant, ostentatious, and creative life of the cities stood out in ever sharper contrast with the austere ethical code sponsored by the government, the reaction of the Tokugawa was not to adjust but to condemn. They were the victims of their own propaganda. They tended to see the breakdown of social classes as a moral problem. At a time when social and economic incentives could not have been less appealing, they increased their moral exhortations to the samurai, the merchants, and the peasants to behave in accordance with the rules that a wise government had laid down for them.

Men rise in hope rather than in despair. By the early nineteenth century there were large numbers of Japanese who were dissatisfied with existing conditions, not necessarily because they were bad, but because it was apparent that they could be improved. Some Japanese felt that they were denied a rightful share in an expanding economy; others, such as the merchants, who enjoyed a much greater share in the economy than their social status prescribed, felt entitled to proportionate social prestige. There were certainly few signs of docility among the peasantry. The whole Tokugawa period is marked by peasant uprisings, never on a national scale and not prompted by any one cause, but all reflecting the stresses and strains that came with the rise of a money economy. The life of the cities had its impact upon the peasant too, for it raised his level of expectation. He saw among other things that wages might be more attractive than farming. Peasant uprisings were almost endemic in the first part of the nineteenth century; and when other groups provided leadership, the peasants provided the man-power with which to challenge the institutions of Tokugawa Japan.

The Tokugawa, who had started the samuari on their road to learning, had as little success in confining them to orthodoxy as they had in stemming the tide of social and economic change. Some of the samurai, especially those of the western clans, turned to the study of their country's history, a seem-ingly harmless pastime. In the eighteenth century, the study of the eighth century texts of Japanese history, the *Kojiki* and the *Nihongi*, was revived under the leadership of the samurai scholar Motoori Norinaga. Scholars stressed the importance of the emperor in early Japan as the head of the state and of society. For this it was easy to argue that the authority of the shogun, which was not given in the text, had been usurped from the emperor and that it was necessary to restore the Japanese emperor to his true position and power.

From their reading of early Japanese history, the samurai scholars drew a picture of an idyllic time in which an all-powerful and benevolent emperor ruled loyal and obedient subjects. At no time had conditions approximated this picture; but it is sometimes more effective to secure acceptance for new ideas if they are presented as old ones. Of this the samurai and the leaders of the western clans were well aware. They found the historical argument a useful weapon with which to challenge the ideological position of the Tokugawa shogunate whose power they later helped to destroy under the pretext of an imperial restoration.

The challenge to the ideological basis of the Tokugawa state came also from another direction. There developed a considerable following for Wang Yang-ming, the idealist Chinese philosopher who held that self-knowledge was the highest kind of learning. Knowledge and practice are inseparable; a man may discover the principles of right behavior by looking into his own nature without wasting time on speculation about the laws of the universe. The effect of this teaching was to encourage an independence of mind that had little in common with orthodox Confucianism. To the Tokugawa it was a dangerous tendency because it led to consideration of the principle of loyalty and therefore raised the question of the legitimacy of the shogunate.

Opposition to the shogunate came also from those who were impressed by Western science and especially by Western military achievements and techniques. It was through the Dutch at Nagasaki that the Japanese had access to such Western books. This group was not so much interested in the question of the legitimacy of the shogunate as in its competence. But as the incompetence of the shogun came to be a constant factor in the situation, this made very little practical difference. As the group was persecuted by the shogun, it became a ready ally of others who opposed the regime on different grounds.

Japan at the beginning of the nineteenth century was very different from the tightly closed feudal kingdom of the seventeenth century. Practically every class in Japanese society had reasons for desiring a change. The simple concept of the division of classes into rulers, warriors, and commoners, had little relation to Japan of the early nineteenth century with its teeming cities, rich merchants, restless samurai, and discontented peasantry. The coming of Commodore Perry did not create the forces that launched modern Japan on her way; it merely released them.

CHAPTER IV

Southeast Asia

1. THE INDO-CHINESE WORLD

Tʜᴇ countries of Southeast Asia have been the cultural borderlands of the great civilizations of India and China. Southeast Asia includes the countries of Burma, Thailand, Annam (Vietnam), Cambodia, Laos, and British Malaya on the Asiatic continent, and the island groups of Indonesia and the Philippines. The influence of China was felt particularly in Indo-China, Burma, and Thailand through migration and various degrees of political control. In the areas which were beyond the political control of the Chinese empire Chinese traders settled and formed important minority groups. The only country, however, which took over the institutions and beliefs of the Confucian state was Vietnam which borders on China and lies closest to it by sea. The other countries of Southeast Asia received their religious beliefs and social customs in the main from India. Traders, priests, and monks from India brought in successive waves of Hinduism and Buddhism—religions which still dominate the civilizations of Burma, Thailand, Cambodia, and Laos. The Indians later brought Islam to Sumatra from where it spread to Malaya, the whole Indonesian archipelago, and even to Mindanao and other islands in the southern Philippines. The spread of Islam might well have led to the establishment of a Moslem empire over the whole area, had its growth not been stopped by the Portuguese and the Spanish in the sixteenth century. In all of these countries, however, Islam has remained a major cultural and political factor. In spite of the modern impact of the Western world the cultural border between Chinese and Indian influence is still apparent.

The countries of Southeast Asia are populated by a variety of peoples, most of whom belong to two major groups: the continental countries of Burma, Thailand, and the states of Indo-China are inhabited chiefly by

87

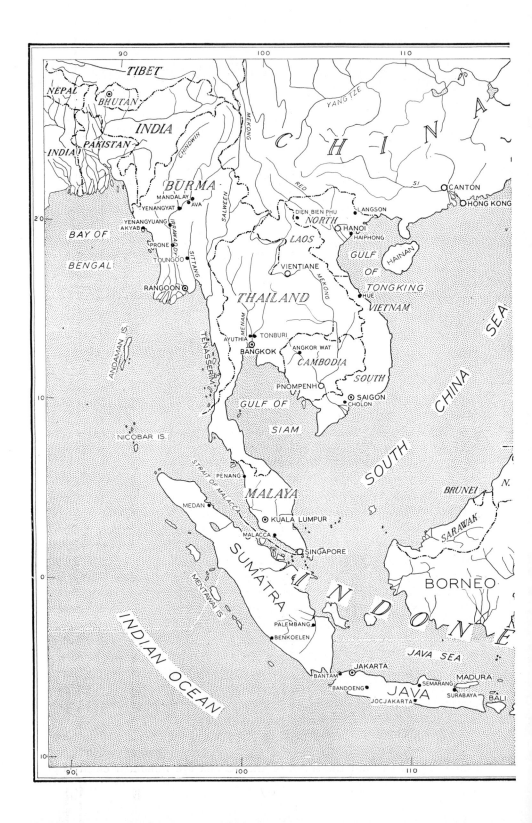

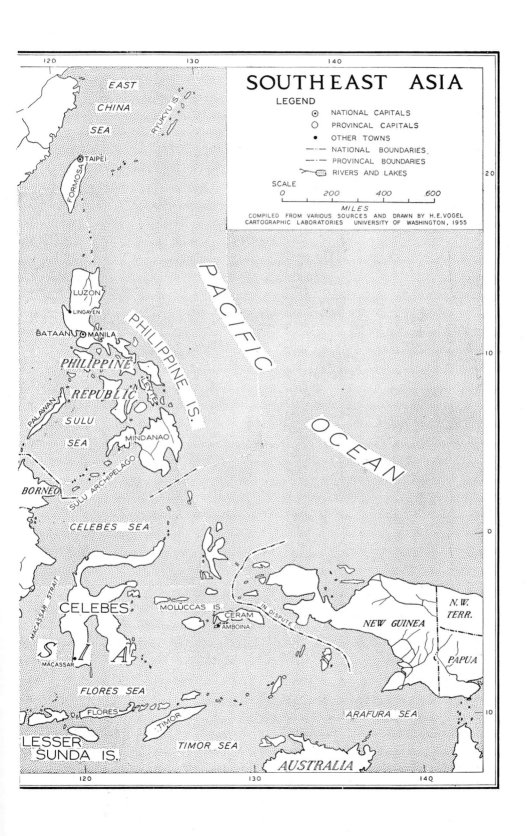

SOUTHEAST ASIA

LEGEND

⊙ NATIONAL CAPITALS
○ PROVINCAL CAPITALS
● OTHER TOWNS
—··— NATIONAL BOUNDARIES
—·—· PROVINCAL BOUNDARIES
RIVERS AND LAKES

SCALE

0   200   400   600

MILES

COMPILED FROM VARIOUS SOURCES AND DRAWN BY H.E.VOGEL
CARTOGRAPHIC LABORATORIES UNIVERSITY OF WASHINGTON, 1955

EAST
CHINA
SEA

RYUKYU S.

TAIPEI

FORMOSA

LUZON

LINGAYEN

BATAAN   MANILA

PHILIPPINE

PHILIPPINE IS.

REPUBLIC

PALAWAN

SULU

SEA

MINDANAO

SULU ARCHIPELAGO

BORNEO

CELEBES SEA

PACIFIC

OCEAN

CELEBES

MOLUCCAS IS.

CERAM

AMBOINA

IN DISPUTE

NEW GUINEA

N. W.
TERR.

PAPUA

MACASSAR STRAIT

S I A

MACASSAR

FLORES SEA

FLORES

TIMOR

LESSER
SUNDA IS.

TIMOR SEA

ARAFURA SEA

AUSTRALIA

20

10

0

10

peoples of Sino-Tibetan stock; the people of the Malay Peninsula and the island belt of Indonesia and the Philippines are mainly of Malay stock, having moved in prehistoric times from the continent to the Indonesian islands and northwards to the Philippines.

The mountain ranges, the river valleys, and the seas of Southeast Asia have helped to carve out natural frontiers for the political units which these peoples established. In central Burma, in Thailand, Cambodia, and Java, for example, there arose kingdoms based on an economy of irrigated agriculture which were the predecessors of the modern states of Burma, Thailand, Cambodia, and Indonesia. It was the ruling classes of these historical kingdoms which adopted the beliefs and institutions of India.

In modern times the whole of Southeast Asia, with few exceptions, was brought under Western colonial control. The Portuguese, Spanish, Dutch, and later the British and French conquerors and traders went there in search of the spices and riches of the East. The colonial powers have since developed this area's resources and raw materials to such an extent that it has become the source of many of the modern world's most strategic goods. Southeast Asia produces such important commodities as rubber, oil, and tin and a whole list of tropical products such as coconut oil, cocoa, quinine, coffee and spices. Southeast Asia, indeed, has played an important part in building up the economies and capital wealth of the European colonial powers. Holland especially derived a great part of her wealth from the Dutch East Indies.

Under the European colonial system there developed a dual economy. The spice gardens, the coffee gardens, and the rubber plantations, for example, were an extension of the Western economic system which remained alien to the native economy. This form of exploitation was carried on side by side with the native economy, with which it was not integrated and which provided only the labor and the raw materials. Eventually colonial rule led to the development of native nationalist movements which drew their inspiration from the influence of Western thought as well as from local cultural traditions. In modern times Southeast Asia has become a key strategic area in the relationships between the Communist bloc and the Free World.

2. THE PHILIPPINES

The Philippines form an island group in the chain that extends along the Asiatic coast from Borneo to the Kamchatka Peninsula. The Philippines consist of over seven thousand islands, but of this large number many are very small and have no population. A few of the large islands have determined the development of the entire group. The two largest islands are Luzon in the north and Mindanao in the south; together they take up 78,000 of the 115,600 square miles of the entire group. Like the neighboring islands to the north and south, the Philippines are mountainous and have numerous volcanos. The Philippines, which lie between the fifth and twenty-first degrees latitude, have a subtropical climate well suited to agriculture; they have plenty of rainfall from the monsoons. Only a part of the arable land has been cultivated, and the islands are one of the few places in Asia where the land and natural resources could support a substantially larger population. Rice has been the staple crop since the time of the early Malay settlers. Other crops grown are sweet potatoes and corn, the latter introduced from Mexico by the Spanish colonizers. Sugar, coconuts, and hemp have been the main cash crops planted in the twentieth century for export overseas. In addition to these agricultural resources, the Philippine Islands possess gold and important industrial raw materials, chiefly iron.

The people of the Philippines are believed to have come from the south in successive waves of invaders of Malay stock; these people either assimilated the original native inhabitants or drove them back into the mountainous inland areas where some of them still survive in various tribal groups. The Malays make up the large mass of the Philippine population which is today about twenty-three million. They belong to the same ethnic group as the people of the Malay Peninsula and Indonesia but have developed differently because of different cultural factors and divergent colonial administrations and policies.

The Filipinos have acquired a Western cultural background. Owing to the Spanish missionary policy, over 90 per cent of the people have become Christians and of these over 80 per cent are Catholic. Their cultural outlook has been influenced not only by Christianity but also by Spanish customs. Christian hymns have taken the place of Malay folksongs, and the young people working in the fields plant their rice to the rhythm of Spanish guitars. Of the Malay heritage little except the language remains. There are a number of Malay dialects, of which Tagalog, spoken on Luzon, is now the official language.

The Philippine population includes a number of ethnic and religious minority groups. In the mountainous country of the interior live tribal groups who are either unassimilated pre-Malay aborigines of the islands or the remnants of earlier Malay immigrant groups. The earliest aborigines are primitive pigmy peoples. Some of these have Negrito, others have Mongoloid characteristics, and others are related to the aboriginal Australians or the Ainu of Japan. These primitive peoples have become intermixed, have lost their original languages, and now speak Malay dialects mingled with words of their own former tongues. Besides these very primitive forest people, there are some tribal groups, largely on the island of Mindanao, which are believed to have belonged to an earlier wave of immigration from Indonesia and are termed "Indonesians." Other early invaders are the tribes of semi-civilized Malays, who live mainly in the mountainous areas of Luzon. Together these tribal groups are estimated to number about half a million people.

In addition to these ethnic minorities, there exists a religious minority in the southern part of the islands, mainly on Mindanao and the Sulu Archipelago. Most of the Malays of this area had accepted Islam before the Spanish occupation and strongly resisted all attempts at Christianization. They have remained hostile to the Spanish and Christian Filipinos and have retained a different culture and economy. The Spanish gave them the name of Moros, after the Moors, whom the Spanish had fought in their own country. The Moros, who make up a population of about 600,000, have posed a much more serious political problem than have the tribal minorities.

The Chinese are another important minority group. They came to the Philippines in early Spanish times and increased considerably in number during the nineteenth century. Today they number about 250,000. They came as traders and took over a substantial part of the retail trade and moneylending business in the Islands. They have frequently been subject to attacks from Filipinos who resented the prosperity of Chinese moneylenders and shopkeepers.

The social and economic structure of the Philippines has been strongly affected by the Spanish colonial system and its traditions. Spanish control over the Philippines was first established in the sixteenth century. In 1521 Magellan came to the Philippines on his famous voyage around the world and perished there. When the news of the islands was brought to Spain, new expeditions were equipped to establish the Spanish in the islands. Between 1556 and 1571 the Spanish set up their rule over the islands which they named the Philippine Islands in honor of the crown prince who later became Philip II of Spain. In 1571 Don Miguel Lopez de Legaspi, the first Spanish governor, established the capital at Manila on the island of Luzon.

When the Spanish came they found on the islands a number of principalities, each ruled by a noble chief or rajah whose position was inherited. The rajahs had their own hierarchy of political authority and loyalty, the lesser principalities being subject to the larger. The followers and subjects of the rajahs were free commoners, but there also existed groups of slaves, who could be bought and sold and who worked either as servants in the households of the nobles and free commoners or as laborers in the fields. Those employed in the fields lived in their own houses and worked for allotted periods of time. These slaves were either prisoners taken in the wars between petty principalities or men who lost their freedom through indebtedness or in punishment for crimes. Intermarriage between free people and slaves resulted for the offspring in conditions of half or quarter slavery, with correspondingly limited terms of work.

The Spanish conquerors of the Philippines came not from European Spain but from Central America, where they had already developed a colonial system. This system was an application of the feudal tradition of Spain to conditions in the New World. The Spanish rewarded their conquistadores, the adventurous soldiers who made up their military forces, by allotting to them native people and territory, a so-called *encomienda*. The people worked for the *encomendero*, who had both economic control and political jurisdiction over his domain. The *encomenderos* thus became the masters of large landed estates.

The *encomienda* system, developed in America, was applied to the Philippines. The Spanish took over the power of the local chieftains and in many cases used them to enforce their own authority. The exploitation of the natives by these *encomenderos* was, however, much harsher than it had been under the rule of the chieftains. The *encomenderos*, therefore, were generally hated and were sometimes even assassinated by the subject people of their domains.

The Spanish throne set up a centralized administration in the islands in order to check the *encomenderos* and to control the collection of taxes and the transportation of commodities. The administration consisted of a governor-general, the highest political authority, and an *audiencia*, or supreme council and court. In view of the importance of the position of the governor-general, the Spanish government set—at least on paper—very high qualifications for this appointment. The governor-general was supposed to be neither too young nor too old a man; he had to be unmarried, neither in debt nor a creditor, neither avaricious nor profuse, but of great courage and tried prudence, a frank and humane cavalier, and above all a man of piety. The governor-general supervised the administration of the provinces and districts, which were ruled by local officials, the *alcaldes*, *mayores*, and *corregidores*. It was through the local administrators that the central authorities supervised and checked the power of the *encomenderos*. The *encomienda* system was the basis of Spanish rule in the Philippines; the central administration was established not to replace it but to prevent its worst abuses.

The Catholic church played a major part in the development of the Philippines; it was the aim of Spanish policy to convert the new subjects to the Christian Catholic faith. Missionary monks came with the first Spanish conquerors, and Manila was made a bishopric as early as 1578. The Church established religious communities on the estates of the new Spanish landowners, sending out parish priests who lived in the Filipino villages and became leaders in social as well as religious affairs. The Christian faith and the pageantry of the Church had a great appeal to the Filipino people, and the influence of the Church spread rapidly in the parts of the Philippines where primitive forms of local shamanism had previously prevailed. The spread of the Christian religion was arrested, however, in the parts of the southern islands where Islam had gained a strong foothold. At the time of the Spanish conquest, Islam was also beginning to penetrate into the northern islands and might in a short time have spread over all the Philippines had the Spanish conquest not interfered. As it was, the Spanish prevented the penetration of Islam into the main islands, and carried on a counter-offensive against the sultans of Borneo and the Moluccas, who were extending their commercial and religious influence to the Philippines. When the religious conflict came to a standstill in the seventeenth century, a small Moslem minority remained in the southern part of the islands, but the rest of the Philippines was almost completely Christianized. The Church became an integral part of the economic as well as the cultural life of the colony. The large stretches of land which were granted for the support of the churches and the monasteries made the Church one of the main landowners in the Philippines.

The Philippine Islands were administered as an appendage to the Spanish colonies in Central America up to the time when Spain lost its

American colonies. The governor-general at Manila dealt with Spain through the Spanish colonial administration in Mexico. Spanish galleons carried the products of the Philippines to the port of Acapulco in Mexico, and the funds to support the colonial administration in the Philippines were sent from Mexico.

During the first century of Spanish rule Manila was a center of Far Eastern trade. The Spanish were all the more interested in making Manila a trading center when they found that the Philippines were rich neither in gold nor in spices, the original objects of their conquest. The products of China, Japan, the Moluccas, Malaya, Sumatra, Siam, Cambodia, Borneo, Ceylon, and other countries were brought to Manila. Traders from China brought silk and many other commodities such as ornaments, jewelry, copper kettles and utensils, furniture, many kinds of fruit, animals, singing birds, gunpowder, and endless varieties of luxury and consumer goods. Portuguese merchants brought spices, slaves, textiles, ivory, wood, and jewelry from the Indies, tea from India, Chinese goods from Macao, and preserves from Portugal. The Japanese brought armor and weapons, salt, meats, and wheat flour. All these and many other products were bought and sold in Manila, from where they were shipped to Mexico. When the volume of trade was especially great, direct shipment to Spain was occasionally permitted. The trading community in Manila—a wealthy group of Spanish and foreign merchants—prospered, and the colonial administration profited from the tariffs which it imposed on both the export and import of goods.

The early trade boom was arrested by the decline of Spain and the consequent growing isolation of the Philippines. It was in the middle of the seventeenth century that the economy of Spain began to decline. Shaken by rebellions at home and spoiled by the riches of the New World, Spain did not progress beyond the trade in spices and luxuries to the trade in industrial products which England and other countries developed. Spain therefore did not share in the new kind of trade between the West and the Far East which developed in the late eighteenth century. Europe's direct trade with China and the Dutch development in Indonesia diverted the commodity exchange from its former center in the Philippines. Japan closed her islands to all outsiders. Finally, at the beginning of the nineteenth century, Spain's American colonies became independent and Manila lost its political and economic link with the New World. In Manila itself, trade rivalries led to several large-scale massacres of the Chinese communities in the city.

Although the world importance of Manila and the Philippines declined, the social and cultural institutions which the Spanish had introduced into the Philippines remained unchanged. The most important of these institutions was the *encomienda* system through which powerful families ruled their separate estates. The *encomienda* institution was abolished at the end of Spanish rule, but the large landowning families continued to exercise economic and political power. The rule of these powerful families has been called *caciquism*, a word borrowed from the former Spanish American colonies. It has been translated as "local bossism." The caciques combined economic and political power; they were landowners, moneylenders, and—through their control of the local police—the local political bosses. These powerful families were of Spanish, or of mixed Spanish and Malay, origin. The Spanish had no racial prejudice against their new subjects. The Church approved of intermarriage between Spanish and Malay if the offspring were baptized in the Christian faith. These families provided the leaders for the anti-Spanish, and later the anti-American, independence movements in the Philippines. Many of the great names of the Philippine national struggle, names such as Manuel Quezon, Manuel Roxas, and Elpidio Quirino, came from these Spanish-Filipino families.

Spanish colonial policy was responsible for the existence of one nation in the Far East with a Western cultural tradition. As a result of Spanish influence the Philippines came to have a new religion and a new ruling class. Spanish influence thus prepared the ground for a nationalism which matured much earlier in the Philippines than in other Malay countries.

3. INDONESIA

Indonesia consists of a large group of islands reaching from the southeast Asiatic peninsula to the continent of Australia. The land area of these islands consists of some 735,000 square miles, one-fourth the size of the United States. With the inclusion of the water area, the island group covers a much larger territory which extends for about 3,000 miles from west to east, and about 1,250 miles from north to south. The western islands were once a part of the Asiatic continent, from which they are believed to have been severed only after the last Ice Age, when the rising ocean waters separated the higher islands from the coast. The plant growth on these islands indicates a previous connection with Asia. The eastern part of Indonesia belongs to the geographical block of Australia, from which it is separated by a shallow ocean. Between the eastern and western islands there is a deep ocean which is dotted with volcanic islands.

The Indonesian islands vary greatly in population density and development, but there has always been a trend towards ethnic and political unity. This has been due in part to the location of the island group across the trade routes of the Far East, and to the ease of inter-island communication. The former Malay rulers as well as the Dutch conquerors controlled the islands of Indonesia as one political unit.

Since the island group reaches across the equator, there are no appreciable seasonal differences in temperature, which has not exceeded 96 or fallen below 66 degrees in the past ninety years. The great humidity and the monotony of the temperature, which changes little between day and night, increase the effect of the heat on the people living in the area. The whole island group is in an area of regular monsoon winds and most of the islands have heavy rainfall throughout the year. The heat and the rainfall create the conditions for tropical jungle growth which covers most of the islands and quickly overgrows any cleared area left untended. Apart from the seaports, the best conditions for human settlement have been in those inland areas where the rainfall is sufficient but not excessive and the soil is fertile. These conditions exist on the island of Java which since early historical times has been the main center of Indonesian development.

At the end of World War II, Indonesia had a population of some 73,000,000 people, making it the third largest nation in the Far East. This population is very unevenly distributed over the island group. The vast majority of over 50,000,000 live on the islands of Java and Madura alone. These islands have the highest population density of any agricultural area on earth with a maximum of over 3,000 people per square mile.

The island group is divided into the Larger Sunda Islands, the Lesser Sunda Islands, the Moluccas, and the island of New Guinea. The Larger Sunda Islands are Borneo, Sumatra, Java and Madura, and Celebes. Borneo, 213,000 square miles in area, is the least developed and has a population of only 2,500,000 people. The interior is mountainous jungle territory, inhabited mainly by primitive tribal people. In modern times some of the coastal areas have been used for rubber plantations, and oil has been found and exploited. A strip on the west coast is British colonial territory.

Sumatra, 167,000 square miles in area, has the somewhat denser population of over nine million people. In modern times it has been important for plantation development, the chief product being rubber, and for its oil wells and tin mines. The eastern part of the island consists mainly of plains, which in the south and towards the coast are frequently swamps and marshes.

Java, only 51,000 square miles in area, is the most important of the islands. Most of the population of Indonesia is concentrated here. In the past it was the seat of Javanese empires which extended at times over the surrounding islands. It also became the center of the Dutch colonial administration and, in recent times, of the Indonesian republic. Jakarta, the Dutch "Batavia," has been the capital since the beginning of Dutch rule.

Celebes, the smallest of the Larger Sunda Islands, has always been important for the coastal trading stations on the tips of its many peninsulas, especially Macassar, the capital, in the south. More recently it has become known for the production of copra. It has a population of 4,500,000.

These four larger islands are the most important part of Indonesia. The Lesser Sunda Islands, which lie to the east of Java, also have a plantation economy but are less populated and productive. The Moluccas, to the east of Celebes, were famous in the seventeenth and eighteenth centuries as the center of the spice trade. The main products of that time, cloves and nutmeg, brought great profits to the early Dutch and local traders, and the control of these spices became a major objective for all the powers with interests in that area. To the east, the large island of New Guinea, the western part of which came under Dutch control, is the least populated and developed of the whole area. In its inland jungles and mountain ranges primitive tribal groups have survived until present times.

The development of the Indonesian islands has been brought about by Malay people who are believed to have come from the Asiatic continent in two main waves of migration. These Malay groups either drove the pre-Malay tribal people of Negrito and other ethnic types into the less accessible mountain areas of the larger islands or destroyed or assimilated them. The Malay people themselves have developed along many different linguistic and cultural lines, retaining, however, an underlying cultural cohesion.

The culture of the Malays has been greatly influenced by India and the Near East, whence Hinduism, Buddhism, and Islam were brought into Indonesia by succeeding waves of immigrants.

The Indians, who came both to the coastal areas of Sumatra and to Java, by the eighth century had established small kingdoms controlled by a Hindu-Indonesian upper class. On Java these states were of two types: the coastal states, which were mainly engaged in commerce, and the inland states, which developed irrigated agriculture. They were ruled by rajahs. Indonesian legends which tell of the introduction of writing and a calendar by a Hindu prince indicate that Indian influence led to the spread of agriculture and irrigation. The Indians brought with them both Buddhist and Hindu religious beliefs. There seems to have been little conflict between the priests of Buddhism and of Hinduism, both of whom assisted in the establishment of princely states. Buddhism affected mainly the coastal areas while Hinduism was most important in the inland areas of central and eastern Java and on the neighboring island of Bali. The ruins of great temples and the remnants of extensive irrigation works are signs of the kingdoms of that time.

From the twelfth century on, commerce gained a new and greater importance when merchants from Persia, Arabia, and India came to the islands for profitable trade in pepper from Sumatra and spices from the Moluccas and other islands. These traders were Moslems and through them Islam penetrated the coastal ports and eventually became the predominant religion on the islands. The trade of that time was unrestrained by systems of international law and order, and no line was drawn between legitimate trading operations and methods of outright piracy and looting. Trading establishments on the coastal ports depended on their military power; the richest and strongest merchants became the kings or sultans of trading empires which extended over the area dominated by their ships and men.

In the fourteenth century the inland agricultural state of central and eastern Java gained control over the coastal trading states and established the great Javanese empire of Majapahit, which unified most of the island group into one political system. This empire not only held direct administrative control over the agricultural inland areas but also had enough naval strength to establish its control of the sea and of commerce and to reduce its commercial rivals to the status of vassalage. In the inland agricultural areas appointed district chiefs were responsible for the upkeep of bridges and roads, the protection of sacred trees and monuments, the tending of rice fields and crops, and the upkeep of dikes. Village elders directed the affairs of the Malay village communities under these district chiefs. At the court, the king had his prime minister and officials who were supervised by both Hindu and Buddhist priests.

The unity of this Javanese empire was not maintained for more than a few decades. The agricultural empire lost control over its vassal states and was itself divided. During the fifteenth and sixteenth centuries Islam spread from Sumatra over the whole of Indonesia. In the sixteenth century Java too became Moslem, but the political division between the agricultural inland state and the coastal trading ports remained.

This division facilitated foreign conquest and control. In 1596 four Dutch ships arrived in Indonesia, and in 1598 no less than five Dutch expeditions with a total of twenty-two ships came to the trading ports of the islands. In 1602 the Dutch formed the Dutch East Indies Company. Before them, Portuguese traders had already begun to play a part in Indian and Indonesian trade and had established their own bases in the Strait of Molucca and on the Spice Islands. The Dutch drove the Portuguese out of the southern Moluccas and established their first territorial possession at Amboina. They gained control over all of the Spice Islands after driving out Spanish garrisons sent from the Philippines. From the beginning, the Dutch aimed at securing a monopoly of the spice trade. They gained this monopoly by treaties with the local sultans, by development of spice gardens under their own control, and by ruthless destruction of spice production on the islands which they could not control. The Dutch succeeded because of their naval power, which they used to exclude European competition and to destroy the naval power of the Malay states. In the destruction of Malay naval power they were aided by the conflicts between the Javanese sultan of the inland state of Mataram and the coastal sultanates of the Javanese north coast. The victories of the sultan of Mataram practically eliminated the sea power of the coastal states, thus greatly facilitating the Dutch rise to power. The sultan of Mataram, who thought little of matters of trade, was willing to give trading privileges to the Dutch in order to weaken the coastal states. Thus the inter-Javanese rivalries helped the Dutch to build up their trading monopoly.

In 1618 the Dutch established a fortress at Jakarta, the seat of a sultanate on the northwest coast of Java, moving there from the former trading center at Bantam, where they had been in competition with the British and other traders. This new fortress was given the name of Batavia. It became the seat of the governor-general and the center from which the Dutch East India Company controlled what came to be called the Netherlands East Indies. The fortress was successfully defended against the British and also against the sultan of Mataram, who eventually became hostile to the growing Dutch power. Thus secured against attacks from within and without, Batavia became in the seventeenth century the center of trade for goods from Persia, India, the Moluccas, and Japan, and the link between this eastern trading world and the Company's base in Holland. Profits increased, especially after 1650 when Dutch naval supremacy was assured. During the second half of the seventeenth century, the Dutch subjugated the inland sultanates one after another by intervening in struggles among members of the ruling houses for succession to the throne. By 1705, the Dutch had control of Java and had secured a monopoly of the spice trade.

In the eighteenth century the Dutch developed a system of agricultural exploitation in the islands. They introduced a system of "contingents and forced deliveries" under which the Javanese sultans and smaller local rulers had to provide a yearly tribute of crops which they were forced to plant in their respective territories. Coffee, which was introduced at the beginning of the century, became the main article of forced production. The Dutch made use of the method of "indirect rule," using the local sultans and the aristocracy in their economic exploitation. In some places the former sultans were retained and in others Javanese "regents" were selected from aristocratic families to administer territories under Dutch control. Dutch control was exercised through a Commissary for Native Affairs, with Dutch supervisors in each of the Indonesian states and territories. These supervisors, known as "coffee sergeants," and the Commissary staff were the beginning of the Dutch civil service in the East Indies. As the regents were appointed by the governor-general, the officers they appointed had to have the governor-general's approval. The peasants were subjected to forced labor in the coffee gardens, for which they received no compensation.

While this system placed a heavy burden on the exploited Javanese population, it also created stable conditions through the imposition of a Dutch-enforced peace. In the preceding period of declining Javanese power and constant wars between the various sultanates, systematic irrigation works had been difficult to maintain. Whole areas had been abandoned and much of the agriculture was carried on in temporary clearings in the jungle. Now that wars were forbidden, irrigation works were built up again. The population grew and by 1780 had reached the figure of three and a half million people.

Under the Dutch administration, the Chinese, who had already played an important part in the preceding century as traders in the ports, became an intermediate economic group in the field of finance. At first some Chinese immigrants were given land in the neighborhood of Batavia in order to increase rice production, and others were given positions as collectors of highway taxes for the Dutch. Later they came to act as moneylenders and owners of pawnshops and took over most of the retail trade. Thus they became an economic buffer between the Malay people and the Dutch upper group, incurring a good deal of Javanese hostility.

In extending their domination over the island of Java, the Dutch became responsible for the supervision of local jurisdiction over the Malay people and also over the Chinese. Finding it impractical to apply Dutch concepts of law to the different societies on the island, they used three legal systems for the different groups of Indonesia. For the Malay population, the Dutch supervised the application of native law, the so-called *adat*. In order to enforce an equal and fair application of this customary law of the islands, the Dutch had to study and develop it. They thus promoted and preserved an Indonesian tradition, a policy which differed completely from the Spanish policy in the Philippines.

The Dutch found it impossible to apply Indonesian or European law to

the Chinese, who clung together in their own social group. To them, therefore, the Dutch applied Chinese law, as interpreted by headmen of the Chinese community. For themselves and other Europeans, the Dutch used
Dutch law. In the group of Europeans they included the offspring of legitimate and illegitimate unions between Dutch and Indonesians.

By the end of the eighteenth century the foundation had been laid for
Dutch colonial rule of the populated areas of Java itself. The Dutch continued their strict control over the eastern islands and in Sumatra their coastal
economic penetration by trade agreements that undermined the independence of the Islamic states. However, they concentrated their main activities on
Java, where they had subjugated the inland states. A large part of the territory was ruled by regents, and the once powerful sultanate of central Java
was divided into the sultanates of Jocjakarta and Surakarta, both dominated
by Dutch residents.

At the end of the century, during the Napoleonic wars, Holland came
under French control and was isolated from her colonial possessions. As a
result all the outlying islands were lost to the British, and finally Java itself
came under British administration. When the oligarchic government in Holland was overthrown in 1795 by Dutch revolutionaries allied with the French,
the new Dutch government wanted the Dutch people to secure a greater
share in the benefits derived from the colonies. The ruling Dutch oligarchy
had based the East Indies Company monopoly on a policy of limited and
controlled trade, high prices, and small capital investment. In 1799 the new
government abolished the East Indies Company and permitted free trade.

When the Netherlands East Indies were restored to the Dutch after the
Congress of Vienna, the economic and political benefits which the revolution
had brought to the people of Holland were not extended to the people of the
colonies. The government felt that even the limited domestic slavery that
existed in the Indies could not be abolished until other European countries
with overseas colonies were willing to give up slavery. In spite of demands for
the introduction of the "free play of economic forces," the system of forced
deliveries and compulsory cultivation was continued and further developed
in the nineteenth century into a system of forced production for the motherland, the so-called culture system, the most extensive form of forced labor ever
devised by any colonial power.

4. ANNAM, CAMBODIA, AND LAOS

On the southeast Asian continent Chinese influence was strong. At one
time or another the countries of this area were in a tributary relationship to
the Chinese court. Of these countries Annam was most closely linked to
China. Like Korea, Annam was a vassal state with its own organization and
administration, loosely related to the Chinese court by tributary missions and
politically dependent upon it.

Annam was the largest and most populous unit of the three kingdoms
which were eventually combined into the colonial territories of French Indo-

China. The name Indo-China describes the area in which Indian and Chinese influences have met. Of the three kingdoms Cambodia and Laos were influenced mainly by Indian culture while Annam was under Chinese cultural influence.

The Annamese populated the lower valley and delta of the Red River—the area known as Tongking—as well as the coastal belt to the south of it, and from there moved into the fertile delta of the Mekong River on the southern tip of the peninsula—the area known as Cochin China. The territory of Annam consists of a strip of land along the coast connecting the rich rice lands of the deltas of the Red River in the north and of the Mekong in the south. The shape of this area has been compared with a coolie's load—a bamboo pole balancing a bucket of rice at each end. The integration of this territory into one political unit was difficult, and the kingdom of Annam suffered from division and inner strife even before the establishment of the French colonial empire. The two kingdoms of Cambodia and Laos are located on the inland border of the Indo-Chinese territory. Mountains and high plateaus occupy most of this inland area which has much less population than the coastal lands of Annam. Cambodia consists of the lower part of the Mekong plain, with the exception of the coastal deltas, which were taken by the Annamese. Laos covers the plains and mountain lands between the upper part of the Mekong and the range of the Annamese Cordilleras which run in a northeastern-southwestern direction and separate the coastal plains of Annam from the inland plains of Laos and Cambodia.

The comparative importance of these three ethnic and political areas can be seen from the relative size of their population figures which after World War II have been about 21,000,000 for Annam, 3,370,000 for Cambodia, and 1,125,000 for Laos. The importance of the river deltas in Cochin China and Tongking is shown by the distribution of the Annamese population which was roughly 9,000,000 for Tongking, 5,000,000 for Cochin China, and 6,500,-000 for the whole coastal area of central Annam.

The Cambodians are the descendants of the ancient Khmers whose former glory and high civilization are still evinced by the magnificent ruins of Angkor Wat. They were forced back from the coastal lands by the Annamese, whose historic capital was Hue, but whose principal modern cities have been Hanoi in the north and Saigon in the south.

More than any other of China's neighbors, the Annamese have been influenced by China both culturally and ethnically. In the second century B.C., Tongking and the northern part of Annam were even part of a Chinese state and were combined with what are now the provinces of Kwangtung and Kwangsi. In this northern part of the Annamese area there was a great deal of early intermixture of Annamese and Chinese people. The area remained under direct Chinese control for most of the time until the tenth century A.D. Later, it was intermittently linked to China in a tributary relationship and served at times as the last base of retreat for defeated Chinese dynasties. Members of the Ming dynastic family, for instance, took refuge there. As a result of this early Chinese influence and the continuing contact, Tongking and central Annam were quite Chinese in character, Chinese immigrants mingled with the Annamese, and no distinguishable Chinese minority remained.

The southern part of Annam—the plains of Cochin China—had a somewhat different cultural development. The Annamese people did not move into this area until the sixteenth century, taking the land away at that time from the Cambodians. China never controlled southern Annam, and no Chinese influence existed there until modern times, when considerable numbers of Chinese merchants migrated there. The Chinese intermarried with the Annamese but have remained a recognizable Chinese minority group, making up almost four per cent of the population.

The society of Annam has many parallels with that of China. The Confucian tradition with its ancestor cult and authoritarian family relations has been strong. Most of the people were peasants living in villages which were also the units for joint labor in irrigation work. The unit of land worked by the peasant family was small and the living standard near the minimum level. In Tongking and northern Annam the land usually belonged to the peasant who tilled it, while in Cochin China, where there was a surplus production, tenancy was the rule. Rice is the staple crop of Annam; and in spite of the density of the population in the cultivated areas, especially in the deltas, southern Annam has been an area of rice surplus and export. As in China there has been little animal husbandry, and pork and fowl make up the meat diet for those who can afford it.

It was the duty of the village elders to collect the taxes, to transmit them, to provide public labor for the upkeep of local irrigation systems and roads and to guarantee peace and order. Above the common peasants and the smaller number of artisans and traders living in the towns was a group of officials appointed by the king. In all this the Chinese influence was evident. The basis of the officials' privileged position was a Chinese system of education that even included periodic examinations. The social structure thus showed the influence of China's Confucian society. There also existed a strong Buddhist influence which expressed itself in the art and architecture of the temples and pagodas.

Under the Manchus the Chinese dynastic control of Annam was reaffirmed and regular tributary relations established. But the unity of the kingdom of Annam was threatened from within by dynastic rivalries, supported by different groups of the leading official elite. In 1673 Annam was divided into the three states of central Annam, Tongking, and Cochin China, and a dynastic struggle ensued which continued all through the eighteenth century. This division and internal struggle invited intervention by the French, who during the seventeenth century first aspired to colonial possessions in India and Southeast Asia. Spearheaded by French Jesuit missionaries, the French moved into Annam which they regarded as a special sphere for their religious as well as their commercial activities. In 1787, when the king of Annam was driven from his throne by his brothers, the French took the side of the deposed king. In 1789 he was reinstated with the help of French troops, led by a Catholic bishop. In exchange the French were granted bases on the southern coast. In 1801, this ruler succeeded in extending his control over Tongking and Cochin China, thus re-establishing the united kingdom of Annam. During the French Revolution the influence of France was arrested for the time being, and Annam remained an autonomous kingdom, tributary to China until the French renewed their expansion in the second half of the nineteenth century.

5. Burma

Burma, the most westerly of the countries of Southeast Asia, is separated from the subcontinent of India by the jungle-covered Arakan and Patkoi Mountains. These mountains have been a barrier in the way of close cultural or political relations with India. To the east, the deep river gorges of the Mekong and upper Yangtze and the high mountain ranges and vast jungles that lie between them have been an equal hindrance to close relations with China. Protected by these barriers, Burma could not easily be absorbed by either China or India.

Burmese society began in the central part of the country. Here, where the Chindwin joins the upper Irrawaddy, plains and low hilly land lie between these rivers and the upper Sittang River. In this rich agricultural area the Pagan dynasty established the kingdom of Burma during the eleventh century A.D. This dynasty extended agriculture by constructing irrigation systems and unified the small states and tribal groups of the valleys and surrounding areas.

The people who were unified by the Pagan dynasty belonged ethnically to the Sino-Tibetan group. The largest and most important group among them had come from the Chinese borderland as late as the eighth or ninth century A.D. and had mingled with related groups already living there. They were hostile to another more highly civilized Sino-Tibetan group, the Mons, who occupied the lower part of the Irrawaddy and Sittang valleys and the Tenasserim range which stretches down the coast into the Malay Peninsula. The Mons were eventually defeated and brought into the Burmese kingdom.

The jungle and mountain areas of the lower part of Burma were inhabited by Karen tribes who were first under the control of the Mons and later under that of the Burmese kingdom. Shan tribes, related to the Thai, moved into the high mountain plateaus to the east of the Sittang and upper Irrawaddy rivers. The northern and western mountains on the Indian and Tibetan borders were occupied by the Chin and Kachin tribes, who had moved there from the Tibetan border area. The Burmese people in the central river valleys were thus surrounded by mountain tribes of varied ethnic origin and of primitive social organization. The territory of this Burmese state covers 260,000 square miles and in 1953 had a population of about 16,000,000 people, of whom the Burmese made up more than two-thirds.

Although the overland approach from India was difficult, the lower river deltas could be reached easily by sea. There was contact between India and the coastal regions since the early centuries of the Christian era when Indian merchant colonies were established along the Arakan and Tenasserim coasts and on the river deltas. These merchants brought with them Hinayana Buddhism, which was accepted by the Mon people. The Indian script used in the Pali Buddhist texts became the basis for Burmese writing; the Indian art and architecture of the time became models for the Burmese. When Buddhist sutras were introduced from Ceylon, the Mons, because of their location in the west, were the first to receive them. It was through the Mons that the Pagan dynasty secured its knowledge of Buddhism, the ideology on which the Pagan government was based. In the eleventh century the Pagan dynasty forcibly seized the sutras from the Mons and established direct contact with Ceylon, the source of the Hinayana Buddhist faith accepted in Burma. The Burmese retained this religious and ideological system, and Hinayana Buddhism has remained the basis of education and cultural development in Burma.

The Pagan dynasty was destroyed by Mongol invasion from China in the thirteenth century. After the Mongols established their dynasty in China, they crossed the border and destroyed the Burmese capital in 1287. Though the Mongols withdrew, they had decisively weakened the central economic area of Burma and had destroyed Burmese unity. The Mons again controlled the south, and Shan tribes took over the upper Irrawaddy River. Burma was again united temporarily under the Toungoo dynasty in the middle of the sixteenth century; but in the seventeenth and the early eighteenth centuries frequent invasions from China and Thailand weakened the Burmese kingdom. Not until the middle of the eighteenth century was Burma again unified. At that time a new government, founded by Alaungpaya, defeated the Mons and re-established Burmese control over the whole area. The government of this kingdom sent tributary missions to the Chinese court but was otherwise independent. This Burmese state, with its capital at Ava, close to Mandalay, lasted until the British conquered the kingdom during the nineteenth century.

6. THAILAND (SIAM)

Thailand has the most central location of the countries of Southeast Asia. The country is formed by the plains and valleys of the Menam River basin and the mountains and high plateaus that surround it. Thailand has been furthest removed in the past from the influence of India or China either overland or by sea. In modern times it has been hemmed in by the British colonies of Burma and Malaya and the French colony of Indo-China. Situated as a buffer state between British and French colonial territories, it is the one country in Southeast Asia which has been able to preserve, at least nominally, her independence. Her rulers succeeded in retaining their freedom of action by exploiting British and French colonial rivalry.

The Thai people are of mixed origin. During the first millennium A.D. groups of Lao people moved in from the north and settled in the river valleys of northern Thailand, whence they spread south and came into contact with

Khmer peoples with whom they intermixed. In the eleventh century an organized state was established in the middle of the Menam River plain. In the fourteenth century the Mongols conquered the Nan Chao kingdom in southwest China and drove another wave of people south into Thailand where in 1351 they set up a new government with the capital at Ayuthia. The Thai people are a mixture of the Khmer and the two waves of immigrants from China.

Thailand has today a population of about eighteen million people of whom about fourteen million are Thai. Small minorities of Laotians, Annamese, and Cambodians in the north and east, of Malays in the south, and about three million Chinese make up the remainder of the population of the country. Thailand has an area of about 200,000 square miles. The central part of the valley and the surrounding plains of the Menam River contain the bulk of the population. This plain has been used for rice agriculture; but only a little over one-quarter of it has been cultivated, great stretches remaining a waste of grass and reeds. This land, if irrigated, could become one of the greatest rice-producing centers in the world. To the east of this central plain is a mountainous plateau, which inclines towards the east and sends its waters into the Mekong. This plateau has an adverse climate and poor soil, except in some small areas, and has therefore a comparatively thin population of a million and a quarter Laotian, Thai, and Cambodian people. The mountainous areas of the north are inhabited by Lao groups under their own tribal chieftains, while the long arm of the Malay Peninsula in the south is peopled by Malays and Thais who live in the small fertile valleys. The political focus of these territories is the area of the Menam River plain; its most important center in the past was the capital of Ayuthia. The surrounding agricultural region, Thailand proper, was divided into provinces under appointed governors, while more distant territories were ruled as vassal provinces.

Thailand was an absolute monarchy in which all power rested in the king. There was no hereditary nobility. The king ruled with the help of appointed officials who held their titles by virtue of office and at the king's pleasure. The salaries of the officials, which were comparatively small, were calculated according to purely nominal rights over rice lands. Officials and their families were exempt from labor service. Any strong personal ties or cliques within this official group were frowned upon as being dangerous to the king's authority. The central government was directed by deputies and royal secretaries and, as in China, divided into six ministries. There was a division between military and civil officials. The governors of the central provinces were also appointed and removed by the king, while those in the vassal provinces farther away were "semi-hereditary" and more or less independent. Under this bureaucratic regime lived a submissive farming population, obliged to give labor service to the king under the direction of the Ministry of Public Service. The people had to render corvée service for public works and paid their taxes largely in commodities. They were also subject to recruiting for the army and navy and for special Imperial Guards maintained at the capital. These Guards formed the hard core of the army and were supplemented during military campaigns by further levies according to need. Service could be avoided by payment of fees. The actual control of the ruler varied according to the internal political situation and the danger of outside attack. Such attacks came from Burma, Cambodia, and once from the Mongols in China. These attacks weakened the government and even led to short periods of foreign domination.

In the second half of the eighteenth century a Burmese attack again threatened the independence of the Thai state. In 1767 the capital, Ayuthia, was taken by the Burmese and destroyed; the Thai king perished, and a Burmese viceroy was left to rule the country. A Thai official who escaped the besieged capital organized another Thai force, defeated and killed the Burmese viceroy, made himself king, and moved his capital to Tonburi on the western shore of the lower Menam River. Consolidating his power, he succeeded in unifying all of Thailand, with the exception of the Tenasserim area, which remained in Burmese hands. He in turn was dethroned in 1781 by a rebellion of officials led by a former minister and officer of the royal armies, who ascended the throne in 1782 and established the present Siamese dynasty, known as the house of Chakkri, from the name of its founder. Under him the capital was moved to the eastern shore of the lower Menam River to the city of Bangkok, which was built to emulate the former capital of Ayuthia and has remained the Thai capital ever since. A new Burmese invasion which started in 1785 was beaten off, and since 1792 there has been no further major conflict between the two countries.

7. British Malaya

British Malaya is located at the southern end of the Malay Peninsula, which stretches from the Asiatic continent to the island group of Indonesia. Because of its location on the Strait of Malacca, which commands the sea routes that connect the Indian Ocean with the Indonesian archipelago and the China Sea, the peninsula has always been a recipient of trading groups, settlers, and cultural influences from all sides.

Thailand pushed southward along the peninsula and appropriated the northern and central part of it. The remaining southern part of the peninsula, which became British colonial territory and is known as British Malaya, has a territory of 52,000 square miles. Like the northern parts of the peninsula it is mountainous country covered with tropical jungle and exposed to two monsoon seasons which bring heavy rain all through the year. The population of the peninsula is largely of Malay stock, but there are two groups which are believed to be remnants of a pre-Malay population. These are the Negritos and the Sakai, the latter taller and somewhat lighter than the Negritos. The Malay culture started in prehistoric times. The early Malays had irrigated rice fields, but they lived primarily by hunting and fishing. The Malays have intermingled with some of the Negritos and Sakai and have also mixed with later immigrants such as the Thai, the Chinese, and the Malays from Sumatra and Java.

The most important ethnic as well as cultural influence on the Malays has come from India. Hindus came to Malaya, as they did to Indonesia, from the beginning of the Christian era. They did not come as invading armies but rather in small groups and as individuals. They were traders and adventurers, priests and scholars. They brought products from India and settled in the ports of the Malacca Strait, which they helped to develop. They intermarried with the leading families of the Malays, establishing a Malay-Hindu upper group. The Hindu and Buddhist priests and monks brought their religious ideas and texts. They also brought Hindu ideas of kingship, and these led to the establishment of agricultural and trading states by the Malay-Hindu upper group. The cultural and political impact of Hindu and Buddhist India was, after the eleventh century, supplanted by a second wave of Indian influence. Islam had become important in India, especially among key trading groups; and merchants like the Tamils and others brought their Islamic religion and institutions to Malaya and Indonesia. The Malay states became Moslem states, the rajahs became sultans, and Islam became in time the dominant religion and cultural tradition throughout the Malay world, with the exception of the Philippines.

The Malay states of the peninsula, based only upon the agriculture of the small river valleys and the competitive trading of the ports, were not powerful enough to be independent. Their sultans, absolute rulers within their realms, had to acknowledge the control of larger outside powers. The sultans of Malacca exchanged tribute and presents with Chinese emperors of the Ming dynasty and asked for protection against Thai pressure. More important still was the control exercised by the Indonesian empires of Sumatra and Java. The Malay sultans became vassals of the more powerful rulers of Palembang and Jambi and, in the fourteenth century, of the Javanese empire of Majapahit. The influence of this connection with Indonesia has survived until recent times.

Among the Malay states themselves relationships of vassalage and dominance were also established. A Malay state at the location of modern Singapore was a flourishing center of trade with China and politically dominated the scene until it was conquered and destroyed by the Majapahit empire of Java in the fourteenth century. With its destruction, Malacca, which had a strong colony of Moslem traders from India and the Middle East, became the most important political and trading center.

The end of this Malay political development came with the European impact which began in the sixteenth century. Three of the early colonizing powers of Europe in turn made their appearance on the Malay Peninsula. In 1511 the Portuguese conquered Malacca and established themselves there. In 1641 the town fell to the Dutch and was put under the same administration as the Dutch possessions on the islands of Indonesia. Later the Dutch were forced out by the British who established themselves on the peninsula around the turn of the nineteenth century. In 1786, the British received the island of Penang from the sultan of Kedah and established their first crown colony. Malacca fell to them during the Napoleonic Wars. After the war,

Sir Stamford Raffles, who had administered the Dutch East Indies until their return to Holland, founded in 1819 the British free port and naval base of Singapore which was soon to become the dominant trading and military center of the area. From these three colonial possessions, known as the Straits Settlements, the British moved inland during the last part of the nineteenth century, to extend their control over the Malay states.

CHAPTER V

Russia in Asia

THE development of Russia as a power in Asia is a vital part of Far Eastern history. From the sixteenth century, when the Russian frontier first began to move into Asia, until the present time, the expansion of Russia across Central Asia to the Far East has been a story of continuous advance. The Russian drive across the continent pushed forward the borders of the Russian empire until they touched on China and on Manchuria, Mongolia, and Turkestan. With the development of Siberia as a part of Russia, Russia became herself a Far Eastern power as well as a major contender among the imperial powers struggling for territorial gains in Asia. As Asiatic Russia grew in population and economic importance, Russian influence in the Far East increased. In recent times the development of Asiatic Russia has been accelerated; and the territorial ambitions of the tsars have been carried on by the Soviet Union within the context of the world-wide Communist movement.

The foundations of the Russian position in Asia were laid during the period between the sixteenth and the early nineteenth centuries. Before this time the Russian state had been limited to Europe, where it had taken shape in the forested plains and river regions between the Black Sea and the Baltic. The cities of Kiev, Novgorod, and Moscow became one after the other the political centers of an agricultural and commercial Slavic society, whose commercial life was patterned after that of the cities of Scandinavia and the Hanseatic League and whose religion and culture were drawn from Byzantium and the Greek Orthodox Church. Old Russia had already developed its own cultural tradition before it fell under the control of Mongol conquerors in the early thirteenth century, when Genghis Khan and his successors extended their empires by sweeping raids across Central Asia, around the Caspian Sea, and into Europe. The Mongols did not follow up their raids into Central Europe, but they established a rule over Russia which lasted from the thirteenth to the fifteenth centuries. During this period the Russians paid tribute to the rulers of the Mongol Golden Horde, who established their capital on the Volga River. The Russian princes, among whom the Muscovites gained the leadership, depended for their positions on the confirmation of the Mongol khans for whom they acted as representatives. Through the Mongols the Russians even acquired some Asiatic institutions and practices, such as the methods of tax and tribute collection and the taking of a census of the population. In the fourteenth century the Mongol power declined because of internal strife between rival steppe empires. At the same time Russian unity grew and led to a Russian counterattack under the leadership of the Muscovite princes. In 1480 the "Tatar yoke" was finally thrown off. A hundred years later the Russians began their drive across Asia which was to bring them to the Pacific in less than seventy years.

Geography of Asiatic Russia

The whole of Russia forms a vast plain which stretches from the Baltic and the Black Sea almost to the Pacific Ocean. It has an area of 8,000,000 square miles, of which two thirds lie in Asiatic Russia. The Ural Mountains, which run north and south, form the dividing line between the European and Asiatic parts of Russia, but they are not an obstacle to the unity of the whole. They do not rise above 6,000 feet, and some of the passes are no more than 1,000 to 2,000 feet in height. The great Eurasian plain is a unit in itself, set apart from the rest of Asia by natural borders. In the north the border follows the Arctic Ocean to the Bering Straits. In the south the plain is bounded by the Caspian Sea, the highlands of Iran, and the ranges of the Hindu Kush, the Pamir, the Tien Shan, the Altai, and Sayan Mountains. To the east, the Stanovoi Mountains form the natural border of this vast territory of plains and high plateaus, but Russian expansion has reached beyond these mountains to the Amur River, the Japanese Sea, the Kamchatka Peninsula, the island of Sakhalin, and the Kuriles.

Asiatic Russia is divided into various climatic belts that lend themselves to very different forms and degrees of human settlement. Much more of Asiatic than of European Russia lies north of the Arctic Circle. In the north and east, along the Arctic Ocean and towards the Bering Straits, is the tundra, a region where the land is frozen almost all the year around and agriculture is impossible. In the past the economy of this area was based on the herding of reindeer. To the south of this zone is the *taiga*, a large forest belt that extends across the central part of Asiatic Russia. This forest belt of coniferous trees covers most of Asiatic Russia. To the south of the taiga is a zone of steppe land which has a temperate climate and sufficient rainfall for agriculture. The bulk of this steppe zone is in central Russia, to the northeast and east of the Caspian Sea. The climatic zones—the tundra, the taiga, and the steppe—have shaped the course of Russian expansion. The bulk of the population settled in the steppe and forest lands of central Asia, but

Russian settlements also stretched beyond this area to the east along the corridor between the tundra and the Mongol-Chinese border.

The Eastward Migration

The movement of the Russians into Asia began in the sixteenth century after the collapse of the Mongol states. The Russians penetrated into Siberia in order to exploit the resources of its forests, especially the plentiful furs—sable, fox, squirrel, and many others. Scores of adventurers came across the Urals into the forest belt and the tundra and reached the Pacific. They were attracted by the furs of the forests, the mammoth teeth found in the tundra, and the seals of the Bering Sea.

The first Russians to move into Asia were small groups of Cossacks. The Cossacks were organized bands of runaway serfs, criminals, and adventurers. Such groups of freebooters had first gathered together in the Don and Volga areas, between the country of Russian settlements and the Tatar states of the steppe. They elected their own leaders—hetmans or atamans—and were largely independent of any government control. They were always willing to penetrate into new areas for new gains, and hearing of rich fur resources in the area of the Ob River and its tributaries, they moved into Siberia. The first group crossed the Urals in 1581 under the Cossack leader Yermak, who has gained legendary fame as the "conqueror of Siberia." Yermak defeated a Tatar chieftain and conquered the town of Sibir on the Tobol River where he established a settlement. From the name of this town has been derived the name Siberia, which is now used for the whole area of Russian Asia from the Urals to the Sea of Okhotsk.

Once established in their new territories, the Cossacks sent emissaries to the tsarist government with gifts of valuable furs. In return the government granted the Cossacks pardon for whatever crimes they had been guilty of and took the territory they had conquered under Russian administration. From this time on bands of Cossacks came into Siberia in increasing numbers and with them came the authority of the Russian state. In rapid succession the Russians moved from the river system of the Ob and Irtysh to the Yenisei and the Lena, and from there across the mountains to the Sea of Okhotsk. In 1588 the city of Tobolsk was established at the junction of the Tobol and Irtysh rivers. From there the Russians advanced to the Ob and established the town of Obdorsk in 1595. In 1604 Tomsk was established on the Tom River near the upper Ob River; in 1619 Yeniseisk on the upper Yenisei; and in 1632 Yakutsk on the Lena. From Yakutsk the Cossacks went northeastward to the Kolyma River and the East Cape, first circled by the Cossack Dezhnev in 1648. The Cossacks moved eastward across the Stanovoi Mountains to the ocean where they founded Okhotsk in 1649, and southward in the same year to the Amur River, where they established only a temporary foothold. Thus in less than seventy years the Russians moved across the entire Asiatic continent to the sea.

The rapidity of the move was all the more remarkable in view of the formidable transportation problems involved. The rivers were the best available means of communication wherever they could be used. Cossacks sometimes dragged their boats across the low passes of the Ural Mountains from one river system to another. In Siberia the three great rivers, the Ob, the Yenisei, and the Lena, flow in a general south-north direction and empty into the Arctic Ocean which is icebound most of the year. The Russians, who were moving across the continent from west to east, could use only portions of these rivers and their tributaries. Only the middle and upper parts of the rivers were useful, but with the help of the tributaries it was possible to narrow the gap between the main river systems. It was still necessary, however, to travel great distances overland by sleigh, horseback, or on foot. In the search for a sea route along the Arctic coast, expeditions were undertaken to explore the waters between the mouths of the rivers. These explorations involved tremendous hardships and great loss of life. No practical use, however, could be made of the Arctic Ocean for sea communication at that time.

In the forests the Russians encountered comparatively little resistance from the scattered tribal population. The possession of firearms gave the Russians an easy mastery over these disunited and backward people. The Russians established a number of forts or blockhouses, the so-called *ostrogs*, from which to control the tribes, and made use of the native people in their economic exploitation of the area. In the name of the tsarist government the Russians imposed on the tribes a heavy tribute in furs, called the *yasak*. In order to get this tribute, which made up a larger part of the fur collection than that provided by Russian hunters and trappers, the Russian officials took advantage of intertribal conflicts and supported chieftains who were loyal to the Russian authority. These chiefs were sometimes treated well and became the heads of petty principalities within their districts. They were responsible for collecting the *yasak* from their tribes. They were bound to the Russian authorities by oaths of allegiance, but the internal affairs of the tribes were left to them. In the earlier period a hostage system was often applied to enforce the tribute payment, but it was finally abolished in 1769. The Russians had no racial prejudice towards the natives. The only barrier was religion. While "pagan" people were often treated with great brutality, especially in the first period of conquest, baptized natives were equal to Russians and even joined Cossack groups or entered the government service.

The first drive through Siberia enriched private traders, individual officials, and the tsarist government through exploitation of the fur resources of the forest country. Ruthless methods of exploitation rapidly diminished the fur resources and eventually exhausted them. Continuing the search for furs Russian adventurers crossed the sea to Alaska to hunt the seals of the Alaskan coast. The Russian-American Company, growing out of an earlier merchant enterprise, was founded in St. Petersburg in 1799 and flourished during the first part of the nineteenth century.

The Cossacks, private traders, and government officials depended at first on European Russia for supplies. As the garrisons moved farther into the forest belt, it became difficult to supply them, and they often suffered from hunger and starvation. In order to provide local food supplies for the Siberian towns the Russian government promoted agricultural settlements around the newly developed towns, especially in the border area of the steppe and the southern fringe of the forest belt. Peasants were assigned to the cultivation of "state land." But most of the peasants who came to Siberia took possession of land, and since there was free land always available the government could not keep them tied to "state land." At first peasants were permitted to work on their own land only if they cultivated "state land" in the proportion of one acre to five acres of their own. Later, these attempts to force the cultivation of "state land" were given up and replaced by a tax on the peasants. From the very beginning the peasant was freer in Siberia than in European Russia.

Serfdom never existed in Siberian Russia. This is the more remarkable because Siberian agriculture developed during the time in which serfdom became finally established in European Russia. In fact, all during the seventeenth and eighteenth centuries the pressure of political and economic conditions in European Russia caused a continuous flight of peasants into Siberia, seeking to escape debt, punishment or servitude. They made up the large majority of the Russian migrants. By 1700 they were already producing enough grain to provide for the population of Siberia As the fur resources of Siberia declined, agriculture came to play a more and more important part in the economy.

Siberian agriculture was very unevenly distributed. The main agricultural production was in western Siberia, and the whole of eastern Siberia, Yakutsk, and Kamchatka had to depend largely on the transport of food and equipment from the western part. To find a food basis for this rich fur country of eastern Siberia, Russian adventurers went first to the Amur area. Nerchinsk was established in 1658 on the Shilka, a tributary of the Argun, itself a tributary of the Amur River. Attempts to control the Amur as an outlet to the sea and a communication link with Kamchatka persisted until they were blocked by the Chinese. In the early nineteenth century the outposts of the Russian-American Company in Alaska also needed nearby sources of supply, and for this reason the Russians moved into California where they established Fort Ross as a base from which to secure provisions.

The Russian penetration into south central Asia began considerably later than that into the forest belt of Siberia. The drive into the Kirgiz steppes and into the Turanian lowlands to the east of the Caspian Sea came at the same time as the Russian move against the Tatar and Kalmuk tribes on the Black Sea and the Caspian Sea. Omsk was founded in 1716, and Semipalatinsk in 1718. Expeditions against the Kirgiz under Peter the Great in the second decade of the eighteenth century were unsuccessful; but before the middle of the century the steppe tribes, later known as the Kazakhs, were brought to submission peacefully. Not until the late nineteenth century did the Russians send military expeditions to the south and establish control over what has become Russian Turkestan.

The Russian population of Siberia had passed the million mark by the beginning of the nineteenth century, and Siberia had become an important part of Russia. The development of Siberia would not have been possible without the backing, the protection, and the military and civil organization provided by the tsarist government. The military expeditions that moved into new territories and established fortified towns went in the name of the tsarist government, even though they operated on their own initiative in this wild and distant country. The towns provided military protection for the traders, hunters, trappers, and settlers who preceded and followed the military units. The towns were the markets and centers of transportation, as well as the centers of the fur tribute and of government administration.

Siberian Administration

The administration of Siberia and the income derived from it was regarded as important enough by the tsarist government to warrant the establishment of a special ministry (*prikaz*) for Siberian affairs. This ministry collected reports from all sources, including official administrators and private merchants, and used them in planning policy. It gave directives to the Russian officials in Siberia and, most important of all, it supervised and managed the fur tribute.

In the early years the local Siberian administration was in the hands of the *voevodas* who were in charge of the various circuits; later, under Peter the Great, a system of provincial administration was introduced, and each province was administered by a governor. There was no governor with viceregal authority over the whole of Siberia. The governors of the provinces, like the *voevodas* before them, were appointed by the imperial government and were directly responsible to it. The officials were paid and supplied from the capital and were appointed for short periods so that they could not build up independent authority. In the early period before the provincial administration was set up, the assistants of the *voevodas* were clerks from the Moscow ministry, and wealthy businessmen were appointed to assist the *voevodas* in the financial administration and the management of the fur tribute. All officials were thus dependent on Moscow and checked and counterchecked each other.

The actual administration was at first military; it was run by men selected from the military nobility. They brought with them troops, mainly Cossacks and *streltsy*, or professional soldiers sent from European Russia to serve in the Siberian campaigns and in the garrisons. In time the *streltsy* merged with the Cossacks who increased their forces with recruits from the growing Russian population of Siberia. For special military undertakings the government enlisted volunteers from the traders and hunters and also used auxiliary native troops. The Cossacks were of two kinds, those who garrisoned the towns, received salaries, and saw active service, and those who were distributed in the settlements as agricultural colonists, exempted from the land tax and under obligation to protect their respective communities.

In the local recruitment of Cossacks and other units, the commanders who were selected first appointed their own lieutenants who in turn selected their men. The whole group was responsible for each member. These forces served in the protection of the settlements and conquest of new territory, in the collection of *yasak*, in the convoying of transports, and in other capacities such as guards or messengers. Siberia was thus first organized as a militarily controlled territory, and the military aspect remained important even after the introduction of a provincial administration.

Siberian Prisoners

From the outset, the Russian government used Siberia for a special purpose. Siberia was known as the place to which prisoners were exiled—a land of ice and snow from which there was no return. Actually, the ordinary criminals and political prisoners who were banished to Siberia played an important part in its development and their life was not always so hopeless as is widely believed. Siberia was used as a place for political exiles since the end of the sixteenth century. During the seventeenth century those who were imprisoned after the rebellions of that time were sent to Siberia. Then came the turn of religious heretics. The stream of prisoners grew larger and continued through the eighteenth and nineteenth centuries. The forms of exile differed greatly. There were those condemned to *katorga*, or forced labor in the mines and the government factories, which had been established in the eighteenth century. After serving their terms they had to remain in Siberia as exiles, sometimes for life, living as settlers near the area of their imprisonment. Some were accompanied by their families, and this kind of life was often not too unpleasant for those who had means of support. The exiles could make a living in the area. Some of those who were highly educated contributed to the knowledge and development of their land of enforced residence. But many others perished en route in the prisoner caravans or died of malnourishment and the strain of forced labor. The government used the prisoners in the mining of salt, the production of which was a government monopoly. From the time of Peter the Great, silver and copper had been mined in the area around Nerchinsk and in the Altai Mountains, and gold was found in several locations.

Russia and China

The Russians continued to push into Asia until they reached the borders of the Chinese empire, where they were faced with an opponent stronger than the tribal peoples whom they had subjugated in their eastward drive. When the Russian Cossacks reached the Sea of Okhotsk and crossed the mountains to the Amur River in the 1640's and 50's, China had just been conquered by the Manchus who established the Ch'ing dynasty in Peking in 1644. Coming themselves from the Manchurian mountain area on the Korean border, the Manchus regarded the Amur and its tributaries as their own preserve from which they could draw recruits for their banners. They were bound to resist the invader in their backyard and had the military strength to repulse the small groups of Cossack settlers. Twice the Russians attempted to establish themselves at Fort Albazin on the Amur River but were forced to give up their position in the face of far larger Chinese forces. Finally the Russians, interested in good relations with China as a market for the fur products of Siberia, were willing to negotiate. At Nerchinsk, where the Chinese envoys arrived with a strong military force to meet the tsarist envoys, a Russo-Chinese treaty was concluded in 1689. The Russians were forced to give up the territory of the Amur River below the mouth of the Shilka; and the border was drawn along the Stanovoi Mountains, which form the watershed between the Lena and the Amur. But the western shore of the Sea of Okhotsk was included in the Russian territory. This Russian setback, accepted for the sake of favorable trade relations, was to last until the middle of the nineteenth century, when the greatly increased Russian military pressure could no longer be resisted by a weakened China.

Relations with the Chinese empire required a further delineation of the border when the move around Lake Baikal brought the Russians into Mongol territory. The Manchu dynasty had extended its control over the Mongols, and in the Treaty of Kiakhta in 1727 Russia recognized that Outer Mongolia was Chinese. The border settlement was accompanied by an agreement on trade relations in which the Chinese designated several places on the frontier as markets for the exchange of goods. China agreed to permit a Russian commercial mission of two hundred merchants to come to Peking every three years and to permit the establishment in Peking of a Russian Orthodox Church with resident priests and language students. Through these contacts the Russians kept themselves well informed of Chinese affairs.

The treaties of Nerchinsk and Kiakhta, which set a temporary limit to Russian territorial expansion, were also the first treaties between China and a Western power. They marked the limits of Russia's first drive across the Asiatic plains to the mountains of the Pacific. There was no more no-man's-land to be conquered. Russia's further moves into Central Asia and the Far East brought her into the international power struggle which focused around the weakening Chinese empire.

PART TWO

The Response to the West

CHAPTER VI

New Forces
in the Far East:
Europe and America

1. FAR EASTERN TRADE IN THE AGE OF MERCANTILISM

IN the nineteenth century the leading Western powers forced the countries of the Far East into the orbit of the Western world and the independent growth of Far Eastern civilizations came to an end. With the opening of China and Japan to the influence of the West there began an entirely new phase in the history of the Far East.

Western countries had been in contact with the Far Eastern world for many centuries, but China and also Japan had hitherto been able to deal with the West on their own terms. Before the nineteenth century the commercial companies and military forces of the West had not been strong enough to impose on China, or even on Japan, the kind of control that they established in India, the East Indies, and the Philippines. Japan permitted a strictly limited trade with the Dutch East India Company at Nagasaki, thus maintaining sufficient contact to keep informed about Western affairs but preventing any inroads on her economy or political system. China, the center of the Far Eastern world, handled her trade relations with the West in accordance with her traditional system. The Chinese government had always controlled trade with foreign countries at officially designated market places at the frontier and under the supervision of special officials. The trade was taxed and regulated and the foreign traders were held to the same inferior position, in relation to Chinese officials, as were the Chinese merchants. No foreigners were permitted to trade within China itself. The tribute missions which came to the imperial court carried on a certain amount of trade, but for the Chinese government the missions were important as an indication of foreign acceptance of the Chinese world order. Trade, therefore, was secondary to the maintenance of the Chinese political system both at home and abroad. For the Chinese to give up the tribute system as a method of dealing

119

with other countries or to permit outside traders to deal with Chinese officials on terms of equality would have undermined the foundations of the existing social and political order.

The traders who came by sea, from the Arabs and Persians to the English and the Americans, had all been dealt with in the same manner. They were allocated to certain designated ports where they could carry on a supervised trade. By 1760 all foreign trade by sea was confined to the port of Canton where local officials and special trade superintendents collected a variety of duties from foreign traders and licensed a number of Chinese merchants to conduct the trade with the foreigners. In Canton thirteen licensed merchant firms were grouped together in 1720 into an organization known as the Co-Hong and were held responsible for informing the officials about the trade with foreign merchants and for the payment of taxes and fees imposed by the government. It was only through the licensed merchants that the officials dealt with the foreign merchants.

Under this system foreign traders were restricted to a small strip of land next to Canton and were allowed to remain only during the trading season. It was here that they had their factories or warehouses and were provisioned by the Co-Hong merchants upon whom they were completely dependent. While the Chinese authorities did not interfere in disputes between foreign traders, they exercised full jurisdiction over all cases involving Chinese subjects. In the Chinese view foreign traders were unruly barbarians who had to be strictly controlled. Whenever a foreigner was accused of criminal action, the Chinese officials compelled his surrender by threatening to take action against the whole group of foreign traders. Their strongest weapon was the threat to cut off all trade, a threat which was always effective because the foreigners were always willing to yield on matters of legal principle in order to continue the profitable trade.

The two most famous cases of this sort involved British and American sailors. In 1784 a gunner of the British ship *Lady Hughes*, when firing a salute, used a loaded cannon and accidentally sank a Chinese boat, causing the death of two minor officials. The Chinese threatened severe reprisals, including the cessation of trade, and the British handed over the sailor to the Chinese authorities, who ordered him put to death by strangulation. In 1821 an American sailor by the name of Terranova was held responsible for the accidental death of an elderly Chinese boatwoman. Feeling that the sailor was innocent, the Americans refused to settle the matter by negotiation. When the case was brought to the Chinese officials, they threatened to stop all trade unless Terranova was surrendered. The Americans complied and Terranova was strangled. Such incidents confirmed the Chinese in the view that they could always control the foreigners, for whom the trade seemed absolutely essential. To the Westerners the conditions of trade and the treatment they received were highly objectionable, but there was little disposition to endanger the highly profitable trade by protesting against the existing relationships.

The Chinese method of trade led to many abuses. As the taxes and fees were collected before the goods were released for trade, the merchants tried to dispose of some of their goods before they were taxed. This illegal trade was carried on with the cooperation of the Chinese merchants and with the connivance of the officials, who received their "squeeze." In the traditional pattern of the trade ". . . the officials partly served the emperor and partly profited themselves, the Chinese merchants partly aided the officials and partly sought to evade them, and the foreign traders did the best they could." [1]

The Western methods of international trade in the eighteenth century were still those of the mercantilist age. International trade was carried on through great chartered companies which attempted to establish as much of a monopoly as possible against the competition of rival trading nations. The most outstanding examples in the Far East were the Dutch East Indies Company, which monopolized the trade of the East Indies and set up the Dutch colonial administration there; and the British East India Company, which conquered much of India and extended its trading operations to China. These companies were incorporated groups of private merchants, licensed by the state, and granted the political and military authority necessary to establish and maintain their trading monopolies. The directors and stockholders of these companies had great political power in the parliaments of their home countries; they were looked on as an arm of government.

In China the British East India Company dominated the trade at the port of Canton although it did not have exclusive trading privileges. The Portuguese, who had an establishment at Macao, the French, the Dutch, and later the Americans, the Prussians, and others also traded there. The British East India Company type of organization fitted into the Chinese system of trade because the officials of the Company had control over its merchants. The Chinese thus had a "headman" with whom they could deal and whom they could hold responsible for the actions of the whole group.

The foreigners came to Canton mainly to buy. The most important item of trade was tea, a commodity which was in great demand in Europe and the sale of which created a great part of the wealth of the British East India Company. Silk, porcelain, rhubarb, and Chinese art objects also entered into the trade. But the foreign traders had no goods which the Chinese would buy in sufficient quantity to balance the trade. The agrarian economy of China was largely self-sufficient and whatever trade with foreigners was permitted was regarded as a luxury which could be dispensed with at any time. China did not need the West as the West needed China. There was in China a limited market for furs and ginseng and, after the development of British control in India, for Indian cotton goods; but the balance had to be paid in cash through the importation of silver. The British secured much of their silver in India, thus linking the exploitation of their Indian colony with the China trade. The Americans secured their silver from trade with Mexico, and the Mexican silver dollar became the first silver coin to be used in China. The Chinese had previously used a silver unit, the tael, which was measured

[1] John K. Fairbank, *Trade and Diplomacy on the China Coast* (Cambridge, 1953), p. 47.

by weight and was the equivalent of U. S. $1.40. For all the foreigners trading with China the one-sidedness of the trade was as irksome as the Chinese attitude towards the trade. These conditions were accepted, however, until revolutionary economic and political changes in the West built up pressures which broke down the old trading system and compelled China to accept new commodities from the West and new methods of trade. These changes were brought about by the economic consequences of the Industrial Revolution and the political consequences of the American Revolution.

The Industrial Revolution

The Industrial Revolution took place first in England in the second half of the eighteenth century. The textile manufacturers of the new industrial cities, such as Manchester and Liverpool, came to be more and more concerned with finding new markets for their products. They brought pressure to bear on the East India Company to find overseas markets for their woolens, especially in China, where the Company merchants were looking for commodities acceptable to the Chinese in order to balance the trade. In 1793 the British government sent Lord Macartney on a mission to the Chinese emperor in an attempt to negotiate a trade agreement. Macartney took with him samples of British woolens which he distributed on his way from Canton to the capital at Peking, much to the surprise of the Chinese peasantry. Macartney's instructions were to ask for one or two cessions of territory "near to the tea- and silk-producing and woolen-consuming areas, where English traders might reside and where English jurisdiction might be exercised," for a commercial treaty and the opening of new ports. He was also to create a taste for British products in Peking.[2] All these demands clearly indicated the new pressures in England to find additional markets for English goods. The Chinese could not accept these demands without giving up the traditional tribute system and the concept of the Confucian state.

On his arrival at the court, Macartney presented to the emperor a letter from George III requesting that a minister be accredited to the Court of Peking and that the conditions of trade be improved. To these requests the emperor replied that

. . . to send one of your nationals to stay at the Celestial Court to take care of your country's trade with China, this is not in harmony with the state system of our dynasty and will definitely not be permitted. . . . . there is nothing we lack, as your principal envoy and others have themselves observed. We have never set much store on strange or ingenious objects, nor do we need any more of your country's manufactures . . ."[3]

The emperor stated very clearly the Chinese attitude towards foreign trade:

Our Celestial Empire possesses all things in prolific abundance and lacks no product within its own borders. There was therefore no need to import the manufactures of

[2] Earl H. Pritchard, *The Crucial Years of Early Anglo-Chinese Relations, 1750–1800* (Pullman, Wash., 1936), p. 307.

[3] Teng Ssu-yü and John K. Fairbank, *China's Response to the West* (Cambridge, 1954), p. 19.

outside barbarians in exchange for our own produce. But as the tea, silk and porcelain which the Celestial Empire produces, are absolute necessities to European nations and to yourselves, we have permitted, as a signal mark of favour, that foreign *hongs* should be established at Canton, so that your wants might be supplied and your country thus participate in our beneficence.[4]

As much as the British wanted a market for their woolens the Chinese had no need to buy. Macartney's demands were thus turned down and the mission was compelled to return to England without having gained any of its aims.

The Chinese had treated Macartney as a foreign tribute bearer and in only one respect did he escape the formalities of submission which such tribute-bearing embassies customarily fulfilled in audience with the emperor; he did not have to perform the *kotow*, which consisted in nine successive prostrations before the throne. By special dispensation Macartney was permitted to indicate his respect to the Chinese emperor on bended knee, the same homage that he would pay his own king. This was an unusual concession on the part of the Chinese who regarded the *kotow* as a part of established etiquette which each performed according to his rank. The emperor himself kotowed to Heaven and to his parents. The refusal to kotow, which in Macartney's mind was an indication of the superiority of the Englishman, was to the Chinese merely an indication of ignorance of good manners.

In 1816 the British sent another mission under Lord Amherst. Amherst was not received by the emperor, ostensibly on the grounds that he refused to go through with the ceremony of the kotow and to appear at an audience to which Chinese officials tried to force him immediately after a hurried journey. Like the Macartney mission the Amherst mission was designated by the Chinese as a tribute mission. Amherst's failure to secure an audience with the emperor made no more difference to the outcome of his mission than did Macartney's success in gaining an audience. So long as there was no change in the Chinese concept of the state and its relationship to trade, the issues of the kotow and of obtaining an audience with the emperor were of no importance. The real differences between the British and the Chinese could not be settled by negotiation.

Under pressure from home, the British East India Company took woolens to Canton where it sold them at a loss, which it could well afford because of the enormous profits made in the tea trade. The Chinese Co-Hong merchants took the woolens as a favor to the British merchants and sold them eventually at a loss which they also could well afford because of the profits they made in the export of tea.

The rise of the Great Industry in England brought with it new political and economic ideas. The English middle class gave to the world the concept of production for profit, of material prosperity as the yardstick and acquisition as the rational end of life. The English first developed the idea of strong property rights in connection with landed property, but with John Locke the concept of the sacredness of property came to be applied to commercial and

---

[4] Harley Farnsworth MacNair, *Modern Chinese History, Selected Readings* (Shanghai, 1933), pp. 4–5.

industrial wealth and thus became a part of the philosophy of capitalism. Under the influence of Adam Smith, eighteenth-century English middle-class liberalism took the position that in the pursuit of commercial freedom it was desirable to limit the powers of the state. The landed interests who controlled the state imposed annoying restrictions on trade and social discrimination on traders. It is not surprising, therefore, that the two-hundred-year struggle of the English middle class to get rid of government restrictions elevated the doctrine of *laissez faire* into a dogma which became the answer to all economic, social, or political problems. It was not until the Reform Act of 1832, which rearranged the electoral districts for Parliament in such a way as to give adequate representation to the new and populous industrial centers of northern England, that the middle class secured a decisive share of political power and used it to destroy the mercantilist system of trade.

The American Revolution

The economic doctrines of eighteenth-century English liberalism found their first political expression in the American Revolution over half a century before they triumphed in England. In their revolt against the British mercantilist system the American colonists relied on doctrines which originated in England. It was mainly by way of the New England Federalists that the contributions of English thought were fitted into the American setting. To the Federalists, the main object of government was to protect property, especially commercial and shipping property; the purpose of the state was to make private enterprise possible and profitable, not to control it through monopolies. The American Revolution was fought to break the British economic monopoly both in the colonies and in international trade and to give Americans the fullest opportunities through private enterprise to build up the economy at home and to share in international trade. Once the Republic was established and was cast off from the protection as well as the exploitation of the British mercantilist trade system, it had to fight for freedom to trade as the first principle of national policy. In the early years of the Republic a Federalist lawyer asserted free trade to be an "inalienable right."

The American republic, a weak neutral with little naval power, immediately lined herself up with other small powers in favor of freedom of the seas, a necessary condition for freedom of trade. The American approach to world problems was shaped by the struggle of the new republic for survival against the naval and commercial might of England. The conflicts of the European powers, extending as they did to every known land and to all the high seas, not only made it possible for the colonists to achieve their independence but also set a world-wide stage for the Republic in its struggle to survive. Economic necessity took Americans to every country where goods could be bought or sold. The New England states, in particular, had to trade or die. Impoverished in the long revolutionary struggle, cut off from the longstanding trade with England, with the harbors full of idle ships, and unable to produce at home the manufactured goods they needed, the former colonies had to sail the seas to get the means with which to buy abroad. If Americans went to China, they also went to Turkey, India, Siam, Muskat, and the East Indies. They bought and sold all over the world to get the necessities of life. Rarely has there been such a demonstration of opportunism, resourcefulness, greed, courage, commercial acumen, and maritime skill.

American trade from the Revolution to the first decades of the nineteenth century had two significant characteristics: it was world-wide and interrelated. What Mr. Morison has said about the trade of Massachusetts is generally true of the whole structure of American commerce:

No one of her sea-borne industries was self-sufficient, and many of the greater merchants were directly concerned in all of them. . . . The outward cargoes to the East Indies were first obtained through trading with the West Indies, the Mediterranean, and Northern Europe; and the success of Yankee vessels in these markets depended as much on their skillful handling of Southern produce, as on the ancient Massachusetts staples of fish, lumber, whale oil and rum. . . . the bulk of the Oriental cargoes brought into Salem and Boston was re-exported. No section of the edifice could be touched without disturbing the rest.[5]

In other words, the maritime and commercial interests of Americans, whether in Turkey or China, would stand or fall together.

Americans succeeded in breaking down many barriers to trade because no one nation was economically self-sufficient, and the great monopoly trading companies, such as the British East India Company and the Dutch East India Company, were in political and commercial competition with each other. In 1798, for example, the Dutch in order to avoid the danger of having their ships captured by British men-of-war chartered an American ship to conduct their trade with Nagasaki. As the French and Dutch had trading settlements in India and for political reasons were willing to help the Americans in order to spite the British, the British East India Company admitted Americans to the India trade, preferring profit where they could not enforce exclusion. A lively American trade developed with India, Africa, Sumatra, Turkey; at one time the pepper trade with Sumatra actually rivalled in value the trade with Canton.

The China Trade

American commerce with the port of Canton began with the sailing of the *Empress of China* from New York in 1784. The Americans were introduced to the Chinese by the French and were allowed to trade as independent merchants. While it is true that the Chinese officials always tried to find one American who would be responsible for the conduct of all the others, they were not successful. In a very short time the China trade became the most important and profitable part of the vast interrelated commerce of the United States. It was in this trade that some of the great fortunes were

[5] Samuel Eliot Morison, *Maritime History of Massachusetts, 1783–1860* (Boston and New York, 1921), p. 161.

made which subsequently were used in the development of New England industry. The trade with China depended in large measure upon adequate supplies of silver to balance the trade. Some of the goods which were purchased at Canton could be paid for by selling to the Chinese ginseng, furs, and Turkish opium. But much had to be paid for in silver, and it is estimated that the export of *specie* to China from 1784 to 1852 amounted to no less than one hundred and eighty million dollars. This silver had to be earned in other parts of the world.

From the beginning the China trade was promoted and protected by the federal government in which the merchant aristocracy of New England was strongly represented. Some of the earliest legislation of the Congress was designed for the benefit of the China trade. As Tyler Dennett has pointed out, those who traded with China

enjoyed the protection of the navigation act of 1789 which imposed a discriminating tonnage tax of forty-six cents per ton on foreign bottoms, and the protection of the tariff act of the same year which gave to the American importer a 12½ per cent protection in duties on East India imports other than tea, and on tea a protection which absolutely excluded importation in any but American bottoms.[6]

The China trade led to great American activity in the Pacific Ocean. Americans established themselves for varying periods in the Sandwich Islands (1787), at Nootka Sound (1788), in the Marquesas (1791), Fanning (1797), and Fiji (1800). An American agent was set up at Honolulu in 1820. In spite of all this activity, however, American trade in the Pacific did not receive adequate naval protection, not because there was lack of will but because of lack of naval power. As early as 1800 the government sent the U.S.S. *Congress* to the Far East to provide what protection it could against French privateers. In 1815 the U. S. sloop *Peacock* was sent to the East Indies to protect American shipping, and in 1819 the *Congress* went to Chinese waters for the same purpose. The *Congress*, obeying the orders of the Chinese, did not force its way up to Canton. With what little force they had the Americans resisted the efforts of the British men-of-war to exercise the right of search but they also, on occasion, tried to enlist the assistance of the Chinese. In 1805 the American merchants memorialized the Chinese officials on the subject of the right of search, using the argument that according to international law,

the persons and property of friendly foreigners within the territory and jurisdiction of a sovereign and independent Empire, were under the special protection of the government thereof, and any violence or indignity offered to such persons or to the flag of the nation to which they belong, is justly considered as done to the government within whose territory the outrage is committed.[7]

This American move, which was not answered by the Chinese, was an example of the American policy of playing one country off against another in order to promote concepts of free trade and freedom of the seas.

[6] Tyler Dennett, *Americans in Eastern Asia* (New York, 1922), p. 8.
[7] *Ibid.*, p. 84.

The Monopoly of the Company Ends

In 1834 the British government abolished the monopoly of the East India Company over the China trade. This was in part the result of political developments in England where, two years before, the parliamentary Reform Act had strengthened the political power of the advocates of free trade. It was also the result of the American example. It was exactly fifty years from the time of the departure of the *Empress of China* from New York in 1784 until the ending of the Company monopoly permitted British merchants to trade as freely as the Americans. The fifty years of American trade had shown that the Chinese were willing to deal with independent merchants and that free enterprise brought great profits. After 1817 American merchants shipped English goods to Canton in competition with the East India Company. Independent English merchants, excluded from this trade, increased the pressure on Parliament to end the monopoly of the East India Company. This is only one of many examples of the way in which American trading practice helped to bring to an end an older system of international commerce. The struggle against the mercantile system was world wide but the China trade was an integral part of it, and a significant aspect of the trade with Canton is the role it played in bringing mercantilism to an end.

The major differences between British and American trading practices disappeared, once the trading powers of the East India Company were transferred to private merchants, although commercial and political rivalry did not diminish. The differences disappeared because the British had come closer to accepting the major policies of the American republic—freedom of the seas, reciprocal commercial opportunity, freedom to trade in any part of the world. On the other hand, American industrialization, although not comparable to the tremendous growth of the Great Industry in England, had gone far enough by the eighteen forties to create a demand for markets for American goods. For American merchants, too, China ceased to be a limited market in which to buy and became more and more, at least in anticipation, an unlimited market in which to sell. By the time the British were ready to bring China into the world market by force of arms, in 1839, the Americans were in agreement with their aims if not with their methods of achieving them.

2. THE OPENING OF CHINA

In the search for commodities which the Chinese would buy, the Western traders finally discovered a very profitable product for the Chinese markets—opium. Opium, which was grown in India by the East India Company and first brought to China in the eighteenth century, became an important item of trade in the nineteenth century. After 1832, the foreign traders, instead of having to pay with silver for Chinese exports, took silver out of China in return for the opium which was imported.

The memorials from the Chinese governors-general to the court in the

1830's complained about the result of the deflation of the currency due to the outflow of silver. The evil effects of opium upon the smoker were also noted and some memorials show that Chinese administrators were concerned with the physical weakening of the laborers used in the public works. These developments led the Chinese imperial government to take various steps towards the prohibition of opium imports. These efforts were largely unsuccessful and led only to an extensive smuggling in which local Chinese officials participated. From any long-range point of view, the opium traffic was harmful even to the Western trade. It clearly eliminated any chance of developing in China that market for Western industrial goods to which the English and others looked forward. Yet the immediate profits of the opium trade were so high that practically all Western traders took part in it, including the Americans who brought their opium from Turkey. What the more reasonable Westerners hoped for was a control and limitation of the trade on the basis of mutual agreement. From the Chinese point of view the decision on the limitation of the trade was a matter of Chinese administrative authority and could not—by definition—be compromised through negotiation.

In 1839 the emperor appointed a special commissioner, Lin Tse-hsü, to enforce the prohibition of the opium trade at Canton. Commissioner Lin, who arrived at Canton before the trading season, forced the arriving foreign traders to surrender all their opium under threat of force and loss of all trade. He then burned the opium which had the very considerable value, for that time, of about six million taels. In addition to this measure Commissioner Lin requested from the foreign merchants the payment of a bond to guarantee against further smuggling. The Americans submitted to the Chinese demands. For one thing, the Americans felt they had more to gain by dissociating themselves from the British and by playing the Chinese against the British. There being very little possibility that the American government would use force against the Chinese government, the Americans did not wish to associate themselves with the British use of force but rather to maintain friendly relations, if possible, with the Chinese. The British refused to accept the Chinese demands and found themselves shut off from the Canton trade. After handling their seasonal business through the Americans, who profited greatly as go-betweens, the British decided on the use of force to obtain satisfaction and reparation from the Chinese. The war lasted from November, 1839, to August, 1842.

The immediate cause of the war had been the refusal of the British to cooperate with the Chinese commissioner in the suppression of opium smuggling. From the Western point of view the issues were much broader and the conflict over opium smuggling was used to enforce demands which had been building up over a period of many years. It was the refusal of the Chinese to accept the new Western concepts of unrestricted trade that infuriated both British and Americans. John Quincy Adams said of China that it was a "noncommercial empire." In his view the cause of the war was not opium but the "Kowtow—the arrogant and insupportable pretensions of China, that she will hold commercial intercourse with the rest of mankind, not upon equal reciprocity but upon the insulting and degrading forms of relation between lord and vassal." In the West the right to trade had almost taken on the quality of an inalienable and natural right. The refusal of the Chinese to accept this view of trade was regarded by Westerners as arrogance and obstinacy. The British and Americans did not realize that it was not a question of arrogance or obstinacy; the whole Chinese social and political order was at stake.

The British Cabinet planned to exert only enough pressure to compel the Chinese to agree to an extension of trading opportunities. This does not mean that the idea of conquering China, which appeared to be very much like another India, did not occur to them. Some years later, in 1857, Disraeli, speaking in the House of Commons, said in effect that the British Foreign Office refrained from embarking on a suggested large-scale military adventure in China because this might have involved them in war either with the United States of America, or Russia, or both. Disraeli remarked that Lord Hastings had offered to conquer China with twenty thousand men in the first decade of the century.

. . . but since the time when our Clives and Hastings founded our Indian Empire the position of affairs in the East has greatly changed. Great Powers have been brought into contact with us in the East. We have the Russian Empire and the American Republic there, and a system of political compromise has developed itself like the balance of power in Europe; and, if you are not cautious and careful in your conduct now in dealing with China, you will find that you are likely not to extend commerce, but to excite the jealousy of powerful states, and to involve yourselves in hostilities with nations not inferior to yourselves.[8]

The British merchants in China and their trade association in London continued to be in favor of aggressive actions in China which might well have involved the collapse of the Manchu government and the assumption of political and administrative responsibility by the British, but they were never able to talk the government into a large-scale military adventure.

When the war started in 1839, it was fought mainly around the Canton area. The local Chinese officials used available troops which, with their outdated equipment, were no match for modern Western military forces. An attempt at Canton to enlist the local population for armed resistance against the foreigners did not get very far. The British took Canton and imposed a local fine of six million taels which corresponded to the value of the opium which had been destroyed. When the British naval forces moved up the Yangtze River, the Chinese government was ready to negotiate for peace because it was afraid that further defeats would lead to a disastrous loss of prestige. The emperor appointed two imperial commissioners, both high-ranking Manchus, Ilipoo and Kiying, to negotiate at Nanking with Sir Henry Pottinger, the British representative. Out of these negotiations came the Treaty of Nanking, August, 1842, which ended the war.

[8] *Ibid.*, p. 298.

The Treaty of Nanking

The Treaty of Nanking in 1842 between England and China was the first in a series of treaties which opened China to the Western world and which have been called by the Chinese the "unequal treaties" because of the one-sided privileges they contained. The Treaty of Nanking provided for the opening of five Chinese ports, Canton, Amoy, Foochow, Ningpo, and Shanghai, to British traders to "reside and carry on trade." It imposed upon China an indemnity of twenty-one million taels, including the six million paid in Canton, and it provided for the cession to England of the island of Hong Kong which controls the sea entrance to Canton. The Chinese agreed to abolish the Co-Hong, and to set up regulations for a uniform and moderate tariff on imports and exports. Any change in duties would be by mutual agreement. Consuls were to be appointed at each of the five ports and there was to be equality between the officials of corresponding rank of the two countries. The Treaty of Nanking did not deal with the issue which the Chinese considered to be of greatest importance, the question of the opium trade. The opium trade continued unregulated until the treaties of 1858 and 1860 when importation was legalized and duties were imposed. Opium remained a major item in Chinese imports until the end of the century by which time domestic production had been developed and opium lost its importance in foreign trade.

The stipulations of the Treaty of Nanking broke down the Chinese system of controlled trade. The Chinese were compelled to give up their system of licensed merchants and to permit the English to trade with anyone they wished. The British, in addition to compelling the Chinese to accept their own trading practices, took away from them the freedom to regulate their own tariffs. Through these stipulations and the opening of new ports, the British removed the obstacles to an increased flow of British goods into China. From the British point of view the main purpose of the war had been not only to enlarge the world market but also to force the Chinese to recognize England on a basis of national equality. The treaty itself was negotiated and written in a form which indicated that China no longer treated England as a tributary state but as an equal. This equality was to be guaranteed by arrangements for official relationships of equality and mutual respect between the English consuls and Chinese officials.

The Treaty of Nanking left undecided the position of other foreigners in China; the British had acted only for themselves but they did not attempt to establish a monopoly. When the Chinese negotiators at Nanking asked Sir Henry Pottinger for his views, he stated that the British "would not be small-minded about it" if others were given the same privileges. In order to protect themselves, however, the British introduced into the supplementary Treaty of the Bogue, concluded with the Chinese in October, 1843, the most-favored-nation clause, so that any privileges which China might subsequently grant to other powers would automatically apply to them. From this time on all treaties with China contained this clause. The fact remained, however, that the British were the only ones with treaty relations with China, and the other powers had to conclude their own separate treaty arrangements to gain the same privileges for their own citizens.

America and the Opening of China

From the moment the British began preparing for hostilities, the American government was put in a position in which it had to take action. American merchants in Canton were the first to see that the old order had gone. While they were willing to make many more concessions than the British in order to continue the trade, once the issue was joined between the British and Commissioner Lin the Americans naturally wanted to be sure of an advantageous position in whatever new order emerged. In May, 1839, the Americans sent a memorial to the Congress requesting that the government take steps to negotiate a commercial treaty with China and to protect American lives and property with naval forces. Unlike the British, however, the American merchants felt that there was no need for war in order to secure the privileges they hoped for. They suggested to the Congress that, if expedient, the United States should take joint action with the British, French, and Dutch, or any one of them to appeal directly to the imperial government at Peking. The Americans felt that a naval demonstration would be sufficient to achieve the objective.

The Congress did not discuss the memorial from the American merchants at Canton until January, 1840. As a result of discussion, the East India squadron under Commodore Kearny was sent to China; but there was no disposition to join with the British in action against the Chinese. The American position was stated by Caleb Cushing, speaking in the House, in terms which were both smug and self-righteous.

But God forbid that I should entertain the idea of cooperating with the British government in the purpose, if purpose it has, of upholding the base cupidity and violence and high-handed infraction of all law, human and divine, which have characterized the operation of the British individually and collectively, in the seas of China.

A policy of protecting American interests but of not cooperating with the British had the support of Boston and Salem merchants interested in the China trade and of public opinion in general. Fear of British imperialism was based upon experience. There were also many who felt that Chinese and American interests were identical in regard to the opium trade; it would be to the advantage of both to have it abolished. American missionaries, though small in number, did a great deal to arouse American opinion against Britain over the opium trade. The United States followed an independent course throughout the war while watching very carefully what the British were doing.

Daniel Webster, Secretary of State, wrote the special message that President Tyler sent to the Congress after the signing of the Treaty of Nanking. It was proposed that a resident commissioner be sent out to attend to American commercial and diplomatic interests.

Being of the opinion that the commercial interests of the United States connected with China require at the present time a degree of vigilance such as there is no agent of this government on the spot to bestow, I recommend to Congress to make appropriation for the compensation of a commissioner to reside in China, to exercise a watchful care over the concerns of American citizens, and for the protection of their persons and property, empowered to hold intercourse with the legal authorities and ready under instructions from his government, should such instructions become necessary and proper hereafter, to address himself to the high functionaries of the empire, or through them to the Emperor himself.

Caleb Cushing, the son of a Newburyport shipowner, was sent to China to secure a treaty. Cushing was instructed by President Tyler to make every effort to secure an audience with the emperor, without performing the kotow, but this was not to be put ahead of his primary purpose which was to secure equal conditions for trade. At the same time America was also anxious to see to it that China should be strong enough to resist further encroachments.

Mr. Forbes of Russell and Company, the head of the leading American firm at Canton, suggested to Daniel Webster that because the Chinese had a great fear of encroachment by other foreign nations it would be useful "if we could, in a quiet way, without infringing upon the courtesies due to Britain, contribute anything to the means of defense against further aggression." In such a way the emperor of China would be led to see the advantages of an alliance with the United States.

The instructions to Caleb Cushing reflect to some extent the same approach. Cushing took with him, among other things, books on fortification, gunnery, ship-building, military and naval strategy, and natural science for presentation to the Chinese. This was the first expression of the American policy of assisting China to maintain her territorial and administrative integrity. Cushing was given explicit instructions about the importance of pointing out to the Chinese the contrast between the United States and England. The Chinese were to be informed that the United States had asserted its independence from England and had no colonial possessions in the neighborhood of China. The British, on the other hand, were well established in India, a fact which the Chinese must have regarded with dissatisfaction.

Before Cushing arrived in China, the imperial commissioners, Ilipoo and Kiying, who had negotiated with the British, had recommended to the emperor that all other foreigners be given the same privileges as the English. Following their advice, the emperor decided that it would be wiser to have the powers indebted to China rather than to the British for the new trading privileges. An imperial edict opening the ports to all comers was actually issued before Cushing's arrival at Macao, but Cushing still threatened to proceed to Peking for an imperial audience as a means of putting pressure on the Chinese negotiator, Kiying. This threat did not help to secure the treaty but probably delayed it because the Chinese would not sign until they were sure that Cushing was not going to Peking.

The Treaty of Wanghia, signed in July, 1844, put American trade relations with China on an independent basis and secured for United States citizens the same treaty port rights as those gained by the British. It was especially important for the formulation of the right of extraterritoriality which had not been explicitly stated in the British Treaty of Nanking. The United States wanted explicit legal protection for its citizens to compensate for the lack of a naval base, such as the British had secured in Hong Kong. Article 21 of the American treaty provided that

subjects of China who may be guilty of any criminal act towards citizens of the United States shall be arrested and punished by the Chinese authorities according to the laws of China, and citizens of the United States who may commit any crime in China shall be subject to be tried and punished only by the consul or other public functionary of the United States thereto authorized according to the laws of the United States; and in order to secure the prevention of all controversy and disaffection, justice shall be equitably and impartially administered on both sides.

The principle of extraterritoriality included both civil and criminal cases. The Chinese were quite willing to accept the system because they assumed that foreigners would be limited to their concessions and that there would be a minimum of contact. They did not foresee the full impact of this stipulation.

The French negotiated a treaty in October, 1844, which covered very much the same ground as the Treaties of Nanking and Wanghia, and secured from the emperor permission for the establishment of Roman Catholic missions in the treaty ports and for the toleration there of Chinese as well as foreign Christians. The French envoy suggested this provision in order to have something to show over and above what the British and Americans had secured and to help his home government out of political difficulties by a gift to the Church.

The British, American, and French treaties set a pattern for China's relations with the Western powers that lasted for a hundred years. Although these treaties limited China's autonomy in the administration of law and the control over tariffs, neither the Chinese nor the foreigners could see the full implications of these steps. As the treaties concluded with the foreign powers contained an unqualified "most-favored-nation" clause granted to these powers unilaterally and unreciprocally, any advantage given to one was immediately shared by all others. The combination of the right to reside in the newly opened treaty ports and exemption from Chinese jurisdiction under the extraterritoriality clause gave the foreign communities a special position in China, which was developed through custom and practice to a point where the foreign communities became autonomous units with very little actual control by higher authority. The Chinese agreed to having the foreigners in limited concessions ruled by their own laws. From the Chinese point of view there seemed every reason to believe that the foreigners would be less of a nuisance if they all lived together on small pieces of undesirable land—the concessions—and did not get mixed up with the Chinese legal system. As first conceived, extraterritoriality was a device by which to insulate the foreign communities from the rest of China. In the event, however, the foreign settlements became centers of new economic development and the base of a new Chinese class outside the control of the Chinese government.

Treaty Ports and Treaty Powers

During the two decades following the Treaty of Nanking the Manchus lost more and more of their control over China, and China had to surrender more and more of its sovereignty to the powers. The British, French, and American merchants and consular officials embarked upon the exploitation of the opportunities opened up by the early treaties with an energy commensurate with their optimism. It seemed as if all obstacles had been removed to a long-sought access to the fabulous market of China. The first stage was the development of foreign national concessions. These were established through agreements between local Chinese officials and foreign consuls which set aside pieces of land for the residence of the citizens of the consul's country. British, French, and later Russian, Italian, German, and Japanese concessions were thus established in Chinese treaty port cities. The respective consul was the highest authority on the spot and the residents regulated their affairs through municipal councils.

A special situation developed, however, in Shanghai. Of all the treaty ports of 1842 and later years, this was the most important because of its location at the point where the main net of inland communications connected with the sea. In Shanghai, French and British concessions had been established as in the other treaty ports, but the pattern was changed between 1848 and 1854 under the influence of American political pressure. The American consuls and commissioners objected to the policy of national concessions, and specifically to the British concession at Shanghai.

The Americans were against the establishment of national concessions, which they regarded as local monopolies which could easily lead to colonial control. The United States, with one short later exception, never attempted to set up American national concessions in the treaty ports. It was naturally feared, however, that Americans would be at a disadvantage if their houses and factories were situated in concessions controlled by other nations. They fought, therefore, for the transformation of the British concession in Shanghai into an international settlement. The international settlement, established in 1854, became a unique international institution. Theoretically, the authority for the extraterritorial foreign community was in the hands of the body of consuls which could make decisions only by unanimous vote. In practice, however, the foreign landowners established a municipal government of their own and were to a remarkable degree free from any control in the pursuit of their economic interests. The French refused to add their concession to the international settlement in Shanghai, and it continued under separate administration. In the other treaty ports, national concessions remained the rule. Through the treaties, therefore, there came to be established in the key cities of China a number of foreign communities which were outside Chinese jurisdiction and not too strongly controlled by the governments of their own countries.

Probably the most important fact to influence policy and opinion after the Treaty of Nanking was the failure of the China market to produce the results which had been expected. When the new ports were opened, the Co-Hong monopoly abolished, a moderate tariff established, and Hong Kong developed as an entrepôt for trade, it was expected that the last obstacles to a limitless market had been removed. Yet ten years after the Treaty of Nanking British exports to China had declined rather than increased. Not only that, the trade was subject to extraordinary fluctuations.

It had been expected that all the mills of Lancashire could not provide for more than a fraction of this fabulous market. What had happened? There developed two main points of view among the British, the views of official London and those of the merchants in China who came to be known as "old China hands." The official view laid the emphasis mainly on economic factors. It was pointed out that the payment for opium imports consumed China's available supply of silver and that tea and silk were the only commodities which could be used to balance the import of foreign manufactures. Yet there was a limit to the amount of tea and silk that China could export or, indeed, that the West could absorb. So long as China's purchasing power was spent mainly on opium, therefore, it would be difficult to increase the sale of manufactured goods. The Select Committee on Commercial Relations with China went on to rap the China merchants over the knuckles.

We feel ourselves warranted . . . in reminding our fellow countrymen residing in foreign countries, that while they are entitled to expect that the whole force and influence of their country should be put forth for their protection, when injured in property and person; yet that the interests of Commerce are best consulted by studying a conciliatory demeanour, and cultivating the good-will of the nations with which they traffic.[9]

The merchants on the spot, however, tended to think that political obstacles were responsible for the failure of the China trade to develop as had been hoped. The merchants felt that the British government did not give them the kind of support that was necessary and, in particular, did not maintain British prestige. Continuing to believe that the potentialities of the China market were without limit, the China merchants saw the solution to their troubles in the extension of trading opportunities. There were not enough ports open to trade, and "without permission to go into the interior of the country trade with China must remain stunted and crippled." Furthermore, the flow of British manufactures into the interior was stopped by the internal tariffs which were beyond the control of the foreign powers. Pressure by the merchants for more and more privileges in China did not enlist the sympathies of the British officials responsible for negotiating the treaties. One British official quite correctly charged that many foreign merchants "under no effective control" were converting "privileges of access and trade into means of fraud and violence." They had "launched into a wholesale system of smuggling and fraudulent devices for the evasion of duties." [10] In his view, the aim of British policy should be to restrict the trade, limit points of contact, and support Chinese authority in its efforts at control.

[9] Nathan A. Pelcovits, *Old China Hands* (New York, 1948), p. 13.
[10] *Ibid.*, p. 18.

The British government decided that British commercial interests in China would never be sufficient to justify large-scale political or military commitments in that country. It was feared that any further concessions forced from the Chinese might result in internal anarchy and that if Chinese authority collapsed the British might be compelled to take over. Hence the support of the Imperial Manchu government when it was seriously threatened by a great internal upheaval, the Taiping Rebellion (1850–1864), and the efforts to restrain the aggressive ambitions of the China merchants during the rest of the century.

The Taiping Rebellion was sufficiently successful to raise the question as to whether or not it would overthrow the reigning dynasty and control the whole of China. The city of Nanking fell in 1853 and by the end of that year the Taipings were well established in the Yangtze Valley, the main area of foreign trade. The question of the future of the Manchu empire acquired additional importance for the foreign powers because of the Christian doctrines professed by the Taipings. Protestant missionaries and many merchants favored the Taiping movement because they believed that it would bring Christianity and a pro-Western outlook to China. The French were opposed to the Taiping movement from the very beginning, partly because its alleged Christianity was Protestant and partly because they were informed by Jesuit priests that the movement would probably fail. The British and Americans agreed on the need to defend the foreign settlement at Shanghai against the rebels, and after securing first-hand information on the Taiping government in Nanking, also came to the conclusion that nothing was to be expected from the Taipings and that the Manchu government must therefore be supported.

In September, 1853, the Chinese city of Shanghai fell to rebels who were associated with the Taipings and the collection of customs by imperial authorities broke down. The English and American authorities agreed that the customs should be collected in some way; and the consuls took from their merchants promissory notes which were to be honored when imperial authority was restored. The promissory notes, however, provided no solution to the problem. Merchants of other countries were not controlled at all, and because of the inequality of the treatment there was the danger that trade might move elsewhere on the coast. Both the British and American representatives were agreed on the importance of respecting the treaties and therefore of maintaining the Chinese authority to collect the customs. In July, 1854, they agreed with the Chinese officials on the establishment of a foreign inspectorate of the customs which would collect the customs for the Chinese government. The Chinese accepted this arrangement on condition that the promissory notes collected by the foreign consuls should be honored. Actually no payment was forthcoming but the agreement remained in force. Thus began a foreign-staffed customs service which, after the Taiping Rebellion, extended its control over the maritime customs of the whole of China. The top positions in the customs service, which remained a part of the Chinese administration, were distributed among nationals of foreign countries according to their share of the trade. The Inspector General was therefore always an Englishman.

The Maritime Customs came to play an important role as a stabilizing factor in the financial administration of China. It provided a non-corrupt service and an assured revenue for the central government at a time when it was losing other sources of revenue because of the growing autonomy of provincial administrators. The treaty powers could also use the customs revenues as a guarantee for the payment of indemnities imposed on China by treaties, and later for loans. These payments were made a first charge on the customs revenues. Many Chinese, therefore, have regarded the management of the customs service by foreigners as a means of exploiting China. On the other hand, Sir Robert Hart, who was Inspector General for the whole period from 1863 to 1908, and his commissioners

became the trusted counsellors of Chinese officialdom. They supplied at first some of the functions of a diplomatic service and supported financially the early efforts to educate and train such a corps. Lighthouses on the China coast, harbor conservancy and aids to inland navigation, hydrographic charts, pilotage and quarantine, the collection of many special dues and taxes were all by degrees added to the Customs' original functions. The great variety of Customs statistical, commercial and scientific publications partially made up for the lack of a modern Chinese government printing office. The Maritime Customs organized and until 1911 financed China's modern Postal Service. Customs commissioners of many nationalities made their contributions to scholarship as well as to diplomacy. But above all the Customs set a standard of incorrupt public service and of devotion to the central administration which has been of incalculable value to the Chinese government. . . .[11]

The treaty port system depended for its smooth functioning on the Maritime Customs, an institution which provided a basis for Chinese and foreign cooperation.

Treaty Revision

Once the powers were all agreed that the Taiping Rebellion had no chance of success, the clarification of treaty relations with the Manchu government became their chief objective. The first set of treaties had not worked out as had been hoped, especially at Canton. At this port the Chinese officials were attempting to continue as much of the pre-treaty arrangement as possible. They continued to control an enlarged group of Chinese merchants, whom they permitted to trade, they put difficulties in the way of foreigners who tried to take up residence in Canton, and they ignored the treaty provision for direct contact with high Chinese officials on the spot. For the foreign merchants, who had expected to expand their trade by leaps and bounds, the obstinacy of the Chinese was so frustrating that they thought more and more of using force to bring about compliance. If the Chinese would not honor the treaties which had already been signed, then they should be compelled to agree to a revised treaty settlement which would remove all remaining obstacles to trade and diplomatic intercourse.

[11] John K. Fairbank, *Trade and Diplomacy on the China Coast*, p. 462.

The legal instrument for treaty revision was contained in the American treaty of Wanghia which provided for the right to revise the treaty after a period of twelve years. The most-favored-nation clause extended this privilege to all other powers having treaties with China. American commissioners had made several attempts to negotiate treaty revision, attempts which the Chinese completely ignored. In this atmosphere two incidents occurred which gave England and France the occasion to force the issue through war. One such incident was the boarding by Chinese officials of the lorcha *Arrow*, a ship which had been registered in Hong Kong and flew the British flag although its registration had expired. The Chinese removed some members of the crew, and a dispute over their return led to hostilities at Canton in 1856. British forces occupied the city in 1857, the lorcha *Arrow* incident was settled on a local basis, and normal relations were resumed at Canton. The British, having settled a local issue by force, now decided to settle the broader issues of treaty revision by the same means. Naval and military forces were therefore sent north to Tientsin.

The second incident involved the French. A French missionary, the Abbé Chapdelaine, was executed by a Chinese magistrate for traveling in the interior, which he had no treaty right to do. To punish the Chinese for what has been called a "judicial murder," the French joined with the British in the attack on Canton and continued their cooperation in the projected campaign to the north. Lord Elgin for the British and Baron Gros for the French traveled with the expedition as plenipotentiaries to negotiate new treaties.

The United States was willing to cooperate with the other powers in peaceful demonstrations against the Chinese but not in actual war. Distrust of the British was obviously a concern that never left the minds of American policy-makers. There was also a reluctance to come to blows with the Chinese and thus forfeit Chinese goodwill. American influence had been at its height up to the Treaty of Paris (1856) which ended the Crimean War and released British and French energies from conflicts nearer home. Once the Russians were disposed of, the British particularly were anxious to restore their leadership and prestige in China.

The American government, which had succeeded in opening Japan without armed conflict, remained adamant in its refusal to cooperate with Great Britain or with France in an aggressive policy, even though many American officials and merchants in China agreed with the British. They claimed that the government of China had not protected American citizens, had evaded payment of reparation claims, and had made communication with the imperial authorities as difficult as possible. A message from President Pierce to the emperor of China had been handled with studied contempt. For these reasons, the United States was willing to go along with the British in giving diplomatic support to their aggressive actions in 1858, but this support had to be short of war.

The Department of State instructed Mr. Reed, envoy extraordinary and minister plenipotentiary, to make known to the Chinese that the United States believed that the objectives of the allied powers were just and expedient. On the other hand, he was to make it quite clear that the United States was not at war with China; he was to develop friendly relations with the Russian representative and to offer his services as a mediator between the allied powers and China in the event that his services should be required. The United States was serving its own interests as effectively in this manner as the British thought they were serving theirs by going to war. The United States was better able to have a restraining influence on the British designs in China by playing the role of a strong neutral than by becoming a junior partner in war.

Russia, like the United States, had a strong interest in the development of treaty relations with China. Count Putiatin for the Russians, like Mr. Reed for the Americans, came as the representative of a neutral power to participate in the treaty negotiations. The Russians shared with the other powers an interest in the approach to China from the sea, an interest which was closely connected with the decline in the overland fur trade.

After military action by the two belligerent powers, the British and French, in which the Taku forts that barred the approach to Tientsin were taken, the Chinese agreed to negotiate and in 1858 concluded the Treaties of Tientsin with all four powers.

The Treaties of Tientsin provided for the opening of eleven new treaty ports. One of these ports was on Formosa, most of the others in north and central China. The most important artery of inland communication, the Yangtze River, was opened to foreign navigation and commerce. Foreigners acquired the right to travel in the interior. China was compelled to agree to the fixing of her tariff rates at 5 per cent ad valorem and could not change them without the permission of all the powers. Opium was included in the tariff schedules and thus became a legal import. Most important of all, the treaties provided for the residence in Peking of diplomatic representatives of foreign countries. The French secured Chinese agreement for toleration of missionaries and converts at all places in China.

When the representatives of the four foreign powers, ignoring Chinese efforts to avoid ratification in Peking, prepared to move on to the capital for the ratifications, a new clash occurred in 1859 at the Taku forts near Tientsin. In the first effort to take the Taku forts the British forces had hard going. The forts had been re-equipped with new guns, probably provided by Russia. In the action the British Admiral Hope was seriously wounded. The American Commodore Tattnall could not resist going over to express his sympathies to Admiral Hope and to get into the action by towing British junks up to the line of battle. He explained his action with the famous phrase, "Blood is thicker than water." The Secretary of the Navy decided to consider Commodore Tattnall's actions as entirely appropriate and no violation of American neutrality. When the Taku forts had been captured, the allies moved on to Tientsin and from there to Peking. The Hsien-feng emperor retired to Jehol, where he died the next year. The British and French forces destroyed the Summer Palace outside the walls of Peking as a retaliation for Chinese atrocities against allied prisoners.

At Peking the Chinese were compelled to exchange the ratifications of the Treaties of Tientsin and in addition to sign conventions which included new stipulations. By the Conventions of Peking in 1860 the Chinese agreed to an increase in the original indemnities to England and France provided in the Tientsin treaties, to add Tientsin to the list of treaty ports open to trade and residence, and to cede to the British the tip of the Kowloon peninsula, which is opposite Hong Kong. The French convention included a clause that read, "It shall be lawful for French missionaries in any of the provinces to lease or buy land and build houses." The Chinese have always claimed that this clause was added to the French text without their knowledge. All other powers secured the same priviliges for their missionaries by virtue of most-favored-nation treatment, and the whole of China was thrown open to missionary endeavor.

Once the treaties were ratified, however, the powers intervened immediately on behalf of the Manchu government, a government in which they now had a vested interest because they needed it to carry out the treaties. A small mercenary force, composed of foreigners and Chinese and financed by the foreign merchants, had been organized in the early years of the Taiping Rebellion for the defense of Shanghai. This force was under the leadership of an American, Frederick T. Ward. Later it was incorporated in the government forces to fight outside the limits of Shanghai against the Taipings. Aside from the high pay which they received, these troops were rewarded with the loot from captured towns. Ward died in 1862 as a result of wounds and was succeeded by another American, Burgevine, who became dissatisfied over arrears in pay and went over to the Taipings. The remnants of his force were reorganized by a regular officer from the British army, Captain Charles George Gordon, later to become General Gordon of the Sudan. Under his leadership the force already known as the Ever Victorious Army played an important role in the fighting although it never operated more than one hundred and fifty miles from Shanghai. The contribution of this foreign force to the defeat of the Taipings in the lower Yangtze area must be weighed against the participation of Burgevine on the Taiping side and the very profitable trade in smuggled arms that British and American merchants carried on to the very end of the conflict.

Foreign intervention was important but not decisive in the outcome of the internal struggle. It was Chinese forces under such regional commanders as Li Hung-chang and Tseng Kuo-fan that finally destroyed the base of Taiping power in Nanking.

The treaties of Tientsin and Peking completed the process by which China was forced to accept the goods and the ideas of the West. The treaties took away from the Chinese government its control over the Chinese economy, and the government was no longer able to prevent the forcing of Western goods on the Chinese people. These goods could be distributed in the interior of China from the greatly increased number of treaty ports. For the foreign manufactures the 5 per cent ad valorem tariff was a very low hurdle indeed, and once over this hurdle they could move freely throughout China without additional charges, a fact which gave them a great advantage over Chinese goods which were subject to innumerable transit charges. The right to travel freely in China, added to the right of extraterritoriality, gave the foreigners an unassailable position independent of Chinese law. Foreign troops and gunboats at the treaty ports were used to back up foreign claims and demands on the spot. Foreign control over the collection of customs, which was not entirely to the disadvantage of the central government, was a further invasion of Chinese sovereign rights. The treaty ports led to a concentration of industry, education, and westernization along the coast and in a few inland centers. The treaty port communities soon came to include Chinese as well as foreigners, and under foreign protection there grew up a new westernized social class of Chinese which was to have a great influence on China's development.

China was practically helpless within the grip of the treaty system. Far from being able to play off the powers against each other, the Chinese were compelled to grant to all of them any concessions, however outrageous, that were granted to any one of them. From 1860 on China was neither an independent state nor a colony. She was responsible to all the powers, yet not one of them was responsible for the well-being or the protection of the Chinese state. The Chinese suffered from most of the disadvantages without receiving any of the advantages of the colonial system.

The Manchu dynasty suffered this blow at a time when it was threatened by the Taiping Rebellion. It was another four years before the rebellion was put down; but even after the rebellion was over, the empire never recovered sufficient strength to reverse the events of 1860. Once and for all the policy of attempting to keep the West at arm's length by making diplomatic intercourse impossible had been shattered. For the Chinese system of treating other countries as tributary nations there had been substituted the systematized inequality of the "unequal treaties." Not until World War II did the Chinese recover their full sovereignty.

3. The Opening of Japan

American Interests in the Pacific

The opening of Japan to commercial and diplomatic relations with the West in 1853 was undertaken by America ten years after the opening of China by the British. The new treaties with China could not fail to raise the hope of increased commerce in America as well as in England. This was the great age of the clipper ships and of high profits from the export of tea and other goods from China. At the same time, however, the American textile industry had developed to the point where it looked for overseas markets, and American cotton manufacturers became interested in China as a potential market for their goods. For American importers and exporters, therefore, the China market was the focus of attention. Japan had no great attraction as a potential market. Americans had visited Nagasaki on behalf of the Dutch in the eighteenth century, but there had not grown out of this contact any dreams of fabulous markets such as there had come to be about China.

Japan's importance was that it lay on the great circle route from the American Pacific Coast to China. By this time many things were happening to increase American interest in the Pacific: the general movement to the West, stimulated in part by the discovery of gold in California; the building of the Trans-Isthmian railroad in 1852; and the spirit of continental expansion. Americans came to look on the Pacific Ocean as a direct highway to the Far East which would take the place of the old sailing routes via the Atlantic and the Indian Oceans. On this highway Japan was bound to become an important way station.

The increase of American interest in the Pacific coincided with the development of steam navigation. In the age of sail it would have been desirable to have facilities in Japan for securing provisions. In the age of steam it became necessary to have coaling stations available, and Japan was believed to have large supplies of coal available. Japan was the logical stopping place for a trans-Pacific line of American steamers on the direct route to China.

The development of the West Coast, the interests of commerce, and the needs of steam navigation led to an increase in the activities and the responsibilities of the American Navy in the Pacific. The Navy was suspicious of British and Russian naval activities in the Pacific. Both of these powers had sent ships to Japanese waters in an effort to open up Japan. This they had failed to do but they succeeded in persuading both the Japanese and the Americans of their aggressive designs. American suspicion of British intentions was a part of the American Revolutionary tradition, and Americans had always distrusted British policy in China. While suspicion of Russia was not, perhaps, as strong as that of Great Britain, the United States was keenly aware of the Russian trading position on the American West Coast and the general expansion of Russia towards the Pacific. As early as 1792, a Russian expedition had landed on Hokkaido, the northernmost of the Japanese islands, apparently for the purpose of establishing relations with the Japanese government. For the American Navy it was important that Japan should not be controlled by either Russia or Great Britain. The Navy therefore promoted, with the Department of State, the idea of American initiative in opening Japan.

Navy Policy

The most important part of American naval policy, however, was the drive to secure naval bases in the Pacific. It was around this time that naval missions were sent to chart the island groups and coastlines of the Pacific and to look for suitable sites for bases. The most articulate of the Navy's policy makers was Commodore Matthew C. Perry, who was entrusted with the mission to establish relations with Japan. Perry was equally interested in securing naval bases. He wanted to see in the Pacific and in Asia a large number of American "settlements," and with this in mind examined the Liuchiu Islands, the Bonins, and Formosa. Perry felt that he should "assume the responsibility of urging the expediency of establishing a foothold in this quarter of the globe, as a measure of positive necessity to the sustainment of our maritime rights in the East." Few men have been more eloquent about the manifest destiny of the United States in the Pacific. Perry argued that it was idle to suppose that the United States could always escape from the responsibilities which its growing wealth and power inevitably fastened upon it. It was necessary to anticipate the need to protect a vast and rapidly growing commerce in the East. "We cannot expect to be free from the ambitious longings of increased power, which are the natural concomitants of national success." Perry was obsessed by the need to oppose the expanding empire of Great Britain which held the most important points in the East India and China seas. "Fortunately the Japanese and many other islands of the Pacific are still left untouched by this unconscionable government; and some of them lay in the route of a great commerce which is destined to become of great importance to the United States." Perry urged, with more eloquence than logical consistency, "though it does not belong to the spirit of our institutions to extend our dominion beyond the sea, positive necessity requires that we should protect our commercial interests in this remote part of the world, and in doing so, to resort to measures, however strong, to counteract the schemes of powers less scrupulous than ourselves." The President and Congress, however, held a tight rein on Perry's ambitions to forestall imperialism by being imperialist, and turned down his proposals for naval bases.

The instructions to Commodore Perry on his mission to Japan directed him to seek the right to purchase coal at certain designated ports, the opening of one or more ports to trade, and guarantees for the protection of shipwrecked American sailors. The last point referred to the bad treatment received by American sailors, mainly from whalers in the Sea of Okhotsk, who had been driven by storms to the shores of Japan. The plan was for Perry to proceed with an imposing force to the capital city of Japan where he would press his demands with firmness and courtesy. In the event that argument and diplomacy did not succeed he was to

change his tone, and to inform them in the most unequivocable terms that it is the determination of this government to insist that hereafter all citizens or vessels of the United States that may be wrecked on their coasts or driven by stress of weather into their harbors shall, so long as they are compelled to remain there, be treated with humanity; and that if any acts of cruelty should hereafter be practiced upon citizens of this country, whether by the government or the inhabitants of Japan, they will be severely chastised.[12]

At the same time Perry was told that he should avoid fighting except in self-defense and that he should remember that the President had no authority to declare war.

[12] *Ibid.*, p. 264; see also Arthur Walworth, *Black Ships Off Japan* (New York, 1946), p. 244.

Perry decided that the best course to follow was

to demand as a right, and not to solicit as a favor, those acts of courtesy which are due from one civilized nation to another; to allow of none of those petty annoyances which have been unsparingly visited upon those who had preceded me, and to disregard the acts as well as the threats of the authorities, if they in the least conflicted with my own sense of what was due to the dignity of the American flag. . . . to practice upon them a little of their own diplomacy, by forbidding the admission of a single individual on board any of the ships, excepting those officers who might have business with me, and the visits of these were to be confined to the flag ship, on board of which they were not allowed to enter until they had declared their rank and the business upon which they came . . . to confer personally with no one but a functionary of the highest rank in the empire.[13]

Perry's squadron, the famous Black Ships, steamed into Yedo Bay on July 3, 1853. When the Japanese, unable to divert Perry to Nagasaki or to obstruct him with low-ranking officials, received him in a manner Perry considered appropriate, they were presented with a letter from President Fillmore to be transmitted to the emperor. The letter stated that the United States was interested in friendship, commerce, coal and provisions for its ships, and protection for shipwrecked sailors. This letter was accompanied by one which Perry himself addressed to the emperor, and in which, following the instructions he had received, he stated:

The President desires to live in peace and friendship with your imperial majesty, but no friendship can long exist, unless Japan ceases to act toward Americans as if they were her enemies.[14]

Having delivered the letters, together with suitable presents to the emperor, Perry departed with his ships stating that he would return for an answer in the spring with even more ships. Actually Perry returned in February, 1854, somewhat earlier than he had originally planned, because he was afraid that he might be forestalled by the Russians or the French. The time between July and February had been used to lay claim to some of the Bonin Islands.

The Japanese received Perry's return visit cordially enough but offered insufficient concessions. Perry put forward further demands, threatening that a bigger force would be brought in if they were not agreed to. The obvious desire to conduct the negotiations peacefully, combined with the willingness to use force if necessary, resulted in arrangements acceptable to both sides.

In March, 1854, Perry succeeded in negotiating a treaty in which the Japanese agreed to open up two more ports in addition to Nagasaki, where ships could coal, provision, and be refitted. They also agreed that the United States should have a consul in residence at Shimoda, one of the ports, to give protection to shipwrecked sailors and to enforce most-favored-nation treatment. In the years 1854–57 the British, Russians, and Dutch negotiated separate treaties which differed very little from the American treaty.

The Perry treaty was far less exacting in its terms than the first treaty with China. While it contained that cornerstone of American policy—the most-favored-nation clause—it did not mention extraterritoriality which the

[13] 33d Congress, 2d Session, Senate Ex. Doc., No. 34.
[14] Walworth, op. cit., p. 252.

first American treaty with China had so carefully defined. The ports were neither very good harbors nor particularly favorable for trade. Nor were supplies of coal made available. There seems every reason to agree with Perry when he called this a treaty of friendship. To naval strategists, thinking in terms of a coming struggle with the British for control of the Pacific and concerned with the long-range relationship between commerce and sea power, it may have seemed more important to have Japan as a friendly base and an ally in the coming struggle than a resentful enemy.

The Perry view of American interest in the Pacific influenced but did not dominate the State Department. Perry wanted the Pacific dotted with coaling stations, ports of refuge, and unfortified commercial settlements. The Navy was not interested in large colonial possessions or territorial acquisition for the purpose of ruling other people. But Perry was impressed with the way the British had taken care of their lines of communication all the way from Gibraltar to Singapore and Hong Kong; and, like the British, he thought the way to get on with Asians was to intimidate them. Perry wanted to have a sort of American Hong Kong in northern waters as a base for commerce and a port of refuge; hence, his interest in the Bonins, in Okinawa, and also in Formosa. If Japan had not acceded to American demands in 1854, it is possible that the American flag might have been permanently established in the Bonins and Liuchius. As it was, the capitulation of Japan spoiled Perry's plans. He wrote to the Secretary of the Navy in January, 1854, stating that if the Japanese government refused to negotiate, he would take control of Okinawa. After the Perry treaty of March, 1854, Secretary of Navy Dobin replied in May to the effect that "The President [Pierce] is disinclined, without the authority of Congress, to take and retain possession of an island in that country, particularly unless more urgent and potent reasons demanded it than now exist." The Perry policy would have had far more chance of becoming the national policy if Japan had been as obstinate as China.

Peter Parker and Formosa

Perry's school of thought was not limited to naval officers. Dr. Peter Parker, an American missionary whose linguistic abilities had been most useful to American officials dealing with the Chinese, was an enthusiastic expansionist who, like Perry, hated and emulated the British. Dr. Parker, who first went to China in 1834 as an eye doctor, moved into the diplomatic service and by 1855 rose to the position of commissioner. While in this position, he became obsessed with the idea of lopping off Formosa from the Chinese empire and putting it under the American flag. The island was rich in coal. Parker even encouraged an American firm, Robinet and Nye, to fly the American flag over its trading establishments in Formosa. They even offered to set up an independent government on Formosa if Washington gave its approval. They already had Parker's approval, which he expressed in high sounding moral and rhetorical terms. Writing to the State Department about the importance of doing something about Formosa, he said,

It is much to be hoped that the Government of the United States may not *shrink* from the *action* which the interests of the humanity, civilization, navigation and commerce impose upon it in relation to Tai-Wan [Formosa], particularly the southeastern portion of it, at present inhabited by savages, to whose depraved cruelties we have every reason to believe many Europeans, and among them our own friends and countrymen, have fallen victims.[15]

A little later he expressed himself in a more straightforward manner, suggesting that in the event Formosa be severed from the mainland "that the United States should possess it is obvious, particularly as respects the great principle of the balance of power." [16] Parker's project was squashed by Secretary of State Marcy under Pierce, and then by President Buchanan, both of whom stated in no uncertain terms that the United States was not interested in territorial acquisition in Far Eastern waters and that the extension of American commerce would be left to individual enterprise. The Parker incident was closed in 1857, one year before Townsend Harris put American commercial relations with Japan on a new basis.

The Harris Treaty

The commercial treaty with Japan of 1858 was the work of Townsend Harris, a New York merchant appointed by President Pierce as consul to Shimoda as authorized by the Perry treaty. Harris arrived in Shimoda in 1856, and during the next two years, for eighteen months of which he was completely out of touch with the American government, he associated with the Japanese without any further benefit of displays of naval power. In spite of the great skill of Mr. Harris, his efforts would have been to no avail if there had not been other weapons at his disposal. A basic argument used by Harris was as simple as it was realistic. He succeeded in persuading the Japanese that it was wiser on their part to sign a treaty with the United States, thus setting up a model for others to follow, rather than to have treaties forced upon them by the British, the French, or the Russians, who fortunately for Harris provided at exactly the right time the sort of evidence (a naval demonstration off Kyushu) to support Harris's representation of their intentions. In 1858 British and French naval forces attacked the Chinese fortifications at Taku, the port of Tientsin. The report that the British proposed to move on immediately to Yedo was sufficient to persuade the Japanese of the advantages of Harris's advice and the shogun signed the treaty.

By the treaty of 1858 the Japanese agreed to the establishment of diplomatic and consular relations, opened four more ports, permitted trade on a non-governmental basis, accepted a treaty-regulated tariff on foreign trade, and agreed to the establishment of the extraterritorial system. The Japanese also agreed to the free exchange of foreign coins in the country and the right to export Japanese coinage. The United States offered to mediate with the other powers in the event that Japan required assistance.

[15] Dennett, *op. cit.*, p. 286.
[16] *Ibid.*, p. 287.

Most of the basic principles of American policy in Asia can be seen in the opening of Japan and in the treaty of 1858. Taking the initiative in good time, the United States was able to do in Japan what it would have very much liked to have seen done in China. The economic and political interests of the United States coincided to a remarkable degree. American economic interests were to keep the world market as open and competitive as possible. In order to keep an open door for trade, it was necessary first of all to compel reluctant countries to accept international commerce. It was to the American political interest that European powers should be permitted to encroach as little as possible upon the independent nations of the Orient. The corollary of this, from the American point of view, was to see that these countries should be strong enough to keep the door open. That is why Townsend Harris offered to the Japanese the services of American military and naval officers as well as shipbuilding facilities. The same idea had been proposed much earlier to the Chinese by Cushing. There was nothing inconsistent about a policy which saw to it that the United States benefited from every advantage gained by other powers, whatever the means employed, and at the same time sought to strengthen and support both China and Japan.

The other powers rapidly signed treaties with Japan on the model of the Harris treaty, which became in effect the basis of Japan's foreign relations for the rest of the century. It was after the signing of the treaty with America that the Japanese had the opportunity of watching the British and the French march to Peking, where they reduced the Summer Palace to ashes in order to enforce observance of agreements which the Chinese had entered into the same year but had shown an apparent reluctance to fulfill. The shogunate had surrendered just in time. It was the good fortune of Japan that after the Harris treaty she was able to resolve her own internal struggles without inviting the degree of foreign control imposed upon China.

The Harris treaty and the treaties with England, France, and Holland that followed were signed by the Tokugawa shogun who was still the actual ruler of Japan. The shogun's power was already weakened, however, by the many changes which had taken place in Japan, and the most dangerous of his opponents, the western clans, exploited the shogun's forced acceptance of the treaties to embarrass him. The leading clans of Satsuma and Choshu were responsible for two incidents that involved Japan in clashes with the Western powers. In 1862 an Englishman, Mr. Richardson, crossed the path of the Lord of Satsuma and his party who were on their return journey from Yedo. The Japanese, who interpreted this action as showing a lack of respect, killed Richardson on the spot. The British demanded satisfaction of the shogun and when this was not forthcoming took direct action against the Satsuma clan by bombarding its capital, Kagoshima. A second incident occurred in 1863 when the Choshu clan attempted to close the passage to the inland sea by firing on foreign vessels entering the straits of Shimonoseki. The foreign powers—the British, Americans, French, and Dutch—decided on a joint expedition to bombard the Choshu capital. These military demonstrations brought home to the two strongest western clans the superiority of

Western arms and the futility of a policy of seclusion. It also made clear to the powers that the shogun was neither the highest nominal authority in Japan nor in full control of the country. They therefore insisted that the emperor ratify the treaties in order to ensure their fulfillment. When the emperor signed the treaties in 1866, the opening of Japan was complete and the stage was set for the modernization of Japan which began with the Meiji Restoration in 1868.

4. The Imperial Powers in China

American Policy: the Burlingame Period

Once the Western powers were established in Peking and Tokoyo, the chief aim of American policy was to preserve the territorial and administrative integrity of both China and Japan. To carry out this policy the United States tried to secure as much cooperation as possible between the powers and to head off a struggle for territorial dismemberment. While the United States was careful to insist upon the most-favored-nation treatment, American diplomats were quick to exploit every opportunity to support the Chinese government.

Anson Burlingame, who in 1862 became the first American minister to Peking, described his policy as one of cooperation with the British and friendship with China. In his own words,

The policy upon which we are agreed is briefly this: that while we claim our treaty right to buy and sell, and hire, in the treaty ports, subject, in respect to our rights of property and person, to the jurisdiction of our own governments, we will not ask for, nor take concessions of, territory in the treaty ports, or in any way interfere with the jurisdiction of the Chinese Government over its own people, nor ever menace the territorial integrity of the Chinese Empire. That we will not take part in the internal struggles in China, beyond what is necessary to maintain our treaty rights. That the latter we will unitedly sustain against all who may violate them.[17]

Cooperation among the powers did not last any longer than the conditions which made it possible. These conditions were the common interest of the powers in the suppression of the Taiping Rebellion and the maintenance of the authority of the Manchu government which had made the treaty concessions. While Burlingame assumed the leadership in securing cooperation among the powers, he also took credit with the Chinese for what he called the "nonconcession doctrine." In other words, he posed as the defender of Chinese sovereign rights.

The imperial government thought so well of Anson Burlingame that it requested him, in 1867, to go on a mission abroad as a representative of the Chinese government. Burlingame was made an official of the highest rank and was accompanied by two Chinese officials of the Tsungli Yamen, the organization set up in accordance with the Treaty of Tientsin to handle foreign relations. Burlingame and his Chinese colleagues were instructed to

[17] *Ibid.*, p. 375.

visit the eleven Western countries with which China had treaties. The mission was wined and dined from San Francisco to the East Coast. It then proceeded to London and St. Petersburg where Burlingame died.

One concrete result of the mission was the so-called Burlingame Treaty, signed at Washington in July, 1868, which consisted of supplementary articles to the Treaty of Tientsin. Burlingame probably exceeded his authority in concluding the treaty, the articles of which are of more interest as an indication of American policy than as an addition to the structure of treaty relations with China. Burlingame was apparently trying to use the authority and prestige of his own government to establish among the powers the American view of relations with China. The point was certainly not lost on either the British merchants in China or on the British officials who, unlike the merchants, had originally been sympathetic to the mission.

The treaty that Burlingame signed stated the United States position in Article 8:

The United States . . . do hereby freely disclaim and disavow any intention or right to intervene in the domestic administration of China in regard to the construction of railroads, telegraphs, or other material internal improvements. On the other hand, His Majesty, the Emperor of China, reserves to himself the right to decide the time and manner and circumstances of introducing such improvements within his dominion. . . .[18]

Rutherford Alcock, Her Majesty's Minister to Peking, a man who had often denounced in dispatches to his government the unscrupulous treaty-breaking greed of British merchants in China and who had at first seen constructive possibilities in the Burlingame mission, was forced to the conclusion that "this public disclaimer of all right to adopt a meddling or coercive policy for the advancement of foreign trade would seem to be especially directed against the mercantile communities in China and perhaps some Foreign States prone to advocate or adopt a policy of compulsion." [19] He saw the possibility that the United States was trying to establish itself as the protector of China and in this manner take away from Great Britain its predominant commercial and political position in the East.

The British home government disliked the American effort to make capital out of protestations of friendship for China because they agreed with the essence of the American position. They would never have stated their policy in the generous terms of the American document, but their general aim was to avoid measures which would involve a weakening of the Chinese government. This meant discouraging the so-called "gunboat" policy of the British merchants and naval officers in China, which was to handle all disputes on the local level on the grounds that referring grievances to Peking was a complete waste of time. It was the official view of the British government that Peking was to be held responsible for the carrying out of the treaties and the protection of British nationals.

The British Foreign Office had its own good reasons for arriving at these

[18] Pelcovits, *op. cit.*, p. 51.
[19] *Idem.*

policies, unpopular as they were with British merchants in China. The Foreign Office was not impressed with the possibilities of the China trade and felt that far too much blood and treasure had been spent already in securing such commercial intercourse as then existed. But the major consideration, not quite so apparent to the merchants, was the international scene and the attitudes of other powers. Among these the United States was obviously one of the most important, and in this connection the statements of American policy in the Burlingame Treaty certainly did nothing to encourage the Foreign Office to support the attitudes of British merchants. For this reason it is probably true to say that the Burlingame mission achieved what the Chinese government hoped that it would achieve. It was one of the factors that made it more difficult for the British merchants to secure treaty revision along the lines they wanted.

There were other aspects of the Burlingame Treaty which were of significance in American relations with Asia. The treaty gave to Chinese coolies or laborers the right to enter the United States, where they were promised the same treatment as that accorded to the citizens or subjects of the most favored nation. This was part of the general policy of treating China as an equal among the powers, a pretension which in this particular instance was mocked by events. A demand for cheap labor on the Pacific Coast had been stimulated particularly by the discovery of gold. By this time Chinese coolie labor, already in demand from Panama to Australia, was an organized traffic in which some Americans shared with great profit. Unscrupulous methods used in China to secure laborers did a great deal to increase Chinese suspicion and hatred of the foreigners. There were about 25,000 laborers in California by 1852, and by the time that Burlingame came to America in 1868 the number had increased to well over 100,000. With the increase in numbers went a sharp decline in popularity.

When the gold rush petered out, unemployed white workers found themselves competing with cheap Chinese labor. Pacific Coast legislatures passed more and more restrictive measures against the Chinese. They were subjected to discriminating taxes and denied citizenship. In violation of the letter and the spirit of the treaty, Chinese, particularly in California, were subjected to every kind of abuse and injustice. In the words of one American historian,

Without offering any justification for this treatment which was brutal and appalling, it is evident from the figures that California was actually engaged in a very elemental conflict for race supremacy. South China had a superabundant population; California was sparsely settled and yielded large returns not merely in its mines but in its agriculture to the plodding, indefatigable labor of the Oriental. If natural laws were permitted, unchecked, to assert themselves it was only a question of time when the Chinese with lower standards of living and lower wage standards, would be able to displace the whites. The condition in the southern states after the emancipation of the slaves was ever before the citizens of California, so many of whom had come from the South.[20]

It was only the employers, always looking for cheap labor, who kept the door open.

[20] Dennett, *op. cit.*, p. 539.

The immigration clauses of the Burlingame Treaty were written by Secretary of State Seward, who seems to have been less interested in establishing
American-Chinese relations on a high moral plane than in the supply of
cheap labor. The supply of labor from China had to overcome two obstacles,
the Chinese legislation against emigration and the abuse and discrimination
faced by the Chinese in the Pacific Coast states. The treaty took care of
Chinese objection to emigration; and it was hoped that by putting the
weight of the federal government behind the articles prohibiting contract
labor and safeguarding Chinese coolies in America, something could be done
to head off discriminatory legislation by the states. The continued growth of
ill feeling towards Chinese in California forced the question of Oriental immigration into national and domestic politics, and both parties, Republican
and Democratic, declared themselves opposed to Chinese immigration.
About 1880 the United States felt it necessary to send a commission to China
to negotiate a new treaty, putting itself in the unhappy position of having to
ask for a modification of the Burlingame Treaty which had been so generous
in the matter.

The Chinese government adamantly refused to surrender to the United
States the right to prohibit immigration but agreed in the Treaty of 1880 that
the United States should have the right to "regulate, limit, or suspend" the
flow of Chinese laborers to the United States. Two years later the Congress
passed a law suspending the immigration of Chinese laborers for ten years
and broadening the definition of the word "laborer" to include both skilled
and unskilled workers. Further restrictions were added in an amendment to
the law in 1884. The Chinese immigration question continued to plague
American-Chinese relations for some time to come, leading ultimately to
more and more unilateral actions by the United States, not only in relation to
the other powers but also in relation to the Chinese government itself. While
in the process of negotiating a new treaty with the Chinese government, the
Senate passed the famous Scott Act of 1888, which among other things prohibited the return of all Chinese laborers who had gone to China for a visit,
even though they held re-entry permits. The Chinese protested but to no
avail.

The continuing friction between the United States and China over the
question of Chinese immigration was the only legacy of Burlingame's diplomacy. The cooperative policy as a means of protecting China was short-lived;
it soon gave place to a new period of imperialist competititon and aggrandizement.

Inroads on the Chinese Empire

The first loss of Chinese territory came with the cession of
the island of Hong Kong to the British at the close of the Opium War and the
Treaty of Nanking. For two decades the major aim of Western policy was the
opening of China rather than the seizure of territories. An exception to this
was the establishment of the Russian border at the Amur and Ussuri rivers in

1858 and 1860. In the following decades of the nineteenth century, however, the Western powers came more and more to invade the territories of the Chinese empire. Manchuria, Turkestan, Burma, Annam, and Korea were the Chinese dependencies and outer territories which came under attack.

The attack from the outside was facilitated by the rebellions which threatened Chinese government control from within. The Moslem rebellions in Chinese Turkestan and in the southwestern border province of Yunnan were especially instrumental in preparing the way for territorial advances by Russia and England. During the uprising in Turkestan, the Russians seized the opportunity to occupy the rich Ili Valley in 1871 under the pretext of preserving it for the Manchu government. The effective Chinese suppression of the Turkestan rebellion forced Russia to return, by the Treaty of St. Petersburg in 1881, the larger portion of this territory including the strategic mountain passes. She still retained, however, some of the rich agricultural sections. During the southwestern rebellion the British, then advancing their position in Burma, established contact with the rebel Moslem leader in China. After the rebellion was suppressed by new Chinese provincial leaders, the British continued their drive for a trade route through upper Burma into the southwestern hinterland of China. A British expedition, advancing in 1876, was met at the border by a British consular official, a Mr. Margary, coming from China. When this British official was assassinated by local border groups jealous of their trading monopolies, the advance of the expedition was halted. This incident was used as a means of diplomatic pressure in the negotiations leading up to the Chefoo Convention of September 13, 1876. The convention itself provided for the extension of British trade, the improvement of official relations, and an indemnity in punishment for the assassination. These concessions could be extracted from the Peking government, but the government did not have sufficient control over the governor-general of the southwestern provinces, who had resisted the British advance, to satisfy the British demand for his removal. The Margary incident slowed down the British advance, but ten years later the British completed their conquest of the whole of Burma.

On China's southern border, the French challenged the Chinese emperor's sovereign rights over the Red River area of Tongking in the kingdom of Annam. In 1874 when a Frenchman attempted to travel from Tongking up the Red River into Chinese territory, the Chinese local authorities resisted. A local French military expedition achieved no results. At the same time the Annamese government sought Chinese aid in its struggle to maintain its independence from French colonial rule, and the Chinese representative in Paris restated China's right of suzerainty. Chinese troops moved into Tongking and guarded the Red River. In 1883 the French government sent troops and in 1884 war broke out between France and China. The fighting on the Yunnan-Kwangtung border was undecisive, but the destruction by French naval action of the French-built and recently completed Chinese naval base at Foochow led to the Li-Fournier Convention of May, 1884. France agreed to respect the Chinese southern frontier while the Chinese gave up their claim to suzerainty over Annam and permitted trade with southern China. After some further fighting on the Chinese border, a new treaty was signed in Paris in 1885 in which the stipulations of the convention of 1884 were confirmed.

Japanese Imperialism

These territorial losses to Russia, England, and France were paralleled by the still more serious Japanese advances on Chinese territory. The Meiji Restoration of 1868, which begins the story of modern Japan, released political energies which found expression in an almost immediate bid to play a part in the imperialist struggle. The first Japanese move, only three years after the Meiji Restoration, was to conclude a treaty with China in which they tried to secure as privileged a position as the Western powers enjoyed. In this they were not successful. The Chinese were particularly adamant in refusing Japan the most-favored-nation treatment and the right for Japanese to travel freely in China. The treaty provided for reciprocal extraterritorial rights and included, on Chinese insistence, an article by which the two countries promised each other mutual assistance or the rendering of good offices in case either was threatened by another power. It was clear that China wanted a policy of equality among Asiatic powers and Asiatic unity against the Western threat, while Japan wanted to assume the role of a Western power. The treaty of 1871 was badly received in Japan because it fell short of the concessions secured by the Western powers in China. When the United States raised the question of the meaning of the stipulation about mutual assistance, the Japanese quickly denied any implication of an alliance with China.

When the treaty was ratified in 1873, the Japanese used the occasion to the fullest advantage. The Japanese ambassador, being the highest ranking representative, took precedence at the reception given by the Chinese emperor at his majority for foreign diplomats. The timing of the ratification had been carefully arranged by the Japanese to coincide with this event. Even more important was the Japanese attempt to gain from the Chinese an admission of their lack of control over the Liuchiu islanders, the natives of Formosa, and the people of Korea by asking the Chinese whether they would be responsible for incidents in these areas. Fearful that they would have to pay indemnities and ignorant of international law, the Chinese did not claim actual control in Korea, ignored the question of the Liuchiu islanders, and gave an evasive answer on Formosa.

The Chinese had good reason to be alarmed. A year earlier, in 1872, the king of Okinawa had been brought to Japan to pay homage to the emperor and be reduced in rank in order to fit into the new administrative system. The Okinawan king had been accustomed to paying tribute to both the emperor of China and the Lord of Satsuma, thus safeguarding his economic and political relationships with both. The unilateral action of the Japanese in bringing the Liuchiu Islands within their domain created an opportunity for further expansion when some Liuchiu islanders who were shipwrecked on Formosa were killed by headhunters. The Japanese had information that the area inhabited by the headhunting tribes was not administered by the Chinese, thus making it possible to send a Japanese expedition there without coming into contact with Chinese-administered territory. The war party in Japan had an expedition to Formosa in mind at the time when embarrassing questions about this incident were raised.

A Japanese expedition left for Formosa in April, 1874. The eastern portion of the island was occupied; there was little fighting and less glory. The Japanese were encouraged to be cautious partly by the concentration of Chinese troops across the Formosa Straits in the province of Fukien and partly by British disapproval of any alienation of Formosa. With British mediation a settlement was reached with the Chinese in October, 1874, the Japanese agreeing to withdraw from Formosa. The important part of the agreement was the article which by implication confirmed the Japanese claims to the Liuchiu Islands. This article stated that the Japanese had acted justly in punishing the Formosan natives who had "unlawfully inflicted injury on the people belonging to Japan." When the Chinese discovered the real meaning of this phrase, they reopened the question, and the sharpness of Chinese protests brought the two countries to the verge of war. Former President Grant on his visit to Japan got into the dispute as a mediator in 1879, using his influence to prevent a conflict which in his view would merely weaken both countries in relation to the Western powers. Negotiations, which looked for a time as if they would lead to agreement on the basis of division of the Liuchiu Islands, were broken off, and China dropped her protests as she became involved in war with France in 1884.

The other question raised by the Japanese related to Korea, long a tributary of China. The Chinese tributary system did not provide for clearly defined responsibilities for incidents occurring in the tributary states that involved other countries, except for the over-all Chinese authority to adjudicate disputes. For the Western powers, who were extending their juridical as well as their economic system to the rest of the world, the tributary system was too vague to be an acceptable basis for international relations. The tributary system could work only so long as China was strong enough to prevent the interference of other powers with different concepts of international relations. The problem arose at this time because of Chinese weakness, which enabled Japan—now one of the modern powers—to exploit the contradictions between the tributary system and international law.

The issue of Korea had been raised by the French in 1866 when some French Roman Catholic missionaries and their converts were murdered by Koreans. The United States, in order to prevent unilateral French action, suggested a joint expedition to Korea. When the French refused, the United States itself tried, unsuccessfully, to open negotiations with Korea in 1868. In 1871 the United States undertook an expedition to Korea which was patterned after the mission of Commodore Perry to Japan. The only achievement of the expedition was a naval engagement with Korean forts and an ignominious retreat after several forts had been destroyed and many Koreans killed.

The initiative which the United States had seized from the French now passed to the Japanese. In 1875 the Japanese sent a surveying party to Korea, which also came into conflict with Korean coastal defenses. A Japanese envoy was sent to Peking where he secured renewed assurances that China was not responsible for such incidents. Japan therefore felt secure in sending a strong naval force to Korea in order to force a treaty upon that country. The Koreans yielded and a treaty was concluded in February, 1876, which recognized the independence of Korea, thus by implication eliminating Chinese suzerainty. The Japanese secured extraterritoriality, the opening of several ports, and regular diplomatic relations. This was as far as the Japanese judged they could go without embroiling themselves in serious conflict with China.

Other powers, led by the United States, made similar treaties with Korea, thus seeming to emphasize Korean independence. The British preferred to see China responsible for Korea, partly because it would be easier to control China, partly to deny it to Japan, and partly because they felt that Korea itself could not protect its own independence. The United States, however, thought that Korea should be independent but was willing to approach Korea either through Japan or China, whichever seemed the more convenient. By this time it looked as if Japan would be the natural ally. United States officials, including no less a visitor to Japan than General Grant, were deeply impressed with the domestic reforms in that country and the success of Japan in the opening of Korea in 1876. In 1880 Commodore Shufeldt was sent to Korea to conclude a treaty but found the Koreans unwilling to negotiate. He was therefore instructed to visit Japan and to secure from the Japanese government letters of recommendation to Korean officials. It soon became clear, however, that the Japanese had no intention of being helpful and had very little desire to share Korea with the rest of the world. Shufeldt therefore accepted the invitation of the prominent Chinese official, Li Hung-chang, to go to Tientsin, where he was promised Chinese assistance in securing a Korean treaty.

The United States and Korea signed a treaty in Tientsin in May, 1882. The Chinese, who negotiated the treaty, failed to secure any statement as to the dependence of Korea on China; but by opening Korea to the other powers they hoped to protect it from the Japanese. The American treaty was followed immediately by similar treaties with England, Germany, Italy, Russia, and France, all of which recognized the government of Korea as that of a fully independent state. The Shufeldt treaty weakened the Chinese claims to suzerainty over Korea, and to that extent prepared the way for eventual Japanese domination.

From this time on, the political struggle at the Korean court became linked with the conflict between China and Japan over the control of Korea. Though China had permitted the conclusion of treaties between Korea and other countries which declared Korea to be an independent state, she was not willing to give up her traditional overlordship over the country. One group in the Korean government took the same view. This group was led by the regent, who was running the government during the minority of the young king. When the king came of age he and his queen, with the backing of the Min clan, to which she belonged, favored the modernization of Korea with Japanese help, while the conservative regent continued to lean on Chinese support. In 1882 the ex-regent attempted a coup in which he hoped to seize the king and queen and eliminate the influence of the Japanese and the progressive group. The royal couple escaped, but the Japanese legation was burned and some Japanese and their Korean allies lost their lives. The Japanese mobilized military forces, sent their minister back, and secured from the Korean government an indemnity and the right to station Japanese troops in Seoul. The Chinese did not interfere with the Japanese but retreated, taking with them the ex-regent whom they held responsible for the failure.

In 1883 Li Hung-chang, the strong man of North China, sent Yüan Shih-k'ai, one of his chief lieutenants, to Korea as Chinese "resident." In 1884 during the Sino-French war the Japanese attempted a coup of their own, seizing the king and queen and compelling them to declare Korea independent of China. Yüan Shih-k'ai moved in with troops, recaptured the palace and the royal couple, forced the Japanese to withdraw, and restored the government under his personal control. A stalemate ensued as neither Japan nor China was ready to fight. In April, 1885, a treaty was concluded at Tientsin by Li Hung-chang and Count Ito, according to which both powers had the right to send troops to Korea when necessary but should first notify each other of such intentions. There was little change in the situation until 1894 when the revolt of a Korean secret society threatened the capital and the government. The king called on Li Hung-chang for military assistance, but the revolt was put down before troops came. However, both Chinese and Japanese troops were sent, the Japanese actually arriving first in Seoul where they held the king under their influence. The Japanese claimed that the Chinese notification of the sending of troops to Korea contained an unwarranted reference to Chinese suzerainty and that it was dispatched too late. Actually these matters had little to do with the Japanese decision to fight. When the Japanese attacked and sank a British ship which had been hired to bring Chinese reinforcements to Korea, the Sino-Japanese War of 1894–95 began.

The war was won by Japan in a very short period of time. It revealed the startling superiority of the Japanese over the Chinese military forces. The Japanese secured control of the seas by defeating the Chinese navy, rapidly took over Korea, and pushed on into Manchuria. The Chinese agreed to come to terms when it looked as if there was nothing to stop the Japanese from moving on Peking. Li Hung-chang and Count Ito negotiated the Treaty of Shimonoseki, April, 1895, which concluded the war.

In the treaty China renounced all claims to suzerainty over Korea which was declared to be an independent state, thus in reality preparing the way for eventual Japanese annexation. Japan's imperialist ambitions were indicated by her far-reaching territorial demands. China was compelled to cede the island of Formosa and the Pescadores. Japan also demanded the cession of the Liaotung Peninsula in the southern part of Manchuria. In addition to further commercial privileges in China, the Japanese demanded a huge indemnity of two hundred million taels. Japan gained extraterritorial rights for her subjects in China and the most-favored-nation treatment, thus acquiring equal status with the Western treaty powers.

Japan's overwhelming success and ruthless exploitation of her victory alarmed some of her competitors in the imperialist struggle. Russia, herself interested in Manchuria, was unwilling to see Japan acquire the Liaotung Peninsula and thus block both Russian expansion to the south and access to Peking. In her diplomatic move to push back the Japanese advance, Russia found herself supported by both France and Germany. The French had the obligation of an ally, and Kaiser Wilhelm II seemed to think that by supporting Russia he could turn her attention more to the Far East and away from Europe. The three powers intervened with diplomatic representation at Tokyo threatening military action if Japan did not relinquish her Manchurian conquest. In the face of this opposition Japan retreated, exchanging the Liaotung Peninsula for an additional thirty million taels indemnity from China.

The defeat at the hands of Japan had revealed China's extreme military weakness. This had not been apparent before. China had long been the leading military power in Eastern Asia, and several of the powers had been involved in the modernization of the Chinese navy and army. The failure of the navy was not due to the quality of the ships or officers, but to corruption in the supply system and the administration. The extent of corruption in the army, as in the navy, could not be measured until the test of war. The powers were quick to see that this turning of the tables was no accident of the battlefield; it revealed a deep weakness in the political structure of China just as it showed the strength of the new Japan. There was no possibility of the Chinese making a quick recovery and reestablishing their dominant position.

The Slicing of the Melon

China's inner weakness was an invitation to the imperialist powers to compete with each other for every kind of advantage at the expense of China. This process is usually known by the somewhat inelegant phrase, "the slicing of the melon." In the eyes of the Western powers, China was not expected to survive much longer as an independent government. It was natural that the Chinese government should try to find support from the outside. Li Hung-chang, to whom the Court still turned to find salvation from humiliation and defeat, approached Russia for support. Russia was the leading power in the triple intervention which had forced the Japanese to give up Manchuria. In 1896 a secret military alliance between China and Russia was concluded, for a price. Russia received the right to build a Russo-Chinese railway through northern Manchuria between the border town of Manchuli and her naval base at Vladivostok, a much shorter route than that around the Amur and Ussuri rivers. The railway cut through territory only thinly populated by non-Chinese Mongol and Tungus tribal people, thus opening up the possibility of incorporating northern Manchuria into Russian territory and replacing the Amur bend by the shortened border across Manchuria.

Such a policy of limited expansion was actually represented at the tsarist court by Count Witte, then Russian Minister of Finance and a leading Russian statesman. Another group of military leaders, supported by the tsar, advocated a more aggressive policy of moving into southern Manchuria and to the ice-free ports of the Liaotung Peninsula. Such a move would bring Russia into territory with a Chinese agricultural population and give her practical control of the area which by this time had become known internationally as Manchuria. The more aggressive course won out, and in 1898 Russia gained from China the Kwantung leased territory including the port of Dairen and the naval base of Port Arthur, and at the same time extended its railroad rights by building a line from Harbin in north Manchuria through the leased territory to Dairen and Port Arthur. Thus Russia secured a T-shaped railroad system in Manchuria from which she could exert strategic control over the whole territory. The railroads were built and run by a Russo-Chinese company to which the treaty of 1896 had given the right of political administration in the railroad zone. This important concession was left out of the Chinese version of the treaty text but was included in the official French text. The treaty of 1898 merely referred to the treaty of 1896 and thus gave Russia the same political rights in the extended railway zone running down through southern Manchuria. The Chinese were paying a high price for Russian help in keeping the Japanese out of Manchuria.

Russian penetration of Manchuria was part of a general threat to Chinese independence. The major Western powers secured bases on the Chinese coast and prepared the ground for the seizure of slices of territory in case of colonial division. Germany used the murder of two German missionaries by the Chinese as the occasion to demand from the Chinese government a ninety-nine year lease of Tsingtao and its surrounding area, the Bay of Kiaochow, a monopoly of railway and mining rights in the province of Shantung, and an indemnity to pay for the cost of the naval expedition which enforced the demands. The monopoly was made specific instead of general, but otherwise the demands were accepted. To balance the Russian position at Port Arthur, the British took over the leased territory of Weihaiwei opposite Port Arthur.

At the same time the British secured from the Chinese an assurance that they would not alienate to another power any of the provinces in the Yangtze Valley and that a British subject would be Inspector General of the Maritime Customs as long as British trade supremacy in China was maintained. In this way the British reserved to themselves the dominant position at Shanghai and in the Yangtze Valley area. They also added the Kowloon leased territories to the crown colony of Hong Kong. South China, on the other hand, had for some time been recognized as an area of French influence. The Chinese had agreed in 1895 not to surrender the island of Hainan to any other power; they gave the French preferential customs rates for goods coming in from Indo-

China; they assured the French special mining and railroad priorities in the southern provinces of Yunnan, Kwangsi, and Kwangtung. In 1898 the French extended these privileges and secured a ninety-nine year lease on Kwangchow Bay. In the same year the Japanese secured from Peking an agreement that no other power should have Fukien province, opposite Formosa. By the end of the century there were few harbors, provinces, or economic concessions worth the having which had not been taken or spoken for.

The powers understood the "leased territories" and spheres of interest as the first steps toward annexation. A sphere of interest, such as Russia's in Manchuria or Germany's in Shantung, was understood to be an area in which the dominant power had prior claims on economic exploitation and development and in which no other power would seek concessions or leased territories. If the dominant power came to exercise any political and administrative control, then the area would be known as a "sphere of influence." This stronger term can be considered a middle step between the "sphere of interest" and outright annexation. In the scramble for China, some of the powers actually reached written or unwritten understandings as to their various spheres, moves which limited China's freedom of action and helped to avoid conflict between the powers themselves. One example of such an agreement was the Scott-Muraviev agreement of 1899 between Britain and Russia by which the British agreed not to seek railroad concessions in Manchuria on condition that the Russians would respect the British sphere of interest in the Yangtze Valley. The spheres in China marked the ebb and flow of the vast world-wide conflict between Russian territorial expansion and British naval power. The complete disintegration of China, which seemed to be imminent, did not actually take place, partly because of events in China and partly because of changes in the international situation.

5. THE UNITED STATES IN THE PACIFIC

In the period following the Civil War, the energies of the United States were occupied mainly in the development of the American continent itself. Such a task, consuming as it was, did not divert all American attention from the Far East. It was during the period from the close of the Civil War to the end of the century that the United States acquired Alaska, the Midway Islands, and Hawaii; assisted in the opening of Korea; annexed the Philippine Islands; and sent troops to help relieve the legations at Peking during the Boxer Rebellion. The second half of the nineteenth century saw the development of an isolationist spirit which was a reflection of the drive to develop the American continent. But at the same time the very strength of the continental America that emerged from this period brought a feeling that the destiny of the country had to be played out on a world-wide stage. In the view of the isolationists, the century closed with unnecessary and rash American commitments in the western Pacific; in the view of other Americans, the second half of the century saw many lost opportunities and a heedless attitude towards the world responsibilities of the United States.

The Acquisition of Naval Bases

The United States Navy continued to press for its policy of acquiring naval bases, which was started at the time of Commodore Perry. In 1867 the United States purchased Alaska. The Russians were willing to sell this distant outpost because of the decline in the fur trade. For Secretary of State Seward the acquisition of Alaska and the Aleutian Islands was a means of strengthening the naval position of the United States in the northern Pacific. In the same year, 1867, the Midway Islands were acquired, and Seward began negotiations for the acquisition of the Hawaiian Islands. He did not succeed, but in American opinion there was no need to hurry toward annexation because American economic and naval predominance was already assured. In 1871 Secretary of State Fish drew attention to the importance of Honolulu as a "resting spot in mid-ocean between the Pacific Coast and the vast domains of Asia which are now opening to commerce and Christian civilization," and again raised the question of annexation. In 1875 a non-alienation agreement gave the United States a preferred status in the islands and assisted decisively in the growth of American investments in the sugar industry. In 1881 Secretary Blaine openly stated America's strategic and political interest in the islands, and in 1884 Pearl Harbor was leased to the United States as a naval base. The annexation of the Hawaiian Islands in 1898 was the conclusion of a long process.

In this same year, 1898, the United States extended its system of naval bases all across the Pacific. Tripartite control over the Samoan Islands by England, Germany, and the United States, which had lasted for nine years, came to an end over a conflict concerning the selection of a new Samoan king. A settlement was reached by which the British withdrew, in return for compensation elsewhere, Germany gained the western islands and the United States the eastern, including Pago Pago on the island of Tutuila. Pago Pago was a coaling station and one of the finest harbors in the Pacific; it was an important strategic base for the American fleet in the South Pacific. The United States assumed formal sovereignty over the islands in 1900. In the central Pacific the United States acquired Wake Island and Guam, which, added to Midway and Hawaii, provided a line of bases to the Far East.

Conquest of the Philippines

The naval policy of acquiring strategic bases in the Pacific was the main reason for the acquisition of the Philippine Islands. The United States found itself at war with Spain in April, 1898, over the question of Cuba, an issue that had nothing to do with the situation in the Far East. The United States extended the war into the Pacific because it presented an opportunity for a vigorous application of the policy, originating with Perry and continued by Seward, of establishing naval bases across the Pacific. In anticipation of the conflict, Theodore Roosevelt, then Secretary of the Navy, had ordered a strong naval squadron to the Chinese coast with Admiral Dewey in command. As was expected, the British, the Chinese, and the Japanese immediately declared their neutrality in the conflict; and the United States fleet had to choose between returning home, leaving American shipping and other interests at the mercy of the Spanish fleet, or of attacking the Spanish fleet in the western Pacific. The decision to attack had actually been made before the war started. Admiral Dewey left Hong Kong at the request of the British and steamed to Manila Bay where he surprised the Spanish fleet and destroyed it completely without loss to his own ships. This was on May 1, eleven days after the outbreak of war.

Dewey, however, was in no position to go beyond naval action. He could not take the city of Manila or attack the Spanish on land until reinforcements arrived. Before the attack Dewey had negotiated in Hong Kong with an exiled Filipino insurrectionist leader, Emilio Aguinaldo, for military cooperation. Aguinaldo was brought to the Philippines on an American ship, established himself on Luzon, and one week before American forces occupied the city of Manila, appealed to the world for recognition of his government. The occupation of Manila was a necessary step to guarantee a base for the American fleet and to anticipate similar action by other powers, particularly the Germans, who had moved ships and troops to Manila Bay. But the occupation of Manila raised the question of the status of the rest of the islands.

The alternatives facing the United States in the Philippines were still being debated in America while the peace negotiations with the Spanish were in progress. The sudden and startling realization of American naval disadvantage in the western Pacific when other powers denied the use of their ports and bases had led immediately to the annexation of Hawaii, a step which was also supported by the newborn fears of Japanese immigration and even of possible Japanese annexation. It also led to the seizure of Guam from the Spanish. The problem of the Philippines was much more complex. Spain was in no position to protect them from any outside power. To leave the Philippines open to international competition might very well lead to world war. While President McKinley's first reaction was to take over the island of Luzon and to leave the rest in Spanish hands, it soon became clear that such a course might involve serious dangers in conflict with other interested powers, such as Germany and Japan, both of which had an eye on these Spanish possessions. There would be an international struggle for ports, concessions, and control over the rest of the Philippine archipelago. Step by step, the McKinley administration moved to the conclusion that occupation of all the Philippines was the only course. McKinley therefore decided to demand from Spain the cession of the whole island group, to which the Spanish agreed in return for the payment of $20,000,000 as compensation for public buildings and the like.

McKinley ordered the extension of American military government over the islands. This move led to immediate conflict with the existing Philippine government under Aguinaldo which had already proclaimed its independence and had expected American support. Fighting started between American troops and Philippine insurrectionists on February 4, 1899, two days before the Senate vote on the Treaty of Paris which ended the Spanish-American War. After American lives had been lost, national pride was involved and to some extent the hand of the Senate was forced. Even at that, the treaty was approved by a very narrow margin.

Not all Americans were unaware of the political issues at stake. Late in 1898 and early in 1899 resolutions were proposed in the Senate designed to bind the United States government to a declaration of policy forbidding acquisition of colonies or other territories unless they were suitable for admission into the Union. Senator Bacon of Georgia brought in a resolution which said in so many words that the United States disclaimed any intentions of ruling the Philippine Islands and intended to hand over to a native government all the rights secured under cession by Spain. The Vice President cast a deciding vote against the resolution. By such a narrow margin the Senate decided against immediate independence for the Philippines. McKinley considered the Filipinos unfit for self-government and predicted that if left to themselves they would relapse into anarchy and misrule. If the wish were father to the thought, it must also be added that McKinley had behind him not only important industrial interests but also the almost unanimous support of the Protestant Church. This was a time when missionary activity depended upon treaties and national prestige, and the prospect of new fields to conquer was tempting indeed.

The American annexation of the Philippines was approved by the British, who did not wish to have the islands in German or Japanese hands, and was accepted by the Germans. Germany had sent naval units to Manila Bay during the war, which she had tried in vain through diplomatic action to prevent, hoping to purchase from Spain the Philippines, the Carolines, the Marianas, and the Palau Islands and thus build up her position in the Pacific. After the conclusion of peace with Spain, Germany actually purchased the Carolines, the Marianas, with the exception of Guam, and the Palau Islands, The Japanese government maintained strict neutrality, but when Aguinaldo resisted the American occupation it did not prevent certain elements in Japan from assisting him. This was done under cover by making use of Sun Yat-sen, the leader of the Chinese nationalist movement, who at that time was also receiving Japanese support for uprisings in China. In the name of Sun Yat-sen Japanese military experts and a supply of arms were sent to Aguinaldo. The officers reached Bataan but the ship, loaded with arms, foundered en route. The Japanese made no further effort to prevent American occupation of the Philippines. But the arrival of American military power in the Philippine Islands only a few hundred miles away from the Japanese colony of Formosa increased the possibility of friction between America and Japan.

The strategic concepts of the American Navy and its supporters at this time were strongly influenced by the doctrines of A. T. Mahan, the American naval officer best known for his book, *The Influence of Sea Power on History*. Mahan provided the theoretical framework for Theodore Roosevelt, Senator Henry Cabot Lodge, and President McKinley, the men who were in favor of what was called the "large policy." Mahan, like many Navy men before him, saw the large policy as one involving the annexation of Hawaii, domination of the Caribbean, and the building of the Nicaraguan Canal; but it was not until after Dewey's victory at Manila that the large policy came to include the Philippines.

The Open Door Notes

The background of military success in the Philippines and the presence in that area of considerable American land and naval forces made it possible for American diplomacy to play an active role in the critical situation that had developed in China. In the closing years of the century the growth of spheres of interest and influence in China and the apparent danger of China's disappearance as an independent state endangered the traditional American policies of protecting the independence of Oriental states and of assuring equality of economic opportunity. These policies were reaffirmed in the Open Door notes of September, 1899, sent by Secretary of State John Hay to the governments of Britain, Germany, France, Italy, Japan, and Russia. In the notes, Hay requested that

each, within its respective sphere of whatever influence:

First. Will in no way interfere with any treaty port or any vested interest within any so-called "sphere of interest" or leased territory it may have in China.

Second. That the Chinese treaty tariff of the time being shall apply to all merchandise landed or shipped to all such ports as are within said "sphere of interest" (unless they be "free ports"), no matter to what nationality it may belong, and that duties so leviable shall be collected by the Chinese Government.

Third. That it will levy no higher harbor dues on vessels of another nationality frequenting any port in such "sphere" than shall be levied on vessels of its own nationality, and no higher railroad charges over lines built, controlled, or operated within its "sphere" than shall be levied on similar merchandise belonging to its own nationals transported over equal distances.[21]

While the notes dealt with the situation within the spheres of interest and of influence, these phrases were always put in quotation marks, or referred to as "sphere of whatever influence," thus indicating an unwillingness to give them formal recognition. The United States did not wish to assist, even by the use of words, the growth of monopoly rights. The United States also tried to preserve, within the areas in question and the leased territories, existing American investments and enterprises as well as equality of treatment in railroad rates and harbor dues. More important still was the stress on the responsibility of the Chinese government in the collection of duties, taking for granted the authority of that government. In this way the United States expressed again its traditional policies of equality of commercial opportunity and protection of Chinese territorial and administrative integrity.

The reception of the notes by the powers can hardly be counted a success. All the powers, with the exception of Russia, agreed to the policies expressed on condition that the others would do the same. Russia in her answer expressed her willingness to treat the citizens of all other countries equally but

[21] John V. A. MacMurray, *Treaties and Agreements With and Concerning China, 1894–1919* (New York, 1921), Vol. I, p. 223.

omitted any promise to give them equal status with Russian subjects. In other words, all other countries would be treated equally badly. The negative Russian reply automatically released all the other powers from their acceptance. Secretary Hay, however, chose to pretend that his notes had been accepted, and no one of the powers was willing to deny the commitment openly.

The Open Door notes had been carefully drafted, and in their preparation John Hay relied heavily on W. W. Rockhill, an American diplomat with considerable Far Eastern experience, and on his friend Mr. Hippesley, an Englishman who had served in the Chinese Maritime Customs. As Hippesley's official life had been largely in the service of the Chinese government, he naturally emphasized the importance of maintaining the integrity of the Chinese government and the Maritime Customs and of continuing the trade with China on the basis of equality of commercial opportunity for all. He was therefore in full agreement with the traditional American position as it was reaffirmed in the Open Door notes.

The American position was cautiously supported by the British government; in fact, the British were seeking, at this time, an alliance with the United States. The Japanese also had everything to gain by opening the door as wide as possible in China as they had neither the military nor the naval strength to oppose the powers of Europe at this time. The Open Door notes were a perfect reflection of the international situation. In their replies the powers gave up nothing except those steps toward the further partition of China which might have involved them in world conflict. Perhaps the most important aspect of the Open Door notes was the indication to all the powers interested in China that the United States had to be counted in as an active agent and that any further efforts to partition China would have to take this fact into account. Although the notes did not attract much attention at the time, at least outside the United States, the Open Door came to be used more and more as an accepted policy in almost all the treaties concerning China in the following years, beginning with the Anglo-Japanese alliance of 1902. The notes succeeded because the powers, with the exception of Russia, agreed on the policies stated by John Hay, and in fact from this time forward the drive for monopolies was arrested.

The Open Door was merely a new slogan for a policy as old as American interest in the Far East, the policy of equal opportunity and of protection of the territorial and administrative integrity of Far Eastern countries. In the critical situation at the end of the century this policy was stated in John Hay's notes with much greater caution and in a much more restricted form than either before or after. However, the restatement of the policy at this time, and the new slogan under which it appeared, served the purposes of American diplomacy. By the end of the century the Open Door policy was closely linked with the other important American policy, that of securing a strong naval position in the Pacific. But while the Open Door policy in China would have been far less effective without naval backing, the naval policy itself had led to the conquest and colonization of the Philippines, a direct violation of the concept of the Open Door.

6. New Alignments in the Far East

Impact of the Boxer Rebellion

The international pressures on China which brought about the Open Door notes had a great deal to do with internal Chinese developments. The Boxer Rebellion (1899–1900), a primitive uprising by a secret Chinese society, was in part directed against the penetration of China by foreign interests and foreign missionaries. Those foreigners who escaped the violent outbreaks against them in the north fled to Peking where they sought protection in the Legation Quarter. In spite of warnings, few precautions were taken by the foreign community until May, 1900, when a stronger force arrived for the protection of the legations just before they were besieged by the Boxers and cut off from all contact with the outside world. On June 11 a member of the Japanese legation was murdered and on June 17 the German minister, von Ketteler, when attempting to open negotiations, was shot in the street by a Manchu sergeant. In June, foreign naval units captured the Taku forts in order to clear the way for a relief expedition; in retaliation, the Boxers attacked the foreign community in Tientsin with the aid of imperial troops. Foreign forces took Tientsin in July, and in August an international relief expedition left for Peking. It included Japanese, Russian, British, French, and Italian troops and an American unit of 2,500 men. These forces took Peking and freed the besieged legations on August 14, 1900. Two months later a German unit was added and all troops were put under the nominal command of Field Marshal Count Waldersee.

Negotiations for an agreement to end the war began in December and the Boxer Protocol was finally signed on September 7, 1901, the delay being caused by disputes between the powers as to the size and distribution of the indemnity. In the Boxer Protocol, China was compelled to apologize for the murder of Baron von Ketteler, punish the officials responsible for the insurrection, and apologize to Japan for the murder of the Chancellor of the Japanese legation. China agreed to suspend the official examinations in those places where foreigners had been attacked, to stop importing arms and materials for their manufacture for two or more years, to pay an indemnity, and to fix customs at a rate of 5 per cent ad valorem. She was compelled to destroy the forts at Taku, permit foreign occupation of sufficient places to protect communications between Peking and the sea, abolish the Tsungli Yamen and create a ministry of foreign affairs.

The most important of these stipulations was the indemnity which was fixed at the enormous sum of 450,000,000 taels, payment of which was to be secured by the maritime customs and the salt gabelle. The United States and Great Britain later returned part of the interest on the indemnity to China to be used for educational purposes. The other important stipulation proved to be the right to station troops between Peking and Tientsin, a right which was later exploited by the Japanese in their moves to secure control over North China. The willingness of the United States to exploit its power and position at this time, short of actual alliances, did much to encourage the trend away from "slicing the melon." In a circular note of July, 1900, Hay restated the American stand in the following words: ". . . the policy of the Government of the United States is to seek a solution which may bring about permanent safety and peace to China, preserve Chinese territorial and administrative entity, protect all rights guaranteed to friendly Powers by Treaty and international law, and safeguard for the world the principle of equal and impartial trade with all parts of the Chinese Empire." [22] This statement of policy set the tone for the negotiations with China that led up to the Boxer Protocol.

Russia had exploited the opportunity created by the Boxer unrest in Manchuria to occupy the whole of Manchurian territory, from which she was not to be dislodged when peace was restored. The expansion of Russian control in Manchuria and the revival of Russian interest in Korea led to growing conflict between Russia and Japanese imperial ambitions which eventually developed into the Russo-Japanese war of 1904–1905. The diplomatic alignment of Great Britain, the United States, and Japan, informal as it was, played something of a role in opposing further Russian expansion. The refusal of the United States, however, to make alliances led the British to conclude an alliance with Japan in 1902 as a counterweight to further Russian ambitions in Eastern Asia. Each party agreed to maintain strict neutrality if the other were attacked by one power but to come to the other's aid if it were attacked by two powers. The Russians and the French, in answer to this alliance, extended their own alliance to cover the Far East; but the Anglo-Japanese alliance actually achieved the localization of war between Japan and Russia when it occurred. It also recognized Japan as one of the great powers of the world.

The Russo-Japanese War

The Russo-Japanese War of 1904–1905 arose directly out of the competing imperialisms of Russia and Japan in Korea and Manchuria. In 1895, the Russians, with the help of France and Germany, had denied southern Manchuria to Japan. Since that time, Japan had to watch Russian expansion in Manchuria and even the extension of Russian moves to Korea, a country whose control was counted among the very first prerequisites of Japanese imperialist expansion.

The secret Russo-Chinese treaty of 1896 had been directed against Japan. The refusal of Russia to withdraw from positions she had taken during the Boxer troubles in Manchuria, the Russian threat to Peking, and the control of the sea approach to the capital via the Gulf of Chihli were of concern not only to Japan but also to other powers, especially England. Hence the British interest in the anticipated conflict between Japan and Russia. By the alliance Japan was assured that the Russians could not count on French and German support as they had done in 1895.

The Anglo-Japanese alliance had the effect of temporarily slowing up

[22] *Foreign Relations of the United States, 1900*, p. 299 ff.

the Russian advance in Manchuria. The Russians made an agreement with the Chinese government to withdraw their troops in Manchuria into the railway zone, from which they had fanned out all over the countryside during the Boxer troubles. Russian troops were actually withdrawn from southwestern Manchuria but remained throughout the rest of Manchuria. In fact, the agreement was sufficiently vague to give the Russians a pretext for remaining. At the same time negotiations were opened between Russia and Japan in which Japan suggested what amounted to a mutual recognition of their respective spheres of interest in Manchuria and Korea. Feeling that they were strong enough to decide what concessions they could or could not make, the Russians avoided the acceptance of any binding limitation of their interests. The Japanese cut off diplomatic relations and began the war in February, 1904, with a surprise attack on the Russian fleet at the naval base of Port Arthur. The Japanese had the advantage of being near the battle area and consequently having the better means of communication. For the prolonged siege of Port Arthur, Japanese supplies could come in by sea, while the Russian position in southern Manchuria depended on the long overland route from European Russia. After taking Port Arthur, the Japanese advanced into Manchuria.

The only way in which the Russians could interfere with the Japanese lines of communication was by naval action. A few cruisers which operated from Vladivostok as raiders were soon eliminated by the Japanese. The main Russian fleet was concentrated in the Baltic on the other side of the world, but the Russian government decided to send the major portion of the fleet to help in the war in the Far East. After an extraordinary voyage through the Baltic, the North Sea, the Atlantic, around the Cape of Good Hope, and then through the Indian and Pacific Oceans, the fleet reached the Straits of Tsushima on its way to Vladivostok. When it was passing through the narrow straits between Korea and Japan, the fleet was attacked by the Japanese navy. In the ensuing engagement, the Japanese under Admiral Togo almost completely destroyed the Russian fleet with very small losses to themselves. After this setback and their retreat in Manchuria beyond Mukden, the Russians were willing to come to terms. The Japanese, whose lines of communication were now greatly extended and who had begun to feel the financial strain of the war, were also ready for peace.

The peace treaty of Portsmouth, signed in September, 1905, was negotiated through American good offices. The Japanese received the Russian rights in southern Manchuria as far as their territorial conquest had taken them. This meant the leased territory with Port Arthur and Dairen and the railway from these cities via Mukden as far north as the city of Changchun. The rest of this railway line from Changchun to Harbin as well as the west-east line from Manchuli via Harbin to Vladivostok remained in Russian hands. Besides falling heir to the Russian position in southern Manchuria, the Japanese finally gained Russian acceptance of their "paramount political, military, and economic interests" in Korea. The Japanese also wanted the Russians to cede the island of Sakhalin and to pay an indemnity of $600,000,-

000 in order to ease the financial crisis in Japan; but the Russians themselves were in a critical financial condition and unwilling to pay. They were also reluctant to make further territorial concessions. As a final gesture, the Russians offered to cede the southern half of Sakhalin without the payment of any indemnity. The Japanese, feeling the financial strain of the war, accepted this offer. Unfortunately for them, oil was later discovered in the northern part of Sakhalin.

President Theodore Roosevelt played an important part not only in bringing the belligerents together but also in the negotiations at Portsmouth. His military advisers warned him that the Japanese were in no condition to keep the war going much longer and that if the tide of battle changed to their disadvantage the possibility of the conflict spreading both in the Far East and Europe would be very much greater. Roosevelt warned Germany and France that America might assist Japan if they came to the aid of Russia, but at the same time he advised the Japanese to come to terms with the Russians without insisting on an indemnity. Japanese public opinion, aroused over what seemed to be a failure fully to exploit a hard-won victory, held Roosevelt responsible for denying Japan the indemnity.

The Treaty of Portsmouth established Japan as a continental Asiatic power. Korea, which became a Japanese protectorate, was finally annexed in 1910. Its rice surplus supplemented the food supply of a rapidly industrializing Japan. But the main gain was southern Manchuria which the Japanese immediately proceeded to develop.

The Struggle for Manchuria

The increased territorial strength and prestige of Japan brought about changes in the relations between the United States and Japan. Japanese resentment over the Treaty of Portsmouth was fed by the further resentment at American racial discrimination on the West Coast, which included, among other things, the exclusion of children of Japanese ancestry from the regular school system. On the American side, the feeling grew that it was now Japan rather than Russia which represented the greater threat to American policies in the Pacific and Eastern Asia. There was a great deal of concern about Japanese designs on the Philippine Islands. In 1907, in a demonstration of American naval power, President Roosevelt sent the fleet on a tour around the world, on which it visited Japan. In November, 1908, there was an exchange of notes between the American Secretary of State, Elihu Root, and the Japanese Ambassador, Takahira, in which an effort was made to delineate the general position of each of the two powers in the Far East. Both parties promised to maintain the "existing status quo" in the Pacific, which implied that the Japanese would respect the American position in the Philippines while America would give Japan a free hand in Korea. The notes also included Japanese confirmation of "the principle of equal opportunity for commerce and industry in China" and respect for Chinese "independence and integrity." The United States had secured a renewed Japanese acknowledgment of the policy of the Open Door, but the way in which this general principle would be applied to specific cases obviously depended on the power relationships at any given time.

Manchuria was the main area in which these policies were tested. At the time when the Japanese took over the Russian rights, Manchuria had a population of some 7,000,000 people and great possibilities for agricultural and industrial development. Railways were essential to bring in the settlers and take out the agricultural surplus. The struggle for Manchuria became a battle for railroads and railroad control. In the treaty of Portsmouth, Russia and Japan had agreed to withdraw their troops into the railroad zone, except for the leased territory, and to put no obstacles in the way of China's economic development of Manchuria.

When the Japanese took over the Russian rights in 1905, both Russia and Japan felt the need to obtain Chinese consent to this transfer of rights which had been granted by China to Russia in 1898. The Chinese government agreed to this transfer in the Sino-Japanese Treaty of Peking, 1905. In addition to this transfer, the Japanese forced the Chinese government to make a further concession which was not included in the Treaty of Peking itself but was attached to it in a secret *procès-verbal*, the minutes of a binding verbal understanding, in which the Chinese promised not to build in Manchuria any railway "parallel to and in competition with" the South Manchurian Railway, now taken by the Japanese. The interpretation of this secret Chinese promise became a major source of conflict between China and Japan.

The Japanese regarded this promise as a legal basis for the economic monopoly which they now tried to establish in the southern part of Manchuria. The railway, when they took it over from the Russians, was an incomplete military field line which would require considerable capital for full development. During the Russo-Japanese War an American railway magnate, Harriman, had become interested in extending his activities to Asia. The Japanese accepted his offer to supply the capital and organization for the rebuilding of the Manchurian railroad. After the peace treaty, however, the Japanese cancelled their agreement and went ahead on their own; but the question remained as to whether Manchuria, together with the rest of China, would be a field of "equal opportunity" for railroad development by all nations. A British-Chinese railway had already been built from North China to Mukden in 1902 before the Japanese conquest. The first test in the Manchurian railway situation came in 1907, when a British company secured from the Chinese government the right to build an extension of this railroad from the city of Hsinmintun in the south to Fakumen in the north. The announcement of this railroad concession brought an immediate protest from the Japanese. They revealed the secret agreement which had been concluded with the Chinese government in 1905 and interpreted it to exclude the building of any such railroad as that contemplated by the British firm. The British government, still allied with the Japanese, gave in and persuaded the British firm to give up its concession.

Another major effort to participate in the railroad development of Man-

churia was made by the United States in 1909. The American railroad magnate, Harriman, had not given up his plans for a round-the-world railroad
under his control, and he had hoped to negotiate an agreement with the Russians on their section of the Manchurian railroad system, following which he
would be able to come to terms with the Japanese. Harriman died in 1909 before completing his plans. An American banking group pursued this interest
in Manchuria and, in its behalf, the American consul in Mukden, Mr.
Willard Straight, succeeded in obtaining from the Chinese government a concession for a railroad all the way across Manchuria from the port of Chinchow
to the city of Aigun on the Amur River.

The American government attempted to use this railroad concession as a
bargaining point with Japan, Russia, and the other powers to bring about a
joint development of the Manchurian railroad system. Instead of conducting
private negotiations with Russia and later with Japan, the American Secretary of State Knox sent public notes to the interested powers. These notes, the
so-called "Knox Neutralization Plan for Manchuria," contained two alternate proposals. The American government declared its willingness to place
its new concession in a general pool if the Japanese and Russians would do the
same with their railroads. The whole railroad system of Manchuria would
then be administered jointly by the powers. As an alternate proposal, the
same suggestion was made for the projected Chinchow-Aigun Railroad alone.
These suggestions were turned down by all the powers. Again Japan referred
to her understanding with China which, according to her interpretation,
prevented the building of practically any railroad in southern Manchuria by
anyone else. After this general refusal, the American government dropped the
issue. The result of the "Knox Neutralization Plan" was thus entirely negative. It had not only strengthened the Japanese and Russian monopoly position in Manchuria but it even brought these recent antagonists closer together.

In 1907 Japan and Russia had concluded an agreement to link the railroad systems between their respective parts of Manchuria. As a result of the
pressure from Knox, they now joined to protect their respective Manchurian
monopolies. In a series of open and secret treaties in 1909, 1911, and 1916,
they delineated their spheres in southern and northern Manchuria and promised to consult each other in regard to outside competition. The agreement
of 1916 actually amounted to a military alliance directed against the United
States. All outside attempts to prevent the growing Japanese and Russian
railroad monopolies in Manchuria had failed. The Japanese, especially, developed complete control of their spheres.

The Japanese attitude became very clear in the negotiations with an
international banking group which was interested in joint economic development on Chinese territory. A four-power banking group had been formed in
1908 by representatives from England, France, Germany, and the United
States. In 1912 this group was extended into a six-power group, the Six Power
Banking Consortium, to include Japanese and Russian representatives. The
Japanese and Russians, however, demanded the exclusion of Manchuria for

economic exploitation by the group. Although the Japanese did not secure an acceptance of their demands, the position they took again indicated their intention to maintain monopoly control.

To counteract the American slogan of the Open Door to which they had repeatedly subscribed, the Japanese used a slogan of their own, the term "special interests." In one form or another this term had already appeared before the First World War in treaties between Japan and England, France, and Russia. The only country which had not acknowledged such Japanese "special interests" in any part of the Far East was the United States. Japan, therefore, had not been able to secure recognition of her Manchurian monopoly in the case of the Banking Consortium or to secure from the United States acceptance of its slogan of special interests for that area.

The great opportunity for Japan to strengthen her position in Manchuria as well as in China in general came with the First World War. England, France, Germany, and Russia were all concentrating their strength and energies on the war in Europe, and the United States was drawing ever closer to the conflict.

World War I

By this time American efforts to preserve the territorial and administrative integrity of China involved much more than the problem of preserving the Chinese state against Japan and other powers; they were concerned with the future of the Chinese Revolution. The Manchu dynasty and the imperial system had disappeared in the Revolution of 1911 which established the Republic. In the years following the emergence of the Republic, a struggle went on between the military strong man and president of the Republic, Yüan Shih-k'ai, and the revolutionary organization of Sun Yat-sen. America joined the Western powers in assisting Yüan Shih-k'ai. This support, which helped Yüan to win the domestic battle, took various forms from official government action to the participation of unofficial American advisers in Yüan's political program. Dr. F. J. Goodnow, a political scientist, wrote a memorandum for Yüan in 1914 in which he suggested that China was not ready for more than a dictatorship modified by an appointed advisory council, a suggestion which fitted in with the ambitions of Yüan Shih-k'ai. A year later Yüan's plan to re-establish the monarchy with himself as emperor was also supported by a memorandum from Dr. Goodnow in which he declared that "the monarchical system is better suited to China than the republican system." Goodnow made his plan for a constitutional monarchy conditional on the acquiescence of the people and the approval of the foreign powers.

Even more important was the financial support which the powers gave to Yüan Shih-k'ai. Shortly after assuming office as president, Yüan began negotiations with the members of the Six Power Banking Consortium—England, France, Germany, the United States, Japan, and Russia—for a reorganization loan of $125,000,000. This loan was granted to Yüan on condition that the Consortium monopolize all loans to the government, that negotiations with other banking interests should be cancelled, and that the loans should be guaranteed by the income from the salt gabelle and other government services. America had participated in the negotiations but refused to sign the loan agreement. President Wilson, who had just come into office, regarded the terms of the agreement as a threat to Chinese administrative integrity and for this reason forced American withdrawal from the Consortium, which then proceeded, as a Five Power Consortium, to conclude the loan.

Foreign threats to the integrity of China became much more dangerous with the beginning of World War I in August, 1914. Japan now became the main aggressor in China and the major challenger of American policies in the Far East. The Anglo-Japanese alliance called for Japanese participation in the war. Although the British did not press the matter, the Japanese were only too eager to come to the aid of their ally, as their status as a belligerent, while not important for the war in Europe, gave then unrivalled opportunities to expand their influence and territorial possessions in Asia. The Japanese, moving freely through Chinese territory with their forces, captured the German leased territory of Kiaochow. They also took over some of the German-owned islands in the Pacific. During this period the Japanese were secretly promised by England and France that at the final peace treaty they would be allowed to retain the former German interests in Shantung and the German islands north of the equator.

The Japanese extended their influence in China in 1915. When Yüan Shih-k'ai's government raised the question of continued Japanese occupation of Chinese territory in Shantung, the Japanese refused to withdraw and in January, 1915, presented the Chinese government with a series of new demands known as the Twenty-one Demands. These demands, secret and far-reaching in their implications, were backed by the threat of military force, against which China had no means of resistance. The demands were divided into five groups; four dealt with the extension of Japanese rights in Manchuria, Shantung, and Fukien provinces and the increase of Japanese control over the Hanyehp'ing Ironworks; the fifth group contained far-reaching proposals for control over the whole Chinese administration and police forces. The fifth group of demands, if accepted, would have given the Japanese complete control of China.

In the negotiations which followed the presentation of these demands, the main Chinese weapon was to reveal them to the world in the hope that other powers would raise objections. It is believed that considerable British pressure was put on Tokyo to modify the demands, and in Peking Yüan found support from the American representative, Minister Paul S. Reinsch. As a result of this pressure, the Japanese modified some of their demands and agreed to postpone, for the time being, the fifth and most far-reaching group. Considering the weakness of China and the reality of Japanese military power, the treaties and exchanges of notes of May, 1915, which were finally concluded between China and Japan were probably about as good as could be obtained under the circumstances.

By these treaties the Japanese greatly expanded their economic and political control over Manchuria. The leases on the Liaotung Peninsula and the South Manchurian railroad rights were extended to ninety-nine years, and the Japanese gained the right to live, travel, engage in business and lease land over the whole of Manchuria. This was the first time that a foreign power secured such privileges outside of the treaty ports, privileges which were especially dangerous because they were linked with extraterritoriality. The Japanese declared that their subjects would register with the local authorities and "submit to the police laws and ordinances and taxation of China." On the other hand,

Civil and criminal cases in which the defendants are Japanese shall be tried and adjudicated by the Japanese Consul; those in which the defendants are Chinese shall be tried and adjudicated by Chinese Authorities. In either case an officer may be deputed to the court to attend the proceedings. But mixed civil cases between Chinese and Japanese relating to land shall be tried and adjudicated by delegates of both nations conjointly in accordance with Chinese law and local usage.

When, in future, the judicial system in the said region is completely reformed, all civil and criminal cases concerning Japanese subjects shall be tried and adjudicated entirely by Chinese law courts.[23]

In other words, the Japanese paid lip service to Chinese authority but made sure that they could operate in Manchuria almost as freely as in their own country. Armed with these privileges, the Japanese were in a position to establish effective economic control over the whole of Manchuria. In order to make it quite clear what they were after, the Japanese specified in an exchange of notes the localities and the types of mines that they intended to develop.

The Japanese also indicated that they intended to keep railroad development to themselves. They secured a stronger control over the Chinese branch line of the South Manchurian Railway from Changchun to Kirin by compelling the Chinese to agree to the refinancing of the original Japanese loan. The Chinese had also to agree that if they needed foreign capital for further railroad construction, they would get it from the Japanese. In this way the Japanese finally acquired the power to prevent the development of any foreign railroad building. Leaving nothing to chance, they also secured from the Chinese the declaration, "Hereafter, if foreign advisers or instructors on political, financial, military, or police matters are to be employed in South Manchuria, Japanese may be employed first." In addition the Chinese agreed to open Eastern Inner Mongolia to foreign trade and residence by establishing suitable commercial ports. At the same time, Japan secured from Russia an agreement that Eastern Inner Mongolia was within the Japanese sphere of interest.

By the treaty relating to Shantung, the Chinese government agreed in advance to any arrangements that the Japanese might make in the peace treaty with Germany. At this time, however, China agreed to a non-alienation clause in regard to Shantung and gave the Japanese further railroad privileges in that province. On her part, Japan promised to return to China

---

[23] MacMurray, *op. cit.*, Vol. II, pp. 1220–21.

the leased territory in exchange for specified commercial privileges in that area.

In regard to Fukien province, important to Japan because it faced Formosa, the Chinese agreed, as they had done earlier, not to give any other country military bases or positions. The Japanese reinforced their control over the Hanyehp'ing Ironworks, and the Chinese government agreed "not to confiscate the said Company, nor, without the consent of the Japanese capitalists, to convert it into a state enterprise, nor cause it to borrow and use foreign capital other than Japanese."

The notes and treaties of 1915 set Japan apart from all other treaty powers in China, not only in the pattern but also in the extent of her imperialism. For China the Twenty-one Demands became the symbol of foreign aggression and the rallying point for student nationalism; there began at this time the long struggle to loosen the stranglehold that Japan had imposed upon Chinese development. Japan had succeeded by force in securing Chinese agreement to her advance in Manchuria and in China proper; it remained for her to secure international recognition of the new position.

The United States, once again, presented itself as the main opponent to the Japanese advance. While not interfering with the Japanese moves, the United States through Secretary of State Bryan declared that it would not recognize any treaty violating American rights or the policy of the Open Door. This statement of 1915 foreshadowed the American policy of non-recognition which came to be applied on many occasions later. From her allies in the war, Japan secured in 1916 and 1917 secret assurances that her newly acquired gains would be recognized. In the Russo-Japanese treaty of 1916, the last before the Bolshevik revolution, the Russians recognized the new Japanese position in China in exchange for Japanese recognition of the Russian advance into Outer Mongolia.

By secret agreements in 1917 the British, French, and Italians promised that in the final treaty of peace Japan would take over German rights and interests in China and the German Pacific islands north of the equator. The United States was the only country which did not accept at this time the new Japanese position. Both the United States and Japan were willing, however, to come to an understanding. The United States, drawn into the European conflict in April, 1917, was anxious to secure from Japan a promise that she would not take advantage of the war to further her position in China. The Japanese were ready to trade such a promise for American recognition of the gains which they had already made. In November, 1917, the two countries came to an understanding in an exchange of notes between Secretary of State Lansing and the special Japanese ambassador, Viscount Ishii.

The Lansing-Ishii agreement was an expression of the stalemate between the policies and slogans of the United States and Japan. For the first time the phrases "Open Door" and "Special Interests" stood side by side in a formal agreement between the United States and Japan. The agreement stated:

The Governments of the United States and Japan recognize that territorial propinquity creates special relations between countries, and, consequently, the Government of the United States recognizes that Japan has special interests in China, particularly in the part to which her possessions are contiguous.

On the other hand, the agreement stated,

The territorial sovereignty of China, nevertheless, remains unimpaired and the Government of the United States has every confidence in the repeated assurances of the Imperial Japanese Government that while geographical position gives Japan such special interests they have no desire to discriminate against the trade of other nations or to disregard the commercial rights heretofore granted by China in treaties with other powers.

The Governments of the United States and Japan deny that they have any purpose to infringe in any way the independence or territorial integrity of China and they declare, furthermore, that they always adhere to the principle of the so-called "Open Door" or equal opportunity for commerce and industry in China.

Moreover, they mutually declare that they are opposed to the acquisition by any Government of any special rights or privileges that would affect the independence or territorial integrity of China or that would deny to the subjects or citizens of any country the full enjoyment of equal opportunity in the commerce and industry of China.[24]

American willingness to admit publicly its conditional acceptance of Japan's policy was based on a secret promise by Japan not to "take advantage of present conditions to seek special rights or privileges in China which would abridge the rights of citizens or subjects of other friendly states." However comforting this secret assurance might have been to the United States, the public exchange of notes came like a bombshell to the Chinese, especially since the Japanese and Chinese translations of the term "special interests" indicated not an abstract general principle but rather concrete and specific Japanese gains. Although it was later denied by Lansing that he had granted the Japanese any advantage and that he had recognized not the new Japanese position but rather an obvious general truth, the agreement accomplished for both sides exactly what each wanted. The Japanese did not go further than the position established in their treaties with China in 1915, but neither did the United States attempt to dislodge them from their new gains.

During the year 1917 the Western allies, including the United States, became interested, for different reasons, in bringing China into the war. The United States was particularly anxious to have China a formal member of the alliance because this would entitle her to a stronger voice in the making of the peace. The British were especially interested in having the Chinese eliminate German commercial competition by interning German merchants and taking over their shipping in Chinese ports. The Japanese did not particularly want China as an ally, but they strongly advised the Chinese to declare war after they had secured international recognition of their special interests in China, thus taking the diplomatic initiative in this matter away from the United States. In China discussion centered not so much on participation, although

[24] MacMurray, *op. cit.*, Vol. II, pp. 1394–95.

there were some fears expressed that the outcome of the war was still uncertain, as on the conditions of participation. After the death of Yüan Shih-k'ai in 1916, the struggle between the parliamentary group and the militarist government had been renewed, the parliamentary group insisting that foreign promises of tariff revision, suspension of payments on the Boxer Indemnity, and other financial advantages should be implemented before a Chinese declaration of war. Under foreign pressure, the military government declared war without having first secured the concessions, thus abdicating its bargaining position. When some of the concessions were actually granted, such as suspension of payments on the Boxer Indemnity for five years and strict enforcement of the 5 per cent maritime tariff rate, they marked no improvement in China's international standing but rather emphasized her dependence. The foreign powers made only those concessions which they felt necessary to keep the Chinese government solvent enough to serve their interests.

The Japanese especially took advantage of the financial dependence of the Chinese government, extending loans in return for which the Chinese were compelled to grant a number of economic privileges and to accept Japanese political influence. These loans became known as the Nishihara loans from the name of the Japanese financier who arranged them. At the same time, the Japanese negotiated financial support for the political opponent of the Peking government, Sun Yat-sen, who was then in Canton. By financial and other agreements they also strengthened their hold over the Chinese administration in Manchuria, then dominated by the warlord Chang Tso-lin. Japan was the dominant power in China until the end of World War I.

The Peace Conference to conclude World War I met in Paris in January, 1919. At this peace conference, the Chinese delegation reopened the question of the validity of the treaties of 1915 with Japan, stressing particularly their claims to the return of the economic as well as political rights of the Germans in Shantung. These claims, backed by strong public sentiment in China, were sympathetically echoed in the American press and played a role in the negotiations and in American domestic politics which was out of proportion to their actual importance. The Japanese had gained American approval of their case in the Lansing-Ishii agreements; but they also raised another emotional issue by demanding the inclusion of the principle of racial equality in the Covenant of the League, which was to become a part of the peace treaty. This was designed to embarrass the United States and certain British dominions which severely restricted Asiatic immigration. President Wilson vetoed the racial equality clause in order to forestall opposition to ratification of the Covenant in the United States. Having weakened President Wilson's position by forcing him to take a stand against racial equality, the Japanese further threatened a walk-out from the peace conference, and Wilson had to yield on the Shantung issue. This led to the refusal of the Chinese government to sign the Treaty of Versailles and also contributed to the refusal of the United States Senate to ratify it. When the Shantung issue was brought up again at the Washington Conference three years later, the Japanese again won their point and the validity of the treaties of 1915 was maintained. They returned the former German-held leased territory to China as they had agreed, but maintained all the rights and interests which the Chinese had been forced to concede.

A matter that attracted far less attention at the time was the great strengthening of Japan's position in the Pacific through the acquisition of the German-held islands north of the equator. These islands, the Marianas, the Marshalls, and the Carolines, which Japan had been promised in the secret treaties of 1917, lay athwart the American lines of communication from Hawaii to the Philippines. Control of these islands, which enabled Japan to cut American lines of communication, changed the whole balance of naval forces in the Pacific to the advantage of the Japanese. This concession had been made to Japan at the expense and without the knowledge of the most interested power, the United States. President Wilson was in no position to unmake these commitments; but after consultation with his naval advisers, he tried to neutralize the Japanese advance. A formula was found by which the Japanese had to agree not to fortify these islands as naval bases and to submit them to the control of the newly established League of Nations. This formula was the so-called mandate system.

The mandate system was invented as a solution to the problem of reconciling the principle of self-determination with the aim of the allies to divide the territories of the Turkish empire as the spoils of war in the Near East. It was applied also to the former German colonies in Africa. As there were differences in degrees of readiness for self-government and independence, the mandates were divided into categories A and B; a C category of mandates for the islands in the Pacific was added to these two categories. These small islands, with little population, were never expected to become independent countries. Their classification as mandated territories was intended to make it possible to impose on the mandatory power the obligation of not using them for military purposes and of administering the islands under the general supervision of the League of Nations. The United States did not ratify the Treaty of Versailles and the Covenant of the League and therefore took no part in the administration of the mandated islands, thus denying herself the opportunity of using to the fullest advantage that instrument for controlling Japan which she herself had helped to create.

CHAPTER VII

China in Trans-
formation

1. THE DOMESTIC CRISIS

I N the nineteenth century the Manchu dynasty no longer ruled the country with the firm grasp and elegant confidence of the Ch'ien-lung emperor (r. 1736–1795). Long before the violent clash with England in 1839, signs of inner decay were evident in the increasing incidence of rebellion, in the weakening of the administrative system and the army organization, and in the cumulative failures of succeeding emperors to handle the worsening economic situation. It is necessary to understand the internal crisis in Chinese society in order to put the events of the nineteenth and even the twentieth centuries in their proper context.

The Manchu Emperors

It may be useful to review the political history of the various emperors before taking up an analysis of the crisis in which they were caught. The Chia-ch'ing emperor, who followed his famous father Ch'ien-lung to the throne in 1796, faced the first large-scale challenge to imperial authority when a secret society, the White Lotus, organized a rebellion in five provinces of west and northwest China during the years 1798 to 1802. Chia-ch'ing left to his successor Tao-kuang (r. 1821–1850) an empire marked by growing rebellion and economic troubles.

In 1832 the Miao tribes of the three southwestern provinces rose against the government. In the same year serious drought affected large areas of central and northern China. Small-scale uprisings continued in several parts of China during the next two decades, and the last years of the reign of Tao-kuang between 1846 and 1850 were marked by drought and flood as well as other natural calamities in most parts of northern and central China. The whole of Honan, for instance, was affected by a severe drought in 1847; and in 1849 the four provinces of the lower Yangtze area were devastated by major floods. During these years an average of more than 500 districts yearly or about one-third of the whole country suffered from such natural catastrophes. The government attempted relief measures for over one hundred of these districts every year but with little effect because of the decline and the increasing corruption of the administrative organization.

In the first half of the century the emperors themselves tried conscientiously to counteract the growing difficulties in the provinces; in the second half of the century, however, the court itself contributed to the growing decay of imperial power. The Hsien-feng emperor (r. 1851–1861) led a life of pleasure and had little regard for state affairs, even though his reign was greeted with the great uprising of the century, the Taiping Rebellion. He died at Jehol where he had fled when the capital was occupied by the British and French forces in 1860. Hsien-feng was succeeded by a child, the T'ung-chih emperor (r. 1862–1874). From that time on the real authority, however, was in the hands of a woman, the young emperor's mother, formerly a favorite concubine of the emperor Hsien-feng. She was the empress dowager, Tz'u-hsi, also referred to as the Old Buddha, who governed first as co-regent (1861–1873; 1875–1881) and later as regent (1881–1889; 1898–1908). Her own son T'ung-chih, like his father Hsien-feng, lived a life of debauchery, with which she did not interfere, and died young, one year after his majority. After his death, Tz'u-hsi placed on the throne another child, her nephew, who ruled as the Kuang-hsü emperor (r. 1875–1908). During his minority the empress dowager continued to direct affairs, and she remained a power behind the scenes even after Kuang-hsü officially took over in 1889. In 1898 she imprisoned the emperor, and resumed the regency, which she retained until her death in 1908, one day after the death of the Kuang-hsü emperor. Her political actions hastened the eventual downfall of the Manchu dynasty. After the short rule of the child emperor Hsüan-t'ung the last of the imperial dynasties came to an end in 1911.

The personalities of the emperors and the struggle for power in the court, however, were only contributing factors to the decline of the dynastic government. Whatever the intentions and qualities of the emperors, throughout imperial Chinese history forces within the Chinese imperial system itself brought about recurring crises which usually led to a change of dynasty. These forces were as obvious in the nineteenth century as in earlier times; but there was a difference, a difference due to the emergence of new phenomena, especially those caused by the impact of the West.

Decline of the Dynasty

After nearly three centuries of Manchu rule the dynastic crisis cycle had almost run its course. In the first half of the nineteenth century it was quite clear that the authority of the central government had declined and that in many parts of the empire the people were impoverished, exploited, and insecure. The Manchu dynasty no longer effectively controlled the vast bureaucratic machine, and bribery and corruption were getting out of hand. The fixed revenue quota for the whole empire, approximately 40,000,000 taels a year, of which two-thirds came from land taxes, became inadequate to meet growing expenditures as prices rose and the population grew. Even this quota, however, was not met. During the years of peace and prosperity the scholar-gentry used their privileges to enrich themselves, first at the expense of the people and then more and more at the expense of the government. Because of the gentry's evasion of taxes the tax burden was concentrated on those least able to pay. The narrowing of the tax base made it difficult for the officials to meet their tax quotas, so rather than deny themselves they robbed the government. Revenue could not be collected from areas in revolt, and the suppression of rebellion, owing to the accompanying devastation, often postponed the recovery of revenue for many years. It was customary for the government to remit the taxes in areas hit by flood or drought. Many officials, however, misrepresented local conditions in order to secure remission of taxes which they had actually collected so that they might pocket the money themselves.

The corrupt officials who were responsible for the reduction in revenue also misused the funds allotted by the government for the maintenance of public works and for other government services. By pocketing the money intended for dike repair, corrupt officials contributed to a decay of public works, which in turn caused floods and famines further destroying revenue at its source. In the Yellow River Administration there were more officials than ever before, and less work was accomplished. The disastrous change in the course of the Yellow River in 1854, which led to the inundation of vast areas of agricultural land and the death of millions of people, was undoubtedly hastened by neglect of the dikes. The campaigns for the suppression of revolts also added substantially to the expenses of the government. Last but not least the indemnities which had to be paid to foreign powers, beginning with the Treaty of Nanking, were an additional burden. Under these conditions neither the collection of revenue nor the expenditure of government funds was effectively controlled. The whole imperial bureaucracy was rotten with corruption.

The administrative weakness of the dynasty was matched by its military decline. The Manchu banner garrisons, which were the final guarantee of Manchu authority, were a loyal but ineffective military force. The dynasty kept the bannermen apart from the Chinese population and forbade them to engage in any gainful employment. They were supported by salaries from the government and income from banner lands. The banner population of the garrisons increased, but as the number of paid soldiers was fixed, more and more banner families became impoverished and demoralized. As prices had increased, even the fixed salaries had decreased in purchasing power. Some of the emperors gave special allocations of money to the bannermen, but these were quickly used up and did not bring about any lasting improvement in the situation. Under these conditions training was neglected and the military value of the garrisons became almost negligible.

The Chinese troops, called the *Lü-ying*, or Green Standard, were not much better. They had been affected by the general corrosive influences of corruption and graft which permeated the administration. It became common practice for officers, who received the pay for their troops, to pocket the money and maintain an army listed mainly on paper. Less than half of the soldiers listed were actually in service, and at times of inspection coolies were often hired to fill the ranks. Arms were put out to pawn and training was greatly neglected. The weakness of Manchu arms was dramatically revealed by the defeat suffered at the hands of the British in the Opium War. This defeat lowered further the prestige of the military branch of the government which became less and less able to maintain internal security.

Condition of the People

The conditions which marked the middle of the nineteenth century were a weakened civil and military administration, widespread rebellion, decaying public works, and a growing feeling that the mandate of Heaven had been exhausted. The decline of the imperial authority and the corruption of the bureaucracy contributed to the economic deterioration which was typical of the advanced stage of the dynastic crisis cycle. After centuries of relative internal order there was usually an increase in the population which put a strain on the available resources. But never before had the population increase been so spectacular as it was during the Manchu dynasty. According to Chinese figures the population had passed the 150,000,-000 mark by the middle of the eighteenth century. By the end of the century it had reached 300,000,000. Even if these figures are not entirely reliable there is no question of the huge increase in population during this period of the highest prosperity and power of the dynasty. The increase in cultivated land did not, however, keep step with the increase in population. The per capita land unit in the middle of the eighteenth century was about 3.4 *mou* (6 *mou* = 1 acre); in the first decades of the nineteenth century this figure had decreased to about 2.0 *mou* per capita. These figures help to explain the existence of vast numbers of peasants who had little to lose by joining in rebellion. While more people were living on less land, less land had to pay more taxes because of the shifting of the tax burden from the gentry to the peasants. Surtaxes and extra fees, allegedly imposed to cover the cost of collecting the taxes or for local needs, multiplied the tax burden many times. Local officials and gentry were able to exercise a freer hand in exploiting the peasantry because of the increased competition for land. For many the burden became unbearable. Large numbers of peasants, forced off the land, wandered from place to place seeking a livelihood, often as coolies in the carrier trade that grew up with the treaty ports or eking out a marginal existence in the towns. The more aggressive organized themselves into bandit groups and added their exactions and violence to the hardships of peaceful communities.

Economic conditions were also seriously affected by the failure of the government to suppress the trade in opium. The value of opium imported into China after 1820 reached an average of 10,000,000 taels a year, representing an import of from 10,000 to over 30,000 cases of opium. The reports from governors-general of various provinces before the war indicated that they had begun to realize the bad effect of opium smoking on corvée labor. More often mentioned was the effect on the exchange rate between silver and copper resulting from the growing outflow of silver in payment for the increased importation of opium. Between 1820 and 1845 the value of silver in relation to copper almost doubled, and this change resulted in a tremendous increase in the peasants' tax burden, which was calculated in silver but paid in copper. The lot of the peasant was aggravated by the deflationary effects of the rising value of silver.

Additional problems arose in South China as a result of the opening of the treaty ports. The former center of trade at Canton declined in importance in competition with Shanghai, and the effects on the hinterland, the provinces of Kwangtung and Kwangsi, were soon felt. An extensive transportation system had been built up during the centuries of trade through the port of Canton, and large numbers of coolies and boat people depended on this for their livelihood. Many of these people now found themselves without employment and turned to banditry. At the same time the British took energetic measures against piracy on the Kwangtung coast, driving some of the pirates inland. The former coastal pirates took over control of the river system of South China and by working in close cooperation with existing bandit organizations terrorized large and important areas. These special conditions added measurably to the economic and political problems of South China.

The Local Corps

The less effective the government became, the more it was necessary for local leaders to take matters into their own hands. Members of the gentry, secret-society leaders, and others organized their localities for defense against bandits. Local military corps emerged. They got financial support from forced contributions, from control over business, and from organized vice, or special enterprises. In this way the local corps leaders usurped the authority of the officials and dominated local affairs. Local quarrels were no longer arbitrated by the officials but fought out; and the line between defense and attack, between protection against banditry and assault on weaker neighbors became fluid. Small-scale warfare, from which the officials tried to abstain, was common all over the country. The local forces on occasion came into conflict with the officials, especially when the officials interfered with their activities. There were many reports on such clashes from the officials of several provinces during the 1830's. These small uprisings either ended in compromise or were suppressed by military force.

Although such clashes with the officials were occasionally started by gentry-led forces, the gentry-led corps were as a rule more easily tolerated by the officials and generally cooperated with them. The secret societies, on the other hand, were always potential opponents of the Manchu government. Out of these local armed groups grew larger organizations, and out of local riots grew rebellions. During the first decades of the century there were several large uprisings, such as the White Lotus and Miao rebellions. Although the government successfully suppressed these rebellions, the process of administrative decay continued.

The most serious consequence of the military decline of the Manchu dynasty was that it could not prevent the growth of local and regional military forces. All it could hope to do was to control them by using one against the other. This policy was successful so long as no issues arose to unite local forces into a political movement directed against the dynasty. Such issues might come from ethnic minority groups resisting Chinese exploitation and discrimination or from religious movements. The White Lotus rebellion was organized by a secret society which was founded on certain Buddhist beliefs; the Miao rebellion was the uprising of an ethnic minority group. The Moslems of China came into conflict with non-Moslem Chinese when the government was not strong enough to protect them. In the nineteenth century the missionaries, whose work was greatly extended by the forced opening of China, provided new beliefs which could be seized upon by those who were in search of a solution for the problems of the time. The Christian ideas of brotherhood seemed to echo the brotherhood ideas which had long been propagated by the secret societies. Pseudo-Christian beliefs were actually amalgamated with existing Chinese beliefs into an ideological system that was strong enough to bring together many discontented people into one great political movement. This movement is known as the Taiping Rebellion.

The Taiping Rebellion

The Taiping Rebellion (1850–1864), one of the greatest rebellions in Chinese history, was an almost fatal challenge to the Manchu dynasty. The Taiping Rebellion arose out of local conflicts in South China but rapidly grew into a vast movement which affected seventeen of the eighteen provinces of China and resulted in a tremendous loss of life, estimated between 20,000,000 and 40,000,000 people. It was an outgrowth of economic deterioration and the widespread suffering of the people and was made possible by the administrative decay and the military ineffectiveness of the Manchu dynasty.

The Taiping movement began in the province of Kwangsi, an area which was the first to feel the economic consequences of the Opium War. Banditry and piracy were prevalent. Many of the villages had their own military forces which frequently fought with each other. Conflicts between tribal groups and the Chinese population were common. In both Kwangsi and Kwangtung the situation was further complicated by the enmity between the local Chinese and the Hakkas, a minority group of later Chinese immigrants from the north. The word Hakka means "guest people" and indicates that the latecomers were not fully accepted by the earlier Chinese settlers. The Hakkas preserved their own customs, spoke their own dialect, and did not frequently intermarry with the earlier settlers. The conflicts between Hakka villages and the earlier settlers frequently took on the bitterness of civil war.

Hung Hsiu-ch'üan (1814–1864), the leader of the Taiping movement, came from a poor Hakka family which lived in Kwangtung province in a district close to the Kwangsi border. As a boy, Hung prepared for the examinations in order to move up to gentry status and official position. He was a candidate in the government examinations several times, but he always failed. In 1836, when he was in Canton taking his examination, Hung was handed a pamphlet, "Good Words to Admonish the Age," written by a Christian missionary. At that time he did not give it much attention. When in 1837 he failed the examination again, Hung had a nervous breakdown and was for weeks seriously ill and out of his mind. He recovered and tried again in 1843, but to no avail. Then, however, he connected his illness with the contents of the pamphlet, with which by now he had become familiar. He believed that during his illness he had ascended to heaven, where he had met God the Heavenly Father and Jesus Christ and had found himself to be the younger brother of Jesus, entrusted by God with the task of establishing a Heavenly Kingdom on earth. Having fought the demons of the other world with the help of the Heavenly Father and Jesus Christ, he returned to earth to continue his work. He made a few converts among his relatives and friends, and together they took up the preaching of his beliefs.

In 1844 he went to Kwangsi province where he gathered followers in several small localities and organized the Society of "God-Worshippers." Hung and some of his friends concentrated their activities as wandering preachers in a number of districts in Kwangsi province, where they gained followers mostly from the Hakka people and from other distressed groups as well. Hung's half-religious and half-political authority was based on his trances in which he claimed to receive heavenly commands. Other leaders also claimed to have trances and considerable conflict ensued during which some of the leaders were purged as pretenders. A hierarchy of rank and authority was finally established.

In the ideology of this group, religious tenets taken from Christianity were mixed with traditional Chinese ideas. The Chinese family system, for instance, was introduced into heaven where the Heavenly Father and the Heavenly Elder Brother Jesus had their wives and families. The Christian concept of brotherhood was linked with the brotherhood ideal of Chinese secret societies. This strange amalgamation of Christian beliefs, traditional Chinese thought, and the fantasies of its leader created a remarkable mixture of political ideology which eventually burned itself out in its own contradictions and inadequacies. But from the outset this movement produced a religious and political fanaticism that carried it beyond the small-scale battles of secret societies and brought it within reach of the establishment of a new empire. It sought the overthrow of the Manchu dynasty, which was to be replaced by a new dynasty, called T'ai-p'ing T'ien-kuo or the Heavenly Kingdom of Great Peace, with Hung Hsiu-ch'üan as the Heavenly King.

In 1850 the leaders gathered together various groups of their followers numbering about 30,000 at Chin-tien in Kwangsi. They eluded the regular government troops that had been sent against them and moved in a growing avalanche of military might through the provinces of Kwangsi and Hunan into the Yangtze area. The discontented peasants in the areas through which they moved joined them in large numbers, swelling their armies to well over the million mark. They moved swiftly down the Yangtze, capturing river boats wherever they could to transport their troops. Coming down the river with a large fleet, they took Nanking and set up their government there in 1853.

The main principles of the Taiping program were community property, the brotherhood of man, and equality of the sexes. Each member of the Taiping forces had to contribute to the group all that he owned or gained, and he received from the public treasury his food and other needs. In this way the Taiping forces were able to maintain their mobile military organization. For the peasantry in the territories which they overran, the Taipings established—at least theoretically—their own land system. The land, nominally owned by the king, was distributed according to need. Rent was abolished. These theoretical principles, however, did not lead to equal distribution or free use of land. The Taiping armies lived on the land, and the peasants had to give what they had. In the Taiping organization itself, the leaders had by far the greater share of the community property and could accumulate great personal wealth. They lived in great luxury while their followers were kept in military and labor camps, rarely under good conditions, and left to starve when supplies ran short. Women were treated the same as men.

The equality of the sexes which the Taipings proclaimed meant in practice that women were organized into working units and at times even into the armed forces. They were always kept apart from the men, except for those who were assigned to the harems of the leaders. Women were made officers and administrators with ranks and titles equal to those of men but were assigned only to special women's camps. The Taipings attempted to enforce among their followers a complete separation of the sexes by the threat of capital punishment for all who violated the rule of chastity which they imposed. Even married couples were compelled to live apart. According to the Taipings, men must treat women like sisters and, at least for the followers, sex must not enter into the relationship. The only real gain for women was the abolition of the custom of footbinding; otherwise equality of the sexes merely meant their separation.

From the outset the movement was marked by weakness in organization, conflicting ideology, and inadequate leadership. Each of the main leaders was given the title of king and each had a full administrative staff. During the first years central direction was in the hands of the shrewdest and most ruthless of Hung's lieutenants, a former leader of the coal miners, Yang Hsiu-ch'in. When Yang attempted to usurp all authority, he was assassinated together with all his immediate family and followers in 1856 by one of the other kings. This king was also assassinated shortly afterward. From this time on the Taiping campaigns continued under very able generals but without strong central direction. The Taiping armies fought vigorous campaigns for the control of the lower Yangtze provinces, especially Anwhei and Chekiang, where they maintained themselves for some time. Hung Hsiu-ch'üan, who remained in Nanking, became more and more deranged and isolated himself in his palace. It was only because of their brilliant military leadership and the demoralization of the government forces that the Taipings were able to maintain themselves until 1864.

The Taiping Rebellion revealed the weakness of the government. The imperial armies, affected by the general demoralization, were not able to stem the rebellion. After many local setbacks the government armies were disastrously defeated in 1856. In that year two large government camps which had been set up in the Nanking area were attacked and dispersed by the Taiping forces. By this time the government could no longer find the funds for financing the war against the rebels. At the height of the government's power in the 1780's, the treasury held a cash reserve of some 50,000,-000 taels, more than the government's total yearly income. By 1814, after the White Lotus Rebellion and its aftermath, this reserve had diminished to 12,400,000 taels; by 1850, at the outset of the rebellion, only 8,000,000 taels were left. The first two years of the rebellion reduced this reserve to 3,000,000 taels, and thereafter it disappeared almost entirely. During the rebellion the regular government income had dwindled as the tax income from the richest central provinces, devastated by the war, was greatly reduced. The government could not meet even the normal expenses, let alone finance the war.

The failure of the government meant that all Chinese who were opposed to the Taiping movement and its ideology had to organize their own defense. But the local forces, accustomed only to fighting each other, were helpless against the Taiping armies. The Taipings could be opposed only by forces as large as their own.

The New Regional Forces and the Fall of the Taipings

The main opponents of the Taiping leaders and their new ideology were the scholar-gentry, who rose to defend the system against this violent and heretical attack. The gentry sponsored and led many of the corps which had been organized for local defense. Although these groups were in general too small and localized to resist the growing Taiping armies, they did have a certain amount of success especially in Hunan province, where they held off the Taiping armies and diverted them from some well defended areas. It was these local corps which served as nuclei for larger regional armies which could match the Taiping strength.

The first such regional force was organized in Hunan by a member of the scholar-gentry and a former high official, Tseng Kuo-fan (1811–1872). Tseng came from a fairly well-to-do farmer family in a mountainous district of Hunan province. One of his uncles had bought a gentry title, but otherwise his family had not had gentry status until the time of Tseng Kuo-fan himself. He passed the lowest examination at the same time as his father, but while his father never rose above this level, Tseng Kuo-fan went on to pass the higher examinations with great distinction and to gain considerable prestige as a Confucian scholar. For several years he served at the capital in high government positions and then returned to his home district upon the death of his parents for the traditional mourning period. This was at the time the Taiping Rebellion was beginning.

When the central government recognized the seriousness of the rebellion and its own desperate situation, it gave members of the scholar-gentry a free hand to organize military resistance in their home areas. Tseng Kuo-fan was entrusted by the government with the defense of his province. Tseng, however, went beyond the system of local corps and built up a regional army in his home province of Hunan. As a nucleus he used those local corps which had been most successful. These he welded into a unified force which he increased by further recruitment from similar local units. Tseng was careful not to enroll the large numbers of roving and unemployed people set adrift by the economic distress and the rebellion itself. His aim was to establish a comparatively small but reliable force recruited from men with a common village background, personally known to each other and to their unit leaders. These men were to be well paid at double the rate then promised—but rarely paid—to the regular soldiers. In the regular army the officers were not highly educated; and although counted as gentry were looked down upon by the scholars. The military profession was thought to be beneath the dignity of the Confucian gentleman, who expected to be in charge of troops as an administrative official, not as a unit commander.

The new Hunan army of Tseng Kuo-fan was led by a new type of officer selected largely from young scholars of the province, who, like Tseng himself, had been serious in their studies and philosophical writings. They professed a type of Confucianism which combined the doctrines of several schools. Instead of pursuing the elegant and rather technical textual studies predominant at the capital, these men tried to synthesize the various Confucian schools and to stress the principles of character formation as well as the practical application of Confucian ideas in the administrative field. This was their answer to the broad attack launched by the Taipings on every kind of Confucianism. A popular version of Confucianism was used for the indoctrination of the army.

Each unit in Tseng Kuo-fan's army bore the name of its officer, to whom the soldiers were expected to be loyal. It was this personal relationship between officers and men, derived from the smaller local units, on which the esprit de corps of the new regional army rested. With this system of personal relationships based on loyalty to the leader of the unit rather than to an impersonal organization or to the government, began the trend toward personal armies.

Tseng Kuo-fan's army was at first supported by contributions from the gentry and the local communities. With government permission additional income was secured by the sale of academic and official titles in the province. On this basis Tseng could finance the comparatively small army of well-paid men which he carefully trained and indoctrinated before committing it to battle. After some initial setbacks the new army was able to hold its own against the forces of the Taipings. As the area of conflict expanded, other such regional armies were set up, the first one being in Anhwei. Tseng's army became the model for the growing number of regional armies which eventually defeated the Taipings.

The central government, which depended more and more on the gentry-led regional armies as the main force for resisting the Taipings, was not unaware that the existence of such semi-independent forces endangered its own military control. For as long as possible the government attempted to treat these armies as irregular forces, but their leaders pressed for official recognition. The more their military task grew, the less it was possible for the armies of Tseng Kuo-fan and his colleagues to operate on the basis of irregular contributions and income and as distrusted rivals of the regular administrative organization. Tseng and other commanders felt it necessary to control the regular provincial administrations of the areas in which they fought.

It was not until 1860, however, when its main armies had been finally defeated and the situation had become desperate, that the central government yielded and appointed Tseng Kuo-fan the regular administrative head of the provinces which his troops were to defend. The appointment, followed by those of other regional and military leaders, signaled the beginning of a breakdown of the centralized system of control with its checks and balances and its functionally divided administrative organization. Regional military power, financial authority, and control over administrative appointments became combined under the authority of one man and one group. A rival source of power had been created; and even after the defeat of the Taipings, the central government never regained the control it had been forced to yield during the time of crisis. In this way the decline of the Manchu government led to the establishment of regional power, a development which had characterized the downfall of dynasties in the past.

Once in authority, the provincial organizations of Tseng Kuo-fan and other regional leaders no longer reported to the central government any details about the military forces they maintained. Appointments to administrative or military positions were controlled by the regional leaders although they still had to be confirmed by the central government. The regular provincial tax income was known to the central government, but most of it was retained by the regional administrations, which gave only the most superficial accounting of its use. These regular taxes were, however, not sufficient to finance the new armies, and the provincial leaders introduced a new type of tax, the administration and the use of which they kept entirely in their own hands. This new tax, which was first levied in 1853, was known as *likin* and was a tax on inland trade and business. Most of the *likin* revenue came from levies on trade which were collected at innumerable inland custom barriers. There was also a tax on merchandise in the stores. The *likin* became a major source of revenue for all provincial administrations, and the central government never gained any real knowledge of the amounts collected. It has been estimated that at the end of the Taiping Rebellion the yearly provincial revenue from this tax amounted to over 10,000,000 taels.

The *likin* was an important indication of the growth of trade and the increased movement of goods since the opening of the country to foreign commerce. From the beginning it was in the hands of the provincial leaders who used it to establish fiscal autonomy. It also provided the means by which they could offer the peasantry temporary tax relief, necessary because of the devastation in the areas of fighting which could no longer provide even the regular tax income. Lower land taxes were also advisable in order to counteract the promises of the Taipings' land program. When the land tax was fully restored, however, the *likin* remained a major source of revenue for the new provincial administrations and was carried over into republican times.

Tseng Kuo-fan was not the only regional leader who successfully organized resistance against the Taipings and other rebellious groups. Hu Lin-i (1812–1861) had organized local corps in the central Yangtze area for defense against the Taipings before Tseng, with whom he later cooperated, had organized his army. He was instrumental in establishing the policy of easing the tax burden on the peasants and in raising funds through the *likin*. More important still was Tseng Kuo-fan's disciple and political ally, Li Hung-chang (1823–1901) who passed the highest examination and studied under Tseng at the capital. Li was from Anhwei province where his father had already established a local corps in the family's home district. After working for some time on Tseng Kuo-fan's staff, Li set up his own regional army in Anhwei modeled after Tseng's army and with Tseng's support. As in the Hunan army, the units of the Anhwei army depended on personal loyalty to the officers, and these officers in turn were loyal to Li Hung-chang who organized and financed the whole force. The two armies continued to cooperate closely in their campaigns against the Taiping rebels.

In 1862 Li Hung-chang moved his army to the lower Yangtze region and established his main financial base at Shanghai, which was just developing as a center of commerce and business. The revenue from the maritime customs and from the newly established *likin* stations plus the official and unofficial income derived from the supervision of trade gave Li a financial foundation which was considerably stronger than that of Tseng Kuo-fan who was in authority in the central Yangtze provinces. Besides paying for his own armies, Li contributed to the financing of the Hunan army of Tseng Kuo-fan. The alliance of two such growing regional organizations further weakened the central government's authority.

Another prominent leader of a military organization was Tso Tsung-t'ang (1812–1885), a Hunanese who also started his career on the staff of Tseng Kuo-fan. Entrusted with his own section of the Hunan army, Tso established his authority in Chekiang province and for a time was in charge of this province and of neighboring Fukien.

These new regional leaders were far more successful in building up administrative and military control over the areas they occupied than were the Taipings. Tseng Kuo-fan in particular succeeded in building up a naval force in the inland waterways which was superior to the fleet of river boats collected by the Taipings. The armies of the Taipings, lacking political direction and organization, could not persist against such regional strength. Area by area and city by city, they were driven back and destroyed until a prolonged siege of the Taiping capital at Nanking ended in 1864 with the fall of the city and the death of the Taiping leader Hung Hsiu-ch'üan. Shortly thereafter the last remnants of the Taiping forces in the rural areas to the south were destroyed, and the Taiping Rebellion was over.

The downfall of the Taipings had been accelerated by their inability to establish relations with the Western powers, some of whom had at first shown an interest in supporting the movement. After the new treaties of 1858 and 1860 between the Western powers and the Manchu government, the West supported the government against the rebels. On a minor scale a Western volunteer force, the "Ever Victorious Army," participated under the command of Li Hung-chang in the regaining of towns in the lower Yangtze area around Shanghai. But foreign volunteers also fought with the Taiping forces.

The Nien and Moslem Rebellions

The Taiping Rebellion was the major outbreak of the time, but it coincided with a number of other rebellions which continued in other parts of the country after the Taipings had been defeated. The Nien Rebellion (1853–1868) took place in the provinces of Anhwei and Shantung. It was started by a number of secret-society leaders who had fortified their villages with earthwalls as a defense against bandits. At first this defense system was approved by government officials, but later the Nien extended their system of interlocking fortifications throughout a large area from which all government control was eliminated and from which the Nien leaders sallied forth to raid neighboring areas. The mobility of the Nien cavalry made it possible for them to evade government forces on their far-flung raids and return to the safety of their home area. The Manchu rulers called in Mongol cavalry forces under their leader Sengolinchin. After initial successes this force was ambushed by the Nien and its leader killed. The government finally had no choice but to call in Tseng Kuo-fan, the victor over the Taipings. Tseng's new strategy of blockading the Nien area was later carried through by Li Hung-chang when he succeeded Tseng as commander of this campaign. The major Nien force was cut off from its home area, bottled up in a narrowing circle, and eventually destroyed.

More removed in their geographic location but no less dangerous were the Moslem rebellions in the southwestern province of Yunnan (1855–1873) and in the northwestern provinces of Kansu and Shensi and in Chinese Turkestan (1862–1877). These rebellions of the best organized and most active religious minority group in China challenged the authority of the government and threatened to eliminate Chinese territorial control over these areas. In Yunnan and in Chinese Turkestan the Moslem leaders made contact with, and were given support by, the British. The Turkestan rebellion served also as a pretext for the Russians to occupy Chinese territory in the Ili Valley. The suppression of these rebellions and the defense of Chinese national interests were accomplished by new regional leaders. In Yunnan, Ts'en Yü-ying (1829–1889) created his own regional army and rose to the position of governor-general of the area. In the northwest the government sent Tso Tsung-t'ang with his regional army to Kansu and Shensi and appointed him governor-general of these provinces. After crushing the rebellion there, Tso marched into Chinese Turkestan in a memorable campaign, provisioning his troops by having them do their own planting and harvesting on the various stages of the march. After thoroughly defeating the Moslem leaders, Tso reasserted Chinese authority over this outlying area.

Regionalism and the Treaty Ports

The Ch'ing dynasty was saved, but the new regional leaders, who had wrenched the key areas of China from the rebels, remained in power. They retained their military forces, their financial resources, and the administrative organizations which they had created in the areas which they had occupied. The central government had no choice but to appoint these men to the positions of governor or governor-general of these areas and thus to sanction the growth of regional power. When the government removed individual leaders, the organizations remained. The government could not destroy the organizational basis of regional power or the personal loyalty of the officers and officials to their leaders. Even when the regional leaders were moved to another province, they brought their staff and some of their troops with them.

Li Hung-chang, for example, was moved from the lower Yangtze region to become governor-general of Chihli, the capital province. He took some of his troops with him and appointed some of his friends to key administrative positions in the north; but he also maintained troops in the south and along the route to his northern base. Li also established new sources of financial support in Tientsin without giving up his old ones in the Yangtze area. The strength of Li's position was indicated by the fact that from then on the government entrusted to this most powerful of the new leaders not only the defense of the north but also the handling of its foreign relations. Between 1870 and his death in 1901, Li became the foremost Chinese diplomat handling treaty negotiations with the foreign powers.

The Taiping Rebellion and the other rebellions of the time had a profound influence on China. The tremendous loss in life accounted for the fact that the population of China in the 1870's was the same as it had been at the outset of the century. Vast areas had been devastated. There was a decrease in cultivated land and in production. Of even greater importance was the shift in power from the central government to the regional administrations. The whole elaborate system of centralized control based on carefully contrived divided authority and overlapping responsibilities almost ceased to function. There developed a new type of provincial governor who had military and financial power of his own and who had to be consulted by the throne on major policy matters. This loss of authority by the central government was also a loss of leadership for the Manchus. The new regional leaders were Chinese and represented a Chinese nationalism. Because some of these men began to deal directly with foreign powers, foreign policy became linked with the inner political struggle.

The price paid by the central government for the suppression of the rebellion was its own administrative disintegration. Attempts were made by the throne to stem this process. In spite of their corruption and uselessness the old regular armies were merged with the new regional forces. The result was a blunting of the new military development without re-establishment of central control. At the time when China faced the fast growing threat of foreign control and colonization it lost authority over its regional administrations and military forces.

The rise of powerful regional administrations is of especial importance because it coincided with the growth of trade and industry both in the treaty ports and in many inland areas. The regional administrations had already secured, through the *likin* tax, an important financial stake in the production and movement of goods. For the regional administrations the new commercial activity was both a source of revenue and a field for patronage; and commercial activities and investment opened up new sources of income for careerist officials.

The first Chinese industries outside the treaty ports were established by the governors-general to support their military and political power. Arsenals, tool factories, shipyards, ironworks, mines, printing presses, and even consumer industries came under this type of official control in the early stage of Chinese industrialization. Li Hung-chang established the Shanghai Arsenal in 1864, and in 1866 Tso Tsung-t'ang built the Foochow shipyards. In 1873 Tso Tsung-t'ang set up a weaving mill in Kansu. In 1878 Li Hung-chang opened the Kailan mines which were to become the most important mining enterprise in China proper. In order to transport coal from the Kailan mines, Li built the first Chinese-owned railroad, the real beginning of Chinese railroad development. In 1872, while still in Shanghai, Li Hung-chang had established the China Merchants' Steam Navigation Company. This shipping line transported Li's troops and also the tax grain of the central Yangtze area to the north in addition to carrying private merchandise. This large and important Chinese steamship company was thus from its inception in the hands of the new type of regional official.

The growth of regional power machines was simultaneous with the development of the treaty ports under the influence of the West. The treaty ports were the vehicles through which the new Western commercial life entered China. The Taiping Rebellion itself contributed to the rapid growth of the new treaty ports as they became places of refuge for large numbers of people, especially the more well-to-do, escaping the dangers of the civil war areas. Shanghai, the most important treaty port, increased in population during the rebellion from about 120,000 people to over half a million.

The growth of the treaty ports deeply affected the Chinese economy. The increase of the import of Western commodities in the second half of the nineteenth century can be measured by the revenue of the Chinese Maritime Customs. While this revenue, based on a 5 per cent ad valorem rate, had averaged 4,000,000 taels yearly at the beginning of the rebellion, it grew to over 10,000,000 taels in the 1870's and over 20,000,000 taels in the 1880's, moving up to 26,500,000 taels by 1900. This increase in trade by six and one-half times had a serious impact upon the Chinese economy. The new machine-made Western products that came into China through the treaty ports increasingly replaced the handiwork of the Chinese artisans. The old, largely self-sufficient exchange system between the small town and its countryside was seriously disrupted. The towns near the treaty ports and along the main arteries of inland communications were particularly affected by the unemployment and economic dislocation created by the import of manufactured goods. On the other hand, agricultural products were sold on the treaty-port markets, and slowly cash crops began to replace the local subsistence system of Chinese agriculture.

The importance of the treaty ports, however, was not limited to the effect they had on trade and production. The Chinese in the treaty ports who were attracted by the opportunities of these new economic centers were the beginning of a new merchant class. At first Chinese merchants and firms acted as go-betweens for foreign business and rural markets. These middlemen working for foreign firms were called "compradores." It was not long before Chinese firms were established, and a new class of Chinese businessmen emerged. The businessmen in the treaty ports were free of the control of the Chinese government, central or regional, which had no jurisdiction in the treaty ports themselves. They did not need to fear government interference and did not have to fight for their freedom. The fact that they enjoyed the protection of the treaty ports improved their bargaining position with the regional power machines with which they did profitable business.

It was very important for the future development of China that the business class did not grow up in conflict with the regional bureaucrats. In fact they worked closely together. Men such as Li Hung-chang and other officials who owned or controlled most of the growing trade and industry outside of the treaty ports worked hand in hand with the Chinese businessmen of the treaty ports. Participation in modern commerce and industry and cooperation with the treaty-port businessmen, both foreign and Chinese, was a new departure for the scholar-officials, who acquired, in the process, a different outlook. The Confucian ideology of the scholar-gentry did not fit into this new type of commercial life. The resurgence of the gentry under Tseng Kuo-fan had been in defense of the Confucian tradition against the Taiping rebels, but Li Hung-chang and his associates were operating in a social and economic milieu which was inhospitable to the Confucian tradition. They were divorced from the social responsibilities which had balanced their bureaucratic privileges and only bureaucratic authority remained. For such men, as for the businessmen in the treaty ports, Confucianism lost its compelling force, and Western education and thought began to replace the Chinese tradition.

Western Thought and the Missionaries

Missionary work had begun to make inroads among the Chinese in the treaty ports. When the treaties of 1860 gave the missionaries permission to carry on their work anywhere in China, they penetrated inland. They did not limit their activities to evangelic work; they compiled dictionaries, translated foreign and Chinese books, and established missionary schools for Chinese students. The missionaries took advantage of the Chinese interest in Western learning which had been awakened by the obvious weakness of their own government and the strength of Western civilization. In the early 1860's the government established a school for interpreters at Peking using some foreign teachers. When the school was reorganized in 1865 into the T'ung-wen College, scientific courses were added to its language work. In 1869 Mr. W. A. P. Martin, an American missionary, became its president; he played an important part in transmitting Western ideas to Chinese intellectuals. In 1872 a Chinese educational mission promoted by Tseng Kuo-fan and Li Hung-chang was sent to the United States for the training of a group of thirty Chinese students in Western knowledge. These students, who enrolled in a number of universities, lived in the homes of missionary families. In these early years the educational influence of the West came largely through the missionaries and was limited mainly to those Chinese who were in contact with foreigners in the treaty ports and at Peking. For most of the scholar-gentry in the interior, however, traditional education remained superior to what the West had to offer, until the end of the century when military defeat and the threat to China's political existence raised the whole issue of the relationship of the Chinese cultural tradition to the new learning of the West.

2. THE ATTEMPTS AT REFORM

China Defenseless

The Manchu dynasty survived but never recovered from the rebellions of the mid-nineteenth century and the wars with the West. The attempts of the dynasty to restore its military strength and political authority never succeeded because of the resilience of the political and military machines which the regional leaders had built up for the suppression of the rebellions. The dynasty still had the authority to move its high provincial officials from one position to another, but they retained the loyalty of their staffs and their military officers and control over their economic resources. There was a political stalemate between the dynasty and the leading Chinese provincial officials. The efforts of the dynasty to curb the military power of men such as Li Hung-chang contributed to the decline of the victorious regional forces without adding to the military strength of the dynasty.

Powerful as they were in building up their organizations, the regional leaders lacked the authority as well as the capacity to plan or to lead in the reconstruction of China. By extending bureaucratic controls over the nascent capitalism beginning in the ports and by establishing their own enterprises they stifled any possibilities there might have been for the expansion of free enterprise from the treaty ports to the rest of China. After the rebellions were over, the armies of Li Hung-chang, now merged with the old-style imperial forces, were corrupted by their association with Li's business empire. Political and military machines of the type constructed by Li Hung-chang were no answer to the problem of creating a modern China.

A different element in the situation was the participation of Chinese in the economic development of the treaty ports. It was in these commercial centers that there emerged a new Chinese business class, influenced by the West and outside the control of the Chinese government. They found it profitable to cooperate on economic matters with the officials of the regional organizations, but they played no part in the political power struggle and provided no new leadership. There was no group in China able to organize a constructive defense against the continuing pressure from the West.

The opening of China was a continuing process. Foreign pressure, which never relaxed even during the Taiping Rebellion, led to more and more concessions. Of special significance for the modern economic development of China was the fixed tariff on imports established by treaty. The tariff, which was fixed at a maximum of 5 per cent ad valorem on all imported goods, could not be raised by the Chinese government unilaterally, and it remained at this low rate until well into the republican period. The low import tariff prevented the Chinese government from getting a larger revenue from the greatly increasing import trade at a time when every possible source of revenue was needed to cover the growing government expenditures. The Western tariff control had still other disadvantages. The government could not use the tariff to protect China's new industrial development against foreign competition. The tariff applied to all kinds of imported goods and did not discriminate between essential commodities, such as machinery, and less necessary consumer goods, such as tobacco and cigarettes, which rapidly increased in sale in China. After the Taiping Rebellion the desperate needs of the central government and the regional administrations caused them to depend on loans from Western banks and governments. These loans and the many indemnities imposed upon China were guaranteed by the customs revenue. The foreign-administered customs service, therefore, came to have the peculiar character of serving Western as much as Chinese interests. The salt administration, which also employed Westerners, later came to be used as another acceptable guarantee for foreign loans.

A new phase of foreign aggression began in the 1870's and 1880's. The colonial powers, England in Burma, France in Indo-China, and Russia in Turkestan, struck at the control of the Chinese government over its dependent areas. In each case some resistance was attempted, but it was largely limited to regional commanders. The climax of this nibbling-away process at the outer territories of the Chinese empire came with the Sino-Japanese War (1894–1895) fought over the control of Korea.

When the modernized Japanese forces attacked the Chinese in Korea, Li Hung-chang's troops and navy, regarded then as the strongest force in China, were stationed largely in the cities of North China, Manchuria, and Korea itself. They had to carry the brunt of the fighting, and the war was regarded by other Chinese regional and central officials as Li Hung-chang's war. The corruption and demoralization of Li Hung-chang's forces, especially of their supply system, was revealed by the overwhelming victories of the Japanese. Li Hung-chang's units were defeated in Korea, driven off the Yalu River, and chased out of Manchuria. In a battle off the Shantung coast, the Chinese navy, although superior to the Japanese in ships and gunpower and commanded by well-trained officers, was defeated because of lack of ammunition, resulting from the "squeeze" in the supply system. The turret guns of the Chinese flagship had only two shots to fire before they had to submit to destruction.

The sweeping victories of the Japanese left North China at their mercy and forced the government to the humiliating peace treaty of Shimonoseki (1895). Li Hung-chang lost the position of governor-general of Chihli and much of his influence. His organization survived and later was taken over by one of Li Hung-chang's former lieutenants, Yüan Shih-k'ai. Although Li Hung-chang's organization had borne the brunt of the conflict, the defeat reflected the conditions of China as a whole. The Western powers did not expect China to survive much longer as an independent state, believing that the time had come for her to be divided into colonial territories.

The Chinese central government tried to find support from the outside. The court held Li Hung-chang responsible for the defeat and expected him to find some way of salvation. Encouraged by the Three Power Intervention, Li looked to Russia for support and in 1896 journeyed to St. Petersburg. There he concluded a secret military alliance between Russia and China. In return China gave Russia her first railroad rights in northern Manchuria. In the years from 1897 to 1899, however, the threat to Chinese independence became more imminent. Germany led the way with the establishment of the leased territory of Kiaochow in 1898 and the securing of railway and mining rights and a "sphere of influence" on the Shantung peninsula. Russia, instead of supporting Chinese resistance, as the Chinese government had hoped, advanced her own interests in Manchuria, where she gained the leased territory of Dairen and Port Arthur and extended her railway rights southward toward these ports. The other powers followed suit with the establishment of their respective "leased territories" and "spheres of interest." These "leased territories" and "spheres" were understood at the time as the first steps towards annexation, and while the Chinese government had been willing only to "lease" for periods of up to ninety-nine years, this term was regarded by the diplomats as veiled language for "cession" of the territory in question.

K'ang Yu-wei

The desperate situation finally stirred the Chinese government to recognize the need for complete reform if independence were to be preserved. The hope of finding security by playing off one Western power against another had ended in complete disappointment. When the German demands came, the court consulted at first the heads of the regional organizations, the governors-general who had the actual power in their respective territories. Their answers showed that they too had neither the modern military power nor the diplomatic plans with which to avoid disaster. After agreeing to the German demands, the emperor turned to his advisers for a program of real reform and for a man to undertake it. This man was K'ang Yu-wei, who was regarded as an outstanding figure by the younger group of scholars who were deeply perturbed about political events and were pressing for changes.

K'ang Yu-wei (1856–1927) was the last great creative thinker in the Confucian tradition. He came from a family of scholars and received a traditional education in his home district near Canton. While still in his twenties, he developed his own interpretation of Confucian philosophy. During a four-year period of retirement in the mountains of his home district, he wrote a philosophical work, *The Commonweal*. In this work he interpreted human history as a process of development from a first period of chaos through one of partial peace and order to a future period of complete peace on earth. Basing his philosophy on one section of the *Li Chi*, the classical text of ceremonial usages, K'ang stressed public-spiritedness as the main principle with which to establish among mankind the great harmony or Commonweal. He disregarded that part of Confucianism which emphasized authority and discipline and substituted the idea that general human love should replace all selfish limitations of human relations, even those of the family relationship. He envisaged a state of great equality and unity between all men, based on unselfishness and human love. All inequalities of high and low and rich and poor, of the races and the sexes, were to disappear; there would be no princes and no state, and all men would share property in common. Selfishness had been the cause of suffering, fighting, and wars among people; and salvation from this suffering was to be achieved through a religion which would make people give up their selfishness in order to serve others. K'ang Yu-wei was interested in Buddhism, which he had studied, and in Christianity, of which he had heard; but he believed that in China, where the people should never give up reverence for ancestral tombs and temples, Confucianism alone could be the basis for such a religion. According to his new interpretation Confucianism should be a religion and not merely an ethical system. Earlier Confucian writers had stressed certain equalitarian tendencies, but Confucianism had never been developed into such an extreme system as that of K'ang Yu-wei, who completely eliminated the authoritarian principles of the orthodox Confucian school and wanted to make of Confucianism a religion.

The Commonweal stage in human development was a dream of the distant future. Fearing that publication would discredit his immediate program K'ang Yu-wei kept his work on his book secret, and not until later were parts of it published. During these early years he was well known for his brilliant philological writings in which he attempted to evaluate the authenticity of the Confucian classics. Politically, he did not go further than to urge changes and reforms that would overcome the decay and deadlock in China and would lead her back to a place worthy of her cultural tradition.

K'ang Yu-wei first went to Peking in 1888. Passing through Hong Kong and Shanghai, he was greatly impressed by the Western life in those cities, and read whatever was available of Western writings in Chinese translations. In Peking he handed his first memorial to the emperor, in which he pointed out the dangers which China faced and the need for changes. K'ang warned of Japan's secret ambitions regarding Korea and the neighboring Chinese territory; of Russia's railroad program and her threat to Manchuria; of England's interest in Burma and her moves towards Yunnan and Tibet; and of France's plans to extend her influence from Tongking to Yunnan and the Kwang provinces through the building of railroads. As China was weak and little able to face these threats, thorough reform of the whole government was urgent. K'ang criticized the division of authority between officials, their lack of education, and the buying of office. The whole system was only a corruption of the true Confucian state. The real institutions of the early imperial Chinese state could well be used for government under modern conditions. In sharp words K'ang demanded a new order in which the people's feelings would be considered and China strengthened to resist the foreign threat.

K'ang's memorial never reached the emperor and his advisers because the transmitting officials were afraid of its tone and language; and K'ang returned to Canton. After the Sino-Japanese War in 1895, when he was back in Peking, he became the spokesman of a large number of young members of the scholar-gentry who were aroused by the dangers of military defeat. Led by K'ang Yu-wei, over 1,200 of these young scholars, who were in Peking for the metropolitan examinations, signed a petition in which they demanded a repudiation of the treaty, a move of the capital to the interior of the country, the formation of a new army, and the total reform of the government. This pressure had no effect, but in 1897, after the German demand for Kiaochow, K'ang submitted another critical memorial to the throne in which he ascribed the causes of the weakness and decay of China to the ignorance and incapacity of its officials. He set forth a whole program of reform which included the promotion of agriculture and industry and a total revision of the educational system. The new education was to be based on a revised Confucianism as well as on Western knowledge. Confucianism was to be strengthened in China and among the overseas Chinese. On the basis of these inner reforms a strong army and armament industry were to be built up. In a number of other memorials K'ang pointed out that with the changed conditions of the world, in which China was no longer surrounded only by small, weak tribes, the concept of the "rule of the world" had to be abandoned and the whole government system reformed.

The pressure for reform led to a reaction at the court. Officials who felt their position threatened grouped together in opposition. At the court itself there was a struggle for authority between the young emperor Kuang-hsü, who took over the government in 1889, and his aunt, the empress dowager, Tz'u-hsi, who until then had been the all-powerful regent and who was still directing matters from behind the scenes. The officials opposed to reform gathered under her protection, and on her request several high officials favorable to the reformers were dismissed. K'ang Yu-wei himself left again for Canton. But when in 1898 the new foreign pressure brought a desperate crisis, K'ang Yu-wei, who had come back to Peking, was received by Kuang-hsü in person on June 16 and given full powers for far-reaching reforms. There followed what later became known as the Hundred Days of Reform. This period ended with the victory of reaction.

K'ang Yu-wei attempted to carry through his program of reform through a large number of imperial edicts which followed one another in rapid succession. His aim was to establish a new type of central administration to replace the old corrupt machine with its many sinecures, and at the same time to regain control of the provincial administrations. In this double attack he intended to use a broad educational, political, and economic approach of a liberal character. He wanted a constitutional monarchy supported by a new type of official. The traditional education and the examination system, which had become entirely formalistic, were no longer producing men who possessed the imagination and initiative necessary to carry out the transformation of the Chinese government. K'ang Yu-wei proposed, therefore, the abolition of the traditional examinations and a complete renovation of the educational system in which the liberal arts and sciences of the West would be combined with the Chinese classics. Agricultural and technical schools were to be founded and a general school organization was to be established. Aside from training officials, the new educational system was expected to prepare the ground for the establishment of a representative system of government. As a part of the education of the public in political affairs, newspapers were to be encouraged and journalists were to be trained. A broader participation in government was to come about through the establishment of elected assemblies in the districts and provinces, on which basis K'ang planned to build a national parliament.

K'ang's general economic plans were designed to develop internal and external trade. Officials were to be instructed to encourage commerce and industry, to help towards the establishment of modern banks, and to give aid to business wherever possible. Bureaus of commerce in Shanghai and Hankow were to serve commercial interests rather than control them. Other bureaus were set up to encourage mining and to promote agricultural improvements. In order to facilitate commercial transportation K'ang planned the construction of railways, especially the completion of the Peking-Hankow Railroad. The government was to introduce a modern national budget which was to be made public. To clear the way for his program, K'ang Yu-wei abolished existing sinecures and tried to weed out useless, old-style officials.

The weakness of this far-reaching reform program was the speed with which K'ang Yu-wei and his colleagues tried to carry it through. His educational and economic measures needed time to mature; and his immediate attack against the old officialdom on the one side and the autonomous regional organizations on the other aroused strong opposition. During this period K'ang himself and a number of youthful friends held a few key positions in the central government, but the rest of the officials in the central government as well as in the provinces remained unchanged. Many were either afraid of the results of reform or incapable of carrying out the ideas of the reformers, and what started with feverish activity at the court was bound to bog down in the administrative organization. Conservative officials and holders of sinecures feared the loss of their position and influence. The growing opposition rallied around the empress dowager who became the leading opponent of the emperor's reform.

K'ang Yu-wei felt that he could overcome this opposition only if he had full control over the armed forces and the national revenue. But these were no longer controlled by the Manchu government. The regional officials, who controlled the largest part of the revenue, provided the bribes that were enjoyed by all the higher officials of the court. When K'ang Yu-wei went to the War Ministry for information on the armed forces, he found that the ministry did not even know the size and the strength of the many armies in existence, let alone exert any central control. But K'ang knew that he needed military force to break the opposition gathering under the empress dowager. On his advice the emperor called in Yüan Shih-k'ai, who commanded the northern military forces.

Yüan Shih-k'ai (1859–1916) came from a Honan gentry family which had been closely connected with Li Hung-chang's military organization. Yüan was himself a protégé of Li Hung-chang, under whom he served as Chinese commissioner in Korea, a post which brought him into prominence. After the war with Japan, Yüan Shih-k'ai was chosen by the court to reorganize and modernize Li Hung-chang's armies. In this way he became the heir to the military power of Li Hung-chang and the strongest of the military leaders of the time. His relations with the Manchu court were particularly close because of his friendship with Jung Lu, one of the leading Manchu princes and a confidant of the empress dowager.

In order to gain the support of Yüan Shih-k'ai and the troops under his control, K'ang Yu-wei had Yüan appointed to a high position at the court.

When the opposition to the reforms became more determined and K'ang Yu-wei learned that the empress dowager planned to resume her power, he attempted to forestall her by making the first move. On K'ang's advice the emperor called in Yüan Shih-k'ai and ordered him to arrest Jung Lu, the main military supporter of the empress dowager. But Yüan Shih-k'ai, though seeming to accept these orders, actually went to Jung Lu and gave the scheme away. The empress dowager, who in turn was informed by Jung Lu, now acted herself. On September 21 she had the emperor taken prisoner, deprived him of the seals of office, and resumed power herself under a new regency. K'ang Yu-wei, warned by the emperor, escaped to Tientsin where he boarded a British ship. Some of his friends and colleagues escaped too, but others remained and were executed. The Kuang-hsü emperor himself was a prisoner of the empress dowager from that time on until his death.

K'ang Yu-wei went to Hong Kong and from there to Singapore, and in the following years traveled widely in the Far East, the United States, and Europe. Though out of power, K'ang continued his political fight under the monarchy and later under the republic. He continued to seek the establishment of a constitutional monarchy and the restoration of the authority of the Kuang-hsü emperor and his successor. K'ang also continued to believe in the necessity of making Confucianism a national religion. He believed that a nation that retained its faith and its culture could preserve its national identity, and therefore regain its political independence if it had been lost. Somewhat prophetically he gave as his examples India and the Jewish people. But if religion was gone, the nation was lost. Of his Chinese opponents, who wanted to abandon the Confucian tradition, he asked in later years:

Those who believe that one can throw away the teaching of Confucius, do they know that the whole Chinese culture is closely intertwined and linked with it, and if one abandons Confucianism, the whole Chinese culture follows it and perishes, and that all groups and clans will follow and be destroyed?

Though K'ang Yu-wei continued his fight as a political exile, he never regained political power after the failure of his reform movement. The empress dowager's seizure of power and the flight of K'ang Yu-wei ended the only genuine attempt to reform China on the basis of the Confucian tradition.

The Empress Dowager and the Boxer Rebellion

From 1898 until her death in November, 1908, the empress dowager ruled as regent for the Kuang-hsü emperor, whom she kept prisoner. All the reform edicts were repudiated. Many of the offices abolished by K'ang were restored. The traditional examination system was re-established and plans for the introduction of new schools were given up. The new agricultural, industrial, and commercial bureaus were abolished. Newspapers were banned and the formation of new political organizations forbidden. The crushing of the reform movement and the re-establishment of the old interests did not, however, solve the problems caused by the grave threat of foreign control and the continuing disintegration and growing discontent within the empire. The inclination of the group of Manchu and Chinese officials who now supported the empress dowager was toward old-style resistance to the West and the prevention of any major change except in the most superficial, technical, military sense—the buying of foreign guns and the training of Chinese troops in their use.

Old-style resistance to the West found support in a peasant movement in North China which had originally both an anti-government and an anti-foreign character—the so-called Boxer Movement. The Boxers, or the "Society of Righteous Harmony," derived their foreign name from their stylized exercises which seemed to resemble boxing. They were a secret-society organization, not unlike the many other secret societies which flourished in China. They had established many branches, particularly in the province of Shantung where they originated. During the critical, uncertain conditions at the end of the century, they had organized a number of local corps. In provinces like Shantung where foreign missionary activities had spread, the Boxer organization took on an anti-foreign character. Missionary work had in many cases disrupted the village communities. Christian converts stopped contributing to those community activities which were classified by the missionaries as "pagan." Converts also sought foreign protection in lawsuits, which became more frequent as a result of the ideological cleavages in the villages. Village feeling turned against the converts and their missionary protectors. From this local bitterness, it was but a step to the feeling that the foreigners were responsible for the economic ills suffered by the peasant population. Certain officials, unable to suppress the secret-society organizations among the discontented peasants, saw in the anti-foreignism of the Boxers an opportunity to divert the movement away from the attack on their own authority. As many officials were themselves hostile to the foreigners and their ideas, they were doubly inclined to encourage the anti-foreign tendency of the Boxers.

In 1899 the Boxers in Shantung began to attack isolated missionaries, railroad engineers, and other foreigners, as well as the Chinese converts of the foreign missionaries. The attacks spread into other parts of North China and into Manchuria. Local Boxer groups banded together into larger forces and converged on Peking where a large group of foreigners had fled from many regions of North China. At the capital the Boxers received support and encouragement from the most reactionary officials, who were ignorant of the real strength of the foreign powers and hoped that this popular movement might free China of the foreign threat. The empress dowager herself was more than annoyed by the policy of the foreign powers which had prevented her from depriving the imprisoned emperor of his nominal position and refused to surrender K'ang Yu-wei and the other reform leaders who had escaped. She was therefore easily inclined to use the Boxers to get rid of the hated foreigners and gave the movement more support than was known at the time. The climax of the rebellion came in 1900 when Boxer forces besieged the foreign legation quarter in Peking.

All the foreign powers sent troops to relieve the legations. The siege was easily broken; and the empress dowager, fearing the consequences of her policy, fled to the Summer Palace in Jehol, taking with her the imprisoned young emperor. Because the Boxer movement dramatized the potential difficulties which the foreign powers would incur if they were to destroy the imperial government, the powers permitted the empress dowager, regarded as the strongest figure of her government, to come back. The Boxer Protocol of 1901 imposed a heavy indemnity and stipulated other conditions which strengthened the foreign position in North China.

Defeated in this primitive resistance against the foreign threat, the imperial government now had no choice but to return to the path of reform. Some of the practical ideas of K'ang Yu-wei, condemned before, were now taken up by the empress dowager's government, although the relationship between these reform measures and those of K'ang Yu-wei was denied. But while K'ang Yu-wei had a far-reaching program, the reforms now undertaken were individual measures forced on the government by the necessities of the situation. These reforms were not a new effort at centralization but piecemeal measures based on acceptance of the regionalism of the time.

The Regional Leaders

The government now depended on Yüan Shih-k'ai, the man who had saved the power of the empress dowager. He initiated the military program which took first place in the reform plans of the government. Yüan Shih-k'ai had the support of the former Anhwei army which he used as a basis for the creation of a more modern force trained by Western advisers in the use of Western arms. In 1901, after the death of Li Hung-chang, Yüan Shih-k'ai was made governor-general of the capital province of Chihli. There he built up, between 1902 and 1905, a force of six divisions commanded by military officers who had formerly served under him. He also devised a program which was meant to raise his force to the standing of a national army by introducing general conscription on the German model. The practical application of his measures would have required the military overthrow or subjection of the armies which other governors-general had built up in central and south China. Yüan faced the problem of centralizing and integrating the military organization of the empire, the key to the restitution of central government control.

The most important competition to this northern military and political machine was still in the central Yangtze area. The leading figures in the provincial administrations of these areas at that time were Chang Chih-tung (1837–1909) and Liu K'un-i (1830–1902). Chang, who was a Confucian scholar of distinction, had held high government office in Peking and had gained experience as a provincial administrator during the years 1884 to 1899 when he was governor-general of Kwangtung and Kwangsi. There he developed an organization which followed the pattern of the regional machines in central and northern China. He made use of the new type of provincial army in the border war against the French in Annam in 1884 and succeeded in repelling French attacks. He also gathered around him as personal secretaries a number of young Chinese students who had been abroad. He established several industrial enterprises, among them an arsenal which became the basis of the military organization of the two provinces. After he had gained this experience, Chang Chih-tung was transferred in 1889 to the position of governor-general of the central Yangtze provinces of Hupeh and Hunan, a position which he held for eighteen years, with the exception of two short intervals in which he served as acting governor-general of the lower Yangtze provinces.

During this prolonged stay in power, Chang became one of the outstanding figures among the new regional leaders. He reorganized the provincial troops, which he trained with the help of German advisers and equipped with modern weapons. He was thus Yüan Shih-k'ai's main competitor for military leadership. Chang also took the lead in the industrial development of the provinces under his control. In cooperation with gentry leaders of the area, he established cotton mills, silk factories, and tanneries. His most outstanding accomplishment was the founding of the Hanyeh-p'ing Iron and Steel Works, which became the most important industrial enterprise of its kind in China proper. In all these activities Chang cooperated with Liu K'un-i, a former officer of the Hunan army who also became one of the new provincial leaders. From 1865 to 1874, Liu was governor of Kiangsi province and later held the important position of governor-general in the lower Yangtze provinces.

The attitude of these provincial leaders towards industry can be seen in the career of Chang Ch'ien (1853–1926). Chang Ch'ien was a high gentry member from Kiangsu province who had taken a typical gentry interest in the welfare of his province. He had been active in the improvement of sericulture, in the building and maintenance of Confucian temples, in the distribution of grain to the needy, and in the fight for tax reduction. He had also been in charge of a local corps for the defense of his home area. In the critical years of the last decade of the century, he turned from these traditional gentry activities to a new interest in industrial development. With the support of Chang Chih-tung and later of Liu K'un-i, Chang Ch'ien established a number of cotton mills and other enterprises in several towns both to the north and south of the Yangtze. The political motive behind this industrialization, sponsored by the provincial leaders and carried out by a leading member of the gentry, was the strengthening of the country in its resistance to outside threat. Chang Chih-tung, Liu K'un-i, and Chang Ch'ien discussed the threat of Japanese competition and planned to combat it by promoting Chinese industrial development. Their aim was to strengthen their home area and thus to enable it to resist outside pressure.

The new economic policies of men like Chang Chih-tung and Liu K'un-i were thus designed to develop regional strength. The attempts of the central government, now in the hands of the empress dowager, to interfere with this autonomy by shifting the heads of the organizations from one provincial position to another and by playing them off against each other met with little success. Chang Chih-tung, for example, had been in Canton until 1889, when he was moved to Wuchang. From 1894 to 1896 he was acting governor-general at Nanking before he returned to Wuchang. In 1902, after Liu K'un-i's death, he again went to Nanking and from there was called to Peking to participate in reform planning. He returned to Wuchang in 1904 and remained until 1907, when he was again called to the capital to join in the discussions concerning railroad development. The central government shifted other provincial leaders around in a similar way in an unsuccessful attempt to restore its control over the political and economic affairs of the provinces.

The empress dowager also began to suspect Yüan Shih-k'ai's growing personal and military power, and as a matter of caution she tried to curtail his control of the northern army by removing two divisions from his personal command and placing them under the direct control of the War Department. This move too had little real effect, as the loyalty of officers and troops remained with Yüan who continued to be the dominating figure in the north. But all these leaders had to guard their steps and to protect themselves by a cautious participation in the policies at the capital.

Chang Chih-tung had originally been in favor of the reformers, but he shifted quickly to the side of the empress dowager when she was victorious in her coup d'état. During the Boxer Rebellion, Chang Chih-tung and Liu K'un-i had disobeyed the empress dowager's edicts which ordered them to support the Boxers. They had dealt directly with the foreign powers and had kept their provinces free from Boxer troubles, but they covered themselves by pretending that the Boxer movement was a "rebellion" directed against the empress dowager who herself was unfree to act. In this way they also facilitated the empress dowager's return to power after the defeat of the Boxers, and earned her gratitude.

The new regional leaders also concerned themselves with education and the problem of adjustment to Western ideas. While governor-general at Canton, Chang Chih-tung became famous for establishing an academy of studies and a printing office for the publication of Chinese works, mostly by authors of the Ch'ing period. In the critical years of the late 1890's, Chang Chih-tung, like all his contemporaries, was concerned with the relationship of Chinese traditional Confucian learning to modern Western knowledge. In 1898 he published a pamphlet "Admonition to Study" which was widely read and became very popular. In this pamphlet Chang took a stand in defense of the traditional Confucian learning. He was in favor of introducing the study of Western science but only as something to be grafted on the trunk of Chinese philosophy. His attitude reflected the general realization among the educated in China that Western science could not be ignored and that the Confucian tradition of learning must adjust to it. In contrast to K'ang Yu-wei's attempt at a profound reform of Confucian philosophy itself, Chang Chih-tung suggested nothing more than the addition of some Western studies to the traditional subjects. After the Boxer Rebellion, when the imperial government turned to reform measures, Chang Chih-tung's proposal for a mechanical combination of Chinese and Western studies found general acclaim and plans were laid for the introduction of a modern school system along the lines of his proposal. Chang was called to Peking to participate in the planning as an adviser to a new ministry of education.

Educational and Constitutional Reforms

As a punishment for the anti-foreignism of the scholar-gentry, the Boxer Protocol had decreed that no state examinations were to be held in the provinces concerned until 1905. Although this suspension of the traditional examination system had been intended as a temporary measure, the institution was now permitted to lapse altogether. At the same time, the first steps were taken to create Western-type educational institutions. The abolition of the examination system was a much more far-reaching step than its instigators may have anticipated. The study of Confucianism no longer had any practical value and the educational reforms prepared the way for an attack on Confucian philosophy. With the end of the examination system, the formal distinctions that had determined membership in the scholar-gentry disappeared and the institution of the scholar-gentry was in fact abolished. This signaled the end of traditional Chinese society.

The abolition of the examination system was followed by a demand for a constitution with a representative system on the Western model. This demand came from the Western-educated students and was supported by the provincial leaders who were interested in limiting the power of the throne.

At first the government resisted, but then the Japanese example convinced the empress dowager that it might be possible to have a constitution without endangering the authority of the throne. As the Japanese constitution had been granted by the emperor, who maintained his position as a sovereign ruler, a constitution in China could also leave the power in imperial hands. The Japanese example became more attractive after the Russo-Japanese War in 1905 when the Japanese victory demonstrated that modernization and political reforms had greatly increased Japan's strength. Japan, an Eastern country with a constitution, had defeated Russia, the largest Western land power and the one which did not possess a constitution. The case for a constitution seemed proved to the Chinese. In 1907 the empress dowager announced a nine-year program for the establishment of a representative system. Provincial assemblies were to be called within one year and the way prepared for a national parliament to be instituted at the end of the nine-year period.

The empress dowager died on November 15, 1908, one day after the death of the imprisoned emperor. The regent who ruled for the new child emperor P'u-yi, known as the Hsüan-t'ung emperor, continued the reform program. The provincial assemblies, called in 1909, were advisory to the provincial governors-general and had no powers of legislation. The assemblies were elected by the educated classes, the very people who had backed the provincial leadership in its opposition to central control. The new provincial assemblies therefore marked the strengthening of the regional forces against the central government. From the moment they were called, the provincial assemblies clamored for their own interests, and the conflict between the central government and the regional leaders moved into a new and sharper phase. This conflict was brought into focus when a constitutional assembly was convoked in October, 1910. Half the members were representatives of the provincial assemblies and half were imperial appointees. The vast majority of the representatives, not only those from the provincial assemblies, were strongly critical of the government. They demanded a shortening of the nine-year period of preparation for a constitution, and the period was consequently reduced to five years with the promise of the establishment of a parliament by 1913. The assembly was also critical of government policies and very nearly impeached the state council. The weakness of the government was indicated by the way it yielded to most of the demands of this assembly. Before the assembly's adjournment in the spring of 1911, the government had accepted the principle of government by a cabinet responsible to the national assembly and eventually to the parliament.

The Railroads and the Revolution

In the years between 1909 and 1911 the conflict between the regional interests and the central government led to a major controversy in the provinces. This controversy arose over the question of the government's railroad policy. In this field too the regional administrations had taken the lead. Li Hung-chang had started a railroad in the north in connection with the opening of the Kailan mines. Chang Chih-tung had promoted the development of the railroads from Peking via Hankow to Canton, and from Hankow into Szechwan province. In line with the regional policy which Chang Chih-tung himself represented, the building and control of these railroads were to be in the hands of the provincial authorities.

The conflict between the provinces and the central government for railroad control was complicated by a variety of factors. Railroads were important for political control. It was only natural that they should become a source of contention in the power conflict between the central government and the provincial administrations. If the loss of railroad control were added to military and financial disintegration, there would be little real authority left to the central government. The government recognized this problem in 1909, towards the end of the reform period, but it had no funds of its own to invest. Its only source of capital was foreign loans, and the Western governments and banks were very interested in financing such railroads provided they had control over them. To these foreign interests, the central government seemed the logical authority in China to which to turn for railroad rights and privileges.

The central government's agreements with foreign powers for the financing of railroads gave the Chinese provincial leaders a new nationalist argument against central control. They began the so-called "Rights Recovery" movement, directed against the foreign influence exercised through the central government. These provincial forces, led by Chang Chih-tung, scored a victory when the right to build and control the respective sections of the main north-south and east-west railroads was handed over to the provincial leaders of Hupeh, Hunan, Kwangtung, and Szechwan. The gentry in each of these provinces founded railroad societies to raise the capital for the construction of their own sections of the road. None of these provinces, however, collected sufficient funds to finance their sections of the railroad. At the same time the pressure increased on the central government to grant railroad rights to the British, French, German, and American banks which in 1908 had organized the Four-Power Banking Consortium to participate in the Chinese railroad development.

Chang Chih-tung had encouraged the provincial gentry groups in order to get their support against the central government. Before his death in 1909, he had come to realize the difficulty of raising enough funds in the provinces and had negotiated for foreign loans. After Chang's death the central government and the gentry organizations of the provinces came into sharper conflict over the railroad issue.

The person who managed the central government railroad policy was Sheng Hsüan-huai (1849–1916). Sheng himself was a gentry member interested in industrial development. He had managed the Wuhan ironworks under Chang Chih-tung, after having managed the China Merchants' Steam Navigation Company and having held other similar positions under Li Hung-chang. In 1911, however, Sheng had gained influence and position in the central government and, as president of the Board of Communications in Peking, stood for central control. His plan was to buy off the provincial interests and build a centrally-controlled railroad system with a large loan secured from the Four-Power Banking Consortium. The foreign loan itself had already caused protests and riots in several of the railroad provinces. This opposition increased when Sheng Hsüan-huai tried to negotiate settlements with the railroad societies. Sheng offered to exchange the railroad shares of these societies for interest-bearing government bonds. At best such settlements reimbursed the provincial societies for their expenses without permitting them any part in the control of the future development. The sacrifice of provincial interests was even greater, however, because of the low value of the shares to be exchanged. At the time of the exchange the shares in Kwangtung province, for instance, were at a discount of over 50 per cent. In Szechwan, where a substantial part of the capital subscribed had been lost in speculations by one of the managers, the shareholders were to be compensated only for the sums actually expended for railroad development. The settlement was protested by the governor-general in memorials to the central government. This official move was followed by demonstrations of resistance, refusal of tax payment, closing of shops, and student strikes. When some of the leaders of this movement were arrested, there was an open outbreak and an attack on the yamen of the governor-general. As a result, the government was forced to send in troops to deal with the uprising.

The uprising in Szechwan and the unrest in the other provinces provided the occasion for the outbreaks that culminated in the revolution of 1911. That revolution had been prepared by the decline of the dynasty and the emergence of regional administrations. Weakened by its loss of control and in conflict with the provinces, the dynasty collapsed when the fight for regional autonomy turned into an attack against the government itself. The revolution, however, was more than the product of inner disintegration; it took its initial direction from a political society which was the first organized expression of the hopes and aspirations of the new social groups which had developed in China as a result of the influence of the West.

3. THE REVOLUTION AND THE REPUBLIC

New Trends

The political revolution that brought about the end of the Manchu dynasty stemmed from the changes brought about by the influence of the West. Western influence on China made itself felt through the influx of Western goods and ideas. The most important centers of this Western influence were the treaty ports and the new educational institutions. The treaty ports attracted the most enterprising people from the inland districts to participate in the new economic and intellectual life; and this loss of the most active and able men helped to weaken leadership in the inland areas where the situation deteriorated into the warlord struggle. The coastal centers, protected by the Western treaty rights, were outside of the Chinese political conflict; and the Chinese residents, much as they might be interested in the political struggle, were not forced into it. The treaty ports were living examples of Western society, enclaves in which Chinese residents could experience Western law, economic practices, and social institutions.

The establishment of the treaty ports brought a large increase in the commodity exchange between China and the Western world. By the end of the nineteenth century the Chinese themselves began to participate in this growing trade, and there emerged in the treaty ports a group which had a distinctly Western outlook on trade and business.

The character of China's trade changed considerably during the nineteenth and early twentieth centuries. The change in trade was closely related to an economic transformation in China itself. The main export products at the time of the Opium War were tea, silk, and porcelain. Aside from some cotton piece goods from India, there was little that the West could sell in the self-sufficient Chinese economy. During the nineteenth century opium was the main item of import and continued to hold this place until the end of the century when it was superseded by other goods. In 1908 and 1911 agreements were made with the British Indian government for the limitation and eventual suppression of the opium trade, but by this time the damage had been done. Opium had declined as an item of import mainly because it was now produced in China itself, where it became a major source of income for later Chinese governments.

By the beginning of the twentieth century, when opium was no longer an important import, the Chinese cities and to a lesser degree the countryside were becoming more and more dependent on Western textiles and other manufactured goods. Cotton goods became the major item of import and, together with sundries, made up more than 70 per cent of the value of imports. The import of such Western goods, as well as of household utensils, hardware, and even food, indicated the growth of new tastes and adaptation to Western ways of living. Kerosene came to replace vegetable oil as the fuel for lighting purposes and kerosene lamps were freely distributed by Western oil companies in order to promote their sales. Tobacco and cigarettes also came into China in steadily increasing quantities.

In the first decade of the century the treaty ports began to develop as centers of industrial production. Like the commercial development, this industrialization was first introduced by foreign interests. Although some factories had been sponsored earlier by men like Li Hung-chang, there was no substantial industrial growth until the turn of the century, when the Westerners, especially the British, began to establish textile mills in Shanghai. Industrialization later spread to other treaty ports, but Shanghai remained by far the most important industrial center. In the years during and after the First World War, when European industry was deeply affected by the war and war production, the textile industry in the Far Eastern countries experienced a boom period. It was during those years that a large number of Chinese textile mills were established, and the Chinese began to invest in industry. At the same time the growing Japanese textile industry set up factories in China and took the lead from the British concerns. The total number of spindles in China's cotton mills increased from 836,000 in 1913 to 3,100,000 in 1920. In addition to the cotton mills there were a large number of silk factories, most of which were Chinese, as well as woolen mills, flour mills, tobacco and paper factories, and chemical plants. China's early industrialization was largely in textiles and consumer goods, iron and steel works being relatively undeveloped. Many of the enterprises had little capital, but taken together they amounted to an important development in Chinese economy. The new industries, financed by Chinese as well as foreign capital, were established almost exclusively in the treaty ports.

The growth of the textile industry changed the nature of the Chinese import trade. Where formerly only manufactured goods had been imported, raw cotton and other industrial raw materials as well as machinery now made up an increasing part of the import trade. At the same time a change in Chinese exports took place. Tea, the main export item in the nineteenth century, steadily declined in importance. This was the result of Japanese, and even more of Indian, competition and also of a change of taste in Europe. Silk remained an important export but was gradually overtaken by soya beans and soya products which were first exported around 1900. A variety of other items such as bristles, tung oil, tungsten, antimony, and tin were exported as raw materials for Western industry. The land, which had formerly been cultivated to produce crops for local consumption and for the tax needs of the government, was now used for the production of raw materials, such as cotton and tobacco for the Chinese factories. In the treaty ports and the neighboring towns, machine-made goods of both foreign and Chinese manufacture began to take the place of handicraft.

The treaty ports grew in importance and population. Here was concentrated the first Chinese industrial labor force, which included many women and children. Except for some skilled workmen, most workers were poorly paid. For the new urban population of entrepreneurs, investors, merchants, bankers, and professional people, who were Western in outlook, the treaty ports provided an opportunity to live and prosper in a new environment. They were beyond the reach of the Chinese government.

It was in the treaty ports that some of the most fundamental changes in Chinese social life first took place. The opportunity for earning independent incomes made it possible to break away from the customary pattern of economic dependence on the family. By the same token women workers in the factories became more economically independent and therefore acquired a social status which they had not enjoyed before. The new opportunities for business and professional men, which gave the individual a chance to establish himself, tended to weaken the authority of the family. The changes made possible by the Western type of economic life were hastened by the pressure of Western ideas on the rights of the individual and the equality of the sexes. Out of this situation there developed a revolt against the authority of the Confucian family. This revolt was expressed most dramatically in a movement for the emancipation of women. Through the influence of the missionaries women first acquired an opportunity for formal education, and eventually women entered the professions. Co-education was gradually accepted in the educational system. Another aspect of the emancipation of women was the revolt against arranged marriages, which played a large part in the break with parental authority. The growing independence of women and the new regard in which they were held led to the abandonment of the habit of footbinding, which had been customary for millions of women since the tenth century. Western dress, especially for men, became more and more common. The Chinese in the treaty ports adjusted more and more to the Western way of life.

The Chinese merchants in the treaty ports were the first to entrust their children to Western missionary schools where they learned English and practical subjects in preparation for business careers. The missionary education in China followed the school system of the West, especially that of the United States from which the majority of the missionary teachers had come. The curriculum and the textbooks were largely more Western than Chinese. Many of the students coming from these schools continued their studies abroad, in the United States, in Europe, and especially in Japan, which had preceded China in modernization and was, after its victory over Russia in 1905, particularly attractive to Chinese students. Japan was also close by and life there was comparatively inexpensive; she accommodated the stream of Chinese students by establishing special schools where the desired modern degrees were provided.

From this educational background came the first group of modern Chinese intellectuals, ardent in their admiration for the West, but for the most part limited in their understanding of the social and ideological foundations of Western society. The limitations of their Western education were not always compensated by a rich knowledge of their own history and the problems of their country, both of which were little stressed in their schooling.

Another group interested in the modernization of China was the overseas Chinese. Many Chinese traders had gone to Southeast Asia in earlier centuries; but the nineteenth century with its vast new business opportunities in Southeast Asia and the Pacific brought a great increase in the emigration of Chinese workers and merchants to these parts. Large Chinese minorities were created in the Philippines, in Indonesia, in Cochin China, and in Thailand. Singapore became a Chinese city, Hawaii soon had a large segment of Chinese population, and tens of thousands of Chinese came to the cities of the American West Coast. Among the overseas Chinese, who best understood the strength of the Western world, many were anxious to have China modernized. The weakness of their country was not only humiliating to them but it also deprived them of any protection against the discriminations to which they were often subjected.

Branches of Chinese secret societies had been formed in the treaty ports and overseas, among the Chinese storekeepers, workers, businessmen, and intellectuals. In moving from the traditional rural background into modern city environments, the secret societies had changed their character. Now functioning among minorities, they had taken on some of the attributes of self-protection groups. Sometimes they functioned like guilds or labor unions, and sometimes they moved into criminal activities which led to rackets and gang warfare. Their branches or "tangs" in overseas communities often represented very local interests. But in China they still maintained broader organizational contact and were an ideal tool for political movements. It was from these groups and organizations that the revolutionary movement drew its supporters and its financial backing.

Sun Yat-sen and the Revolution of 1911

The organizer of the Chinese revolution was Sun Yat-sen. Sun was born on November 12, 1866, in a rural area near the city of Canton. His home district, Hsiangshan, was later renamed Chungshan after the official personal name of its famous son. Sun was one of the Chinese who had received a Western education and was not entirely at home either in the West or in the world of traditional China. Sun was of commoner peasant origin and his education had been very uneven, consisting of occasional studies in a private village school. In his later writings and political speeches, Sun showed little grasp of the Confucian scholar tradition and, for a boy coming from a peasant family, little understanding or real concern for the agrarian problems of China. His interest was directed towards Western knowledge. At the early age of twelve Sun was taken out of his Chinese environment to go overseas. This chance was given to him by an older brother who had emigrated earlier to Hawaii as had many younger men from the Canton area. This brother had done well in business and owned a small plantation. In the tradition of family loyalty he had helped to support his parents, brothers, and sisters in the village near Canton by sending them money. But he wanted to do more and decided to bring his younger brother to Hawaii, where he received his education in a British missionary school. As Chinese was a part of the school's curriculum, Sun also received a Chinese education, though it was through the medium of a Western school. Sun became an ardent believer in the West and also accepted Christianity. On a visit home at the age of sixteen the zealous young Christian and a like-minded friend went out to the village temple to do damage to the idols. After this behavior Sun and his friend had to leave the village.

Sun Yat-sen continued his education in Hong Kong, where he studied Western medicine and then practiced medicine in Macao until his license was withdrawn because he was not a resident. During this time he was full of ideas on how to improve and westernize his country, and he discussed them with a few student friends of similar outlook. Sun later stated that his ambition to overthrow the Manchu government began after the humiliations of the Sino-French war in 1885, which left a deep impression on him. He also claimed to have used his medical practice in Macao for spreading anti-Manchu propaganda. On the other hand, in 1894, before the calamities of the Sino-Japanese War, Sun traveled north and tried to hand to the governor-general, Li Hung-chang, a reform memorandum. This was ignored, and any hopes which Sun may have had of employment by Li vanished. After this disappointment Sun began to work seriously for the overthrow of the existing government and organized a secret revolutionary group. This organization was made possible through secret-society support which Sun gained with the help of a student friend and secret-society member. The group which Sun organized in 1894 was called the *Hsing-chung-hui* (Revive China Society). In 1895 this secret conspiratorial society prepared an uprising in Canton and an attack against the yamen there. The coup failed. Some of the young conspirators lost their lives and Sun had to flee, becoming from that time on a fugitive from the Chinese government with a price on his head. He began to travel abroad, collecting funds and members for his group.

Sun's travels during the coming years took him to Japan, the countries of Southeast Asia, Hawaii, the United States, and Europe. Wherever he went he tried to gain support for his plans and organization among overseas Chinese communities, which were growing fast in some of these countries, and from Chinese students abroad. During the first years Sun Yat-sen's activities were not so successful as those of another political movement that relied on overseas Chinese support. K'ang Yu-wei, himself a refugee from the imperial government after the failure of his reforms in 1898, traveled among the overseas Chinese communities. He was widely honored and celebrated and gained much support for his program of constitutional monarchy which had a greater appeal than the radical ideas of Sun. But after 1905 attitudes changed. Japan's victory over Russia, which made many Chinese impatient for action, had a strong impact on Chinese students abroad. At a meeting in Tokyo in that year Sun's organization was broadened and reorganized into the *T'ung-meng-hui* (the Combined League Society). This meeting was attended by a large number of Chinese students, over 600 of whom joined the new society. The *T'ung-meng-hui* was made up of a number of secret-society groups that joined with the *Hsing-chung-hui* in a common revolutionary effort. Sun Yat-sen remained the head of the new organization and attempted to formulate a political program.

Sun Yat-sen's leadership in these revolutionary organizations was based on his personality, his sincerity and integrity, his revolutionary fervor, and his sense of personal destiny, all of which commanded loyalty. Wherever he went on his journeys, Sun gathered around him students and secret-society leaders who were assigned such different tasks as preparing uprisings, collecting men and arms, or promoting revolutionary ideas through newspapers and journals. But most important was Sun Yat-sen's ability to secure financial support for the revolutionary organization. Sun himself collected most of the funds and administered them. Contributions came mainly from overseas Chinese businessmen—from the life savings of laundrymen as well as from Singapore millionaires. To persuade these overseas Chinese to support his cause, Sun Yat-sen explained his aims to individuals and small groups in the homes and business places of the Chinese he visited. There he formulated phrases, slogans, and illustrations which he used later in making up his political program.

The program was stated officially for the first time at the mass meeting in Tokyo in 1905 when the *T'ung-meng-hui* was founded. It included the main points which later were formulated as the Three People's Principles. Sun used the three Chinese slogans, Min-chu or "People's Rule," later translated as "Nationalism"; Min-ch'üan or "People's Authority," rendered as "Democracy"; and Min-sheng, or "People's Livelihood," sometimes called "Socialism." Aside from these three principles in slogan form, Sun claimed six objectives which dealt with the overthrow of the Manchu dynasty, the establishment of a republic, the promotion of world peace, the nationalization of land, good relations between China and Japan, and the quest for the support of the powers. The program and the slogans remained rather general and vague. The only definite goal was the overthrow of the imperial government and the establishment of a republic by Sun's group which was then expected to bring the solution to all problems of modernization.

Sun Yat-sen's methods were conspiratorial. The *Hsing-chung-hui* and, after 1905, the *T'ung-meng-hui* attempted a number of local putsches, consisting of armed attacks by small groups of men on government offices in various cities, mainly in South China. These attacks—ten of them are generally listed—all failed. Some of the military support for these attempts came from foreign countries. One uprising in 1900 in Kwangtung province was engineered from Formosa with the support of Japanese military adventurers. It collapsed when, because of a change in government in Tokyo, the promised delivery of arms did not take place. Other uprisings in South China were planned in French Indo-China with the connivance of French officers. None of these uprisings succeeded, but they indicated Sun's willingness to accept foreign help, an attitude which permitted the exploitation of Sun's political movement by foreign interests.

Sun's organization also received another type of military support which was to be a decisive factor in the eventual success of the revolution. Among the students who joined the *T'ung-meng-hui* in Japan there were cadets of Chinese military schools, sent overseas by several regional armies to study. In this way the *T'ung-meng-hui* and Sun Yat-sen gained adherents in various regional military forces. One of the cadets who joined the party was Chiang Kai-shek, who had been sent to Japan from Yüan Shih-k'ai's military academy at Paotingfu and who was at a later time to become a key figure in the party. Other officers who joined the *T'ung-meng-hui* belonged to the armies of Chang Chih-tung. These military men created a link between Sun Yat-sen's organization and the rising regional resistance against central control.

In the fall of 1911, when the railroad struggle in the central Yangtze provinces led to the first open outbreaks in Szechwan, the branches of the *T'ung-meng-hui* had been prepared for uprisings in the major cities of these provinces. At Wuhan an accident occurred that precipitated an uprising and started the revolution. An explosion in a house in which *T'ung-meng-hui* members prepared bombs resulted in a police search and the discovery of a membership list of the society which included the names of officers of the local army. These officers, in danger of their lives, forestalled the government's prosecution by forcing their own commander, a Colonel Li Yüan-hung, to lead an uprising of the troops against the dynasty. The uprising spread quickly to other cities of central and south China where the government officials surrendered or fled without offering much resistance to the rebellious troops or *T'ung-meng-hui* groups. The outbreak at Wuhan, which occurred on October 10, 1911, has been regarded as the starting point of the Chinese revolution.

Sung Chiao-jen and Yüan Shih-k'ai

Preparations for the uprising of the *T'ung-meng-hui* in the Yangtze provinces was largely in the hands of Sung Chiao-jen, a Hunanese, who was to play a major part in the next two years of the revolution. Sung Chiao-jen (1882–1913), was one of the organizers of a secret society in Hunan which joined with Sun Yat-sen in the founding of the *T'ung-meng-hui* in Tokyo in 1905. In 1911, when Sun Yat-sen was traveling in the United States, Sung Chiao-jen was left in charge of the *T'ung-meng-hui* activities in

China. Following a plan of his own which discarded the strategy of isolated outbreaks, Sung prepared a coordinated uprising in the key cities of the Yangtze area in which active party branches had been newly established. This plan proved successful and Sung, as one of the leaders of the revolutionary group in Wuhan, called a meeting of the branch leaders. He drafted a provisional constitution for the revolutionary government providing for the establishment of a parliamentary system. The new government was to be responsible to an elected assembly and dependent on the support of a majority of the representatives. Before any decisions were taken on the form of government, the leaders of the revolutionary forces had moved to Shanghai and a plan was prepared to establish a government in Nanking. When Sung Chiao-jen had left for Nanking to prepare the ground, the representatives in Shanghai elected Li Yüan-hung as generalissimo of the revolutionary government. However, no agreement was reached on leadership or form of government. During this political stalemate, Sun Yat-sen returned from abroad and arrived in Shanghai in December, 1911. He was immediately elected president of the republic by all the leaders of the *T'ung-meng-hui*. Sun Yat-sen's election to the presidency, however, did not end the conflict for leadership, which now revolved around the key position of prime minister of the new government. A full agreement among the revolutionaries was never reached, either on the type of government or on the relative position of the leading figures under Sun Yat-sen. Before these questions were solved, the intervention of the northern army brought an altogether different solution.

The Manchu government, faced with the collapse of authority and the growing revolution in the Yangtze Valley and the southern provinces, tried to recover its position by calling for help from the strongest military man of the time, Yüan Shih-k'ai, who could count on the loyalty of the officers of the northern army. At this time Yüan Shih-k'ai was no longer in office. In 1908 the imprisoned emperor, Kuang-hsü, had demanded on his death bed that Yüan Shih-k'ai be brought to justice. The regent, who was the father of the child emperor, and the brother of Kuang-hsü, wanted to carry out this demand; but he did not dare to touch Yüan personally and so only had him removed from public office. Now, in 1911, the regent's government was faced with outbreaks in central and southern China, and with increasing demands for wide political reforms from the assembly in Peking. The only man who could save the dynasty was Yüan Shih-k'ai because he alone could provide the support of the northern army. Yüan was called back but he accepted the invitation only after having received the most far-reaching powers, which included the position of governor-general in the central Yangtze valley, his election as prime minister by the National Assembly in Peking, and full authority over the northern army and navy, which were still loyal to the government.

Assured of his demands, Yüan Shih-k'ai began his military campaign against the revolutionaries. He not only prevented them from moving north, but also defeated them in the central Yangtze area and captured Wuhan. He did not, however, push his campaign so far as to destroy the revolutionary forces but negotiated for a political compromise, first with Li Yüan-hung and later with the representatives of Sun Yat-sen. The reason for the willingness of the revolutionaries to compromise was not only their military inferiority but also their inner rivalries and lack of agreement on the form of government. The revolutionary leaders obviously counted on being asked to participate in Yüan's government.

In February of 1912 the negotiations resulted in a settlement in which Sun Yat-sen resigned from the presidency in favor of Yüan Shih-k'ai. In exchange for this resignation Yüan promised to bring about the abdication of the Manchu dynasty. The dynasty, having surrendered whatever actual power it had held to Yüan Shih-k'ai, had no choice but to give up the throne in exchange for a guarantee of personal protection and a financial settlement. In abdicating, the emperor transferred his authority to Yüan, whose position was therefore legitimized by both sides, much to the annoyance of the revolutionaries.

The establishment of the republic was the one achievement of the *T'ung-meng-hui* which represented the political objectives of the westernized Chinese. The presidency of Yüan Shih-k'ai was a logical outcome of the preceding regional disintegration. On the collapse of the dynasty, the strongest regional military figure was accepted as the head of the Chinese Republic. The *T'ung-meng-hui* itself, lacking a practical political program and torn by divided leadership, had not been able to maintain a government of its own. The revolution removed the dynasty, the traditional focus of ideological and political unification, but did not put in its place a viable political system.

Yüan decreed in February, 1912, that everyone exercising power at that moment in any provincial or regional position was to continue and to become the recognized legal authority. The only men who exercised power were those in control of military forces.

There remained for Yüan Shih-k'ai, as well as for his opponents in the *T'ung-meng-hui*, the problem of finding new ways of integrating the Chinese political system. At first both sides collaborated. Sung Chiao-jen and a number of other *T'ung-meng-hui* leaders became members of Yüan Shih-k'ai's first cabinet under the premiership of T'ang Shao-i, an American-educated supporter of Yüan Shih-k'ai who had been in favor of the revolution and the *T'ung-meng-hui*. Not much was accomplished by this cabinet, which fell in August, 1912. The coming conflict between Yüan Shih-k'ai and the revolutionaries had already been indicated by the quarrel over the location of the capital of the new republican government. The *T'ung-meng-hui* leaders wanted the capital at Nanking, the area where they had their strongest political organizations and military friends; Yüan Shih-k'ai wanted to remain in Peking, where he had his armies and could count on political support. Under the pretext of having to stay in Peking in order to control mutinous troops, Yüan won this first tug of war and forced the revolutionaries to come to Peking to participate in the government. As the conflict sharpened, Sung Chiao-jen brought together several of the revolutionary groups in a new type of political organization. In August, 1912, Sung succeeded in forming the

Kuomintang, or Nationalist Party, through an amalgamation of five political groups of which the *T'ung-meng-hui* was one.

Sung Chiao-jen organized the Kuomintang as an open political party, with open membership in contrast to the secret-society character of the *T'ung-meng-hui* and other similar groups. Sung thought of this as the first step towards free elections and a parliamentary form of government. His ideas had already been indicated in the provisional constitution which he had drafted in 1911. These were revolutionary moves which, if successful, would would have given the Western-educated Chinese a responsible political role. As Sung Chiao-jen was an able party organizer and public speaker he could himself expect to play a leading part in a representative system. During the elections of 1913 for parliament, Sung campaigned for the Kuomintang which was opposed mainly by the Progressive party, led by Liang Ch'i-ch'ao, a follower of K'ang Yu-wei. As a result of the elections, the Kuomintang became the strongest single party. Sung Chiao-jen was recognized as the party leader and his influence both in the party and in the country grew rapidly. As Sung's power grew, the animosity between him and Yüan Shih-k'ai increased. Sung had already openly attacked Yüan for his "unconstitutional" activities. When Sung became a real threat to Yüan Shih-k'ai, Yüan decided to destroy his main rival. He called Sung to Peking for consultations before the opening of parliament, which was to convene there in April. On March 20, 1913, as Sung boarded the train in Shanghai, he was assassinated by two men in the pay of Yüan Shih-k'ai's officials. Sung's assassination was the decisive blow against the parliamentary movement which he represented.

Sun Yat-sen and his friends had never been in favor of a parliamentary type of government. Indeed, Sun had opposed the founding of the Kuomintang. He had continued to favor a closed, secret-society type of organization, loyal to himself. But as long as Sung Chiao-jen was alive he was able, with his persuasive and powerful personality, to gain the support of the rank and file of the *T'ung-meng-hui* for his parliamentary plans, and Sun Yat-sen had been forced to yield. In many of the official histories of the party Sung Chiao-jen is strongly attacked for this "mistaken" policy of an open party which brought him into conflict with Sun Yat-sen and his chief lieutenants.

Yüan Shih-k'ai's Monarchical Program

After the death of Sung Chiao-jen, for which Yüan Shih-k'ai denied any responsibility, the parliament convened in Peking. A battle soon developed between Yüan Shih-k'ai and the parliamentarians, who sought to establish their power by drafting a constitution in which the executive authority would be in the hands of a prime minister responsible to a parliamentary majority. This system would leave the president with little real authority. While the parliament debated the constitutional draft, Yüan Shih-k'ai tried to fortify his position by extending his control over the administrative organization itself. He began to replace those military leaders in the Yangtze Valley who were friendly to the Kuomintang with men of his own choice. This provoked a break with the Kuomintang. An open rebellion against Yüan occurred in August, 1913, when Yüan replaced the military governor of Kiangsi, a supporter of the Kuomintang, with one of his own men. The rebellion was quickly suppressed by Yüan's forces, and in November, 1913, he declared the Kuomintang illegal. A few months later he dissolved the parliament altogether. Having destroyed the opposition, Yüan Shih-k'ai set about the establishment of his own organization.

Yüan's power was based on his control of the northern army which was stationed north of the Yangtze and guaranteed to Yüan the tax revenue of this area. Once established in power, Yüan had the support of the officials and of the Chinese businessmen of North China. As president, Yüan Shih-k'ai also gained strong support from the foreign powers. By the foreign representatives and business communities Yüan was regarded as the "strong man" best suited to re-establish and retain the peace and order necessary to the development of their commercial and other interests.

Yüan had taken over a government without financial reserves. In order to pay the staff and the armies, to undertake all the new tasks of the government, and to win the battle with the Kuomintang, he needed funds. These he acquired through loan agreements with the foreign powers. In the spring of 1913 he concluded an agreement for a reorganization loan of $125,000,000 with the Six-Power Banking Consortium. The parliament refused to ratify this agreement; but the foreign powers, satisfied with Yüan's signature, ignored the parliamentary protest, and Yüan received the vital financial support. After dissolving the parliament in January, 1914, Yüan established his own political organization, the so-called "Constitutional Council." This body consisted of a number of men selected and appointed by Yüan himself. The constitutional draft, which the now defunct parliament had formulated and which provided for a parliamentary government and a weak president, was replaced by a constitutional compact concentrating all powers in the hands of the president. Yüan had himself elected president for life as the first step towards his final aim, which was to establish a constitutional monarchy with himself as emperor.

Yüan was seeking more than the gratification of personal ambition. His plan for a constitutional monarchy included a serious program for the re-integration of the Chinese political system. The peasants of rural China, still bound by tradition, were expected to accept the Confucian imperial system. But the political institutions were to be modern, not traditional. Yüan wanted to introduce a modern system of law to take the place of the former imperial institutions which had disappeared with the ending of the scholar-gentry and the examination system. He therefore ordered the drafting of Western law codes which would enable him to establish a constitutional monarchy of a Western type.

Yüan's position was weakened in 1915 when Japanese military pressure forced him to make major political concessions. During World War I the preoccupation of the Western powers with the war in Europe gave Japan the opportunity to present the Twenty-One Demands. When Yüan was forced to accept most of them, a wave of national indignation swept the Western-educated groups in China, and Yüan's position as a national leader was damaged. More than ever Yüan Shih-k'ai needed an indication that Western political thinkers were not adverse to the establishment of a constitutional monarchy as a practical solution for China's problems. Such an indication, especially if it were to come from an American, would be helpful in affecting the thinking of the Western-minded Chinese students. Yüan got academic approval of his plans from an American political science professor, Dr. F. J. Goodnow, later president of Johns Hopkins University. Dr. Goodnow, as Yüan's political adviser, wrote a memorandum in which he stipulated the constitutional monarchy as the ideal form of government for China at this stage, provided that it found public approval.

Yüan now took the final steps. Through selected "citizens representatives," he let himself be urged to restore the monarchy. These representatives met in a convention, surrounded by soldiers with fixed bayonets, and voted in favor of the monarchy. Their ballots were carefully checked by Yüan's men, and the vote for the monarchy was unanimous. With apparent reluctance Yüan accepted and proceeded to conduct sacrifices at the Altar of Heaven.

Yüan had underestimated the opposition to this move. Sun Yat-sen and his group, who had been eliminated temporarily from the political struggle, raised their voices again. Even Liang Ch'i-ch'ao and his friends, the followers of K'ang Yu-wei, who had formerly supported the idea of a constitutional monarchy, now spoke out in defense of the republic. What was more important, the military rulers who had accepted Yüan's dissolution of the parliament and elimination of the party opposition to his regime, revolted against this attempt to establish a monarchical, central authority that would eventually have threatened their own local, military power. The military governors rose against Yüan, whose own men in Szechwan and Hunan joined the opposition. The fatal blow came when Yüan was deserted by some of his own military underlings in North China.

Faced with the collapse of his authority, Yüan Shih-k'ai attempted to retrace his fatal step. He stated that he had been mistaken in interpreting the people's will and attempted to retreat to his former position of president. The military opposition had joined with the party groups of the former parliament and they sought to force the complete retirement of Yüan Shih-k'ai. Before any agreement could be reached, Yüan died on June 6, 1916.

Emergence of Warlordism

The opponents of Yüan Shih-k'ai tried to return to the political situation as it was in 1913. The old parliament was reinstituted with the same members and the constitutional draft, ignored by Yüan Shih-k'ai, was revived. The actual conflict between the military organizations in the provinces and the parties in the parliament remained as before although a temporary compromise was effected. Li Yüan-hung, who had been vice-president and was a strong supporter of the parliament, became president. T'uan Ch'i-jui, who had been a military leader in Yüan Shih-k'ai's army but had deserted Yüan at the time of his monarchical plans, became prime minister. He represented the regional military faction in the north. As the draft constitution had relegated the presidency to a figurehead position, the actual power was in the hands of the prime minister and his cabinet. The same conflict between the military and the parliament which had characterized Yüan Shih-k'ai's regime soon reappeared. In the struggle for power the two sides could not agree on the method of appointing provincial governors. The military wanted to have the provincial authorities appointed by the central government, the parliamentarians wanted them elected. As a result, the whole section on provincial government was taken out of the constitutional draft and the local military leaders continued in authority.

Two cliques had been formed among the military governors, the so-called Chihli group from the north with Feng Kuo-chang as the principal figure, and the Anhwei group with T'uan Ch'i-jui as the leader. Both men had been adherents of Yüan Shih-k'ai, but with Yüan gone they fought each other for control over the country. They were united, however, against the parties and the parliament. The conflict between the parliament and the military men came into the open over the question of the declaration of war against Germany in 1917. There was no real disagreement over the desirability of declaring war, but the high-handed behavior of the prime minister, who acted without parliamentary approval, brought a demand for his dismissal. President Li Yüan-hung sided with the parliament and dismissed T'uan Ch'i-jui.

When the conflict between the parliament and the prime minister sharpened, the military governors of the provinces, known under the official title of "Tu Chun," formed a "union." The military governors of the northern and central provinces held a conference at Hsuchow in which they expressed their joint opposition to any threat from the parliament and formed a league for joint action.

T'uan Ch'i-jui's dismissal resulted in the open rebellion of the military governors. They gathered at Tientsin, set up a counter-government, and prepared for a military march to the capital. The president called for the assistance of another militarist who was outside the "union," General Chang Hsün. After occupying Peking with his army, General Chang took matters into his own hands. He dissolved the parliament in June, 1917, and, being a monarchist of the old school, brought back the child emperor to restore the Manchu dynasty. Such a crude anachronistic attempt to restore the old dynasty, unacceptable both to the assembly and to the military governors and supported only by the troops of one small army, could not succeed. But it gave the military governors in Tientsin an excellent opportunity to continue their march on Peking in order to drive away Chang Hsün and his forces and "restore the Republic." In assuming power the military men eliminated every parliamentary leader from the government which they established. Feng Kuo-chang, who had been vice-president, replaced Li Yüan-hung as president and T'uan Ch'i-jui returned as prime minister. From this time on the government remained in the hands of the military leaders but as these leaders were not controlled by one outstanding man with superior military forces, they soon became divided among themselves. Each regional group and military organization asserted itself, and a struggle for power ensued in which alliances were constantly formed and dissolved. The next decade of civil war has become known as the period of warlordism.

Sun Yat-sen Seeks Support

During these years Sun Yat-sen and his political organization had reached the low point of their influence. Sun Yat-sen himself had taken no active part in the battle of the Kuomintang with Yüan Shih-k'ai for a parliamentary government. Sun had never been a believer in the open political party and the parliamentary system. After Yüan Shih-k'ai became president, Sun Yat-sen came to Peking for a visit and was very cordially received by Yüan who flattered and honored him. Yüan Shih-k'ai put Sun in nominal charge of the planning of China's future railroad development, a position for which he was to receive a monthly remuneration of 30,000 dollars. Sun Yat-sen, who had always been interested in railroad development, drew up plans for a future Chinese railroad system which was to have 75,000 miles of track and be constructed at the cost of three billion U. S. dollars. These amateurish and unrealistic plans, however, remained on paper.

In 1913, after Yüan Shih-k'ai had defeated the parliamentary movement and crushed the rebellion of the Kuomintang, Sun Yat-sen tried to re-establish himself as the leader of the revolutionary movement. He abolished the open party and established the *Ko-ming-tang*, or Revolutionary party. This was again a secret organization whose members were loyal only to Sun Yat-sen. The membership of this group was much more limited than that of the Kuomintang had been. Sun required all members to take an oath of personal allegiance to him, sealed with a fingerprint. Some of Sun Yat-sen's personal followers refused to do this and left China to study in Europe or the United States. It was with this new organization that Sun Yat-sen attempted to regain control in China. First of all, he needed financial support to oppose Yüan Shih-k'ai. He sought this support abroad, especially in Japan and the United States.

Sun Yat-sen had never been reluctant to exchange important economic concessions for financial assistance. In 1912, during his short period as president before he resigned in favor of Yüan Shih-k'ai, Sun Yat-sen had mortgaged the Wuhan ironworks to the Japanese as security for loans they were to grant him. This agreement was not realized because of Sun Yat-sen's resignation. In 1914, when Sun became desperate in his attempt to defeat Yüan Shih-k'ai, he tried again to attract foreign support by making far-reaching promises. The offers he made to some of the Japanese leaders were very far-reaching and indicated that Sun Yat-sen was willing to accommodate the Japanese in China if the Japanese would support him rather than deal with Yüan Shih-k'ai. Sun Yat-sen's offers to the Japanese were made in two letters, one to Prime Minister Okuma in 1914, and one to the head of the political affairs section of the Japanese Foreign Office in 1915. These letters were secret, but their contents leaked out. The letter to Okuma, later found in Okuma's papers after his death, was published by an English newspaper in China. In this letter Sun Yat-sen promised that in exchange for Japanese help "China would throw open all the trade centers in the country to Japanese labor and merchants, and enable Japan to monopolize the commercial field of China." In return for Japanese support in the diplomatic negotiations to free China from the unequal treaties, the Japanese would be permitted to live in the interior of China. A commercial alliance with Japan would result,

whereby Japanese manufactures imported into China and Chinese raw materials imported into Japan will be exempted from paying duties. The prosperity of Japanese commerce and industry will go hand in hand with the development of the national resources of China. . . . Japan could, therefore, without incurring the trouble and expense of stationing troops, as Great Britain did in India, acquire big commercial marts in China. . . . [1]

All these advantages, though, would depend on Japan's turning her back on Yüan Shih-k'ai and giving her support to the revolutionaries.

As an argument for such a Japanese policy Sun stated in this letter his firm conviction that China can never have peace unless the governmental powers are in the hands of the Mintang. The reasons are that the Chinese are roughly divided into three classes, to wit, the official class, the Mintang, and the masses. The last take no active part in politics. The official classes make energetic efforts to protect their personal interest, but their energy only lasts as long as they are in power. . . . Such was the conspicuous example of Yüan himself. . . .

The Mintang, however, is composed of persons of different type; its members are fearless and determined to attain the aim they have in view. . . . Anyone who has studied the conditions in China will realize that, as long as the Mintang fails to attain its object, China will never have peace. . . .

Though it is an extraordinary matter for a Government to support the people of another country to overthrow their Government, yet extraordinary men accomplish extraordinary deeds in order to attain extraordinary results. . . . [2]

In March, 1915, when the Japanese brought pressure on Yüan Shih-k'ai to accept their demands in Manchuria and other parts of China, Sun Yat-sen sent another letter to the head of the political affairs section of the Foreign Office. Having learned of the negotiations with Yüan Shih-k'ai, he warned the Japanese of the bad faith of this "evil government." He claimed that his revolutionary group favored friendly relations with Japan, that a Sino-Japanese alliance was necessary for the freedom of Asia, and that the European war provided an excellent opportunity to destroy Yüan Shih-k'ai's regime if the revolutionaries received Japan's support. To indicate what he

[1] Lyon Sharman, *Sun Yat-sen, His Life and Its Meaning* (New York, 1934), p. 188.
[2] *Ibid.*, p. 189.

was willing to concede, Sun included in the letter the draft of a Sino-Japanese treaty which included the following points:

1. Japan and China to consult together before either concluded important agreements with a third power on matters relating to Asia.
2. To facilitate military cooperation, China to use Japanese style arms, ammunition, and equipment for both army and navy.
3. For the same reason, China to give priority to Japanese officers when employing foreign military advisers for army and navy.
4. To effectuate political coalition, China to give priority to Japanese when employing foreign specialists in the central and local governments.
5. To develop economic cooperation between China and Japan, a Sino-Japanese Bank, with branches, to be established in all important cities of both China and Japan.
6. For the same reason, China to consult Japan first if outside help and capital is needed for mining, railroads, and coastal trade, and outside help to be invited only if Japan cannot supply it.
7. Japan to provide the necessary help for removing the evil government of China.
8. Japan to help China reform her government, adjust her military system, and establish a sound nation.
9. Japan to support China in the changing of the treaties regulating customs independence, extraterritoriality, etc.
10. The contents of the foregoing articles having been agreed to by the proper authorities in China and Japan and by those initialing the treaty of alliance, neither party to form an alliance with any other power.
11. From the day this treaty is signed until its expiration cooperation is to extend, and thereafter it can be renewed according to the desires of the two parties. (Marius B. Jansen, *The Japanese and Sun Yat-sen*, Cambridge, 1954.)

Sun Yat-sen had thus compromised his position as a nationalist leader and he lost a great deal of support as a result. To cover up, he not only denied the authenticity of the news about his offers to Japan but also accused Yüan Shih-k'ai of having invited the Japanese demands in order to gain Japanese support for his own imperial aspirations.

Sun's willingness to use economic monopolies as pawns for financial support was shown in similar negotiations with other foreign groups. Shortly after his negotiations with his Japanese friends, Sun Yat-sen had considerable correspondence with a representative of American interests, a Mr. Dietrich, to whom he offered a monopoly of department store development in Chinese cities. The monopoly was to be given to an American group in exchange for financial support in the amount of $10,000,000, which was to be advanced immediately. Sun thought the store project would also be a stimulant to Chinese modern economic development in general. When no acceptance was forthcoming he reduced his price to $1,000,000. This plan, which came to nothing, was a clear example of Sun Yat-sen's policy of gaining whatever financial backing he could get at the price of promising a share in Chinese development. As Sun lived in Japan from 1913 to 1916, his main contact was with the Japanese. According to Japanese reports of conversations with Sun Yat-sen, Sun even offered vast political concessions, such as Japanese control in Manchuria, claiming that the Japanese government would fare better with him than with his opponent, Yüan Shih-k'ai. Taken together, all these documented examples of Sun Yat-sen's bargaining reinforce each other too well to be discarded as mere forgeries and falsifications.

After Yüan Shih-k'ai's death, Sun Yat-sen attempted in 1917 to reestablish his own organization, first at Shanghai and then at Canton. He succeeded in setting up a government in Canton for a short time. Sun's Canton government was dependent on the favor of the warlords of Kwangtung and Kwangsi provinces, to whom Sun's name and organization gave additional political prestige. In 1920, Sun's party was again reorganized into a Kuomintang and the personal oath of allegiance to Sun was discarded. But no party organ was created for the discussion and determination of policy; the party was still the instrument of Sun Yat-sen's personal political power. During these years at Canton, Sun Yat-sen maintained himself not only by negotiating with the warlords of the south but also by participating in the warlord struggle of the north where he sided with T'uan Ch'i-jui's Anfu clique.

Sun Yat-sen saw himself as the destined leader of the Chinese revolution. He always insisted on personal control of his political organizations. The short parliamentary period of the early Kuomintang of 1912 to 1913 had been initiated by Sung Chiao-jen, contrary to the will of Sun Yat-sen. When this movement was defeated, Sun returned to his type of secret organization obedient to the will of its leader. In the early years of the *T'ung-meng-hui* he personally collected the funds for his organization and its activities; in later years he tried to attract financial and military support in exchange for the promise of economic and political advantages under a future Chinese government which he would form. As he had been defeated and was out of power, he was no longer very successful in gaining support. Sun's revolutionary organization seemed on the decline until he found a different outside source of support in the newly established Soviet Russian government. This contact with Soviet Russia, which began in 1923, led to a total reorganization of the Kuomintang on the model of the Russian Communist party.

4. THE INTELLECTUAL REVOLUTION

Nationalism

The problem that the West forced on China was that of adjustment to the concept of the modern nation state. By the treaties of the nineteenth century the Chinese were compelled to give up their traditional idea of the world state and to accept the Western concept of the equality of sovereign states. They were forced to agree to foreign diplomatic representation in Peking, the establishment of a foreign office, and the maintenance of Chinese diplomatic representation abroad. Acceptance of Western forms of international life brought more than a modification of China's relations with other powers; it negated the mandate of Heaven and the principles of the Confucian political order. It destroyed the position of the scholar-gentry, the organizing and controlling group in China. After China was forced into contact with the modern world, the educational system in which the gentry were trained was no longer adequate and was eventually abandoned. The revolutionary concessions to the West which brought about the negation of the mandate of Heaven and the undermining of the scholar-gentry shattered the whole structure of authority and consent upon which the Confucian state was based.

Having been compelled to accept the Western concept of the legal equality of sovereign states, the Chinese had no choice but to adopt the Western type of nation state. China had most of the components that in varying measure are regarded as necessary for the formation of a nation: a well-defined geographical home, ethnic unity, a common language, and the bonds of a common history and cultural tradition. The one element she did not have was the sentiment of nationalism which unites the people in loyalty to each other and to the state and which gives to all a feeling of participation in a common destiny. The problem for China was that of accepting and integrating the concept of nationalism in a new social and political order. The question was who would take the lead.

The violent impact of the West brought about certain reactions in imperial China which presaged the later growth of the sentiment of nationalism. During the Opium War, for example, the gentry organized local resistance against the British, whom they denounced for their disregard of the laws, institutions, and principles of China. When the imperial powers threatened China's dependencies, regional leaders took the initiative in defending the territory of the empire. They also initiated the Self-Strengthening Movement which was designed to modernize China's military and economic systems in order to resist the West. The more the pressure on China mounted, the more the spirit of resistance grew among the scholar-gentry. When the government decided to negotiate for peace with Japan in 1895 after a humiliating defeat, some 1,300 young scholars led by K'ang Yu-wei publicly protested in Peking and signed a petition demanding a continuation of the war, removal of the government from Peking, and popular resistance.

The first real attempt to create a nation state in China had been that made by K'ang Yu-wei in 1898. K'ang, who was very conscious of the modern world to which China had to adjust and of the main currents of Western thought, also believed that a Chinese national spirit could emerge only if the essence of Confucianism were preserved. He had attempted to transform Confucianism into a religious movement to provide the ideological basis for a modern state, to modernize the educational system, and to establish representative institutions. This unsuccessful attempt to set up a Confucian nation state had been made by a group of the younger gentry under the leadership of K'ang Yu-wei. The Reform Movement of 1898 marked the last attempt of a gentry group to adjust Confucian China to the West. For the next decades the role which the gentry had ceased to fulfill was not taken over by any other social group.

Yüan Shih-k'ai, who fell heir to the Republic, was the leading figure among the military men who now controlled public affairs. The military had a tradition of their own; their Chinese models were the regional leaders such as Tseng Kuo-fan and Li Hung-chang; their foreign models were Germany and Japan, countries in which a national army played a strong role. Yüan Shih-k'ai used German military advisers to help train his officers at his military academy at Paotingfu and to assist in building up his army on the German model. He tried to establish a modern state on the basis of the imperial tradition, a national army, and a Western legal system, but he did not secure support on a nation-wide basis and failed in his efforts. The military, however, remained a decisive factor in the situation. Their nationalism was too narrow and limited for them to appeal successfully for broad popular support, but as they controlled the armies no other group could do anything without their backing.

Even more futile than Yüan Shih-k'ai's experiment were the efforts of Sun Yat-sen to organize political revolution through secret societies and with the help of military officers. The parliamentary approach had no chance of success after Sung's assassination. Both Sun and Sung in their different ways were influenced by the important changes which were taking place in the social and intellectual life of the country.

Ever since the failure of K'ang Yu-wei the disappearance of the gentry had revealed the steady growth of new social classes in those areas of China where the influence of the West was most directly felt. These classes were the businessmen and workers of the treaty ports and the overseas Chinese communities, and the Western-educated intellectuals of the modern educational institutions in the capital and the treaty ports.

Trade and business, which had been looked down upon in Confucian society, came to be respected activities in the westernized society of the treaty ports. The new social class of Chinese businessmen was not vitally interested in the political struggle so long as the Western powers provided it with a sanctuary. These men had their economic interests to defend. They were concerned with Western, especially Japanese, competition and with the recovery of tariff autonomy. They participated in the political boycotts of foreign goods. The first such boycott, in 1905, was a protest against American exclusion of Chinese immigration. One of the most important boycotts was that directed against Japanese goods in 1915 over the issue of the Twenty-One Demands. The boycotts were used to encourage the purchase of Chinese manufactures and to support Chinese industries. While they supported boycotts and gave money to political movements, the businessmen rarely played an active part in political leadership. The other new social class, the workers, had little interest in nationalism during these early years.

The tradition of an educated ruling elite survived the dissolution of the gentry as an institution. The new intellectual elite which had been brought up in a westernized educational system had a high opinion of its own importance. The intellectuals, who were excluded from the struggle for power, searched for philosophical ideas and political systems which would solve China's problems and which would enable them to play their leading role in a new China.

The Influence of Western Thought

The intellectuals hoped to find many of the answers to their problems in Western thought. The missionaries and the missionary educational institutions did much to introduce the Western intellectual tradition. In the first decades of the twentieth century many missionary societies began to put much of their effort into education, especially higher education. Indeed, it was largely through Christian colleges which were established in the first years of the twentieth century that Western higher education was brought to China. Its growing popularity stimulated the flow of Chinese students to Japan, the United States, and Europe. In the years just before the revolution Chinese student enrollment abroad reached a high level which was maintained during World War I. Scientific studies were regarded as the most important contribution the West had to make to China. The curriculum of the Chinese colleges stressed chemistry, physics, engineering, and other technical subjects. There was also great interest in Western government and institutions. To students of history and philosophy scientific method became an end in itself, and a whole generation came to believe in science and progress. Educational work was also carried on by the YMCA and the YWCA. The YMCA organizations became independent of the missions and were mostly run by the Chinese themselves. Their educational program included many courses in practical training for business purposes. This practical approach was also applied in the YMCA's "citizen education campaign" which gave instruction in the mechanics of representative government.

One of the first to advocate the acceptance of Western virtues was Liang Ch'i-ch'ao, the leading disciple of K'ang Yu-wei. In 1902 Liang started a journal in which he published a series of sixteen articles on "The Renovation of a People." He believed that such Western virtues as civic morality, nationalism, regard for people's rights and freedoms, a sense of duty, self-discipline, self-respect, the spirit of adventure, the willingness to fight, the ability to unite and organize, and the general attitude of progressiveness should be accepted and cultivated in China. But he thought that they should be added to the Confucian morality which he still regarded as the foundation of Chinese culture.

The idea of combining Western thought with traditional Chinese beliefs, however, was given up by most of the Chinese intellectuals in the years after the revolution. The new group of young Western-minded intellectuals carried on a campaign against the intellectual standards and moral values of the Confucian tradition. The fall of the Manchu dynasty and the political weakness of China discredited the official Confucian philosophy in the eyes of young students while the impressive strength of the Western powers commanded their interest and admiration. In these years of political and moral disintegration respect for the Confucian tradition reached a low ebb and it was thought that Confucianism no longer suited the needs of a rapidly changing society. This was the time in China when the belief in science and in the possibility of solving all human problems through science became the predominant school of thought. Science was expected to make possible the material progress which alone could create a better society. As American influence was predominant in the new education, the pragmatism of John Dewey gained many adherents in China. A number of Chinese students who studied under Dewey in the United States later became leaders in China's intellectual life and were influential in spreading his philosophy. Dewey himself was invited to China where he lectured in Peking in 1919 and 1920. As a result of his influence pragmatism became one of the dominant philosophical trends among Chinese intellectuals. Although the German and French philosophers Driesch and Bergson had their Chinese adherents, the main stream of Chinese thinking came to be pragmatic and materialistic.

It was during the First World War that an ideological struggle arose between those Chinese intellectual leaders who wanted to merge the methods of Western science with the Chinese cultural tradition and those who believed in the possibility of a scientific civilization. K'ang Yu-wei and Liang Ch'i-ch'ao urged that the draft constitution of 1916 should include a clause making Confucianism the basis of moral education. This suggestion was defeated by those who were exclusively interested in Western thought. Among these were such men as Wu Chih-hui, a key figure in the Kuomintang and a strong believer in science as a panacea for all problems, and Ts'ai Yüan-p'ei, who had passed the highest examinations of the old system and then acquired a Western education. Ts'ai became Chancellor of Pei Ta (National Peking University), the first great non-missionary institution of higher learning and a center of new Chinese thought. In a lecture in 1917 Ts'ai stated that religions were obstacles to human progress and suggested that they should be replaced with a universal education in esthetics for the cultivation of an appreciation of the beautiful and the sublime.

The Literary Renaissance

The main attack against the Confucian tradition in China was the Literary Revolution which came during the last years of the war and culminated in the so-called May Fourth Movement of 1919. The leaders of the Literary Revolution aimed at the abolition of the literary language of the past. Chinese education had preserved the form of the Confucian writings as well as their content. The classics were written in an abbreviated style and used a different syntax and vocabulary from those of the spoken language. The written language was changed and developed through its use in political and administrative documents and historical writings, but it retained its abbreviated form and special structure. As time went on the written language became far removed from the living language. Traditional education in China required not only the memorizing of the characters, each standing for a word, but also a knowledge of the classical written language and its form of expression. The examination system itself helped to make writing more artificial. In the examinations a special style was introduced for use in the answers to the thesis questions, a style called the "eight-legged essay," in which the emphasis on form tended to overshadow the importance of the content. The abolition of the examination system in 1905 was a fatal blow to this classical literary tradition.

The problem of the form of writing became more acute with the introduction of Western education. The vocabulary of the Confucian classics was not well suited to the exact sciences. A new written language was therefore needed to express the thoughts gained from Western education. The attack against the written language and the classics went hand in hand with the attack on their content, and the effort to modernize the written language was a part of the struggle for a scientific education.

The new written language was the spoken language written in the characters of the classical language. There were some experiments with phonetic writing but very little came of them. The leading proponent of the new written language was Hu Shih, a philosophy student in America who studied under Dewey and became his strong admirer. Hu Shih was born in 1891 in Anhwei province and came from a gentry family. His articles proposing the use of the new written language, called *pai-hua*, appeared in journals in the United States and in China. His position was supported by Ch'en Tu-hsiu, who at that time was head of the literature department at National Peking University. On Hu Shih's return to China in 1917 the new writing spread rapidly among the Western-educated Chinese. It was used even in poetry, the field in which classical tradition had been most entrenched, and Hu Shih himself published a "book of experiments" which contained poems written in the new language.

Hu Shih claimed that this use of the spoken language for writing was not entirely new. The popular novels of the past were written in this way but had never been accepted by the classical Confucian scholars. For Hu Shih this movement was a restoration of the true Chinese tradition, a "Chinese Literary Renaissance," as the movement came to be called. But the movement was much more than a change in the style of writing; it was closely linked to the whole social and ideological revolution that broke out in China at that time. In the words of Hu Shih the leaders of the Renaissance movement wanted

. . . a new language, a new literature, a new outlook on life and society, and a new scholarship. They want a new language, not only as an effective instrumentality for popular education, but also as the effective medium for the development of the literature of a new China. They want a literature that shall be written in the living tongue of a living people and shall be capable of expressing the real feelings, thoughts, inspirations, and aspirations of a growing nation. They want to instill into the people a new outlook on life which shall free them from the shackles of tradition and make them feel at home in the new world and its new civilization. They want a new scholarship which shall not only enable us to understand intelligently the cultural heritage of the past, but also prepare us for active participation in the work of research in the modern sciences. This, as I understand it, is the mission of the Chinese Renaissance.[3]

The Literary Renaissance reached its height in 1919 when the new writing became the vehicle for the expression of Chinese nationalism. Chinese na-

[3] Hu Shih, *The Chinese Renaissance* (Chicago, 1934), p. 46.

tionalist feelings were aroused by the failure of the Chinese delegates at Versailles to recover the German rights and leased territory in Shantung province which had been taken over by Japan. The nation-wide demand of the Chinese intellectuals for the restoration of Shantung led to an outbreak in Peking on May 4, 1919. This demonstration, later known as the May Fourth Movement, was started by students and professors at Peking University, from where it spread among students all over China. In a short time over four hundred newspapers and journals appeared using the new written style. The new writing became a tool for the new nationalism. A year later the Ministry of Education decreed the introduction of textbooks for the primary schools in the new writing. In 1922 this decree was extended to include books for secondary schools, and from that time on the new writing became the vehicle of Chinese education. At the same time book publishers began to accept novels and general writings in what had now become the "national language." Together with the new writings in Chinese there appeared a wave of translations of Western literature.

Pragmatism, Materialism and the Question of Metaphysics

The leaders of the Literary Renaissance gained a complete victory in bringing about a general acceptance of the new style of writing but they met with considerable opposition to their attack on the Confucian tradition. An orthodox Confucianist such as Chang T'ai-yen was interested in the study of Western scientific thought but did not give up his belief in the most conservative approach to Confucian learning. Others, like Liu Ch'iu-an, warned against the acceptance of Western utilitarianism and the indiscriminate adoption of a Western civilization which had its vices as well as its virtues. He stressed the importance of maintaining the ethical principles of the past. The position of those Chinese scholars who held up the West as the model of science and progress was weakened by the impact of the First World War and the spectacle of the West engaged in self-destruction. There was widespread skepticism of the superiority of Western civilization, especially of the materialistic philosophy of progress. In 1919 Liang Ch'i-ch'ao warned against the uncritical acceptance of the so-called scientific view:

These materialistic philosophers, in the name of science, have established a purely materialistic and mechanical philosophy of life. They have subsumed under the "necessary laws" of matter in motion all activities of life, whether inner or outer. . . . Not only so, they identify psychological [processes] with what is spiritual, and on the basis of experimental psychology, arbitrarily assert that human spirit is nothing but a kind of matter, and is, like matter, under the control of the "necessary laws." For this reason, they cannot but deny the free will of men. If there is no free will, would there be any [point in talking about] responsibility of [doing] good and evil? . . .

With such a materialistic and technical philosophy of life . . . [man's] only aim would be struggle for bread . . . what interests would we have in life? What value could we attach to mankind? . . . [Science] has achieved in the last one hundred years several times as much progress in materialistic [civilization] as in the previous three thousand years. [Yet] not only does it not bring us, mankind, any happiness; on the contrary, it brings us calamity . . . the Europeans have had a great dream about science, dreaming that it is omnipotent, but now they are shouting that science has met with bankruptcy.[4]

Liang Ch'i-ch'ao did not attack science as such but rather the belief that science was the answer to all human problems. For him, "problems relating to the intellectual aspect of life must be solved by the scientific method: those related to emotions necessarily transcend science." These views, however, did not appeal to the rising generation of Chinese students who were turning to the proponents of a philosophy of science.

An uncritical acceptance of "science" as the key to all human problems prepared the ground for belief in a system which claimed to provide scientific answers to social problems. The Russian Revolution had left a deep impression on Chinese intellectuals. In the spring of 1918 a society for the study of Marxism, in which Ch'en Tu-hsiu took an active part, was established at Peking University. At first this society took a critical view of Marxism, which it approached as an academic study. This attitude remained unchanged even during the May Fourth Movement when the society published a special number of its magazine, *New Youth*, devoted to Marxism. When John Dewey lectured in Peking in 1919 and 1920, Ch'en Tu-hsiu and others of the Marxist study group were interested in his view that the democratic life must develop from the local village and town communities; it could not be imposed from above. Dewey's message was that democracy could be achieved only through a slow process and that social objectives were relative. He was particularly interested in the scientific approach which he described as the search "for concrete methods to meet concrete problems according to the exigencies of time and place." In contrast to the apparent indefiniteness of this general social philosophy the Communist theory provided the Chinese intellectuals with a system which also claimed to be scientific and to be based on a materialistic and antimetaphysical interpretation of human life. In addition, Communist theory provided a program of action, definite goals, and an historically determined role for the elite. Lenin's theory of imperialism as the by-product of world-wide capitalist exploitation linked the Communist doctrine to Chinese nationalist feelings. The role assigned to an intellectual elite in the vanguard theory of the Communist party was a special inducement to Chinese intellectuals, because the educated had always been a privileged ruling elite. By the end of 1920, Ch'en Tu-hsiu and his group had accepted Marxism-Leninism.

The period of the Literary Revolution also brought forth a revival of Buddhism and other forms of religious life. Buddhist study groups, such as those of Ou-yang or Abbot T'ai Hsu, attracted a small number of followers. The revival of interest in Buddhism, however, did not alter the general trend towards the belief in science.

The omnipotence of science was the issue in a philosophical controversy in 1923. The dispute began with a lecture at Tsing-hua College given by Dr.

4 "Ou-yu hsin-ying chieh-lu," in Liang Ch'i-ch'ao, *Yin-ping shih he-chi* (Shanghai, 1936), pp. 11–12.

Carsun Chang (Chang Chün-mai), a follower of K'ang Yu-wei and a student of Eucken and Bergson. In his lecture on "The Philosophy of Life" Carsun Chang asserted the need for metaphysics. In his view the exact method of the natural sciences could not be applied to the social sciences and humanities because the latter dealt with human problems. All human problems must be approached from a subjective, intuitive, and synthetic point of view, which recognized free will. Because of these characteristics the problems of life could never be solved by science, no matter what progress might be made in its method. Solutions for problems of this kind depended exclusively on man himself, as science could never bring life under its control.

Carsun Chang was immediately attacked by the many proponents of the scientific school, and a lengthy debate resulted in which a number of leading Chinese intellectuals participated. A large majority sided against Carsun Chang who was supported only by a few scholars such as Liang Ch'i-ch'ao and Chang Tung-sun, the translator of Bergson. All those who believed that metaphysics was unscientific and nothing but superstition scorned the views of Carsun Chang who was declared to have been "seized by the devil of metaphysics," who, after haunting Europe for over two thousand years, was supposed to have disappeared from there and now to have reappeared in a new guise in China.

The opponents of Carsun Chang came from several different schools of thought but they all shared a belief in the omnipotence of science. Ting Wen-chiang, a geologist and a follower of the English sensualist, Charles Pearson, opened the attack. Following Pearson, he denied all metaphysics and held that the content of psychological processes and concepts and inferences about truth were, without exception, the subject matter of science. The problems that had not yet been solved would be solved by science in the future. The belief that science could solve all issues was itself a necessary incentive that drove men to seek scientific answers. Ch'en Tu-hsiu shared in the attack against all Confucian tradition before he was a Marxist. Now his Marxist belief that "mind is but an expression of matter . . ." excluded any acceptance of Carsun Chang's metaphysical views.

Materialism was the dominant trend among the leading Chinese intellectuals—pragmatists as well as Marxists. It was perhaps most strongly pressed by Wu Chih-hui, one of the leading figures of the Kuomintang, who, like many of the proponents of the new role of the exact sciences, was not himself a natural scientist. For Wu science provided "a new conception of the universe and of life based on a new belief" which "ruled out the term 'God' and banished the soul or the spirit." Wu regarded man as a tool-making animal and science as the means of improving man's life, making him better and more moral. Wu Chih-hui firmly stated his belief in the words, ". . . the more material progress is achieved, the more goods will be produced, the more needs will be met, and the more easily will men be in a position to solve all the most perplexing problems of the world." [5]

Wu Chih-hui's view was shared by Hu Shih who at the time of the dis-

[5] Hu Shih, *op. cit.*, p. 92.

cussion was professor of philosophy at Peking University and recognized as the leading exponent of pragmatism in China. In a lecture series in Chicago in 1933 Hu described this ideological struggle in which he himself had participated. In his lectures Hu Shih refuted the Marxist view that economic forces were the only decisive factors in human development, but acknowledged that he shared Wu Chih-hui's materialistic and mechanistic approach which he termed the scientific view of life. In his lecture on religion, he tried to show how earlier in Chinese history Buddhist mysticism had been overcome by Chinese rationalism. After pointing to Wu Chih-hui's statement as an example of the combination of the rationalist tradition of the West with that of China, Hu Shih stated his own position as follows:

it is that combination [of the Western and the Chinese rationalistic traditions] which makes us feel completely at home in this world; and it is that which has led some of us better to appreciate the intellectual and moral significance inherent in Western civilization which the Western philosopher, because of the tremendous weight of a religious tradition, has not always been willing to recognize.[6]

In the debate of 1923 Hu Shih joined in the attack against Carsun Chang with an article entitled "The Monkey." In this article Hu Shih told the Buddhist fable of the monkey who tried to jump away from Buddha's realm but who, no matter how often and how far he jumped, when he landed, always found himself in the hand of Buddha. Hu Shih used this fable to illustrate his belief that no matter how far the human mind might jump, it would always find itself within the realm of science.

Those who upheld the "scientific philosophy of life" captured the younger generation which had come to think of metaphysics as coming close to idolatry and superstition. The controversy of 1923 revealed the thinking of the dominant groups among the Chinese intellectuals. Although every important Western philosophy found its advocate in China, pragmatism and materialism ruled the field.

The Chinese accepted and understood these two philosophies better than any other religious or philosophical systems they received from the West. The pragmatists held a naturalistic view of life and the universe and believed, with Dewey, that truth is an instrument changing with circumstances. There were many bridges between pragmatism and materialism. Around the time of the Literary Revolution the Chinese materialists followed the school of critical naturalism and were influenced by Haeckel's writings on the monism of substance.

This materialist school was later replaced by the Marxist school of dialectical materialism. The founder of the Chinese Communist party, Ch'en Tu-hsiu, who became one of the chief exponents of dialectical materialism, was once an exponent of the earlier school of materialist monism. The Chinese pragmatists were not hostile to either of these materialist schools; in fact the pragmatists and materialists joined forces in a bitter attack against Confucianism. The pragmatists tended to be tolerant of dialectical materialism and therefore of Communists, whom they saw as ardent champions

---

[6] *Ibid.*, p. 93.

of science and technological progress. The Communist movement was represented as an integral part of the Western civilization they admired, a logical development of the democratic ideal, supplementing democracy's so-called earlier individualistic stage.

The pragmatists helped to prepare the way for the spread of materialism in the next decades. By joining in the attack against Confucianism they discredited the traditional value system but themselves offered no new system of values. They proposed solutions to the problems of the day according to what Dewey called "the exigencies of time and place." Because the pragmatists themselves tended towards a materialistic and utilitarian interpretation they offered little resistance to Communist doctrine.

The two main philosophies of the Renaissance Movement inspired the thinking of the students of China. The ideas of the Renaissance were not limited to academic discussion; they were expressed in a mass movement propagated through a mass literature. In a popularized form they were used to express the emotions and aspirations of youthful nationalists. The country was flooded with pamphlets and writings on materialism, but the greatest impact on the thinking of the young intellectuals came through the vast new literature of essays, poems, novels, and dramas that followed the Literary Renaissance and expressed the intellectual ferment of the time.

CHAPTER VIII

The Modernization of Japan

1. THE MEIJI RESTORATION

THE beginning of the modern period in Japanese history is usually dated from the Meiji Restoration of 1868. At this time the long rule of the Tokugawa regime came to an end and the imperial institution, in the person of the new Meiji emperor, was ostensibly restored to its ancient glories. The men who came into power in 1868 were responsible for that extraordinary development which in the short space of half a century took Japan from seclusion to a position of world power. Fifty years after the Perry expedition Japan had undergone revolutionary changes at home, had expanded her dominions abroad, and was linked with Great Britain in the Anglo-Japanese alliance on terms of equality. During this time Japan had defeated her mighty neighbor China and had cast a shadow over the political independence of Korea. Japan's adjustment to the modern world passed through two stages: the development and triumph of the Restoration movement of 1868; and the events which led up to the granting of the Constitution of 1889. It was during this period that feudalism was abolished and some of the institutions of the modern state were established.

The Japan of late Tokugawa times was a society in process of change. All the political devices and social policies of the Tokugawa shoguns to preserve themselves in power were becoming less effective because that society did not remain static. The shogunate was not able to find solutions to pressing economic problems which it did not understand or to control social changes which it did not approve. The policy of isolating Japan from all foreign contacts had prevented an alliance between internal enemies and foreign powers, but it had not prevented contact with foreign ideas. For more than two centuries the shogunate had maintained the fiction that the emperor ruled and the shogun carried out his wishes, but this was recognized by everyone as a mere political device. Opposition to Tokugawa rule had been growing during this period, but it was not until the nineteenth century that there emerged several ideological lines of attack on the shoguns which could be used to challenge their position. From these various lines of attack, the Restoration leaders chose to emphasize one above all, the theory that in ancient days the imperial institution had enjoyed great power and prestige and that the shogun was a usurper who had taken all real authority away from the emperor.

The demand was for the shogun to surrender the power which he had usurped and to restore to the emperor his original and traditional authority. Such a line of attack on the shogun became more and more effective as Tokugawa power progressively declined. When Perry arrived in 1853, the shogun, faced with a foreign military force which he could not successfully oppose, felt it necessary for the first time to turn to the emperor and to the daimyo for political support. He wanted the throne associated with him in accepting the terms insisted upon by the West. The emperor and the court nobility were in no mood to help the shogun out of his difficulties or for that matter to come to terms with the Western powers. They were naturally supported by the leaders of the western clans who had been enemies of the Tokugawa from the very beginning of their rule. The shogun had to sign the Harris Treaty of 1858 without the emperor's support, a step which was an open reversal of the policy of isolation which the Tokugawa considered one of their main devices for keeping themselves in power. As the foreign powers came to realize that their treaties had not received imperial sanction, they put the shogun in a more and more embarrassing position by pressing for the emperor's signature and in this way played an important role in the development of those internal events which led to the overthrow of the Tokugawa shogunate some ten years after the signing of the Harris Treaty.

The Restoration Leaders

It was during these ten years from 1858 to 1868 that the combination of forces which finally overthrew the Tokugawa and their allies came into being. These forces included the four great western clans of Satsuma, Choshu, Hizen, and Tosa, which provided the armies and the territorial base of operations; the emperor and the court nobility, who served as the ideological justification for the overthrow of the "usurping shogun"; the merchants, who contributed money to the revolution which made their creditors solvent; and the peasants, who not only provided soldiers for Choshu armies but whose general discontent weakened the Tokugawa fiefs. Direction of this alliance came from the samurai, some of whom were the actual administrators of their fiefs, some of whom were intellectuals or new-style warriors, and all of whom were convinced that the Tokugawa had to go.

It has been estimated that about one hundred men actually directed the Restoration movement and set the policies of the new Meiji government. They were young men. Kido Koin, a samurai of Lord Mori of Choshu, was thirty-four at the time of the Restoration. Saigo Takamori, a samurai of Satsuma was forty-one, and his fellow clansman Okubo Toshimichi thirty-two. Sanjo Sanetomi and Iwakura Tomomi, two important members of the court nobility, were thirty-one and forty-three respectively in 1868. These were the most outstanding of the Restoration leaders but there were others who played an important role at the time and an even more important one after the Restoration. Ito Hirobumi, for example, was the son of a farmer who was adopted into samurai status in the fief of Choshu under Lord Mori. Like most of his contemporaries he was brought up in the Chinese classics and military science, but after the arrival of Commodore Perry's black ships in Tokyo Bay he took up the study of English. In 1863, at the age of twenty-two, he and his clansman Inoue Kaoru went secretly to England where they acquainted themselves with the material progress of the West. Ito returned to Japan in 1864 and had great influence on Lord Mori. Kido Koin, referred to above, was the son of a physician in the fief of Choshu; he also was brought up as a scholar in the Chinese and Japanese classics and was twenty years old when Perry came to Japan. Unlike Ito he had no personal experience in the West but like him believed that the Tokugawa had to go. Kido Koin performed the very important task of bringing together the fiefs of Choshu and Satsuma—the two most powerful enemies of the Tokugawa.

The young men who led the Restoration movement knew a great deal, either from personal experience or from reading, about the organization of Western states and in particular about the sources of their military strength. One important indication of this is that the fief of Choshu departed from the tradition of a privileged warrior class by recruiting well-to-do peasants into a modern army which was drilled and trained along Western lines. The young men who came to power in 1868 had thus initiated important changes in the territories of the western clans and knew in general what kind of government and society they wanted.

The various elements which combined to make the revolution were so disparate that it was no easy task to bring them together. Some of the daimyo of the western clans were interested only in replacing the Tokugawa, others, thinking that everything would remain the same except that the clans would live happily under the emperor instead of the shogun, took seriously the propaganda about returning to the ancient glories of the imperial institution. Others were genuinely anti-foreign and were quite serious about the second half of the famous slogan which the extremists developed: "Revere the emperor. Expel the foreigners." The Restoration leaders were quite willing to go along with any groups they could use so long as they fitted into the strategy of destroying the power of the Tokugawa which was for them the first step towards abolishing the institutions of feudalism.

The task of bringing the various groups together would have been much more difficult had it not been for the pressure from the West. After the signing of the Harris Treaty the shogun agreed to send a mission abroad to ratify the treaty in the city of Washington. A Japanese mission came to the United States, arriving in San Francisco in March, 1860. From there it proceeded to Washington, where it was very well received and given every opportunity to study American institutions and material achievements. A similar mission was taken to Europe by the British in 1862, where it studied everything from military installations to manufacturing methods and trade regulations. The willingness of the shogunate to send these missions abroad and to follow them with students for further study indicated that at this time the shogun was more willing than were the emperor and the daimyo to learn from the West.

In 1862 there occurred an event which had considerable influence on the course of domestic politics—the so-called Richardson affair. An Englishman by the name of Richardson, with some companions, found himself in the path of the daimyo of Satsuma. Not knowing the etiquette the situation called for, Richardson gave offense to the daimyo and was cut down. The retaliatory action taken by the British Navy included the bombardment of forts in Kagoshima Bay, a demonstration which persuaded many young samurai of Satsuma that existing Japanese weapons could not be successfully opposed to modern arms. Satsuma decided to begin the construction of a modern navy, for which the British offered their assistance.

In the same year the emperor's advisers persuaded him to put pressure on the shogun by announcing that on June 25, 1863, a decree calling for the expulsion of the foreigners would go into effect. As it was obvious that the shogun could not enforce the decree, the court expected that this would advertise his weakness and further damage his position. As the shogun showed no signs of enforcing the edict, the daimyo of Choshu took it upon himself to do so and began by firing on an American ship near the entrance to the straits of Shimonoseki. French and Dutch ships received the same treatment. In retaliation a joint naval expedition, in which the Americans took part, bombarded Shimonoseki. Choshu reacted in the same way as Satsuma before it, deciding to take up the study of Western military arts and to rebuild its armies along Western lines. The anti-foreign movement had been broken.

In 1865 the foreign powers sent a naval expedition and diplomatic representatives to Osaka to demand the immediate opening of the port of Hyogo. This time the court reprimanded the shogun's representatives for even considering the signing of a treaty without imperial sanction, and demanded their dismissal. The emperor finally gave his sanction to a treaty with the foreigners but the prestige of the shogun had been given another blow. In 1866 the shogun tried to recover his position by sending troops to punish Choshu for its earlier disobedience, only to have them defeated by the now much better trained and led Choshu forces. The peasant army fought the aristocratic warriors of the Tokugawa to a standstill.

Those who now rallied more and more around the emperor changed their estimate of the military strength of the West but did not give up their antagonism to the Tokugawa. On the contrary, they were well content to let the shogun bear the consequences of his inability to defy the European and American powers, for this played into their hands. The imperial party, therefore, continued to saddle the Tokugawa with their own traditional policies of excluding the foreigner and revering the emperor. At the same time the revolutionary leaders proceeded to secure the support they needed for the final blow. They got the necessary financial help for their movement from the merchants, particularly those of Osaka, by promising to further the aspirations of the merchants for social recognition. They also made full use of the discontent of the peasantry in the domains of the Tokugawa, promising the peasant title to land and freedom as a citizen—freedom which included the privilege of bearing arms.

The Restoration

The shogun and the emperor died in 1867. The simultaneous accession of a new emperor and a new shogun created an opportunity for the western clans to present the new shogun with an ultimatum demanding that actual power be restored to the emperor. The shogun resigned, apparently confident that he would be called back to high position by the emperor. He discovered very quickly that the western clans had no intention of permitting this and were instead intent upon his removal from power. The Tokugawa tried to restore their position by force of arms but were defeated and their two hundred and fifty years of rule came to an end. The Meiji emperor was restored, at least in theory, to full authority.

The attitude of the Restoration leaders was shown very clearly by the way they handled the Tokugawa after their defeat. They took over some, but not all, of their fiefs and administered them directly as the property of the central government rather than leaving them under the usual feudal arrangements. The leaders obviously had something in mind other than the restoration of feudalism under the emperor. The men who led the revolution could not have anticipated all the measures which were to be taken after 1868, but men who were able to bring together such disparate elements as the western clans, the merchants, peasants, samurai, and court officials in such a way as to have them all believe that their material and social interests would be furthered by the overthrow of the Tokugawa were lacking neither in a sense of direction nor in the skills of the professional revolutionary. Their brilliant opportunism stemmed from their sense of dedication and from their clear view of personal and national objectives.

The real leadership of the Restoration movement remained in the hands of the samurai from the four great western clans, who by and large kept themselves in the background and manipulated the affairs of state through officials with high-sounding names and titles just as they had done formerly in their own fiefs. They understood what their masters failed to perceive, that there was no future for feudalism. A new kind of state organization had to take its place if there was going to be a modern army and a modern economy to make Japan a strong nation.

The Reforms

The Restoration leaders moved rapidly and skillfully towards the abolition of feudalism. In 1868, the year of the Restoration, they sent government officials to each fief as representatives of the central authority. They then persuaded their own masters, the lords of the western clans, to hand over their domains, with the land registers, to the emperor. This precedent was then used to compel the other feudal lords to do the same. By 1871 the leaders felt strong enough, having behind them the troops of the western clans and those of some of the Tokugawa clans whose fiefs had not been taken over after the suppression of the Tokugawa revolt, to issue an imperial rescript abolishing the feudal fiefs and clans and putting an end to feudalism. The rewards for the western clans were high, for they were in a position to gain much more from office and power in the new government than by returning to their old domains. But the Restoration leaders saw to it that all the feudal lords, not only those of the western clans, were well compensated for the loss of their feudal rights, which had long been mortgaged and actually represented little but indebtedness. They were granted an annual pension of one-tenth the nominal income of the estates which they returned to the emperor. This was a very profitable exchange because the feudal lord was no longer responsible for his samurai, his debts were largely taken over by the government, and in terms of actual income he was better off than he had been before. The daimyo also were well taken care of when the government later established its new aristocracy with such new orders as baron, count, marquis, and prince by the Peerage Ordinance of 1884. To these new titles the government appointed the former daimyo, the court nobility, and those men who had been active in the Restoration movement, whatever their previous status. In this last group were some wealthy merchants and a few leading samurai.

The government did not provide as handsomely for the two million or more members of the former samurai class as it did for the daimyo. In 1872 the old class distinctions based on occupation were abolished, and the samurai lost their privileged position. This involved an adjustment which not all were able to make. The pension scheme for the samurai reduced their actual incomes by half, which in effect meant that they had to find some other way of making a living. The more enterprising and able samurai either found positions in the new administration or moved into commerce and industry, but for the bulk of them the revolution seemed to have brought little reward. The government was not indifferent to their fate; in fact it gave them preferential treatment in its own enterprises, including land settlement in Hokkaido, and pushed them into commerce and industry. They naturally gravitated to the army and navy, to the police corps—to which they brought the samurai contempt for common people—to teaching and to less respectable occupations. The samurai tradition lasted longer than the class. It was a tradition of valor and sacrifice and also violence. For many years there were always available to unscrupulous men, political parties, and even the government, men who would do anything from starting a riot to committing assassination.

The government rewarded the wealthy merchants of Osaka, such as the Mitsui and Sumitomo families, by making their debts a governmental obligation. More important than this, it legalized the mortgages held by the merchants on the feudal farm lands which up to this time could not be alienated. By a stroke of the pen large numbers of peasants became tenants and many merchants became landlords. The peasant, whose riotous discontent had assisted the Restoration movement, became a free man, able to move and to own land. Everyone, therefore, except the samurai went up in the social scale.

The introduction of a national conscription law was one of the most fundamental changes introduced by the Restoration leaders. The development of a national army struck at the very roots of the old society in which the bearing of arms had been a jealously guarded privilege. The Restoration leaders were spared the problem which had faced many other revolutionaries, that of external military intervention. They had the rare opportunity of putting their house in order without having to defend it at the same time. But the leaders were not spared the other and possibly more critical test of all new revolutionary governments, the economic test. It was one thing to transfer to the imperial government the personal debts of the daimyo, to establish pensions, to pay back the merchants who had financed the revolution, and to equip a national army with modern weapons; it was another thing to find the money.

The foreign powers had imposed upon Japan, as they had upon China, a tariff so low that the maritime customs could not become a significant source of revenue. Even more important, the tariff could not be changed without the permission of the powers, a permission which they were not easily persuaded to give. So pressing was the need for money that a mission headed by Prince Iwakura and including such important Restoration leaders as Kido, Ito, and Okubo proceeded to America and Europe in 1872 to study the West and bring about a revision of the treaties. The mission failed to secure any revision in the treaties which would have made it possible to raise more revenue from the maritime customs, but it learned a great deal about Western politics and the whole world balance of power. This information was actually more important than treaty revision would have been, for it gave these leaders the ammunition with which to crush the reckless expansionist policies of some of their more eager and less informed colleagues.

Failure to secure a revision of the treaties made it more necessary to take drastic measures to solve the financial problem. It was costing the government twenty million yen a year merely to meet the bill for pensions for the feudal lords and the samurai. The most important step in the modernization of Japan's financial structure was the institution in 1873 of a nationwide tax on land which actually became the main basis of the state revenue. In contrast to the feudal system of rice dues and labor service, this tax was paid in cash.

The Restoration leaders inherited a very confused currency situation, for several of the feudal fiefs had issued their own currency. In an effort to control the currency situation and to finance the government, Ito started the first national bank in 1873, copying American models. The Bank of Japan was established in 1882. Modern banking institutions and practices developed slowly because the government continued to expand the currency with inconvertible paper. It was not until nearly twenty years after the Meiji Restoration that Japan was in a position to establish a convertible currency and it was another ten years before she could establish herself among the eminently respectable by going on the gold standard. This was no small achievement. National control of the currency and regulation of banking is an essential feature of the modern state.

The financial burdens of the government were only partly eased by the establishment of banks and national control over the note issues. More drastic measures were necessary in the early days to cut down expenditures. Count Okuma, the Minister of Finance, made a tentative move in 1873 to cut down the largest burden on the government, the pensions paid to lords and samurai. On an optional basis, samurai whose pensions came to less than one hundred *koku* of rice (one *koku* equals five bushels) were given the opportunity to commute these pensions for a single payment, half in cash and half in government bonds bearing 8 per cent interest. The commutation was to be at the rate of six years purchase for hereditary pensions and four years for life income. It was not until 1876 that the government felt strong enough to make a similar plan compulsory.

The Samurai and the New Society

In this same year, 1873, in which the government started the national tax on land, opened the first national bank, and suggested the commutation of pensions, the problem of the samurai came to the fore in another form. It was far too soon for the social energies of the samurai to have been redirected with complete success into the building up of the new state. The natural bent of the samurai was to make a living as warriors; this was the only profession most of them knew. Many of them had taken very seriously one of the important elements in the ideology of the Restoration movement, the appeal to the ancient glories of Japan and in particular the doctrines of that great prophet of ultra-nationalism and expansionism, Yoshida Shoin, the patriot and royalist who had been executed by the Tokugawa shogun not long before the Restoration. Ignorant of the relative strength of Japan and other countries and of the facts of international life, a considerable group of samurai were in a mood where they sought not the long-range interests of the state but the short-range satisfaction of engaging in war.

Many of these conservative samurai were particularly angry at the refusal of the most important Restoration leaders to embark upon punitive action against Korea in 1873. Trouble with the mainland had started very early in the career of the new government. Taking over the claims of the

Lord of Satsuma to the Liuchiu Islands, the Japanese government made claims on China for reparations when some Liuchiu sailors, shipwrecked on the coast of Formosa, were murdered by the aboriginal inhabitants. At the same time the Korean government refused to receive a Japanese mission or to resume the custom of paying tribute. This might not have aroused so much feeling had not the Korean government answered one of the Japanese commissions in a very aggressive and insulting manner. The Japanese felt that the Chinese government was encouraging Korea in its resistance to Japanese overtures. On hearing of the rising demand among the samurai for war, the Iwakura mission returned hastily from Europe and proceeded to block the war party. As a sop to the advocates of war a small expedition was sent to Formosa, but this did little to satisfy and nothing to appease the conservative samurai.

The government proceeded to take further steps to absorb the samurai into the new social order. In 1876 it issued a ban against the wearing of swords in public, a traditional samurai privilege and the distinguishing mark of the class. In the same year the tentative plan of 1873 for the commutation of pensions was made compulsory. Frustrated by the decision against war in 1873, angered and warned by the measures of 1876, the samurai of Satsuma came out in open revolt against the government. They were led by Saigo Takamori, one of the young samurai who had played a part in the Meiji Restoration but who had not gone along with the revolutionary changes which followed it.

Saigo had offered to go to Korea in 1873 at the head of a mission which, he argued, would be insulted by the Koreans and thus provide occasion for war. Saigo felt that the best way to take care of the demoralization of the samurai, which followed their loss of status and privilege, was to occupy them in war. In this first great clash between the military and the civilian approach to national problems, the Saigo military faction lost to the Iwakura group. The most outstanding leaders of the Restoration, it will be recalled, were five men—Kido, Saigo, Okubo, Sanjo, and Iwakura. As a result of the clash over the Korean issue one of them, Saigo, left the government and went into opposition. He retired to Kagoshima in Satsuma where he opened a school for the training of officials and officers. In 1876 his own followers involved him in fighting with government forces, and the die was cast. Saigo led a large-scale rebellion. He is estimated to have opposed 40,000 troops against the government's 60,000. After eight months of civil war, during which Saigo's army suffered 20,000 casualties, the conscript armies of the government inflicted upon the rebels a defeat so crushing and final that never again was the government challenged by force. Saigo died on the field of battle. Another Satsuma man, Okubo, stood firm against the last flare-up of military feudalism, led by his childhood friend Saigo, in his own home territory of Satsuma, and remained a dominant figure in the government.

The strength of the young reformers was that they had a firm grasp of the essentials of power. No revolution can be brought about without violence or the threat of violence, and the Meiji Restoration was no exception. If a strong army had not been built up, all other things would have failed; but the Restoration leaders knew that a new military system could not be maintained without a new political and economic system. They acquired from the West all the knowledge they needed for their own specific purpose of building up the national strength of Japan. The introduction in 1872 of compulsory elementary education for a four-year period showed remarkable perspicacity. Universal education would be valuable for the new kind of army, necessary for the development of modern industry, commerce, and banking, a prerequisite for government propaganda, and a further means of undermining the class position of the samurai who had long monopolized learning. The Restoration leaders also understood that to get rid of extraterritoriality they must have a modern legal system. They proceeded to develop one on continental models. A desire to learn from abroad was not only openly professed, it was carefully organized. The Japanese tried to take from each of the Western countries those things in which it most excelled. Their students were not allowed to wander the world in the free pursuit of knowledge as were Chinese students later on. They were sent abroad to study specific things where they could best be learned. The government decided what things Japan wanted from the West and what things she should adopt. Men who were interested in military strength and national unity were quick to see the importance, for example, of the telegraph, which they brought in as early as 1868, and of railroads. The first railroad was constructed and opened for use as early as 1872, and by 1894 there were over two thousand miles of road in operation. They were quick to add a modernized postal and police system, to train a civil service, to create ministries in various administrative fields, and even to adopt the Western calendar. By and large they chose well, selecting what they wanted with the trained eyes of men who had not only seized, but were creating, power. The oligarchy did not merely order and dragoon the Japanese people into a new state and society. It released enormous social energies by changing the relationships between classes and by setting up a new institutional pattern within which those energies could find expression. An important part of that institutional pattern was the Constitution of 1889.

2. THE CONSTITUTIONAL MOVEMENT

The Satsuma-Choshu Oligarchy

From the time of the Meiji Restoration the government of Japan was in the hands of a small group of ex-samurai and court nobility, an oligarchy with unlimited powers. This oligarchy took over the Tokugawa administration intact and filled all positions with men from the four western clans, the highest offices going almost exclusively to the biggest clans, Satsuma and Choshu. Given the continuing strength of personal and clan loyalties, it is clear that the Restoration leaders had to fill every post with men they could trust. New ministries, new boards, and new missions were created as the unfolding program of modernization demanded them. The oligarchy could neither anticipate events nor control all the forces it had released, but because it was generally in agreement about the direction in which it wanted to go, it could usually maintain the initiative. Nowhere is this more clearly seen than in the events leading up to the granting of a constitution in 1889.

The first step toward the constitution was taken at the time when the oligarchy crushed the power of the Tokugawa. When the shogun was under pressure from Perry to open up the country, he put his problem to a group of feudal lords and imperial councilors, thus sanctioning the principle of a deliberative assembly which was then pressed by the anti-Tokugawa forces and became part of their propaganda. When the Restoration was completed, however, the leaders sought to modify the implied intention of continuing the assemblies, which some of the samurai of Tosa had made quite specific—suggesting an upper house of the fiefs and a lower house of the samurai—and set up a very narrowly based ruling oligarchy. The new government, however, put into the mouth of the young emperor the famous Charter Oath of April, 1868.

1. Assemblies shall be widely convoked and all measures shall be decided by open discussion.
2. The government and the governed shall be of one mind, and the national economy and finances shall be greatly strengthened.
3. Civil and military officials as well as the common people shall achieve their aims, and thus the people's minds shall not grow weary.
4. All absurd customs of olden times shall be abandoned, and all actions shall be based on international usage.
5. Knowledge shall be sought for all over the world and thereby the foundations of Imperial rule shall be strengthened.[1]

Part of the purpose of the Charter Oath was to give imperial sanction and prestige to the decision to open the country to the modernizing influence of the West. At the same time it was an appeal for support to all the classes which had assisted in the revolution as well as those who opposed it, but the appeal was for support without representation. It was to satisfy the pride and prestige of the feudal lords and the higher samurai that the government set up, after some experimentation, a deliberative assembly (*Dajokwan*) which consisted of two houses, an upper house or council of state made up of court nobility, feudal lords, and high samurai, and a lower house or assembly made up of representatives of the samurai in general. The lower house had no authority and the upper house was in practice merely the administrative committee of the oligarchy.

All might have gone well if the oligarchy had remained united, but it did not. The Korean issue of 1873 split the oligarchy wide open, and such was the determination of these unusual men that in the case of Saigo, the issue had to be settled by armed conflict. Itagaki and Kido, who left the inner councils at the same time as Saigo, adopted different tactics. Itagaki tried to secure his objective by political methods, the most obvious of which was to revive the idea of a deliberative assembly. For this purpose it was

[1] Nobutaka Ike, *The Beginnings of Political Democracy in Japan* (Baltimore, 1950), p. 438.

necessary to devise ideological weapons which could be used to embarrass the ruling oligarchy. Some of these weapons were borrowed from the concepts of Western liberalism which by this time had come into Japan through translations of Western books or via students returned from abroad. There was a broad familiarity with the political theory and practices of the Western countries, particularly England, France, and America. To those who were now the "outs" liberal ideas were useful weapons with which to fight the "ins."

Political Parties

Immediately after leaving the oligarchy over the Korean issue, Itagaki and his followers turned to the idea of organizing political groups to adapt Western liberalism to their purposes. In 1874, Itagaki formed a small group called *Aikokukoto*, the public party of patriots. For the first time they brought into Japanese politics the idea of human equality and popular rights; in fact the party pledge began with the words, "When men were created by heaven, there were attached to them certain fixed, inalienable rights, and these rights, having been bestowed upon men equally by heaven, cannot be usurped by human power." In practical terms they asked the government for a popularly elected assembly, charging that the government power rested not with the imperial house, to which they themselves remained loyal, or with the people, but with the oligarchy.

The most obvious connection between Western liberalism and Japanese conditions was the idea of an elected assembly. Stimulated by Itagaki's activities in the former fief of Tosa, from which he had originally come, political schools and associations spread so rapidly all over the country that it was possible to hold a meeting of their representatives in Osaka in 1875. In order to head off further growth of libertarian ideas, the government sent Okubo to meet with Kido and Itagaki. This meeting, the famous Osaka Conference, led to two concessions on the part of the government. One was to establish what was known as the *genro-in*, or council of elder statesmen, and the other was to set up a *daishin-in*, or supreme court, to "consolidate the judicial authority of the courts." Kido and Itagaki agreed to return to the government.

Repressive measures followed rapidly on the heels of these concessions. A new press law in 1875 increased the danger of publishing attacks on the government. Later the same year Itagaki again withdrew from the government. The Satsuma rebellion of 1877 was followed by even more repressive measures restricting freedom of the press and of speech. Such measures limited the expression, but did not limit the growth, of discontent. The movement for a national assembly continued to grow until the government countered with the "law of public meetings" of April, 1880. This law gave the police complete control over political meetings and speakers. All military and naval personnel, including the reserves, police officers, teachers, and some apprentices were forbidden to join political associations. The oligarchy apparently intended to make it impossible to form any political associations on a national scale or to conduct any political discussion in which its agents were not represented. Political parties were to be strangled at birth.

The anti-government ex-samurai were not easily intimidated. In spite of this pressure from the oligarchy the *Jiyuto*, or Liberal party, was brought into being by Itagaki in 1881 and issued a party platform calling for an extension of civil rights and constitutional government. The oligarchy was narrowed again by the resignation of Okuma, a Hizen man, who had chosen to press the issue of a constitution beyond the patience of his colleagues and to object to the apparent intention of the government to turn over a costly colonization project in Hokkaido to private interests at a fraction of its cost. The public scandal was so great that the government was compelled to retreat.

The resignation of Okuma became the occasion for the first really important step towards a constitution. Within twenty-four hours of his resignation the emperor announced that plans would be drawn up for a national assembly to be called nine years later, in 1890. Prince Ito was sent to Europe with instructions to study constitutions so that on his return he could draft a new constitution for Japan.

The breach between the oligarchy and Okuma could not be healed. When Okuma told the citizens of Tokyo about the Hokkaido scandal, mobs set fire to police boxes and destroyed government property. Having discovered the potentialities of public demonstrations, Okuma in 1882 established the progressive party, *Kaishinto*, a precursor of the *Minseito* party of the twentieth century. It was typical of Japanese politics that Okuma did not join forces with Itagaki's *Jiyuto*, the forerunner of the modern *Seiyukai*. Parties were groupings based on personal loyalties, and these still tended to run along clan lines. Now that Okuma of Hizen was out of the government and Itagaki of Tosa was in opposition, the conflict took on some of the aspects of a quarrel between the Satsuma-Choshu and Hizen-Tosa clans, the original four western fiefs whose alliance had provided the backbone of the revolution.

Preparation for a Constitution

The time had obviously come when the oligarchy must formulate its own philosophy of government and crush all competing ideas. Prince Ito, to whom the nine-year task had been given, proceeded to Europe in 1881 to study constitutions. He stayed there until 1883. Ito decided that the best model for Japan was Prussia, a part of Germany—a state which was only ten years old and which also had the problem of forcing the pace of industrialization. He brought back with him to Japan German constitutional experts who played a very important role in drawing up the constitution.

Ito proceeded step by step towards the constitution. In 1884 five orders of nobility were created in preparation for a house of peers. In 1885 a cabinet was established with ten ministers. Ito was the first premier and was made directly responsible to the emperor. Taking advantage in 1884 of riots which came about in protest against rising inflation, the oligarchy blamed them on the political parties, which were forced into temporary dissolution. A very important next step was to start a civil service, a move which indicated a willingness to broaden the basis of the bureaucracy beyond the four great western clans. In 1887 a supreme war council was set up to advise the emperor on the armed forces, and in 1888 a privy council with Ito at its head was established and given the job of reviewing the proposed constitution. In order to make quite sure that the constitution would be promulgated to an acquiescent people, a peace preservation ordinance designed to eliminate any possible opposition before it could get started was issued to reinforce the hands of an already powerful police. By this ordinance the police were empowered to remove anyone considered to be a potential troublemaker from any place within seven and one-half miles of the imperial palace and therefore out of the capital.

Constitution of 1889

On February 11, 1889, the new constitution was revealed, not to the general public but to a small group of carefully chosen officials. Newspapers were forbidden to comment. This was a constitution granted to the people by the emperor as a gracious gesture; it was not, as in Anglo-Saxon countries, an expression of the will of the people. The preamble of the constitution pointed out that the emperor had ascended the throne in a lineal succession unbroken for ages eternal—in fact it was claimed that this was the 2,549th anniversary of the founding of the Japanese empire and that "The rights of sovereignty of the State, We have inherited from Our Ancestors, and We shall bequeath them to Our descendants. Neither We nor they shall in future fail to wield them, in accordance with the provisions of the Constitution hereby granted." This was a constitution to end all constitutional discussions; it was a series of arrangements regulating the manner in which the oligarchy would rule the country in the name of an emperor who theoretically was the source of all power, whose position was "sacred and inviolable." The emperor was the supreme commander of the armed forces and he alone could declare war, make peace, and conclude treaties. He appointed and controlled all administrative offices, made laws with the consent of an imperial Diet, laws which were not effective without his sanction, and kept to himself important ordinance powers. The legislative body, the imperial Diet, was to consist of two houses with equal powers, the House of Peers and the House of Representatives. The House of Peers was partly appointed and partly elected by the lower orders of nobility and the highest taxpayers in the country. The House of Representatives, elected by the people, was the only body in which political parties could operate. The Diet, of which the House of Representatives was one part, could initiate legislation, but only the emperor could make it law. The Diet could stop legislation initiated by the administration, but it could not throw out a hostile cabinet which was responsible to the emperor alone. The Diet had the power to approve the budget, but the budget of the previous year came automatically into effect if the Diet refused to accept an increase. The Diet approved constitutional amendments by a two-thirds vote of members present in both houses, but only the emperor could initiate them.

The actual exercise of power was carried out through a number of organs grouped around the emperor. The two most important of these organs had been created before the constitution itself and were written into it. The council of ministers or the cabinet, under the direction of the prime minister, was one and the privy council the other. The cabinet had the actual duty of carrying out administrative affairs, while the privy council was more of a policy-making group centered around the emperor. Policy-making and administration were thus directed from above without any serious check by the people at large. There was added to the processes of government by unwritten tradition an institution which came to be important and influential, the group called the *genro* or elder statesmen. The *genro* were the political leaders of the Meiji period who, after an active political life, became the highest advisers to the emperor and formed an inner core of political power. This group of elder statesmen dominated the political scene for some thirty years after the granting of the constitution. It provided practically all the premiers and most of the presidents of the privy council. Leading military men, such as Field Marshal Yamagata and Oyama, were also *genro*. Few men have dominated the Japanese army or any other army quite so long and so thoroughly as did Field Marshal Prince Yamagata until his death in 1922. The *genro*, through the Satsuma clan, also dominated the navy and could count on it for obedience.

It is no exaggeration to say that the actual rulers of Japan for the last twenty years of the nineteenth century and the first twenty years of the twentieth century were the *genro*. Seven of them were samurai from the clans of Satsuma or Choshu, and the eighth, Saionji, a court noble, was a friend of Prince Ito. The *genro* provided the answer to the problem of running an absolutist administration within a framework of representative government.

The oligarchy might not have made even the limited concessions to popular government included in the constitution had it not had a healthy respect for the strength of the demand for broadening the base of government. The electorate that sent representatives to the lower house was limited by qualifications of sex, age, and income. Only men of twenty-five could be voters and there was the additional requirement of a minimum income tax, a limitation which was not removed until 1925. The requirement of a certain income level eliminated from the very beginning the radical elements in the political parties. The *Jiyuto*, for example, which had drawn considerable support from radical peasant movements, became, through the working of the constitutional system, a more conservative party. It was only by threatening to withhold approval of the budget that the political parties could exert any pressure whatsoever on the government. As this was a time of constantly growing government expenditures this power became more and more the means by which the parties gained their bargaining position in the political process.

There was still another way in which power was kept in the hands of the men around the emperor. This was in the field of military affairs. There was established an almost complete dualism between military and civil affairs. The movements of the military forces were not under the control of the cabinet but under the authority of the so-called Supreme Command. The Supreme Command of the armed forces was theoretically another aspect of the power of the emperor himself but in practice was exercised by a group of high military officers who were usually members of the *genro*, acting in the name of the emperor. This independence of the military authority could be, and was on occasion, exploited by the Japanese government to its general political advantage. If military adventures in the field failed, they could be blamed on the autonomy of the military; if they succeeded the government could take advantage of them. The military power in the governmental structure was not, however, limited only to the control of troops.

Though not required by the constitution it became a practice at the end of the nineteenth century for the ministers of war and of navy in the cabinet to be approved by the armed forces of which they had to be active members. Being in uniform they were under the authority of the Supreme Command and the chiefs of staff of their respective services. The military could at any time force these men to resign their positions or could order members of the services to refuse cabinet positions. The military could therefore bring about the downfall of any cabinet or prevent the formation of a new cabinet by refusing the cooperation of members of the armed services. They thus had a most far-reaching negative control on the process of government and the formulation of policy. The only way in which the military could be restrained by other political forces was through the Diet control over additions to the budget. As the main reason for the continual increase of the budget was the demands of the army and navy for funds, the military authorities were in constant conflict with the leaders of the political parties.

The decision to regulate the affairs of state through a constitution and the steps by which the decision was implemented illustrate the political agility as well as good luck of the small group of revolutionaries who built up the modern state in Japan. Although major changes, especially on the economic side, were still planned or in process, the revolutionaries had now become the nucleus of a new oligarchy which was as much concerned with political conservation as with economic innovation. The oligarchy had created a new aristocracy which reflected the social and economic changes which had taken place in late Tokugawa and early Meiji. It was composed of representatives of all the main groups which had come together to put through the Restoration—the imperial family and the court nobles, the territorial lords and samurai who had played an important part in the Restoration, and the newly created aristocrats from the wealthy merchants who had contributed money to the revolution. The oligarchy, however, did not limit the membership of the House of Peers to the aristocracy. As set up by imperial ordinance it was a mirror of the new social order. It included princes of the blood and all princes and marquises over the age of twenty-nine. Counts, viscounts, and barons elected representatives of their orders for seven-year terms. All these together added up to about 200 members. The emperor, on appropriate advice, appointed up to another 125 persons for life membership. The Imperial Academy, a scientific body, elected four members for seven-year periods and the highest taxpayers of each prefecture elected from among themselves around sixty or seventy members of the House of Peers. Such groups not only reflected the great social changes which followed the elimination of feudal institutions but also were well chosen to preserve those changes and see that they should go no further. The House of Peers had legislative powers equal to those of the House of Representatives, and its members often served as premiers and cabinet members.

The oligarchy could count on the general support of the aristocracy, which it had either created or brought to new heights of prestige, and through the powers of the emperor could always co-opt into its ranks the cream of Japanese leadership from any important class or group. But the development of the institutions of the modern state, together with the vastly extended area of government penetration into society, brought about an enlargement of the civil responsibilities of government that was to have important consequences. The oligarchy sprang from a military class, even if all its members were not professional warriors, and its success had depended very largely on its ability to organize and use a revolutionary army which crushed all opposition to the new order. When the Restoration took place the distinction between military and political measures was hard to make, but the development of a complex government structure involved differentiation of function. Most of the original leaders probably took for granted the dualism between military and civil affairs which the constitution so clearly recognized, control over the army being the decisive element in control of the country. The differentiation in function, however, brought out differentiation of outlook because matters of personal prestige and political influence were closely connected with types of responsibility. The split in the oligarchy between the Satsuma-Choshu monopoly and the Hizen-Tosa "outs" continued for some time along these clan lines but came to be more and more submerged in a deeper struggle between the civil and military branches of government. In this struggle the civilian oligarchs, who loved representative institutions no more than did the military, turned for support to the political parties, the wealthy family trusts, and finally to the people themselves. While it is true that the elder statesmen, the giants of the Restoration, ruled Japan to the end of World War I, they ruled over a rapidly changing society.

3. THE EMPEROR IDEA

The Constitution of 1889 was only the public and written description of the way in which the oligarchy proposed to rule Japan. It helps to explain how, but not why, the elder statesmen could maintain themselves in control for so long and with such effectiveness. Because government ultimately rests on opinion, as the oligarchs well understood, the reasons why the system worked as well and as long as it did must be sought elsewhere. The Meiji Restoration was almost a silent revolution; it released great social energies but not great slogans formulating the longings of the inarticulate masses. Men rallied around the cry of "Revere the emperor," it is true, but the increase in reverence did not bring any increase in power any more than the cry of "Keep out the foreigner" brought continued seclusion. Peasant and merchant got land and citizenship, social outcasts got equality, and men of low birth or great wealth broke into the aristocracy without the inspiration of universal appeals such as those which marked the French Revolution.

In Japan the revolution came from above and the new oligarchs differed from the old, not so much in their views of the relationship between governers and governed as in their understanding of the need for the creation of a new kind of power. It was due to peculiarly Japanese conditions that so much that was new could be introduced in the name of so much that was old, in particular, the institution of the emperor. The intellectual preparation for the Meiji Restoration had revolved around restoration of the ancient glories of Japan and of the emperor institution. It was the institution rather than the person of the emperor which was important, for the institution, with all the myths that went with it, was a symbol of unity to a clannish and warring people. The Tokugawa shoguns had carefully kept alive the myth that the emperor was the source of all power and that each shogun was invested by the emperor. The Restoration leaders developed the emperor institution as the central symbol in their ideological system. The emperor became the object of national worship, he acquired great wealth—in fact the imperial family became one of the richest in Japan—and he had to be accepted by all as the absolute ruler of the nation. His prestige had never been greater but his personal power remained very limited. The greater the reverence for the emperor and the more absolute his power, the greater the authority of those who ruled in his name. The Restoration leaders, therefore, deliberately set out to develop the cult of emperor worship, to make the emperor the symbol of national unity, to transfer to his person the strong feudal loyalties which all the social changes of Tokugawa times had not seriously weakened.

The attempt to develop personal loyalty to the emperor was the more necessary because of the destruction of feudal institutions. The Tokugawa had thought of an hierarchy of loyalty according to which, stated in over-simplified terms, the peasant was loyal to his feudal lord, the lord to the Tokugawa shogun, and the shogun to the emperor. To the peasant, if he had ever heard of him, the emperor was far away indeed. When the territorial lords were divorced from their lands, their retainers, and their peasants, a vacuum was created which had to be filled. The Restoration leaders filled the vacuum with a much enlarged emperor idea: all Japanese were to be equal in at least one respect, reverence for the emperor and obedience to his commands. As the emperor and the state were considered to be one and the same thing, and the emperor could be worshipped as the theoretic head of the state, Japanese nationalism took a form which was not common, at this time, in the West. For the first time in Japanese history the emperor was built up as an object of national worship, because for the first time there had arisen the need for mass allegiance; the new state could not operate through a tangled maze of petty individual loyalties; there could be no delegation of obedience.

Several important steps were taken to build up the emperor idea. His powers were defined by law in the constitution. Because the emperor promulgated the constitution himself, and he alone had the power to initiate amendments, the constitution itself was beyond the bounds of criticism, for no one was permitted to criticize the emperor. As the "rights of sovereignty of the state" had been transmitted from emperor to emperor, it was logical that ministers should be responsible to him rather than to the people. It is difficult to see how the oligarchy could have secured its position more thoroughly than it did by monopolizing access to absolute authority. Prince Ito, the chief architect of the constitution said, "The Emperor is Heaven-descended, divine and sacred; He is pre-eminent above his subjects. He must be reverenced and is inviolable. He has indeed to pay due respect to the law, but the law has no power to hold Him accountable to it. Not only shall there be no irreverence for the Emperor's person, but also shall He not be made a topic of derogatory comment nor one of discussion." According to the constitution the emperor was sacred and inviolable. He was also in supreme command of the army and navy, a power which Ito pointed out was to be exercised with the advice of ministers but like the imperial military command "nevertheless belongs to the sovereign power of the emperor, and no interference by the Diet should be allowed."

The emperor was such a valuable piece of property for the oligarchy that great care was taken to avoid disputes over the succession. The Imperial House Law laid down rules for everything from court etiquette to regency and succession. A special minister, independent of the fate of cabinets, the Minister of the Imperial Household, was appointed to regulate the affairs of the emperor and the imperial family. As Japanese politics came to be almost literally a struggle for the body of the emperor, the imperial household ministers, who controlled access to him, were obviously important people, chosen with great care by the oligarchy.

Definition of the emperor's position in the constitution was not enough. In order to have it accepted there had to be an emotional basis for the necessary reverence and obedience. The oligarchy attempted to do this by making the emperor the central figure in a revived and officially sponsored Shinto religion. In preparation for this Buddhism was disestablished after the Restoration and Christianity kept out as long as possible. Buddhism had received state support under the Tokugawa who thought it wise to sponsor a religion which kept people calm and peaceful, an outlook that hardly fitted the new regime. Temples were torn down and lands taken away from the Buddhist church during the early Restoration period although later in the seventies and eighties Buddhism came back quietly with a strong lay movement and without government opposition. When Christian missions were again tolerated in Japan in 1873, Christianity continued to be looked upon as an alien and dangerous challenge to the ideological basis of the state. In building on Shintoism the oligarchy was using what is generally thought to be the earliest religion of Japan.

Shinto, the Way of the Gods, is really an elaboration of the idea of ancestor worship. It is concerned with the divine origin of Japan, its people and its emperor as described in old documents. According to the legend the Sun Goddess, Amaterasu-O-mikami is the ancestress of all the Japanese people, and the emperor, a direct descendant of the Sun Goddess, is the father of his people. The ancestral deities who created the "land of the gods" continued to protect it and to guide the destinies of its people. Such divine guidance and guardianship imposes an obligation which requires the most unlimited loyalty to the emperor, who expresses the will of the gods. It is a short step from all this to the conclusion that those who are so divinely blessed should share their blessings with others; the emperor, in other words, should ultimately rule the world and establish therein the divine institutions. Such was the mixture of myth and history, of legend and reality, from which the Restoration leaders molded an extraordinary instrument for creating a mass loyalty to the imperial institution and the person of the emperor. In this way they gave Japan a unity which she could hardly have achieved in any other way and a sense of uniqueness which afforded some protection from foreign ideologies.

The imagination and vision of the Restoration leaders should not be underestimated. The problem of developing unity in Japan, of arousing an ardent and reliable patriotic spirit was not an easy one. Japanese history shows the Japanese to have been a warlike, factional, bickering people who at times exhibited a contemptuous disregard for personal or institutional loyalties. The idea of raising the person of the emperor to a sacred and inviolable status, of merging the imperial household, as it were, into the very bloodstream of Japanese history and tradition, of making an object of national worship out of something so little known and so recently insignificant, was the only solution sufficiently bold and dramatic to meet a situation in which an old moral order was dying and the people were open to foreign ideologies. The emperor idea was big enough to fill the need. It exploited existing Japanese values of loyalty and obligation, it was simple enough for everyone to understand, it could be related to every aspect of life and daily living, it was easily identified and not easily confused with anything else in the world.

The next problem was to get the people as a whole to understand and take a positive attitude towards the emperor idea. The establishment of universal elementary education was undoubtedly designed to provide enough literacy, not only for the training of a technically competent population, but also for the indoctrination of the Japanese people in the highly doctored version of Japanese tradition that went with the doctrine of the divinity of the emperor. Every child was brought up to believe that the emperor was divine and that all Japanese shared in the common descent from the Sun Goddess. As it was naturally more difficult to secure active acceptance of this mythology from the intellectuals, the state used all its police power to prevent criticism of the whole imperial line and to suppress anything else which looked like a "dangerous thought." The imperial portrait was displayed in all school houses and other public institutions, and deference was paid to the august presence as part of the routine of daily life. This was especially true in the capital, Tokyo, the former center of Tokugawa power, where all who passed the imperial palace removed their hats and bowed before the main gates. The emperor was the spiritual and temporal head of the state, and ministers were responsible to him—not to the people.

There was enjoined upon all citizens a common responsibility for the welfare of the nation. Society came first. It is easy to see that there was little fertile soil for the growth of movements such as liberalism and socialism, which flourished in the secular states of the West. In political thought no line was drawn between the rights of the individual and the authority of the state. The constitution itself underlined the traditional Japanese idea that moral and political philosophy are one. The preamble to the constitution, a document which could have been written in no other land, expresses better than any paraphrase the spirit that informs Japanese political thought.

Having, by virtue of the glories of Our ancestors, ascended the Throne of a lineal succession unbroken for ages eternal; desiring to promote the welfare of, and to give development to the moral and intellectual faculties of Our beloved subjects, the very same that have been favoured with the benevolent care and affectionate vigilance of Our ancestors; and hoping to maintain the prosperity of the State, in concert with Our people and with their support, We hereby promulgate, in pursuance of Our Imperial Rescript of the 12th day of the 10th month of the 14th year of Meiji, a fundamental law of State, to exhibit the principles, by which We are to be guided in Our conduct, and to point out to what Our descendants and Our subjects and their descendants are forever to conform.

The rights of sovereignty of the State, We have inherited from Our ancestors, and We shall bequeath them to Our descendants. Neither We nor they shall in future fail to wield them in accordance with the provisions of the Constitution hereby granted.

We now declare to respect and protect the security of the rights and of the property of Our people, and to secure to them the complete enjoyment of the same, within the extent of the provisions of the present Constitution and of the law . . .[2]

With this in mind it is possible to follow the definition of the Japanese government that was written by a former president of the privy council, Baron Hozumi, at the end of the century.

The Emperor holds the sovereign power, not as his own inherent right, but as an inheritance from his Divine Ancestor. The government is, therefore, theocratical. The Emperor rules over the country as the supreme head of the vast family of the Japanese nation. The government is, therefore, patriarchal. The Emperor exercises the sovereign power according to the Constitution, which is based on the most advanced principles of modern constitutionalism. The government is, therefore, constitutional. In other words, the fundamental principle of the Japanese government is theocratic-patriarchal constitutionalism.[3]

[2] In J. M. Maki, *Japanese Militarism, Its Cause and Cure* (New York, 1945), pp. 114–15.
[3] In Baron Hozumi, *Ancestor Worship and Japanese Law* (Tokyo, 1901), pp. 87–88. Quoted in Robert K. Reischauer, *Japan, Government—Politics* (New York, 1939), pp. 75–76.

The synthetic ideological structure built up by the Restoration leaders served its purpose, especially in the early years, but it was severely tested by the Japan which they actually created. From the very beginning it was more easily accepted in the villages than in the towns; it was especially suitable for a peasant army whose loyalty was of first priority. The formidable power of the state was strong enough to enforce the system to the very end of World War II, but long before that time the social changes that came with industrialization and the intellectual influences which no censorship could keep out had eaten into the tough fabric of emperor worship and all that went with it.

4. THE GOVERNMENT AND THE DIET

The Oligarchy and the Parties

By the time of the granting of the constitution the leaders of the Restoration were middle-aged and as a group had come to be known as the *genro* or elder statesmen. They continued to monopolize the highest offices of state under the new constitution up to the end of the First World War in 1918. From the time of the establishment of the premiership in 1885 until 1918 there were only one or two cases when it was out of the hands of the *genro*. The office rotated between Ito, Yamagata, Katsura, and Terauchi of Choshu; Kuroda, Matsukata, and Yamamoto of Satsuma; Okuma of Hizen; and Saionji, a former court official and a friend of Ito. The same men dominated, for most of this period, the privy council, the army and the navy. The dominance of the Satsuma and Choshu clans is obvious.

Even before the Diet met for the first time in 1890, the government was facing opposition owing to its lack of progress in revising the unequal treaties. The frantic efforts which had been made to develop a judicial system satisfactory to the Western powers had not yet borne sufficient fruit to persuade the powers to give up extraterritoriality. With the help of the French jurist Gustave Boissonade, Japan's court system had been reorganized along the lines of the French system. The first new penal code and code of criminal procedure, based on French models, were promulgated in 1880 and put in operation in 1882. A code of civil procedure, taken from the German system, was ready by 1889 and was put into operation two years later. But new civil and commercial codes were not introduced until the years 1896 and 1899.

Most of the reforms thus far were on paper because Japan did not yet have the trained lawyers to put them into practice. The government could point to treaties with America in 1878 which gave Japan its tariff autonomy and control of all coastwise traffic. But even though the State Department took the precaution of insisting that these concessions should not go into effect until other powers had made similar agreements, the United States did not yet consider the time ripe for the abolition of extraterritoriality. Count Inoue, foreign minister in 1882, approached the foreign ambassadors in

Tokyo on the subject of treaty revision but achieved nothing more than an extradition treaty with the United States.

Count Okuma, who succeeded Inoue as foreign minister in 1887, again tried to bring about revision of the treaties by negotiating with the powers one by one. All he secured was a treaty with Mexico in 1888, negotiated on the basis of equality. After his failure Okuma was the victim of an attack by ultranationalist Japanese in which he lost his leg, and Premier Kuroda resigned over the issue of treaty revision. Yamagata, the Choshu samurai, a purposeful and ruthless militarist, accepted the premiership. The two important parties among the nine which had representatives in the Diet, Itagaki's *Jiyuto* and Okuma's *Kaishinto*, led the stormy criticism of the government and openly defied the Satsuma-Choshu oligarchy. Count Ito, as president of the House of Peers, was able to neutralize the attempts of the lower house to cut the budget but the government's complete absence of party support left the field wide open to its critics.

The main motivation of Itagaki and Okuma was to oppose, as representatives of Hizen and Tosa, the Satsuma-Choshu monopoly. In order to do this they needed weapons, and the weapons came to have considerable importance. The main weapon was the demand that the cabinet should be responsible to the Diet, a direct challenge to the constitution itself. When the second session of the Diet met at the end of 1891 with the premiership now in the hands of Matsukata, the two party leaders launched an attack upon the government that was designed to hold up the working of the constitution until the parties should have a share in political control. The government resorted to a device which it came to use a great deal during the next decade; it dissolved the House of Representatives and forced a new election.

The efforts of the government in the elections of 1892 to tip the scales in its own favor by using the police power of the state were met by riots, especially in Tosa, Itagaki's birthplace, and the new Diet was still overwhelmingly against the government. Count Ito took over the premiership from Matsukata and, finding himself facing an uncontrollable lower house, took the extreme step of securing an imperial rescript in order to break its opposition and secure his budget. The impact of the imperial rescript did not last very long. The political parties, especially Okuma's, returned to the attack and embarrassed Ito to such an extent that he resigned for a brief period. He came back very quickly, however, armed with another statement from the throne, this time to the effect that the emperor alone could appoint or remove ministers of state. The unruly Diet was dissolved and new elections were held in March, 1894. In spite of the use of its police power the government was still unable to secure a majority in the Diet and had to face further attack. Refusing to pass any legislation, the Diet insisted upon first sending to the emperor an address to the throne but the oligarchy chose to have the emperor refuse to accept the address and again dissolved the Diet.

Count Ito, the framer of the constitution, found himself in a position where something drastic had to be done to make the instrument work. So long as the oligarchy refused to yield on the question of Diet control of the cabinet,

Okuma and Itagaki continued to obstruct all legislation. It was at this time that Ito, possibly because his personal prestige was at stake, made a decision which solved the problem of the Diet, at least for the time being. In 1894 Ito came out in favor of war with China over the Korean issue.

Events in Korea for a period of over ten years had led to increasing demands in Japan for war. Ito had a choice of continuing to block the war party in the oligarchy, of resigning and leaving the field to Prince Yamagata, who was the chief protagonist of war, or of uniting both the oligarchy and the nation by precipitating conflict with China. He chose the last course of action, with the anticipated result of bringing the whole country for the first time to the support of the government. There was no trouble with the new Diet, which voted to give the government any amount of money it required for the purposes of the war.

Ito and Yamagata

The rivalry between Ito and Yamagata, which now came out into the open, had very important consequences for Japanese institutions. The personal rivalry dramatized the struggle between the civil and the military branches of the oligarchy which gradually merged into a conflict between the military and the parties. Both men came from the same clan but each had made different contributions to post-Restoration Japan. Ito's prestige rested upon his abilities as a statesman, on his knowledge of foreign countries, and on his reputation as the framer of the constitution and the architect of the imperial idea. He was not a man to shrink from the use of violence or police repression; he was autocratic by nature and no admirer of democracy. But he knew more than most of his colleagues about the power of the West and did not wish to see his handiwork in Japan thrown away in reckless adventures abroad.

Yamagata's first contribution to the Restoration was the organization of a military force in Choshu which included peasants. He took a leading part in the fight against the Tokugawa. A year after the Restoration he went to Europe to study military matters and on his return began the organization of the new Japanese army. He was mostly responsible for the introduction of conscription, and it was he who put down the Satsuma rebellion of 1877. His views on democracy were expressed in a letter to Ito in 1879 in which he said ". . . every day we wait, the evil poison [democracy] will spread more and more over the provinces, penetrate into the minds of the young, and inevitably produce unfathomable evils." [4] Yamagata was Minister of State for Home Affairs in the years immediately before the promulgation of the constitution. It was he who used the army and the police to restrict the activities of the political parties and who enforced the peace preservation law of Christmas Day, 1887, by which the government cleared 500 of its political opponents out of Tokyo. Yamagata was the first premier under the constitution, a document which he had slowly and reluctantly come to accept

[4] Ike, *op. cit.*, p. 93.

as a necessary evil. From the time of his first experience with the unruly Diet, Yamagata determined that party politicians should never, if he could prevent it, interfere with the interests of the army. It was his determination to put the interests of the army above everything else that led him into conflict with his old friend Ito.

Prince Ito remained premier while Yamagata and Oyama took charge of the military expeditions, which were successful. They returned as heroes. Ito negotiated the Treaty of Shimonoseki with China and the terms which he secured were acceptable to Japan, but when Russia, France, and Germany compelled Japan to give up the Liaotung Peninsula, it was Ito who had to take the blame. To the Japanese military and even to the political parties, it seemed that Japan had come out of the war with little to show for her victories.

Ito had to face the Diet again in December, 1895, after the Treaty of Shimonoseki had been signed. Under attack from Okuma, Ito accepted the support of Itagaki and his party, and for a time it looked as if the rival oligarchies would form alliances with the parties. Matsukata, who succeeded Ito as premier, made Okuma the Minister of Foreign Affairs in order to secure the support of Okuma's political party now called the *Shimpoto*. The Satsuma-Choshu oligarchs rapidly closed ranks again, however, on the issue of refusing to make the cabinet responsible to the lower house, and by December, 1897, the government found itself facing the combined forces of Okuma's *Shimpoto* and Itagaki's *Jiyuto* in the Diet, which was dissolved for the fourth time.

There would have been considerable danger to the program that the oligarchy had outlined for Japanese economic development if the political parties had secured control over the cabinet in these early years. The election law provided for only 460,000 voters, with high property qualifications, in a population of fifty million people. The voters were mainly landlords, many of whom were also interested in local industries such as sake brewing. The political parties, which depended on their votes, reflected their grievances. The vehemence of the attack on the government, especially by the *Jiyuto*, was mainly due to resentment against high taxes on the land and local industries and government use of this money for the financing and construction of big industries, for government policies hurt the *Jiyuto* supporters both ways—as landlords and as small local industrialists. The parties defeated the government land tax bill in 1898, and the Diet was again dissolved. So bitter had become the opposition to the government that Okuma and Itagaki amalgamated their followers to form a new party, the *Kenseito* or constitutional party.

The elder statesmen met to consider the situation. Ito wanted to make the constitution work by organizing a government party, but this idea ran into opposition from Yamagata, a blunt and uncompromising enemy of all political parties. Yamagata also possibly saw in this device, if it were successful, a means by which Ito, who would control a party, could remain in power indefinitely. Yamagata also opposed Ito's next move, which was to suggest that the political parties be invited to form a government, but the proposal won out in the end. The party leaders were taken by surprise when they were ordered to form a government, but as they controlled two-thirds of the members of the lower house, they seemed to be in a strong position to do so. Okuma became premier and Itagaki, home minister.

It seemed to Ito that by one stroke, Yamagata had been restrained and the constitution made to work. There followed two years of party government which ended in a complete collapse of the coalition and the failure of this first attempt at party rule. If Yamagata had consented to a party government in the hope that it would be discredited, he could not have had his wishes better fulfilled. The party leaders fell out over the division of the spoils; Itagaki's followers resigned from the cabinet and Okuma had to give up the premiership. Yamagata moved in quickly and formed a new ministry before Ito could return from a trip which he was making to China. Yamagata bought a majority of votes in the lower house by bribing Itagaki's followers to cooperate with him. Such an alliance could not last too long, however, because the government needed more and more money for the army and navy, and there was only one source from which it could be readily raised— the tax on land. Yamagata, therefore, sought to redress the balance of political forces in the Diet by proposing to increase the number of representatives from urban areas. It was in these areas that Okuma, whose party was now called the *Kensei-Honto*, found its greatest strength. The *Kensei-Honto* naturally supported the government's new election law which increased the membership of the lower house from 300 to 381 and doubled the electorate. Yamagata, who hated political parties, recognized that he needed their support. The House of Peers was just as angry with Yamagata for allying himself with political parties as it had previously been with Ito.

When Ito returned from China in 1900, he realized that he would need powerful allies in order to counterbalance the increasing influence of Yamagata and the military. In an open bid for the support of the political parties he came out in favor of party government, a move which succeeded in breaking the alliance between Yamagata and the *Kenseito*. In fact the *Kenseito* dissolved itself and emerged again as the *Seiyukai* of which Ito himself became the leader and organizer. As this put Ito at the head of the majority party in the Diet, Yamagata withdrew as premier and turned the office over to Ito. Okuma came back as the head of the only other large party, the *Kenseihonto*. Ito was in a difficult position because Yamagata had entrenched himself with the House of Peers by playing on the prejudices of the peers against a leading oligarch who had given prestige to one of the political parties by becoming its leader. Ito was forced to resign, and Yamagata promoted one of his own men, Katsura, to the office of prime minister. In 1903 Ito persuaded his friend Prince Saionji to take over the leadership of the *Seiyukai* and retired from active participation in party politics by accepting the presidency of the privy council. Ito's last act as the head of the *Seiyukai* had been to compel it to vote in favor of the government's taxation bill in order to strengthen the armed forces for the coming war with Russia.

The more Japan increased her foreign commitments, the stronger became the influence of the military branch of the oligarchy. When he was premier in 1898, Yamagata attached a supplement to the imperial ordinances for army and navy matters in which he indicated that the only persons eligible to become ministers of war and navy should be high officers on the active list. No opposition was raised to this rule, which became effective in 1900, and from then on Yamagata and his military successors could make or break a cabinet by appointing or refusing to appoint ministers of war and navy.

The political parties had created a great deal of trouble and embarrassment for the government, but they had lost the battle to change the constitution in the direction of cabinet responsibility to the Diet and they had failed to make the constitution unworkable. As the threat of war with Russia grew greater, the parties could hardly put themselves in the unpatriotic position of refusing to vote increased appropriations for the army and navy. The political parties tended more and more to give up the effort to control the cabinet and instead competed with each other in making political bargains with the government in power. If the spoils of office were the chief objective, more were to be obtained this way than by perpetual opposition.

The head-on collision between the oligarchy and the lower house which marked the first decade of constitutional rule was followed by a period, lasting from 1901 to 1912, in which the government had the support of the *Seiyukai* party. Two men, Katsura and Saionji, alternated the premiership during these years, and in spite of their differences both drew parliamentary support from the same source. The war with Russia (1904–05) brought with it a surge of patriotism which obliterated all outward signs of party difference and the government had no difficulty in raising all the funds that it needed. At the end of the war, however, the lower house reflected public disappointment over what seemed to be a small return for so large an outlay, and the government came under strong attack. The militarist Katsura skillfully maneuvered the civilian Saionji into the premiership in order to avoid the damaging blasts of public criticism and the financial difficulties following the war. Ito was sent to Korea as the first resident-general. He accepted this post in the hope that he could prevent the annexation of Korea, feeling that this would get Japan into waters beyond her depth, give more prestige and power to the military, and divert the capital resources and industrial development of Japan into purely military channels.

In 1908 Saionji could no longer solve Japan's acute financial problems, at least not to the satisfaction of the military, whose demands were constantly increasing. In spite of the fact that Saionji came out of the elections of 1908 with his *Seiyukai* party in complete control of the lower house, the oligarchs replaced him with Katsura so that they could move on to the annexation of Korea without the embarrassment of forcing Saionji to go against the wishes of his friend and sponsor Prince Ito. Ito was removed from the resident-general position in Korea and sent on a tour of Korea and Manchuria in order to keep him away from Japan. He never came back alive. He was assassinated by a Korean in the city of Harbin. Yamagata, now operating from behind the scenes, used the national indignation over the murder of Ito to bring about the very thing that Ito had least desired, the annexation of Korea, in 1910. There was now no one to challenge the enormous influence of Yamagata, not even Saionji, who came back to the premiership again. When he tried to resist further increases in the size of the army, Saionji was elevated to the position of *genro*, the last to be appointed to this exclusive group. The influence of Yamagata lasted until his death in 1922, by which time great changes had taken place in Japan's internal and external position.

5. ECONOMICS AND POLITICS 1889–1922

Impact of Economic Change

The Restoration leaders needed all their tremendous political power in order to push through the economic changes which they had in mind. They had been determined from the first to construct an economy sufficiently industrialized to enable Japan to hold her own in the modern world. The oligarchy was agreed on the general direction. Ito and Yamagata differed on the question of how much of the national resources should go into strengthening the military forces, and how much should go into developing the economy, but both wanted the same kind of Japan.

The Restoration leaders had forced through most of the measures necessary for the development of a capitalist economy before they were compelled to grant a constitution. They had abolished feudal institutions, legalized private property in land, started a Western-style legal system, established compulsory education, organized modern departments of central and local government, and removed the legal barriers between social classes. The government had built railroads, opening the first eighteen-mile stretch in 1872, had introduced the telegraph for commercial use, started a postal system, set up banks, reformed the currency, permitted foreign travel, allowed newspapers and magazines to be published, and encouraged the idea that business was a respectable and desirable occupation. The Restoration leaders very adroitly used the prestige of the emperor, who became a very rich man, and the imperial family soon extended their holdings in practically every important business enterprise in Japan, and later in the colonies. Rich merchants became aristocrats, and peers of the realm were permitted to become capitalists. Manners and customs changed dramatically. Samurai were ordered to remove the knot of hair worn on the head and to wear their hair in Western style; swords could not be worn on the streets and European-style clothes were given official blessing. The Gregorian calendar came into force on January 1, 1873, changing holidays and festivals.

The chief opposition to Western customs and to the forced pace of industrialization came from the rural elements, the noisy and articulate landlords, who found a leader in Itagaki and who even dominated Okuma in

spite of his connections with urban elements and his genius for appealing to
to the city crowds. The daimyo with their commuted pensions and the ex-
samurai with their enterprise and native ability went into trade and small-
scale industry, such as sake-brewing, with considerable success, but they were
not willing to be heavily taxed, if they could prevent it, for the purposes decided on by the oligarchy. But at this stage the oligarchy refused to solve the
problem of capital accumulation by involving the country in heavy foreign
loans on the grounds that this would bring with it foreign control. The money
had to come from the only major source of revenue in an agricultural country, the land taxes. The political problem and the economic problem were
therefore inextricably intertwined—how to rob the country in order to build
up the towns.

About the same time the government announced that it was prepared to
grant a constitution, it began the process of selling to private owners all those
state enterprises which did not relate immediately to military needs. Several
reasons have been offered by Japanese economic historians for this decision,
such as the high cost of operating government-owned factories, the possibility
that model factories had already done their work of demonstration, and the
suggestion that by selling government properties at low prices to ambitious
and able ex-samurai the opposition of this discontented class could be diverted or divided. The process began in 1881, and in 1887 the government
encouraged private enterprise even in railroad construction. But when the
first Diet met, the agrarian interests had by far the largest representation in
the lower house, and a government which wanted to increase land taxes found
itself in constant trouble. Of the 300 electoral districts only seventeen were
urban and in the first election the commercial and industrial classes had only
nineteen representatives, a number which increased steadily but which even
in 1898 was no more than forty-two. The lower house attacked the government on practically every issue it brought up; in fact it set out on a deliberate
campaign to make the constitution unworkable, but its main concern was
with the economic issues of taxation, prices, and government subsidies.

The representatives of agrarian interests in the lower house were aware
of the poverty and depressed conditions of the peasant, but they were elected
only by those who paid high taxes. The agrarian revolution which had come
with the institution of private property and the legal equality of peasant and
samurai brought with it serious changes in the countryside. In general the
tendency was for the division between landlord and peasant to grow sharper,
both economically and politically. Landholdings in Japan were not on a very
large scale but the economic differences between the top and the bottom of
the scale were very considerable. The policies of the oligarchy tended to make
them greater. The number of tenants increased and the number of landlords
decreased. The hierarchy of ownership had many stages. There were those
landlords who lived on the land and supervised their tenants, those who were
half landlords or even cultivators and half entrepreneurs in rural enterprises,
those who were absentee landlords, those who were part owners, part cultivators, those who were pure tenants, and at the bottom of the scale the land-

less agricultural laborers. The simple device of demanding land tax in cash, instituted after the Restoration, had several consequences. Although the tax was at first actually lower than in Tokugawa times it forced the landlord to get cash and therefore to be more dependent on city markets, a trend which he disliked. The tenant, however, continued to pay his rent in kind on the basis of a percentage of the main crop, a custom which worked to the advantage of the landlord and the disadvantage of the peasant. The tenant was almost invariably in debt and therefore had to sell his rice crop long before harvest. And once in debt to a usurer the peasant rarely got out again. In a period of rising prices—and there was a general tendency for prices to rise—the landlord with his fixed money tax stood to gain, while the tenant paying his rent in kind profited not at all from the high prices and had to pay more for manufactured goods. The depressed condition of the peasant inevitably led to landlord-tenant disputes and sporadic peasant outbreaks.

The fact that the agrarian representatives put up such a bitter struggle against the oligarchy in the first decade of the constitution was mainly due to the stresses and strains that came with the revolution in agriculture. The political battle should not obscure the fact that the oligarchy got many of the things that it wanted. For one thing the growing commercialization of agriculture, the increase in the size of holdings and therefore of the unit of production, the gradual application of science to agriculture, all combined to bring about an increase in the production of rice per unit of land under cultivation. According to official figures the production of rice increased from 10,692,000 *koku* in 1882 to 50,222,000 in 1913. This achievement was partly due to the operation of forces set in motion by the government, such as changes in the tax structure, subsidization of urban industry and the consequent demand for cash crops, and partly due to direct government action.

The government took the initiative in making available to the farmer better seeds, implements, and fertilizers, in setting up rural banks, agricultural schools, and experiment stations. Much of the government interest was motivated by the desire to secure goods for export; hence the encouragement of tea and silk production, which paid off very well later on. Japanese export of silk caught up with that of China by 1910, a remarkable development considering the relative sizes of the two countries, and one which indicated the extent to which the Japanese farmers, two-thirds of whom were engaged in the raising of silkworms, had come to be tied in with the world market. The close relationship between agriculture and the world market, through silk and tea, was a tremendous risk, as the sharp decline in American buying of silk was to demonstrate, but while the export market was maintained the Japanese farmer lived somewhat better than his Chinese neighbor. It took government action to bring about this economic pattern, for the first tendency after the Restoration had been to follow the Tokugawa pattern of supplementing agriculture with local industries, such as the manufacture of soy sauce, bean paste, and silk, owned by local landlords to serve a local market. It was this pattern that the lower house tried unsuccessfully to keep.

There was one crop, however, which the government discouraged. Finding that Indian cotton was superior to Japanese, the government set about the mechanization of the spinning industry on the basis of Indian rather than Japanese cotton, a decision which led to the rapid decline of the cotton-spinning handicraft industry. In the decade before the Sino-Japanese War the development of the spinning industry was indicated by the increase in the number of factories from twenty to forty-five, of spindles from 71,604 to 530,074, and of bales of raw cotton used from 16,757 to 322,250. When the Japanese government decided on the use of Indian cotton and started the cotton-spinning industry, they added to their achievements in railroad building and banking that additional element which gave life and direction to the new economic structure. The textile industry helped to set the pattern of relations between town and country by drawing on cheap labor from the villages and thus establishing a low level of wages for other industries. It forced the pace in the development of merchant shipping and foreign commerce; it was an important factor in capital accumulation. The textile industry in particular benefited from the commercial privileges in China which were secured as a result of the Treaty of Shimonoseki. By 1895 the Industrial Revolution had been put in motion.

In the drive for treaty revision the cabinet was goaded on by the Diet, for the lower house criticized it loudly for the slow progress which had been made. The earliest agreements were made with the United States, but they were nothing more than moral victories. In 1894 the foreign minister adopted the different approach of trying first to secure British assent to treaty revision on the grounds that the other powers were more likely to follow if the British gave the lead. In a treaty signed that year the British agreed to most-favored-nation treatment for both countries, to the abolition of extraterritoriality, to reciprocal rights of travel, residence, navigation, and religion, and to far-reaching tariff concessions. The treaty was to go into force in 1899 on the condition that the other powers agreed, which they did, although the United States made fewer concessions on the tariff. To all intents and purposes, however, the Japanese secured tariff autonomy in 1899, and all restrictions finally ended in 1911.

The government drive to mechanize industry was intensified during and after the Sino-Japanese War. The government now felt strong enough to accept foreign loans, which were necessary to take care of the indebtedness and inflation caused by the war, and to assist by credits, subsidies, and protective legislation the new industries it so strongly desired. In 1896 Japan went on the gold standard with the help of the huge indemnity paid by defeated China.

The results of Japan's efforts to industrialize and to expand her foreign trade can be indicated in several ways. The figures show a tendency for manufactured imports to decline and for exports to increase. In the decade before the Sino-Japanese War the percentage of imported manufactured goods (measured in money value) dropped from around 45 per cent to 33 per cent, and the percentage of exports rose from around 6 per cent to 24 per cent. In round figures the volume of trade, both imports and exports, rose from 66,000,000 yen to 230,000,000 yen in ten years. Before 1895, to take an arbitrary date, Japan's imports were those of an agrarian country—fully manufactured items. After 1895 they tended more and more to be raw materials and partly finished goods in exchange for which Japan exported finished and partly finished manufactures. It took some time for Japanese industry to acquire all the capital equipment and machine tools it needed to take care of the domestic market; in fact the balance of trade remained unfavorable until the First World War.

According to Japanese economists, when Japan went to war with China in 1894, there were around 800 companies with a capitalization, in round figures, of 45,000,000 yen; ten years later there were nearly 2,500 companies with a capitalization of 170,000,000 yen. At the same time the number of prime movers in Japanese industrial establishments grew considerably as a result of the government drive for mechanization; for example, the number of machine looms increased steadily in proportion to the number of hand looms. During the decade 1895–1905 between the Sino-Japanese and the Russo-Japanese War there was a steady expansion of industry; after 1905 industrialization proceeded by leaps and bounds.

Japanese capitalism developed, not as state capitalism nor as unfettered private enterprise, but as a specific mixture of the two. Immediately following the Restoration the oligarchy had to do almost everything—find the capital, select the enterprises, train the managers and workmen, secure the raw materials, import the foreign consultants and directors, and brush aside all opposition. It looked for a time as if the state planned to own and control everything of importance, but all except the most strategic industries were turned over to private enterprise, usually to political associates at a very low price. The government continued to direct, stimulate, subsidize, protect and control, but not to own and manage, the new industries except those important for purposes of war. Thus Japanese business came to depend on government policy and government aid.

Emergence of the Zaibatsu

There are two main reasons why businessmen were peculiarly dependent on government. The process of industrialization had to be forced by all the power of the state; resources were limited and had to be expended according to a plan in order to avoid waste; the pressure of the foreign powers was too great to be warded off by unprotected private enterprise. That dependence continued, however, when the process of industrialization was well under way and Japan had achieved equality with the powers.

The second reason was that the old commercial class which had grown up under Tokugawa rule did not establish its economic leadership in spite of its important role in the Restoration. The leadership of the industrial movement came more from the old warrior than from the pre-Restoration commercial class. There had been some movement of daimyo and samurai into business connections and activities before the end of Tokugawa; in fact there had been intermarriage between samurai and merchant families. It was the deliberate policy of the Restoration oligarchy to make business respectable for the ex-samurai and to seek strong leadership from this class. The reasons for this are not far to seek. The prestige of the warrior had not been shattered by the fall of the Tokugawa; on the contrary it had been built up by the ideology of the Restoration movement, and the warrior code had been extended to the raw peasant conscripts in the national army. The Restoration leaders understood and trusted men of their own sort. Being an entrepreneur in early Meiji Japan required more than commercial skill; it required also high qualities of leadership and the confidence and support of the government. Leadership came more naturally to ex-members of a ruling class of warriors, however impoverished they might be, than to the socially despised merchants, in spite of their wealth and newly granted social equality. The government was very much concerned with the economic problem of the ex-samurai and daimyo. In the Restoration settlement they had been paid off for their loss of feudal incomes, but what they did for a living was up to them. Many could not readjust themselves to the times. For those who could there was the choice of industry, government service, or politics. The policy of selling government plants to private entrepreneurs was probably part of a more general policy of making business respectable for members of the old warrior class and of giving some of them a flying start, in order to encourage the others.

The recruitment of ex-samurai into the ranks of commerce and industry, banking, and foreign trade brought into these fields men whose values differed little, if at all, from those of the one-time samurai of Satsuma and Choshu who were now the ruling oligarchy. They were men who transferred to economics the views they had of politics and who saw nothing unusual in the close association between a political and an economic oligarchy. They did not want to restrict and control the power of government; rather they competed for its strong and paternalistic protection.

In spite of the official encouragement of private enterprise the structure of Japanese economy, therefore, was marked by a high degree of centralization. In the period from the Restoration to the Russo-Japanese War there emerged a group of financial cliques, or *zaibatsu*, whose relationship with the government was extremely close and almost entirely subservient. The best known names among the zaibatsu are those of Mitsui—one of the few houses from pre-Meiji times—Mitsubishi, Sumitomo, and Yasuda. Mitsui, Mitsubishi, and Sumitomo were involved in commerce, banking, and both light and heavy industry. Yasuda, Kawasaki, and Shibuzawa concentrated more on finance and banking, Asano and Okura on industry. These great houses, which came to wield enormous economic power, carried over into the economic field patterns of paternalism and centralized control which they took for granted in the political field. If they turned to their friends in government for support, they also used the bonds of family and kinship to keep together their sprawling combines. Some zaibatsu were organized purely as family trusts, the entire stock being in the hands of one family, a peculiarly Japanese adaptation of the joint stock company to national conditions; others reached out to all sorts of enterprises in a series of alliances, in which strong feudal obligations and loyalties formed the working basis of what looked, on the outside, like an American holding company. Many agreements between units in such zaibatsu organizations were unwritten, the obligations assumed by members of the group being enforced by social pressure in terms of a code of honor which stood in sharp contrast to the unscrupulous and ruthless economic warfare that went on between rival companies. The zaibatsu played a role in Japanese politics and economics second only to that of the government.

From the government point of view the big financial and industrial houses had a double role. They were necessary economic spearheads in the process of modernizing industry and agriculture. It is difficult to see how much of the technological progress made by Japan could have occurred if there had not been organizations with great economic strength and powerful government backing. The zaibatsu were not the whole of Japanese business— but they were the most easily identified and certainly the most convenient channel of communication. The second role in which the oligarchy tried to cast the zaibatsu was that of a new political force brought in to redress the balance of the agrarian landed interests in the Diet. Ito, the framer of the constitution, faced with the opposition of the lower house, early indicated concern over the dominance of the agrarian interests and suggested an increase in the representation of the urban groups. His rival Yamagata actually pushed through the new election law in 1900 which led to slightly higher representation of non-agrarian interests. But the businessmen were not anxious to play a strong political role. One of their greatest friends among the oligarchs, Ito, thought of the businessmen as the possible nucleus of a government party; in fact he took over the presidency of the *Seiyukai* with this in mind, but after the election of 1902, which followed the new electoral law, he expressed his disappointment at the reluctance of the businessmen to enter politics. The businessman depended so much on government support for his economic survival that he was unwilling to run the risks involved in independent political leadership.

The zaibatsu repaid their political debts in two ways, by enriching their sponsors and by forming a bridge between the oligarchy and the party leaders. Most of the zaibatsu had political connections which can be identified. The House of Mitsui counted on the friendly support of Ito and Inoue among the oligarchs and Goto and Itagaki among the *Jiyuto*, later the *Seiyukai*, party leaders. The Furukawa family was in much the same position. Mitsubishi, on the other hand, was closely connected with Matsukata in the oligarchy and Okuma in the Diet, and constantly challenged the political ascendancy of Mitsui. Whatever the rivalries, the great business houses played a role which smaller ones had perforce to follow. It was a role sufficiently important by the turn of the century to explain, in some measure, the relative political peace which marked the relations between Katsura and Saionji, as premiers, and the lower house. It was not that the *Seiyukai*, which put its majority in the lower house at the service of the government during the years 1901 to 1914, had become overwhelmingly urban in representation; it was rather that the zaibatsu were by now rich and powerful enough to bridge the gap between government and party. The price, in terms of corruption and public scandals, was high, but not higher than the country could bear and perhaps not out of the ordinary when compared with the record of other developing industrial societies.

The final steps in the change from an agrarian to an industrial society came in the years 1905 to 1920. This meant that the decisive period in the growth of Japanese capitalism came after the strength of the civil branch of the oligarchy had been weakened and the influence of Yamagata, now exercised from behind the scenes, had become dominant. The majority party, the *Seiyukai*, had found a way of coming to terms with the government, to which it lent its support. Instead of trying to make the constitution unworkable the parties competed to secure as large a share as possible of the growing wealth of the country for themselves and their friends. The development of Japanese capitalism up to this time had been along lines which did not include the emergence of a middle class of the sort known in the West. In addition to the zaibatsu there were many small industries and small businessmen, but their economic independence was limited by the fact that credit, management, and political influence were concentrated in the hands of the few big combines. As the zaibatsu held the same theory of the state as the oligarchy, the lesser businessmen were not likely to challenge it. The tremendous industrial strides made by Japan during this period did create new social and economic groups, but it was not until after World War I that these groups had an influence on the political scene that even mildly reflected their real significance.

Economic and Social Changes

The most important characteristic of Japan's industrial growth was the emphasis on heavy rather than light industries; iron and steel, chemicals, shipbuilding, and machine tool industries account for the continued importation of foreign-made machinery and the unfavorable balance of trade. According to Japanese economists there were in 1905 some 2,500 industrial companies with capital assets of 189,000,000 yen; in 1920 there were nearly 12,000 companies with capital assets of over three billion yen. During the same period the number of factories increased from a little under 10,000 to a little under 46,000 and the labor force from half a million to a million and a half. This development was made possible by protective policies, by foreign and domestic loans, and by direct foreign investment. Nor was the advance limited to heavy industry. The increase in the number of machine looms, especially during World War I, put Japanese textiles in the forefront of world production. The increase in foreign trade and the change in the nature of imports and exports were both apparent by 1895. The total value of imports and exports in 1894 was a little under 240,000,000 yen; in 1919 it had risen to over four billion yen, which, even allowing for the rise in prices, is a considerable increase. Another index of the growing industrialization of Japan is the increase in public expenditures which went up from somewhere around 300,000,000 yen just before the Russo-Japanese war to well over a billion yen after the First World War. The percentage of this budget spent for military purposes was never below 33 per cent during this period and actually reached 49 per cent in 1921 at the end of it. Borrowing for war and for railroad development on the continent increased the national debt at least five times.

With industrialization came a steady rise in the size of the population. In a fifty-year period ending in 1920 the population had gone up from around 35,000,000 to 56,000,000, the average yearly rate of increase being 437,000. From 1920 to 1940 the annual rate of increase went up even higher, to 800,000. The population in 1920 was almost double what it was when Perry came to Japan in 1853, and in spite of improvements in agriculture it outstripped the food supply of the Japanese islands.

The government was aware of the pressure of people on the available land resources and made various efforts to find a solution to the problem. In 1869, one year after the Meiji Restoration, a Colonial Development Office had been created when the government of Hokkaido was reorganized. Interest in Hokkaido was stimulated by fear of Russian designs. American consultants were imported to help develop the island by building railways and developing coal mines. As part of the program an American-style agricultural college was set up in Sapporo, the capital, and American agricultural staples were grown there. The population rose steadily but slowly from an estimated 58,000 in 1869 to a little more than 2,500,000 in 1925. The inducements to settlers were high but apparently not high enough to overcome the dislike of the Japanese for the cold climate. Karafuto, or South Sakhalin, is even colder than Hokkaido, and by 1925 had a population of only 197,000 Japanese, who worked the fisheries, mines, and forests. When Japan annexed Korea, she took over an already heavily populated country with a lower standard of living. The Japanese farmer or worker could not compete with the Korean unless given special privileges. Half of the 400,000 or more Japanese who had moved to Korea in the decade following annexation lived in the principal cities, where they were officials, petty administrators, merchants, or bankers. Formosa, with its hot, moist climate, to which the Japanese are not accustomed, had not absorbed even 200,000 Japanese by 1920, and at that time the population of the island was only 4,000,000.

When the Treaty of Portsmouth gave Japan a grip on Manchuria the government announced that over a ten-year period it would send one million colonists into that part of Manchuria which was under Japanese control. Twenty years later there were less than 70,000 Japanese in Kwantung, most of them in Port Arthur and Dairen, and no more than a quarter of a million in the whole of Manchuria, whose Chinese population was rapidly approaching 30,000,000. Actually more Koreans than Japanese emigrated to Manchuria during this period. It is small wonder that by the early twenties the Japanese government had given up any real hope of solving its population problems by emigration even to its own colonies. A little more than half a million had settled abroad, but most of the suitable countries closed their doors one by one to Oriental immigrants and in 1926 a Japanese premier stated that the danger of arousing the suspicions of other countries was greater than the advantages to be secured by pressing the Japanese people to emigrate.

The increase in population brought with it problems which were complicated by the growth of social distinctions along lines common to highly industrialized countries. There was a broadening of the base of ownership in industry and commerce, not because the zaibatsu became weaker but because the extension of their activities stimulated other businesses. The World War I years in particular saw the emergence of large numbers of new rich or *narikin*. The elder statesmen of Japanese capitalism, like those of politics, were dying off and a new generation was coming to the fore, often trained abroad and more open to ideas from the West. Natural science and technology were the order of the day. Thousands of Japanese who had been abroad as diplomats, merchants, administrators, or soldiers were exposed, in varying degrees, to new ideas and ways of life. Japanese literature brought in concepts which the educational system was well designed to exclude. The greatly increased commercial, banking, and industrial classes became more aware of their comparative standing in society, and some looked wistfully on the greater prestige and political power enjoyed by their opposite numbers in other lands. The impact of Woodrow Wilson's ringing phrases was felt in many quarters of Japan and even in her colonies, as Korea was to show. Democracy was in the air; it had just won a world war with Japan as an ally. At last there was a social base, however narrow, in which it might take root in Japan.

The increase in the size of the business community was matched by the growth of a large laboring class in the cities and the factories. As in many other countries where agriculture was based on intensive methods of farming which called for the application of large quantities of human capital to the land, the conditions in the factories were no better than those in the fields. Japanese industry was marked by low wages, long hours of work, the use of large numbers of women, especially in the textile mills, and the system of farming out work to small establishments. As early as 1900 the government anticipated the tendency of workers to organize and passed the "Peace Preservation Law" which threatened anyone who tried to persuade others to strike. The pressure of the police power of the state and the strongly traditional views which workers fresh from the farms brought with them combined to make such labor organizations as there were too weak to be taken seriously at this time. There were many strikes for higher wages, but they did not spring from, or contribute to, the strength of labor unions; they were local, spontaneous, and uncoordinated.

The worker had found no way of communicating with his government except through strikes and riots. The Japanese, who are often painted as a docile people hesitant to challenge authority, have a long history of peasant rebellions and city riots. The rice riots of 1918, at the very height of the wartime boom, are an excellent illustration of the relations between government and people at this time. The government failed to prevent the riots but did succeed in preventing them from being exploited by left-wing leadership. The story of the rice riots begins with the 1916 rice harvest of 58,000,000 *koku*, the highest in Japanese history. The two succeeding crops were poor, supplies ran low, and in 1918 the price of rice skyrocketed. Government edicts against the fixing of rice prices had no teeth in them, and a few big exchange houses soon monopolized the market. The riots began in a small village in the northern part of Japan where some housewives demonstrated in vain against the shipping of rice from the local storehouses. The riots spread all over Japan to thirty-three cities and 201 villages. The government issued statements calling for a revival of ancient virtues, blamed the press for its incendiary headlines, collected rice by force in Korea, called out the troops—who in some cases refused to march out of sympathy for the rioters—and finally shipped in large quantities of rice from Southeast Asia. The riots died out as fast as they had started, once there was rice to be had. The incident is interesting because it was marked by an almost unanimous and unprecedented antigovernment reaction in the press and because the nationwide reaction indicated that a national economy had come into being. This last phenomenon was not lost on Katayama Sen who had tried to organize a Social Democratic party as early as 1901 and was later Japanese representative on the Comintern. He pointed out that this was a revolutionary situation which was not exploited because of the lack of organization.

The government's chief approach to the problem of social change was to anticipate and prevent the organization of labor and peasant unions and radical political parties. It is true that factory legislation was passed in 1911, becoming effective in 1916, which at least on paper provided for certain improvements. The employment of children under twelve, with some exceptions, was forbidden in factories having fifteen or more workers and in certain dangerous industries. Hours of work for women and children under fifteen were restricted to twelve hours a day. In every month there were to be two days of rest. The law was not vigorously enforced and in any case was full of exceptions; it could not be taken seriously.

The peasants were always easier to control than the workers. They were split up into small villages, had less access to newspapers, and their every move was a matter of public knowledge. It was during the period under discussion that the agrarian sector of the economy definitely lost first place. The tenant farmers and small owner-cultivators probably gained less than any other class in society from the process of industrialization. According to government statistics, by the nineteen-twenties nearly one-half of all cultivated land was farmed by tenants, and more than 68 per cent of all farming families were either full or part tenant. Of those who owned land nearly half held less than one and one-fourth acres. The distribution of wealth in the countryside matched that in the cities where great possessions stood out in sharp contrast with great poverty.

The impact of modernization on the countryside was very complicated.

Agricultural production was both changed and improved. There was an increase in rice yield per acre, more land was brought under cultivation, and diversified crops were introduced; fertilizers came into common use and rural banks provided an alternative to the usurer. The gains in agriculture, however, like those in industry, barely kept up with the rising population and permitted no perceptible improvement in the standard of living for the masses. At the same time there was no mechanization of agriculture as there had been of industry, and small-scale cultivation continued to be the rule. The diversion of most available capital to industrialization meant that there was not the means to modernize agriculture in any revolutionary manner. The pressure of people on the land, though lighter at times of great industrial expansion, was always sufficient to make it less profitable to use machines than men. Irrigated agriculture presents a difficult problem for the modernizer, even where there are both the will to mechanize and the necessary capital.

The farmer lost his independence as cash crops, such as silk, became more common and as the economic condition of the village was tied in with world markets. Industrialization and cash crops both tended to undermine village handicrafts, thus robbing the farmer of subsidiary sources of income. The towns, with their banks and brokers, seemed now to control the life of the farmer and determine his economic status, a fact which caused both bewilderment and resentment. Those who owned land and paid money taxes to the government had the advantages as well as the disadvantages of the right of ownership which came with the Restoration. But for the tenant, who paid sometimes as much as 50 per cent of his main crop to the landlord as rent, the situation was very different. He always stood to lose, for he had been deprived of traditional rights and protection and forced to compete for land under capitalist rules. The economic foundations of the old relation between master and peasant retainer had gone, but the old attitudes did not disappear immediately. Although now without any obligations to their tenants, the landlords still expected to control the villages and usually did.

The peasants blamed most of their troubles on the cities and developed anti-capitalist attitudes which strengthened a predisposition to fear and dislike the West. The West was associated with the cities and with all those changes in dress, in attitudes towards the family and to women, which seemed much more out of place in the village than in the town. In the villages the influence of the military was also stronger than in the towns. The retired army officer tended to play a role in the village in relation to old and prospective peasant soldiers very much like the one he had in the army.

Considering the strength of tradition, it is surprising that peasant unions made any headway at all. It is claimed by Japanese historians that at the end of the First World War there were a little over one thousand peasant unions claiming a membership of over 132,000. Disputes between peasant and landlord became more and more common, leading in many cases to violent measures. There was no question about the existence of agrarian unrest, but the peasants were not strongly organized; the unions were numerous and the membership small.

The Government and the Parties 1908–1922

During the decade preceding World War I the party struggle in Japan was largely a struggle for a share in the increased wealth which had been created by the Industrial Revolution. The *genro*, who still exercised great influence, had accepted the support of the political parties in the lower house as a necessary part of the process of government. Since the turn of the century the parties had been willing to cooperate with the government in return for financial gain, a development made possible by the role of the zaibatsu, who bribed and supported politicians of every party. In this way the party politicians shared in the profits of the zaibatsu which they helped to provide through their legislative action. The wealth of the zaibatsu served as a bridge between the parties and the bureaucrats. There were few Japanese politicians who did not accept bribes, and corruption was taken for granted as a part of the system.

The members of the *Seiyukai* party, which had been in power since 1901, profited most from this system. On occasion bribery was exposed and made the basis of a great political scandal. One example was the case of the Greater Japan Sugar Refining Company, which bribed members of the Diet in 1907 and 1908 in an effort to have legislation passed which would make sugar a state monopoly. Such a monopoly would have enabled the officials of the company to cover up their frauds by selling the bankrupt company to the government at an inflated price. For this case of corruption, which was revealed because the bribery did not work, many others went unrecorded because they were successful. The sum of money spent on bribes to members of all parties has been variously estimated but it appears to have been considerable.

Corruption was revealed by rival political groups which had not shared in it. The behavior of the *Seiyukai* in supporting any government that came into office and its attempts to monopolize the spoils presented other political parties with little choice but to follow its example. The *Kenseihonto* could secure a share in political power and financial rewards only by playing the same game. To have adopted any other course would have been to stand alone in opposition to both the bureaucrats and the *Seiyukai*. In an effort to consolidate opposition to the *Seiyukai* the *Kenseihonto* was dissolved and a new party called the *Kokuminto*, Constitutional Nationalist party, was formed in 1910. The party platform called for party control of cabinets, but this seems to have been merely a bargaining point for the real objective of replacing the *Seiyukai*, not of changing its role. The struggle of the parties was closely linked with the struggle within the oligarchy. The army and navy fought each other for the lion's share of the budget while the parties tried to resist increases in taxation.

The year 1912 marked the end of the Meiji period. The emperor died on

July 30, 1912, and was succeeded by the new Taisho emperor. The death of the emperor, whose name is given to one of the most remarkable periods in Japanese history, did not affect the political struggle, although some high patriots, such as Nogi, of Russo-Japanese war fame, and his wife, committed suicide in order to avoid the disgrace of outliving the emperor.

Relations between the army and the parties came close to the breaking point over Yamagata's insistence on adding two divisions to the armed forces. Saionji, in spite of his huge *Seiyukai* majority was compelled to give up the premiership, to which he never returned. It was at this time that he was appointed a *genro* and thereupon removed from active politics. The political parties raised such a hue and cry about the fall of the Saionji cabinet, for which Yamagata was so largely responsible, that it was difficult to find anyone to take over the premiership. The *genro* finally solved the problem by having the emperor order Katsura, then Lord Chamberlain, to become premier in the face of what seemed to be the united determination of all the parties to fight for constitutional government.

Katsura tried to break the opposition of the parties by using his great wealth to buy a majority. Pulling to his side the more opportunist elements of the *Kokuminto*, which had been formed three years before for the announced purpose of fighting for party control of cabinets, he set up a new party called the *Doshikai*. But he failed to cajole or purchase sufficient members to secure a majority in the Diet. Katsura was attacked in the Diet for using imperial rescripts for personal aggrandizement, and the whole history of the use of the throne by the Satsuma-Choshu oligarchs was bitterly attacked. The oligarchs were accused of using the throne as their rampart and rescripts as their missiles. Katsura again tried to bring the Diet majority to heel by using the power of the throne but was defied by the *Seiyukai*, which was not normally in the habit of disregarding the imperial wishes. Such actions did not bring down on the parties the wrath of the oligarchs because they were only too happy to see the personal power of Katsura broken, but once the fight was over and Katsura had retired from the scene, the old *Seiyukai* alliance with the oligarchy returned, and the outcry of the parties was a thing of the past. Although party control of the cabinet seemed no nearer achievement, the emperor tended from this time on to avoid direct intervention in party struggles. Party leaders came from the career bureaucracy rather than from the elder statesmen and were included in many cabinets. The parties had not secured control of the government, but their support was essential to any ambitious man who had political aspirations.

Admiral Yamamoto, who took over from Katsura at the command of the *genro*, lasted only a short time and achieved very little. The civil service was opened up a little more to party patronage, the number of civil servants cut down by something over 6,000 positions, and the war and navy cabinet positions opened to retired as well as active officers. Yamamoto's cabinet fell in April, 1914, over the famous naval scandal, sometimes called the "Siemens Affair," which involved the German firm by that name, the English Vickers Company, and the House of Mitsui. Several high naval officers apparently

accepted bribes from foreign firms in return for arranging contracts for building battleships. Popular indignation ran so high that troops had to be used to
control street rioters. The lower house cut 30,000,000 yen from the naval
budget, and the peers capped this by cutting the budget another 70,000,000.
The government was compelled to punish the ringleaders.

The *genro* were hard put to it to find a successor to Yamamoto until the
name of Okuma was suggested. The old man, from whose *Kaishinto* party of
1882 had stemmed one of the two great political traditions, had seen so little
of high office that his reputation for honesty and devotion to political principles was comparatively high. The founder of Waseda University in 1882,
Okuma had been its chancellor since 1907 when he retired from politics. He
used this platform to keep up a steady attack on the self-seeking politics of the
Seiyukai, the representative of the rival political tradition started by Itagaki
as early as 1874. In the election of 1914 the *Kenseikai*, a successor to Okuma's
original party, secured enough seats to bring to an end the *Seiyukai*'s long
control of Diet majorities.

Okuma accepted the premiership, but it soon appeared that his reputation as a tribune of the people was the luxury of the man who stood apart from
politics. Okuma carried out the wishes of the *genro* in pressing ahead with the
bill to add two army divisions and played politics in much the same way as
the *Seiyukai* whose conduct he had previously criticized. Elections were held
again in 1915, and turned out favorably for Okuma, but it was soon discovered that the Home Minister Oura had not only interfered in the elections
but had also bribed members of the Diet to vote for the army's two divisions
bill. There was nothing unusual about the methods employed by Oura,
except perhaps that they continued under the great Okuma who was so critical of them when used by the *Seiyukai*, but they became so notorious that Oura
was permitted to resign from the cabinet. The dismissal of Oura pleased
Kato, the leader of the *Kenseikai* majority and Foreign Minister, who had
criticized the Home Minister with some bitterness, but Kato himself was the
next to go. The *genro* were not at all happy about the way in which the cabinet
had handled the Twenty-one Demands on China, or with the storm of
criticism from the *Seiyukai*, which demanded a cooperative policy with that
country, and as in most cases where Japan did not get all that she wanted
abroad, someone had to be the scapegoat. In this situation Kato was sacrificed to the *genro*. Okuma, after pushing through the bills for more men and
money for the army, resigned in October, 1916, having destroyed his earlier
reputation of honesty and devotion to party government and having become,
while in office, wealthier than before.

The *genro* brought in as premier General Terauchi, a Choshu samurai
and a protégé of Yamagata, who dissolved the Diet in January, 1917, and
used the full powers of the government to influence the election. With the aid
of the government Kato's *Kenseikai* lost its majority and the *Seiyukai* was once
more back in the saddle. After the rice riots of 1918 the Terauchi ministry
came to an end.

In September, 1918, the premiership was taken over by Hara, the so-called "Great Commoner," the first man without a title to occupy the premiership, a man who had risen through the ranks of the *Seiyukai* party, and the first premier who held a seat in the lower house. As at all times the appointment was made on the advice of the *genro* of whom there were now three living members—Yamagata, aged eighty-one, Matsukata, aged eighty-four, and Saionji, aged seventy. Okuma, who had been officially nominated as a *genro* had continued to refuse the honor. It was Saionji who nominated Hara after refusing to accept the premiership again for himself. In spite of the *genro* selection, however, Hara insisted on appointing a party cabinet, an objective which he achieved except for the ministries of war, navy, and foreign affairs. It looked as if Japanese politics had entered on a new era.

CHAPTER IX

Colonialism and Nationalism in South-east Asia

1. THE NEW IMPERIALISM

THE most important influence on Southeast Asia during the nineteenth century was the expansion of European colonial rule. The British conquest of Burma and Malaya and the French conquest of the countries of Indo-China brought all of continental Southeast Asia under colonial rule. The single exception was Thailand, which maintained its independence as a buffer zone between the British and French colonial domains. While Dutch rule in the East Indies and Spanish rule in the Philippines had been established much earlier, both were greatly modified by the economic and political forces of nineteenth-century Europe.

The colonial policies of the imperial powers in the nineteenth century had their origin in the changes brought about in Europe and America by the French Revolution, the Napoleonic Wars, and the Industrial Revolution. The new industries in Europe and America required markets and access to raw materials which were plentiful in Southeast Asia. Westerners had the capital and the managerial ability to develop the resources of the countries of Southeast Asia, and the Industrial Revolution provided them with the precision weapons and the military power with which to enforce colonial rule. These developments came at a time when China, the leading Far Eastern power, was in decline and in no position to counteract the Western onslaught on her southern neighbours.

The expansion of Europe affected every aspect of life in the colonial countries. The forms of colonial rule varied from country to country, but in all cases Western types of political organization were established. Western types of economic organization were also imposed upon the colonies, in most of which a dual economy developed. There was superimposed upon the native economy a Western owned and operated economy which produced for the world market. As a consequence the balance of the native economy was seriously disturbed, and integrated development of a modern national economy prevented.

The social consequences of Western imperialism were equally serious. The foundations of native culture were steadily undermined by the political and economic institutions imposed by the imperial powers. The leading imperial powers introduced a small number of their colonial subjects to Western education. This was done for the practical purposes of administration and economic management as well as for religious and humanitarian motives. Through those who were educated in Western-type schools or abroad the colonial peoples had a limited access to the whole range of Western thought. The liberal, democratic, and nationalist ideas of the time had as great an impact upon educated men and women in the colonies as they had had upon the peoples of Europe and the United States. As in Europe, these ideas were merged with the traditional beliefs of each people to form new patterns of nationalism. Nationalist movements in the colonies drew heavily on these Western ideas but necessarily revived and restored respect for their own native cultures. Eventually the nationalists were strong enough to challenge colonial rule and to fight for the establishment of their own nation states.

2. INDONESIA (THE NETHERLANDS EAST INDIES)

In the period from the beginning of the Napoleonic Wars to the end of the First World War there were three important developments in the history of the Indonesian islands. The Dutch East Indies Company, which had built up the Dutch empire in the East Indies, was abolished and the Netherlands government took over political control and direct economic exploitation of the islands. This development was a direct consequence of the French Revolution and the Napoleonic Wars. In 1795 the French conquered Holland, overthrew the oligarchy, and set up a new government which was in effect a satellite of France. As a result of the revolution in Holland, the directors of the East Indies Company in 1796 handed over its administration to the new government, and the charter of the Company, which expired in 1799, was not renewed. The Netherlands government introduced a new era in the colonial administration of the Indies.

The second important development, which occurred later in the century, was the transfer of the economic exploitation of the Indies from the government to private enterprise. The government monopolies, which had been held by the Crown, were taken over one after another by Dutch capitalists who introduced the plantation system. This development was also a consequence of changes in Holland. The revolution of 1848 led to constitutional changes, as a result of which the Dutch Parliament secured the legal right to interfere in the administration of the colonies. Over a period of more than half a century the Parliament gradually gave up the economic monopolies of the government. By the time of the First World War Dutch capitalists were in control of the production of all the important raw materials of the East Indies.

The third important development, last in time, was the emergence of an Indonesian nationalist movement. This development was a reaction against Dutch colonial rule and was in part stimulated by Western ideas of nationalism which were introduced through Western education. It was this nationalist movement which prepared the way for the eventual establishment of the Indonesian republic after World War II.

When the Netherlands government took over the administration of the Indies from the Company in 1796, it set up a Committee for East Indian Affairs as the policy-making body controlling the governor-general and the administration of the colonies. The committee soon made it clear that the benefits of the French Revolution were not to accrue to the colonies. It declared that "the doctrines of liberty and equality . . . cannot be transferred to nor applied to the East Indian possessions of the State as long as the security of these possessions depends on the existing and necessary state of subordination [of the Indonesians] and as long as the introduction cannot take place without exposing these possessions to a confusion, the effect of which cannot be imagined." The change from company to government rule was not intended to change the relationship between revolutionary Holland and the colony.

The extension of the Napoleonic system to Holland, however, led to the adoption by the Dutch of French bureaucratic methods of administration which the Dutch applied to the colonies. In 1808, when Napoleon's brother had become king of Holland, a new governor-general, Herman Willem Daendels, was sent to the Indies and given dictatorial powers. Daendels, who was once a revolutionary leader, had developed into a typical officer of the Napoleonic system. During his rule in the Indies from 1808 to 1811, he attempted to carry through an administrative reorganization. He replaced the system of indirect rule through the sultans with a more direct administration under central control. The sultans became appointed officials deprived of most of their authority. The smaller sultanates were reduced to regencies, several of which came to be combined in one prefecture, administered by a Dutch official. At the courts of the larger sultanates the Dutch residents were raised in rank to ministers and received priority in status over the sultans. In addition to this administrative reorganization, Daendels carried through judicial reforms. He established a system of local and prefectural courts to handle the cases of Europeans and set up a clear division of laws—Western law for the Europeans and Adat law for the Indonesians. Daendels also investigated the system of compulsory cultivation which had been imposed on the princely states, and finding it useful for his purposes, he extended it.

Daendels did everything in his power to strengthen the Indies as a military base in the war against England. Until this time the British, who had taken some of the outer islands, had left Java alone as they did not consider it a threat and had few troops to spare. Daendels' military preparations, however, provoked the British to the conquest of Java and the occupation of all the Dutch East Indies. The British rule lasted from 1811 until the islands were returned to the Dutch in 1818. The British conquest and administration were both carried out, under the direction of Lord Minto, by Thomas Stamford Raffles, who later became famous as the founder of Singapore and of British rule in Malaya.

Raffles completely reorganized the administration of the islands. He continued some of the measures of Daendels, but whereas Daendels had aimed at an efficient bureaucracy of the Napoleonic type, Raffles held English ideas on local self-government and tried to introduce them as far as was compatible with the traditions and customs of the Indonesians. He deprived the sultans and princes of all their authority and of their revenues, leaving them only in nominal control and putting them on the government payroll. Only four sultanates remained in central Java, and these continued to exist until their incorporation into the government of the Indonesian Republic after World War II. In the regencies the ruling regents lost their hereditary authority and became regular officials whose function was to carry out the orders of their administrative superiors, the British "residents" of the provinces. The Indonesian aristocracy was still used; it was merely robbed of its hereditary authority and put in an administrative relation to the British officials. The people of each village elected their own village headmen who were responsible for the local administration. This measure of local self-government in the village communities in Indonesia was later continued under the Dutch. Raffles also tried to encourage Indonesian participation in the administration of justice by the establishment of a jury system after the English example. This idea, which was counter to the Dutch tradition, was immediately discarded by the Dutch after their return to power.

Raffles not only ended the autonomous rule of the sultans and princes but also abolished the system of tribute and corvée labor which they had enforced on their people. The Dutch had developed this system to impose on the princely territories the compulsory cultivation and forced delivery of coffee, spices, and other products. Raffles replaced the princely right of tribute and labor with a tax. According to his interpretation the princely right of sovereignty was a form of landownership which had been transferred from the princes to the colonial government. The government therefore owned all the land, which it leased to the village communities whose headmen sublet plots to the villagers. State ownership remained, however, a mere theoretical concept and the individual farmer gained a definite right of usufruct which came close to practical ownership. The farmer was to pay a rent in money or kind, which varied according to the value of the land and its production from one-quarter to one-half of the main crop, which was rice. This rent—which in reality was a land tax—amounted to about two-fifths of the yield. The new tax law, together with the administrative reforms, might have freed the Indonesian farmer from the oppressive rule of the princes as well as from the extreme forms of exploitation by the colonial governments. But the British administration under Raffles lasted for too short a time to bring permanent political changes or to guarantee those benefits which the farmers might have derived from the recognition of their rights to use the land. After the return of the Dutch, Raffles' system of taxing the individual farmer was eventually abolished. The Dutch made the villages responsible for tax in kind and labor service—a system which combined the worst features of the princely privileges of the past with exploitation by a colonial bureaucracy.

When the Dutch took over again in 1818, they intended at first to pursue a policy in harmony with the liberal ideas of Europe at the time. The king, to whom the constitution of 1815 gave control of the colonies, declared that his aim was "to promote the interests of all his subjects, without any exception." The king's government thus professed to be as much concerned with the welfare of Indonesian as of Dutch subjects. Three commissioners-general were sent out from Holland to study conditions and to make recommendations on administrative reorganization and to draw up an organic law for the colony. On their recommendation the land rent was maintained, and in addition the buying of estates by Europeans was prohibited in order to protect the Indonesian farmers. The commissioners proposed that the islands be thrown open to private enterprise and that a department of agriculture, art, and education be set up to acquaint the Indonesians with Western methods of agriculture. It was hoped that an increase in production would bring greater profits to the government's treasury. The commissioners also urged the establishment of a school system and held that instruction ought to be carried on in Malay, Javanese, and other local languages, with the aim of maintaining an Indonesian culture. These recommendations actually set the policy of supporting the Indonesian cultural tradition, a policy in which the Dutch took special pride.

The economic ideas of the commissioners and of the first administration after the Dutch return were, however, soon discarded and the policy of monopoly exploitation was reintroduced. The largest possible profits were extracted from the colony for the benefit of the king. The reason for this policy can be traced to the strengthening of royal authority after the change in the political scene in Europe. The constitution of 1815 had placed the control of the colony in the hands of the king and his ministers, and the income from the colony went into the royal treasury. The war in Europe and its aftermath left the royal treasury empty, and the financial needs of the government were increased by the policy followed in the islands themselves. The reform measures of the government aroused the resistance of the Javanese princes, who started an uprising in 1825 under the leadership of a pretender to the throne of the sultanate of Jocjakarta. This aristocratic leader, Dipa Negara, believed that he was selected by Allah to drive out the foreigners and restore the glory of the Moslem state. He became a popular figure about whom there were many legends. He withdrew with his followers into the mountains and engaged in guerrilla warfare which he carried on until 1830. With the help of some of the Javanese princes who had remained loyal to them, the Dutch suppressed the uprising but at great cost of life and treasure. After the fighting, some of the territory was taken from the sultans and brought under the

Dutch government; only a small area in the center of the island of Java remained under the sultan of Jocjakarta.

The prolonged military campaign and some minor ones on the coast of
Sumatra enabled the Dutch to complete the reorganization of their colonial
government. Most of the territory was divided into administrative areas under native "regents." These regents, selected from aristocratic families, administered their districts under the supervision and direction of a Dutch
"resident" who governed the province. The last surviving sultanates of central Java were controlled by a Dutch adviser or minister. The Dutch system
still remained one of "indirect rule." But in contrast to the former method of
forced deliveries, in which the Dutch had only checked on the production
within the sultanates, the Dutch now managed the administrative system
themselves and derived their income from direct taxation. In fact, the sultans,
as well as the regents, were but figureheads—useful tools who enabled the
Dutch to impose their administration without having to interfere with the
cultural tradition and customs of the Indonesians.

After the establishment of this system, the royal Netherlands government
used colonial revenues to meet the debts it had incurred in Europe as well as
in the final conquest of the islands themselves. A theoretical discussion as to
how the islands could provide the greatest profits had been going on in Holland for some time. According to the new liberal belief in Europe, if the
Indonesians were permitted to develop undisturbed, they would greatly increase their agricultural production and the home government could profit
through taxation. The opposite opinion was that the Indonesians were hopelessly lazy by nature and that if they were not forced to work, nothing much
could be expected from them. A new variation of this latter theory was then
used to justify a departure from the liberal policy and a return to forced
labor. According to this view it was not laziness but ignorance which prevented the Indonesians from doing their best in cultivating the fields. They
had to be taught to work and they could be taught only if they were ordered.
This argument was used to introduce the *kulturstelsel* or culture system
through which the Indonesian peasants were forced to plant crops for export
and sale in Europe for the benefit of the royal treasury.

The culture system was introduced in 1830 by Governor-general van
den Bosch, who had been a social reformer interested in finding new employment and income for the large numbers of impoverished and unemployed
people in the cities of Holland. The industrial competition of England and
the decline of the Dutch merchant fleet, not yet recovered from the Napoleonic Wars, had helped to bring about this economic misery. With his Indonesian policy van den Bosch aimed at solving not only the problems of the
colony's economy and of the king's treasury but also the problem of unemployment in Holland.

When the culture system was introduced, the Indonesian farmers
were led to believe that it would ease their tax or rent burden, which had
amounted to about two-fifths of their main crop. Instead of paying this tax
through their headmen, the Indonesian villages were now required to set

aside one-fifth of their land for the production of export crops determined by the government and to spend at least one-fifth of their labor on the cultivation of these crops, for which the government would pay what it considered a fair price. In theory the arrangement was to be a free contract and the villagers were to receive the value of the export crops in excess of the rent which they formerly paid. The system was actually inspired by the American slave plantations, and in practice turned out to be very different from what it purported to be in theory. The economic power was too unevenly divided between the two sides to give the Indonesian farmers a chance to uphold their position, and the system resulted frequently in excessive exploitation of the Indonesian population. In fact it became one of the harshest and most profitable systems of colonial exploitation ever devised.

The commodities produced by the culture system, such as coffee, indigo, sugar, tea, tobacco, and cinnamon, brought high prices in Europe. The more profitable they became, the more the Dutch demanded increased production. In some of the most exploited areas the Indonesian farmers had neither enough time nor land left over to raise food crops for themselves, and the soil became exhausted when it had to produce crops year after year without receiving enough care. As the price paid for these export crops was extraordinarily low, the farmers did not have enough income to buy the food they lacked. As a necessary part of the system, groups of villagers were sent to work out their quota in the factories where sugar, indigo, and other products were processed and prepared for export. The factories were managed by European or Chinese owners, who sometimes received government credits for these enterprises. The working contracts of the villagers were in theory free and their labor was to be paid. In practice they had to work at very low wages, under conditions which amounted to compulsory labor.

To enforce this system and to make it as productive as possible, the Dutch and the Indonesian administrators had to play a more active role than they had previously done. The regents gained a new importance and their hereditary rights were restored. They met once a month with the chiefs of the villages of their districts to discuss the production problems. The regents were checked by Dutch inspectors, the former "coffee sergeants" who now were given the title of controllers. The whole administrative responsibility remained in the hands of the Dutch residents. This system created a condition of semi-starvation, which became permanent in many areas, and on occasion there was actual famine. But the royal treasury profited greatly. In the years between 1831 and 1877 a total of 823,000,000 guilders was earned for the motherland, a fantastically large amount for that time, providing nearly one-third of the Netherlands' budget. Additional profits accrued from the revival of Dutch shipping which was used for the transport of colonial products to Europe.

The culture system led to an increase in the production and the population of Java. Because of the pressure from the Dutch for more production, more land was brought under cultivation and there was a considerable increase in population. In 1815 the population of Java had been 5,000,000 people; by 1860 it reached the figure of 11,000,000. The rise in production, not only of crops for export but also of food, was balanced by a doubling of the population and not by a rise in the living standard. This population growth occurred on Java where enforced production under the culture system was centered. As a consequence of the culture system Java remained the agrarian, economic center of the islands, and it was here that over two-thirds of the total Indonesian population lived. The culture system also led to the introduction of new agricultural plants to Indonesia. Among them were tea, tobacco, and the cinchona tree, from whose bark quinine is derived. Quinine eventually became a near monopoly of Indonesia.

The reaction against this form of exploitation came not from the Indonesian people, who had been reduced to practical slavery, but from Holland, where there was a revival of the spirit of liberalism and of free enterprise and an open challenge to the economic principles on which the culture system was based. The reaction began in the revolutionary year of 1848, when a new constitution gave the Dutch parliament the legal right to interfere in the administration of the colonies. In 1854 this parliament undertook the writing of a colonial constitution. It imposed limitations on the use of forced labor, abolished slavery, and cleared the way for reintroduction of the land tax. The constitution provided for establishment of schools for the Indonesians, a policy which had been proposed by the commissioners in 1818 but had not been carried out. The colonial constitution provided also for the leasing of unused land to European estate owners, thus preparing the way for private enterprise in colonial agriculture.

The attack against the culture system was continued by those who believed in private enterprise and wanted to open the East Indian islands for the investment of private capital. Together with this economic attack against government monopoly came a moral condemnation of its abuses. A Dutch clergyman, who as a pastor in Batavia had seen the misery caused by the system, and who later became a member of the Dutch parliament, raised his voice for reforms. The greatest effect on public opinion in Holland, however, came from a novel, *Max Havellar*, published in 1860 by Edward Douwes Dekker, under the pseudonym "Multatuli." Dekker described the greediness of the Dutch administration and the misery of the Indonesians, and aroused a moral indignation against the existing colonial system which fitted well with the new economic ideas of the time. Not until 1860, however, when a liberal cabinet came to power, were the first steps taken to abolish the culture system. Between 1860 and 1865 tea, indigo, tobacco, and cinnamon were excluded from the system. By 1870 it applied only to sugar and coffee—the most important products. The use of forced labor in the production of sugar was gradually given up between 1878 and 1890, and in the production of coffee between 1900 and 1915.

The last remission to Holland of the results of forced labor took place in 1877. The culture system was dealt a heavy blow by the agrarian law of 1870, which prepared the way for the establishment of the new system of private plantations. This legislation was also intended to protect the Indonesian farmers against the dangers of becoming as much exploited by private estate owners as they had been by the government monopoly. The agrarian law forbade the sale of Indonesian land to non-Indonesians. Foreign plantations could be set up only through leases for a maximum period. For government land, that is, uncultivated land, the maximum lease was seventy-five years, but cultivated land owned by the village communities could be leased for only twenty years or five years according to the type of land. As a limited amount of the total land of a village could be leased in this way, enough land for the food production of the villagers was assured. Indonesian landowner-ship was thus protected at the time when Dutch plantations were developing. With the introduction of these measures the Dutch strengthened the tradi-tions of communal ownership and thus continued to prevent the develop-ment of ideas of private ownership which Raffles had once emphasized in his reforms. This problem of landownership remained an important one in Indo-nesian politics. The agrarian law protected the village lands in order to guarantee sufficient food production, but in doing so it bound the farmer to the village community and thus prevented the emergence of an independent Indonesian farmer class. The plantation system brought tremendous profits to European estate owners and commercial enterprises but did nothing to raise the living standards of the Indonesian farmers.

In the period from 1870 to 1900 the production of export crops greatly increased under the new plantation system. The production of sugar more than doubled and some of the crops, such as tobacco and tea, which had been introduced under the culture system but had brought no great profits, now brought high returns to the plantation owners. The change of the economic system in the East Indies coincided with the increased demand for the prod-ucts of the colonies that resulted from the industrialization of Europe and of the United States. Communication between the East Indies and the Western world was greatly facilitated by the opening of the Suez Canal. Dutch in-vestment was promoted by a number of trading companies and banks which lent the necessary capital to foreign planters. The increase in cultiva-tion brought the tax income of the colonial government to the point where it made up for the decline of income from government products under the cul-ture system. But as the actual yearly income increased in later decades so did the expenses of the colonial government. Instead of being able to transmit large amounts to Holland, the colonial government found it so difficult to meet its own expenses that eventually the idea of transmitting profits to the home government was given up. It was now through the private profits of the planters, the banks, and the trading companies that the wealth of the East Indies flowed to Holland and became the real source of Dutch prosperity.

Dutch investments went not only into plantations but also into the ex-ploitation of all the raw material resources in which the islands were rich. Tin mining became one of the most profitable industries and provided vast profits for the mining companies. The islands of Bangka and Billiton, to the east of Sumatra, were rich in tin. Of greatest importance were the oil re-sources of Eastern Borneo and Sumatra. The Royal Dutch Oil Company, founded in 1890, was later combined with British interests to form the Royal Dutch and Shell Company which became one of the largest oil concerns. Plantations, banking, and mining were the main fields of private economic enterprise after the opening of Indonesian economy to private investment.

The New Dutch policy affected every aspect of Indonesian life. The native aristocracy, used by the Dutch in their administrative system, became more and more separated from its traditional role in Indonesian society. The earlier warfare between the princes had hampered economic development and kept down the population. After the Dutch had crushed internal resistance, they were able to maintain law and order and thus made it possible for the population to increase. The population of the island of Java was 11,000,-000 in 1860, 28,000,000 in 1900, and 34,000,000 in 1920. The Dutch also constructed irrigation works in the original areas of the old Javanese agricultural empires, thereby increasing the food supply. Under colonial rule Java became a rich agricultural country whose wealth made Holland prosperous. With the increasing prosperity questions were again raised in Holland concerning the Dutch obligations toward the Indonesian people.

The legislation of the 1860's on education was not followed up as the colonial government found the expense of setting up a general school system prohibitive. Even the lowering of educational requirements decreed in a reform of 1893 did not make it possible to support more than a very small number of schools. In 1899 an article was published in a Dutch periodical under the title "A Debt of Honor." The author, Van Deventer, argued that Holland should educate the Indonesian people as repayment for the many million guilders which she had extracted from them. This article had a strong effect on Dutch opinion and was in part responsible for the government's recognition of 1901 of the "moral duty of the Netherlands toward the people of the Indies." This policy of "moral duty" has also been called the "ethical policy." In 1905 the Dutch treasury gave 50,000,000 guilders to the Indies for the general improvement of conditions. In the first decade of the twentieth century the Dutch established village schools for elementary instruction at comparatively little cost. The government provided the buildings and the wood for the furniture, and paid the salaries of young teachers who had graduated from the schools established earlier. The villages were responsible for the upkeep of the schools, and the students had to pay a small monthly fee. But the development was slow and the level of education not very high. By 1913 there were only 7,000 schools in the Indies, half of which were village schools. The total enrollment was 227,000 students. Vocational schools were also established, but in general higher education was neglected. For higher education young Indonesians had to go to Holland or other Western countries. Actually the increase of school enrollment fell behind the growth of the population, and the educational record of the Dutch in the years of their colonial rule does not compare favorably with the Spanish or American record in the Philippines.

During this whole period the development of Indonesian economy was in foreign hands and the Indonesians were only the workers in an economic system which supplied raw materials for the Western markets. Their plane of living was little improved by the advances resulting from industrialization of the West. The land legislation and other measures of the Dutch which were meant to preserve the Indonesian cultural tradition actually froze the communal status of the villages and prevented any economic initiative on the part of the Indonesians. In the village economy some of the handicrafts of the past survived. The villagers continued to wear their traditional garments made from batik, a type of textile material made by a special technique in which color patterns on cloth are produced. Even much of the batik industry was taken over by non-Indonesians during the nineteenth and twentieth centuries. The Chinese gained a virtual monopoly of this industry, controlling the sources of raw materials and organizing the production of Indonesian workers under Chinese entrepreneurs.

By the time of World War I the pattern of the Indonesian economy was one in which the Dutch and other Europeans controlled the capital; the Chinese were a middle group, taking some part in plantation development but concerning themselves mainly with retail trade, moneylending and pawnshops, and with entrepreneurial activities in local industries, such as batik; and the Indonesians were the workers except for the members of the aristocracy whom the Dutch used in the government.

The plantation economy spread from Java to the outer islands. The land available for planting on densely populated Java was limited. The protective Dutch legislation prevented the plantations from expanding their control of village land because it would cut down the rice supply for the population. Sumatra, Borneo, and the islands to the east of Java were the main regions where land was available, and it was there that the plantation economy as well as the mining industry came to be largely centered. During the second half of the nineteenth century the Dutch moved inland on these islands from their coastal possessions. In the eighteen seventies the Dutch brought most of northern Sumatra under their control with the exception of the state of Atjeh on the northern coast of the island. This area, like most of the coastal states of Sumatra, was strongly Moslem. Its people were seafarers, trading or engaging in piracy on the trade routes in the Malacca Straits. In 1893 the Dutch started a war against Atjeh to eliminate the piracy and bring the state into submission. But since the sultan of Atjeh had little control over the traders and the local population, the Dutch had to subdue many fanatical Moslem forces led by local leaders and religious teachers who carried on a prolonged guerrilla war. Not until 1908 was Atjeh finally brought to submission. Between 1896 and 1900 the interior of Borneo was explored and Dutch control extended. In these islands the Dutch established the political order which made possible the plantation development of the early twentieth century. At the end of World War I more than 60 per cent of the plantation economy was concentrated on Sumatra, a little more than 20 per cent on Java, the rest on the other islands of Borneo and the east.

Indonesian nationalists first began to express themselves in the first decades of the twentieth century. Their opposition to the Dutch differed completely from the earlier resistance of the sultans, princes, and merchants of Mataram, Jocjakarta, and the Sumatran states against the Dutch East Indies Company or the colonial government of the nineteenth century. The nationalists of the twentieth century aimed at self-government, independence, and freedom from foreign economic control. Nationalism began as a cultural movement and was founded by modern, Western-trained intellectuals. A society *Budi Utomo* (High Endeavor) was organized in 1908, with the primary purpose of establishing Indonesian schools and promoting a program of Indonesian culture and social and economic progress in general. It soon had more than 10,000 members among the leading Indonesian intellectuals, officials, and aristocracy. The *Budi Utomo* wanted to provide educational opportunities for Indonesians so that they would be treated as equals by the Europeans. The Dutch had not only neglected Indonesian education but had also made little use of educated Indonesians in higher positions in government, industry, or business. Higher educational standards, it was thought, would strengthen the Indonesian claim for participation in political and economic positions of responsibility. The leaders of *Budi Utomo* stressed a revival of the Indonesian cultural tradition as the basis for the new education.

The *Budi Utomo* movement developed on Java and Madura, where the old Hindu tradition among the upper social groups had not been entirely displaced by Islam, as it had been on Sumatra and where at this time the ideas of Gandhi and Tagore had a great influence. This educational movement, limited largely to the intellectuals, was soon superseded by the more popular *Sarekat Islam*, founded in 1910. The *Sarekat Islam*, as its name indicates, was a movement which aimed at strengthening the Islamic religion. At the outset the movement led the fight of the batik industry against the exploitation of Indonesian workers by Chinese entrepreneurs. It stood for the promotion of commercial enterprise among the Indonesians and of cooperative effort for mutual economic support.

The *Sarekat Islam* was behind a number of anti-Chinese riots in Soerabaja and Soerakarta in 1911 and was temporarily suppressed by the government. But in 1912 it was reorganized and became the first mass movement in Indonesia. At the first congress of the *Sarekat Islam* in 1913 its leader declared that the organization was not a political party and that it was loyal to the government. At the national congress in 1916, however, resolutions were passed which demanded an evolutionary development of self-government within the framework of the Dutch empire. After 1917 *Sarekat Islam* became more radical, but at the Congress of 1921 the radical leadership was purged. After that time the organization declined in membership and influence. The *Sarekat Islam*, however, was the first indication of the strength of Islam as a basis for a political organization in Indonesia.

In answer to the nationalist movement in the Indies, the Dutch government introduced the first steps toward self-government. A law of 1903 had provided for the establishment of local and city councils, but these had a very limited authority. It was only the strength of such movements as *Sarekat Islam* which forced the Dutch government to make concessions permitting

Indonesians to participate in the colonial government. During World War I, when the trend toward national self-government was strengthened in both Europe and the East, the Dutch government yielded to the agitation for greater Indonesian autonomy, and in 1916 established the so-called Volksraad or People's Council. The Council, which met first in May, 1918, originally had 39 members, of which the majority were Europeans. The number of Indonesian members was later increased, and by 1928 the Volksraad consisted of thirty Indonesians, twenty-five Dutch, four Chinese, and one Arab. Twenty Indonesians, fifteen Dutch, and three Chinese were elected; the rest were appointed by the governor-general. The Volksraad, which at first had only an advisory function, was eventually given a decisive voice in the determination of the budget and had to approve many other measures undertaken by the governor-general's administration. Popular representation was thus established after World War I, but it provided very limited participation in government for the Indonesians, who held only half the seats of the council and only one-third of the elected seats. The small European ruling group, with twenty-five representatives, held a disproportionate share of the seats. The power of the Dutch colonial government was assured by its right to appoint a large number of representatives. Nationalism had made a start in the first decades of the twentieth century, but the colonial government retained its control.

3. THE PHILIPPINES

Until the nineteenth century Spain ruled the Philippines as a sub-colony of the Spanish-American colonial empire. The products of the colony were shipped from Manila to Acapulco in Mexico and from there to Europe. The loss of the Spanish-American colonies in the first decades of the nineteenth century therefore destroyed the base from which Spain controlled and exploited the Philippines, and the successful revolt of the colonies set a dangerous example for the Philippines. Spain found it necessary to readjust both its economic and political relationships with the Philippines.

The need for readjustment came at the time when new ideas were abroad in Europe as a result of the French Revolution and the Napoleonic Wars. The mood prevailing in Spain at that time favored the development of free trade rather than the continuation of the Spanish government's monopoly. In 1830 the Spanish opened Manila to foreign trade, an act which resulted in a new prosperity for Manila. As a result of this experience and the continued pressure of Philippine merchants, five additional ports were opened to general trade between 1855 and 1862. The new commercial activities brought wealth to a growing number of merchant families which became influential in the trading ports and were interested in political developments. It was this group which accepted and propagated European ideas of nationalism and progress and pressed for their application in the Philippines.

The new economic relationship with the Philippines was not matched by equally liberal political attitudes on the part of the Spanish government. The more the Filipino commercial and intellectual leaders prospered on free trade and revolutionary European ideas, the more the Spanish reverted to the traditional policy of strict political and cultural control. Weakened by the loss of the American colonies and stagnant in her own economic and political development, Spain tried to hold back any move in the Philippines towards greater economic and political autonomy.

At the beginning of the nineteenth century, Filipinos joined with some of the liberals in Spain in an attempt to bring about Philippine participation in the government of Spain as well as reform in the Philippines themselves. In the first decades of the nineteenth century, a Philippine delegate was sent as a representative to the *Cortes*, the Spanish legislature, which the liberals hoped would come to play a greater part in the government of Spain. But the representative was a Spaniard rather than a Filipino and was appointed by the governor-general, so that in fact he did not represent the new national aspirations in the Philippines. In 1836 the *Cortes* discussed the question of instituting the election of a Philippine delegate. But this proposal was defeated, and a year later even the representation through an appointed delegate was discontinued. This attempt to strengthen the Philippine voice in Spanish politics failed and was never renewed.

The new business group in the Philippines combined with the Western-educated leaders to press for reform of the educational system. Education in the Philippines was entirely in the hands of the Catholic Church. Following the European trend of the secularization of schools, the new Filipino nationalists pressed for a separation of the school system from the church. In this they were only partially successful. A public school system was introduced in 1863, in which education was removed from the monopoly of the church. Secular and religious subjects were separated in the schools, and although the clergy still remained influential in education, it was no longer in complete control of teaching.

The economic concessions and the compromise on the system of education were as far as the Spanish government was willing to go in loosening its colonial rule. While the Filipino drive for greater freedom increased towards the end of the century, the Spanish government became more conservative, and the contrast between Spanish policy and the aspirations of the new Philippine nationalists sharpened. Their demands were at first for reforms and autonomy rather than for independence. But as the Spanish resisted the changes they requested and began to suppress their activities, the Filipinos turned from reform to revolution. Their aim was the complete separation of the Philippines from Spanish rule. Their fight was directed against the policy of the Spanish governor-general, which was dictated from Spain and supported by Spanish troops, and also against the Catholic Church, which had large landholdings and participated in the Spanish exploitation of the colony. It is significant that the fight against the church lands, or the so-called "friar lands," was not extended to all landed estates, as this would have affected the landholdings of the Philippine upper group itself. The new liberal ideas of

Europe were used as a weapon with which to fight for political freedom and economic independence from Spain, but the Philippine nationalists did not apply these ideas to their own disadvantage in domestic affairs.

The symbol of the fight for freedom in the Philippines was Jose Rizal y Mercado (1869–1896). Rizal was partly Chinese and came from a family that had been fairly well off. Like other well-to-do young people he had gone abroad to study, in Spain, France, and Germany. While studying for a degree in medicine Rizal read widely in the liberal and socialist literature of the Europe of his time. In his writings Rizal attacked the stagnation and backwardness of the Spanish government, and urged political and educational reforms. He attacked the all-pervading political influence of the Spanish friars, who in his opinion were the main obstacle to reforms. In 1886, while he was still in Germany, Rizal wrote a political novel, *Noli Me Tangere*, in which he attacked Spanish tyranny and suppression of free thought. This book and a second novel, *El Filibusterismo*, of similar content, published in 1890, expressed the mood and thinking of his contemporaries in the Philippines and had a vast influence on them. When Rizal returned to the Philippines in 1892, he was already regarded as a national leader by the Filipino intellectuals and at the same time treated with suspicion by the Spanish officials.

In the year of his return Rizal organized the *Liga Filipina*, which he intended to be a social as well as a political movement. He wanted to bring together young men from different social strata, educated or uneducated, to organize cooperative groups for agricultural, commercial, and handicraft enterprises and to train them in these fields. The *Liga Filipina* was also to provide general educational facilities and to promote the establishment of liberal political institutions. This movement had no more than a start, however, when Rizal was arrested and deported to the island of Mindanao, where he remained for three years as a virtual prisoner. In 1895 he petitioned the Spanish governor-general to let him leave for Cuba, where he was willing to serve as an army doctor. This request was entirely acceptable to the authorities. Shortly after Rizal arrived in Cuba the revolution of 1896 broke out. Rizal was accused of participation, taken prisoner, brought to Spain, and executed there on December 30, 1896. With his death Rizal became the hero of Philippine nationalism, and his statue in Manila testifies to his place as the founder of the liberal nationalist tradition.

The independence movement had taken a more radical turn after the arrest of Rizal. A secret society was founded, the *Katipunan*, which advocated a sweeping reform of the government and the elimination of the influence of the Spanish friars. One of the aims of the *Katipunan* was to distribute among the tenant farmers the vast landed estates which the church had accumulated and from which it derived its main income. This program of land distribution provided the secret society with broad popular support from the tenant farmers in many of the agrarian areas of Luzon. It is believed that in 1896 the society had over 50,000 members. The Spanish government and the church attempted to suppress the movement, and several of its leaders—as well as some other outstanding Filipinos who were not politically involved—were arrested and executed or exiled.

This attempted suppression caused an open military outbreak. The *Katipunan* organized its own local militia and in August, 1896, attempted to capture Manila. The attempt failed and several local outbreaks were suppressed by the Spanish with the help of military reinforcements. The membership and power of the *Katipunan* continued to grow. In 1897 Emilio Aguinaldo became the head of the organization, and a proclamation was issued demanding: (1) that the Spanish friars be expelled and their land be returned to the communities; (2) that all persons be equal before the law; (3) that parliamentary representation be granted to the Philippines, and freedom of assembly, of the press, and of religion be established; and (4) that Spaniards and Filipinos be equally treated and equally paid in civil service positions. These demands were disregarded by the government and the fighting continued. In December, 1897, a truce was concluded between the rebels and the government. The government promised to institute reforms, to grant political amnesty to the rebels, and to compensate the rebel leaders with a cash payment. The reforms did not materialize, however, and the persecution of rebellious leaders continued. Aguinaldo and his followers, who had gone to Hong Kong, continued their political activities until the Spanish-American War gave them and their movement a new opportunity.

The Philippine nationalist movement began with a program of political and social reforms and was not originally anti-Spanish. In fact, most of its leaders were Spanish or partly Spanish by origin and came from the *encomienda* and merchant families which had flourished under the Spanish system. Stimulated by the economic changes of the nineteenth century and influenced by nationalist and liberal ideas, these leaders came to demand a reformed government of the Philippines in which they would have a voice. It was only when they saw that their hopes could not be fulfilled that they turned to rebellion against Spain and took up the fight for independence. Once political independence became their goal, they never gave it up and the fight for independence continued against the new colonial power—the United States.

At the outset of the Spanish-American War, American plans for the Philippines were not clear. Even after Dewey's victory over the Spanish fleet in Manila Bay on May 1, 1898, it was uncertain how far the drive for naval expansion would go. In his efforts to defeat the Spanish Dewey was willing to cooperate with the Philippine insurrection leader Aguinaldo but was cautious enough not to make him any definite promises. Discussions with the American consular representative in Singapore, however, gave Aguinaldo the impression that the Americans would support his plans for independence. After the battle of Manila Bay an American ship brought him back to the Philippines where he arrived on May 19, 1898. There Aguinaldo organized a military force, supplied with the help of the United States, and with this force drove the Spanish from large parts of Luzon. On May 24 he established a provisional government and on June 12 he declared the independence of the Philippines. On August 6 Aguinaldo called on the foreign governments to recognize the independence of the Philippine Republic and its status as a belligerent in the war against Spain. Aguinaldo took these actions before American troops were on the scene. When they arrived, American and Philippine troops together attacked Manila and forced its surrender on August 13. After the capture of Manila Aguinaldo continued to organize his new government. In September a congress was called to draft a constitution, which was completed in November and promulgated by Aguinaldo on January 21, 1899.

While Aguinaldo was setting up his republican government, the political battle over the fate of the Philippines was fought in public debate in the United States and in the Spanish-American negotiations for the Treaty of Paris. The American decision to request from Spain the cession of the whole island group destroyed the chances of the Philippines for independence. But the signing of the peace treaty in December, 1898, did not stop the Philippine leaders from completing their constitutional work or from continuing to fight for their independence.

There was considerable opposition in America to the annexation of the Philippines. The platforms of both political parties included promises for their eventual independence. The conflicting emotions and motivations are reflected in a statement made by President McKinley in August, 1898, to a group of Protestant clergymen:

> The truth is I didn't want the Philippines and when they came to us as a gift from the gods, I did not know what to do about them. . . . I sought counsel from all sides—Democrats as well as Republicans—but got little help. I thought first we would take only Manila; then Luzon; then other islands, perhaps, also. I walked the floor of the White House night after night until midnight; and I am not ashamed to tell you, gentlemen, that I went down on my knees and prayed Almighty God for light and guidance more than one night. And one night late it came to me this way—I don't know how it was, but it came: (1) that we could not give them back to Spain—that would be cowardly and dishonorable; (2) that we could not turn them over to France or Germany—our commercial rivals in the Orient—that would be bad business and discreditable; (3) that we could not leave them to themselves—they were unfit for self-government—and they would soon have anarchy and misrule over there worse than Spain's was; and (4) that there was nothing left for us to do but to take them all, and to educate the Filipinos, and uplift and civilize and Christianize them, and by God's grace do the very best we could by them, as our fellow-men for whom Christ also died. And then I went to bed, and went to sleep and slept soundly. . . .[1]

This statement is all the more remarkable in view of the fact that the Filipinos were Christians of the Catholic faith. Filipino leaders felt ready to assume the responsibility of self-government and protested the transfer of authority from Spain to the United States, claiming that since they had established their own *de facto* government, Spain had lost her authority in the Philippines and could therefore not transfer any rights to the United States. When their protests were disregarded, they started military action against the troops of the United States.

[1] *Christian Advocate* (N. Y.), Jan. 22, 1903. Quoted in Thomas A. Bailey, *A Diplomatic History of the American People* (New York, 1942), p. 520.

From February to November, 1899, the American forces fought an open war against the Philippine troops, driving them from one area to another. But the war did not end with the defeat of Filipino troops in the field and the occupation of government headquarters. The Filipinos turned to guerrilla warfare, and all over the country secret military units were organized which constantly attacked and harassed American forces. The garrisoning of all the troubled areas placed a strain on American military resources. In the spring of 1900, General Arthur MacArthur was given command of American forces fighting the Filipinos. During the next half year little military progress was made. Filipino resistance was not suppressed until military action was combined with political measures. The United States promised the Filipinos participation in the new civil government which it would establish.

The new civil administration in the Philippines, which was to replace American military government, was worked out by planning commissions from the United States. The first commission was sent in 1899 and was replaced in 1900 by a permanent commission under the chairmanship of Judge William Howard Taft, who later became the first governor of the Philippines. Following the recommendations of the commission a new administration was established in which Filipino officials were elected to municipal and provincial governments. The electorate consisted of men who were over twenty-one years of age and who could read and write English or Spanish, or who had taxable property. All the justices of the peace, half the justices of the court of first instance, and three of the seven justices of a newly established supreme court were Filipinos. The introduction of these measures giving the Filipinos immediate participation in their local government contributed as much as the military actions to the suppression of Philippine resistance to American control. Many Filipinos deserted Aguinaldo and took the oath of allegiance to the United States. Aguinaldo himself was captured in March, 1901, but the last of his followers did not surrender until June, 1902.

In July, 1901, Taft became civil governor and continued the organization of civil government as outlined by the commission. His program included the establishment of a department of public instruction and the building up of a system of primary, intermediate, and secondary schools patterned after that of the United States. A large number of American teachers were brought to the Philippines. At the same time a normal school was established in Manila to train Filipino teachers who could eventually replace the American staff. In 1908 the University of Manila was founded. The school system which the Americans established in the Philippines considerably expanded the opportunities for education. Over a third of the children of school age were enrolled in schools, a higher percentage than in any of the other colonial countries of the Far East, though still far below the high record of modern Japan. Governor Taft also established a bureau of public health to provide for modern sanitation and to take measures to control the existing danger of smallpox and cholera epidemics.

The Taft administration undertook an agrarian reform program under which 430,000 acres of friar lands were taken over by the government and sold to the tenants. These land measures were politically important because Aguinaldo's fight against the landholdings of the church had been an important aspect of his revolutionary movement. This agrarian reform program affected somewhat less than 10 per cent of the cultivated land but did not include all the church lands nor did it touch upon the larger question of the landed estates that had been created by the *encomienda* system. The issue of landlordism and tenancy remained a major problem of the Philippines.

The Taft administration had given the Filipinos a chance to participate in their government. But the Filipino leaders, in spite of their willingness to cooperate with the American administration, continued to struggle for full independence. As in other parts of the Far East, the victory of the Japanese in the Russo-Japanese War had a profound influence on the nationalist leaders in the Philippines and strengthened the nationalist movement. The nationalist pressure within the Philippines was met by an American program which provided for the first representative Philippine assembly, elected in July, 1907. The existing Philippine commission of five Americans and four Filipinos, all appointed by the President, became the upper house of the bicameral legislature. Political parties were organized, some of which stood for immediate independence while others were willing to accept the American administration of the time with the understanding that independence would come in the not too distant future.

The representative system of government was greatly expanded during the period of World War I. The Democratic party in the United States had stood for Philippine independence even before it came into power with the election of President Wilson. President Wilson appointed Francis Burton Harrison as governor-general of the Philippines. The period of his administration has sometimes been described as the time of "Filipinization" of the government of the islands. A great number of American officials were replaced by Filipinos. At the end of Harrison's tenure very few Americans remained in positions of authority and the actual management of affairs had become a Philippine responsibility. The addition of two Filipino members to the commission gave the Filipinos a majority in the upper branch of the legislature. Governor Harrison stated that he would accept the decisions of the legislature as binding on him, thus transferring the actual responsibility of political decisions to the Filipinos.

The Jones Act, passed in August, 1916, by the American Congress formalized these administrative moves. This act contained the first official promise of eventual independence for the Philippines. The act provided for a new legislature of two houses, a senate and a house of representatives. The Philippine Congress had full legislative authority limited only by the powers of the governor-general and the President of the United States. The President of the United States held the right to veto in certain specified instances, and the governor-general held the same veto powers in the Philippine system as the President in the American system. The legislature had no power to deal with the trade relations between the Philippines and the United States or to disregard a Philippine bill of rights included in the Jones Act. A Philippine executive authority was added in 1918 by the creation of a council of state, consisting mostly of the chairmen of executive departments. This council of state was to determine administrative policies while the governor-general came to act principally as an adviser. In 1919 President Wilson, on the advice of Governor-general Harrison, recommended to Congress the initiation of legislation giving the Philippines complete independence. But with the change of administration in 1920 the policy of maintaining effective American control was resumed and the fulfillment of the promise for independence had to wait another quarter of a century. However, during the entire period of American administration and guidance American political institutions were introduced and political parties formed which provided a strong base for the Philippine government when independence was finally attained.

American control of the Philippines brought the two countries into close economic relationship. When America took over, she promised in an "open door" declaration to permit other countries to participate in the economic development of the Philippines. Furthermore, the peace treaty with Spain provided that for a period of ten years the islands were to be kept outside of the United States tariff system. After this treaty obligation expired in 1909, the enclosure of the Philippines in the American system brought very important changes to her whole economy. The duty-free import of Philippine products into the United States made it profitable to invest in Philippine plantations producing sugar, copra, tobacco, hemp, and flax. The new plantations that were created converted a substantial acreage from rice cultivation to the production of cash crops for the American market. This colonial type of economic development caused a number of serious problems in the Philippines. The position of the tenant farmers in the estates producing the cash crops became worse because they no longer produced their own food and were therefore all the more dependent on their landlords. Tenancy contracts were shortened and gave less and less protection to the peasants. Little incentive remained for the short-term tenant farmer to improve his holding by investing his labor or capital. Tension between landlords and tenants increased and prepared the ground for political conflict and open rebellion.

The close trade relationship also had the effect of making the Philippine economy almost completely dependent on the United States. After 1909 the Philippines came to trade principally with the United States. The import of American manufactured goods, which had amounted to only $1,150,000 in 1899 had reached a figure of about $5,000,000 in 1908 just before the treaty with Spain expired. After 1909 this import increased rapidly until after the First World War it reached a figure of over $50,000,000 or more than 60 per cent of the total Philippine imports. At the same time the exports to the United States, which had been negligible at the time of the annexation, made up about 80 per cent of the total Philippine exports. This trade was only a very small percentage of America's total commerce and did not mean a great deal to her, but to the Philippines it became of vital importance. The problem of political independence indeed came to be closely linked with the economic dependence of the Philippines on the American market.

4. FRENCH INDO-CHINA

The French penetration into Indo-China dates back to the seventeenth century, when French Jesuits went to Annam, Tongking, and Cambodia and helped to open them to French commercial enterprise. During the last part of the seventeenth century the French extended their interest to Siam, but when their attempts at political control were defeated in 1688, they concentrated again on Indo-China. During the early eighteenth century French activities there were limited to missionary work, but in 1787 a political struggle took place in the kingdom of Annam which presented an opportunity for French intervention. A fight among several brothers for the succession to the throne provided the French with the chance to support one of the brothers who had been driven out by the others. At the suggestion of a missionary bishop a small French expeditionary force was sent and with its help the defeated candidate was restored to the throne. This king, who reigned under the title Gia-long, established his capital at Hué and by 1801 had united under his rule the whole of Annam, including the northern and southern areas of Tongking and Cochin China. For their help the French received the bay of Tourane and an island group at the mouth of the Saigon River. The French Revolution and the Napoleonic Wars prevented any further French expansion, and the king of Annam ruled undisturbed over all of Annam and continued to acknowledge his tributary relationship to the emperor of China.

Although Gia-long had been placed on the throne with the help of a French missionary bishop, the royal government was suspicious of missionaries. This suspicion, more political than religious, led to occasional persecutions. The fear that missionaries were the spearhead of Western aggression increased after the Opium War, and in 1858, as a result of the Anglo-French war in China, new attacks were made upon French and Spanish missionaries. Both France and Spain sent in troops, but the Spanish soon withdrew. French troops captured the city of Saigon in 1859, and in 1860 they occupied the three provinces of eastern Cochin China. In 1862 a treaty was signed in which the king of Annam was forced to cede the area of Cochin China, which became a French colony. From Cochin China the French moved up the Mekong plain into Cambodia, over which Siam claimed suzerainty. The French counted on the possibility that Siam would intervene in defense of Cambodia and thus give France the opportunity to invade Siam itself. But the Siamese government relinquished Cambodia without a fight, and the French established their protectorate over it in 1867. A French move into Siam was averted by a strong indication of British opposition, and the French instead turned north towards Annam and Tongking.

The Franco-Prussian War of 1870–1871 delayed for a few years further French moves into northern Annam. In 1871, however, a French merchant,

Jean Dupuis, made a commercial agreement with the Chinese provincial administration in Yunnan for the delivery of arms to the troops fighting against the Moslem rebels in southwest China. When he arrived with his merchandise in 1873, the Annamese officials at Hanoi refused him passage through the Red River Valley. Thereupon, Dupuis brought in a mercenary force of Chinese and Filipinos with which he occupied part of Hanoi and called upon the French government for help. French troops occupied Hanoi and the neighborhood, but were not strong enough to hold the area and were withdrawn. In a treaty of 1874, however, the Annamese government was forced to give the French the right to trade at Haiphong, Hanoi, and throughout the Red River Valley. The treaty also provided extraterritoriality for French citizens and protection for missionaries.

To resist further French advances the Annamese officials called in Chinese regional troops from the border area. These were the so-called Black Flags who moved into Hanoi and the Red River area and from 1881 to 1885 fought the French from Tongking to the Yunnan border. By 1882 the French troops had taken Hanoi and much of the Red River delta. They also occupied the capital of Hué, and when the king fled, they placed on the throne first his brother, and after he had been assassinated, his nephew. In 1883 the French concluded a treaty with this king by which Tongking was separated from the rest of Annam and became a French protectorate, while Annam itself was placed under French protection. But the French troops did not succeed in breaking the resistance of the Black Flags on the border or in forcing Chinese acceptance of the French protectorates over Tongking and Annam. A war with China resulted. The Chinese regional troops had some success against the French on the Chinese border, but the French fleet destroyed the new Chinese fleet and arsenals at Foochow and blockaded the China coast. In the treaty of Tientsin in 1885, which ended the war, China gave up her claim to suzerainty over Annam and recognized the French protectorates. French and Chinese were permitted to travel across the Tongking-Chinese border which was opened to trade. The French secured the right to build railroads in Tongking and were to be called upon when the Chinese needed foreign capital to build a railroad in Yunnan.

After gaining control of Annam, the French consolidated their position. In 1884 they concluded a second treaty with the king of Cambodia, leaving the latter only in nominal control of the country. In 1893 they moved on to Laos and occupied most of that mountainous state. Some local resistance and small-scale warfare continued, but by 1907 the French had completed their conquest of Indo-China.

The French colonial possession of Indo-China consisted of one colony, Cochin China, and four protectorates, Cambodia, Annam, Tongking, and Laos. Of the two Buddhist states, Cambodia and Laos, Cambodia had been a unified kingdom whereas Laos had been divided into several political units. Under French rule Cambodia remained united and Laos was made into one kingdom. In contrast, the kingdom of Annam, which had been unified, was divided into three parts by separating the rich agricultural river areas of the north and south from the long, central, coastal strip of the kingdom. The French combined the five sections into one colony and called it French Indo-China.

The French system of centralized government, derived from the Napoleonic tradition in France, was applied to Indo-China. The head of the French administration was a governor-general who resided in Hanoi, the capital of French Indo-China. The governor-general was a political appointee and usually had no previous experience for the position. The average term of office, about two years, gave the governor-general little time to acquaint himself with the problems of the colony. He was therefore at the mercy of the permanent French officials. Any willingness to act on his own initiative was further restrained by his dependence on the Ministry of Colonies in Paris. Under this ministry there was established a Department of Direction of Control, which consisted of a number of inspectors who regularly visited the colonial governments. Their reports remained secret, and out of respect for their authority and that of the ministry in Paris, the local administrator was little inclined to do anything but carry out instructions from home.

Under the governor-general, there were the governor for Cochin China and the *résidents supérieurs* for each of the four protectorates. The colony of Cochin China had an almost entirely French administration, the official hierarchy, down to the minor positions, consisting mainly of Frenchmen. An advisory privy council was consulted by the governor on executive matters. A colonial council, partly appointed and partly elected by French citizens and a small number of influential Annamese, controlled taxation and had advisory functions in other matters. Cochin China was actually a part of the French metropolitan administration. The close relationship of Cochin China to France was indicated also by the election of one deputy from Cochin China to the French chamber. This deputy was elected by the French citizens in Cochin China.

The same general type of organization applied to the protectorates. The highest French officials in the four protectorates were the *résidents supérieurs*, responsible to the governor-general at Hanoi in the same way as was the governor of Cochin China. Each *résident supérieur* ruled with the help of an appointed executive council. The kings of Cambodia, Annam, and Laos received ample salaries and retained elaborate ceremonies at their courts but the actual administration of revenues and public works and the maintenance of peace and order were under the control of the chief residents. The protectorates were subdivided into provinces, each under a resident. The French used a greater number of native officials for local government in the protectorates than they used in the colony of Cochin China. But these native officials were French appointees and were paid by the colonial government upon which, as they well knew, their positions depended. On the village level, elected headmen carried out tax collection and police control. These headmen too were responsible to their French superiors, upon whom they were in fact dependent. Whether through French and native officials in the protectorates or through French officials in the colony, the French administration in Indo-China was a strongly centralized system, directed through the governor-general by the metropolitan government of France. This system was not changed by the introduction of protectorate councils, or, as in Cambodia, by a consultative native assembly. Such bodies were elected mostly by the officials and notables in French service, and had only advisory functions. The Cambodian assembly, for instance, was expressly forbidden to debate political subjects.

It was the French policy to grant French citizenship to a very limited number of their colonial subjects, as an honor bestowed for meritorious service to France. It permitted participation in the French political system rather than in that of the colony. Its purpose was to create a special loyalty to France and to discourage local responsibility and leadership. This system of centralization was a special characteristic of the French colonial policy. Although the French drew no color line and were comparatively free from racial prejudice, the distinction which they made between a small number of French citizens and a large number of French subjects resulted in another form of discrimination.

The French colonial government was concerned with the development of production for the world market. Rice became one of the main export crops. In the Tongking area of the Red River delta, production was mainly in the hands of small owners. The landholdings of the peasants were very small with 60 per cent of the peasant families owning less than one acre. Although the peasants owned their land, they were generally in debt to Chinese middlemen who controlled the rice crops. Overpopulation prevented any large surplus, and in bad years the Tongking area actually imported rice from Cochin China where the French had built large irrigation works. In the Mekong delta the area under cultivation was more than doubled in the period between 1880 and 1937. Here the land was owned largely by landlords and worked by tenant farmers. Agricultural indebtedness in the north and the estate system of the south created a measure of agrarian discontent. This discontent was often directed against Chinese moneylenders who controlled the rice market and against the whole Chinese minority in Cochin China, which numbered only some 300,000 people but played an important economic role. French Indo-China also provided rubber and a number of raw materials for French industries. Coal, tin, and zinc were mined mainly in Tongking. Iron ore, bauxite, and manganese were also produced. It was French policy in Indo-China to favor these French economic interests. Aside from the opportunity provided for French mining companies, rubber plantations, and other enterprises, there was a protected market for industrial exports from France. The French discriminated against the Annamese both politically and economically.

The first signs of a new Annamese nationalism came in the first decades of the twentieth century. The influence of liberal thought from France and from other countries of Asia had its effect on a small group of Western-trained Annamese intellectuals. The Japanese victory in the Russo-Japanese War showed that an Asiatic people was capable of a modern development and provided stimulation for a latent anti-foreignism. The years following 1905 became known as the "Era of Plots" in which a number of local uprisings directed against French control were suppressed. A group of "young Annamites" compiled a list of grievances against the French regime. Under the influence of the reform movement of K'ang Yu-wei and Liang Ch'i-ch'ao in China, Annamese intellectuals began to read translations of European philosophers of the eighteenth and nineteenth centuries. Names like Rousseau and Montesquieu became familiar and their ideas were discussed. One main grievance of these intellectuals, who had acquired their knowledge abroad, was the lack of educational opportunity provided by the French. As a result of their pleas the French opened a university at Hanoi, but it was closed again in 1908 in reaction against anti-French uprisings.

The French position in Indo-China improved at the end of World War I when France was one of the victorious powers. The original attraction of Japan was weakened when Japan herself followed a course of imperialism. But the war also created new elements of discontent. After 1915, over 100,000 Annamese workers were drafted for labor in France; some were also used as soldiers. On their return these men brought back to Annam a knowledge of the West and a desire to improve their own condition.

After World War I the trend towards nationalism began to make itself felt in French Indo-China. The economic conditions caused strong grievances which were aggravated by an awareness of the possibilities of better standards of living. A growing number of intellectuals were acquainted with Western ideas of nationalism and self-rule but had no openings for their talents under the centralized French colonial system. Some French critics pointed out the danger of such a policy of "education without application," but the French continued their political system and blocked opposition by a policy of divide and rule, through which they prevented the splinter groups of intellectuals from combining into any large party formations. The intellectual elite, educated under the French system but finding no place in it, created an atmosphere of dissatisfaction out of which grew an anti-French nationalist movement which had no strong leader or organization and which the French administration did everything in its power to divide and disorganize.

5. BURMA

At the beginning of the nineteenth century the Burmese kingdom was at the height of its power. Secure in its inland position and in its bureaucratic agricultural tradition, this kingdom had a Chinese contempt for commercial ventures and commercial powers. Burmese political control went beyond the mountain ranges which protected the basins of the Irrawaddy and Sittang rivers. It included the Arakan area on the coast of the Sea of Bengal and the Tenasserim region on the western upper arm of the Malay Peninsula. The Burmese had also invaded and retained a part of southeastern Assam. As a result of this penetration into Assam, the Burmese state faced the domains of the British East India Company, which was expanding its control over

Indian territory. Border conflicts between Burmese forces and the British East India Company at Chittagong and in eastern Assam broke out in 1823 and were used by the British as an excuse for a war against Burma in 1824. In this war British forces drove the Burmese out of Assam and also took the coastal stretches of Arakan and of Tenasserim. The British army captured Rangoon in May, 1824, and marched overland against the Burmese capital at Ava. In February, 1826, a peace treaty was signed in which the Burmese kingdom yielded the coastal territories of Arakan and of Tenasserim and the Assam border area.

The Anglo-Burmese War of 1824–1826 was but the first of the three stages by which the British incorporated the whole of Burma into their colonial empire. Arakan became a part of Bengal and was developed as a major rice producing area. Tenasserim, which was at first an unprofitable acquisition, eventually became a source of income for British firms which exploited its teakwood production. The treaty of 1826 also provided for a British residency at the Burmese capital of Ava. The resident attempted to negotiate for the opening of Burma to British commercial enterprises, but the Burmese continued to oppose all attempts at further British economic penetration. Dissatisfied with the negative results of their negotiations and aware that the teak resources at Tenasserim were dwindling, the British started a new war in 1852. British military expeditions were sent up the valleys of the Irrawaddy and the Sittang rivers and drove back the Burmese forces. They did not move farther than halfway to the Burmese capital, which had now been moved near Mandalay, for the farther the expeditions moved into the interior, the more the Burmese resistance increased. The East India Company contented itself with annexation of the province of Pegu in the lower southern valleys of both rivers. This annexation brought British control to the towns of Prome on the Irrawaddy and Toungoo on the Sittang. But the British had to fight for eight years to overcome local resistance and have their rule accepted.

The kingdom of Burma came to an end in 1885 after a third British-Burmese war. The British military action was in part precipitated by the fear that the French might move in first and take over. The French were at that time establishing their protectorate over Annam, and the Burmese government attempted to negotiate with France in order to counter the British threat. A quick military campaign ended with the British conquest of Mandalay. The Burmese king was captured and exiled to India, and his country was annexed. But the opposition had not ended and a strong British-Indian army had to continue fighting for over four years to suppress Burmese resistance. Guerrilla warfare in upper Burma continued until 1895. This prolonged Burmese resistance, which followed each British conquest, was an indication of the will of the Burmese people to maintain their independence, even before modern nationalism made itself felt.

As the Burmese kingdom was a vassal state of the Chinese empire, it was necessary for the British to make a settlement with China in which the Chinese government would accept the British conquest. To make such a settlement easier, the British promised, in an agreement with the Chinese government in 1886, to continue the traditional tribute missions which had been sent to Peking every ten years. A Burmese tribute mission was actually sent in 1895, but after that the British discontinued this practice. Two years later, Burma was included in the administration of the Indian colonial government.

The British created a profitable colonial economy in Burma, but the Burmese people profited little. The British colonial government, by providing the opportunity for private investment in Burma and protecting this investment with a Western legal system, made it possible for Indian merchants and businessmen to take over much of the country's modern economy. The fact that Burma was administered by the British-Indian government facilitated the movement of Indians to Burma as entrepreneurs and as laborers. The Chettyars, a Hindu caste of bankers and moneylenders from Madras, came to control a large section of Burmese agriculture; their investments were estimated to be larger than all British investments in the country. Much of this investment was in the lower Irrawaddy delta where rice production increased tremendously in the last decades of the nineteenth century and the beginning of the twentieth century. Rice became one of the main exports and was sold mainly to India and Southeast Asia. The Burmese who brought the land under cultivation were given loans by Indian moneylenders who eventually came to own much of the land. The land was worked by Burmese peasants and by migratory Indian coolie labor. Between World War I and World War II, over a quarter of the land in the main rice districts belonged to Indian landowners, and a large number of Burmese peasants who had become landless moved from village to village as itinerant laborers. These homeless people provided an element of restlessness and insecurity which helped to undermine the traditional foundations of Burmese society and later became an explosive political factor.

The principal economic value of Burma for British firms was in its oil and teakwood resources. There was also considerable investment in lead, zinc, wolfram, and tin mining, in steamship companies, and in other enterprises. Oil was discovered and exploited at Akyab, Yenanguang, and Yenangyat. Teakwood production was regulated by a system of licensing introduced by the colonial government. This ended the wasteful and indiscriminate exploitation of the teak forests which in the early period of British control had endangered the resources of Tenasserim and lower Burma. The British created the means for a modern commercial development. Railroad lines were built; steamship companies were organized on the rivers; a modern postal service and telephone and telegraph service were established; and a Western legal system was introduced, in the framework of which this economy functioned.

The Burmese considered these Western measures a mere foreign importation. They did not share in the economic benefits, and remained antagonistic. The property laws of the West, which legalized mortgages on land and the right of foreclosure, were contrary to the Burmese tradition, according to which the ancestral lands could not be alienated. The introduction of

Western law might not have been so obnoxious to the Burmese had it not led to the loss of economic control to foreign moneylenders. As it was, the property laws of the West fed Burmese hatred of the Indians as well as of their British rulers.

The British also imposed upon Burma a new political system. After their conquest the British removed the district headmen who had led the prolonged Burmese resistance against British control. In their stead the British introduced a highly centralized colonial rule. Burma, as a province of the British-Indian government, was under a governor who controlled all local administration and had British deputy commissioners in the districts who were responsible to him. The deputy commissioners appointed headmen who were in charge of the villages or of wards and blocks in the towns and cities. These local headmen were responsible for tax collection and for supervising the policing of the villages. They maintained registration records for the villagers and could themselves enforce minor police regulations. They were thus an arm of the central government rather than local leaders. When the modern nationalist movement began they were forbidden to participate in political activities. British administration was thus kept apart from the local aspirations and national aims of the Burmese.

Under the British government the Buddhist orders, formerly so closely allied with the government of the Burmese kings, lost their official backing and functions. Without government authority it became more difficult to maintain discipline within the orders themselves, monastic rules were often not strictly enforced, and sometimes the monasteries became places of refuge for outlaws. The decline of the influence of the Buddhist orders led to a weakening of their educational role. Modern Western schools, introduced by the government or the missionaries, competed with the traditional Buddhist education which had stressed a philosophy of life rather than practical skills. The monasteries became centers of resentful opposition to the West and thus remained close to the Burmese people who were themselves resentful of Western economic and political domination. Although they did not maintain the standards of the past, the monasteries kept alive Burmese cultural resistance to Western civilization.

Western influence was much greater among the tribal groups. Missionary work, which had little success among the Burmese, was very effective among the Karens. The British found support among the chieftains of the Shan tribes who were better off under the British than they had been under the Burmese kings. Some of the tribal people also profited from the economic development of Burma. The Karens, for example, greatly raised their standard of living and level of education. They were given an opportunity under the British which they had never had under the Burmese and therefore tended to be pro-British in attitude. Having no advanced culture of their own, the Karens were all the more receptive to Western civilization. In contrast, the Burmese remained restless, economically dissatisfied, and culturally hostile. Their social traditions were undermined by the destruction of village cohesion and the increasing numbers of landless and homeless people. The bitterness eventually found an outlet in the struggle for national independence.

Burmese nationalism was first expressed after the Russo-Japanese War which gave to the Burmese and other Asiatic peoples the example of an Asian nation defeating a Western military power. Burmese nationalism became more pronounced during and after World War I, when President Wilson's call for self-determination was echoed all through the Far East. The Burmese movement combined opposition to British colonial rule with a bitter hostility to the Chettyars and the Indian laborers. It emphasized the cultural past of Burma and especially its Buddhist tradition. Buddhist religious groups took the lead in this movement.

As Burma was a part of British India, it claimed a share in the political reform measures which the British introduced in India at the end of World War I. The British were at first unwilling to extend to Burma the reforms resulting from the Montagu-Chelmsford report of 1919. When this became known in Burma, a representative General Council of Buddhist Associations protested, demanded self-government, and refused to accept any measures which did not give Burma the same position as India. As a result of this pressure the new form of government was applied to Burma in 1921, giving it the same position as the other provinces of British India. These reforms provided for the establishment of a legislative council through which the Burmese people would participate in their own government. In fact the provisions for Burma were actually more favorable than were those for the other Indian provinces. In Burma 80 per cent of the members of the legislative council were elected as compared with 70 per cent in India. In addition to these legislative councils the Montagu-Chelmsford reforms provided for a dyarchic system in the executive branch of government by which half the members of the governor's cabinet were responsible to the legislative council while the other half were appointed by the governor and responsible to him. In this way the British tried to reserve for themselves some of the most important controlling functions, such as finance and police, while transferring some of the other functions, such as education, to a representative government. In Burma, the important Forest Department was transferred to Burmese control, a concession which had not been given to the Indian provinces.

The dyarchic system did not, however, gain the support of the Burmese religious and nationalist leaders. The governor found it extremely difficult to find Burmese willing to accept cabinet positions or other high offices and had to turn to the Karens, Indians, Chinese, or British to fill these positions. The governor's cabinet could do little more than continue to maintain the status quo through orderly government and cautious administration of finances. The whole system of dyarchic government became thoroughly discredited in Burmese eyes and the General Council of Buddhist Associations by majority decisions boycotted the elections. In the districts, indirectly elected councils were given authority in the fields of education, health, and the maintenance of public roads. This was as far as the British could go in giving the Burmese a share of political responsibility without having to face the great political issues of Indian landownership and immigration, of tenancy and rent control, and of the whole economic situation of the Burmese. These were to be the major issues in the continuing struggle of the Burmese for independence.

6. THAILAND (SIAM)

By the end of the eighteenth century Thailand had been reunified by the royal house of Chakkri. The capital was moved to the city of Bangkok which has remained the political center of Thailand. In the past the main danger to the Thai government had come from the neighboring country of Burma which invaded Thailand for the last time between 1785 and 1792. In the nineteenth century the British conquest of Burma eliminated this danger but created another threat, the loss of Thai independence to the British. The history of Thailand in the nineteenth century and in the beginning of the twentieth century is in part a story of successful resistance against this threat of colonial rule. It was to the advantage of Thailand in its struggle for survival that the British advance on its western frontier was matched by the French conquest of Indo-China to the east. England and France were jealous of each other's expansion and it was this mutual jealousy which helped to preserve Thailand's independence. It was the policy of the Siamese kings to contribute to this British-French stalemate through skillful diplomacy. The kings also carried out reforms and provided economic opportunities for the Western powers which left them no pretext for moving in.

While she maintained her political independence, Thailand lost some of her border territories to England and to France. In the south, England forced several of the sultanates on the Malay Peninsula to sever their ties with the kingdom of Thailand and to become a part of British Malaya; to the southeast, the French added the provinces on the Cambodian border to their protectorate. With the exception of the losses on the border, Thailand survived as an independent country as a result of her location as a buffer country between English and French colonial territory, her skill in making necessary diplomatic concessions, and her timely domestic reforms.

An Anglo-Siamese treaty was concluded in 1826 immediately after the first British war with Burma. Thailand granted liberal trading concessions to the British but it permitted neither extraterritoriality nor the establishment of a British consulate at Bangkok, both of which rights the British sought to acquire. This British treaty attracted the Americans, who had traded with Thailand before, selling mainly Mexican silver coins and firearms, but who had been hampered by high duties and the king's monopoly control over business. The new British privilege stimulated the American government to send a mission to Thailand in 1833, headed by Edmund Roberts, who concluded a more extensive treaty than the British had been able to secure. The American treaty, like the British treaty, did not include extraterritoriality, and the Americans agreed to operate under Thai laws; but the price monopoly of the king was ended. All ports were opened to American ships, and the American commercial representatives could trade with any Thai merchant.

The duties were fixed at a maximum of 15 per cent. The American treaty stipulated that opium was to be contraband and provided that arms were to be sold only to the king's representatives. This last provision was entirely in line with the American policy of supporting governments of Far Eastern countries against falling prey to inner attack or outside colonial conquest. Another stipulation of the American treaty provided that the Americans should profit from any reduction in duty granted in a future treaty to any foreign nation. Here, as elsewhere, the Americans were anxious to secure most-favored-nation treatment.

In the following decades Thailand was also opened to Christian missionary work. Catholic missions were established under the auspices of a French society, while Protestant missionaries came mainly from the United States. These first contacts with the Western world were broadened under the rule of Mongkut, who reigned under the name of Rama IV from 1851 to 1868. On the death of his father, King Mongkut had been excluded from the throne by a younger half-brother who had gained the political support of the court officials. During his brother's rule Mongkut had retired into a Buddhist monastery where he not only studied Sanskrit and Buddhist sutras but also learned English, French, and Latin with the help of Protestant and Catholic missionaries. When he ascended the throne in 1851, King Mongkut initiated the westernization of the existing bureaucratic government of the country. He hired Western advisers and with their help reorganized the army and navy; he established a mint and introduced a modern currency; he founded an academy of foreign languages to provide for a Western training of his official staff; he established a modern postal and telegraph service and constructed railroads; on the advice of missionaries he built modern hospitals. At the same time he strengthened the agricultural economy by building new irrigation works.

King Mongkut was willing to conclude new treaties with the Western powers. A model treaty was signed with England in 1855. In the negotiations preceding it, the British envoy, Sir John Bowring, had indicated to the king that increase in trade with the West depended on the provision of opportunity for Westerners to live in Thailand, free from the control of its laws and according to their own customs. As a result the treaty with England provided extraterritoriality for British subjects. It also set a tariff of 3 per cent and permitted the importation of opium. British merchants were given the right to trade in all ports but had to live in Bangkok where a British consulate was established. The treaty also included a most-favored-nation clause for the British. Following the English treaty, the French and Americans concluded similar treaties in 1856 which gave them all the rights that the British had acquired. The French added stipulations to their treaty which gave them extensive privileges to conduct missionary work and maintain establishments throughout the country.

King Mongkut's son and successor, Chulalongkorn, who ruled as Rama V from 1868 until 1910, continued the reform measures of his father. He created a cabinet and attempted to have the work of the ministries based on a modern budget. He reorganized the tax system and abolished the farming out of taxes. He strengthened central control over the administration by appointing provincial officials from members of the Chakkri family. He also used Western advisers. The king, who had received a Western education under an English tutor, encouraged Thai students to study in foreign countries. The most important reforms were the codification of laws, the establishment of schools for Western law, and the setting up of a modern system of law courts. On the basis of these measures, the king began to negotiate with the foreign governments for the relinquishment of extraterritorial rights. In 1909 extraterritoriality was modified but was not actually abolished until after World War I.

The king was modern in his thinking and travelled abroad, but in his palace he led the life of the traditional Siamese monarch. He was addicted to the smoking of opium and maintained a large harem. Vajiravudh, the son and successor of Chulalongkorn, ruled as Rama VI from 1910 to 1925. The king was known in the West for his interest in art and literature and his expensive style of living. Under his rule the policy of westernization, carried on by his father and grandfather, was finally successful. Extraterritoriality was abandoned, the regulation of the tariff by foreign treaties was given up, and Thailand regained her full sovereignty.

With King Vajiravudh ended the period of "enlightened absolutism" that brought westernization to Thailand as a gift of her kings. The kings had succeeded in carrying out a minimum of reforms and westernization which, combined with skillful diplomacy, had enabled Thailand to survive as an independent state. As a result of the reforms civil and military officials and intellectuals were educated along Western lines. When they rose to positions of influence, they attacked absolutism and forced the acceptance of a constitution which made the kings mere figureheads.

Thailand's political independence was also protected during these critical decades by her comparative lack of economic attraction for Western interests. Her agricultural, tropical products could be obtained as easily elsewhere. Teakwood became a major export item, but the most important export was rice, which went mainly to India and other British possessions. As England controlled 75 per cent of Thailand's overseas trade, she became the dominant Western power in Thailand's economy. Within Thailand the influential position of the Chinese minority in the control of local trade was instrumental in giving the emerging Thai nationalism an anti-Chinese character. On the whole Thailand remained economically underdeveloped. The autocratic policy of westernization by the kings remained limited in scope and there was no stimulus to evoke among the Thai people a real drive for social and economic changes.

7. British Malaya

The establishment of the British hold over Malaya was largely the work of one of the most active, adventurous, and far-sighted empire builders whom the British East India Company ever produced, Sir Thomas Stamford Raffles. Raffles was of humble origin, and it was only his service in the company which gave him the opportunity for an outstanding career as a colonial administrator. His ability and brilliance were recognized by the company directors who, however, were afraid of his aggressiveness and his unwillingness to submit to direction. In 1811, Raffles, under the direction of his protector, Lord Minto, led the British conquest of the Dutch East Indies and carried out British reforms in this Dutch colonial area. He dreamed of British rule in Indonesia as the beginning of British expansion into Southeast Asia and was greatly disappointed when the islands were returned to the Dutch in 1818. For two years he had tried to hamper the restoration of Dutch authority in the hope that the British government would change its mind. When authority was restored to the Dutch, Raffles directed his energy to the neighboring area of the Malay Peninsula.

During the French wars the British bought the island of Penang from the sultan of Kedah in 1786 for use as a British base. To this acquisition was added, after a few years, the territory opposite the island, later known as the province of Wellesley. This British base was a commercial disappointment and had little strategic value as it did not control the Strait of Malacca, which was the main shipping route to the East Indies and to China and was frequently endangered by pirates. It was no substitute for Malacca, the principal port in the strait, which had been taken from the Dutch by the British in 1795 and returned to the Dutch in 1818. A year later Raffles gained permission from Lord Hastings, then governor-general of India, to establish another British post on the peninsula, further south than Penang. With this authority Raffles negotiated with the sultan of Johore for the cession of the island of Singapore, then practically uninhabited. In the following years Singapore developed under Raffles into one of the most important British commercial and strategic centers. The island's location on the southern tip of the Malay Peninsula made it ideally suited as a trading entrepôt on the route between Europe and the Far East and a center for the local trade of the Malayan islands. Singapore was also of foremost strategic importance because it controlled the Malacca Strait and defended the eastern approach to the Indian Ocean.

Raffles' policy fully exploited the favorable location of Singapore. He made Singapore a free port in which foreign traders could store their goods and reship them without payment of tariff and with a minimum of official interference. This gave the new port a great advantage over the established Dutch trading ports. For the rapidly growing international community of Malays, Chinese, and Europeans, Raffles instituted a uniform codified law and a court system which protected property and business enterprise without distinctions. Raffles was also interested in providing educational opportunities for the Chinese and Malay youth under his jurisdiction. The East India Company, at first hesitant about Raffles' moves, soon saw the importance of the new establishment and ignored Dutch protests over the British acquisition of Singapore.

The British hold over the Malay Peninsula was rounded out in the Anglo-Dutch agreement of 1824, by which the Dutch gave up the port of Malacca in exchange for the British surrender of Benkoelen on Sumatra. With this exchange each party gained complete control over its side of the Malacca Strait. In 1826 the British combined the so-called Straits Settlements under a single administration which was placed under the government of British India in 1830. The Straits Settlements consisted of Singapore, Malacca, Penang, the province of Wellesley, and the small area of Dindings to the south of Penang. These Malayan colonial possessions remained linked with the Indian government until 1867, when they were separated from it and formed into a crown colony under a governor who worked through an appointive legislative council.

From these coastal possessions of the Straits Settlements, the British extended their control inland into the Malay states. This penetration was at first of an economic nature. British and Chinese trading and mining interests were established, and the Straits Settlements functioned as an outlet for the inland economy. From the beginning this economy was mainly in the hands of British, Chinese, and Indian firms which took advantage of the opportunities provided by the commercial freedom and the protection of Western property under British law. Until the 1870's this protection was limited in theory to the Straits Settlements. In the Malay states the sultans still ruled, and investment and commercial development depended on their cooperation. In the last decades of the nineteenth century, when the great possibilities for a growing plantation economy and further promotion of the mining industry were realized in British Malaya, the political control of the British was extended into the Malay states. The first treaties were concluded with the sultans in 1874. British resident administrators took over most of the government authority, such as the collection of revenues and the general administration, and a little later they also assumed political jurisdiction. The sultans retained their titles and income as well as their authority over religious affairs and Malay customs. The transfer of power was justified by the claim that arbitrariness and misrule by the sultans should be replaced by a modern administrative and legal system with equality and justice for all. This transfer of authority extended the area under British law and order and enabled foreign enterprise to move in and dominate most of the new economic development in the sultanates. Plantations, mining companies, and commercial houses were mainly foreign owned and the Malays had little share in the new economy of British Malaya.

The British divided the Malay states into two groups, the Federated and the Unfederated Malay States. Those states in the southern part of the peninsula, which came first under British domination were joined, with the exception of Johore, into a federation in 1896. The Federated Malay States were the five states of Negri, Sembilan, Selangor, Perak, and Pahang. In each Federated state a British resident took over the actual administration from the sultan, but he was responsible to a British resident-general who was located at the federation capital of Kuala Lumpur. In the first two decades of the twentieth century the power of the government in Kuala Lumpur was steadily increased; the resident-general was named chief secretary of the federation and a civil service came into being. The federation government handled the development of communications and the promotion of mining and plantation agriculture and represented European-Chinese economic interests. After 1920 the centralization of authority in the hands of the federation was opposed by a Malay movement for returning more authority to the sultanates.

In the latter part of the nineteenth century the British established protectorates over the four sultanates of Trengganu, Kelantan, Kedah, and Perlis, and separated them politically from the kingdom of Thailand. In each of these so-called Unfederated Malay States administration was taken over by British resident ministers, while the sultans retained their control over Malay customs and religion in the same way as they had in the Federated Malay States. The Western economic penetration of these Unfederated Malay States came later and never went as far as it did in the federation. In 1914 a British protectorate was also established over the sultanate of Johore. Johore, next to Singapore, had long been exposed to Western investment and business development. It owed its status of formal independence to the special relationship between the British government and the sultan of Johore, who was accepted in British society and was well acquainted with Queen Victoria. Even after 1914 Johore was not included in the federation.

By the beginning of the twentieth century there were three different patterns of British rule over Malaya. There were the Straits Settlements, the Federated Malay States with their capital at Kuala Lumpur, and the protectorates over the Unfederated Malay States. The government of these three parts was united in the person of the British governor of the Straits Settlements, who, as High Commissioner, directed the federation government at Kuala Lumpur and the resident ministers of the Unfederated States.

Under this British system tremendous economic, social, and ethnic changes took place all over British Malaya. The government provided both the technical means and the legal framework for changes. Modern means of communication such as the postal service, telegraph, telephone, and roads were a special concern of the government. A railroad was built along the length of the peninsula from Singapore through Thai territory up to Bangkok. A department of medicine carried on research and performed great service in the fight against tropical diseases; research departments for forestry and scientific agriculture were of help in plantation development. In the twentieth century a school system was established. An irrigation system was constructed to provide a water supply for new agricultural areas. This technical progress took place under a regime of peace and order in which piracy and lawlessness were stamped out and legal protection was provided for private investments. The introduction of Western law led to the abolition of debt slavery and of the arbitrary power of the sultans and the protection of the rights of the individual, all of which was new to the Malays. But the freehold landownership, which the law recognized and protected, resulted in the Malays losing much of their land to Chinese and Indian money-lenders, to whom the Malays became indebted. In this way a serious problem of tenancy came into existence.

Under British rule there were two decisive developments—the growth of a plantation economy and a change in the ethnic composition of the population. The increase in the development of rubber plantations began in 1900, and in the years that followed they swallowed up most of the land. Sugar, coffee, and coconut plantations followed, but they were of secondary importance. All this plantation economy was in the hands of foreigners while the labor was exclusively Chinese or Indian. Together with the growth of the plantation economy there was a steady increase in the number of extractive industries. The Chinese controlled the early development of mining between 1874 and World War I, but from that time on the largest mining concerns were established with British capital, and only the smaller enterprises remained Chinese. The most profitable tin mines were in the state of Perak and in the neighboring area of Kuala Lumpur; the tin was processed in large smelters at Singapore.

Under British rule tin and rubber were the main exports of British Malaya and rice the main import. As the production of tin and rubber increased, the area left for rice cultivation became inadequate to supply the food requirements of the population, and rice had to be imported, as local production provided only one-third of the needs of the country. Tin and rubber, however, brought great profits to the plantation owners, the trading firms, and the British government, which derived its main income from export duties on these commodities.

Under British rule Malaya ceased to be a Malay country. Chinese and Indians came to live in the Straits Settlements and to work and own plantations and mining enterprises. In the first three decades of the twentieth century the total population grew to a figure of over 5,000,000. The Chinese and the Malays each made up two-fifths of the population but the Chinese were rapidly outnumbering the Malays. The Indians were the next largest population group with about 14 per cent of the total. By the end of World War I the population of the Straits Settlements was largely Chinese, Singapore was almost 80 per cent Chinese, and the Chinese made up more than half the population of most of the Federated Malay States. Only in the Unfederated Malay States did the Malays still constitute the majority.

The ethnic composition of the population soon influenced Far Eastern politics. The Chinese community of Malaya for many years looked to China as its homeland. The Chinese regarded their years in Malaya as a temporary period in which they would make a fortune and return to China. This feeling of living in a foreign country often persisted even among the Chinese born in Malaya, and only slowly did some of them come to regard British Malaya as their home and begin to fight for participation in its political development. The Malays, on the other hand, regarded the Chinese and the Indians as invaders and resented the loss of their land to the Chinese and Indians, who dominated the economy. By World War I, Malay feeling against the Chinese and the Indians reached considerable intensity; the Malays wanted a greater share in the development of the country. This early expression of Malay nationalism coincided with the movement for a Moslem religious revival which, after World War I, spread over all the Moslem countries from the Near East to Indonesia. The British supported this Moslem revival by helping in the building of mosques and by permitting religious instruction in the schools.

The British made of Malaya a peaceful country and a source of great profits to themselves. The island of Singapore became one of the great ports of the world and a naval base for British sea power in the Far East. In the process of building up the plantations, the mining, and the trade of Malaya the British encouraged Chinese immigration which provided cheap labor and the commercial enterprise which the Malays seemed to lack. By doing so they changed the composition of the population of Malaya. The Chinese, who came to outnumber the Malays, incurred their enmity by becoming the dominant economic group. Under these conditions the growth of Malay nationalism was diverted into the ethnic rivalry between the Malays and the Chinese. In order to compensate for the influence of the Chinese the British favored the Malays culturally and politically. This policy was successful so long as China was not in a position to give the Chinese of Malaya strong political and military support.

CHAPTER X

Expansion of Russia
Under the Tsars

1. THE SETTLEMENT OF SIBERIA

IN the nineteenth century there was a new Russian drive into Asia. Asiatic Russia, which had first been penetrated and conquered by the Cossack adventurers, fur traders, and the peasants who followed in the wake of official and private exploration, was settled and developed. The way was prepared by the work of Count Michael Speransky, a political reformer who was sent to Siberia as governor-general in 1819 and held this post until 1821. He took a personal interest in Siberia, about which he became well informed, and introduced there some of the social, economic, and political ideas of Europe in the period of the Enlightenment. Speransky was instrumental in preparing the legislation of 1822 which brought to Siberia an orderly bureaucratic administration, protective laws for the natives, less control over trade, and a loosening of restrictions on the immigration of peasants into Siberia. Siberia was separated into two governor-generalships, a western one with its center at Tobolsk and an eastern one with its center at Irkutsk. While control of over-all policy-making was retained at St. Petersburg, Siberia was given a local administrative subdivision and a decentralization of responsibility that provided greater freedom of local development.

Russian peasants continued to move into Siberia in ever increasing numbers without regard to government policy, which wavered between restriction and support of the peasant movement. Even in the last decades of the nineteenth century and the first decades of the twentieth century, when the government gave more support to migration, well over half of the peasant settlers were irregulars who did not make use of government-provided facilities.

Russian peasant migration was the greatest single factor in the development of Asiatic Russia in the nineteenth and the beginning of the twentieth centuries. At the beginning of the nineteenth century the Russian population of Siberia had already passed the million mark and was twice as large as the native population. By the end of World War I there were over ten million Russians in Siberia as compared to about a million native people.

The largest part of the Russian population in Siberia were peasants. During the first half of the nineteenth century the volume of peasant migration into Siberia had been surpassed by the number of prisoners banished to Siberia by the tsarist government. The stream of prisoners to Siberia continued all through the tsarist regime and reached a total of about a million people during the period from 1800 to the Russian Revolution. But the number of peasant immigrants steadily increased and from the 1880's on was more than double that of political exiles. Peasant immigrants numbered over one million people in the 1890's and over two million in the decade from 1900 to 1910.

Siberia had always seemed like a promised land to the serfs and state peasants of European Russia. To them migration to Siberia meant free land and the end of serfdom, since serfdom never existed in Asiatic Russia. The temptation to move was therefore great, but so were the obstacles for getting away and for undertaking the long journey. In the second half of the nineteenth century however, it became much easier for the peasants to move. One reason for this was that in 1861 serfdom was abolished in Russia and with it went the legal restrictions on the peasants' personal freedom to move. The legislation which abolished serfdom also settled the question of the ownership of the land which the unfree peasants had worked. The lords retained their personal estates, amounting to about half of the total cultivated land but surrendered their control over the lands of the village communes. The peasant was freed of his obligation to work on the lord's land and acquired a right to his share of the land of the commune. This settlement left the peasant with a unit of his own, but as it was too small for his needs, he had to rent more land from his former lord and thus continue a relationship of dependency. On the other hand, his newly-gained freedom permitted him to sell his share in the commune's land and to move to other areas where free land was available. The abolition of serfdom thus loosened the bonds that had restrained the peasant of European Russia and precipitated a large migration into the freer lands of Russian Asia. The tsarist government decided after some hesitation to support this movement of peasants into Asiatic Russia.

The other reason which made it much easier for peasants to move to Siberia was the building of the Trans-Siberian Railroad. The construction of a transcontinental railroad was first suggested in 1858, but by 1890 the line had barely crossed the Urals. In 1891 an imperial edict authorized continuation of the line to the Pacific, and in that year construction was also started at Vladivostok. The Trans-Siberian Railroad was a technical accomplishment comparable to the great transcontinental railroads in the United States. The construction of the section around Lake Baikal alone was a major engineering feat. For a number of years the trains were taken across the lake, by ferry in summer and over the ice in winter. Construction of the section through the mountainous territory around the shores of the lake involved the building of over forty major viaducts and tunnels. The Trans-Siberian Railroad was finally completed in 1905.

The railroad line channelled the stream of migration and stimulated an enormous increase in the movement of peasants to Russian Asia. It provided the first direct west-east line of communication across the whole extent of Russian territory and shortened the time of travel and facilitated the movement of goods. It made possible a more direct political supervision over the whole area and was of obvious strategic importance. It vastly improved Russia's military position in the Far East and thus strengthened her imperialist policy.

2. Russia Expands Her Borders

The borders of Russia in Asia had been drawn by the Treaty of Nerchinsk in 1689. At this time the small vanguard of Russian settlers and Cossack adventurers who were seeking an outlet to the Pacific by way of the Amur River was thrown back by the then powerful Manchu dynasty, to a border that followed the line of the watershed between the Amur and the Lena rivers. In 1727 the Treaty of Kiakhta extended this border south of Lake Baikal along the ranges of the Sayan, Tannu, and Altai mountains, to form the frontier between Chinese Outer Mongolia and Siberia. In the nineteenth century, when peasant settlers poured into Asiatic Russia, the frontier question was reopened. By this time the technical superiority of the West and the decline of China had shifted the balance of power in favor of Russia.

The expansion of the Russian frontier was largely the work of one man, Muraviev, who was appointed governor-general of Siberia in 1847. Muraviev renewed Russian interest in the Amur region. He sent an expedition to the mouth of the Amur River; on receiving favorable reports he decided to take over the area and in 1850 founded the town of Nikolaevsk at the mouth of the Amur. He also established a number of settlements in the lower Amur region, explored and occupied the island of Sakhalin, and founded there the town of Alexandrovsk. In order to compel the Chinese to accept Russian territorial expansion and the opening of the Amur to Russian shipping Muraviev moved a fleet down the Amur River over the protests of Chinese officials whom he forced to conclude the Treaty of Aigun in 1858. By this treaty the Amur River became the new border between China and Russia. Not satisfied with this gain Muraviev also moved into the territory bounded by the lower Amur, its tributary—the Ussuri, and the Pacific Ocean. This coastal strip of land, which reached down to the Korean frontier, became at that time a Russo-Chinese co-dominion.

The Russian move coincided with the Anglo-French War against China (1858–1860) and the Treaties of Tientsin and Peking of 1858 and 1860 which were concluded with China not only by the two belligerent powers, England and France, but also by the United States and Russia, whose diplomatic representatives followed the British-French forces. During this period the Russians posed as friends of the Chinese government and provided it with modern weapons for defense against the Western powers. This pretense of friendship was designed to weaken the Western competitors of Russia and to facilitate Russia's own gains on the Chinese border. In 1860 by the Treaty of Peking the coastal area between the Amur and the Korean frontier was fully ceded to Russia, and at its southern tip the Russians founded the port and naval base of Vladivostok. The name of this Russian base, which means "Ruler of the East," indicated the Russian political ambitions.

The drive into the Far East, for which Muraviev received the honorary title of Count Muraviev-Amursky, gave Russia an outlet to the coast from her landlocked and icebound Asiatic territories. She had extended her control beyond the Stanovoi Mountains and by gaining the right to navigate the Amur had secured a waterway to the sea. The Trans-Siberian Railroad connected the Russian base in Europe with the rapidly developing area of Central Siberia, the corridor of settlements along the Chinese-Mongolian border, and the Far Eastern territory down to Vladivostok. Russia's new position made her a Far Eastern power and brought her into the area of international conflict. A short time later Russia had to settle her claims to the Kurile Islands and to Sakhalin with the newly emerging Japanese empire. In the treaty of 1875 a compromise was effected; Russia retained Sakhalin and the Kurile Islands went to Japan. The settlements with China and Japan consolidated Russia's territorial position in the Far East and gave her a new base from which to carry forward her imperialist policies.

As she strengthened her position on the Pacific coast of Asia, Russia abandoned her holdings on the American continent. The Russian-American Company had declined as a result of the exhaustion of the seal hunting grounds and the deterioration of the fur trade, and the company gave up its possessions on the American west coast. Alaska had lost its importance for Russia and was sold to the United States in 1867. At this time Russia was concentrating her efforts on the international struggle in China and on the consolidation of her new position on the Pacific.

Manchuria

In Europe Russia had long sought to gain access to the sea. The traditional "two-window" policy was to secure control of the Gulf of Finland and of the Dardanelles as outlets to the Baltic and the Mediterranean. In the Far East Russia sought a third window, a warm-water port on the Pacific. In tsarist times the frozen Arctic was useless for practical navigation, and the Sea of Okhotsk was frozen during a large part of the year. The acquisition of the Amur River, the harbor at Nikolaevsk, and the coastal area to the south had improved that situation, but even the base of Vladivostok was icebound during four months of the year. Russia began to look for ports farther south in Manchuria.

When the Sino-Japanese War had ended with a Japanese victory in 1895, the three-power intervention of Russia, France, and Germany prevented Japan from taking southern Manchuria. Russia, the leading intervening power, was already interested in moving into Manchuria herself. China was incapable of resisting further Japanese aggression and sought the protection of her powerful Russian neighbor, who had saved her from Japan. In 1896 China concluded an alliance with Russia, the price of which was the admission of Russia into Manchuria.

The treaty of 1896 gave Russia the right to build a railroad through northern Manchuria from the border town of Manchuli to the Russian port of Vladivostok. This railroad was a much shorter route than that of the railroad around the Amur bend and along the Ussuri River. As the new railroad cut through territory which was only thinly populated by non-Chinese Mongol and Tungus tribal people, the suggestion was made in St. Petersburg that Russia should limit her railroad expansion to this northern part of Manchuria and eventually annex it. A further move to the south would only endanger this possibility.

This view was represented at the tsarist court by Count Witte, then Russian Minister of Finance and a leading Russian statesman. A group of military leaders, supported by the Tsar himself, advocated a more aggressive policy of moving into southern Manchuria and the ice-free ports of the Liaotung Peninsula. Such a move would bring Russia into territory with a Chinese population and give her practical control over all of the region which became known as Manchuria. The more aggressive course won out. In 1898 Russia secured from China the Kwantung leased territory with Dairen and the naval base of Port Arthur, and at the same time extended her railroad rights down into southern Manchuria. She was permitted to build a line between the leased territory and her railroad through North Manchuria, connecting at the city of Harbin. This gave Russia a T-shaped railroad system in Manchuria from which she could exert strategic control over the whole territory.

The railroads were built and run by a Russo-Chinese company, which, by the treaty of 1896, secured the right to administer and guard the railroad zone. This important Chinese concession was left out of the Chinese version of the treaty text but was included in the decisive French text. The treaty of 1898 simply referred to the treaty of 1896 and thus established the same political rights for the extended railway line.

In 1900 Russia expanded her control beyond the railroad zone and the leased territory and occupied Manchuria as a whole. The Boxer unrest had spread to Manchuria and served as a pretext for this move. When the Boxer movement was suppressed and the Boxer Protocol of 1901 was signed, Russia refused to evacuate the occupied territory. An agreement concluded with the local Chinese officials provided for Russian withdrawal after peace and order had been secured by Chinese authorities. But the Russians did not allow the arming of Chinese forces in the area and so prevented any enforcement of order by the Chinese.

The Russian move into Manchuria was supported by France and Germany and opposed by Britain and Japan. Japan had been defeated in her own ambitions in Manchuria and regarded the Russian position there as a threat to Japanese control of Korea. The tsarist timber concession at the Yalu River on the Korean border, which was worked by Russian soldiers, indicated the nature of Russian ambitions. England had established her leased territory at Weihaiwei in 1898 to counter the Russian position at Port Arthur. The new Russian threat brought England and Japan together in the Anglo-Japanese alliance of 1902 which caused the Russian government to slow down in Manchuria. An agreement was concluded with the Chinese in which the Russians promised to withdraw in three stages from Manchurian territory outside the railroad zone. The first stage, the withdrawal from the southernmost part of Manchuria, was actually carried out. But the troops withdrawn from this area remained in other parts of Manchuria and there was no further withdrawal. The tension increased and an attempt was made to settle the conflict by Russo-Japanese negotiations. In these negotiations the Japanese indicated at one time that they would accept the Russian position in Manchuria in exchange for a clear Russian recognition of the Japanese position in Korea. The Russians, however, were reluctant to accept any binding limitations on their advance, believing that they were under no compulsion to accept such a compromise. While they evaded a decision, the Japanese took the initiative and started war.

The Russo-Japanese War of 1904–1905 began with a Japanese surprise attack, not preceded by a declaration of war, on the Russian fleet at Port Arthur. The siege of the naval base of Port Arthur followed, ending in its capture by the Japanese, and the Russians were forced back from southern Manchuria. The war ended in a Russian defeat. In the peace treaty Russia lost the Kwantung leased territory and her railroad rights in southern Manchuria. The loss of southern Manchuria cut Russia off from the ice-free port of Dairen and forced her to give up her ambitious plans in the Yellow Sea and instead to concentrate on consolidating her remaining position. Russia also ceded to Japan the southern half of the island of Sakhalin, an area of no great economic importance to Russia, for even when oil was discovered later on Sakhalin, it was found only in the northern, Russian part of the island. To the Japanese, however, southern Sakhalin was of considerable strategic importance since it strengthened their control over the Sea of Japan.

After the war tsarist Russia concentrated on the development of northern Manchuria and strengthened the defenses of her Far Eastern line of communications by extending her control into Mongolia. In the years between 1905 and the Russian Revolution, the Russians were particularly active in northern Manchuria and Outer Mongolia. Regarding northern Manchuria Russia concluded a number of treaties with Japan in the years 1907, 1909, 1911, and 1915. The former enemies arranged for cooperation in the development and mutual defense of their interests in Manchuria. The railroads were linked, telephone and telegraph communications were connected, and a line was drawn across the whole territory of Manchuria delimiting the interests of each power. When the two powers felt that their monopoly positions were threatened by the American policy of keeping Manchuria open to all comers, they came to an understanding, and eventually, in 1915, to a practical alliance for a joint defense of their positions against any such pressure from the United States. In these Russo-Japanese agreements, western Inner Mongolia and Outer Mongolia had been left on the Russian side of the line dividing Russo-Japanese areas of interest. Having reached this understanding with Japan, Russia was then able to advance her own plans for the political penetration of Outer Mongolia.

Mongolia

The opportunity for this new Russian move came with the Chinese Revolution of 1911. Even before the revolution, Russian agents had been active in Outer Mongolia. The Chinese government, worried over this threat to its territorial control, had attempted to strengthen the military defense of Mongolia by training and equipping Mongol forces under Chinese officers. The financial burden of this military effort fell on the Mongols and increased the already existing discontent and irritation with Chinese rule.

There were many reasons for this discontent. The last two decades of the Manchu dynasty had brought an increasing number of Chinese into Inner Mongolia. Chinese settlers took over some of the best Mongol pasture land and brought it under cultivation. The growth of Chinese administration that came with this agricultural settlement brought other forms of financial and political control so that in Inner Mongolia the Mongols were forced to fight for economic survival.

In Outer Mongolia the Chinese influence took other forms. The Mongols came under the financial control of Chinese merchant houses to whom whole tribes became indebted. At the beginning of the twentieth century, Outer Mongolia became the source of wool and hides and other animal products exported through China to Europe and the United States. This connection with the world market brought to the Mongols only a growing indebtedness to Chinese merchants. When the new burden of a military reorganization was added to this private financial exploitation, the Mongols began to resist; and the Chinese Revolution gave them an opportunity to throw off the Chinese authority altogether. Claiming that their loyalty had been to the Manchu dynasty rather than to a Chinese national state, the Mongols rose against the Chinese, and Outer and Inner Mongolia declared their independence. The Chinese garrisons were driven out and the Mongols turned to Russia for help against the expected Chinese retribution.

The Russian government had helped to instigate this Mongol uprising in Outer Mongolia. In 1912 after the Chinese had been driven out, the Russians, through their agent Korostovetz, concluded an agreement with the Mongol leaders in which they gave their support to the Mongol aspirations and established their own controlling position. The Mongols were promised protection but were told that they could not ask for independence but only for autonomy within the Chinese state. Mongolia was thus to remain nominally within Chinese territory, but any actual Chinese authority was eliminated. This anomalous political situation made it easier for Russia to carry out her own plans for establishing a practical protectorate over Outer Mongolia. The Mongol leaders were also told that this autonomy was to be limited to Outer Mongolia, where Russia did not fear Japanese and Western objections; and that Russian support would not be given to Inner Mongolia which was closer to the Western interests. Consequently, the Mongols of Outer Mongolia were not permitted by the Russians to come to the support of the Mongols of Inner Mongolia, who were left to their fate when their revolt was suppressed by Chinese provincial troops.

The Russian assistance to Outer Mongolia was both military and financial. Russian officers were sent to Outer Mongolia to train Mongol troops which were equipped with Russian weapons, and a Russian loan of 4,000,000 rubles was used for these purposes. A Russian telegraph line was established with Urga, the capital of Outer Mongolia, and the seat of the Khutukhtu, the Living Buddha and head of the Mongol Lamaist church. Russia also received the right to be consulted first on railroad development in Outer Mongolia. She did not intend to use this right to develop railroads of her own but rather to prevent a railroad connection between Mongolia and China. Tariffs on Russian goods at the Mongolian border were abolished.

The move into Outer Mongolia had become possible with the intensification of the Russian development of Asia. The economic development of Siberia and the building of the Trans-Siberian railway made it easier for Russia than for China to extend her trade and influence into the nomad territory. At the same time, Mongolia had become strategically more important to Russia. The Russian settlements through which the railroad ran formed a corridor along the Mongolian border. Any power in control of the plateau of Outer Mongolia could threaten the flank of the whole Russian Far Eastern territory and cut its line of communication. When the Japanese moved into Manchuria and the British extended their influence into Tibet through the Younghusband expedition in 1904, the control of Mongolia by another power had come into the realm of possibility and the establishment of a Russian protectorate in Outer Mongolia was thus part of a pattern of competitive imperialist policies.

The uprisings in Outer Mongolia which occurred during the Chinese Revolution were settled in negotiations between China and Russia. In 1913, when the confusion of the Chinese Revolution had been ended with the establishment of Yüan Shih-k'ai's government, a Russo-Chinese treaty was completed in which China accepted the situation and granted Mongol autonomy in exchange for Russian recognition of a nominal Chinese "suzerainty" over Outer Mongolia. In 1915, when Russia was already involved in the war in Europe, a tripartite pact was concluded between Russia, China, and Outer Mongolia, in which the autonomous status of Mongolia was recognized by all parties.

Chinese Turkestan

In the second part of the nineteenth century Russian military campaigns succeeded in breaking the resistance of the Moslem state to the east of the Caspian Sea, in taking the cities of Samarkand and Tashkent and in pushing the Russian border to the Hindu Kush, the Pamir plateau, and the Tien Shan. Russia reached the borders of Chinese Turkestan. In the 1860's, this Chinese dependency was drawn into the series of rebellions and uprisings that shook the entire Chinese empire, and the opportunity arose for foreign powers to exploit China's troubles to their own advantage. The Moslems of Chinese Turkestan had risen under the leadership of Yakub Beg, defeated the Chinese administration, and set up their own government. The fate of Chinese Turkestan then became of interest to the Russians as well as to the British, ever concerned with the protection of the Indian frontier. For a while British policy was inclined to support Yakub Beg in the hope of encouraging the formation of a buffer state in Southern Turkestan. The Russians took advantage of the chaotic conditions to occupy the Ili Valley, the most fertile and populated part of northwestern Chinese Turkestan. The Chinese military campaign for the suppression of Yakub Beg's rebellion was also designed to discourage these British and Russian aspirations. The Chinese commander, Tso Tsung-t'ang, one of the ablest regional leaders, knew as well as the government in Peking that the defeat of Yakub Beg had to be convincing enough to persuade Russia and England that China was able and determined to defend her position in Turkestan. This aim was accomplished, and in order to strengthen Chinese authority Turkestan was formed into a Chinese province in 1878 under the name of Sinkiang or "New Frontier." In the Sino-Russian Treaty, which was negotiated shortly thereafter in 1879, Russia retained a part of the Ili Valley. The treaty was not ratified by the Chinese government, and a new treaty was concluded at St. Petersburg in 1881, by which Russia returned the larger part of the territory including the strategic mountain passes in exchange for an increased indemnity payment. Certain privileges were also granted to Russian traders in Chinese Turkestan.

This first advance into Chinese Turkestan was followed by further Russian activity there after the Russo-Japanese War. It was at this time, when Russia was also exploiting the anti-Chinese sentiments of the Mongols, that she sent her agents into Turkestan. Russian activity in Chinese Turkestan aroused British concern. By the beginning of the nineteenth century conflicts in the Far East were a part of the worldwide conflicts that stemmed from the European power groupings. In opposition to the German-Austrian Alliance and the later German-Austrian-Italian Triple Alliance, Russia, France, and England came together to form an Entente. In the Anglo-Russian agreement of 1907, which completed the Entente, areas of possible conflict between the two countries were adjusted. Both powers agreed that Chinese control should be retained in Turkestan, thus setting up a practical barrier between British and Russian territory.

By the time of World War I Russia had consolidated her position in northern Manchuria, extended her control into Mongolia, and agreed to the neutralization of Chinese Turkestan. The Russian defeat and collapse in the war, followed by the Russian Revolution, completely undermined Russian power in the Far East and Central Asia, and destroyed the Russian position in Manchuria and Mongolia. Foreign troops came into Russian Far Eastern territories, which were the scene of civil strife. Within less than a decade, however, Soviet Russia had regained control over all this Russian territory, pushed beyond her borders in Central Asia and the Far East, and set in motion the forces of international communism.

PART THREE

The Far East in World Conflict

CHAPTER XI

Communist Russia and the Far East

THE Russian Revolution and the advent of Communism brought to the international struggle in the Far East and the internal development of Far Eastern countries a new and dynamic force. Communism transformed Russia and had a decisive impact on the Far East. Communist doctrine and the story of the Russian Revolution made a tremendous impression upon the educated elite of many Far Eastern countries. This was especially true in China, which at the end of World War I was in one of her worst periods of political chaos and confusion. China's educated elite, now out of power, had become aware of the staggering problem of modernizing the country, of recovering national independence, and of regaining control over political affairs. To this frustrated group of men the Russian Revolution provided a successful example of how to seize state power and drive out interfering imperialist countries. It also contained the promise of abolishing tsarist imperialism and of solving the problems of a backward economy through science and industrialization. This picture of Russia and of Communism was reinforced by the dissemination of Communist literature and propaganda. It was a picture which enlisted the sympathy and even the admiration of many men who had no intention of becoming Communists. There was no great difficulty, therefore, in finding a small number who could be induced to form a Communist group. It was for the purpose of creating such groups all over the world that Moscow organized the Communist International, or Comintern. The Comintern trained Asiatic leaders, founded Communist parties in Far Eastern countries, and directed their policies. The new political ideology and the new type of political organization which Communist doctrine and the Comintern brought to the world were powerful enough in themselves to inflame the Far East, but behind them there was the growing power of the Soviet state, its expansion into Asiatic Russia, and the influence of Soviet power politics beyond Soviet borders.

1. THE DOCTRINE, THE PARTY, AND THE COMINTERN

The Importance of Doctrine

Communist doctrine and achievements did not affect every country in the Far East at the same time, in the same degree, or in the same manner; the attraction of Communism varied with the differing conditions in each country. The greatest immediate impact of doctrine and example occurred in China where the old moral system was breaking up and no alternate system of beliefs had come to be generally accepted. The old values had been abandoned most completely by the educated minority which had long been under the influence of Western thought. The technical superiority demonstrated by the Western powers made Western knowledge very appealing to intelligent men from an older culture who had experienced the military might and political power made possible by this scientific knowledge.

This was a period in which science was overrated even in the West. It had revolutionized the ways of life in Europe and America, and even to many Westerners held the promise of solving all the mysteries of life and the problems of human existence. This enthusiastic belief in science came to be linked with the idea of "progress." Man's lot was to become better and better, not only in regard to his material conditions but also in the development of his moral and mental capacities. Science would provide an open sesame to the unknown forces behind man's history and fate.

Belief in the omnipotence of science was held even more strongly by some intellectuals in Asiatic countries than by their Western contemporaries. While science in the West had grown up within a cultural pattern of which it remained a part, it came to the East from outside as a system which could free an Eastern society from the stagnation of its own cultural patterns. In China, as in many other countries, a small educated elite held sway over the large mass of the people. Its traditional system of education and the beliefs on which that education was based were largely replaced by the imported scientific education, but the new system did not give the educated elite the authority to rule as they had in the past. Science, which is a method of inquiry and a body of knowledge, provided many hopes and many answers but by its nature could not provide the one thing which was necessary in order to take advantage of its potentialities—the authority and the method of establishing political institutions suitable for the modern world. Yet a new political structure and a new way of life were the most urgent of China's needs. Western societies had already broken away from the structural rigidity of the past and set up political institutions in which there was a free interplay of social and economic forces. The institutions of democracy held great attraction for many Chinese intellectuals, but it is not surprising that they were initially more impressed with science, whose results were all around them, than by democracy, which was a way of life difficult to achieve. For some, therefore, the temptation was very great to seek a short-cut to political power which would give to them, the intellectuals, the means by which to regain the dominant role they had played in the past and to manage social and economic changes with all the power of the state and the authority of established dogma. To a few Chinese intellectuals Communism, which had the prestige of coming from the West and of claiming to be a scientific system, seemed to provide some of the answers to national problems. To some Chinese it provided all the answers, for here was a body of doctrine and a tested formula for the seizure of power by a small group of disciplined men and women. For those Chinese, few at the time, who wanted a formula, both for taking over the power of the state and for managing it, Communism provided a pseudo-scientific body of doctrine which exploited the high prestige of the West and of Western science.

Marx and His Theories

This is not the place for a detailed description of Marxism or of Communism, but it is necessary to mention a few main facts and doctrinal points in order to clarify the theoretical and political struggles of the Communist parties in the Far East. Soviet Communism stems from the Marxian theory of history, but it is only one of the several schools of thought that are based upon the writings of Karl Marx (1818–83). Clashes over various interpretations of Marx have been of great importance in the history of Communism in the Far East.

The theory of Karl Marx, "dialectical materialism," was developed on the basis of events and of thought in Europe in the middle of the nineteenth century—the *Communist Manifesto* was published in 1848, *Das Kapital* in 1859 and following years. At the time when he formed his ideas, Marx was impressed with the misery of the workers caused by early industrialism in England, to which country he had fled after the failure of the mid-century revolutions on the continent. Marx's theory was derived from the French school of materialism which taught that the mind is formed by, and is dependent upon, matter, and the German philosophy of Hegel who believed in a dialectical process in history. Hegel was not a materialist, but an idealist who thought that history was an expression of a struggle between ideas. A given system of ideas—a thesis—would create its own opposing system of ideas—the antithesis. Out of the conflict of thesis and antithesis, a synthesis would emerge as the starting point of a new system which in turn created a new antithesis, thus continuing the struggle of ideas. This was called a dialectical process. Karl Marx put the dialectical method of Hegel to work in a materialist context to create the concept of dialectical materialism. Where Hegel had regarded human history as emerging out of a process of conflicting ideas, Marx and his colleague Friedrich Engels (1820–95) looked upon human history as a struggle of material forces. This concept is known as that of historical materialism. According to Engels: "The causes of all social changes and political revolutions are to be sought, not in men's brains, not in Man's better insight into eternal truth and justice but in changes in the modes of production and exchange. They are to be sought not in the philosophy but in the economics of each particular epoch." [1] In other words Marx and Engels believed that the world of ideas, of the intellectual life, including all religious beliefs, was but a superstructure of the material world, by which it was determined. Marx conceived of an historical development in which social classes fought for control of the main economic factors. A struggle between a controlling and an exploited class led in a dialectical process from one stage of economic development to another. At each stage one social class was in control of the "means of production," regarded as the decisive factor in the economy. This control of the "means of production" led to the accumulation of all "surplus value" in the hands of the ruling class, while the exploited class lived at a subsistence level. Out of the tension between these classes developed a class struggle in which the ruling class was overthrown and a new class emerged, thus providing the stages of thesis, antithesis, and synthesis of the dialectical process.

Describing the Western development, Marx differentiated various stages of historical development of human society, such as primitive society, slave-owning society, feudal society, capitalist society, and finally socialist society, which was the aim of his political program. The progress from one society to another was the historical process of human development. In the socialist society which Marx predicted there would be no more private ownership of the means of production. The control of the means of production would be in the hands of society as a whole, ending the rule by any one class and bringing about a classless society. Marx believed that private ownership of the means of production gave the ruling class its power. Even the very existence of social classes depended upon private ownership of the means of production. The abolition of this ownership would therefore remove the factor that distinguished one social class from another, its relationship to the means of production. Consequently there would be no more classes.

Marx was chiefly concerned with the European, and in particular the English, society of his time, which was in the stage of capitalism. A class struggle between the workers and the capitalists would lead, in his opinion, to an overthrow of the capitalist system and to a victory of the workers, whom he regarded as the leading class in the historical process at that time. It was the political action and organization of the workers with which he was therefore concerned. This political organization of the workers was to lead to a workers' party, the Communist party.

Lenin: The Vanguard and Imperialism

These political concepts of Marx were carried further by Lenin (1870–1924), the leader of the Russian branch of the Marxist political movement. Lenin believed that the victory of the workers in the class struggle

[1] *Encyclopedia of Social Sciences* (New York, 1930), Vol. IX, p. 215.

could be accomplished only by a disciplined, highly organized group of revo-lutionary leaders. For this purpose he conceived the idea of a "vanguard," which would be a group of people who, understanding the historical process, could act for the workers, organize the revolution, and lead the workers in their historical mission. The vanguard, set apart from the workers and acting for them, was itself to be organized according to the principle of so-called "democratic centralism." In theory the members of the vanguard were to participate in free political discussion to formulate policy for the workers. But once the political decisions were made by the leaders, the followers were to carry them out without question. Thus the Marxian interpretation of history as a struggle of social classes had led to a highly centralized revolu-tionary organization.

The appeal which Marxism had for the intellectuals of Far Eastern countries was greatly enhanced by the vanguard theory. Here was the con-cept of an intellectual elite which had a theory of government and of society and was entitled to rule by virtue of its knowledge, a concept familiar in the Far East where intellectual elites had governed imperial China and the royal states of Southeast Asia. The tradition of the dominant role of such an ed-ucated group retained a good deal of its force in Buddhist, Hindu, and Moslem countries but not in the Confucian world. In China the Confucian educational system had been given up and its last vestiges had been attacked as unscientific by the new Western-trained intellectuals. The majority of the Chinese intellectuals were not won over to Communism. But some Chinese intellectuals, who had become impatient with the political chaos of the Re-public, were attracted by the idea of a vanguard, of a group that had scientific answers to the problems of society. The importance attached to intellectual leadership and its special mission seemed worth the risks and sacrifices of the political fight.

The vanguard concept permitted the organizers of the Communist Revolution to act independently of the workers although ostensibly for their benefit. This concept became all the more important in Far Eastern countries where no significant working class had yet appeared, because it permitted Communist parties to maintain the fiction that they expressed the will of the workers even where no workers existed. The idea that a Communist party could exist in a country where there were hardly any workers was made more plausible by Lenin's theory of imperialism. According to Lenin imperialism was the process by which the capitalist system assured its own survival by the exploitation of native races. Imperialism was an extension of the capitalist drive for monopoly motivated by the need to export capital to backward countries because of the alleged decline in investment profits at home. Lenin stated that capitalism in its latest stage—monopoly capitalism—depended for survival on colonial exploitation. He described the colonial countries as the victims of the capitalist struggle for markets and the objects of capitalist exploitation. In effect Lenin projected the class struggle between the pro-letariat and the bourgeoisie on to the international plane. The colonial peoples took the place of the proletariat, and the capitalist countries that of the bourgeoisie. To drive the imperialist powers out of the colonial countries was therefore regarded as a part of a worldwide struggle against the capitalist system. As Lenin's theory of imperialism stressed so-called economic exploitation rather than political domination, China could be counted, in Communist parlance, as a colonial country. The idea that subjection to imperialist exploitation was the fulfillment of the inevitable historical process was used by the Communists to harness colonial nationalism to their own purposes. The feelings of humilation of leaders in the colonial countries could be channelled into positive hatred of the capitalist system. Lenin's theories of the vanguard and of imperialism were peculiarly appealing to the Chinese who had been shaken out of their traditions by the Western impact and were now in a state of confused transition.

In Russia, the Bolshevik Revolution succeeded by making use of peasant discontent. The revolution was started by the factory workers of Leningrad, but it succeeded only when the Russian peasants stormed the manors of their landlords, took the land, and helped to form the soviets of workers and peasants. This peasant movement was consciously exploited by Lenin for the seizure of power. Once Communist authority was established, the peasant ownership of land was to be destroyed by collectivization. In the agricultural countries of the Far East this strategy of exploiting peasant discontent was even more important because the support of factory workers was practically non-existent. Professional revolutionaries, armed with the vanguard theory, were free to use any social conflict for their avowed end. The Russian Communist revolution provided the organizational pattern and the doctrinal elasticity by which the Communist movement could exploit the social, political, and intellectual problems of the twentieth-century Far East.

Oriental Societies

One of the major inadequacies of Marxian theory was revealed when it was used to explain traditional Far Eastern societies. Marx argued that the power of the ruling class stemmed from its ownership of the means of production and that the abolition of private ownership would lead to the disappearance of classes. In China, as in other ancient empires of Asia, such as Egypt and Mesopotamia, a society existed in which the ruling class did not base its economic power on private property. In China a scholar-gentry class did not derive its power or its main income from private property but rather from the management of people and affairs. This type of society could not well be fitted into the pattern which Marx drew up for the societies of the Western world.

Marx himself, following the classical economists before him, noted that Eastern countries differed from those of the Western world. He spoke of "Asiatic society" or the "Asiatic mode of production" as one in which the state or government played a major role in controlling the means of production. But he avoided a discussion of the class structure of such societies in terms of his own theory. This omission was of vital importance. Marx could not admit that in these Oriental societies the ruling class was a bureaucracy which, to use his terms, did not own but still controlled the means of production. To do so would have been to admit that there could be a ruling class which did not own the means of production. A ruling bureaucracy could then be equally powerful in any other society where private property did not extend to the means of production.[2] A theoretical admission that in such societies a ruling bureaucracy was the dominant class threatened the Communist doctrine at its most vital point. If a ruling bureaucracy could dominate the traditional Asiatic societies based on irrigated agriculture, it could play an equally dominant role in a socialist or Communist society based on modern industry. Any elite, whether owning property or not, could become an exploiting class. And therefore the transfer of the means of production from private ownership to ownership by the state was no guarantee of a classless society.

Marx did not indicate the danger of an exploiting bureaucracy; he avoided the problem. In his allusions to the "Asiatic mode of production" Marx remained ambiguous enough to enable later Communist theoreticians to deny any significance to the term, and to proceed with the classification of Far Eastern societies under the same categories of economic development that Marx used for the Western world. According to the official Communist line Asiatic countries were supposed to go through the stages of primitive society, slave society, feudal society, capitalist society, and arrive eventually at the socialist or classless stage. All societies followed a unilineal course of development leading to socialism, and this socialism was to be brought about by the Communist party as the vanguard of the workers—the historical force of the time. In order to uphold this doctrine it has been necessary for all Communist historians to describe the history of Oriental countries in these terms, however difficult it may be to reconcile the dogma with the historical data. Imperial China, for example, is classified by Communists as feudal. The elimination from Communist doctrine of all consideration of a society in which a bureaucratic ruling class controlled the means of production was designed to avoid the embarrassment of the obvious parallel between the bureaucratic societies of the past and those ruled by the Communists today.

The Communist Party

Since the Russian Revolution, Communist doctrine cannot be considered apart from Communist party organization. The Russian Communist party did not adopt that name until March, 1918. It emerged from

[2] This Marxian omission or ambiguity has been pointed out by Dr. Karl August Wittfogel who, building on the ideas of several predecessors, developed a theory of "Oriental society" in which the control of waterworks was a decisive factor in determining the rule by a bureaucratic official class. The main writings of Wittfogel developing this theory are his early *Wirtschaft und Gesellschaft Chinas, Erster Teil*, Produktivkräfte, Produktions- und Zirkulationsprozess (Leipzig, 1931); his article, "Die Theorie der Orientalischen Gesellschaft" in *Zeitschrift für Sozialforschung*, No. 7, 1938, pp. 90–122; and recently, "The Historical Position of Communist China: Doctrine and Reality," in *Review of Politics*, XVI, No. 4, October 1954; and *Hydraulic Society and Oriental Despotism*, soon to be published.

the Russian Social Democratic party which had been split into two groups, of whom the majority, the Bolsheviks, stood for the use of force and violence in the seizure of power and the accomplishment of social change. The minority, the Mensheviks, stood for social reform by peaceful means and democratic procedure and actually had a much greater popular following. The Bolsheviks, who seized power in the revolution of November 1917, defeating the Mensheviks in the process, indicated their break with the Socialist party tradition and the international socialist organization by changing the name of their own organization to that of the Communist party of Russia, the first Communist party to come into existence. This party became the model for the Communist parties in other countries, which it sponsored and directed.

The Russian Communist party, the brain child of Lenin, is a tightly disciplined organization. It is not a political party in the usually accepted sense of the term but rather a new kind of political weapon well designed for the specific purpose of carrying out the design of a small group of men to seize state power and to force through a social and political revolution. The condition of membership is strict obedience to the will of the party, once policy has been determined. The party is built on the basis of a large number of cells which are organized among the members of any functional group of people working together or, in other cases, living in the same neighborhood. Such cells are organized in factories, in villages, among professional and business groups, women's associations, or youth groups—practically any social unit that seems useful for the purpose. These cells hold meetings which the members must attend and in which the issues of party policy are supposed to be debated and the orders of the party leadership are actually made known. In theory the results of discussions in the cells are communicated to higher party levels and are supposed to be the basis on which the leaders make policy decisions, which, once made, are binding on the membership. This method of formulating policy is called "democratic centralism." In practice, however, there is no free discussion in the cells, for even the topics to be raised in cell meetings are prescribed from above and the outcome of the debate is predetermined.

The hierarchy of the party, starting from this cellular structure, proceeds through several organizational stages up to the Party Congress. The Party Congress, in theory the highest policy-making body, elects a Central Committee. Soon after the Revolution the Party Congress decreased in importance, and actual authority has rested in the hands of the standing committee of the Central Committee of the party. This standing committee, which has consisted at times of as few as five members and at others of over twelve, has been known as the Politburo (recently changed in Russia to Presidium). It is this small group which really holds the party in its hands. In theory each unit of the party, beginning with the cell, elects its delegates to the next larger unit above it, thus supposedly assuring active participation in the formulation of the party's policies. In practice, however, party representatives down to the lowest level are selected from above. The Politburo, through the party secretariat, controls the files on all party members, on whom it secures information through informers and through mutual informing, a system of control which the Communists have brought to a state of great refinement.

The principles of party organization which produced the disciplined group that seized power made the party an extraordinarily effective instrument through which the same small group of men, the Politburo, could rule the state and remake society according to its plans. The Communist party itself remained a tiny minority among the Russian people, whom it dominated. At the time of the Russian Revolution no more than 200,000 men and women made up the party membership. After the seizure of power the party grew to around four million members but in the purges of 1936–38 was reduced to a million and a half. At the outbreak of World War II it had grown again to around three million and by the end of the war had reached the total of six million, but even this was a small group compared to a total population of over two hundred million. Communist party members occupied all key positions in the state, which meant that they controlled every aspect of the life of the nation. They in turn were but the tools of the party leaders, who were therefore the real source of all authority. Besides the party, these leaders relied upon a powerful secret police organization, which used terror to intimidate and control, and upon the loyalty of the Red Army, itself a privileged group.

The authority of the leaders was based on more than the political machinery of party and state: it derived its ultimate sanction from the body of doctrine of which they were the self-appointed guardians. The essence of this doctrine was that in the present stage of human history the workers were the molders of the future, that the Communist party was the only true agent and interpreter of the will of the workers, and that therefore the Communist party leaders were themselves the agents of history. The workers, as a social class in action, were called the proletariat, and in order to carry out their historically determined mission they were empowered to use violence to seize power and to set up a dictatorship of the proletarian class. In practice the dictatorship of the proletariat meant a dictatorship of the Communist party, or rather, of its leaders. It was they who decided on matters concerning every sphere of human existence. There was therefore only one right way not only in politics and economics, but also in painting, sculpture, music, and architecture, in literature and in science itself. Individuals might err, but the party, by definition, could not. A faithful Communist who found himself out of step with the party line had therefore to confess his guilt, for any deviation was heresy. Those leaders who won out in the political struggle for power always justified themselves with the authority of the dogma and, in order to establish the righteousness of their triumph, spared no pains in going through the forms of elaborate trials in order to secure appropriate confessions of guilt and so maintain the myth. So much did the authority of the leaders depend on matters of faith that top leaders were compelled to demonstrate their mastery of the dogma through their own theoretical contributions in speeches or in writing. This was true not only of the relations between Russian Communist leaders and the Russian party but also of the relations between the Russian Communist party and the vast network of Communist parties, all over the world, which it came to control.

The Comintern

The Comintern, a Communist international organization, was established in March, 1919, at an international conference called in Moscow by the Soviet government. At the time of its establishment the only Communist party which existed outside Russia was in Germany, but Moscow invited to the conference all sorts of radical socialist leaders from other countries. From the outset the Comintern was an instrument, in the hands of the Russian leadership, for the establishment of Communist parties all over the world. This was done by declaring open war on those socialist movements which held so-called "reformist" attitudes and by enlisting the more militant radical leaders. The Communist International, or Comintern, was the international organization which in theory represented all Communist parties for joint action and policy, but in practice it both created and controlled them. Potential leaders were brought from all parts of the world, including Asia, for training and indoctrination in special schools in Moscow.

The governing body of the Comintern was the Executive Committee of the Communist International, which handed down its political directives to the national Communist parties subordinate to the Comintern. The same principle of democratic centralism was applied to justify control from the top. The theory that there was only one correct "line" was used to enforce the discipline of the Comintern which got its "line" from the leaders of the Russian Communist party. In this way the Comintern could be used to promote the aims of Soviet foreign policy as well as those of the Russian-sponsored world revolution. The Comintern held occasional congresses, frequently at first but later at greater intervals, and transmitted Communist policies through conferences of various sorts, such as international youth conferences, international labor conferences, and peace conferences. The Comintern continued until 1943 when it was dissolved as a Soviet gesture to wartime allies purporting to demonstrate Soviet willingness to cease the infiltration and subversion of friendly governments. The Comintern was reborn in 1947 under a different name, the Cominform, or Communist Information Service. This organization continued to operate in a similar way as the Comintern, working through its agents abroad and through international conferences, such as the Democratic Youth Meeting held in Calcutta in 1948. The Cominform published a journal under the title *For a Lasting Peace, For a People's Democracy*, through which it transmitted its policy directives.

Communist doctrine, Communist party organization, and the directing force of the Communist International combined to bring to the Far East after World War I a new and disturbing element. The Communist movement provided organization, methods, and a trained band of professional revolutionaries at a time when there was already more ferment in the Far East than ever before.

It was after World War I that Asian nationalist movements took on new hope and that native leaders pressed the struggle against colonial rule. The failure of the Communist revolutions in western Europe turned the attention of Russian leaders to the possibilities of exploiting the growing conflicts in the colonial world of Eastern Asia and the Middle East. At the Second Congress of the Communist International in July, 1920, Lenin shifted the emphasis of Communist strategy from the classical struggle of the oppressed classes against the oppressing classes to the struggle of the oppressed nations against the oppressing nations. Counting China as a part of the colonial world, he spoke of the 70 per cent of the world population which was suffering from imperialist oppression. Lenin even declared that the colonial countries could, "with the aid of the proletariat of the most advanced countries" be guided into Communism "without passing through the capitalist stage of development." The Second Congress of the Communist International called for a policy of supporting all risings and revolts against colonial rule and imperialism. This shift of Communist policy was further dramatized by the Congress of the Peoples of the East, called at Baku, September, 1920, and by a later congress, held at Moscow in January, 1921, which dealt almost exclusively with the Far East. Of this whole Far Eastern area the Communist leaders selected China as the main target of the new strategy. China was the biggest and the most populous country of the Far East, its traditional cultural center, and—at this time of warlordism—extremely vulnerable. As if to dramatize the swing to the East the Comintern sent to China its former emissary to Germany, Adolf A. Joffe, who initiated Soviet cooperation with the Chinese nationalist movement.

2. THE RETURN OF RUSSIAN POWER TO THE FAR EAST

Civil War and Intervention

The Bolsheviks inherited from the tsars an empire whose eastern borders were bounded by the Pacific Ocean and whose influence had long been felt in the power politics of Northeastern Asia. The expansion of Russia under the tsars left a legacy of imperialist concessions and special privileges in Manchuria, of rivalry and war with Japan, and of constant friction with China over the long borders of Inner Asia. Japanese victories in the war of 1905 had pushed back the wave of Russian imperialism from Korea and robbed the tsars of their warm-water port on the gulf of Pechili, but had not confined the Russians to their own borders. The collapse of the Russian government during the First World War gave the Japanese an opportunity to consolidate further their position in Manchuria and aroused among some of the Japanese military the hope of expansion on the continent at Russian expense. Russian power had never been weaker in the Far East than it was at the time of the Bolshevik Revolution. Russian influence ceased in Manchuria and Mongolia. American and Japanese troops moved into Siberia where some of the most important battles of the civil war were being fought. It was several years before the Bolsheviks recovered control over Russia's Far Eastern provinces and once more extended Russia's power and influence beyond the old borders.

Admiral Kolchak, the leader of the White forces in the civil war in Siberia set up an anti-Bolshevik Siberian government at Omsk in June, 1918. At the beginning Kolchak's government was supported by local political factions, and for a while he controlled Central Siberia and even gained some military victories over the Bolshevik troops. But in November, 1918, Kolchak made himself military dictator and started an all-out battle with the Bolsheviks. The behavior of the troops on both sides of the civil war was atrocious, and the ruthlessness of his own forces cost Kolchak much of whatever local support his regime had enjoyed. Eventually he was defeated by the reorganized and strengthened Red troops and was captured and executed. Kolchak's political base had been the central part of Siberia. In the Far Eastern Russian territory, at Chita, to the east of Lake Baikal, another White Russian leader, the Cossack ataman Semenov, had established another regime. Eventually he too was driven from Russian territory by the Bolshevik troops.

During the civil war the Far Eastern and Siberian territory of Russia was the scene of intervention by foreign troops. The Siberian intervention, which started in 1918 and ended in 1922, was carried out by Japanese, American, British, and French forces. The reasons for this intervention were complex. To the Japanese the Russian civil war was a chance to expand their position on the continent. The naval base of Vladivostok, so close to the Japanese home islands, seemed a constant threat. The opportunity to support any separatist movement that might emerge from the civil war was an obvious temptation.

The United States was traditionally opposed to intervention but was also opposed to any Japanese advance on the continent. In order to stop Japan from taking advantage of the situation the United States was eventually compelled to send troops to Siberia. During the early part of 1918 the American press and the American public became interested in the fate of the Czech legion which was trapped between the fronts of the Russian civil war. The founding of the Czechoslovakian state out of the Austrian empire was a favorite American objective in the war. Towards the end of the war a Czech legion had been organized in Russia from Austrian prisoners of war to fight with the Allies for the establishment of such a Czechoslovakian state. When the Bolshevik government concluded the Treaty of Brest-Litovsk, which ended the Russo-German fighting, the Czechs were cut off on the west. The only way out of Russian territory was towards the east across Siberia. Negotiations between the Czechs and both factions in the Russian civil war had paved the way for a Czech retreat along the Siberian Railway, but distrust on both sides prevented the smooth execution of the agreement. The American press and public came to believe that the Czechs needed help from the outside in order to escape from Russia. The American sympathy for the Czechs was further aroused by a rumor, played up in the American press, that German prisoners of war in Siberia had organized and armed themselves into a force to block the Czech withdrawal and establish themselves in that area. This rumor, though completely unfounded, played a large part in promoting an American opinion favorable to intervention.

Another consideration was the problem of salvaging war material which had been sent to the Russians via Vladivostok and the Siberian Railroad. Considerable stocks of war material had accumulated along the line, and it seemed important to prevent them from falling into the wrong hands.

The main motivation behind American policy was, however, concern over possible unilateral Japanese action. American participation in a joint Allied intervention would make it possible, or so it was argued, to limit the operation to assisting the Czech withdrawal and to evacuating military stores. An understanding was reached between the United States and Japan, and both declared that the intervention would not lead to interference in the internal affairs of Russia and would be carried out with full respect for Russian territorial integrity. When the object of the intervention was accomplished, the military forces would be withdrawn immediately. The United States and Japan each agreed to send approximately 7,500 men, and England and France were to participate with smaller contingents. When the troops were sent, the United States force was approximately of the agreed size, but the Japanese forces numbered about ten times the original figure.

The commander of the American forces, Major General William S. Graves, followed closely the instructions not to intervene in the civil war and attempted to restrain his Japanese partners. But the Japanese, who advanced along the Siberian Railroad from the Amur area westward, were intent on exploiting the civil war situation for their own advantage. They made every effort to assist Kolchak as well as Semenov.

This Japanese policy placed the White Russian leaders in a dilemma. If they accepted Japanese assistance, they would be regarded as traitors to the Russian cause. But if they refused, they would have difficulty in getting necessary support over a railroad line held by foreign troops. The behavior of the Japanese troops and the Japanese policy of control did great harm to the White Russian cause as the Bolsheviks could appeal to the Siberian population to resist the Japanese invader.

In this situation Kolchak, a Russian patriot, attempted to maintain an independent position until the end. But Semenov cooperated closely with the Japanese and, after the defeat of his forces, retreated with the Japanese into Manchuria, where he met his fate years later when Soviet troops captured Manchuria at the end of World War II.

The avowed purpose of the intervention was accomplished early in 1920 when the Czech legion had been successfully evacuated. The American forces withdrew, together with the English and the French, and the Japanese were left to carry out their own aims. But if the Japanese commanders had imagined that the removal of the restraining American influence would leave them free to accomplish their aims of fostering separatism in the Russian Far East, they had underestimated Russian resistance. The Japanese attempt to take over control and, incidentally, the ruthless behavior of their troops, led to mounting guerrilla warfare.

The new Soviet regime however was cautious in its political handling of the Japanese threat. Central Siberia as far as Lake Baikal was occupied by Red troops who cooperated with the guerrilla bands which had brought the area under Soviet control. But in the region east of Lake Baikal, where the Japanese troops remained in occupation, the Soviet government had to compromise. It had to cooperate with non-Bolshevik groups in order to secure a broader base for national resistance against Japanese intervention, and it had to accommodate itself to the Japanese demand for a buffer state, independent of Moscow.

The main organizer of this Soviet-dominated buffer state was one Krasnoshchekoff, a Communist working in political contact with Moscow. He organized a state in the area to the east of Lake Baikal, which was called the Far Eastern Republic of Siberia. The Bolsheviks, who dominated the new state, permitted Mensheviks to hold government positions and adopted a constitution in 1921 by which non-party members could be elected as representatives in the legislature. The territory of the state excluded Kamchatka, which was directly controlled from Moscow, and for a time the maritime province between Nikolaevsk and Vladivostok, which was controlled by local Russian administrators under Japanese direction until it also adhered to the Far Eastern Republic.

The success of this Russian political reorganization, directed by Moscow, made it easier for the Japanese to abandon their intervention, which had become costly and was unpopular at home. In 1922 the Japanese withdrew from the mainland, maintaining their occupation in only one part of Russian territory, the northern half of the island of Sakhalin.

The Far Eastern Republic had thus served its major purpose of facilitating Soviet Russian control of the Far Eastern territory. There had also been the hope that the powers might recognize the republic and thus enable Russia to be indirectly represented at the Washington Conference in 1921–1922. When this hope proved futile and the Japanese had withdrawn, no further reason existed for continuing the autonomous regime, and in November, 1922, the Far Eastern Republic was fully incorporated into the Soviet Union.

The Treaties with China and Japan

By 1922 the Soviet government was thus in full control of Russian Asiatic territory with the single exception of Sakhalin. It was still necessary to restore diplomatic relations and to settle certain political issues with China and Japan. In 1924 and 1925 the Soviet government concluded treaties with China and Japan which re-established the former Russian position in the Far East.

In the treaty with China in 1924 the Soviet government renounced the unequal privileges which the tsarist government, like the Western powers, had held in that country. Soviet Russia followed defeated Germany in giving up extraterritoriality and the former treaty port rights in China; and great emphasis was placed by Communist propaganda on the new equality in the relations between the Soviet Union and China. But when it came to the frontier areas, Manchuria and Mongolia, the Soviet government followed the Tsarist example, and demanded the re-establishment of former Russian rights, though in somewhat modified form.

The Russian rights and interests in the Chinese Eastern Railroad in northern Manchuria had been taken over by the Chinese government. During the Russian Revolution the railroad had been run for the Chinese by an international railroad administration, in which American engineers played the main part. At the end of the intervention this group was withdrawn and the Chinese took over. In July, 1919, at the height of the civil war, the Council of People's Commissars issued a manifesto drawn up by Leo Karakhan which promised the return to China of the Chinese Eastern Railroad and of Russian mining rights in Manchuria without compensation. When the manifesto was published in the Soviet press a month later, it no longer contained this promise, probably because the improvement of the Bolshevik position in the civil war made it more likely that the Soviets would soon return to the Far East. The Soviet Union still denies that the promise was ever made. There seems no reason to doubt the authenticity of the original version, which circulated in China early in 1920, as the Soviets had discussed the possibility of giving up Russian imperialist privileges in Manchuria before the manifesto was drawn up. This was at a time, however, when the Bolsheviks were fighting for their lives and needed all the support they could get. When the Soviet Union emerged as a Far Eastern power, it dropped its policy of offering revolutionary concessions and insisted on the maintenance of Russia's imperialist rights and interests. In the treaty of 1924 the Soviet Union obtained the restoration of Russian railroad rights in Manchuria and the establishment of a joint Soviet-Chinese Company to administer the railroads.

The Soviet regime gained actual control of Outer Mongolia during the civil war. The collapse of the tsarist government had brought the Chinese back to Urga in 1918, but in 1920 the White Russian general, Baron Ungern-Sternberg, retreated with his troops from Russian territory to Urga. He slaughtered the Chinese garrison and established a rule of terror using the Urga Khutukhtu, or living Buddha, as nominal head of his government. In reality this White Russian general ruled the country until 1921 when he was in turn attacked by Red Russian troops, defeated, and killed. Once in military control of Outer Mongolia, the Soviet regime established a Mongolian People's Republic and organized a Mongolian People's party which it put in power. Though nominally independent, this party was close enough to the Russian Communist party to follow its political line and to participate in the various purges of party leadership. While tsarist Russia had worked through the Mongol princes and the Lamaist Church, Soviet Russia used the party, a far more effective instrument, as its means of control. Where the tsars had attempted to bring Outer Mongolia into the orbit of the Russian economy by eliminating customs barriers and giving preferential rights to Russian traders, the Soviets established a complete economic monopoly over the Mongolian market, eliminating all Chinese and Western competition. For all practical purposes the Mongolian economy became a part of that of Soviet Russia and was later to be included in the calculations of the Five-Year Plan. The Soviets, continuing tsarist practice, established a Mongolian army, trained by Russian advisers and provided with Russian equipment; and Urga, now renamed Ulan Bator, was soon linked with the Siberian Railroad by a telegraph line and later by a branch railroad.

In the treaty of 1924 with China the Soviets forced the Chinese to recognize the Soviet position in Outer Mongolia in a formula similar to that used by the tsars in their Chinese treaty of 1913. The Soviets also recognized nominal Chinese overlordship which they honored with the name of Chinese "sovereignty." Outer Mongolia remained Chinese on the map, but Soviet Russia demanded from China the recognition of Mongol autonomy, which in practice excluded the Chinese from any influence in the country. The Soviets on their side promised the withdrawal of Soviet Russian troops, which they carried out, retaining their hold through the Mongolian People's party, the Soviet-sponsored Mongolian military organization, and the secret police, which remained in Soviet hands. The Soviets had thus regained and extended the tsarist position in the Chinese border areas and had opened the way for the political and ideological penetration which was soon to follow.

In 1925 a Soviet treaty with Japan finally ended the Japanese intervention by arranging for the complete withdrawal of Japanese forces from Russian territory in northern Sakhalin. In exchange for this withdrawal, Soviet Russia granted Japan oil development and exploitation rights in northern Sakhalin. The Japanese also received the right to lease fishing lots along the coast of the Russian maritime provinces and Sakhalin. These leases were to be determined by auction every year. Later Japanese attempts to come to a permanent arrangement failed, and the yearly fight for the Japanese fishing lots continued to cause friction in Soviet-Japanese relations.

In the treaties of 1924 and 1925 Soviet Russia gained recognition from her Far Eastern neighbors and re-established her position as a power in Far Eastern affairs.

3. Soviet Development of Asiatic Russia

Industry and Communications

The Soviet government, having survived the chaotic years of the civil war and having regained control of the Siberian and Far Eastern territory, turned to the economic development of the whole of Russian Asia. From 1925 on, the various five-year plans placed special emphasis on the development of this vast area. Soviet policy in the Far East was deeply affected by the tremendous industrial and agricultural expansion and population growth which Soviet planning promoted in Russian Asia. Russia became much more of an Asiatic power and therefore a stronger neighbor of China and Japan, as well as of India and the countries of the Middle East. In 1940, before the Russian involvement in World War II, almost a third of the Soviet population lived in Russian Asia. The decentralization of industries, an important part of the Russian planning, had brought about the growth of over a hundred cities east of the Urals, each with a population of over 100,000. Whole new centers of industrial production were created, the most notable of which was the Kuznetsk Basin, close to the cities of Novosibirsk and Stalinsk in Central Siberia. The best coal in Soviet territory was discovered in this area, which also came to have the largest output. Combined with the iron ore resources and the iron and steel mills of the Ural centers of Sverdlovsk, Chelyabinsk, and Magnitogorsk, the Kuznetsk coal became the basis for a key industrial region. The later discovery of iron ore in the Kuznetsk area itself strengthened its industrial importance. The Kuznetsk Basin was also important because it was located as far away from any source of outside attack as Russian industry could be. The air distance from Berlin or Tokyo is about 5,000 miles. In addition the southern location of the basin gives it the greatest possible protection from air attacks across the Arctic. The only close foreign territories were Outer Mongolia, a few hundred miles away, and Chinese Turkestan. Russian policy in Mongolia and Turkestan was obviously affected by their closeness to this new industrial center.

An equal increase in industrial and also in agrarian production took place in the southern bulge of Russian Asia, in the territories of Kazakhstan, Tadzhikistan, Uzbekistan, and Turkmenistan. This area of the southern steppes and border mountains was linked with the Trans-Siberian Railroad through the Turk-Sib Railroad, stretching from Novosibirsk and the Kuznetsk Basin along the Chinese-Mongolian-Turkestan border through Semipalatinsk and Alma Ata to Tashkent, and from there to the Iranian border and the Caspian Sea. At Tashkent a line also ran to Orenburg, connecting with the railroad system in European Russia. These railroad lines linked an area of new industrial cities and large, newly irrigated, agricultural plains with the main centers of Soviet industry. Russian Turkestan became the cotton belt of the Soviet Union, as important for her as the South is for the United States. In addition, the coal and iron of Tadzhikistan and the fruit, wine, and tobacco of Uzbekistan and Turkmenistan gave this area a special place in the Soviet economy.

The five-year plans also affected the Russian Far East and the northern forest and tundra belts. The government promoted the growth and industrialization of cities on the Trans-Siberian Railroad to the Japan Sea and the Sea of Okhotsk. Cities like Irkutsk, Chita, Blagoveshchensk, Khabarovsk, Nikolaevsk, and Vladivostok received new industrial plants, and the Russian Far East became independent of European Russia in some of its key supplies, especially those related to military defense.

In the northern forest belt and in the Russian sub-Arctic region, new emphasis was placed on mining and lumber, and Yakutsk, on the Lena River, became a new center for both industries. The region of the Kolyma River became an important mining center and one of the world's main gold-producing areas. To provide food for these northern regions, agricultural experiment stations were set up to develop fast-growing grain suitable for the short season during which the soil was unfrozen. These experiments produced grain which was suitable for the Russian settlements on the middle courses of the Ob, the Yenisei, and the Lena Rivers. The new economic activity in the northern parts of Soviet Asia was dependent on better means of communication. In the 1930's the Trans-Siberian Railroad was double-tracked. In addition, a branch line was built to the north of Lake Baikal as a link with the river system of the Lena. More important still was the attempt to establish communications between the northern areas and the European part of the country. The Soviets pioneered in Arctic weather stations to prepare the way for airlines serving the Arctic ports. The rivers were also given a new role in the over-all communications system. Because they flowed into the Arctic Ocean, the usefulness of these rivers had been limited in the past to their upper courses. Under the five-year plans a seasonal convoy system was organized. Each summer fleets of transports moved down these rivers and then, with the help of icebreakers, continued along the Arctic coast to the ports in European Russia. These seasonal convoys led to the establishment of ports and weather stations throughout the Arctic territory.

National Minorities

There are two important aspects of Soviet expansion in Asiatic Russia—Communist policy towards non-Russian national minority groups and the large-scale use of forced labor. When Soviet power was established in Asiatic Russia, the Communists proclaimed a program of cultural equality and autonomy for the national minorities. Schools were established and the level of literacy in the native languages rose considerably, thus providing, among other things, a necessary medium for spreading Communist ideas. By encouraging a degree of cultural autonomy, admitting the native language in the courts, and permitting the publication of books, magazines, and newspapers and the presentation of native movies and plays in the local languages the Russian Communists gained goodwill. The introduction of public health measures on a large scale and of veterinary services for the livestock of the nomadic peoples brought immediate results and created a favorable impression. At the same time the Communists began to gain political influence by working with special groups among each of the national minorities. They directed their appeal mainly to the underprivileged. They also began the training of local leaders by selecting likely candidates to be educated in Moscow, mostly at the Communist University for the Toilers of the East. After a two-year course of training the graduates were sent back and were expected to set up Communist cells at home and to form a core of Communist leaders.

After 1922 when the Russian Socialist Soviet Federation was changed to the Union of Soviet Socialist Republics, the states of the union were set up as administrative areas which corresponded, in the main, to ethnic divisions. Many of the minorities became either union republics or autonomous republics within a union republic. Each of the republics had its own Communist party, Supreme Soviet and government, whose members were chosen mainly from local native Communists. But after the great purges of the thirties the all-powerful party secretaries were largely replaced by Russians, which meant that all traces of genuine autonomy disappeared. At the same time the Russian Communists accelerated the cultural sovietization of the minorities.

Among other things a significant change took place in the writing of national languages. In 1926 the Latin alphabet had been introduced in order to facilitate the spread of literacy and to separate the minorities in the Soviet Union from related peoples outside the borders. When Turkey adopted the Latin alphabet, this purpose was no longer served, and it was feared that Latinization would strengthen ethnic nationalism. The scholarly members of the Central Committee of the Latin Alphabet in Moscow, which had been set up to promote the Latin scripts, were therefore accused of fomenting nationalism and were shot. The Russian alphabet was hastily substituted in order to create a stronger link between the minorities and the Russians and to aid in spreading knowledge of the Russian language. Russian technical terms were introduced into the local languages.

Such measures were mild, however, when compared with the actual extermination of the intelligentsia of the national minorities, the writers, artists, and scientists who might have kept alive a local cultural tradition. They were sacrificed to the cause of cultural uniformity; whatever the language, the content of literature was to be the same all over the Soviet Union. It was to deal with Communist propaganda and the greatness of the Russian people.

Slave Labor

The other special aspect of Soviet expansion in Asiatic Russia was the use of a large-scale system of forced labor. Political prisoners and criminals had contributed to the development of Siberia in tsarist times. The *katorga* system of forced labor in the mines and industries of tsarist Siberia had become known as a ruthless form of exploitation and had been attacked by various opposition groups, including the Bolsheviks. But forced labor had played only a minor part in the economic growth of Asiatic Russia under the tsars and did not compare in extent or ruthlessness with its use by the Soviets.

When the Soviet government first came to power it introduced a legal system in which the term "prison" was abolished as implying an idea of punishment which, the Bolsheviks claimed, was connected with the capitalist system of the past. Those who committed crimes had been forced to their acts by society and not by their own fault. They could be brought back into society through "corrective labor." This labor was to be limited and paid for. The early Bolshevik concept of criminal law broke down when criminal actions increased rather than decreased and when the prisons or "corrective institutions" overflowed. At the same time another institution had emerged from the civil war. The defeated anti-Communist forces had been placed in camps and many of those who were not executed remained prisoners in these camps. Soon camp labor was introduced to provide for and pay for the upkeep of the camp. The practice of establishing concentration camps and the breakdown of the utopian prison system led to the institution of forced labor camps. All who were regarded as dangerous to the Soviet state and were not exterminated outright were placed in forced labor camps where they served the economic purposes of the Soviet regime.

The system of forced labor was applied to European Russia as well as to Russian Asia, but was used most extensively in Central Asia and the Russian Far East in the construction of the huge projects that were decisive in the economic development of that area. The canals and the railroad lines of the new communications systems were built almost entirely with forced labor. Hundreds of thousands of prison laborers were used to build the irrigation system of Russian Turkestan. Even in the industries of Kuznetsk, slave labor was used in some plants. The lumber camps and the mines of the Soviet Arctic were nothing but a slave labor economy. In the thirties even the terminology of tsarist times came back. The term "prison" was used again and *katorga* became the punishment for the enemies of the Soviet state. But now prisons and forced labor became part of a whole economic system.

The real expansion of this forced labor economy came after 1928 when it was discovered that large labor forces were needed to build many of the projects included in the Soviet five-year planning. This labor could not be had voluntarily, and enticement by advantages such as good wages was out of the question. Many of the projects could be operated or constructed only by the most ruthless exploitation of human labor. On the other hand, Soviet domestic policy made it possible for large groups of people to be condemned as "enemies of the Soviet people" and imprisoned and enslaved for the purposes of the Soviet state. Many of the workers came at first from the farming population which had resisted the collectivization drive. Whole villages and population groups were uprooted and sent away for forced labor. Many other groups were attacked because of their potential opposition to Soviet aims. National minorities and religious communities and many Communist officials themselves and members of the professional groups who had become suspect were imprisoned and served as workers or as staff, engineers, and managers of the projects. Large masses of people, soon to amount to several millions, were thus placed in camps all through the Soviet Union. The most important of these camps were in Soviet Asia and the Far East. Each camp had its special economic task or tasks, such as the building of railroads, canals, or highways, the establishment of lumber industries, the building and working of mines, of oil wells, or of factories.

The slave labor system was managed by the Soviet political police, which through it gained not only political power but economic power as well. At first it was the OGPU, but after 1934 it was the NKVD, the Commissariat for Internal Affairs, whose police force handled the whole forced labor economy. After 1946 it was the Ministry of Internal Affairs, the MVD, which ruled over this economic empire. The slave labor force was composed of a smaller number of ordinary criminals who were better treated and often given positions of responsibility, and of a larger mass of political prisoners, the "enemies of the people," the "socially dangerous groups," who were regarded as hostile to the Soviet mode of life. All these prisoners were classified according to their ability to work, and were given fixed food rations according to the work they delivered. The food rations, based on a starvation diet, forced the prisoners to exert their utmost in order to receive enough food to keep alive; the vast majority fell behind and perished. The system thus involved the elimination of large numbers of persons whom the Soviets regarded as potentially hostile but whom they exploited to the limit of human endurance.

The system had many variations, from forced migration and settlement to the forced labor of the camps, where the prisoners were kept in barbed wire enclosures with watch towers and guarded by MVD guards and police dogs. In the northeast of Russia the whole administration of the area was under such a police system. Magadan, on the Sea of Okhotsk, was founded by slave labor under the MVD and became the capital of the northeastern police economy. From here, with tremendous loss of life, roads were built across the forbidding frozen mountains and swamps to the Kolyma River and a vast gold mining project established to provide gold reserves for the Soviet government. For the administration of this project a special organization, the Dalstroy, was set up, first under the OGPU and later under the MVD. The Dalstroy planned, managed, and executed the whole enterprise from the shipping between Vladivostok and the new city of Magadan to the gold mines and other mining and industrial enterprises on the Kolyma River and in the sub-Arctic region of the northeast.

The forced labor system resulted in tremendous destruction of life. No figures have been revealed by the Soviet government, which has tried to conceal the existence of this modern slave system. Estimates as to the total number of prisoners and forced laborers vary, but the most conservative calculations give a figure of at least five million people at the outbreak of World War II. Since World War II this figure is believed to have grown. The large majority of those involved do not survive the years of forced labor to which they have been condemned, but the gap is always filled by the arrests and deportations of people from Russia and, since the war, from the European satellite countries.

Unlike the traditional corvée of China, the modern Soviet system of forced labor is not a temporary burden on the peasant from which he returns to his fields; it is the removal of a whole group of people from society, the ruthless and systematic exploitation of men and women doomed to die. The Soviet Union has shown that forced labor can be applied to modern industrial and communications developments. The Soviet forced labor system is an institution which can be exported to any Communist country and especially to those such as China, which face the task of building huge modern communication systems and other public works without adequate capital resources.

The steady accretion of Soviet power in Asiatic Russia from the Urals and the Kuznetsk Basin to the cold seaports on the Pacific slowly changed the political and economic face of the Far East. The vast hinterland of the Chinese and Russian empires, and the area which only the Mongols had known how to conquer, was now to see the addition of modern means of transport, the growth of industrial towns, the influx of millions of people, and the growth of a military power which could be applied to the still undeveloped neighboring provinces of China and Mongolia without drawing on the faraway resources of European Russia. As the years went by this economic and military growth gave to Soviet diplomacy in the Far East a powerful backing which the overextended imperialist diplomacy of the tsars had never enjoyed.

4. Soviet Far Eastern Policy

The Soviet State and the World Revolution

The containment of the revolution within the borders of the former tsarist empire compelled the Bolsheviks to give up their hope of immediate world revolution and to accept at least the form and conventions of international relations and diplomacy. The Bolsheviks took over and continued the interests of the Russian state and pursued many of the aims of tsarist foreign policy. Certainly they were no less interested than were the tsars in territorial imperialism. But the world revolution was not forgotten; in fact it was institutionalized in the Comintern and from the beginning was under the control of Russian leaders. Lenin had already discarded the original Marxist idea that socialism could be victorious in all advanced capitalist countries at the same time, arguing that the uneven development of capitalism would bring socialism to different countries at different times. To promote the spread of revolution, however, was to be the prime task of the new Soviet state.

When the expected revolutions in Europe did not occur in the early twenties, the Bolsheviks concentrated more and more on building up the position of the Soviet Union itself. When Stalin came to power he made it very clear that "the defense of the Soviet Union must be considered paramount" and therefore that international Communism must serve the interests of the Soviet Union. The first condition of successful world revolution was that the one Communist government which had succeeded in coming to power should be strengthened and protected, if necessary at the expense of Communist parties abroad. The world revolution was to be under Russian direction. Any addition to Soviet political or territorial power could therefore be explained and justified as ultimately serving the world revolution. From the point of view of the Soviet leaders the expansion of the Russian state and the promotion of world revolution were both aspects of the same policy.

The Comintern and the Far East

Soon after the founding of the Comintern in Moscow, Communist agents went to the Far East to organize Communist parties. The impact of the Bolshevik Revolution and Communist literature had been strong enough in many areas to pave the way. But conditions varied considerably from place to place, and there was not always a group which was willing to accept the guidance and direction of the Comintern. Communist parties, therefore, emerged at different times in Far Eastern countries.

In June 1920, Voitinsky, a Comintern agent, went to China where he got in contact with a group of Chinese intellectuals who had already shown an interest in the theories of Marx and Lenin. Lenin's book on imperialism had had a particularly strong appeal to the Chinese. Voitinsky carefully and painstakingly taught Communist doctrine and discipline to a small group of Chinese, the most prominent of whom was Professor Ch'en Tu-hsiu of Peking University. Under Voitinsky's direction this group accepted the authority of the Comintern, and by the summer of 1921 a Chinese Communist party was organized. In the meantime, another Comintern agent, Janson, was working in Japan, where a group of students with radical leanings had already been deeply impressed with the Bolshevik Revolution. The Japanese Communist party was formed in 1922.

After the establishment of the Chinese Communist party, Comintern agents in China also organized Korean and Vietnamese Communist parties. Ho Chi Minh, who was secretary to Michael Borodin, the Russian Comintern agent in China, set up a Vietnamese Youth party in Canton in 1925. The Indonesian Communist party was formed by the Comintern in 1920, but in other countries of Southeast Asia formal Communist parties were not organized until the thirties, or later.

While Comintern agents were working abroad, schools were set up in Moscow specially designed to train young men and women as potential leaders of Asiatic Communism. These were the University of the Peoples of the East, established in 1921, and the Sun Yat-sen University, established a few years later. Some Orientals were admitted to the Lenin Institute designed mainly for Western students. In these colleges large numbers of Oriental students and Russians who were intended for liaison work were taught the doctrines, the strategy, and the tactics of the Communist party. Here they learned to become skilled professional revolutionaries who knew all there was to be known about sabotage, espionage, and infiltration. They also studied the art of war, especially civil warfare, and some of them even had experience as officers in the Red Army. They were taught by the highest political and military leaders in Russia, on occasion including Stalin himself.

The most spectacular opportunity for the Comintern was provided in

China. Soon after the establishment of the Chinese Communist party the Soviet Union negotiated an alliance with Sun Yat-sen, the leader of the nationalist movement. The agreement, negotiated through the Comintern agent, Joffe, provided for Soviet help in reorganizing the Nationalist party, the Kuomintang, along Communist lines. A swarm of Russian political and military advisers came to Canton. Great hopes were aroused among Communist leaders that a successful revolution in China would help to break the isolation of the Soviet Union and weaken the capitalist countries in one of the most important colonial areas. So important did the progress of revolution in China become to the Russian leaders that the strategy to be followed there became a chief point at issue in the bitter struggle for power which followed the death of Lenin in 1923. Stalin had authorized the agreement with the Kuomintang. His theoretical justification for an alliance with this non-Communist organization was that China was in a stage of development half-feudal and half-colonial. It had not yet gone through a complete capitalist revolution, nor was this necessary. According to Stalin a capitalist and socialist revolution could be combined in China. The Kuomintang, he argued, was a dictatorship by all the classes which shared in the joint revolution. The members of the Communist party, which was by definition the vanguard of the workers, could therefore join the Kuomintang and work within it.

Trotsky, on the other hand, thought that China was in a more advanced stage of development. She was already sufficiently capitalist to move directly into the socialist revolution. For him, therefore, the Communist party should take the lead and work by itself. He ridiculed Stalin's concept of the multi-class dictatorship under one party and insisted upon the policy of establishing soviets in China. After the break between the Kuomintang and the Communists in 1927 and the expulsion of the Russian advisers, the Comintern had to give its blessing to the policy of establishing soviets in China, but it explained this as a new stage in the development of the Chinese revolution rather than as an acceptance of Trotsky's policy. Actually, hidden behind this doctrinal battle was a personal struggle for power in which the winner, by definition, would be right. As Stalin prevailed, it is his version of the role of the Comintern and of the history of the revolution that has become official. But whatever interpretation Communist theoreticians give to events, the facts are that Comintern policy in the Far East, by the end of the twenties, had suffered a serious setback. When cooperation with the Kuomintang came to an end, the Communists were reduced from a group which was sharing in the leadership of the revolution to a few isolated pockets of military resistance.

Failure in China was the major defeat of Soviet Far Eastern policy in this period, but matters were no better in other parts of the Far East. In Indonesia and Vietnam the Dutch and French administrations succeeded, in a time of economic prosperity, in driving Communist and radical organizations underground and reducing their influence to negligible proportions.

In Japan the Communists had some influence for a period, but they remained a very small group, carefully watched by the police and never permitted to become a threat. By the end of the twenties the Comintern was on the defensive.

At the Sixth Congress of the Comintern in Moscow in 1928 Communist leaders drew up plans for a renewal of the attack. As a result of experience in China a greater emphasis was placed on the role of the peasantry but always with lip service to the leadership of the proletariat. The Sixth Congress also reasserted the policy of fostering anti-colonial movements in order to weaken the imperialist powers and thus strengthen the Soviet Union. Communists were to associate themselves with nationalism and to exploit any local conflicts, whatever their origin. Communist parties, while maintaining their own independence were to cooperate with what was described as the bourgeois democratic revolution, if conditions permitted such a course. In these and other plans the real instructions were to exploit every favorable situation for the furtherance of Communist aims and the advantage of the Soviet Union. As a result of the Sixth Congress new attempts were made to organize Communist parties. In 1930 Ho Chi Minh organized the Vietnamese Communist party in Hong Kong, but it became inactive when the British put Ho into jail for two years. In May 1931, a Communist party was founded in the Philippines but was dissolved again the same year. The Comintern had established in the Far East a foothold which it never lost, but until the coming of large-scale war no important advances were made.

Soviet Policy in Manchuria, Mongolia, and Turkestan

The world revolution was only one arm of Soviet policy. While agents of the Comintern were operating in Far Eastern countries, Moscow was re-establishing Russian political influence in the areas close to her borders. The treaty with China in 1924 gave the Soviet Union rights and privileges in Manchuria and Mongolia which closely paralleled those held by the tsars before the revolution. This policy was carried out by some of the same men who in 1905 had welcomed the Japanese defeat of Russia in Manchuria because it assisted their own revolutionary aims. The treaty of 1924 provided for the return of the Chinese Eastern Railroad in Manchuria to joint management. The Chinese warlord in Manchuria, Chang Tso-lin, however, tried to restrict the Russians by various measures. During the years 1925–27 he closed the Sungari River to Russian navigation, shut down the land offices of the railroad, and demanded that half the revenue of the railroad be placed in Chinese banks which he controlled. The Russians, on the other hand, prevented the joint Soviet-Chinese Board from functioning, so that all authority remained in the hands of the Russian manager who took his orders directly from Moscow.

Friction did not cease with the death of Chang Tso-lin in 1928 and the succession of his son Chang Hsüeh-liang, known as the Young Marshal, who raised the flag of the new National Government and accepted the control of Nanking. By this time the Kuomintang had turned against the Soviet advisers and the Chinese Communists. In May 1929, the Young Marshal raided the Soviet consulates in Manchuria and arrested a large number of Soviet agents. He also took over the railroad administration and arrested over two hundred Soviet employees. This led to a break in diplomatic relations and eventually to military action by the Soviet Union. In November the Soviet Union moved in troops under General Blücher (also known as Galen) who had been military adviser to the Kuomintang, seized the railroad, and compelled the Chinese to come to terms. Soviet control of the railroad was fully restored. The attempt of the Chinese National Government to apply against the Soviet Union the policy of using force to get rid of imperialist rights and interests had been defeated by the very power and the same military adviser who had trained the Chinese revolutionaries in anti-imperialist tactics. In Manchuria the Soviet Union had held its own as tenaciously as any other imperialist power.

In Outer Mongolia the treaty of 1924 had restored the old formula of nominal Chinese sovereignty and so-called Mongol autonomy, which meant, in practice, complete Soviet control. The affairs of the country came more and more into the hands of the Mongol People's party, which was in effect a branch of the Russian Communist party. The influence of the Lamaist Church was completely undermined, mainly through indirect attacks. In 1925, when the highest living Buddha and former ruler, the Khutukhtu, died at Urga (now called Ulan Bator) the Soviets simply declared that he had at last entered Nirvana and was not going to be reincarnated. In this way the leading religious figure of church and state in Mongolia was eliminated. The lamaseries were depopulated by arrests and persecutions and by refusing to allow new students to enter.

Outer Mongolia, after 1928, was included in the Soviet's five year plans. An attempt was made to collectivize the Mongol herds, but this measure was opposed by a great many Mongols who preferred to slaughter their animals rather than surrender them to the authorities. The loss of livestock forced the Soviet Union to restore private ownership of herds temporarily in order to recoup the losses, but in 1936 the drive for the collectivization of the herds was resumed. Soviet interest in the economy of the country led to the introduction of a number of measures to improve the animal stock, such as providing veterinary services, enforcing large-scale pest control, and introducing hay for winter feed. The Soviets also attacked the problem of venereal disease, which was very prevalent among the Mongols, with a great deal of success. They greatly increased literacy by setting up a school system which was also an essential instrument for indoctrination. By the beginning of the thirties the sovietization of Outer Mongolia was well under way.

The position which the Soviet Union had established in Mongolia and Manchuria was seriously threatened by Japanese aggression on the continent. On September 18, 1931, the Japanese began the conquest of Manchuria and within a year set up the puppet regime of Manchukuo. It was much more difficult for the Soviet Union to maintain its imperialist privileges in Manchuria against the pressure of the Japanese than it had been against that of the Young Marshal and his father. Rather than risk attack by Japan on the exposed Soviet position in Manchuria, the Soviet government decided to retreat to its frontiers and offered to sell its share of the Chinese Eastern Railroad to the Japanese. In 1935, after prolonged negotiations, Japan and Manchukuo purchased the Soviet railroad rights for 170,000,000 yen. The Chinese government protested to Moscow, which pointed out that the Chinese were in no position to enforce their own rights and that the Japanese and their puppets were about to seize the railroad. At the same time Soviet Russia strengthened its military position along the whole Amur frontier and at Vladivostok by improving communications, building fortifications, and establishing military settlements.

The Japanese thrust into the Inner Mongolian provinces of Jehol and Chahar threatened the Soviet position in Outer Mongolia and therefore the defense of the Trans-Siberian Railroad. An informal agreement between the Soviet Union and Outer Mongolia in 1934 was the signal for the return of Soviet troops to positions on the Manchurian border. In March, 1936, these troop movements were formalized by the conclusion of a mutual assistance pact between the Soviet Union and Outer Mongolia. Once more Nanking protested to Moscow against an invasion of Chinese sovereignty, pointing out that by the Sino-Soviet treaty of 1924 Outer Mongolia was still under Chinese sovereignty. The Soviet Union denied that its treaty with Outer Mongolia violated Chinese sovereignty which it still claimed to recognize.

The Japanese drive into Inner Mongolia came just after the Soviets had established friendly relations with the Chinese administration in Sinkiang. During the time of the Russian Revolution, a strong Chinese administrator, Governor Yang Tseng-hsin, disarmed the White Russian forces that retreated there from the civil war. He kept Soviet forces out of his province by establishing a policy of neutrality. The assassination of Governor Yang in 1928 by Chinese political rivals gave the Turkish population an opportunity to rise in revolt against Chinese rule. It was not until 1932 that a new Chinese governor, Sheng Shih-tsai, succeeded in suppressing local rebellions and regaining control over the province. This he did with the aid of the Soviet Union, which used this opportunity to establish its influence in Sinkiang. Governor Sheng had to rely heavily on Soviet support because the faraway Nanking government, fighting to consolidate its own power, could give him no assistance. In exchange for its support the Soviet Union secured economic concessions in Sinkiang. Soviet experts moved into the province, helped to establish a number of factories, opened mines, and began drilling for oil. The building of the Turk-Sib Railway across the mountains in Russian Turkestan drew the products of Sinkiang into the Soviet orbit. The economy of Sinkiang thus became linked to that of the Soviet Union, and Soviet influence in Sinkiang had already been established before the Japanese moved into Inner Mongolia. The Soviet Union stationed a garrison at the oasis city of Hami in order to block any Japanese advance along the strategic road to Turkestan.

The United Front Policy

Japanese aggression on the continent was made more serious by the rise of German power under Hitler. By 1935 the Russian leaders were concerned about the threat of a two-front war and began to look around for further means of defending the Communist motherland. The Seventh Congress of the Comintern, held in Moscow in the summer of 1935, announced the so-called policy of the "United Front," and initiated new tactics for Communist parties. For the purposes of Soviet foreign policy it was now necessary to build up as many allies as possible against the immediate enemies, Japan and Germany. All Communist parties were now instructed to cooperate with any political group or government which was opposed to German national socialism or Japanese militarism. Both of these phenomena were classified as fascism. In order to secure the help and the confidence of democratic countries, Communists were ordered to play down the anti-democratic slogans and actions of their program and to stress "national pride," national interests, and the need for military strength in a common fight against Fascist countries. The United Front policy became both more important to the Soviet Union and more acceptable to the Western world when Germany and Japan concluded their anti-Comintern pact in November 1936. The two signatories claimed that the pact was directed only against the Comintern, a supposedly independent international organization, but it was generally regarded as an alliance which could be turned against both the Western world and the Soviet Union.

The policy of the United Front had its greatest success in the Far East. Immediately after the Moscow Congress the Chinese Communist party began to clamor for an end to the civil war and for national resistance against Japan. In view of the intensity of Chinese nationalist feelings against Japanese imperialism, it was extremely difficult for the National Government to press the military campaign against the Communists at a time when they declared themselves willing to join in the resistance against Japan and accept the leadership of Chiang Kai-shek. It was not until December 1936, eighteen months after the initiation of the United Front policy, that Chiang Kai-shek was forced to accept a truce with the Communists as a result of his kidnapping at Sian. Six months later China was at war with Japan, and the National Government accepted the aid of the Communists. By the United Front policy the Soviet Union had succeeded in strengthening Chinese resistance to Japanese imperialism, thus reducing the capacity of Japan to engage the Soviet Union. At the same time the Chinese Communists lost nothing by their nominal acceptance of the leadership of Chiang Kai-shek. On the contrary, the war gave them the opportunity to increase their military forces, to extend their territorial control in the rural districts behind the Japanese lines, and to set up regional governments over a vastly increased number of people. By the time the war was over the internal balance of power in China had shifted in favor of the Chinese Communists.

Once China and Japan were at war, it was to the interest of the Soviet Union to support China in her resistance. Russian military supplies to the National Government came in through Turkestan and the Burma Road. These supplies were of great importance to the Chinese war effort, especially during the period between the fall of France in June 1940, and Hitler's attack on the Soviet Union in June 1941. At this time the Western powers had little to spare for China but the Soviet Union was not yet involved in her own struggle for survival.

Soviet support of China brought about a worsening of relations with Japan. From the time of the Manchurian incident, there had been friction, not only over Manchurian problems but also over such questions as Japanese fishery rights in Russian coastal waters and Japanese oil concessions on Sakhalin. The Soviet Union had made it difficult for the Japanese to exploit the fishing rights which they had secured in the treaty of 1925 by reducing, year by year, the number of fishing lots available to the Japanese. Japanese companies which had received oil concessions in Northern Sakhalin on the basis of the same treaty were constantly harassed by labor troubles but were not permitted to bring in their own labor force. The Japanese retaliated by holding back payment of the purchase price for the Chinese Eastern Railroad. These issues were under negotiation, but after the outbreak of the war with China the tension grew so serious that there were large-scale military clashes on the Soviet-Manchurian border. Ever since the establishment of Manchu-kuo there had been many small border actions designed to test the strength and disposition of Soviet forces. After the China war, however, engagements of considerable size, involving fully equipped armies, took place as a result of disputes concerning strategic frontier areas. The first major clash occurred in July 1938, at Changkufeng, a hill near the Russian, Manchurian, and Korean frontiers. After a prolonged battle Soviet forces remained in control of the hill, and the Japanese agreed to negotiate. More serious still was the incident of May 1939, on the Mongolian border at Nomonhan. Here the Soviet forces gained a decisive victory, partly because of their technical superiority. The Japanese admitted the loss of 18,000 men in the battle. The Soviet Union retained the contested border position.

A complete shift in the international situation in the summer of 1939 brought the frontier battles between Japan and the Soviet Union to a close. In August the Soviet Union concluded a non-aggression pact with Nazi Germany which led to Hitler's attack on Poland and resulted in the division of Eastern Europe between the two partners. This meant the end, for the time being, of the United Front policy. The Soviet Union called the war which broke out in Europe a conflict between capitalist powers, a label which remained until the Soviet Union was attacked by Germany in 1941. At that time the Communist leaders described the conflict as one between fascist and democratic powers. In the meantime the Japanese, caught by surprise at the

German shift to an alliance with the Soviet Union, hastened to adjust their own policy to the new situation. In September 1940, the Japanese formed the Tripartite Pact in partnership with Germany and Italy, an alliance which was designed to carve up vast portions of the world into areas for German, Italian, and Japanese aggression. The Japanese hastened to conclude an agreement with the Soviet Union in order to protect their northern frontier while attacking to the south. In April 1941, after long negotiations, Japan and the Soviet Union concluded a neutrality pact at a time when Hitler, without Japan's knowledge, had already prepared his secret plans for an attack on the Soviet Union.

In the decade which preceded World War II Japanese aggression in the East became linked with German and Italian aggression in the West. The reaction of the Soviet Union to this international aggression revealed the stark opportunism upon which Soviet policy was based. The sole aim of the Russian Communist leaders was to secure and strengthen the power of the Soviet Union. After first seeking support from all those governments and peoples who were opposed to Nazism and militarism, they changed sides when it enabled them to carry out their own plans and share in the spoils.

Soviet Russia and the Far Eastern Front

The military forces of the Soviet Union were not involved in the Far Eastern conflict until the last days of the war. As every available resource was needed for the desperate struggle with Hitler, supplies to China had to cease. While the Soviets withdrew some of their troops from the Far East, Japan, for her own good reasons, honored the neutrality pact. It was only in the province of Sinkiang that the Soviet Union had to give up a position of influence and this was in the face not of Japanese but of Chinese pressure. The Chinese governor, Sheng Shih-tsai, who had come into power with Soviet support, now used the opportunity created by Soviet weakness to drive out his Russian advisers and technicians and to turn again for support to the Chinese National Government, then in Chungking. When challenged in Sinkiang, a position of secondary importance, the Russians did not put up a fight, and left Sinkiang, taking with them all their equipment and installations. The withdrawal of the Russian garrison from Hami left the province open to Japanese attack, but Japan was too busy in the Pacific to exploit the opportunity at this time, and was probably unwilling to run the risk of endangering her relations with Soviet Russia in the later years of the war. The Chinese administration, replenished with Kuomintang officials, soon faced large-scale unrest among the Uighur population of the province. A few years later this unrest was to lead to Soviet-supported uprisings in the whole area west of Urumchi, uprisings which ended with the Chinese losing control over that region. After the war the Chinese attempted to placate the Uighur opposition by transferring the provincial administration to Uighur leaders who were friendly to China, but the Chinese-sponsored administration did not recover control over the rebellious groups.

Until the last days of the war the Soviet Union maintained a policy of strict neutrality towards Japan and refused to participate with its allies in meetings involving China. The furthest she went in associating herself with the Chinese government was the Four Power Declaration of November 1, 1943, by which the United States, Great Britain, the U.S.S.R., and China pledged a united conduct of the war against the powers with whom the signatories were severally engaged and promised cooperation in establishing a postwar security system. This declaration was largely the result of American diplomacy, which sought to substitute China for Japan as the leading Far Eastern power. The elevation of China to the status of one of the Big Four was accepted most reluctantly by the Russians and the British. From this time on Soviet relations with China were inextricably mixed with Soviet relations with the United States.

In spite of the correctness of Russian relations with Japan, Moscow indicated to the United States as early as August 1942, that the Soviet Union would eventually be willing to take part in the war with Japan. In fact Soviet propaganda stressed the old nationalistic ambitions of Russia in the Far East. Russian novels, dramas, and political statements glorified the tsarist position in Manchuria, the defense of Port Arthur, and the battle of Tsushima in the Russo-Japanese War. The United States was particularly anxious to assure itself of Russian support in the conquest of Japan. Stalin promised this support at the Foreign Ministers conference in Moscow in October 1943. At the Teheran Conference in November–December 1943, Stalin repeated his promise but pointed out that the necessary strengthening of Russian armies in Siberia could not take place until after the defeat of Germany in Europe. There was some discussion, in an informal way, of Russian territorial interests in the Far East, particularly of a warm-water port at Dairen in Manchuria, but nothing was settled at this time. In 1944, when the tide of war turned decisively against Germany in Europe, Soviet interest in the war against Japan was strongly indicated to the American and British governments. In October 1944, the Soviet Union promised to enter the Far Eastern war three months after the defeat of Germany but stated certain conditions. Stalin demanded that American supplies be delivered to his armies in the Far East and that his political terms be met. In December 1944, he presented to the American government his specific conditions for Soviet participation. In general these conditions amounted to the re-establishment of the former tsarist position in the Far East, and in addition, the cession of the Kurile Islands "in order to protect Soviet outlets to the Pacific." These demands were the basis for a secret agreement on the Far East which was concluded at the Yalta Conference in February, 1945.

The Yalta Agreements and the Sino-Soviet Treaty

The Yalta agreement, signed by Stalin, Roosevelt, and Churchill, provided that the Soviet Union would participate in the war against Japan two or three months after German surrender, on condition that:

    1. The status quo in Outer-Mongolia (The Mongolian People's Republic) shall be preserved;

    2. The former rights of Russia violated by the treacherous attack of Japan in 1904 shall be restored, viz.:

    (a) the southern part of Sakhalin as well as all the islands adjacent to it shall be returned to the Soviet Union,

    (b) the commercial port of Dairen shall be internationalized, the preeminent interests of the Soviet Union in this port being safeguarded and the lease of Port Arthur as a naval base of the U.S.S.R. restored,

    (c) the Chinese-Eastern Railroad and the South-Manchurian Railroad which provides an outlet to Dairen shall be jointly operated by the establishment of a joint Soviet-Chinese Company it being understood that the preeminent interests of the Soviet Union shall be safeguarded and that China shall retain full sovereignty in Manchuria;

    3. The Kuril Islands shall be handed over to the Soviet Union.

It is understood, that the agreement concerning Outer-Mongolia and the ports and railroads referred to above will require concurrence of Generalissimo Chiang Kai-shek. The President will take measures in order to obtain this concurrence on advice from Marshal Stalin.

The Heads of the three Great Powers have agreed that these claims of the Soviet Union shall be unquestionably fulfilled after Japan has been defeated.

For its part the Soviet Union expresses its readiness to conclude with the National Government of China a pact of friendship and alliance between the U.S.S.R. and China in order to render assistance to China with its armed forces for the purpose of liberating China from the Japanese yoke.

The southern half of Sakhalin and the Kurile Islands were occupied by Soviet forces at the close of the war. The stipulations of the Yalta agreement on China were incorporated into a treaty between the Soviet government and the Chinese National Government. The Sino-Soviet Treaty of Friendship and Alliance, actually signed on August 14, the day of Japan's surrender, contained a Soviet promise "to render to China moral support and aid in military supplies and other material resources, such support and aid to be entirely given to the National Government as the Central Government of China." Soviet Russia promised to respect China's full sovereignty and territorial and administrative integrity in Manchuria. According to the treaty, Dairen was to become an international free port under Chinese administration but the Soviet Union was to have a lease on half the port facilities. Port Arthur was to be a joint Sino-Russian naval base. The T-shaped trunk line of the Manchurian railroad system from Manchuli to the border near Vladivostok and from Harbin to Dairen was to be managed as a joint Soviet-Chinese enterprise in which Russian and Chinese presidents and vice presidents would alternate in the managerial and technical direction. These railroad rights did not include the political and administrative privileges which the tsars had exercised in 1904; China was given the responsibility for the security of the railroad. On the other hand, most of the subsidiary enterprises, such as the industrial plants, mines, and other concessions, were to be included in the joint administration. These Soviet rights and privileges were to continue until 1975.

The treaty also included a Soviet declaration in regard to Sinkiang, that it had no intention of interfering in China's internal affairs. But on Outer

Mongolia the treaty went beyond the Yalta agreement, which had called for a continuation of the status quo. It arranged for a plebiscite in which the people of Outer Mongolia were to vote on the question of independence from China. The outcome of this vote was a foregone conclusion, as the Soviet Union was already in complete control. The plebiscite was actually held at the end of 1945 and Outer Mongolia became "independent" in January 1946. The Chinese felt compelled to agree to this concession, as indeed to many others because the Russian occupation of Manchuria, during the negotiations, made it urgent to secure in writing whatever limits on their demands the Russians were willing to accept. At the request of the Chinese the Russians agreed, orally, to complete the withdrawal of their troops from Chinese soil within three months of the surrender of Japan. The Sino-Soviet Treaty provided for the re-establishment of the economic as well as the naval position of Russia in Manchuria. In return for these concessions the Chinese National Government felt that it had secured from the Soviet Union an agreement to respect its sovereignty, to recognize no other Chinese government, to provide support, and to refrain from interfering in Chinese internal affairs.

The Soviet Union in Manchuria

In order to declare war on Japan the Soviet Union had to denounce the Neutrality Pact of 1941 a year before it could be legally terminated. Soviet troops entered Manchuria on August 8, 1945, and rapidly overran the Japanese armies, inflicting at least 80,000 casualties and capturing almost 600,000 men. Once in control of Manchuria the Russians began a systematic looting and destruction of Manchurian industrial and mining establishments, removing to the Soviet Union stockpiles of industrial material, valuable electrical and generating equipment, and machine tools. They demanded of Nationalist China a joint Sino-Soviet management of the remaining plants, but the Chinese refused. The demand was renewed again in March 1946, in a formal proposal for joint management of the main industrial and mining enterprises and airfields by Sino-Russian companies in which each government would own 50 per cent of the stock. These companies were to be managed on the pattern of the Chinese Eastern Railroad—a Chinese chairman, Soviet vice chairman, Soviet manager, and Chinese deputy manager. The Chinese again refused. The Soviets therefore continued to remove and destroy equipment, and the loss suffered by Manchuria was later estimated by an American investigating committee at two billion dollars.

The Russians were in an excellent position in Manchuria to assist the Chinese Communists in their struggle with the Nationalists for control of Manchuria. Soviet forces were in a position to affect decisively the outcome of the race for Manchuria. The Russians assisted the Chinese Communists by putting obstacles in the way of the Nationalist troops which were sent to take over control of Manchuria. The Russians denied the use of the port of Dairen and of the Russian-controlled railroad to the Nationalist armies, which were transported in American ships and had the help of American technical officers. They agreed to hand over the port of Yingkow to the Nationalists but they evacuated the port five days earlier than had been arranged, thus enabling Chinese Communist troops to slip in, and the Nationalists could not use the port until they drove the Communists out. The main Nationalist forces had to be landed at Chinwangtao, south of the Great Wall, from where they had to force their way overland into Manchuria in the face of determined opposition, thus losing a great deal of valuable time. After hampering the return of the Nationalists to Manchuria, the Soviets carried out their obligation to hand over the key cities to Nationalist forces. When the Nationalists were unable to get there in time to meet the schedule, the Soviets agreed to a three months' postponement of their withdrawal from key cities such as Mukden and Changchun in order to enable the Nationalist troops to arrive and take over. But the Communists had already gained valuable time in the race for territory, time which they used to occupy and organize the countryside. When the Nationalist armies moved into the cities they were soon surrounded.

The most decisive assistance that the Soviet forces gave to the Chinese Communists was to permit them to gain control of large stocks of Japanese military equipment which had been accepted in the surrender of Japanese troops. This equipment gave the Chinese Communists the heavy armament necessary to enable them to shift from guerrilla warfare to frontal battles with concentrated use of artillery and tanks. By the time the Russian forces withdrew from Manchuria, leaving garrisons only at Port Arthur and Dairen, the advantage in Manchuria had shifted to the Chinese Communists. The actions of the Soviet Union, in violation of treaty obligations to the National Government, made possible the victory of the Chinese Communists in Manchuria, a victory that proved decisive for the outcome of the Chinese civil war.

The assistance which the Soviet Union gave to the cause of the Chinese Communists in Manchuria seems hard to reconcile with the thorough looting of that country and the destruction of industrial plants which the Russians carried out before their withdrawal. It is possible that the Soviet Union did not anticipate a Communist victory in the near future and wanted to deny to the Kuomintang the industrial resources of Manchuria. A weakened Nationalist China would be less able to suppress the Communists and less valuable as an ally of the United States. In any case the Russians were desperately hungry for industrial equipment to make up their own losses, and this in itself could be sufficient explanation for the removal of equipment, though not for its destruction. On the other hand, it has been thought possible that the Russians, anticipating a Communist victory, ruined Manchuria in order to increase the dependence of the new Communist regime in China upon the Soviet Union. Whatever the reasons, the Chinese Communist leaders were hard put to explain the Russian depredations in Manchuria to their followers. At no time did Soviet actions indicate that the Soviet government expected a quick Communist victory. As the Chinese Communists moved steadily southward, the Soviet Union maintained the diplomatic proprieties with the Nationalists to the end. The Soviet Embassy was the only one to follow the National Government in its retreat from Nanking to Canton, keeping up the pretense of dealing with the collapsing National Government until the establishment of the Communist regime in Peking, which the Soviets were the first to recognize.

Soviet Attack on United States China Policy

While the Soviet Union was giving covert assistance to the Chinese Communists in building up an army and a territorial base in Manchuria, it was concerned, on the diplomatic front, with the American political and military position in China. As early as December, 1945, at the meeting of foreign ministers in Moscow, the Russians raised the issue of the withdrawal of American troops from China, especially the marines who had been stationed at Tientsin and Peking to assist in the disarming of Japanese troops and in the transfer of this territory to the Nationalist forces. The Soviet government tried to put pressure on the American government by linking the withdrawal of Russian troops from Manchuria with that of American troops from China proper. The communiqué of the Moscow conference, in which the foreign ministers agreed on the "desirability of withdrawal of Soviet and American forces from China at the earliest practicable moment consistent with the discharge of their obligations and responsibilities," [3] was frequently referred to later by Moscow in order to attack American policy in China. In the same communiqué the Soviet Union and the United States agreed on the "need for a unified and democratic China under the National Government, for broad participation by democratic elements in all branches of the National Government, and for a cessation of civil strife." [4] Both sides agreed not to interfere in the internal affairs of China. This agreement must be regarded as a diplomatic success for the Soviet Union because later it enabled Moscow to accuse the United States of breaking the agreement by interfering in Chinese affairs. The communiqué also indicated that the National Government should bring in what the Russians called "democratic elements," which were understood to include the Communists.

At the time of the Moscow conference of Foreign Ministers, General George C. Marshall was sent to China by the American government to assist in the prevention of civil war. At the time it appeared that the Soviet Union, the United States, the National Government of China, and the Chinese Communists were all agreed upon the importance of preventing civil war and upon representation of the Chinese Communists in the government. It soon became clear, however, that Manchuria was not to be included in the cease-

---

[3] Quoted in Max Beloff, *Soviet Policy in the Far East* (Oxford University Press, 1953), p. 46. Text in Royal Institute of International Affairs, *United Nations Documents* (1946), pp. 263–64.

[4] Beloff, *op. cit.*, p. 45.

fire arrangements that Marshall secured, a significant omission, and that the two Chinese parties could not come to a workable agreement. By the summer of 1946 the Soviet Union joined with the Chinese Communists in a propaganda offensive against the National Government and the United States. The National Government was now referred to as the "Kuomintang Government" and the Chinese Communists army became the "United Democratic Army." But the main attack was directed against the United States and its continued support of the National Government, which was condemned as "direct interference in the internal affairs of China" and a violation of the Moscow agreement of 1945.

During the year 1947 the Soviet Union developed the case against American intervention in China into an all-inclusive attack on American policy in the Far East. Isolated as the main enemy, the United States was presented as an imperialist power. America was accused of reviving Japanese militarism and of building up the military strength of the National Government of China for American imperialist purposes. Cushing, who had concluded the first American treaty with China, and Perry, who had opened Japan, were painted in new colors as the early representatives of American imperialism, of which the annexation of Hawaii and the taking of the Philippines were other important examples. While the Soviet Union used all its propaganda resources to discredit America as an imperialist power, the Chinese Communists in their propaganda described Chiang Kai-shek as the running dog of American imperialism.

The Soviet Union in Korea

The year 1947, which marked a turning point in the relations between the Soviet Union and the United States and in the progress of the Chinese Communists in China, also marked the end of negotiations for a united Korea. At the close of the war Korea had been divided along the 38th parallel, Russian troops taking the Japanese surrender to the north and American troops to the south. The Cairo Declaration, which had promised freedom and independence for Korea "in due course," had been incorporated in the Potsdam Declaration, to which the Soviet Union affixed its signature. At the Conference of Foreign Ministers (U. S., U. K., U.S.S.R., China) at Moscow in December, 1945, it was agreed that there should be a Joint Commission formed by the American and Soviet occupation forces to set up a Provisional Government for the whole of Korea, in consultation with "the Korean democratic parties and social organizations," and to submit a plan for a Four-Power Trusteeship of Korea for a period of up to five years. When the Commission met in 1946, it became clear that the Soviet Union wanted to base the Provisional Government only on those parties which it controlled. The Commission continued to meet occasionally until August, 1947, but finally could agree on nothing, not even on submitting two separate reports with a joint letter stating that no agreement had been possible.

The Soviet Union, after the surrender, had sealed the border at the 38th parallel to practically all contact with South Korea. While the Russians could not prevent the flight of North Koreans to the south, they would not permit representatives of the American government or even of the United Nations to visit North Korea. The non-Communist press was also kept out. In the meantime the Russians set up in North Korea a government to their own liking. For this purpose there were in reserve a large number of Koreans who had been trained in the Soviet Union. Some of their leaders had worked with the Chinese Communists during the war. With the help of these Koreans the Soviet forces set up "People's Committees" to take over the local administration. Within a month of the surrender more than a thousand delegates from these committees had been elected and dispatched to Seoul, where they in turn elected a "Central People's Committee of the Korean Republic" which they tried to foist on the American command as a Provisional Government for the whole of Korea. In this they were not successful, but in North Korea the People's Committees, with Russian support, ran the country on the provincial, district, and local levels. The Russians also set up a popular front organization called the People's Party, soon to be merged with the Korean Communist Party into the Workers Party, and formed mass organizations for workers, peasants, women, and youth. In February 1946, the Russians set up a Provisional People's Committee of Northern Korea. Kim Il Sung, a member of the Communist party since 1930, became president of this provisional government.

Once in power the provisional government began to carry out the classical Communist policy. First came the redistribution of the land. In March 1946, the government distributed to agricultural laborers and smallholders all land belonging to Japanese and to "traitors," all land held under lease, and all land holdings in excess of 5 *cho*, about 12¼ acres. The purpose of the land redistribution was to build up political support for the new regime among the peasantry. Next came the workers. In June 1946, the government passed labor legislation to prepare the way for government-controlled labor unions. Then, in August, there followed the nationalization, without compensation, of all enterprises formerly owned by the Japanese or by "traitors." These enterprises were sufficient to give the government decisive control over the economy.

After these measures had been taken, elections were held in November 1946, on the provincial, town, and district level for the selection of people's committees. Elections followed on the village level early in 1947. The voters could choose only those candidates listed on a single slate for what was called the Democratic National Front. The candidates were not all Communists but they were all hand-picked by the Communists. From the committees delegates were selected to attend a Congress, which met at Pyongyang, the capital of North Korea, in February 1947, to elect a People's Assembly of North Korea. In a one-day session this assembly immediately elected a Presidium, a Supreme Court, and a new People's Committee or Cabinet, for North Korea. This cabinet was again headed by Kim Il Sung. One year later, in May, 1948, the People's Assembly adopted a Soviet-type constitution in preparation, presumably, for the unification of the whole of Korea under Soviet domination.

The Soviet Union recognized the North Korean government in October 1948. Some time earlier, in November 1947, the United Nations Assembly had accepted an American resolution for the holding of elections and the setting up of a Korean government. The Soviet Union, however, did not admit to North Korea the United Nations Temporary Commission, which had been sent there in 1948 to carry out this resolution. As a result of the work of the Commission the Republic of Korea was set up in the south and a government elected. To this government the American forces transferred full authority in August 1948, and the American government recognized the Republic of Korea on January 1, 1949. There were now two Koreas.

The Soviet Union withdrew its forces from North Korea at the end of 1948 in order to put pressure on the United States to withdraw its forces from the south. The last American regular troops were withdrawn in June 1949, leaving behind a military mission for the training of the South Korean army. One year later, on June 25, 1950, the North Korean army invaded South Korea, thus beginning the Korean war. The buildup in North Korea, from the establishment of the government to the training and equipping of the army, had been the work of the Soviet Union. But when the forces of North Korea were defeated, it was the Chinese Communists, who had in the meantime conquered China itself, who came into the conflict and took over the direction of the Communist program in Korea.

The Red Army and the Cominform

The establishment of a Communist regime in North Korea would have been impossible without the presence of the Red Army. In fact the Russians wrote into the Korean nationalization law a statement glorifying the role of the Red Army, which, "having entered the territory of Korea with the object of destroying the Japanese army, liberated Northern Korea from Japanese slavery, assured democratic freedoms for the Korean people, took under its protection the private and public property of the Koreans, preserved national property and created the opportunity for the most rapid economic and cultural rebirth of the Korean State." [5] The Red Army also played an important role in China through the assistance it gave to the Chinese Communists in the conquest of Manchuria. In both cases the Soviet Union used the Red Army as a political weapon in supporting Communist expansion in the Far East.

In 1947 the battle against the whole Western world was extended to another front, that of India and Southeast Asia. In these areas, where the Red Army was far away, other methods had to be used. The Cominform, or Communist Information Bureau, was set up on October 5, 1947, as an organization of European Communist parties, including that of the Soviet Union.

[5] Shabshina in *Krisis Kolonialni Sistema*, pp. 264–65. Quoted in Beloff, *op. cit.*, p. 165.

Through the Cominform the Soviet Union directed the strategy of Far Eastern Communist parties, especially those in Southeast Asia. This was done in various ways. For example, at the opening of the meeting of the Cominform the Soviet chairman, Zhdanov, stressed the line that Communist parties must support what he called the national liberation movements. The Cominform also used its own journal, *For a Lasting Peace, For a People's Democracy*, to give direction to Far Eastern Communist parties. The journal frequently dealt with Chinese affairs during the rise of the Chinese Communists to power and on one occasion attacked the Communist leadership in Japan and ordered a new political strategy.

Another method was to call special regional conferences. In February, 1948, only two months after the formation of the Cominform, a Youth Conference of the countries of Southeast Asia was called in Calcutta. It was sponsored by the World Federation of Democratic Youth and the International Union of Students. This type of conference permitted the inclusion of delegates from non-Communist organizations in what were classified as colonial countries. The Calcutta meeting implemented the national liberation policy of the Cominform. It is believed to have initiated the Communist rebellions in such countries as Burma, Malaya, and Indonesia, all of which followed within six months of the conference. These rebellions were only partly successful. In Burma and Malaya they caused serious complications but did not lead to seizure of power, while in Indonesia the rebellion failed completely. The strategy staged at Calcutta did not achieve the hoped-for results. In the meantime the Chinese Communists were conquering China and a new center of Communist power came into being. The Chinese Communists immediately capitalized on this victory by arranging for another conference, this time in Peking. In November 1949, there met in that city a Trade Union Conference of the countries of Asia and Australia sponsored by the World Federation of Trade Unions. This conference indicated that China would play a leading role in the promotion of Communism in the Far East now that the Chinese Communists had come to power.

The Moscow-Peking Alliance

The victory of Communism in China changed the character of the world Communist movement and the power position of the Soviet Union. There was now a new, if secondary, center of Communist power which modified the picture of a Soviet motherland standing out alone against the capitalist world. While the addition of China to the Soviet orbit obviously increased Communist prestige and power, the fact that a non-Russian Communist elite now ruled a vast territory and controlled a large army, and had national interests of its own, meant that there were new problems to be faced in the relationship between Russian leaders and Chinese Communists. This relationship differed radically from the kind to which the Moscow-dominated Cominform was accustomed. The question was not one of whether the Chinese Communists would work within the general framework of Soviet policy but rather of what role they would play within the Communist power structure.

The new relationship began with the Sino-Russian Treaty of Friendship, Alliance, and Mutual Assistance, of February 1950. The agreements which flowed from this alliance covered every important aspect of Sino-Soviet relationships—political, economic, military, and cultural. The fact that Mao Tse-tung, the head of the Chinese Communist party and the new government, himself went to Moscow and stayed there for six weeks is itself an indication of the importance and perhaps the difficulties of the negotiations. This was a long time for the leader of a new government which was still in the process of being organized to spend in Moscow. The most important aspect of the treaty concluded in Moscow was the military alliance which created a military partnership. The alliance was ostensibly directed against renewal of Japanese aggression, not only by Japan but also by "any other State which should unite with Japan, directly or indirectly, in acts of aggression." In other words, this alliance could be invoked against the United States if she undertook any action which the Communist world chose to describe as aggression. The military details of the implementation of this treaty remained unknown, but it was quite clear that large numbers of Soviet military advisers and technicians immediately began to train the Chinese Communist army in the use of modern weapons provided by Soviet Russia in considerable quantity. The treaty also provided for "economic and cultural ties" and the rendering of "every possible economic assistance" as well as the carrying out of "the necessary economic cooperation."

At the same time the Soviet Union undertook to return to Chinese control the Manchurian railroad rights, the naval base of Port Arthur, and the Soviet holdings in Dairen. The return of these rights and interests, which the Soviet Union had secured in the 1945 treaty with the National Government, was to take place on the conclusion of the peace treaty with Japan, or at the latest by the end of 1952, if a peace treaty had not been signed by that time. The promised economic aid was to be a five-year credit of U. S. $300,-000,000 to pay for Soviet deliveries of industrial equipment and materials. Peking was to pay for this through the export of tea and raw materials to the Soviet Union. Peking and Moscow also agreed to set up four joint Sino-Soviet companies for the exploitation of oil and minerals in Sinkiang and for the operation of airlines and shipbuilding plants in Manchuria. The stock of these companies was to be held on a fifty-fifty basis between the two governments and the companies were to be under joint management. The arrangements relating to Manchuria and Sinkiang were concluded by the separate delegations from those areas to Moscow, who stayed on after the main Chinese delegation had left. This followed a precedent which had been set in the summer of 1949, when a Manchurian delegation to Moscow had independently concluded a special economic arrangement by which the Russians agreed to return some of the looted Manchurian factories and to deliver other Russian industrial equipment in return for agrarian products from Manchuria.

The cultural provisions of the treaty of 1950 merely gave an official sanction to already existing activities. Shortly after their victory, the Chinese Communists had set up, in October 1949, the Sino-Soviet Friendship Association in order to promote among the Chinese people a receptive attitude towards Soviet influence. This government organization established branches all over China down to the ward and precinct level. The association distributed Soviet literature, films, newspapers, art and school textbooks; it arranged for Soviet professors and artists to visit China and for Chinese to visit the Soviet Union. All this activity was designed to lay the ideological foundation for support of the close cooperation between the Soviet and Chinese Communist governments.

The new agreements were heralded by Peking and Moscow as the beginning of a new relationship based on friendship and cooperation. In view of the Communist victory in China it was obviously difficult for the Soviet Union to cling to its imperialist privileges in Manchuria, especially as the West had pointed to them as the only remaining example of foreign imperialism in Chinese territory. The projected withdrawal from Port Arthur and the Manchurian railroads was clearly in recognition of the new situation. On the other hand, there were indications that the Soviet Union was still intent on maintaining special economic interests. Of these the most important examples were the joint Sino-Soviet companies in Sinkiang and Manchuria and the special trade agreement with Manchuria, both of which had been negotiated with special delegations from these regions. The Soviet press found it necessary to explain that these companies were based on a relationship of real equality. The credit extended to China did not compare favorably with Soviet credits granted to East European satellites. In the years following, however, the Chinese Communists pressed successfully for more economic support and the surrender of the remaining Soviet economic privileges. In fact the later agreements and negotiations seemed to indicate that the bargaining position of Peking in relation to Moscow had considerably improved.

In 1952 the Manchurian railroads were returned to Chinese management, but the Russians retained, at least temporarily, their naval base at Port Arthur "on the invitation" of Peking, presumably because the Korean conflict had not yet been concluded. The Chinese made new demands on the Soviet Union when they started their Five Year Plan in 1953 at a time when their trade with the West had been severely restricted. In September 1953, Moscow promised equipment and technical aid for the establishment or reconstruction of 141 large-scale industrial enterprises as a contribution to the Five Year Plan. Included in this program were plans for the expansion of the steel mills at Tayeh, near Hankow, and at Paotou in Suiyuan province. It was expected that Chinese steel production would be increased from one million to three million tons. The agreement of September 1953, like the agreements of 1950, was concluded in Moscow after equally prolonged negotiations. When a new Chinese-Soviet accord was concluded in October 1954, it was negotiated in Peking and the Russians indicated their respect for the increasing prestige of the Chinese Communist government by the strength of their delegation. Nikita S. Khrushchev, the first secretary of the Central Committee of the Russian Communist party, himself headed the delegation, which also included several cabinet ministers.

The treaty of October 1954, ended the special privileges which the Soviet Union had held in Manchuria and Sinkiang. The Soviet government promised to return the naval base of Port Arthur to Chinese control on May 31, 1955, and to sell to the Chinese government, on easy terms, its share of the four joint Sino-Soviet companies established in 1950, both of which promises were duly carried out. At the same time the Soviets greatly increased their economic aid. They agreed to add fifteen more enterprises to the 141 already under way and also promised another long-term loan of U. S. $230,000,000. The two governments signed a Technical Assistance Pact by which there was to be an exchange of scientific and technical personnel and information for a period of five years in the first instance. Perhaps the most important aspect of the 1954 treaty was the agreement between the two governments to construct two large new railroad lines connecting China and the U.S.S.R. through Central Asia. The Russians agreed to build a line from Ulan Bator, capital of Outer Mongolia, to the Chinese border where it would connect with a railroad to be built by the Chinese from Chining in Suiyuan province to the border, thus linking the Chinese railroad system directly with the Trans-Siberian Railroad which already had a spur line to Ulan Bator. The other railroad was to lead from Alma Ata, on the Turk-Sib Railroad, to the Sinkiang border from where the Chinese would build a line via Urumchi to Lanchow, in Kansu province, which was to be linked to Sian. The line through Outer Mongolia was completed in 1955, while the line through Sinkiang was scheduled for completion in 1961.

The two great railroad lines are of obvious economic and military importance. They are clearly related to the industrial planning of both countries, the Soviet Union's development of the Central Asiatic border regions and the Chinese plans for the development of the northwest. One great region of new industrial and communications growth in the Soviet Union was now to be made even more important by the addition of another industrial region, across the border in China. The economic and military significance of the opening of the inner Asian frontiers of China and Russia can hardly be exaggerated. This is the first time since the Mongol conquests in the thirteenth century that these areas have been connected. The important fact is that Russia and China are cooperating not only in the removal of a buffer zone but also in the development of an industrial and communications complex. This type of planning between the two big Communist powers may provide the physical basis for their close military, economic, and political cooperation, a cooperation carried on within a common ideological and organizational framework; that such long-range commitments have been made is in itself an indication that the Communist elites of Russia and China have accepted an intimate partnership.

CHAPTER XII

Nationalist and Communist China

---

1. THE NATIONALIST REVOLUTION

Warlordism

THE end of World War I found China in almost complete political disintegration. The attempts of Sun Yat-sen and his political party to gain control of the revolutionary government had ended in total failure. China was in the midst of the period of warlordism. The government was in the hands of military leaders, and these leaders, not being controlled by one outstanding man with superior armies at his disposal, became divided among themselves.

Leaders of regional military organizations and cliques fought among themselves for power and for control of the central government, which had become merely a pawn of these military forces. In 1917 the leaders of two of these cliques, both former followers of Yüan Shih-k'ai, shared the power and together formed a government. T'uan Ch'i-jui was prime minister and Feng Kuo-chang the president of this government in Peking. But this co-operation did not last. In 1918 the followers of T'uan, who were organized as the so-called Anfu Club, ousted their opponents from the capital and installed in the presidency a candidate of their choice, Hsü Shih-ch'ang.

While this conflict was going on in the north, military leaders maintained their power in the south. They fought among themselves for territorial gains and had little respect for the authority of the government in Peking. To counterbalance the prestige which the control of the capital and the government gave the northern leaders, some of the southern militarists in

Kwangtung and Kwangsi allowed Sun Yat-sen's party to establish a government at Canton. Although no real unity was possible under these conditions there was enough agreement among the military men to permit the fiction of a government in Peking which could carry out those essential functions of government about which there was no conflict. During this time of inner disunity, China was ably represented in her negotiations with foreign countries and in the international conferences at Versailles in 1919 and at Washington in 1921–22. The voices of her leading diplomats were much stronger in the international conferences of the time and in the world capitals than was warranted by the inner Chinese situation. These diplomatic representatives stood for Chinese national interests, and Sun Yat-sen, already on the sidelines of the inner Chinese power struggle, could not even play the role of an unofficial international spokesman for the Chinese nation.

The regime of the Anfu clique in Peking lasted until 1920, when two military leaders, who had in the meantime built up stronger regional power of their own, became dissatisfied with their share of the spoils. One of these was Chang Tso-lin who controlled Manchuria. Of bandit origin, Chang and his men had fought on the side of the Japanese in the Russo-Japanese War; and after the war his troops were merged into the Chinese army in Manchuria and were recognized by Yüan Shih-k'ai. The other leader was Ts'ao K'un whose military power was established in central China. These two combined forces in 1920 and drove T'uan Ch'i-jui's group from Peking. But the fight continued among the winners. New warlords and super warlords emerged from the regional armies. A former lieutenant of Ts'ao K'un, Wu P'ei-fu, who was by origin a scholar of the old school, became for a time the key figure in Peking. Wu was eventually forced to retreat when deserted in his battle with Chang Tso-lin by one of his own officers, Feng Yü-hsiang. Feng was a former soldier in the Anhwei army, who had moved up from the ranks to his commanding position through his shrewdness and ability. He was a disciplinarian but popular with his troops, as he made it a point to share their hardships and live the life of a "soldier's general." He had also become a Christian, had his armies sing Christian hymns, and was for a while the hope of some missionaries as the "Christian general" in China.

For a time the conflict in the north focused on these three men. Chang Tso-lin was in control of Manchuria, Wu P'ei-fu of central China, and Feng Yü-hsiang of the northwest. In addition, each of the three men enjoyed some foreign support. Chang Tso-lin was supported by the Japanese who were building up their position in Manchuria; Feng Yü-hsiang was given some Russian aid through Outer Mongolia; while Wu P'ei-fu had the financial and political backing of the British, the Americans, and the French. None of these men had broad popular support or a political program that could claim any revolutionary appeal. The battle among these key figures, as among the lesser military leaders, was for power and for territory from which to obtain the tax income to maintain their armies. Those who controlled what remained of the central government had the additional advantage of claims on customs income and other foreign support.

The revolution thus dissolved into a purely military struggle, each military leader became autonomous within his area, and the government disintegrated. The party of Sun Yat-sen, which had no important hold outside the treaty ports, had little part in this development. Sun was permitted to establish a government in Canton only because the local warlords found him and his party useful for prestige purposes of their own. Sun himself became involved in warlord politics.

Kuomintang-Communist Alliance

In this time of general chaos Chinese intellectuals were greatly impressed by the news of the Russian Revolution. In 1921 the Chinese Communist party was founded in Shanghai, but the successes of the Communists in Russia affected a much larger number of Chinese than those formally organized in this way. During this time of political disorder and intellectual ferment, any revolution that had succeeded, any force that was certain of its direction, would immediately attract the interest of those in China looking for an answer to their own seemingly insoluble problems. Russian propaganda skillfully exploited this interest by appealing to Chinese nationalism. Soviet spokesmen proclaimed Russia's readiness to give up the rights and privileges gained in China by tsarist Russia and to support China in her fight to regain her equality and sovereign rights from the imperialist Western powers. In August, 1922, the Comintern agent Joffe came to Peking, where he gave public lectures at Peking University on the new Soviet policies. In 1924 the Soviet government concluded a treaty with the Chinese government in Peking in which the Soviets relinquished the right of extraterritoriality and the Russian concessions but retained Russian railroad rights in Manchuria and practical control of Outer Mongolia.

Before this treaty with the Chinese government, Soviet agents had already established relations with Sun Yat-sen's party. In 1923 Joffe met Sun Yat-sen in Shanghai where they concluded an agreement for Soviet support of Sun's organization. Both men stated that the purpose of the cooperation was not the establishment of Communism in China, for which China was supposedly not ready, but Soviet assistance to the Chinese national revolution in the fight against Western imperialism. The leadership of this revolution was to be in the hands of the Kuomintang. Individual Communists could join the Kuomintang whose policies they were to support, but the Chinese Communist party was to remain a separate party. As a result of this fateful agreement, Soviet advisers came to Canton where they remodelled the Kuomintang and built up a revolutionary army.

Sun Yat-sen had never favored a Western type of political party. His first political organizations, the *Hsing-chung-hui* and the *T'ung-meng-hui*, had been secret societies, loyal to their leader who controlled their finances and directed their affairs without being accountable to anyone. The Kuomintang had been founded in 1912 as an open party against the will of Sun Yat-sen, and when the parliamentary experiment failed, Sun went back to his own type of party organization in which the leader, Sun himself, could demand unquestioning loyalty from his followers. An authoritarian party was therefore not objectionable to Sun Yat-sen; and when his appeals for Western support, during the Yüan Shih-k'ai regime and later, found no response, Sun saw no reason to decline the Soviet offer to reorganize and revive his party, as long as his own position as leader was guaranteed. The Joffe agreement seemed to be the perfect formula for such cooperation. The Soviet advisers who were sent to Canton were under the direction of Michael Borodin, who became a very influential figure in the Kuomintang from 1923 until the break between the Kuomintang and the Communists in 1927.

Under the direction of Borodin and the Soviet advisers, the Kuomintang was changed from a group of personal followers of Sun Yat-sen into a party organized on the model of the Russian Communist party. According to this pattern the highest authority was nominally the Party Congress, made up of representatives of local cells. The Congress elected a Central Executive Committee in which the real discussion of political affairs took place and through which all control of party affairs was handled. In fact the Central Executive Committee dominated the party. In the Kuomintang, as in Communist parties, policy and membership, as well as representation, were controlled from the top according to the system of "democratic centralism." All political conflict expressed itself in the struggle for power between members of the Central Executive Committee. In the first years of its existence Borodin attended almost every meeting of the Central Executive Committee and had great influence on its decisions. To placate Sun Yat-sen's feelings, Sun was made the party's president for his lifetime. The reorganization of the party was approved by the first Party Congress which met in January, 1924.

After the adoption of these organizational changes there was a purge of the party membership directed against those who opposed cooperation with the Communists and Soviet Russia. Communists did not become members of the Central Executive Committee, which was made up of old followers of Sun Yat-sen, but some of them held key positions in party agencies or were secretaries to leading Kuomintang officials.

The reorganization of the Kuomintang into a totalitarian type of party was accompanied by a broadening of the party's program. Under the influence and example of the Soviet advisers and Comintern agents, the party concerned itself with organizing workers in Canton and Shanghai and peasants in Kwangtung province. Agents were trained to spread the party's ideas and to prepare the ground for military conquest. This program of organizing workers and peasants was at the time not limited to the Communists; it was actively promoted by some of the leaders of the Kuomintang. The Kuomintang thus gained the organization and technique which transformed it from a small group of followers of Sun Yat-sen into a disciplined party which could lead a mass movement.

Chiang Kai-shek and the Whampoa Academy

Even more important than the reorganization of the party was the creation of a revolutionary army. For this purpose there was set up at Whampoa, near Canton, a new military academy for the training of an officer corps. At this academy classes of cadets were trained by a Chinese staff under a group of Russian military advisers. They received political indoctrination as well as technical military training. The president of this military academy was Chiang Kai-shek, who from the time of his appointment played a decisive role in the Kuomintang and in the political history of China.

Chiang Kai-shek was born on October 30, 1887, in the small town of Ch'i-k'ou in the district of Fenghua in Chekiang province. Chiang came from a family of modest means; his grandfather supplemented the farm income by selling tea and food to travelers at roadside stands. His father, a minor imperial official, died when Chiang Kai-shek was still a child. It was through his mother's work and the help of relatives that young Chiang was given an opportunity for an education. After his initial schooling Chiang went in 1906 to Yüan Shih-k'ai's military academy at Paotingfu to prepare for a military career. Being a good student, Chiang was sent to Japan in 1907 for additional military training. There he joined Sun Yat-sen's revolutionary organization, the *T'ung-meng-hui*. In 1911, after his return to China, he took part in the military activities of the revolutionaries in Shanghai. During the following years of political chaos he lived mostly in Shanghai where he established contacts with Shanghai business groups. Little has been recorded about his life during this time. He kept in touch with Sun Yat-sen, and when Sun attempted to establish his southern government in Canton, Chiang Kai-shek came there several times for political consultations. During these visits Sun had been impressed by Chiang's strong personality; and when the Whampoa Academy was set up, Chiang Kai-shek was Sun Yat-sen's choice for president.

When appointed president of Whampoa, Chiang brought with him for the higher teaching positions a number of his classmates and fellow students from the academy of Paotingfu, some of whom had also studied in Japan. The common school background provided the basis for the personal relationship between Chiang Kai-shek and his fellow officers in the years to come. In selecting students for the academy Chiang attempted to overcome the danger of regionalism by taking students from all parts of the country. So many high school students applied for admission to the Academy that it could afford to select only the best qualified. The Academy welded the cadets into a cohesive group with a strong esprit de corps, and throughout their careers the members of each graduating class kept a sense of group loyalty. Most of them were also personally loyal to their former president, Chiang Kai-shek.

A struggle for control of the Whampoa Military Academy was carried on from the very beginning between the Soviet advisers and Chiang Kai-shek. The Soviet advisers wanted to be more than consultants—they expected to dominate the Academy. It was only by using the threat of resignation that Chiang Kai-shek kept control in his own hands. But since the Russians were providing the weapons on which the army depended, they were able to exercise strong pressure. In fact, Chiang Kai-shek, on the advice of Sun Yat-sen, visited Moscow for three months in the fall of 1924. In these early years of the Academy Chiang apparently kept things together by adopting a politically neutral attitude and thus bridging the conflict between the non-Communist and Communist groups. There was no question, however, as to the division among the cadets. The non-Communists formed a Sun Yat-sen society while the Communists were organized into a Union of Youth. Among the cadets at this time were some of the leading Communist generals of later years, such as Chu Teh and Lin Piao, and leading political commissars such as Chou En-lai. Chiang Kai-shek tried to keep the two groups working together but attempted to keep Communists out of the higher staff positions in the Academy and later out of the officer ranks of the First Army.

The training of the cadets was under the general direction, but not control, of the Soviet military advisers, who were headed by General Galen, alias Blücher. Under Russian influence the technique of group conferences was introduced as a method of teaching. While the Soviet advisers had a great deal of influence on the curriculum and the techniques of teaching, the spirit of the Academy was inspired by Chinese tradition. Chiang Kai-shek himself particularly stressed the spirit of personal sacrifice and loyalty, for which one of the great Ming dynasty commanders was famous. It was expected that soldiers and officers would be mutually responsible to each other in battle. Death was the penalty for units which retreated in battle without their officers and for officers who left their units. It was this traditional spirit of loyalty, coupled with the idea of sacrifice for the cause of the national revolution that made the young cadets a formidable force. Shortly after its formation the cadet corps was used to establish the authority of the Kuomintang in the Canton area. The cadets, at great cost in life, won decisive victories over much larger warlord forces. The cadet corps became the nucleus of a new army which expanded by absorbing units of provincial troops whose commanders joined the Kuomintang. Most important of these were the military leaders of Kwangsi province, men like Li Tsung-jen, Li Chi-shen, and Pai Chung-hsi, who were to play an important part in the history of the Kuomintang. By 1925 this army numbered over 100,000 men.

The San Min Chu I

The reorganization of the Kuomintang after the model of the Communist party and the creation of an officer corps and an army made the Kuomintang into an entirely new political force. But the reorganization had to be matched by a program which would give the party its political direction. In 1924 Sun Yat-sen attempted to formulate the necessary program in a number of lectures which were collected and edited under the title of San Min Chu I, The Three People's Principles. Some of the main points of this program had already been stated by Sun in 1905 at the founding of the T'ung-meng-hui. These points were now expanded by Sun Yat-sen in a number of weekly lectures given to an audience of party members. These lectures clearly show the personal inadequacy of Sun Yat-sen for the decisive task of formulating the theoretical basis for the beliefs and the policies of the group he represented. From the beginning the weakness of the Kuomintang was in the field of ideology.

The Three People's Principles have been translated as "nationalism," "democracy," and "socialism" or "livelihood." They expressed a number of the ideas that Sun Yat-sen gathered through his varied readings of Western writings. He had read the works of some of the main political theorists of Western history and also the writings of fashionable reformers of the time, such as the German *Bodenreformer* Damaschke or the American Henry George with his program designed to abolish the evils of real estate speculation in the growing American cities. The ideas of these men and of such unknown writers as the American dentist, Dr. Maurice William, whose booklet fell by chance into Sun's hands, were mixed rather indiscriminately in Sun's program.

Nationalism

In his first group of lectures on nationalism, Sun stressed the need for a nationalist spirit in China and for a fight against foreign control. In this appeal for a national spirit and for a fight against the threat to China's national survival, Sun Yat-sen echoed the feelings of the Western-educated Chinese. Sun's principle of nationalism was the most easily understood and readily accepted part of his program. When he described the evils of Western economic control, he dealt with a genuine obstacle to Chinese national independence. According to Sun, China was worse off than a colony because China was a "hypo-colony," a country in which many foreign powers had practical control without any one of them accepting responsibility. To overcome this foreign domination and to regain her economic freedom, China must develop her national spirit. Some of the points which Sun Yat-sen made in his argument for national survival were obviously wrong. For instance, he compared the Chinese population, which he believed to have been static for the last two hundred years, with the population of other countries, which had increased many fold, especially the population of the United States. His fear was that China, because of her static population position, would eventually be swallowed up and subjugated by countries with a much larger population. Sun Yat-sen called for a policy of population increase to fight this imaginary danger.

Sun had derived his main organizational support from the secret societies, and it was therefore no wonder that he saw in them the true representative of the nationalist tradition. In his eyes the scholar-gentry were discredited by their support of the Manchu dynasty, which Sun had fought. According to Sun a feeling of nationalism was nothing new in China, but it had been undermined by the alien dynasty and was endangered by the preaching of cosmopolitanism. For Sun nationalism was a necessary stage in human development before internationalism could be achieved. This point he illustrated with a story—the story of the coolie water carrier. It is perhaps significant that all the illustrations in Sun's lectures came from Westernized city life in China and not from traditional rural society, and the stories frequently have little meaning. The water carrier of Sun's story had bought a lottery ticket with the few dollars of his savings. As he had no place to keep it, he memorized the number and put the ticket in the bamboo pole on which he carried his two water buckets. When the drawing was held, the coolie's number won the first prize of $100,000. Delirious with joy, the coolie took the water pole, the symbol of his slavery and threw it into the water—together with the ticket which was thus lost. This was the story used by Sun Yat-sen to point out the need for nationalism in China. The bamboo pole represented "nationalism—a means of existence"; the lottery prize represented the Chinese chance of participation in a world of cosmopolitanism, a chance thrown away together with the bamboo pole.

These lectures were given five years after World War I, and Sun Yat-sen speaks about this war as a struggle of imperialist powers. Wilson's fourteen points, and especially the point of self-determination, had given the war the character of a fight for a "noble theme," a theme that was betrayed, however, when the war was over. Imperialism survived, "but," says Sun Yat-sen, "from the war there was unconsciously born in the heart of mankind a great hope —the Russian Revolution." And he goes on to compare the Russian Revolution with Wilson's principles of "the right of self-determination and freedom." "When the Russian people awoke and saw that imperialism was wrong, they started a revolution within their own country, first overthrowing their own imperialism . . ." Lenin, described as a "prophet and seer of mankind" had encountered the opposition of the powers because of his fight against imperialism. In these sentences Sun expressed the broad anti-Western and pro-Russian leanings of China at this time. His lectures on nationalism demanded devotion to traditional Chinese virtues; but they also dealt with the need for the improvement of the table manners and the social behavior of Chinese in Western company. Although Sun may have aroused the nationalist feelings of his audience, his varied ideas can hardly be described as a political philosophy.

Democracy

Of greater consequence from the point of view of future political development were Sun's lectures dealing with the second of his three principles, "people's authority," or as it has been rendered, "democracy." In his lectures Sun discussed this topic in the light of his own rather naive interpretation of human history. He discerned various periods in human development, first, an age of wilderness in which man struggled with the beasts; second, a period of struggle between man and nature and the rise of civilizations; third, a period of struggle between man and man, and the rise of autocracies; and finally the modern period which brought the struggle for a democratic government. This primitive lecture on history contained arguments and comparisons concerning historical events in the West and in China which clearly showed Sun's limited understanding of the matter with which he was dealing. In his discussions of the problems of the French Revolution he contrasted the European desire for liberty with the Chinese desire for wealth. According to Sun nothing in China corresponded to the tyranny of European governments. The example of the treatment of Chinese immigrants by Dutch immigration officials in Indonesia served to indicate "what the old European autocracy was like." The principle of liberty, the product of the fight against such tyranny, had no place in China where, in Sun's opinion, liberty had always been taken for granted, like "breathing the fresh air." This example gave Sun the occasion to elaborate at length on the fact that breathing is necessary but can be had free; and he concludes that the Chinese "have had an excessive degree of liberty," but have given it "no concern, just as when there is plenty of fresh air in the room, we do not realize its value. . . ." So more liberty, in the European sense, was not needed in China. According to Sun,

the aims of our revolution are just opposite to the aims of the revolutions of Europe. Europeans rebelled and fought for liberty because they had had too little liberty. But we, because we have had too much liberty without any unity and resisting power, because we have become a sheet of loose sand and so have been invaded by foreign imperialism and oppressed by the economic control and trade wars of the Powers, without being able to resist, must break down individual liberty and become pressed together into an unyielding body like the firm rock which is formed by the addition of cement to sand.[1]

And again, "on no account must we give more liberty to the individual; let us secure liberty instead for the nation."

Equality, too, takes on another meaning in Sun Yat-sen's mind from that expressed by the philosophers of the French Revolution. The inequality of hereditary social and political position of the Europe of feudal times was unknown in China, and therefore the fight for equality did not have for China the meaning it had for Europe, or for America in her struggle against slavery. The only problem for China was the introduction of a political democracy through the principle of the people's sovereignty.

Sun's interpretation of "democracy" and of "people's sovereignty" differed fundamentally from what is understood by these terms in the West. According to Sun, equality was abused in the West. True equality meant giving the wise men and the sages the chance to move up to leadership. They helped the people to organize for the defense of their freedom, and the people must not forget that. As an example of the misuse of equality, Sun cited the labor unions.

[1] Sun Yat-sen, *San Min Chu I*, tr. Frank W. Price (Shanghai, 1932), p. 210.

In the old days workers were ignorant and had no group consciousness; they did not realize that their position was unequal or that they were being harshly oppressed by the capitalists. . . . Workers in all countries had no conception of their own positions until from without came to them men of good will, who were dissatisfied with labor conditions and who proclaimed among the workers the inequality of capital and labor, the need for organization, and the duty of resistance against nobles and capitalists. . . . Because the workers had these friendly intellectuals from outside as leaders to guide them and to show them how to organize strongly and how to strike, they were able to display great power as soon as they rose up in society. With their great, newly acquired power the workers began to be self-conscious and to talk of equality. The British and French workers then noticed that the leaders and teachers within their organization were all men of different occupations from themselves, either nobles or scholars all from outside, so they expelled them. . . . So the unions, although they themselves did not possess the necessary intelligence for leadership, gave up their wise guides.[2]

This refusal to accept the leadership of the wise resulted, in Sun's opinion, in the unions' disintegration and loss of strength. The trend spread to China where "Chinese workers are also abusing the idea of equality," and were fighting against long-gowned leaders and their politics. So democracy in Sun's mind became a matter of government and of government leadership.

Sun divided the people into three groups, the "discoverers," the "promoters," and the "practical men." Sun's democracy is a state, in which the "discoverers" play the directing and the "promoters" the managing role over the vast number of "operators," but they do it in the spirit of "service" rather than of selfish "exploitation." From this standpoint, Sun arrived at a critical if simple, interpretation of Western democracy and its shortcomings, and advocated for China a system of government by specialists who know best what is good for the people. He claimed that the "rise of democracy has developed an attitude of opposition to government among people," and that the result was a weak government, whereas a strong one was needed. Therefore he proposed a method of government which he described as his own "new discovery and political theory and a fundamental solution of the whole problem . . . namely, that a distinction should be made between sovereignty and ability." Sun's three groups, the "discoverers of mankind" who as "men of vision and foresight are the creators," and the second group, the "promoters" who "cannot create and discover but can only follow and imitate," and the third group, the "operators" who "do not understand even though one tries to teach them" but "simply act," ought each to play its respective role. Government was to be in the hands of those with the ability to govern, or as he put it, "we" meaning his party, "must create democracy and then give it to the people, not wait to give it until the people fight for it." Sun used examples of good rulers of China in the past to describe the functioning of a government by men of ability working for the people. As the king in the past could dismiss a government, so in Sun's concept of people's sovereignty, "if the government is bad, we 400 millions can exercise the privileges of kingship, dismiss it and take back the sovereignty into our own hands." Sun compared his government system with a business company

[2] *Ibid.*, pp. 239–40.

in which "the people of the republic are shareholders, the president is general manager, and the people should look upon the government as an expert." Sun accused the Westerners of using experts only for such matters as training soldiers or running factories but not in the administration of government. "They have not succeeded in doing so because they are not able to change the old, deep-rooted habits of the people." For another comparison, taken like most of Sun's illustrations from Westernized, treaty-port life, Sun used the example of an automobile owned by a wealthy but untrained person— the people—who engages an experienced expert—the chauffeur—to drive and maintain his car. This specialist, however, will have to be given a "complete authority" in the driving and the choice of roads and be held responsible only for bad results, as was the imperial government in the Chinese past.

From this distinction between ability and sovereignty was derived the theory of the people's right of sovereignty and the government's right to govern, a theory which was accepted and continued as the basis of government under the Kuomintang. In its origin this theory contained a strange combination of the idea of the responsibility of the educated scholars of the imperial time and the idea of the vanguard role of the party elite in the Communist system.

For this system, which he called democratic, Sun devised what he believed to be a new machinery of government. The people's control over it was to be expressed by the four powers of suffrage, recall, initiative, and referendum. But these people's powers were to be separate from the powers of the government. Sun Yat-sen had read Montesquieu's theory of the division of powers. This division was, in Sun's opinion, to be applied to the government's power to rule and was not connected with the separate people's right of sovereignty. Sun wanted to improve on Montesquieu and divided government authority into five powers—the executive, legislative, judicial, civil service examination, and censoring powers. The last two of these "powers" he claimed to have taken from the Chinese imperial tradition in which the scholar-gentry were controlled through the examination system and the officials through the censors. It was only natural that Sun Yat-sen wanted to retain such institutions since he believed in rule by an elite and a division between the government's right to govern and the people's right to sovereignty. According to Sun the four powers of the people and the five powers of the government formed a nine-power system: "With these nine powers in operation and preserving a balance, the problem of democracy will truly be solved and the government will have a definite course to follow."

It was the aim of Sun Yat-sen's revolution that this system should be "given" to the people by the party. Even in 1911, when Sun's party was still the *T'ung-meng-hui*, Sun had issued a manifesto in which he conceived of a revolution by stages. The party was to seize control and to establish a military government which, Sun believed, would last for three years. There would follow a six-year period of political tutelage by the party government under whose direction self-government would be established from the district level upward. This theory of a revolutionary change by stages with its period of

tutelage under one-party rule was reaffirmed in 1924 during the reorganization period. Sun did not describe this process in his lectures on the Three
People's Principles, but in his *Outline of National Reconstruction*, published in
that year. In it Sun Yat-sen spoke of the three stages of development, but
they were no longer marked by a definite number of years. In the first or
military stage the party was to seize power through military conquest. In
the second stage the party was to carry through its self-assumed responsibility for educating the people for democracy. This was the period of "tutelage," of one-party rule. The purpose of one-party rule was to prepare the
way for the third stage, the political system which Sun had invented and
which he called democracy.

Livelihood

The third principle, the principle of "livelihood," took Sun
into a field in which he was totally inexperienced. He attempted to provide
an economic program for his movement at a time when the Kuomintang had
been reorganized under Soviet advisers and when Communists were among
its members. He tried to give the term *min-sheng* or "livelihood" a meaning
which would satisfy all of his followers, which would differentiate it from
the program of the Communist party and yet not be hostile to it. Stating
that his "livelihood" was a form of socialism, Sun struggled with a clarification of terms. He explained in his lecture the difference between sociology
and socialism, dealt with Utopian socialism, and then moved on to a discussion of Karl Marx. Sun had great respect for Marx who, according to
him, reached his scientific conclusions by spending the best energies of his
life studying for twenty or thirty years all the writings on socialism. This he
could do in England, "the most cultured nation of the modern world" which
"had a great library of several million volumes covering fully every possible
subject. In this library Marx studied daily. . . . he brought together all
the writings on socialism by ancient as well as by contemporary authors,
compared them in detail and then tried to deduce a conclusion. This was
the scientific method of studying social problems, and so Marx's proposal
for social reconstruction was called scientific socialism." In this way Marx
worked out his theory of history which, as Sun recognized, "gravitated about
material forces."

Sun Yat-sen disagreed with this materialistic theory and sought another
definition for his interpretation of human development. In his search for an
authority to quote, Sun used a booklet, "Social Interpretation of History,"
by an American dentist, Dr. Maurice William, in which, according to Sun,
the author expressed the view "that the social problem, not material forces,
is the center which determines the course of history, and that subsistence is
the heart of the social problem." Sun continued, "the problem of livelihood is
the problem of subsistence," and felt that "the new theory of this American
scholar tallies exactly with the third principle of our party. William's theory
means that livelihood is the central force in social progress, and that social

progress is the central force in history; hence the struggle for a living and not material forces determines history." Having thus satisfied himself that he proclaimed a new theory differing from Marx, Sun tried to show how historical development had shown Marx to be wrong. After attempting a theoretical explanation of his point, Sun developed what he called methods of procedure for his economic program.

The key point in this program was "equalization of landownership," an idea taken from Henry George, the American political reformer, who dealt with the real estate problems in the American cities. According to Sun, China in the past had had many small landowners rather than a few large ones and "most places in China had been quiet and content under this system and no trouble has arisen between the people and the landowners." Only under the Western impact had China experienced a land problem. This land problem was created by the tremendous rise in land values in the commercial cities, such as Shanghai and Canton. Sun Yat-sen told in his lecture the story of the Australian drunkard, who in his intoxicated condition, bid for and bought a piece of land, which was located in what became, decades later, a metropolitan center. Without any efforts of his own, the man became a multi-millionaire, the wealthiest man in Australia. This, in Sun's opinion, should not be; and he compared this Australian example with the rise of real estate values in Shanghai and Canton, values which should be shared by all the people. The "unearned increments" which Sun did not want to have confused with "the profits which industrial and commercial manufacturers get, by dint of hard mental and physical labor . . ." should belong to all.

To solve this land problem and to equalize landownership, Sun Yat-sen suggested that the government buy back the land. To establish a fair price, the landowner was to declare the value of his land, leaving the government a choice of either buying the land or taxing it according to this declared value. If the value was too high, the government would tax it accordingly, if too low, it could buy cheaply, thus forcing the landowner to name a fair price. After this arrangement of land values all future unearned increments should revert to the community.

This proposal of "equalization of landownership" was a "form of the *min-sheng* principle," which, said Sun Yat-sen, "is Communism . . . —a share in property by all." In order not to frighten the property owners among his audience and followers, he continued

The communism which we propose is a communism of the future, not of the present. This communism of the future is a very just proposal, and those who have had property in the past will not suffer at all by it. . . . When the landowners clearly understand the principle involved in our plan for equalization of landownership, they will not be apprehensive.[3]

This abolition of future "unearned increments" of city real estate Sun Yat-sen believed to be the solution of the land problem in China, and the answer

[3] *Ibid.*, pp. 434–35.

to half the problem of livelihood. It is hard to understand how a man who came from one of the farming communities of China could have had so little knowledge and understanding of China's agrarian problems. The answer to the other half of the problem of livelihood lay in industrialization. In Sun's view China needed to develop state capital and to promote industries.

If we do not use state power to build up these enterprises but leave them in the hands of private Chinese or of foreign businessmen, the result will be simply the expansion of private capital and the emergence of a great wealthy class with the consequent inequalities in society. So in working out our principle of livelihood we cannot use or apply in China the methods of Marx, although we have the deepest respect for his teaching.[4]

It is difficult to follow Sun's logic in this argument. He was apparently under the impression that the Soviet Union had given up Marxism in favor of the New Economic Policy and that Marxism, for which even the Soviets were not ready, was even more inapplicable to China. Yet he stressed the need for state control and development of industry, mining, and communications. For these purposes China did not have sufficient capital and must rely upon foreign capital. "If we use existing foreign capital to build up a future Communist society in China, 'half the work will bring double the results.'" If the state controls and owns the industries, then the benefits will accrue to all the people and conflicts with capitalists will be avoided.

In the lecture given a week later Sun came back to what he called the food problem of China. After distinguishing between the four most important kinds of food, namely air, water, meat, and plant food, such as grain and vegetables, Sun dealt with the improvement of agricultural production. By now Sun had been made aware of the agrarian issue by a meeting of farmers and the launching of a farmers' movement, which had not been of Sun's making. Now Sun began to discuss landlordism and the share the farmer retained of the harvest he produced. In contrast to his earlier pronouncement that landlordism was no problem of China in the past, Sun discovered the plight of the peasant. "A large majority of the people in China are peasants," he said, "at least nine out of every ten, yet the food which they raise with such wearisome labor is mostly taken away by the landowners. What they themselves can keep is barely sufficient to keep them alive. This is a most unjust situation." Sun therefore asked for laws to protect the peasant and to give him a larger share of the fruit of the land. This was somehow to be accomplished through the "equalization of landownership," the result of which would be that "each tiller of the soil will possess his own field."

Then Sun Yat-sen repeated the problem:

Although China does not have great landowners, yet nine out of ten farmers do not own their fields. Most of the farming land is in the possession of landlords who do not do the cultivating themselves. It seems only right that the farmer should till his farm for himself and claim its products, yet farmers today are tilling for others and over half of the agricultural products from the farms are taken by the landlords.[5]

[4] *Ibid.*, pp. 438–39.
[5] *Ibid.*, pp. 456–57.

And again Sun declared that "we must immediately use government and law to remedy this grave situation." Sixty per cent of the crops went to the landlord and only 40 per cent to the farmer. As a result farms were abandoned and fields became unproductive. Thus Sun at last admitted the existence of an agrarian problem and offered to solve it with his strangely unrelated program of land equalization. But he turned immediately to a discussion of technical methods of increasing production, such as the "use of machinery, use of fertilizers, rotation of crops, eradication of pests, manufacturing, transportation, and prevention of natural disasters." He then elaborated on the usefulness of these various technical measures. In the following lecture Sun dealt with the "problem of clothing," and used the opportunity to speak for the protection of the Chinese cotton industry against foreign competition. At this point Sun's lectures were interrupted and owing to his death were never resumed.

Sun's lectures were full of commonplace statements, of inaccuracies, and of naïveties. Sun liked to show his knowledge of affairs of the world, but in trying to do this, his limitations became apparent. In a political speech to an uncritical audience his ideas must have been effective, but as a political philosophy, they were woefully inadequate. But they were accepted as a political program and were later taught in schools and in colleges, quoted and revered as the philosophy of the Nationalist revolution. There was nothing else to express the beliefs for which the Nationalist leaders stood; and the Nationalist party continued to suffer from this ideological weakness.

Sun died on March 12, 1925, in Peking, where he had gone to participate in negotiations for a political settlement between the various warlords. Before his death he had dictated a political testament in which he appealed to his comrades to follow his program of revolution and bring it to completion. After his death, his lectures on the Three People's Principles, his political testament, and his plans for reconstruction became the theoretical platform of the Kuomintang, and Sun himself became the worshipped hero of the revolution. The reverence paid to the figure of Sun Yat-sen and to his words has been described as "Sun Yat-senism," a set of beliefs and principles which were intended to give direction to the Chinese Revolution and the actions of its leaders.

Sun's Death and the Struggle for Power

With the death of Sun Yat-sen, the latent problem of leadership in the reorganized Kuomintang became acute. Among Sun's close followers, none was strong enough to assert himself immediately as Sun's successor. In this Communist-type party the leadership issue had to be fought out at the top level among the members of the Central Executive Committee and the commanders of the military forces. For a while the leadership struggle was focused in the Central Executive Committee. Key members of this group were Wang Ching-wei, a traditional scholar from Kwangtung province who had gained his early political laurels through his attempt to assassinate the

Manchu regent, and who had been close to Sun and had written Sun's last testament; Hu Han-min, another member of the scholar-gentry from Canton, who had been entrusted by Sun with the Kwangtung governorship and other high offices; and Liao Chung-k'ai, an American-born Chinese who had studied in Japan and was the organizer of the peasant and labor movements of the Kuomintang. The most important military figure was Chiang Kai-shek, the president of the Whampoa Academy. Borodin, the chief Soviet adviser, who was on close personal terms with all the leading Chinese figures and a regular participant in the meetings of the Central Executive Committee, was an influential promoter of the interests of the Soviet Union.

Cooperation with the Soviet Union had aroused some opposition even before Sun's death and there was a struggle within the Kuomintang over the direction of policy. The so-called left wing of the Kuomintang had a most remarkable leader in the person of Liao Chung-k'ai. Liao, who lived in the United States until the age of seventeen, had joined the *T'ung-meng-hui* in Japan where he had gone to study political science. On the strength of his familiarity with the American scene he became a close adviser of Sun Yat-sen in matters of American political institutions and translated a book by Delos Wilcox, *Government by All the People; the Initiative, the Referendum and Recall as Instruments of Democracy*, which provided Sun with the necessary information for his adoption of these principles in his political program. Liao had also studied economics and became the financial expert of the party. In 1924 he was appointed financial commissioner and governor of Kwangtung province and so became a political rival of Hu Han-min. Liao was an ardent supporter of the Russian alliance but was no Communist. He favored a radical policy which, if it had been carried through, would have placed the Kuomintang in strong competition with the Communist party in securing support from peasants and workers, the main fields of Communist activity. Liao was the organizer of the peasant movement sponsored by the Kuomintang which was started in August, 1924. He was active also in the establishment of labor unions and of an aggressive labor policy in Canton. Liao rejected Communism for China and advocated industrialization under a capitalist system, but he argued at the same time for what he called the immediate liberation of the peasants and workers from economic oppression. Because of this program and of his personal power in the financial administration in Kwangtung province, Liao created a number of powerful enemies, both within the party leadership and without. This opposition led to Liao's assassination on August 20, 1925. The assassination is believed to have been directed by the brother of Hu Han-min, himself an important financial figure in Canton, and supported by some of the local warlords. To what degree Hu Han-min himself was involved in the assassination remains unknown. Liao's death was doubtless caused by rivals jealous of his financial and political control, but the murder was also motivated by the general opposition against the policy of peasant and labor organizations which Liao represented. After Liao's death no leader of the party concerned himself with this vital field of reform, later to be exploited by the Chinese Communists for their own political advantage.

Liao's death did not change the Kuomintang policy of cooperation with the Soviet Union. In January, 1926, a second Party Congress was held which voted for the continuation of the Russian connection. The right-wing leaders of the Kuomintang met at the Western Hills Conference near Peking to express their opposition to the left-wing policy and the continuation of this alliance. They called a rival Party Congress at Shanghai, thus leaving the left-wing leaders in control at Canton. In the meantime the decision was taken at Canton to launch a military expedition to the north, in order to defeat the warlord armies and bring about the military conquest of China by the Kuomintang. Such a campaign would secure for the Nationalist armies the arsenals of central China and free them from exclusive dependence on Russian arms. The decision to start the campaign was opposed by the Russian advisers who felt that the reorganization had not gone far enough and that a premature campaign might endanger Soviet control of the revolution. Under the influence of the Russian advisers the northern campaign was temporarily delayed. During the following weeks, however, a struggle for power ensued which was brought into the open when the authority of the left wing was challenged by Chiang Kai-shek's coup d'état in the spring of 1926. Suspecting that the Communists intended to get control of a gunboat and seize political as well as military power, Chiang Kai-shek, in the temporary absence of Borodin, placed the Russian political advisers under arrest and took over military control. After Borodin's return unity was restored through a compromise agreement. Russian advisers continued their work, but some of them were replaced; and it was agreed that no Communists were to head executive agencies. As a result of the coup Borodin altered his policy and decided in favor of starting the northern campaign immediately. He hoped that this action would forestall the danger of a real split.

The Northern Campaign and the Break with Moscow

The northern campaign started in the summer of 1926. Under the supreme command of Chiang Kai-shek the Kuomintang armies marched north in two columns toward the Yangtze. At first this march was eminently successful. The ground had been prepared by the propaganda agents of the party who had worked among the peasants in the line of march and among the troops of the warlord armies of Wu P'ei-fu. As a result of this propaganda the Kuomintang troops were supported by the people of the villages and towns through which they marched, and were enthusiastically received as an army of liberation. Some costly battles were fought, especially by the Kwangsi armies, but many of Wu P'ei-fu's troops defected and the warlord resistance collapsed.

When the Kuomintang forces marched toward the north, the left column of the army moved down the Siang River valley, through Hunan province toward the city of Wuhan, which was taken. The right column went through the Kan River valley and Kiangsi province to occupy the city of Nanchang. Chiang Kai-shek, in command of the whole expedition, moved with the right wing to Nanchang, while the members of the Central Executive Committee with Borodin went with the left wing to Wuhan. The political division between Chiang Kai-shek, as the leading military man and right-wing member of the party, and the left-wing leaders, who were under Russian influence, was emphasized by this geographic separation. Each side attempted to force the other to come to its headquarters. Chiang Kai-shek tried to call a meeting of the Central Executive Committee at Nanchang, where he could assert his influence. Instead the Committee remained at Wuhan, and when Chiang Kai-shek refused to appear at its meetings there, the Committee deprived Chiang of his chairmanship of the standing committee of the Central Executive Committee and of his position as Commander-in-chief. With this decision the fight for control between the left-wing leaders and Chiang was in the open. The campaign was halted and an inner conflict for control ensued. The left-wing leaders of the Central Executive Committee held the Wuhan cities, a key industrial and commercial center. Chiang held a small arsenal at Nanchang, but in order to strengthen his position he began to negotiate with the Chinese business leaders of Shanghai.

The success of the march north had given the Kuomintang a new importance in the eyes of the Western powers. The anti-imperialist and anti-foreign attitude of the party had greatly alarmed the Western powers, and excesses committed by Kuomintang troops against foreigners had resulted in a policy of withdrawing foreign subjects from the provinces involved in the Kuomintang campaign and of strengthening the foreign forces defending the international settlement at Shanghai. A similar concern over the Kuomintang policy and its radical trend was felt among the Chinese business groups at Shanghai and the lower Yangtze area. When the split occurred between the left and the right, these groups were ready to support a nationalist organization which would break with the Russian Communist advisers. It was therefore possible for Chiang Kai-shek to secure the support of the foreign communities and of the Chinese businessmen and bankers in Shanghai, including those right-wing Kuomintang leaders who had left the party because of its left orientation. The party leaders in Hankow tried to prevent this rapprochement by provoking anti-foreign incidents during the capture of Nanking by troops nominally under Chiang Kai-shek's command. These incidents were settled through negotiations, and Chiang went directly to Shanghai where he succeeded in gaining the support of the business community and non-Communist labor leaders. After securing control of Shanghai through negotiation, he broke the Communist stronghold in the industrial parts of the Chinese city by arresting and executing a large group of Communist leaders and supporters. This victory at Shanghai, which has been violently denounced by Communists ever since, decided the power struggle within the Kuomintang in favor of Chiang Kai-shek, but only after a period of confusion.

Chiang Kai-shek established a government at Nanking under his own direction. In Hankow the non-Communist left was alienated from the Soviet advisers and Chinese Communists. Communist attempts at violent land reform measures and at nationalization of Hankow industries, taken over by the workers, had backfired. When a Comintern agent, the Indian M. N. Roy, committed the indiscretion of showing the Kuomintang leaders a telegram from Stalin demanding acceptance of Russian policy, these leaders turned against the Soviet advisers. The Communists were expelled from Hankow and the Russian advisers were sent home. The Hankow leaders then began to negotiate with Chiang Kai-shek at Nanking. After the break with the Communists and the Russians, personal rivalry among the political and military leaders of the Kuomintang continued. Among the latter were the Kwangsi generals, such as Li Chi-shen, Li Tsung-jen, and the Moslem general Pai Chung-hsi, who had established a strong and efficient administration in their home province. Control of Kwangsi gave them an independent political and financial base, and their Kwangsi troops maintained their identity within the Kuomintang army. These military men joined forces with the leaders of the Central Executive Committee, such as Wang Ching-wei, who had broken with the Communists. At the same time Chiang Kai-shek had military reverses in the fight against warlord armies to the north. Therefore he resigned from his government position at Nanking and withdrew temporarily to Shanghai. Thereupon the Central Executive Committee members moved from Wuhan to Nanking in September, 1927, and attempted to set up the government there with the support of the Kwangsi generals. By that time Chiang Kai-shek found a military ally in Feng Yü-hsiang, the warlord of the northwest who had joined the Kuomintang. This military combination was too powerful for the Kwangsi generals, who withdrew from Nanking to their province. As a result the political leaders at Nanking opened negotiations with Chiang Kai-shek who was brought back to Nanking. By the end of 1927 Chiang Kai-shek was finally in control of the new National Government which had chosen Nanking as its capital.

2. THE NATIONAL GOVERNMENT IN POWER

Military Unification

When the National Government was established at Nanking under Chiang Kai-shek, there still remained the task of continuing the march north and crushing the power of Chang Tso-lin, the warlord who controlled the government at Peking. This campaign was begun in the spring of 1928. The Nationalist army, reinforced by the troops of several warlords who had come into the camp of the Kuomintang, moved northward in two columns along the railroad routes. One column drove from Hankow to Peking and the other from Nanking to Tientsin. The second column, under the direct command of Chiang Kai-shek, was held up at Tsinan as the result of an incident manufactured by Japanese troops still stationed there as a result of the expansion of Japanese influence in Shantung province after World War I. This incident was settled through diplomatic negotiations, but it prevented the troops of Chiang Kai-shek from moving on Peking. Peking was taken by the armies of Yen Hsi-shan, the warlord governor of Shansi province who had joined the Kuomintang. Chang Tso-lin retreated with his troops to his home territory of Manchuria. On this retreat he was assassinated by the Japanese, who mined a bridge near Mukden over which his train was passing.

Chang Tso-lin's assassination was planned by the Japanese military as the first move in an attempt to take Manchuria. Alarmed by the Nationalists' success, the Japanese military in Manchuria believed that the time had come to secure Japanese domination by a formal separation of Manchuria from all Chinese control. The Japanese government was not willing to follow up this lead by the military and the "Manchurian incident" was postponed for another three years.

Chang Tso-lin was succeeded in Manchuria by his son, Chang Hsüeh-liang. The younger Chang asserted his authority by assassinating those of his father's generals whose ambitions he did not trust. The Japanese attempted to prevent the Nationalists from gaining control of Manchuria by prohibiting the entrance of Nationalist troops into the territory and advising Chang Hsüeh-liang not to accept Nationalist authority. Chang Hsüeh-liang, however, formally recognized the Nationalist government and placed himself under its direction. Nominally, at least, China was thus united in 1928 under the Kuomintang government led by Chiang Kai-shek, with its capital at Nanking. The former capital Peking, meaning "northern capital," was renamed Peiping, "northern peace."

Organization of the National Government

Military unification was followed by formal establishment of the National Government of China. Now that military conquest was completed, the second of Sun Yat-sen's three revolutionary stages could begin. This was the period of political tutelage in which the Kuomintang monopolized all authority and was supposed to prepare for the third and last stage—democracy, as the term was defined by Sun Yat-sen. The Organic Law of the National Government, promulgated in October, 1928, provided the institutional framework of government. The Political Council of the Central Executive Committee of the party was to "guide and superintend the execution by the National Government of important national affairs." The policy decisions of the Political Council were to be translated into action by the government agencies named by the Organic Law. These were the Five Yüan or branches of government, namely the Executive Yüan, the

Legislative Yüan, the Judicial Yüan, the Examination Yüan, and the Control Yüan.

The government was headed by a president who was also chairman of a State Council. The president had the official position of head of the state in foreign relations and of commander-in-chief of the military forces, but the limitations of his actual power remained undefined. All governing powers were in the hands of what the Organic Law called the "National Government," and this National Government was to be composed of the Five Yüan. However, national affairs were to be conducted by the National Government through the State Council. The chairmen and vice-chairmen of the Five Yüan belonged to the State Council. All laws and mandates issued by virtue of a decision of the State Council were to be signed by the president of the National Government and countersigned by the chairmen of the Five Yüan. This system made it possible for Chiang Kai-shek to exercise almost dictatorial powers. As president of the National Government from 1928 to 1931 he not only dominated the civil government but also controlled the national army independently of any check by the civil government. The national army was the key to the personal power of Chiang Kai-shek and the basis of the authority which the National Government exerted over military leaders who had joined the Kuomintang but retained their own armies.

Although in theory the chairmen of the Five Yüan were supposed to be equal in authority, in practice their power differed greatly. As all of them derived their authority from the Kuomintang, a true check and balance system could not come into existence. They merely carried out the policy formulated by the party leaders. The Executive Yüan, which had the largest responsibility, became by far the most important agency. The Legislative Yüan was a technical agency of legal experts, entrusted with the preparation of modern Western codes of law and later with the drafting of a constitution. The Judicial Yüan was to carry out these modern laws through the development of a system of modern courts, but only a beginning had been made in the rule of law. The functions of the other two Yüan were still more limited in importance. Under the Executive Yüan, however, a growing number of ministries were established which carried out the main business of government. In fact a multiplicity of agencies emerged, which gave the impression of a great division of government activities, while in reality many of the top positions were filled by a comparatively small group of men who held different titles and performed various functions in party and government agencies. A committee of the Kuomintang kept the records of the party members and determined decisions on personnel within the party and the government. This ministry, therefore, was a key agency of control.

A special law of October, 1928, determined the structure of the provincial governments. A provincial administration was established under the Executive Yüan consisting of provincial councils, the chairmen of which filled the role of governors of the provinces. The chairmen and the members of the councils were appointed by the Executive Yüan. In theory, at least, a centralized system of control over the provinces was erected. But in practice, the National Government enjoyed full authority over the appointment of provincial officials only in the lower Yangtze provinces. In the remaining provinces the central government could only confirm the existing authorities who had accepted Nationalist rule but continued to enjoy autonomous control of the local military forces and financial resources of their area. The regional political councils which were established at Mukden, Peiping, Taiyuan, Hankow, and Canton were another concession of local autonomy. The Organic Law and the law on provincial governments thus formalized the political power situation under which the National Government had complete control only over the lower Yangtze area, basing its power on Shanghai and Nanking and administering directly the provinces of Kiangsu, Anhwei, Chekiang, and Kiangsi. The influence of Nanking over the remaining provinces varied according to their closeness to the central regime and to the military power of the provincial administrations.

The Provisional Constitution

The Organic Law of 1928 was replaced in May, 1931, by a provisional constitution. This provisional constitution was drawn up by a National People's Convention, the members of which were appointed by the Kuomintang. The political structure of the old Organic Law was continued under this constitution. A major change occurred only with regard to the position of the president of the National Government. The supreme command of the military forces was transferred from the president to the National Government as a whole, and the president retained merely the formal functions of representing the government internally and internationally. This legal shift reflected the change of position of Chiang Kai-shek who in 1931 gave up the presidency. That office was given to an elderly, dignified member of the Kuomintang, Lin Sen, who held it until his death in August, 1943, when Chiang Kai-shek again took over, giving the presidency a renewed importance.

Chiang Kai-shek maintained his power through his chairmanship of the newly established National Military Council and his position as Chief of the General Staff. He kept to himself the same military leadership which had formerly been connected with the office of president at the time when he held it, and his military power remained unchecked by government or party control. Chiang set up in Nanking a Central Military Academy which continued the tradition of the Whampoa Military Academy; he was president of the Academy and had a house on its campus. He was also president of the newly established Central Political Institute where the future government officials were trained. Chiang Kai-shek was also chairman of the Central Executive Committee of the Kuomintang and of the Political Council and for a time even held the chairmanship of the Executive Yüan. The secret of Chiang's power, however, lay not so much in his many positions as in his personal control over the appointment of military officers in the national army and in the loyalty which he received from the graduates of the Whampoa and the Central Military Academies.

The provisional constitution was also intended to give the Chinese National Government a more dignified legal basis. It contained a chapter on general principles, giving the territory, the citizenship, the flag, and the seat of the capital of the Chinese republic. Another chapter dealt with the rights and duties of the people. This chapter provided all the legal guarantees of the rights of citizens, and a "bill of rights." The freedoms enumerated in this chapter were protected against arbitrary action but not against abridgement by ordinary law. A chapter on "people's livelihood" promised the development of many parts of the economy by the state. The chapter on education promised all children of school age a free education and state support for various fields of educational activity. Another part of the provisional constitution attempted to define the powers of the central and the local governments. All these general stipulations of the constitution remained, however, on paper; the constitution was important only because it replaced the Organic Law and registered a change in the position of the president.

Political Groupings and Alignments

Almost constant warfare was necessary to maintain the government's authority against inner opposition and outside attack. The National Government dominated only the lower Yangtze area, and its nominal control over the warlord regimes in northern, western, and southern China could be challenged at any time. The main potential opponents of the National Government were the Kwangsi generals in the south and Feng Yü-hsiang in the northwest; Yen Hsi-shan, the governor of Shansi province, was also practically independent of central control and Chang Hsüeh-liang's allegiance was personal and voluntary.

In addition to this array of warlord forces Chiang Kai-shek faced opposition and a struggle for power within the party itself. In order to strengthen his position Chiang Kai-shek tried to consolidate his control over the party machine. As a young man in Shanghai, Chiang had been a protégé of Ch'en Ch'i-mei, the revolutionary military leader of that city, who like Chiang himself was from the province of Chekiang. Ch'en gave Chiang the command of a brigade of his troops and later introduced him to Sun Yat-sen. Ch'en was assassinated in 1916 by agents of Yüan Shih-k'ai. Before his death he asked Chiang Kai-shek to take care of his two nephews, Ch'en Kuo-fu and Ch'en Li-fu. These two brothers were given important positions by Chiang Kai-shek and remained loyal to him. Under the Nanking government they controlled at various times the important Organization Committee of the Kuomintang and its Social Affairs Board, which kept the records of all party members and decided all appointments; the Central Political Institute, which trained new officials; the Ministry of Education, which determined the educational policy of the government; and other important offices. The two brothers exercised considerable power within the party by their control of the files and secret supervision of the members. Ch'en Kuo-fu and Ch'en Li-fu belonged to the right wing of the Kuomintang; they and their followers became known as the "C. C. Clique" and were important supporters of Chiang Kai-shek in the party. The Ch'en brothers were also in charge of the so-called "Blue Shirts," a secret group within the party organized to maintain party discipline and fight any radical opposition.

Another mainstay of Chiang's power was his relationship to the Chinese banking houses and business firms of Shanghai. This relationship was helped by his marriage to Soong Mei-ling in 1927. Madame Chiang, as she became known in the West, was a member of what came to be the most influential family in Chinese financial affairs. She was the youngest of three sisters, the oldest of whom was married to Kung Hsiang-hsi, known as H. H. Kung, who became one of the most important Shanghai bankers and was for a time governor of the Central Bank of China. The second sister was the wife of Sun Yat-sen. A brother, Soong Tze-ven, known as T. V. Soong, was the first minister of finance of the Nanking regime and, like H. H. Kung, became one of the wealthiest financiers of China. At the establishment of the government in Nanking, Soong was mainly responsible for securing the support of the Shanghai financial circles for Chiang Kai-shek's regime and later carried through some of the chief financial reforms.

The opposition to Chiang Kai-shek within the party included so-called "leftist" as well as "rightist" leaders. Those who were described as "leftists" called themselves the "reorganizationists" as an indication of their claim that they carried on the tradition of the party reorganization in Canton in the years after 1923. According to them, the main party leadership had abandoned this tradition, which included a program of land reform and the organization of the farmers and the workers, as undertaken by Liao Chung-k'ai before his assassination. The left wing also advocated party control over the military arm, which meant that they wanted to subordinate Chiang Kai-shek and his friends to the control of a group of party leaders among whom they hoped to prevail. The leading figure in this group was Wang Ching-wei, who had no military support and therefore had to depend on gaining political control through the party itself. Wang Ching-wei, a scholar educated in Chinese as well as Western learning, had been close to Sun Yat-sen whom he assisted in writing some of his plans for reorganization and his political testament. Wang Ching-wei's main strength was his ability as an orator, which he used in party meetings and in addressing groups of intellectuals who were among the main supporters of the party. His stand with the reorganizationist group was not so much a matter of principle as it was a method of gaining the kind of political support which would strengthen him in his struggle for a leading role in the party. His political opportunism was demonstrated later during the war when he went over to the Japanese side to serve as the head of the Japanese-established puppet regime.

Another opponent of Chiang Kai-shek was Hu Han-min, a Cantonese scholar who had also been one of the closest associates and supporters of Sun Yat-sen. Hu Han-min's political inclinations were at the outset as vague as Wang Ching-wei's; at first he belonged to the leftist group of the Kuomintang and supported cooperation with Soviet Russia, but later he assumed the leadership of the right-wing opposition to Chiang Kai-shek and allied himself with the Kwangsi generals. He too supported the principle of civilian control of the party as a means of strengthening his personal position in relation to Chiang Kai-shek. During the first years in Nanking, Hu Han-min was the chairman of the Legislative Yüan. The struggle for power between Chiang Kai-shek and these so-called "left" and "right-wing" leaders within the party continued during the years of the Nanking government with alternating periods of conflict and reconciliation. Through all this time Chiang Kai-shek remained the victorious and dominant figure.

A more dangerous element of opposition to the Nanking government than the surviving warlord regimes and the political rivals within the party was the Communist movement. After the break at Hankow in 1927, it established itself as a guerrilla force in the mountains of south central China, where it remained a territorial as well as a political foe of the National Government.

The most serious opposition to the National Government at this time came from the outside. Japan's expansionist plans on the Asiatic continent could be carried out only at the expense of China and of Chinese national aspirations as represented by the National Government. Japanese interference with Nationalist military campaigns, political organization, and economic plans, and the Japanese attacks in Manchuria and at Shanghai, and finally the attack in North China that led to World War II blocked the program of the National Government and eventually undermined its position to such a degree that the way was prepared for the victory of Chinese Communism. Through all these years Japanese aggression was closely connected with the inner conflict between the Nationalist regime and its various Chinese opponents.

Chiang's Struggle for Supremacy

After the National Government had been established at Nanking, a military conference was called in January, 1929, to discuss the disbandment of the various military forces. As no agreement was reached, there remained a latent possibility of clashes between Nationalist troops and the various warlord armies. Two months later the manipulation of the elections for a third Party Congress of the Kuomintang led to a political break between Chiang Kai-shek and the leaders of the Kuomintang "left." In the same month the first open conflict broke out between the Nanking government and the Kwangsi generals, who had occupied Wuchang with their troops. They were defeated by Chiang Kai-shek with the support of Feng Yü-hsiang who again, as in 1927, was the decisive factor in shifting the balance in favor of Chiang Kai-shek in his struggle with the Kwangsi generals and the Kuomintang "left." But after the defeat of the Kwangsi generals there followed a struggle for power between Chiang Kai-shek and Feng

Yü-hsiang. This conflict became a long-drawn-out struggle in which the other leaders of the north became involved. Yen Hsi-shan, the governor of Shansi, sided with Feng Yü-hsiang, while Chang Hsüeh-liang, the warlord of Manchuria, who at first remained neutral, later gave his active support to Chiang Kai-shek.

While this major power contest was shaping up in the north in 1930, the "leftist" opposition in the Kuomintang tried to establish its own new regime in the south. It attempted to set up a government at Canton with the help of an insurgent Kwangtung general, Chang Fa-kuei, who tried to capture that city. This attempt failed, however, and the left-wing Kuomintang leaders negotiated with Feng Yü-hsiang and Yen Hsi-shan and joined them in setting up a government at Peiping. Peiping was recaptured by the troops of Chang Hsüeh-liang, who joined the fight on the side of Chiang Kai-shek. After taking Peiping, Chang Hsüeh-liang remained in control of that city and thus held in North China and Manchuria the same position that his father had held before him, with the difference, however, that Chang Hsüeh-liang accepted the authority of the National Government at Nanking. The main battle between the Nationalist troops of Chiang Kai-shek and the armies of Feng Yü-hsiang remained undecided, but after the loss of Peiping Feng Yü-hsiang withdrew to the northwest and Chiang Kai-shek was left in control.

The left-wing Kuomintang leaders, after the loss of Peiping, set up a new government at Canton with the help of the Kwangsi generals. They called for a new northern campaign, this time against Chiang Kai-shek, but their plan was blocked and they remained in Canton. The secessionist move in the south coincided with the calling of the National People's Convention by Chiang Kai-shek for the writing of the new provisional constitution. The members of this convention were selected and appointed by Chiang Kai-shek's group within the party. This action aroused the vocal defiance of the left wing of the Kuomintang at Canton; but it also caused the determined opposition of the right-wing leader, Hu Han-min, who was chairman of the Legislative Yüan at Nanking. Hu also feared the concentration of power in the hands of Chiang and declared that Sun Yat-sen had never spoken of a provisional constitution as a step in the political development of the government. Chiang thereupon ordered the arrest of Hu Han-min, who was for weeks imprisoned in his own home. In the meantime the provisional constitution was passed. When Chiang Kai-shek released him, Hu Han-min left Nanking for Hong Kong, never to return. Chiang Kai-shek had thus eliminated his competitors in Nanking, but the opposition group at Canton, backed by the Kwangsi generals and other provincial forces, remained.

The Manchurian Incident and Chinese Politics

                     The Japanese attack on Manchuria in 1931 interrupted the inner struggle for power and added a new factor to the confused situation. The Japanese military action in Manchuria, which started on September 18,

1931, was opposed only by the provincial troops of Chang Hsüeh-liang. After a surprise attack on the Mukden garrison, the Japanese drove most of Chang's troops south into China proper. These troops were later garrisoned at Sian in northwest China where they were destined to play another role in the inner Chinese political struggle. The Chinese military resistance against the Japanese attack was overcome without great difficulty, but the resentment of the students and business groups led to a boycott of Japanese goods which proved to be more effective. In the first three months of the conflict, Japanese exports to China shrank to about a third of their previous value. In the face of this serious threat to her economic interests in China, Japan shifted her military activities from Manchuria to Shanghai which was the center of the boycott movement. In January, 1932, the Japanese sent warships to Shanghai, but their attempt to break Chinese resistance by a show of force led to a major land battle in which the Japanese found stronger opposition than they had anticipated.

The Japanese attack in Manchuria forced a temporary unity on the contending factions in China. In November 1931, the southern leaders came to Nanking to negotiate an end to the inner conflict. Chiang Kai-shek, forced to discontinue his struggle for supremacy, resigned the presidency in December. The main brunt of the battle at Shanghai was carried by the Nineteenth Route army, a provincial army under a Cantonese general, and the valiant fight of this army greatly raised its prestige. The political negotiations between the opposing groups finally led to the establishment of a government in Nanking in which the main political antagonists joined forces. A committee of three, composed of Chiang Kai-shek, Wang Ching-wei, and Hu Han-min, was to control the government. Hu Han-min never came to Nanking, and the cooperation lasted for only a short period before Chiang Kai-shek resumed sole authority.

When Chiang Kai-shek resigned, he had left his real power well anchored with the military commanders of the Nationalist armies who were loyal to him. The civilian heads of his government—among them T. V. Soong—resigned with Chiang. When the southern leaders came to share the authority with Chiang Kai-shek, they attempted to take over the chairmanship of the Executive Yüan and the Ministry of Finance and other key positions. From February until August, 1932, Wang Ching-wei was chairman of the Executive Yüan. But the southern group could not secure the support of the Shanghai bankers. Lacking military force and financial resources, the southern leaders had to give up their attempt to establish themselves in power. When Wang Ching-wei resigned in August and left Nanking, T. V. Soong again took over the chairmanship of the Executive Yüan and the management of the financial affairs of the National Government. From that time on Chiang Kai-shek and his group remained in firm control of the National Government, even when, at the outbreak of World War II, they admitted the members of the political and military opposition to a share in power.

The loss of Manchuria was a serious blow to China. The incident at

Shanghai was settled with a local armistice arranged with international as-sistance in May, 1932. By its stipulations the Chinese government agreed not to garrison or fortify the Chinese city of Shanghai. More serious still were the stipulations of the Tangku armistice agreement signed on May 25, 1933, which ended the conflict over Manchuria itself. The attempt of the Chinese government to gain international help by appealing to the League of Nations had led nowhere, and after the Japanese extended their conquest to the pro-vince of Jehol, the Chinese government was forced to come to terms. The Tangku truce did not contain any Chinese recognition of the Japanese con-quests beyond the fact that the fighting had ceased, but it sealed the loss of Manchuria and Jehol, and prepared the way for the next Japanese move into North China. The Tangku truce established a neutralized military zone between the Great Wall and Peiping from which the Japanese at any time could move unopposed into North China.

The Military Program

Chiang Kai-shek and the National Government, in spite of the loss of territory, emerged from the Manchurian incident stronger than before. The warlord opposition had been weakened or eliminated and the political competitors within the party had largely lost their influence. For a few years the government at Nanking had another chance to carry through its program of economic, social, educational, and military reforms which had been stalled by civil wars, political struggles, and outside aggression. As a military man, Chiang Kai-shek was most interested in creating a modern army. The beginnings had been laid at the Whampoa Academy, where the officer corps had been trained under Russian advisers. After the split with the Communists, a new group of advisers was needed and Chiang Kai-shek turned to Germany, where the limitations of the Versailles Treaty had excluded many professional soldiers from positions in the reduced German army. A number of these took service with the Chinese government to train the national army along German lines. The emphasis was now on a profes-sional, not a revolutionary, army. After the Manchurian incident a formal German military mission was established, organized by General von Seeckt, the officer who had created the postwar modern German army. Von Seeckt first came to China on a fact-finding mission in 1933 to draw up the plans for the reorganization of the Chinese army and returned to China in 1934 as head of the mission. He devoted most of his time to equipping the Chinese army with German material and to initiating the construction of a Chinese armament industry. Von Seeckt stressed the importance of rapid industri-alization for China. He stayed for only a year but left behind him a strong German advisory group which remained in China until after the outbreak of World War II.

The diversified training for army officers which was introduced by the German advisers was designed to build up an effective professional officer corps. The plan was to make the army a national institution. It was expected that ability, not simply personal loyalty, would be the basis of promotion. Great progress was made in the training of such an officer corps, but Chiang Kai-shek continued to favor old colleagues above others and to rely on their personal loyalty. In order to carry out the recommendations of the German advisers for rapid industrialization a National Resources Planning Commission was set up. The military thus took an active part in the sponsoring of industrialization, a task for which it was not too well qualified.

The creation of a modern army was the key to Chiang Kai-shek's whole reform program. Military considerations were predominant in the construction of highways, railroad lines, harbors, and airfields, and in all financial and economic planning. The military build-up could be justified by the urgent need to strengthen China against the aggressive moves of Japan. In violation of the truce that ended the fighting in Shanghai in 1932, the Chinese government secretly fortified the Chinese city of Shanghai and prepared fortifications between Shanghai and Nanking for the defense of this vital area against future Japanese aggression. The Japanese attack on China, in 1937, however, came before Chinese military plans had had time to mature. The program of the German advisers called for two more years of time in order to complete the training and equipping of the new divisions in the army and to start the organization of a navy and an air force. When the Japanese attack came it tested more than military strength, it tested the political and economic foundations of the National Government.

The Fight for Equality

The program of the National Government was also strongly affected by the support which it received from the Western-educated intellectuals, the businessmen, the city population of the treaty ports, and the overseas Chinese communities. These were the men and women who staffed the technical and administrative branches of the government. Like the military they were strongly nationalistic. In domestic affairs their aims differed from those of the military, but in foreign affairs, at this time, they differed more in approach than in objectives. They accepted the need for military preparations and pressed the fight for abolition of the "unequal treaties" and for the recovery of full sovereignty and economic independence.

The National Government had a large measure of success in the reassertion of China's position in international relations. Before it came to power the Kuomintang had drawn heavily on the anti-imperialist feelings of its supporters. In 1925 and 1926 there were several demonstrations against foreign privileges which led to serious incidents in Shanghai, Hong Kong, and Canton. One of these, the May 30th incident, took place in 1925 when newly organized workers in Shanghai started a strike in the Japanese cotton mills and the municipal police under an English officer fired on a procession of demonstrators and killed a number of people. This incident had repercussions in strikes and boycotts not only in the cities but also among the peasantry of central and south China. In Canton the unwillingness of the

British director of the Chinese Maritime Customs to hand over the customs revenue to the Nationalist regime caused a serious anti-British outbreak; and a British gunboat shelled the Chinese village of Wanhsien from which shots had been fired on a British ship. All these and a number of other incidents arose from a mounting wave of nationalism which was directed in the main against England and led to the first widespread and successful boycotts of British goods.

These expressions of nationalism gave vent to the deep feelings of bitterness over the humiliation that Chinese had suffered for many years at the hands of the foreigners in the treaty ports. The superior attitude of the foreigner was expressed in many ways, from the social distinctions in the treaty ports, where Chinese were not allowed in parks or restaurants, to the condescension of some of the missionary educators. The legal privileges, treaty port rights, extraterritoriality, tariff limitations, foreign troops and gunboats, were the outer manifestations of an attitude of superiority on the part of many foreigners which was deeply resented by the Chinese.

The effort to get rid of foreign rights and interests began with the Washington Conference at which the Chinese representatives fought for the abolition of extraterritoriality, tariff limitation, and other treaty-port rights. Though the Western powers indicated a willingness to negotiate these issues, they felt that in each case conditions were not yet ripe for a change—the surrender of extraterritoriality must wait until a modern legal system emerged in China; the restoration of full Chinese tariff control should wait on the elimination of the inland tax on trade, the *likin*. All that the Chinese gained at the Washington Conference was a promise to send a committee to study Chinese conditions with a view to preparing the return of the sovereign rights to the Chinese government. The committee report was on the whole unfavorable, and action was delayed.

The national outburst in 1925 and 1926 and the seriousness of the boycotts changed foreign attitudes. At the end of 1926 the British suggested to the other powers that as a first step towards a more conciliatory policy the immediate collection of a $2\frac{1}{2}$ per cent customs surtax should be permitted (a move on which the Washington Conference had agreed in principle), and that full Chinese tariff control should be recognized as soon as a tariff law had been drawn up by the Chinese government. When Nationalist troops took over the British concessions at Hankow and Kiukiang in 1927, the British began negotiations for their surrender and Chinese authority was restored. The way was therefore prepared for an entirely new approach to the question of Chinese sovereignty once the Kuomintang had broken with the Communists and set up a responsible government. In 1928 treaties were concluded between the Nanking government and all the Western powers, including the United States, in which China regained her full tariff autonomy. These treaties were to take effect in January, 1929. After a short delay caused by the Japanese, the treaties took effect early in 1929.

This was a major victory in the economic field. Tariff autonomy enabled the National Government to introduce protective tariffs for industry and agriculture and to increase its own revenue. The increase in revenue more than matched the payments on foreign debts formerly guaranteed by the Maritime Customs and now taken over by the National Government. Other Chinese gains followed. After giving up their concessions in Hankow and Kiukiang, the British also returned to Chinese control their concessions at Chenchang and Amoy. In October, 1930, the British gave up the leased territory of Weihaiwei. This British naval base, originally secured to counterbalance the Russian lease at Port Arthur, had lost its importance to England. Its return to China again emphasized the fact, already demonstrated at Tsingtao, that the leases remained Chinese territory and that China could claim their return as a part of the restoration of her sovereign rights.

The other leased territories and national concessions remained in foreign hands with the exception of the Belgian concession at Tientsin, which was returned to China in 1931, and the German, Austrian, and Russian concessions, given up after World War I and the Russian Revolution. The international settlement at Shanghai retained its unique position; but in 1928 a number of Chinese representatives were admitted to the municipal council, and in 1930 this number was increased. Little further progress was made towards the restoration of full Chinese jurisdiction in the treaty ports until World War II. Many of the important concessions and the international settlement at Shanghai remained autonomous islands within the area of Chinese jurisdiction.

Even slower were the gains in the fight for the abolition of extraterritoriality. Some major gains on this front had already been made during the warlord period. After World War I Germany had lost the rights of extraterritoriality for her citizens in China. Though China had not signed the Versailles Treaty, a Sino-German treaty of 1920 had formally surrendered the German concessions in the treaty ports and the German rights of extraterritoriality. In the treaty of 1924 Soviet Russia had given up the Russian concessions and extraterritoriality. The extraterritorial rights of the other major Western powers remained undisturbed. Chinese pressure at the Washington Conference had led to an acceptance in principle of the abolition of extraterritoriality, but such a change was to be dependent on the emergence of an effective modern legal system. The political pressure which the National Government exerted in 1929 did not change the policy of the leading Western powers—the United States, England, and France; and when in December 1929, the Chinese government announced that beginning with January 1930, extraterritoriality would be abolished by Chinese mandate, the Western powers accepted this date only for the beginning of negotiations. These negotiations led to no agreements and were interrupted in 1931 by the Manchurian incident. With the growing threat of Japanese aggression the Chinese National Government did not resume its pressure on the Western powers, but the process of creating the legal conditions required for the abolition of extraterritoriality continued.

Introduction of Western Law

Economic and social reconstruction also depended on the introduction of a Western legal system that would provide the framework for property ownership and contract relations necessary for the new economy. The old property relations, restricted by official control and privileges as well as by family authority, had to be changed to a regulated system with legal guarantees. The development of business and industry required protection of contracts and property based on enforceable laws. A system of civil law was therefore as essential for the growth of commerce and industry in China as for the removal of extraterritoriality.

Work on the preparation of a civil code had already been started at the end of the Manchu dynasty and continued, with interruptions, under the government of Yüan Shih-k'ai and the warlord governments at Peking. After the establishment of the National Government this work was taken over by the Legislative Yüan, under the presidency of Hu Han-min. The model for the Chinese civil code was the Swiss code, which itself was closely related to the German code, which in turn derived its main principles from the Code Napoleon. In the choice of the continental German code as their model, the Chinese legislators were influenced by the example of Japan which had also accepted the German code.

The Chinese civil code included in its five books many of the principles of contract relations and property ownership that were necessary for modern commerce. The fourth and fifth books on Family Law and Inheritance aimed at establishing a compromise between Western concepts and Chinese tradition. The five books of this major legal work were passed by the Legislative Yüan and promulgated between the years 1929 and 1931. They became the foundation of the new Chinese legal system. During the same years a great deal of commercial legislation was passed relating to banking, stock exchanges, chambers of commerce, copyright, and, most important of all, commercial companies. Laws of mining, forestry, and fisheries, were also promulgated. Labor legislation, initiated during the same period, reflected a mixture of traditional Chinese concepts of social organization and modern ideas brought in from the West and Soviet Russia. The labor laws dealt with the organization of labor unions, collective bargaining, and arbitration, and included a factory law. But much of this labor legislation had little bearing on actual conditions, expressing rather an ideal to be aimed at. A penal code on which previous governments had already done considerable work was promulgated in March, 1928, but went through considerable revision until its final acceptance in January, 1935. At the same time, codes of procedure were set up and a system of modern courts established, from district courts up to the supreme court at Nanking whose decisions became the accepted interpretation of the laws.

Much of this legislation was accepted slowly, both by the general public and by the courts themselves. The law of inheritance, for instance, which provided equal shares for both sons and daughters, was rarely fully applied, and the legal equality of women, recognized by the law, was not fully accepted even in the cities. As far as procedure was concerned, judges were reluctant to apply injunctions unknown to Chinese tradition. But in the realm in which they functioned, the new Chinese laws and courts were on the whole effective and a legal tradition developed which could be compared with that in the West.

The problem remained, however, of applying this legal system on all levels. There were wide areas in which the courts had no jurisdiction; the courts had no power to check the military, who often took the law into their own hands, or the government which was beyond the restraints of the legal system and used legal procedure only as far as it saw fit. In political life the provisions of the constitution for a bill of rights within the framework of the laws remained largely on paper. But in commercial and in general economic affairs the law codes provided a framework in which modern economic transactions could take place.

Of equal importance to modern commercial and industrial development were the financial measures undertaken by the National Government. The person mainly responsible for the establishment of a modern financial system was T. V. Soong. In the Canton days Soong had set up a budget system by which the revenues from the area under Nationalist control had gone to the Nationalist regime rather than to the local army commanders as had been the case under the warlord regimes. In the negotiations with the foreign powers following the anti-British boycott of 1925, Soong succeeded in forcing the Maritime Customs administration at Canton to hand over its receipts to the Nationalist regime. In Nanking, Soong became the finance minister of the National Government and at the same time the vice-president and, after Wang Ching-wei's resignation in August, 1932, the acting president of the Executive Yüan.

T. V. Soong was the key figure in the economic reorganization that took place in Nanking. His main efforts were directed towards the introduction of a national budget, and of modern budgetary procedures. He did not succeed in convincing Chiang Kai-shek that military expenditures should be limited to a fixed budgeted amount, and under these conditions it was impossible to have a completely balanced budget. The vast expenditures on the military reform program and the services on foreign debts, for which the government was now responsible, made it necessary to finance approximately one quarter of government expenditures through borrowing. The revenues available to the government were limited to the Maritime Customs, the salt tax, and the consolidated taxes. After the National Government recovered tariff autonomy in 1929, it was able to secure much larger income from that source. The Maritime Customs, administered by an effective staff, still headed by foreign experts, provided the largest source of income for the new government, bringing in well over 50 per cent of its total revenue. The salt tax was next in importance, providing about one-third of the total. The consolidated taxes on wines, mining, tobacco, and other products provided most of the rest. The government did not receive any income from the largest potential source of revenue, the land tax, which remained in the hands of the provincial authorities where it had been since the last years of the Manchu dynasty. Partly in order to compensate for this the government introduced a tax on income, but by the time of the outbreak of war, in 1937, it had brought in little revenue.

The deficit in the government's finances was made up by borrowing from the four government banks: the Central Bank of China, the Bank of China, the Bank of Communications, and the Farmer's Bank of China. These banks, which controlled all important monetary activities were the only banks capable of large-scale credit operations. The fact that they used most of their resources to finance government expenditures slowed down capital formation for private economic development. The government gave these banks a monopoly of note issue and used them to introduce a modern national currency system. In the spring of 1933 the traditional tael system, which was based on a silver unit counted by weight and varied in different localities, was abolished, and a new coinage was introduced by law. The new silver dollar was minted at Shanghai.

The transition to the new coined silver currency was at first highly successful but was soon endangered by the silver policy of the United States under the Silver Purchase Act of 1933. The American silver policy was to set an artificially high price for government buying of silver in order to profit the silver-producing states in America. The artifically high rate for American silver purchases greatly affected the economies of the few countries whose currencies were based on silver. Of these, China was the most important. In the early 1930's, when all the major countries had gone off the gold standard and devaluated their currencies in order to enable their export industries to compete in a shrinking world market, China's silver currency was kept artificially high through the American silver price regulation. The American senators who had proposed the silver policy had argued that it would enrich China, thus increasing the sale of American products. But as China produces little silver, the higher silver price and the rapid outflow of silver from China resulted in a serious economic deflation, which soon required urgent measures. China went off silver, abolished its silver currency and set up a government-controlled paper currency. After an unsatisfactory attempt to impose an export duty on silver, the government ordered in November, 1935, a complete change of the currency system. Silver was nationalized and had to be turned in to the government, and the notes issued by three of the four government banks were made full legal tender. These measures were possible because the United States purchased from the National Government substantial amounts of silver at the artificially increased price, thus giving the financial support necessary to back the Chinese new currency. As a result of the silver crisis the Chinese government established a sound currency system which greatly helped to stimulate a favorable development of industry and commerce during the last years before the outbreak of World War II.

Communications

China's modern economic development and central political control over the country depended on a rapid extension of the communication system. In 1928 a Ministry of Railways was established to administer the existing railroads and to plan and carry out new construction. This railroad administration was headed for fourteen years by a former Shanghai banker, Chang Kia-ngau, and he was largely responsible for the rehabilitation and extension of the Chinese railroad system. By restoring the financial credit of the existing railroad system he was able to raise the money with which to complete the main cross-country lines. Before the establishment of the National Government most of the railroad development had been concentrated in North China and Manchuria. Now railroads were built to expand the system in central and south China. By 1937 the opening of the Canton-Hankow and Canton-Kowloon railroads had completed the main north-south connection from Peking to Canton and Hong Kong. Several east-west lines had also been built and extended. The Lunghai Railroad from Haichow on the coast to Sian had been extended further westward to Paoki. The Chekiang-Kiangsi railway had been completed, and a large section of the Hunan-Kwangsi railroad had been built connecting the southwest with the main north-south railroad system.

Of equal importance was the road-building program of the National Government. The National Roads Planning Commission, set up in 1929 was changed in 1932 into a Bureau of Roads under the newly-established National Economic Council. This office carried out a speedy extension of motor roads, providing by the summer of 1937 a total of over 100,000 kilometers of highways. The work began in the southeastern provinces where road-building was of great political importance in connection with the anti-Communist campaign. From here construction was extended to the southwest and to the northwest until highway networks existed in practically all provinces. At the same time a system of airlines was organized for domestic and overseas travel. The China National Aviation Corporation was first founded in 1929 as a Sino-American enterprise and was reorganized in 1930. In 1931 the Eurasia Aviation Corporation was set up as a Sino-German enterprise and operated in western China.

The National Government took over and improved the modern postal system which had been set up under the Manchu dynasty. During the confused years of the warlord times, the postal service had become known for its efficiency and reliability, even though civil wars and banditry interfered frequently with regular service. Under the National Government the postal administration gained a high reputation and, together with the telephone and telegraph services helped to facilitate modern development.

Chinese shipping, which also grew rapidly, was limited almost entirely to coastal and inland waters. Though the main Chinese shipping companies remained under private ownership, they had official connections and in some cases the capital invested belonged to high officials. The China Merchants'

Steam Navigation Company, which was originally founded by Li Hung-chang, remained the leading Chinese shipping company. Its ships plied the coastal trade routes and the lower Yangtze ports up to the gorges of Ichang. Another private shipping company was established in 1924, the Ming Sheng Industrial Company, which limited its activities mainly to the upper Yangtze and the rivers of Szechwan province. These and other smaller inland shipping companies competed with the traditional river boats which still carried the bulk of the inland freight on waterways and were an important part of the modern Chinese communications system.

Education and Ideology

A modern Chinese educational system had already been started at the end of imperial rule and had been stimulated in part by missionary institutions. After the establishment of the republic, modern education spread rapidly and the number of schools and colleges increased. When the National Government came to power there were in existence over fifty national and private universities and colleges, among which were such leading national institutions as Peking University. The National Government reorganized the institutions of higher education, classifying them into universities, independent colleges, and technical colleges. An institution had to consist of at least three colleges to be counted as a full-fledged university. A number of new institutions were founded and the quality of university teaching steadily improved until the leading national universities had higher standards than the missionary institutions which had led the way earlier. The Academia Sinica, set up in 1928, became an internationally known body of scholars in all fields of research.

Modern Chinese education had a more rapid growth in the field of higher learning than it had in the broadening of primary education. The tradition of leadership by an intellectual elite may have been responsible for this somewhat unbalanced development. But an effort was made under the National Government to increase the number of secondary and primary schools and to introduce normal schools for the training of much-needed teachers. Vocational schools were also established by provincial governments. Primary and secondary schools each provided a six-year period of education. In 1935 the National Government introduced a five-year plan which, it was hoped, would broaden compulsory education and substantially diminish illiteracy. However, in the few years remaining until the outbreak of World War II, progress remained limited. Although the official school attendance for 1936 was given as over 21,000,000 pupils, the percentage was still low in comparison to the total population, and the quality and results of primary education remained uneven. Nonetheless, a great effort was being made in the field of education. The aims of education, which stemmed from the Chinese literary revolution of 1919, were the promotion of a unified literary language, a national spirit, and the principles of Western science.

The program of the National Government was always stated in terms of the Three People's Principles of Sun Yat-sen. The personality of Sun Yat-sen remained above any criticism and he continued to be the revered hero of the revolution. His Three People's Principles were taught in schools, and his last will was read at official meetings in government and educational institutions. But these manifestations of patriotism did not compensate for the ideological weakness of Sun's doctrines. Chiang Kai-shek was aware of this problem. In 1934 when the first military campaigns against the Communist opposition had failed and when left-wing Kuomintang leaders attempted to set up a rival government in Fukien, based on the Nineteenth Route army that had so successfully fought the Japanese at Shanghai, Chiang Kai-shek tried to start an ideological movement of his own.

The so-called "New Life Movement" was initiated by Chiang in a speech at Nanchang in September 1934. Chiang stressed the need for a return to the Confucian virtues in order to restore to the Chinese people a self-respect and a feeling of self-importance which would awaken them out of their apathy. Chiang listed the four Confucian virtues of propriety, righteousness, integrity, and a sense of shame, which were to provide a new discipline of body and mind. In its practical application the New Life Movement was mainly concerned with the reform of daily living habits such as the unbuttoning of coats and spitting on the floor. It was hoped that the preaching of the above-named virtues through posters and pamphlets and the enforcement by the police of rules of daily behavior would provide a strengthening of the moral character of the Chinese as well as an acceptance of the authority and responsibility of the government. In this new preaching of morals Chiang Kai-shek found support among some of the missionaries, but his attempt to reintroduce some of the disciplinary aspects of Confucianism was largely ignored and eventually given up.

Literature and Society

During these years the imagination of China's intellectual youth was captured by the new literature which followed the Literary Renaissance. At a time when Chiang Kai-shek was sponsoring a movement which was based on an orthodox interpretation of Confucianism the intellectual climate was dominated by the "scientific philosophy of life" which completely rejected the traditional thought and social customs of China. The essays, novels, poems, and dramas that poured out in these years from a new generation of writers dealt with the problems of the individual and the family in the conflict between the old and the new in China and were full of social criticism.

The best known of the new Chinese writers was Lu Hsün (Chou Shu-jen), whose stories and essays satirized existing institutions and society. Lu Hsün's most famous book, *The True Story of Ah Q*, was a satire on the general outlook of the Chinese people and an attempt at a soul-searching self-criticism of the Chinese. It described the miserable life of a village pauper who has no ambition but accepts his fate with resignation and the consolation that he has the honor of being the most persecuted. Ah Q portrayed the mental climate of China at the time, echoing the West without understanding it. Ah Q's lot is for the satirical author "the proof that Chinese civilization is the first of the world." Comes the revolution, and Ah Q is dreaming of pillage and dictatorship in the village. After a night of such drunken dreaming, he wants to begin the revolution the next morning in the local nunnery, only to find that others had preceded him. Ah Q's fate was to be caught by the military and shot. The general apathy towards the real issues is suggested by the description of the great disappointment of all those who felt cheated by this simple and vulgar death after having looked forward to an old-style and dramatic form of execution.

Lu Hsün died in 1936. His stories made a profound impression on Chinese youth and he later became a hero of the political left. In the words of a French student of Chinese literature, "he may well become tomorrow the Chinese Gorky, the official idol of a new China . . . which he can no longer criticize." This prophecy has been fulfilled.

Among the new Chinese writers were men like Kuo Mo-jo, a versatile writer, a poet, essayist, historical scholar, and political figure who started out as a romanticist and later turned to socialism. Other outstanding writers of the Left were Pakin (Li Fei-kan), who was influenced by Russian authors, and Mao Tun (Shen Yen-ping), a novelist. One of the most important modern novelists of this Chinese generation was Lau Shaw (Shu Ch'ing-ch'un), a humanist concerned with the hardships and sufferings of the individual. Several of his books have been translated into English, the best known appearing under the title *Rickshaw Boy*.

This generation of writers set out to introduce to China Western thinking and the Western type of literature and to use them as an instrument to overcome Confucianism and to change traditional Chinese attitudes. They soon became involved in a struggle among themselves over the ideological trend which their writing was to express. Two main schools emerged, one emphasizing the development of art for art's sake, and the other the use of art to serve a practical purpose for the betterment of society. Two organizations of writers, the group called "Creation" and the "Society of Literary Research," represented these different views, with Kuo Mo-jo and Mao Tun as their respective leaders. At the end of the twenties, however, under Russian influence, the main trend shifted altogether to the Left. Kuo Mo-jo spoke of the shift from the Literary Revolution to revolutionary literature, and participated in a drive against "individualism and the bourgeoisie," and for "collectivism," "new realism," "materialism," and the "dialectic method." Against this trend, writers like Hu Shih and others, who called their group "The Crescent," spoke up for freedom of thought and freedom of the press. Others like Lu Hsün, believed that writing had to serve a political purpose, but still should remain free from political supervision and control. In 1930, the League of Leftist Writers was founded by Kuo Mo-jo, Mao Tun, and Lu Hsün; in opposition to it the humanists and moderates gathered in 1932 under the chairmanship of Lau Shaw in a group called the "Contemporaries."

Under the National Government there was a tremendous amount of publication in many fields outside of literature. Hundreds of textbooks and scientific treatises, and a vast number of translations of Western works were brought out. Many great publishing houses, of which the most important was the Commercial Press in Shanghai, flourished during this period. Particularly significant was the high proportion of Marxist writings among the books published; in fact it was so substantial that they were listed by the publishing houses under a special category. As most of the publishing houses were located in the treaty ports they enjoyed complete freedom, but in fact the government did not attempt to interfere with literary production and tolerated a great deal of criticism.

Agriculture

The National Government paid a great deal of attention to agriculture but very little to the critical problem of tenancy. This neglect was all the more critical as the modern economic development brought an aggravation of the problems of tenancy inherited from imperial times. According to the *China Handbook*, a publication of the National Government, there was an increase in the number of tenant farmers

due to: (1) the increase of production, (2) the development of commercial economy and the invasion of rural society by commercial goods followed by commercial capital in the form of large-scale purchases of land by merchants, (3) the pressure of high interest loans, and (4) high rents. As a result, landownership became more and more concentrated in the hands of a small section of the people.[6]

Estimates varied as to the actual proportion of tenancy among the peasants. According to the *China Handbook*, "almost two thirds of Chinese farmers rented land from others, to whom they must pay heavy rents." An earlier study of the problem, made between 1929 and 1933, estimated that "Somewhat less than three-fourths of the farmland is owned by the farmer himself and over one-fourth is rented." [7] This study recognizes that the proportion of tenancy was higher in the rice region of central and south China. What mattered was not so much the proportion of tenancy as the proportion of the crop which the peasant—whether tenant or owner—had to pay in rent or tax.

The original land program accepted by the Kuomintang at Canton was followed in 1930 by the land law of the National Government. Its most important stipulation was that land rent should not exceed $37\frac{1}{2}$ per cent of the main crop. Enforcement of this stipulation would have eased considerably the rent burden of the tenant farmer who paid on an average about 60 per cent of the main crop to his landlord. But like many other government measures, this rule about maximum rent remained on paper. The rent burden of the tenant farmers was matched by the tax burden of the small farm owners. The land tax had been heavily increased under the warlord regimes and was

[6] *China Handbook, 1937–1943* (New York, 1943), p. 605.
[7] Lossing Buck, *Land Utilization in China* (Chicago, 1937), p. 196.

left in the hands of the provincial administrations when the National Government was established. The lot of the peasant in Nationalist China was thus even worse than it had been in previous times, and the failure of the National Government to institute an effective agricultural program was all the more critical because of the use made of agrarian discontent by the Communist opposition.

The worsening of peasant conditions came at the time when Chinese agriculture changed from the production of food for local consumption by the farm communities to the production of cash crops for industry and the world market. Cotton and tobacco were introduced; the Manchurian soya bean became a major item of Chinese export, and the commercialization of agriculture and absentee landlordism aggravated the traditional Chinese agrarian problem.

In the absence of a program to ameliorate the increasing evils of tenancy or to lighten the tax burden, the National Government concentrated its efforts on technical improvements. Experimental stations of the government and agricultural departments of the colleges and universities studied the improvement of cotton, silk, and tea production and advocated better seeds, the rotation of crops, and the use of chemical fertilizers. This work showed results, but it did not alleviate the main problems of the Chinese farmers.

The opening of China to Western industrial products and the beginning industrial development of China herself added a further factor to the deterioration of the rural economy. Machine-made products began to eliminate the homemade goods of the farmers and caused a decline of rural industry which further affected the income of the peasant families. These products also destroyed handicrafts in the small towns, and the decline of these local centers of trade and exchange also had bad effects on the villages. In some cases the home industries were replaced by the "putting-out" system, in which an entrepreneur farmed out work to peasant families, providing the raw material and selling the finished product. But from this system the peasant profited little. On the whole the destruction of home industries and the shift from a consumer to a market economy worsened the lot of the peasants.

3. THE GROWTH OF COMMUNISM

Moscow and the Chinese Communists

When the empire came to an end, the legal privileges of the scholar-gentry ended too, and the cultural and social responsibilities of this group evaporated. In the villages nothing replaced the gentry and what remained was the economic power of the landlords. The increase of tenancy and the commercialization of agriculture gave the landlords greater power in the countryside without a corresponding responsibility. Rural conditions deteriorated further owing to overtaxation by the local administrations at the very time that the disappearance of the traditional position of the gentry left no group interested in the welfare of rural society. Conditions of tenant farmers and peasant owners varied in different areas and had not grown worse everywhere, but in general economic tension increased. The agrarian policy of the government, directed mainly towards technical improvements and the establishment of a few experimental model districts failed to provide the social and political institutions to replace those which had disappeared with the gentry.

The institutional failure of the National Government was exploited by the Communist opposition. The defeat at Hankow had been a serious setback for the Communist party. The Russian advisers had gone home. Whatever hold the party had had over labor organizations in Shanghai was crushed with the loss of the lives of many leaders. The orthodox labor program of the party was thus destroyed, and the party could survive only through a change of strategy. The Chinese Communist party was a creation of the Communist International and was closely controlled by Moscow from the first. The original small group of founders, mainly a number of professors and students from Peking University under the leadership of Ch'en Tu-hsiu, had been persuaded by Comintern agents into acceptance of the Soviet-directed party line. Disgusted with the political chaos in China in the warlord period and impressed by the success of the Russian Revolution, these intellectuals were led to overcome their original hesitations and to accept fully the Soviet doctrine and the discipline it demanded. They learned the Leninist theory that the Communist party was the vanguard of the working class and the expression of its political will, and they began their political activities by building up Communist-controlled labor organizations among the railroad workers, in the steelworks at Wuchang, and in the factories of Shanghai and Canton. The Chinese Communist leaders believed, as they had been taught, that these organizations were to prepare for the socialist revolution soon to come. Lenin's theory of imperialism, according to which the misery of the colonies and colonially-exploited countries of Asia was entirely caused by exploitation by "monopoly capitalism," appealed to the Chinese feelings of humiliated nationalism. This theory also explained the possibility of an immediate proletarian revolution in China. China was still predominantly agricultural, but Lenin's theory permitted the participation of a Chinese Communist party in what was claimed to be a world struggle between workers and capitalists.

The first shock to these new converts came with the Soviet decision to cooperate with Sun Yat-sen and the Kuomintang. To explain this decision of Soviet Russian power policy in theoretical terms, the Comintern agents proclaimed Stalin's verdict that the Kuomintang did not represent any one social class; in contrast to the general party doctrine which regarded each party as a political expression of one social class, the Kuomintang was supposed to express the coalition of a number of classes and to fight for a joint revolution in which the Communists could participate. In terms of the traditional Communist doctrine this was a theoretical monstrosity which was opposed by the Trotskyist opposition in Russia and was hard for the Chinese Communists to swallow. Ch'en Tu-hsiu and his group had been contemptuous of Sun Yat-sen and his party and were reluctant to accept the Soviet-enforced coopera-tion. But they yielded to the orders from Moscow and carried out the policy of cooperation in which their task was to maintain the "workers' hegemony" in the coalition, in other words, to attempt to insure the Communist control of the Kuomintang.

When this policy failed in 1927, the blame was not permitted to fall on Moscow, whose theoretical line could not be wrong since it represented the ruling historical force. Rather, the failure had to be the result of faulty local leadership. Ch'en Tu-hsiu, who had been trying his best to carry out the directives from Moscow, was accused of "right-opportunism" and purged from the party leadership, as were many others after him who were caught in the contradictions of party doctrine and in the conflicts between reality and the theory of infallibility of the Communist party and its top Russian leaders.

After the failure of 1927, the party continued for a time to place its main emphasis on organizing labor to prepare a workers' revolution which was to start in the cities and be supported by peasant uprisings in the countryside. Under the direction of Moscow this policy was continued by a number of new general secretaries of the Chinese Communist party, among whom Li Li-san was the best known. Li directed party affairs from 1928 to 1930, when he was purged for "left deviationism" and recalled to Moscow. In spite of all the Russian pressure to promote labor organizations and workers' strikes and uprisings, these efforts ended in complete failure. The Kuomintang itself had begun successfully to take over labor organizations. The Communists, who opposed any policy which aimed at improving the workers' economic posi-tion, or what they called "reformism," lost ground with the Chinese workers, who did not want to be sacrificed for Communist political purposes. Indeed, the Chinese Communist party, claiming to be the vanguard of the workers, never regained a hold over even the small number of industrial workers until its military conquest of the country in 1949. When these failures, which were blamed on the theoretical deviations and ineptitudes of the local leaders, came into sharp contrast with Communist success in rural China, Soviet policy shifted quietly away from this emphasis on the workers to the peasants, among whom another type of Communist organization had been set up.

Communist exploitation of peasant discontent for the seizure of power was nothing new. Lenin had used the land hunger of the Russian peasant in the Russian Revolution of the "workers and peasants," and the peasant was to play a similar role in future Communist victories. Indeed, without the use of this entirely "non-proletarian" and "non-socialist" element, the Com-munist party might not have been successful anywhere. In exchange for their assistance in the Communist conquest of power the peasants were given land —only to have it taken away later through collectivization. This un-Marxist procedure was concealed behind the theory that the peasants were under the leadership of the workers with whom they made common cause. In Russia, where the workers played an active part in the October Revolution, this theoretical fiction could be maintained. But in China the workers' vanguard had no workers. All the efforts made by the Chinese Communist party to continue the workers' uprisings were an attempt to provide some basis for this theoretical fiction. Even when the Communists in China turned entirely to the exploitation of the agrarian issue, the fiction of the "workers and peasant party" was never given up, and the idea of a proletarian vanguard that still claimed to express the political will of the workers was carried to its full logical absurdity. The Chinese Communist party depended entirely on the exploitation of peasant discontent and used the peasants as the basis of a military organization with which to seize power.

Mao Tse-tung

The man who led the party to power was Mao Tse-tung. Born in 1893 in Hunan province, Mao came from a fairly well-to-do peasant family which he left to become a student. At the end of World War I he worked in the library at the University of Peking at the time of the Literary Renaissance and the May Fourth Movement. The University was itself the center of the intellectual ferment of the time. Under the influence of his professors Mao became a student of Marxist thought, and when the Comintern agents organized the Chinese Communist party, Mao became one of its first members. Like the others Mao accepted the doctrine of the proletarian revolution and participated in the work of labor union organization.

The first indication of the importance of the peasantry came to the Communist leaders when the strikes and boycotts organized in 1925 against the British in Shanghai and Canton as a result of the "May 30th incident" had been echoed in the villages of central and south China. In 1926 Mao Tse-tung was sent to Hunan to organize peasant associations for the party. This journey left with him a lasting impression of the importance of the peasant movement. On his return, he made a "Report on an Investigation of the Agrarian Movement in Hunan" published in March, 1927, which was a passionate description of the importance of the peasants in the revolution.

The outbreaks in Hunan which Mao examined were started by the poorest section of the peasants. They were marked by violence and some of the landlords were killed. These excesses were condemned by the Kuomintang and Communist leaders at Changsha and Wuchang, who were then still united in the northern campaign. The violence frightened some of the Kuomintang leaders and threatened the cooperation between the Kuomintang and the Communists. There was so much resentment among the Nationalist officers who came from landlord families that the military campaign itself was endangered. As a result of these political complications the peasant uprisings were classified by the Communist party as a "*p'i-tzu* movement"— a movement of peasant loafers, gamblers, and paupers, a sort of "lumpen-peasants."

Mao Tse-tung argued passionately against this classification. He described the events of the peasant outbreaks and their success in sweeping away the privileges and prerogatives of the landlords and in taking over authority in the villages. "The patriarchal, feudal *t'u-hao* [local bullies] and bad gentry, together with the illegitimate landlords, were not only the foundation of the dictatorial regime of the past several thousand years, [but also] the tools of the imperialists, warlords, and corrupt officials." [8] Their elimination was "very good" and not at all "bad" or "very bad," as the situation had been described by the leaders of the party. Mao Tse-tung described how the poor peasants had taken the lead in the movement and how most of them had become "reformed, able and hardworking people," abandoning former bad habits, gambling, and loafing. They deserved support, rather than repression, because: "*This leadership by the poor peasants is very essential. Without the poor peasants, there will be no revolution.*" [9] And Mao predicted: "Within a short time, hundred of millions of peasants will rise in Central, South, and North China, with the fury of a hurricane; no power, however strong, can restrain them. They will break all the shackles that bind them, and rush towards the road of liberation. *All imperialists, warlords, corrupt officials, and bad gentry will meet their doom at the hands of the peasants.* All revolutionary parties and comrades will be judged by them. *Are we to get in front of them and lead them or criticize them behind their backs or fight them from the opposite camp?* Among these three alternatives every Chinese can choose freely, but the current situation demands a quick decision." [10]

Mao allotted the peasants seven out of ten points in the accomplishment of the democratic revolution, and it has sometimes been held that by making the peasantry the main force of the revolution—he diverged from the dogma of the Marxist-Leninist school. It is pointed out that Lenin, in spite of his reliance on the support of the peasants, had regarded the peasantry as only an auxiliary force in the proletarian revolution and that Mao, by giving the peasant the main role, had diverged from Lenin and made a new contribution. But Mao, in his report, was not speaking of the proletarian revolution. He was speaking of the "democratic revolution." What he called the "historic mission" "of the vast peasant masses" was in his words "the rising up of the democratic forces in the countryside who overthrow the feudal forces in the villages, which is the true goal of the national revolution." The "national" and "democratic" revolutions are synonymous and, according to Mao, represent the goal for which Sun Yat-sen had worked for forty years. When Mao spoke of the "democratic revolution" in which the peasants were to play the major role, he did not have in mind the dogma of a proletarian dictatorship, but rather the theory of a multi-class dictatorship, a dogmatic concoction of Stalin's which was used as a cloak to cover many theoretical sins. The fiction that the Communist party itself represented the urban proletariat, or somehow, its interests, was never given up by Mao even when he based his power entirely on the exploitation of peasant discontent. The significance of Mao's report is that he realized the importance of peasant support. His prediction of

[8] Conrad Brandt, Benjamin Schwartz, and John K. Fairbank, *A Documentary History of Chinese Communism* (Cambridge, 1952), p. 83.

[9] *Ibid.*, p. 88.

[10] *Ibid.*, p. 80.

the rising of "hundreds of millions of peasants" was a fantasy. But Mao saw the possibility of using the peasants, a policy which became highly important for the Chinese Communist party and which was made theoretically possible by Stalin's contributions to party doctrine.

In spite of the opinions expressed in his report Mao went along with the peasant policy of the Communist party, which, during the spring and summer of 1927, continued to disapprove of the "excesses" of the peasant movement and attempted to stop them in order not to endanger the cooperation with the left wing of the Kuomintang. Mao Tse-tung, at that time head of the National Peasant Federation, himself carried out the policy of the party as derived from the directives of the Comintern.

As a result of his interest in peasant organization Mao Tse-tung was sent to Hunan in 1927, after the split with the Kuomintang, to foment peasant uprisings there. By this time the Communist party was ready to incite peasant revolts in order to support its plans for workers' uprisings in the cities. Mao Tse-tung tried to instigate uprisings during the period of the harvest, when the collection of tax and rent was expected to create the necessary climate of peasant hostility. But Mao's ideas of the "hurricane"—a broad sweep of peasant uprisings—had been illusory, and the "autumn harvest uprisings," as they were called, were a complete failure. As a result, Mao was dismissed from the Politburo of the Communist party and, according to one story, was even placed on probation as a party member.

From the defeat Mao salvaged a small military force, consisting of armed peasants and deserters from Kuomintang troops. With this force he retreated in the winter of 1927 into the Chingkan Mountains on the border between Hunan and Kiangsi provinces. This small military force in the mountainous hinterland was the beginning of a new military base. Mao Tse-tung was not the only and not the first Communist leader to set up such a military organization in a peasant area, but he became the dominant organizer, political leader, and military planner of this Communist strategy.

During the following years the Communist forces under Mao extended their control in the rural areas south of the central Yangtze. In May, 1928, Mao's army was joined by the forces of Chu Teh, which included some Communist officers trained at the Whampoa Academy. While Mao became the political leader of the group, Chu Teh became its top military commander, and both continued in these positions until after the establishment of the Chinese Communist government in 1949. Mao's personal alliance with Chu Teh was the basis of his power in the party; it gave him the necessary force to eliminate or absorb his competitors. Mao did not rise to power as an ideological innovator or as the leader of a peasant revolution but through the possession of military force. The fact that Mao had no ideological line of his own made it possible for him to adhere to the Stalinist line and while doing so consolidate his power. With the expansion of the area controlled by the Communist forces, a conflict of power began among its political and military leaders. With the support of Chu Teh, Mao eliminated a large number of rival officers within the Communist forces and broke the opposition of political leaders by having them arrested and liquidated. A major clash occurred in December, 1930, when a political faction opposed to Mao's machine and supported by a military unit set up its own rival local organization. After considerable fighting the revolt was quelled and its leaders executed; and with this victory Mao emerged as the main leader of this rural Communist base.

The Chinese Soviet Republic

During these years the party leaders in Shanghai continued to direct the policy prescribed by Moscow's Comintern agents. Mao's activities were tolerated because they were the only successes the Communists could point to, but it was felt that peasant organization must at least be complemented by a workers' revolution in the cities. All attempts at urban uprisings, such as the Canton commune of December, 1927, ended in defeat. For a time the party leaders pressed Mao Tse-tung to attack cities and in this way gain the urban basis on which the theory depended. In July, 1930, a section of the Red Army made an attack on the city of Changsha in Hunan, where it was hoped that an urban center could be established for the Communist movement. But the city could not be held and Mao Tse-tung ignored further orders by the party leaders to attempt the capture of other industrial cities. The strategy of seizing cities was given up and the shift to a rural base became complete when in November, 1931, a Chinese Soviet Republic was set up at Juichin in Kiangsi with Mao Tse-tung as chairman. The party leaders now joined Mao. From that time on, Mao's military organization became the Chinese Communist headquarters and Mao and Chu Teh the top Chinese Communist figures, but Mao still had to reconcile his local strategy with the directives of the Comintern.

The Chinese Soviet Republic issued its own constitution and its own land law which provided for land redistribution to the advantage of the landless poor and middle peasants. A labor law was also promulgated in order to maintain the fiction of the leadership of the proletariat although this law could have no application in the area controlled. The constitution claimed the establishment of "the democratic dictatorship of the proletariat and peasantry. . . ." The theoretical confusion was apparent in the statement of the aim of this dictatorship which was

. . . to destroy all feudal remnants, eliminate the influence of the imperialist powers in China, to unite China, to limit systematically the development of capitalism, to carry out economic reconstruction of the state, to promote the class-consciousness and solidarity of the proletariat, and to rally to its banner the broad masses of poor peasants in order to effect the transition to the dictatorship of the proletariat.[11]

The fiction of the dictatorship of the proletariat and the peasantry was thus proclaimed. Even in its rural surroundings the party was still concerned with the promotion of proletarian class-consciousness and solidarity, and the

[11] *Ibid.*, p. 220.

dictatorship of the proletariat was to be brought about through the "broad masses of poor peasants."

At the time of the establishment of the Chinese Soviet Republic, Mao Tse-tung's military organization had already survived three offensives by armies of the National Government. The Nationalist armies, which moved against the Communist forces in traditional closed columns, expecting frontal battles, were met by a strategy of guerrilla warfare which was developed by Mao Tse-tung and his military commanders. Through their organization of the peasantry the Communists were able to build an excellent intelligence service which kept them well informed about the moves of the government forces. In retreating from concentrated attacks of Nationalist troops, the Communists bore down on the Nationalist lines of communication and supply. Their tactics of retreat, of long marches, and of surprise concentration of forces at points of Nationalist weakness foiled the Nationalist offensives. At times the Communists succeeded not only in forcing the retreat of the Nationalists but also in isolating and destroying large government units.

In the meantime Communist territory and power grew, especially in 1932 when the Japanese attack on Manchuria and the fighting at Shanghai disrupted the National Government and halted all anti-Communist campaigns. After the Manchurian incident was over, the government returned to the anti-Communist campaign in November, 1933, but with a new strategy. Instead of attempting to move into the Communist territory with Nationalist army units, the government threw a blockade around the whole territory in order to make the Communist position untenable. A ring of blockhouses was erected, controlling all roads and passages, and cutting off all communication. Part of this blockade was taken over by regional military leaders who had to follow the government move in order to protect their own territories to the south of the Communist area. This blockade was highly successful in withholding from the Communists vital supplies which their mountain areas did not provide. A specific item of shortage for the Communists was salt which was essential for the vegetarian diet of this rural area.

In November 1933, a revolt against the National Government was started at Foochow in Fukien province by a leading Kwangsi general and several other Kuomintang renegades with the help of the Nineteenth Route army. A "People's Government" was set up and attempts were made to establish cooperation with the Communists. This opportunity was not exploited by the Chinese Soviet regime which, under orders from Moscow, continued to follow the current policy of going it alone. At that time the Communist line had not changed to the "united front" policy of 1935, and the Chinese Communist leaders had to reject the possibility of allying themselves with the Fukien revolt. Such an alliance would have provided the Communists with an outlet to the sea. It might have made unnecessary the costly Long March in which the Communist forces shortly thereafter moved from their southern base to the northwest, a move which was later regarded as a strategic mistake by Mao Tse-tung himself. The Fukien revolt was quickly suppressed by Chiang Kai-shek. Whether the Communists could have maintained themselves successfully in south-central China or not, the refusal to follow this course of action is one of the examples of the victory of dogma as interpreted in Moscow over the realities of the Chinese political situation. However successful Mao Tse-tung was in developing his strategy, he had to remain within the framework of Moscow theory and policy.

The Long March

In 1934 under the pressure of the Nationalist blockade and a new attack, the Communist position in southern Kiangsi and the border areas of the neighboring provinces became untenable. In October, 1934, they broke out of this encirclement to the west. This break-through began the Long March of the Communists which has been celebrated in their writings as a tremendous accomplishment. The march took the Communist armies over a distance of more than 6,000 miles, covered on foot, through the whole of West China. They touched the territory of twelve different provinces, passed over eighteen high mountain ranges, some permanently snow-covered, and went through some of the most forbidding territories of the Chinese-Tibetan borderland. Their march lasted just a little over one year, less than a third of which was spent in stops along the way, many of which were made necessary by military battles. The average daily distance covered on the march was twenty-four miles, all the more impressive considering the difficulties of the terrain. Minor skirmishes took place almost daily, and over fifteen major battles were fought with provincial armies, and Nationalist troops, who continually followed the moving Communist forces. The Communists attempted to exploit their march for propaganda purposes. In the towns they passed through, the Communists held mass meetings with political speeches and theatrical performances. They took clothing and grain from the merchants and distributed them among the poor. In some places they armed the peasants and left agents behind. They also brutally killed some of the officials and wealthy people whom they captured, and held others for ransom; but whatever goodwill they may have gained among the poor peasants in the areas through which they marched was counterbalanced by the loss in military power which their march brought about.

The march greatly weakened the Communists. Over ninety thousand men had left the Soviet area of southern Kiangsi, and new men had been recruited on the way to replace the losses. But only twenty thousand men, with some of their families, reached northwestern Shensi, where the Communist forces established their new headquarters at Yenan in October 1935. Almost fifty thousand people had perished in the high steppe lands and mountains of northwestern Szechwan alone, where they had been forced to go when tribal armies blocked their way. Northwestern Shensi, into which the Communists had been driven, was a poor base for their political organization because of its poverty. To the National Government it seemed possible that here the Communists would be further whittled down. A way of retreat had been left to Outer Mongolia, so that the Communists could be driven off to Russian-controlled territory without the necessity of a do-or-die stand, and the National Government seemed near its goal of eliminating the Communist opposition and consolidating its military power.

The area through which the Communists moved had not been under the direct control of the National Government but under that of local military leaders who had only nominally accepted the government's rule. Most of the Communist battles were with provincial troops who sometimes suffered considerable losses, which was to the advantage of the Nationalists. The Communists' march through the areas of these local warlords gave the National Government the additional advantage of being able to move in legitimately and take over the area from the Communists. The National Government thus gained its first real foothold in many important areas of the western hinterland though it did not succeed everywhere in taking over authority from the local warlords. The Long March had thus greatly weakened the Communists and had strengthened the control of the National Government over the inland areas.

The march had brought other important changes. Mao Tse-tung, who was already the chairman of the Soviet Republic in Kiangsi, became now the undisputed leader. In January 1935, at a conference in Kweichow he formally became chairman of the Central Committee and of the Politburo. When the first units arrived in Shensi in October 1935, the area was already in the hands of local Communist forces which had been organized under the leadership of Kao Kang, but Mao's political machine took over control. Kao Kang, however, always remained a rival for power.

The United Front Policy

The combined Communist forces, now confined in an impoverished area, were in a difficult position to carry on the civil war, and the end of Communist power in China might have been near had it not been for another decisive change which occurred during the Long March and which was to bring about a temporary cessation of the civil war. In 1935, during the Long March, the international line of the Moscow-dominated Comintern had changed. Russia had joined the League of Nations and had begun to develop the strategy of the united front to face the mounting threat of Nazi Germany. The Chinese Communists, who had been clamoring for the execution of Chiang Kai-shek, now followed the change in the line and advocated a united front, under Chiang's leadership, to resist Japanese aggression. During the Manchurian incident the Chinese Soviet Republic had declared war on Japan from the safety of its southern mountain area, and a year later several propaganda appeals were made by the Communists for resistance to Japan. But with the change of the Soviet line, the Communists were serious in their offer to cooperate with the National Government for joint anti-Japanese action. Already on the Long March in the summer of 1935 the Communists, at a conference at Szechwan, had called on "all classes" to fight against Japan, and when they were settled in northern Shensi they bent their main efforts toward setting up an "anti-Japanese national united front."

The Communist argument was strengthened by the seriousness of the Japanese threat against China. Two years after the close of the Manchurian incident and the establishment of the puppet state of Manchukuo, the Japanese prepared the ground for their next move in North China. Their attempt in 1935 to separate the five Chinese provinces north of the Yellow River from the National Government and to set up a puppet organization under their own control was not very successful, but their move resulted in political and military ventures, of which one of the most threatening was in Inner Mongolia, close to the newly Communist-controlled area in Shensi. The seriousness of the Japanese attack outweighed the problems of the Chinese civil war and thus gave the practical basis for the Communist argument. The slogan, "Chinese should not fight Chinese at a time of Japanese aggression," had a strong appeal for non-Communist Chinese. In December 1935, there was a patriotic movement among the students in Peiping to resist Japan. The Communists exploited these nationalist feelings. Their claims to be the most energetic defenders of the nation against the Japanese attracted many intellectuals and put Chiang Kai-shek on the defensive.

In August 1936, the Chinese Communists presented to the Central Executive Committee of the Kuomintang another formal "proposal of a united front against Japan." This proposal remained unanswered. In carrying out his anti-Communist campaign, Chiang Kai-shek refused to listen to the arguments for a united front. His aim was to destroy the Communists and their weak northwestern base or to drive them back to Russian-controlled territory. This would eliminate his main opposition and facilitate Nationalist resistance against the Japanese aggressor, for which he had prepared by the modernization of the Nationalist army, the building of fortifications around Shanghai, and the strengthening of Nationalist control over Chinese territory.

The Sian Crisis

In fighting the Communists, Chaing Kai-shek's government attempted to use provincial troops, as far as was practical, rather than its own well-trained central forces. A weakening of such provincial armies as a by-product of the attack against the Communists was not undesirable from the point of view of the central government. The attack against the Communists in north Shensi was to be carried out by the Manchurian troops of Chang Hsüeh-liang. After having been forced out of Manchuria by the Japanese attack, these troops were garrisoned at Sian, the capital and strategic key city of south-central Shensi. These troops, cut off from their homeland, were especially susceptible to the propaganda for the united front against Japan. When Chiang Kai-shek ordered them to attack the Communist armies, they stalled and finally refused to carry out the orders of the central government.

In December 1936, Chiang Kai-shek flew to Sian to enforce obedience. When he attempted through threats and promises to force the troops to move against the Communists, the troops mutinied, kidnapped Chiang Kai-shek, and held him prisoner.

The dramatic story of Chiang Kai-shek's kidnapping is known as to its outward events, but the details of the political negotiations that were carried on in Sian are still unknown. Before the kidnapping, Chiang Kai-shek had himself, through his own representatives, begun negotiations with the Chinese Communists, and a secondary purpose of the flight to Sian had been to receive the report of his negotiators. This background of preliminary negotiations facilitated the solution of the very complex kidnapping affair. The kidnapping created tremendous excitement. Many forces worked for a compromise solution to maintain Chinese national unity and provide a basis for Chinese resistance against the Japanese threat of attack. Chiang Kai-shek himself remained stubborn at first. He had been taken outside the city of Sian, after most of his bodyguards had been killed in defending him and in covering his attempted escape. He had fallen and been seriously hurt and at first refused to cooperate in any way with his captors. At the same time some of the leading members of the National Government at Nanking prepared plans to attack the mutinous troops at Sian with military force. An air fleet actually set out for a bombing attack on the city of Sian and turned back only at the last moment. It was well understood that such an attack would directly or indirectly endanger Chiang's life, but the argument was raised by some of the Nanking leaders that discipline had to be restored even at such a risk. To avoid endangering Chiang Kai-shek's life, negotiations were started by Chiang's close relatives and political assistants. T. V. Soong, Chiang's brother-in-law, flew to Sian and was followed by Madame Chiang Kai-shek. Their arrival in the mutinous city made any further Nationalist attacks impossible, and negotiations began.

In these negotiations the Communists took part as mediators. With their new policy of the united front, the Communists now felt that it was essential to retain Chiang Kai-shek because they believed that only under his leadership could such a policy succeed. This consideration outweighed the advantages of having him eliminated as their main opponent in the civil war. Their aim was not to get rid of Chiang Kai-shek but to make him give up his policy of destroying the Chinese Communists before pressing the war against Japan and to accept instead the policy of a united front. Whether a formal political settlement was reached is unknown, but the National Government's policy changed, and the Communist influence with the mutinous troops is believed to have been of considerable importance in effecting Chiang Kai-shek's release.

On December 25, 1936, Chiang Kai-shek flew back to Nanking. He was greeted by a tremendous outburst of national rejoicing which took the form of spontaneous celebrations in many cities all over the country. This was an indication of the great popularity of Chiang Kai-shek at this time as well as of the general relief that the civil war seemed to have been terminated. The mutinous troops were no longer forced to carry out the order of attack; some of their officers received a money payment while their chief commander, Chang Hsüeh-liang, followed Chiang Kai-shek to Nanking. He has remained, through all the years of the war and postwar period and after the retreat to Formosa, a politely treated prisoner of the National Government.

The Sian kidnapping and the release of Chiang Kai-shek ended the civil war. A truce prevailed between the National Government and the Communists, and after the Japanese attack in July 1937, there was a period of closer cooperation, and the Communists remained in undisturbed control of the territory which they held. In February 1937, the Communists sent a telegram to a meeting of the Central Executive Committee of the Kuomintang at Nanking. They called for an end of civil war and a concentration of all strength against foreign aggression. They also called for a "National Salvation Conference" and economic reform measures. In exchange, the Communists promised to stop their armed uprisings, to change their independent Soviet government into a regional government and the Red Army into a "National Revolutionary Army" under the leadership of Nanking, to enforce universal suffrage in their area and to discontinue land confiscations. The Kuomintang did not formally accept these Communist suggestions but issued a resolution which in part restated the Communist points. The Communists would be given a chance to "reform" on condition that they abolish their army and Soviet government, end their propaganda and accept the Three People's Principles, and stop their call for a class struggle. The aim of the Kuomintang was still the elimination of Communism, but Chinese unity was to be achieved through "peaceful means."

The Communist and Nationalist statements indicated the main bases of the understanding. The civil war ended and Communist land confiscation was discontinued. Communist propaganda stressed the need for a united front against Japan. The National Government called a People's National Congress for November 1937, which was to prepare a new constitution, and many political prisoners were released. Negotiations for an agreement were continuing when on July 7, 1937, the Japanese attack at the Marco Polo Bridge (Lukouchiao) near Peiping started the undeclared war.

4. THE WAR WITH JAPAN

Chinese Resistance

The Japanese attack on July 7, 1937, was the latest military move in a policy which, since the conclusion of the Manchurian Incident, had aimed at the separation of North China from Nationalist control and the establishment of a Japanese puppet regime there. Since 1935 the Japanese had restricted Nationalist control in the provinces north of the Yellow River. They had set up several local regimes which they expected to run. In Peiping the Hopei-Chahar Political Council was set up to govern these two northern provinces. Officially it yielded to Japanese demands, but under the surface it remained loyal to the National Government with which it maintained secret connections. In addition to the Hopei-Chahar Political Council the Japanese set up two smaller political organizations on the flanks of their position in North China. They established an autonomous Inner Mongolian regime in Suiyuan province and an East Hopei Autonomous Council in the coastal area to the south of the Great Wall. Through East Hopei, which was completely under Japanese control and independent of the new Chinese customs system, vast amounts of Japanese goods were dumped into the Chinese market, seriously affecting the tariff income and economic stability of the National Government. These Japanese moves, clearly leading to an attack on North China, had created a climate of national emergency which made the political compromise for united resistance inevitable.

The Japanese attack at the Marco Polo Bridge struck at the one open railroad not controlled by the Japanese which still linked Peiping with Central China and the national capital. In the negotiations that followed, the Chinese government under Chiang Kai-shek was willing to make economic and other concessions, except the decisive one of giving up North China. Since the main Japanese aim was the control of North China, the negotiations failed, and once the war had started, the Chinese government had the broadest popular support in its fight for North China. Not only were the Communists now willing to cooperate with the National Government, but also all the other military and political groups which had been opposed to Chiang Kai-shek came to the immediate support of the government at Nanking. Among these were Feng Yü-hsiang and the Kwangsi generals whose well-trained troops substantially strengthened the Nationalist forces in the first and most critical phase of the war. In fact the national crisis led to a general political strengthening of the National Government.

In addition to the Kuomintang and the Communist party a number of other political groups and parties supported mainly by Western-educated intellectuals, businessmen, and bankers had come into existence. These minor parties differed from the Kuomintang and from the Communist party in that they had no extensive political machine or organization and, most important of all, no armed forces of their own. They merely represented in varying degrees, the views of the intellectuals and business groups. Some of these parties, like the Youth party, originally founded by Chinese students in France, and the National Socialist party, which later changed its name to the Social Democratic party in order not to be confused with the Nazis, had distinctive political identities and aims. Several minor political groups were later combined in a "Democratic League." All these so-called middle parties were opposed to one-party government by either the Kuomintang or the Communist party; they could exercise an influence by taking advantage of the rivalry between these two major parties. In the months before the end of the civil war, many of the small political groups took up the slogan of a united front for resistance against Japan, thus in effect giving their support to the Communist line. A number of influential non-party public men founded a National Salvation Movement which followed the same line. Some of them were imprisoned by the government. When the war started, the government released these men and accepted the cooperation of the middle parties.

China thus entered the war with a large measure of political unity. In September, 1937, the Communist party issued a manifesto abolishing the Chinese Soviet government and the Red Army, and accepting Sun Yat-sen's Three People's Principles as China's paramount need of the day. It called for the convocation of a National People's Congress and the enactment of the promised constitution. This manifesto was welcomed by Chiang Kai-shek in a formal statement as the fulfillment of all the essential conditions for mobilizing China's national strength and as a sign of a united war effort. The course of the war and the retreat of the Chinese forces made the calling of a National People's Congress impossible. Instead, in March 1938, at an extraordinary congress of the Kuomintang in which the Communist leader Chou En-lai participated as a member of the Presidium, a People's Political Council was organized. This People's Political Council was to consist of 200 members appointed from all political parties and groups, including the Communists and the middle parties. It was to be an advisory body which had the right to discuss and question all government measures and to make proposals to the government. Its establishment and early functioning marked the high point of political unity in China.

The political and general economic developments in China were, however, seriously affected by the course of the war itself. Although the war had started in North China and for the defense of the North, as a result of Japanese-provoked incidents it soon involved Shanghai and the Yangtze area and then the whole of China. The Chinese defense of the Shanghai area was well prepared, and the three months' stand of the Chinese troops against the Japanese attack from land, sea, and air with superior artillery and equipment was a great boost for Chinese morale.

The Chinese strategy, however, was not one of positional warfare. The Nationalist aim was from the beginning to take advantage of space in order to counter the technical superiority of the Japanese. This implied an elastic warfare of slow retreat into inland areas which, because of their mountainous character, could more easily be defended. The great distances of China would force the Japanese to extend their lines of communication and to spread their forces. This would enable the Chinese to attack the Japanese lines of communication and carry on a guerrilla warfare in which space and time would help to wear down Japanese strength. The success of the first defense at Shanghai encouraged the Chinese command to delay too long the general plan of retreat. When at the end of October 1937, the Chinese troops after great losses tried to fall back, the Japanese succeeded in outflanking them and in overrunning the next line of defense. The retreating armies lost all their equipment and a great many of their troops. The remainder narrowly escaped being bottled up at Nanking, which fell into the hands of the Japanese in December. Thus the capital was lost and the Japanese had come close to accomplishing their strategic aim of destroying the main Chinese armies. The Japanese spoiled this chance by pausing at Nanking where their soldiers got out of hand and went on a wild outburst of pillage, murder, and rape.

They behaved the same way in other towns which they captured. These atrocities strengthened the Chinese will to resist and gave the Chinese armies valuable time for recuperation and reorganization. Then began the famous retreat which took the National Government via Hankow to Chungking, which at the end of 1938 became the wartime capital. With the government went a few of the factories needed for war production, the machinery being carried on river boats and on the backs of coolies. The retreat inland was also joined by the leading Chinese universities, which set up free centers of higher education in the towns of west and southwest China.

The retreat was covered by a delaying action fought by the Kwangsi armies under General Li Tsung-jen, which were thrown into a decisive battle at Hsüchou, the key railroad junction on the Tientsin-Nanking line. For three months the Kwangsi troops prevented the northern and central Japanese armies from joining forces and gained one of the first Chinese victories in the battle of Taierchuang in April 1938. When the Kwangsi armies were forced to retreat, the government decided to mine the dikes of the Yellow River, thus causing a flood in the Huai area which destroyed the equipment of the advancing Japanese armies and gained another valuable span of time at great expense of Chinese life and property.

The Japanese failed in their attempt to destroy the Chinese government and military forces while they were within easy reach of the coastal areas. The war developed into a war of attrition in which the Japanese came to hold the plains of north and central China and the coastal areas, while most of the mountainous areas remained outside their grasp. After the fall of Hankow and Canton in October 1938, a stalemate was reached and very little territory changed hands until early 1945.

The occupation of Chinese cities and lines of communications in so vast a territory was a costly undertaking, and the main effort of the Japanese command was directed toward the economic exploitation of the occupied territory, a task for which they needed Chinese cooperation. They attempted to set up puppet governments and gain collaborators. In October 1938, Wang Ching-wei, a leading Kuomintang politician, went over to their side and after lengthy negotiations formed a puppet government in Nanking in March 1940. In spite of this limited success the Japanese did not bring about the collapse of the National Government, nor did they overcome Chinese popular resistance, and the largest part of inland China remained under Nationalist control. The Chinese living in Japanese-occupied territory remained in close touch with those in free China. Chinese resistance was continued on a broad scale, but the stalemate led to an economic decline on the Nationalist side and to a renewal of the fight for control between the National Government and the Communist opposition.

The National Government and the Communists

The kind of small-scale warfare and economic struggle that ensued behind the Japanese lines depended on effective participation by the peasant population. When it became necessary to organize rural communities against the Japanese, the Communists, with their previous experience in organizing the peasantry, had a definite advantage over the National Government. The National Government had derived its main financial support from the cities of the coastal provinces. After the capture of all these larger cities by the Japanese, this support was cut off, and most of the income from the Maritime Customs, which had been the largest item of revenue, was lost. The salt tax and eventually the land tax became the main sources of income for the government. Because it was compelled to rely so heavily on the land tax, the government did not try to experiment with land reform measures as it did not wish to antagonize the landowners through sudden measures of land reform. The National Government therefore had to rely on the most conservative element, the landlords, who were especially strong in the province of Szechwan where the wartime capital was established. The political implications of this dependence on agrarian China were accentuated by the fact that the most influential leaders around Chiang Kai-shek, the C.C. group, controlled the Farmers' Bank which provided the credits for the landowners. On the other hand, the industrial development of West China was very limited and slow and those Kuomintang leaders who depended on urban business and the intellectuals for support became less influential. Whatever industrial activity was established in the west of China was necessarily for war purposes and was controlled by officials.

The Japanese attack and the move inland thus changed the character of the National Government. It was deprived of the urban business support and had to depend more and more upon conservative rural support controlled by the party machine. The previous failure to develop new institutions in the countryside now became of fatal importance, and to undertake such a task would hardly have been possible in the midst of war. Even the newly created institutions of central government were under severe strain and without its sound urban support the Kuomintang could not risk a political and economic upheaval in the rural hinterland.

The Communists, on the other hand, were free to operate without the responsibilities and expenses of a national government. They concentrated on building up political support among the poorer peasants in the areas which they controlled. They broadened their rural support when they changed their line from civil war to the united front policy. Instead of killing the landlords and distributing their land they now introduced a reform policy under which landlordism was continued, but the rent was fixed at a maximum of 37½ per cent of the main crop. This reform policy was taken by the Communists from the original program of the Kuomintang which, however, had never been carried out. When the regular authorities had to flee before the Japanese and guerrilla warfare could be started, the Communists had their chance. With their new moderate policy they could organize behind the Japanese lines a united resistance under their own management and control. A typical example of the Communist organization was the Border Government established in the rural districts of the Hopei-Chahar-Shansi border area. Here the Communists imposed rent restrictions on the landlords who remained, but the land of those landlords who had become collaborators or who stayed in the Japanese-controlled cities was expropriated and distributed. In this way the Communists gained the support of large portions of the population of the rural guerrilla areas. The local government which the Communists established was made up officially of only one-third Communist members; another third consisted of the representatives of the small peasantry, while the last third was reserved for representatives of those landlords who had remained and were cooperative. Though they gave this self-imposed limitation a great deal of publicity, the Communists, who approved all candidates, were clearly in control.

With this program the Communists set up regimes for guerrilla warfare in north and central China and extended their political influence over vast areas where they had had no hold in the past. The National Government became alarmed over this threat and attempted, not very successfully, to compete in the field of guerrilla organization. A conflict for territory again ensued, and it became clear that the Communists were using the war against Japan to extend their own territorial and political control.

The Communist penetration of territory and extension of power soon ended the cooperation between the National Government and the Communists in the war against Japan. From the end of 1937 until the fall of 1938 there existed a common war strategy under which the Communists coordinated their moves and attacks with those of the Nationalist troops. In August 1938, the National Government, still at Hankow, outlawed the mass organizations through which Communists were attempting to gain influence in Nationalist territory. It also became apparent that the abolition of the Communist Soviet government in Shensi and of the Red Army and the political and military submission to the National Government had been only a formal gesture and that the Communists had no intention of submitting to real direction and control by the National Government.

The situation was also affected by the German-Soviet non-aggression pact in 1939 and the consequent ending of Japanese attacks on the Soviet Mongolian border of Manchukuo which had caused serious border incidents earlier in 1939. The period of the united front had ended, and the war in Europe was a "capitalist war" according to the propaganda line of the Comintern. The doctrinal basis for the Chinese Communist cooperation with the National Government had therefore disappeared, and the Communists were free to follow a policy of expansion. It was to their advantage that, though small-scale battles in the Communist areas continued, the Japanese concentrated their major front-line units against the armies of the National Government. While the war with Japan continued, both sides in China began to watch each other guardedly and to reserve a part of their military strength for the anticipated inner struggle.

The first major clash between the National Government and the Communists occurred in January 1941 in the lower Yangtze region. The Communist-controlled New Fourth Army had successfully established its guerrilla bases in the triangular area between Nanking, Hangchow, and Shanghai, the former main base of the Kuomintang. The loss of this territory to the Communists was something that the National Government would not accept. Orders were given to the New Fourth Army to move north across the Yangtze River to Anhwei. The New Fourth Army command objected to this move and pointed to the difficulties of moving a peasant guerrilla organization and to the absence of other forces which could take over. The order to move was resisted as long as possible. When finally the move was undertaken, troops of the National Government surrounded and destroyed the rear guard of the New Fourth Army. This clash marked the end of the period of cooperation.

In the years from 1941 to the end of the war an uneasy truce prevailed interrupted by periodic minor clashes over territory. But in spite of this military friction both sides still sought a negotiated settlement. Chiang Kai-shek frequently denied any notion of using military force to "suppress the Communists." He formulated the policy of the National Government in September, 1943, stating "that the Communist problem is a purely political problem and should be solved by political means," and this statement remained the basis of policy of the National Government. Consequently, discussions were started between government and Communist representatives in May, 1944, which dealt with the following issues:

(1) The disposition, size, and training of the Communist armies, (2) the relationship between Communist-organized regional governments and the national government, (3) problems connected with civil rights and especially the legalization of the Communist Party, and its activities in Nationalist areas.

Although these negotiations did not lead to an agreement at the time, they did lead to an exploration of the possibilities of finding a settlement through a new form of constitutional government on which all sides could agree.

The Weakening of the National Government

While this power struggle continued, the Communists were growing stronger and the National Government was growing weaker. With the fall of Canton and the coastal blockade initiated by the Japanese, the National Government was cut off from most of its outside contact and faced a war of attrition in increasing isolation, especially after Pearl Harbor, when the Chinese-Japanese war was merged into World War II. French Indo-China, through which supplies had come in for a while, had already surrendered to the Japanese in 1940, and the rapid Japanese victories in 1941 and 1942, which established their mastery on Burma, Thailand, and the whole of southeastern Asia, completed the isolation of the Chinese government. When the contact between China and the outside world was slowly re-established, first through the air connection via India—the flight over the Hump—and then through the opening of the Burma Road, the disintegration of the forces of the National Government had already become serious. The last offensives of the Japanese armies through southwestern China in 1945 almost succeeded in destroying the last territorial stronghold of the Chinese government.

Economically strangled by the Japanese blockade and deprived of its main former sources of income and support, the National Government in Chungking faced a steadily deteriorating situation. Thrown on the resources of western China, the government had tried to develop some industrial production in order to maintain itself and to provide for the large number of refugees that had moved inland. The industrialized part of China had been lost to the Japanese, and it became necessary to produce in western China at least some of the simple equipment needed for the war and to maintain some exports to pay for the Western equipment which came in until the lines were cut. To promote production, several commissions on industry, mining, trade, and agriculture were set up, of which all but agriculture were grouped under the National Resources Commission, responsible for the development of natural resources in western China. Most of the new enterprises and organizations were undertaken by the government and were run by officials. This gave a number of high officials of the Kuomintang a personal stake in the key industries, a stake which they maintained after the war.

The measures undertaken to alleviate the economic pressure could not go very far. The longer the war lasted the greater the shortages became, and the rapid rise of prices created all the hardships of a serious inflation. The inflation accelerated a serious deterioration in morale and lowered standards of honesty and integrity among officials.

At the same time the government became alienated from the intellectual elite which had been a major source of strength for the Kuomintang. In the first years of the war the intellectuals moved inland with the government and were in the forefront in maintaining the spirit of resistance. The economic difficulties were especially hard on the faculty and students of the universities who were dependent on shrinking salaries and government rice allowances. The whole intellectual group also became increasingly critical of the government's internal policy. The government's policy of containing the Communist opposition was accompanied by a growing censorship of all critical attitudes towards the government. When the police and the Kuomintang Youth Corps, founded by Chiang Kai-shek in 1938, used repressive measures on the campuses to intimidate opposition, the former cooperation was replaced by an increasing hostility between the government and large sections of the academic and literary world. Out of these wartime developments began the alienation of the business groups and intellectuals from the Kuomintang.

The worse the general situation became, the more Chiang Kai-shek tried to draw all authority into his own hands. At the outset of the war he had established a Supreme Military Council which not only directed all military affairs but also concerned itself with industrial planning and administrative details. Through this Council Chiang Kai-shek personally interfered in all matters of policy and military strategy. This led to conflicts and confusion in the executive agencies as well as in the military conduct of the war. Chiang Kai-shek gave direct orders to units engaged in battle which were often in contradiction to those of the commanders in charge. After many of the best trained officers and troops had been sacrificed in the first years of the war, army organization deteriorated rapidly. There was little time for training, and large numbers of raw recruits were constantly thrown into battle with tremendous sacrifice of life. The conscription of these recruits was badly organized and corrupt, and large numbers deserted or perished of malnutrition or disease on the way to their units. There was little medical care. In the military as in the civil administration the effectiveness of the government declined.

Growth of Communist Power

While the strength and morale on the side of the government declined, the Communists gained not only territory but also organizational strength during the later war years. In Yenan, which had become the Communist capital in December 1937, Mao Tse-tung built up a disciplined party organization loyal to him personally. He himself used the first years in Yenan to get thoroughly acquainted with the writings of Lenin and Stalin and became the chief interpreter of the Stalinist doctrine in China. In 1939 he wrote an interpretation of the Chinese situation which was published in January 1940, under the title of *On the New Democracy*. This adaptation of Stalinist doctrine to the Chinese situation did not contribute any new theoretical concepts. But it was claimed to be a new contribution to "Marxist-Leninist theory" and to provide a special theoretical interpretation of "the historic peculiarities of the Chinese revolution." In this way Mao assumed the role of the leading theorist among the Chinese Communists, a necessary prerequisite for dictatorial authority. Mao's writings, which never departed from the Stalinist line, also established him as the accepted interpreter of Moscow's doctrines and strategy in China. Such a position in the Communist hierarchy, established at the time of the Soviet Union's greatest weakness, freed Mao from dependence on the orders of Comintern agents, so long as he did not depart from the international line established in Moscow. Mao's assertion of his authority as the source and arbiter of all doctrine in China marked his consolidation of power over the Chinese Communist party.

The theoretical basis of the "New Democracy" was the Stalinist theory that the "bourgeois-democratic" revolution and the succeeding "socialist" revolution could be merged. China was still in the "bourgeois-democratic" stage, but this "bourgeois-democratic" revolution in China was taking place within the orbit of a "proletarian-socialist" revolution of the world. It was therefore led by the "joint dictatorship of all revolutionary classes." Such a joint revolution was the "transitional form of the state in the revolutionary colonies and semi-colonies." This joint revolution was to take into consideration the peasants who were "80 per cent of the Chinese population." Mao used a Stalin quotation: "the question of the colonies and semi-colonies is in essence a peasant question," and then continued: "that is to say, the Chinese revolution is in essence a revolution of the peasantry." Mao went on to claim that "the second [largest] section of the Chinese population consists of workers" who according to him made up "several millions of industrial workers." These workers "are the leaders of the revolution and have the highest revolutionary spirit," a claim which gave the Communist party as the vanguard of the workers its leading role in this joint revolution. "The culture" of the New Democracy was claimed to be "scientific" and "should serve the toiling masses of the workers and peasants" who, it was claimed, together "represent more than 90 per cent of the whole population." Thus, by a stroke of the pen Mao increased the number of workers from "several millions" to over 10 per cent of the population, or over 50 million. The "culture paves the way for it [the revolution] by spreading revolutionary thought." The Communist party, in other words, claimed to have complete authority over "culture" because the party represented the workers, who were the leaders of the revolution. It was therefore the task of the party to be the sole interpreter of ideology, the supreme arbiter of all thought and action.

On the New Democracy was one of the most important of the theoretical statements made by the Chinese Communist party and Mao Tse-tung. It provided the theoretical justification for the claims of the Communist party to leadership at this time in Chinese history. According to Communist doctrine China was classified as a feudal society, or as a feudal-bureaucratic society, which would mean that China must complete the capitalist stage before reaching the socialist stage. The New Democracy showed how the two stages, capitalist and socialist, could be merged under the leadership of the Communist party. As the capitalist stage had not yet been completed, it was implied that there would be a need for private enterprise in commerce and industry. The Communists suggested that this stage might continue for a long period in order to allay the fears of the businessmen and of the intellectuals, many of whom came to believe that the Communist aspects of the revolution were a matter for the remote future. The New Democracy called for a "joint dictatorship" of several revolutionary classes thus making room for all who were willing to work along with the Communists. Those classes which have awakened or were awakening included "the Chinese proletariat, peasantry, intelligentsia and other petty-bourgeois elements" whom Mao describes as "the main force on which the fate of China depends." In his economic program Mao called for the nationalization of big banks, big industry, and big business and for confiscation and distribution of the land of the big landlords. In outlining his proposals Mao was able to use the language of the Kuomintang on the subject of nationalization and that of Sun Yat-sen—"the tiller should own his land"—on the subject of landownership. Mao even claimed that his whole program was a reinterpretation of the Three People's Principles. All this was designed to make Communist leadership acceptable and to prepare the way for isolating Chiang Kai-shek and the Kuomintang. The New Democracy induced some of the middle parties to consider cooperation with the Communists and neutralized the opposition of many intellectuals, businessmen, and even Kuomintang members.

Mao Tse-tung assumed the authority to translate the doctrines of the New Democracy into political action and cloaked his personal dictatorial power by representing it as "scientific truth." Mao's claims to doctrinal authority and infallibility were further expressed in a statement *On Contradiction* which was published after the war but which was claimed to have been issued for inner party use in 1937. In this statement, Mao, following Stalin, reinterpreted dialectics as a mere clash between opposing forces in which the decision as to which issue was to be taken up at what time was left to Mao himself. Anyone who fought an issue at the wrong time or in the wrong way was a deviationist from the right line as determined by Mao Tse-tung. This assumption of theoretical infallibility within the framework of Stalinist political doctrine was used by Mao in the following years to tighten the discipline in the Chinese Communist party and to strengthen his personal leadership. In 1942 and 1943 there was a "Cheng-feng" or Party Reform Movement in which rightist and leftist "deviationists" within the party were purged or brought into line. Mao consolidated his authority not only by means of the purges but also through a program of intensive indoctrination of rapidly growing numbers of party members. The party grew from 40,000 members in 1937 to about 1,200,000 in 1945. The increase in the number of party members and in the population and territory under the control of the Chinese Communists, and the difficulties in communicating between one area and another, made it all the more essential that the party should be welded together into a well disciplined and well indoctrinated body. For the purposes of indoctrination Mao used the techniques of group discussion, criticism, and self-criticism, backed up by the threat of violence.

Mao emerged from the war as the undisputed leader of a greatly strengthened Communist party, a disciplined party of professional revolutionaries. He claimed to control about 90 million people and had an army of over half a million men. His power extended across the North China plain from the mountains of Shensi to the Shantung promontory, thus cutting off central China from overland access to Peking and Manchuria. Mao was in a position to exploit every conflict and difficulty in China for the conquest of power. Before the war was over the balance of military and political power had actually shifted to the side of the Communists. Japanese aggression had undermined the very foundations of the National Government, leaving behind it low morale, economic dislocation and misery, and tremendous problems of reconstruction.

5. THE CIVIL WAR

The Nationalist Program

The end of the war in the Far East in August, 1945, found the National Government exhausted by the long struggle and opposed by a Communist party which had grown in military and territorial strength. The National Government was in poor condition to undertake the two main tasks which now faced it—to deal with the Chinese Communists and to restore the economy of China. The real weakness of the National Government in

1945 lay in the inadequacies of the Kuomintang, the party which controlled it.

The National Government was at the height of its influence and power in 1937 when it led the nation in resistance to Japan. Chiang Kai-shek, the head of the government, was recognized as the only man who could unite the country in this resistance. Even the Communists, who had been driven by Chiang Kai-shek, their archenemy, into the poorer sections of the northwest, had had to accept him as the national leader. At Sian they used all their influence to protect his life and secure his liberation. When the war began, Chiang was at the height of his power and prestige, but his consolidation of power had been at the expense of the development of the Kuomintang, which had made his career possible. Chiang Kai-shek's domination of the party eliminated all competition for leadership and helped to subordinate the growth of political institutions to that of military strength.

In the revolutionary years the Kuomintang had represented most of the articulate nationalism of China and in 1937 had no serious rival. It was not a mass party and had never pretended to be one; it drew its support from businessmen, intellectuals, and soldiers, and subscribed to the view that government should be in the hands of the expert elite.

The war with Japan had an important impact on the social basis of the Kuomintang. The influence of businessmen and intellectuals on the central government was undermined by economic dislocation, by the complete economic dependence of the intellectuals on government subsidies, and by the pre-eminence of military considerations. Leadership passed more and more into the hands of Chiang Kai-shek and a very small group of men around him. The change in the outlook of the Kuomintang was clearly shown in Chiang Kai-shek's book, *China's Destiny*, published in March, 1943. It was written during the time of the greatest isolation of China and in a period when the fortunes of war looked blacker than ever before. To some extent it was an effort to draw spiritual consolation and strength from the greatness of China's past. It blamed the misfortunes of China during the past hundred years on the foreign powers and rejoiced in the recent abrogation of the unequal treaties. In January, 1943, the American and British governments concluded treaties with the National Government renouncing extraterritoriality and surrendering the concessions and settlements. These gestures were meant to strengthen Chinese morale in the most critical years of the war. Chiang Kai-shek regarded the end of the unequal treaties as a turning point in the Chinese Revolution.

Under the oppression of the unequal treaties, the people fell into decadent habits and evil practices in their daily life. Each person took his own selfish interests as the basis for determining right or wrong; his selfish desires as a basis for determining good or evil. As a result, depraved and frivolous persons attained power in the villages, and scheming citizens pursued their lawless way in the towns and cities, sacrificing public welfare and other people's happiness for their own selfish ends. Furthermore, literary theories and political writings were used to conceal, or even to justify the evils of this way of life. These writings glorified selfish desires and the quest for profit in order to incite social struggle. The tradition of emulating the sages, worshipping the heroes, and following the precepts of our forefathers not only tended to perish but was despised by the people. They even praised foreign figures and scorned the history of their own country. Confidence in the state declined, and the self-confidence of the people lost its center of gravity. As a consequence, the nation became like a pan of loose sand, and the state fell into disintegration and disunity; the people failing to realize that when the nation and the state are in danger of dismemberment, there is nothing that the individual can depend upon for his own existence.

The ancient sages said: "Propriety, righteousness, modesty, and honor are the four pillars of the state. If the four pillars are not strong, the state will perish." When we think and speak of the future, must we not tremble? Must we not be ashamed and disturbed? [12]

To Chiang Kai-shek the foreign concessions were the source of many evils such as prostitution, narcotics, gambling, thieving and banditry; they undermined the old traditional ethics of human relations, and imposed a stranglehold on China's economy. Hence the degeneration of the state and the decline of the nation.

China's Destiny bitterly attacked those Chinese who accepted foreign theories because they facilitated the cultural imperialism of the powers and assisted in the decay and ruin of Chinese civilization. Chiang Kai-shek's attack on the Chinese intellectuals was directed as much against liberalism as against Communism; in fact it included all foreign theories. For him

Those that admired Westernization abandoned China's own culture in favor of allegiance to foreign theories. Those that upheld the national culture reverted to an isolationist chauvinism. The scholars were careless and irresponsible in their lectures, uncritically echoing the popular trend in order to court favor with the people. [13]

Chiang castigated the irresponsibility and shallowness of the scholars of China, whom he held responsible for the insuperable difficulties in the way of reforming social and political customs.

Now that the unequal treaties were abolished the reconstruction of China could begin. Chiang Kai-shek outlined a program for reconstruction in *China's Destiny*. First there must be psychological reconstruction, which was to be based on the development of an "independent ideology" emphasizing China's ancient culture and the "cultivation of genuinely scientific knowledge." This task was to be carried out by the middle and primary school teachers who were advised to "bury themselves in hard work and devote themselves to cultivating the abilities of their students; . . . refrain from seeking fame, social reputation and lofty careers." Second, there must be ethical reconstruction. Here the ethics of the past, filial piety, loyalty, and obedience were stressed. The new ethics were to be based on the supremacy of the state and nation. Third, there was social reconstruction which was to be based on the New Life Movement. The basis of local self-government was to be the ancient organization of the state which began with the relation of the individual to the family, progressed from the family to the clan, from the clan to the *pao-chia*, then to the village community, and from there to the

[12] Chiang Kai-shek, *China's Destiny* (New York, 1947), p. 90.
[13] *Ibid.*, p. 203.

counties and provinces, all being held together by mutual assistance and joint responsibility. This system, which went to pieces during the Ch'ing dynasty, must be reconstructed. Fourth, there was political reconstruction, many of the tasks of which Chiang claimed to have accomplished since coming into power. But he pointed out that "China's democratic system will certainly not be patterned on the nineteenth-century theories of individualism and class-consciousness of Europe and America." Lastly, there was economic reconstruction which was to follow the lines of Sun Yat-sen's *Industrial Plan*. This program called for an industrialized economy, and for the equalization of land rights and the restriction of private capital. "We must adopt a planned economy" and eventually transform all "capital into state capital." Economic reconstruction, it was expected, would take from thirty to fifty years.

China's Destiny was published two years after *On the New Democracy* to which it was in many ways an answer. The Kuomintang, like the Communist party, had increased its membership during the war years and *China's Destiny* was used in party schools and institutes to indoctrinate the new members. It is clear that the outlook of *China's Destiny* was utterly at variance with the intellectual climate of the prewar years and that it would antagonize the Western-minded intellectuals who were so severely castigated. Nor did the book hold much promise for the Chinese businessmen of the former treaty ports who were scolded for their profit seeking and Western style of life and were asked to envisage a planned economy and the restriction of private capital. Nor was there any message in *China's Destiny* which could capture the imagination of China's youth, which was asked to live a life of frugality and obedience. Mao Tse-tung, in contrast, soft-pedaled the ultimate intentions of the Communists and opened the door for cooperation with businessmen and intellectuals by promising them business opportunity and responsibility. The point of view of *China's Destiny* was that of a military man who was moved by an intense and narrow nationalism, who assumed that he would have military control of the situation and wanted to restore social and political stability according to a very conservative pattern. He neither understood nor sympathized with the intellectual ferment of modern China and thereby lost many potential allies in his struggle against the Communists. The point of view of *On the New Democracy* was that of a professional revolutionary who was drawing up a program for the exploitation of social discontents and the manipulation of social classes.

When the National Government returned to Nanking and reoccupied the coastal cities at the close of the war, it was a different government from that which had retreated before the Japanese armies in 1937. It had changed in outlook, in composition, and in the social basis of its support. For the time being the potential conflicts between the government and those upon whom it formerly counted for support were hidden behind the general jubilation over the victory, and Chiang Kai-shek's prestige was high because he had been proven right in his decision to resist to the bitter end. He had also been given international prestige; China was a founding member of the United Nations and a member of the Security Council. Nor was the outlook for the economic recovery of China necessarily gloomy in spite of the destruction and dislocation caused by the war.

The financial problems of the government were many but did not seem insoluble. In Chungking the war had been financed largely by printing paper money, a policy which had resulted in serious inflation; but when the war ended the government could draw upon the revenue of the rich and productive coastal areas and could also expect the revenue of Manchuria and Formosa, which had been assigned to it by the Cairo Declaration. Its foreign exchange position was extraordinarily strong. The government's holdings in gold and U. S. dollar exchange were estimated to amount to over U. S. $900,000,000, due largely to the accumulation of unspent American credits and payments for American military expenses in China. There were also very substantial private Chinese holdings in foreign currencies.

The problem of restoring production, especially for export, had to be faced, but the level of production in most of the Japanese-occupied area was as high as before the war, and the government could count on immediate technical and financial assistance from abroad. There had been little fighting in many parts of China during the last years of the war, and the Japanese, for their own purposes, had encouraged and organized production. They were successful in increasing the production of coal and iron, but the electric power supply had gone down because of wartime destruction. Both cotton production and the cotton textile industry had declined considerably. Food production in many areas was up to prewar levels, but as China had been a net importer of food for many years, immediate relief was necessary, especially in the cities, because of the disruption of communications. UNRRA (United Nations Relief and Rehabilitation Administration), largely supported by American funds, poured food into China at the close of hostilities and assisted in the re-establishment of power stations, means of communication, and industrial installations and in the rehabilitation of agriculture. The United States contribution to China through UNRRA was U. S. $474,000,-000, out of a total contribution of over $650,000,000. Whatever the prospects for recovery from the devastation of the war might have been, they were shattered by the grave weaknesses within the National Government itself and the formidable position of the Chinese Communists.

The strategic importance of the Communist position was that it barred the government from full control of North China and blocked the way to Manchuria. If the government were to occupy Manchuria it would divide its forces and extend its lines of communication dangerously far into Communist-controlled territory. Generals Wedemeyer and Marshall both advised against this course. On the other hand, to refrain from the attempt to occupy Manchuria would be to surrender the most valuable industrial area in China to the Communists without a fight. Faced with this difficult choice, the government decided to occupy Manchuria. From that time on every move in the struggle with the Communists was affected by this fateful decision.

The PCC Agreements

The sudden collapse of the Japanese forces was the signal for an immediate struggle between the Nationalists and Communists for control of the territory which the Japanese armies now were to surrender. The Communists in North China were much closer than the Nationalists to the territory which the Japanese had to return to Chinese control. The Communists held that the Japanese should surrender to the nearest Chinese troops, a plan which would have given the Communists most of North China. The government held that the Japanese were to surrender only to Nationalist troops, and it ordered them to hold their positions until its troops arrived. Owing to American assistance the National Government was able, with some exceptions, to enforce this rule. American airplanes and ships transported Chinese Nationalist armies from west central China to the coastal cities of the Yangtze area and north to Tientsin and Peking to take over these main centers. Tientsin was taken over temporarily by American Marines until Nationalist troops arrived.

Some awkward situations developed, however, in which Japanese forces had to fight off Communist attacks in order to hold their positions and surrender to the Nationalists. In preparation for the surrender the Japanese pulled their troops into the main cities, leaving the countryside unoccupied. When the Nationalist troops arrived and fanned out from the cities, there was a race for territory with the Communists. Each tried to occupy and hold the areas evacuated by the Japanese. In several places the conflict broke into open fighting which threatened to spread into civil war.

While these military developments were taking place, negotiations were being carried on for a political solution of the conflict. Chiang Kai-shek had promised several times that a solution would be reached "by political means." These negotiations had begun in 1944 when the growing hostility between the Nationalist and Communist forces became a concern of the American government, which was worried about its harmful effect on the Chinese military effort in the war against Japan. The American government offered to assist in the negotiations and for this purpose sent General Hurley as special ambassador to Chungking in September 1944. In a statement of November 1944, the Communists indicated that they did not wish to join the National Government but wanted a new coalition government, to be formed by all political parties including the Kuomintang, the Communists, and other political groups. They were willing to submit their armies and political organization to the control of such a government. The Nationalists, distrustful of this Communist proposal, were willing to incorporate the Communist organization in the existing National Government and accept Communist members into the National Military Council. These Nationalist counterproposals were rejected by the Communists who refused to accept a modification of the existing government controlled by the Kuomintang and insisted on a coalition government. The Communist proposal was unacceptable to Chiang Kai-shek. Chiang stated that the existing political parties, including the Kuomintang, constituted less than two per cent of the Chinese people, and that therefore it would not be in the best interest of China to turn the government over to the control of any political group or coalition of groups. He called for a democratic constitution adopted by a convention in which all the people, not merely the organized political minorities, would participate.

In the negotiations the National Government indicated its willingness to "invite the representatives of the Kuomintang and other parties, and some non-partisan leaders to a consultative meeting." This Political Consultative Conference was to discuss the establishment of a constitutional government as well as military unification and the participation of members of parties other than the Kuomintang in the National Government. Though the Communists at first accepted this invitation to a Political Consultative Conference they broke off negotiations in March 1945, when Chiang Kai-shek made it clear that while the government was willing to invite others, including the Communists, to participate in the government, there was no question of the "relinquishment by the Kuomintang of its power of ultimate decision and final responsibility until the convocation of the People's Congress (for the establishment of a new constitution)." Negotiations were resumed in June with the help of the middle parties. In these negotiations the Communists came closer to accepting a limited participation in the National Government, on the basis of Chiang's promise of a constitutional government in which all parties would participate. Both sides now agreed on the calling of a Political Consultative Conference. This modification of the Communist position came after the conclusion of the Sino-Russian Treaty in August, 1945, in which the Russian government promised to deal only with the Chinese National Government.

The sudden Japanese collapse and the end of the war came before the negotiations had led to an agreement. While the race for territory was on, the Communists delayed their final acceptance of participation in the planned conference. The conference finally met in Chungking in January 1946, soon after the arrival of General Marshall, who had been sent by President Truman on a special mission to assist in the negotiations to prevent civil war. He participated in the discussions for a military settlement. The Political Consultative Conference led to the three major military and political agreements of January 10, January 31, and February 20, 1946, in which the policy previously outlined by Chiang Kai-shek was accepted. The agreements seemed to provide a possible political settlement in China. The first agreement was for a military truce. Both sides were to remain in the area which their troops had occupied by that time. Local clashes and further struggle over territory were to be prevented by truce teams of three men each, consisting of a Nationalist, a Communist, and a neutral American officer, which were to be sent to the areas of fighting. This plan was at first fully successful and temporarily ended the conflict.

On the basis of this military truce a second agreement was reached which included a short-range and a long-range political solution. The short-range solution provided for a division of territory according to which each faction—the government and the Communists—would remain in control of the territory it held. Negotiations continued over the question of the governors and vice-governors in the provinces militarily divided between Communist and Nationalist forces. In addition to this territorial settlement there was introduced into the National Government a new State Council, in which all political groups were to be represented. Under the Kuomintang constitution, the State Council had only a nominal function but now it was to become the key policy-making body. It was to be composed of twenty Kuomintang members and twenty representatives of the middle parties, the independents, and the Communists. The Communists would thus be able to make their wishes felt in central government decisions, but as the independents and some of the middle parties' representatives were closely allied with the government, the government could still count on a safe majority in this State Council.

The long-range part of the agreement embodied new constitutional concepts. In its plan for what it called the third, or the "democratic," stage of the revolution, the Kuomintang had provided for a National Assembly which would be elected every three years and would meet only once to elect the members of the government. This system was replaced in the PCC agreement by a Western-type parliamentary system. Instead of the National Assembly, there was to be an elected legislature which was to remain in session and have control over a cabinet responsible to and dependent on majority support of the legislature. Such a system, if it could have been realized, might have provided a middle way between the alternatives of Communist dictatorship and one-party government by the Kuomintang.

The third agreement, dependent on this political settlement, provided for a military reorganization in which the Communist army was eventually to be integrated into a Chinese national army. The agreement determined the actual strength and distribution of existing units of government and Communist forces. In time these forces were to be reorganized with assistance from the United States in training and equipment. As a part of this agreement, American military missions were sent to the troops of the National Government and for a short time to the Communist troops as well. These three agreements formed a unified whole, and if any part were violated, the whole structure would collapse.

Disagreements soon emerged about various aspects of the settlement. No final understanding was reached, for instance, on the division of provincial authority in the areas contested between the Communists and Nationalists. Nor was any agreement reached on the Communist demand for fourteen representatives in the State Council, which number would have given them a veto power. But the greatest problem arose over control of Manchuria, which was included in the agreement on the distribution of military forces but not in the truce arrangements. The race for Manchuria was soon to begin.

When the war ended, Manchuria was in the hands of the Russian army which had defeated the Japanese forces there in the last days of the war. The number of Nationalist and Communist troops to be stationed in Manchuria was specified in the military settlement, but these units were not yet there. The Communist forces immediately prepared overland moves into Manchuria, and since their forces were so close they got there first and with much stronger units than the PCC agreement had specified. They began immediately to organize local forces in Manchuria with the toleration of the Russians. When the government armies were ready to move, the Russian occupation forces denied them the use of Dairen and its railway communications, and permitted the harbor of Yingkou to fall into Chinese Communist hands. Government troops had to fight their way into Manchuria where the fighting continued. The Soviet Union respected its agreements and surrendered the main cities and railroad lines to Nationalist forces but permitted the Chinese Communists to obtain the arms and equipment surrendered by the Japanese, thus providing them with a vast stock of artillery and heavy equipment. With this equipment the Communists were able to change from small-scale guerrilla warfare to field battles in which they could match the artillery strength of the Nationalist armies, if not their air force.

On the political front, the right wing of the Kuomintang had from the beginning opposed any settlement with the Communists and had disregarded the PCC agreements. This group succeeded in bringing about a decision of the Central Executive Committee of the Kuomintang, disavowing the PCC agreements to which the Kuomintang negotiators and Chiang Kai-shek had bound themselves. This action gave the Communists the opportunity to blame the government for abrogating the agreements. Negotiations continued during the summer of 1946 with the assistance of the American special ambassador, General Marshall. The negotiations on local administration broke down during the summer over the Communist demand for participation in the provincial government of Kiangsu. General Marshall went home in January 1947. The tensions sharpened until the open break came with the expulsion of the Communist delegation from Nanking in February 1947, and full scale civil war was resumed.

Economic and Political Setbacks

The civil war began at a time when the position of the National Government had considerably deteriorated. Most of the advantages enjoyed by the government in 1945 had been dissipated by 1947. The financial reserves in foreign exchange had been largely spent without having brought about any economic improvement, and instead of economic reconstruction there had been further destruction. Inflation had reached dangerous proportions and the national budget was hopelessly unbalanced. The government was losing the confidence of businessmen, professional classes, and intellectuals. According to American observers Nationalist China was suffering from a general decline in morale, widespread corruption, and governmental waste. These conditions were also present in the Nationalist army upon which the power of the government rested.

Not all of these difficulties were of the National Government's own making. It was part of Communist policy to create as many difficulties as possible for the National Government. The Communists deliberately destroyed communications, especially railroads, and sabotaged mining equipment. They expected to profit from economic stagnation or chaos. In Manchuria the first blow was struck by the Russians, who systematically looted Manchurian industry, removing valuable equipment to the Soviet Union and leaving behind a crippled economy. What Chiang Kai-shek had expected to be an asset was now a liability. The second blow was struck by the Chinese Communists who moved their men into Manchuria, where they sabotaged communications and contested Nationalist control.

The conflict with the Communists also forced the government to maintain large armies and to make large military expenditures. To meet these expenses the government issued more paper money, inflating the currency to such an extent that by the beginning of 1947 the exchange rate between Chinese national currency and U. S. dollars on the open market was over 7,000 to one. From then on it rapidly got out of hand. In February, when the exchange had risen to 18,000 to one, the government took drastic police action against speculators but without lasting effect. By August the open market rate of the U. S. dollar was 45,000 and it continued to rise rapidly.

The impact of inflation was felt in many different ways. Inflation seriously handicapped legitimate business and brought about a tremendous boom in speculation. Goods and raw materials were used for speculation rather than put into production, a process which in turn accelerated the course of inflation. Perhaps the most devastating effect of inflation in the long run was that it led directly to widespread corruption. The purchasing power of fixed salaries was so far behind the devaluation of the currency that most officials could not survive if they were honest. The hardest hit were the lower officials, the intellectuals, and the soldiers, who had no way of manipulating funds and depended on declining incomes.

The financial policies of the government contributed to the process of inflation. The government received only part of the tax revenue because of the corruption and speculative activities of the tax officials. Government expenditures remained entirely uncontrolled and were met largely through the printing of paper money. There was no fixed budget, and once inflation got under way there was no way of keeping accounts. The military, who handled most of the funds, were particularly wasteful in their use, partly because there was no competent administrative organization in the army. According to American observers, the National Government entered into full-scale civil war without any fiscal program adequate to the situation and American aid was not effectively used.

The lack of confidence in the government brought about by the inflation and economic chaos was aggravated by the government's attitude towards the business community. After the government's return to Nanking the officials who had run the wartime economy in Chungking soon extended their economic controls to the liberated cities. The government immediately took over all the industrial property formerly owned by the Japanese and ran the industries as state enterprises. In this way the government became a powerful competitor to private enterprise. The Chinese industrialists were opposed to this privileged competition and many were particularly resentful because some of the Japanese property which was seized by the government had originally been Chinese-owned. Chinese industrialists who had remained in cities such as Shanghai and Tientsin had had to get along with the Japanese and were therefore open to the stigma of being looked upon as collaborationists. This put them at a disadvantage in protesting government competition.

The businessmen were at an even greater disadvantage because they no longer possessed the protection from official pressures and exploitation which the treaty ports had provided. In the former treaty ports, now under Chinese administration, private business could operate only on terms established by government officials. It was widely believed that large government monopolies were under the control of leading officials such as T. V. Soong and H. H. Kung and their families. The shift of economic power from private industry and business to the monopolies was facilitated by the take-over of all the Japanese-owned industrial enterprises by the government. In this way, for instance, the National Economic Reconstruction Commission, under the direction of T. V. Soong, took over the cotton mills formerly owned by the Japanese in Shanghai and Tientsin. This gave T. V. Soong's organization control of the greater part of China's most important consumer industry. Since the government controlled export and import licenses and the allocation of raw materials and credit, the National Economic Reconstruction Commission offered serious competition to the remaining private Chinese mill owners. Private industrialists protested against this monopoly and suggested the resale of mills to private owners, but no practical plan was suggested by the government. The competition of official monopolies with private enterprise was all the more serious as the government received the full benefit of the foreign assistance which was given to China after the war through American loans and through UNRRA.

UNRRA cooperated with a Chinese National Relief and Rehabilitation Administration (CNRRA). UNRRA accepted the Chinese government's contention that support should be given partly through the delivery of raw materials such as cotton, tobacco, and coal, and that these commodities should be sold on the open market, the proceeds to be used for the expenses of the Chinese relief organizations and in part for the relief itself. In this way the government could use its official power in the allocation of raw materials to favor officially-controlled enterprises. The direct American support of $400,000,000, voted by Congress in April 1948, was also managed by the Chinese government. American aid, in effect, assisted the government in its competition with private industry and thus helped to alienate the businessmen, who had formerly supported the Kuomintang.

The intellectuals, already embittered by Chiang's attacks on them in *China's Destiny*, resented the government's disregard for them. Many of them suffered badly from the inflation and were opposed to a continuation of the civil war. A considerable section of this group was in favor of the compromise represented by the PCC agreements. As the civil war developed, the government attacked those intellectuals who were in favor of compromise with the Communists and expressed opposition to the policy of the regime. In 1947 these attacks took the form of military and police actions on the campuses of many of the leading Chinese universities. There was a large-scale dismissal of faculty members, and some faculty members and students were arrested. On some occasions the police invaded the campus to make arrests and in one such incident protesting students were killed. Two outstanding professors were assassinated. The result was a fear of police terror which turned many Chinese intellectuals away from the Kuomintang and made some of them at least temporarily willing to accept any solution—even the Communist—in preference to what they regarded as the corruption, the inefficiency, and the terror of the National Government.

Political Reforms

To counteract the loss of popular support and to reassure its American friends who pressed for reforms, the National Government introduced a constitutional change which took effect after the final break with the Communists. In November 1946, a National Convention was called at Nanking. Over 2,000 representatives were invited. The Kuomintang and some of the middle parties participated, but others of the middle parties as well as the Communists, to whom seats had been allocated, refused to attend. Under the firm leadership of Chiang Kai-shek the National Convention adopted a constitution broadly resembling the principles agreed upon by the PCC. This constitution, which was to go into effect in December, 1947, provided for a parliamentary system with a cabinet responsible to a legislature. The legislature was to be directly elected, but its size—over 700 representatives—made it a more unwieldy body than had been provided for in the original PCC agreement. In any case parliamentary responsibility was reserved for the future, and far-reaching special powers were given President Chiang in the emergency situation.

The acceptance of this constitution, like the acceptance of the constitutional principles in the PCC agreement, had been in the main the work of the leader of the Social Democratic party, Dr. Carsun Chang, who had hoped to overcome party dictatorship and military rivalry, as well as the Communist threat, through the introduction of a Western parliamentary system. Without changing the terminology of Sun Yat-sen's program, he had succeeded in bringing about the formal acceptance of a democratic parliamentary system very different from the rule by experts which Sun Yat-sen had had in mind and which had remained the ideal of the Kuomintang. The modified form of the plan as accepted by the National Convention, however, did not prepare the way for an effective representative system. Two elections were held, one for a National Assembly, which still had the function of electing the president and vice president, and one for a parliament. These elections, however, were prearranged and manipulated and had very little to do with an actual expression of the popular opinion of the large mass of the people. In the election for parliament, for instance, seats had been assigned beforehand to members of the cooperating middle parties who possessed no organization in the provinces capable of competing with the Kuomintang. When, in spite of these political agreements, the local Kuomintang candidates who were expected to give up their candidacies in favor of middle party candidates refused to do so and had themselves "elected," a conflict arose within the Kuomintang. The party decided in favor of the middle party candidates, whereupon the elected candidates of the Kuomintang started a protest march to Nanking and had to be pacified. But in spite of this tragicomic procedure, the elections gave members of the Kuomintang the opportunity to resist the discipline of the until then all-powerful leadership of the party machine. Dissatisfaction with the Kuomintang leaders came into the open in the battle for the election of the vice president. Chiang Kai-shek was elected president without any difficulties, but after a bitter fight the opposition elected as vice president the Kwangsi general, Li Tsung-jen, over Sun Fo, the candidate of Chiang Kai-shek and the right-wing Kuomintang.

A new government was set up in accordance with the constitution. Two of the middle parties participated in the government, the Youth party, and the Social Democratic party, which made their cooperation dependent on the acceptance of the constitutional system. The other middle parties, combined in the "Democratic League," went over to the Communists. As a result the "Democratic League" was officially outlawed. In spite of the formal acceptance of the new constitutional procedures, the government remained in the hands of Chiang Kai-shek, who continued to control the armed forces and to exercise the emergency powers provided by the constitution.

Defeat of the Nationalist Armies

The National Government embarked on full-scale conflict with the Communists in 1947 in high confidence. In view of the lack of any comprehensive financial and economic program with which to back up the armies and of the contraction of its political support, this confidence was misplaced. Most serious of all were the weaknesses in the army itself. American military observers deplored the inefficiencies of the army administration, the inadequacy of supply, the poor quality of many of the highest officers, and the confusion in the chain of command. Chiang Kai-shek in particular was accused of choosing his commanders more for their loyalty than for their ability, of shifting commanders in the midst of battles and campaigns, and of interfering directly in military operations. All these factors had their effect on the morale of both officers and men.

The civil war was primarily a military conflict; it was decided by strategy and generalship in a few major battles. The attitudes of the Chinese people were important but not decisive. In spite of its economic and political weaknesses the government had the men and the arms with which to hold the Communists at bay if they had been wisely used. From the very beginning the Nationalists were burdened with a mistaken strategic concept. The general approach was to take and to hold as many key cities as possible rather than to seek out the Communist forces and destroy them. This meant attempting too much with too little. The original decision to move into Manchuria, strongly opposed by all American advisers, was beyond the capacity of the Nationalist forces, but any chance of success that it might have had was dissipated by inept generalship, including that of Chiang Kai-shek. Manchuria became the decisive theater of the war, for it was here that Chiang's best armies, trained and equipped by the United States during the closing years of the war, were committed. Nationalist troops, after fighting their way into Manchuria occupied the cities of Mukden, Changchun, and Kirin and attempted to hold the railroad lines that connected them in a countryside controlled by the Communists. The Nationalists fought a stationary war while the Communists used the time to build up their strength with the Japanese equipment turned over to them by the Russians. The Communists had two years in which to train their armies while Nationalist troops garrisoned the cities. These troops were entirely dependent on the railroad line for their supplies. As the Nationalists could not garrison the whole line sufficiently, the Communists succeeded in cutting the line of supply to the Nationalist armies stationed in the cities. From the summer of 1948 on, the garrisons in Mukden and other cities had to depend on an air lift for their military supply. As the cities were cut off from the Communist-held countryside, the garrisons and even the civilian population had no food supply. To bring in all the food in addition to military supplies was far beyond the capacity of the Chinese air force. The Nationalist forces were permitted neither to attack nor to retreat. The position of the government garrisons eventually became untenable, but in his attempt to hold on to Manchuria, Chiang Kai-shek delayed all withdrawals until it was too late. Changchun was given up early in the summer of 1948 and Kirin shortly thereafter with the loss of a considerable part of the garrison. When in November, 1948, the order was finally given for the evacuation of Mukden, practically the whole garrison and all its American equipment fell into the hands of the Chinese Communists. As this had been the strongest Nationalist force in the whole north, it was a military disaster of the first order and prepared the fall of all China to the Communists.

North China could no longer be defended. General Fu Tso-yi, a military commander in the northwest who did not belong to the Kuomintang inner group, did not receive the equipment and funds for which he had asked and made an agreement with the Communists for the surrender of Peking. The National Government attempted to stem the tide of the Communist forces that moved down to central China by concentrating most of its remaining armies at Hsüchou. In the battle of Hsüchou, December 1948, in which each side concentrated more than a million men, the government was still superior in equipment and also had the advantage of an air force. But the superiority of the Communist strategy, which was one of rapid maneuver and flank attack, as against the government strategy of fixed position in cities, was demonstrated in an amazingly rapid rout and annihilation of the large mass of government forces. With the destruction of the government armies at Hsüchou and the loss of their equipment to the Communists, the Nationalist position seemed hopeless.

Yielding to the criticism of his catastrophic failure and to the demands for negotiations, Chiang Kai-shek retired from the presidency in January, 1949. Vice-President Li Tsung-jen took over as acting president. A three months' lull in the fighting was used for negotiations, during which the Communists regrouped their forces for the move south, while the government prepared the defense of the Yangtze line. In the negotiations the Communists demanded practical surrender by the government and emphasized their request by listing as war criminals all the main figures on the government side. While the negotiators sent north by the government remained in Peking and eventually went over to the Communists, the latter renewed their attack in April, 1949, breaching the government's Yangtze line without difficulty and spreading southward to Canton and westward into Szechwan where the last refuge of the government on the mainland was abandoned in December, 1949. Chiang Kai-shek flew to Formosa where he had been preceded by members of the government and many of his troops.

During the last months of fighting on the mainland the direction of affairs was ostensibly in the hands of Acting President Li Tsung-jen. General Li was a political moderate who had for some time been urging military and political reforms without success and was now willing to negotiate with the Communists in order to gain time. But Li Tsung-jen was in no position to continue resistance on the mainland because he was not in full control of the Nationalist armies and the national treasury. He could expect obedience only from the Kwangsi troops and was therefore not able to organize a sound defense of China south of the Yangtze River. Many of the Nationalist troops did not follow Li Tsung-jen's orders but embarked instead for Formosa. Acting President Li's difficulties were further aggravated by the fact that Chiang had sent to Formosa the remaining financial reserves of U. S. $300 million and Li was unable to pay his own armies which were putting up a successful defense of Szechwan and were expected to defend their native province of Kwangsi. In this way all hope of holding a position on the mainland was shattered and resistance collapsed. Chiang Kai-shek thus retained actual power in his own hands and resumed the presidency on Formosa in March, 1950, while Li Tsung-jen, who considered himself betrayed by Chiang Kai-shek, went to the United States.

The National Government was not overthrown by a "popular revolution" or by the defection of the Chinese "people" as has been so often stated. The National Government had alienated important sections of the politically articulate minority—the intellectuals, students, professional classes, businessmen, and even officials—but very few of these turned to Communism. Many of them lost confidence in the ability of the government to handle the situation after the war and in their despondency and bitterness became indifferent to the outcome of the civil strife. Their neutralism was cultivated by the Communists who carefully concealed, in their public statements, the real nature of their intentions. This neutralism was sufficiently widespread to permit the Communists to take over the cities, the universities and schools, and the power and transportation facilities. The peasants were tired of war, of conscription and taxes, and had no reason to feel that the government was vitally interested in their welfare. But there were no peasant uprisings against the government although there were some against the Communists. To speak of the Communist triumph as a "popular revolution" is not only to misread the facts but also to misunderstand the nature of the Communist movement.

The victory of the Chinese Communists was a victory of military organization and strategy. The Communist armies, which differed radically from those of the Nationalists, were used as the main instrument in bringing about a social revolution and were organized along entirely new lines. The Communist military forces were divided into three main types. At the top was the regular army, organized into divisions and equipped with heavy arms. In the middle were the guerrilla forces which operated in a more restricted area and were used for mobile warfare. At the bottom were the militia organized on a local level and enlisted from the elements in the villages which had come to the top in the Communist-inspired social upheaval. The militia units controlled the villages and the movement of people from place to place; they were a recruiting ground for guerrilla forces, which in turn filled the ranks of the regular army. When the Communists took over an area they immediately imposed their new institutions. The militia and guerrilla forces were strong enough to control lines of communication and to release the regular army from garrison duties. The Communists, therefore, could make the most effective use of their regular armies while the Nationalists had to use their regular troops to garrison the areas they occupied and to protect their lines of communication. When the Nationalist troops had gone, political authority went with them. The superiority in numbers of the Nationalist troops over the regular Communist forces was therefore compensated for by guerrilla and militia units in the Communist military organization. The Communists succeeded, where the Nationalists had failed, in integrating their military organization with new political and social institutions.

Formosa

The National Government had assumed administrative authority over Formosa and the Pescadores immediately after the Japanese surrender. The legal transfer of sovereignty, as promised in the Cairo and Potsdam Declarations, was expected to take place at the time of the signing of a peace treaty. In 1952, when a peace treaty was concluded with Japan,

Japan formally relinquished sovereignty over Formosa but it was not transferred to the Republic of China. The United States had planned to administer Formosa until a peace treaty was signed, but when Formosa was
by-passed in favor of Okinawa as a staging area for the final assault on
Japan, the United States lost interest and the National Government took
over Formosa with American approval and assistance.

General Chen Yi was appointed "Administrator General and Concurrently Supreme Commander in Taiwan Province." The mainland
Chinese were welcomed as liberators by the Chinese people of Formosa who
were expecting to be incorporated into the Republic on the same basis as
all other Chinese. But in fact the people of Formosa were treated as a conquered people; all Japanese-owned enterprises were taken over by the National Government, and prominent Formosans were regarded as collaborators. Japanese enterprises, which included nearly all the economic life of
the island, were organized into government monopolies and staffed with
Chinese from the mainland. The wealth of Formosa was systematically
looted, production went down, and rice shortages soon appeared. It soon
became clear to the Formosans that a small number of Chinese officials were
to monopolize the economic life of the island and that they did not even
have the property rights which they had enjoyed under the Japanese. The
government neglected public services such as health and education. It announced that the new Chinese constitution would not apply to Formosa
until the end of 1949.

The resentment of the Formosans at their treatment led to a revolt in
February 1947. The police fired on an orderly demonstration which was
protesting the killing of a woman for hawking cigarettes on which the tobacco monopoly tax had not been paid. In retaliation the Formosans attacked mainland Chinese but ceased their violence on assurances from Chen
Yi that their demands for certain reforms would be met. In March, when reinforcements arrived from China, Chen Yi broke his agreement, and Formosans were massacred in many parts of the island. It is estimated that
10,000 Formosans were killed, including many of their leaders. After American diplomatic intervention Chiang Kai-shek recalled General Chen Yi and
made Formosa one of the thirty-five provinces of China, and the "pacification" was declared to be at an end. The Formosans were given a share in the
administration of the province, and an effort was made to repair the damage
which had been done. After a short interval during which private enterprise
was given a little encouragement and some steps were taken towards reconciliation, the situation changed again. In 1948 Chiang Kai-shek began to
prepare for eventual retreat to Formosa and sent General Ch'en Ch'eng to
the island to take over control. General Ch'en Ch'eng re-established martial
law and ordered further arrests and executions to eliminate Communist
sympathizers.

The Government of the Republic of China began to function on Formosa in December 1949. In spite of the rapid collapse on the mainland, close
to one million civilians and an army of over half a million troops retreated to

Formosa. By 1954 the total population on the island, which is about the size of the state of Maryland, was well over eight million. Many important officials, both civil and military, had not come to Formosa, either because they deserted to the Communists, or were opposed to Chiang Kai-shek. Of the 3,000 representatives of the National Assembly some 1,200 came to Formosa. More than ever before, Chiang Kai-shek came to dominate the government and the party. He was at the same time president, head of the Kuomintang, and commander-in-chief of the armed forces. He controlled the finances and placed his own men, including his son Chiang Ching-kuo, in charge of various branches of the secret police. One of his first steps was to streamline the party organization by abolishing the Central Executive Committee for which he substituted a Central Reform Committee of sixteen high-ranking party members and charged it with the tasks of reorganizing the party and reformulating its doctrine. One aspect of this work in which Chiang himself collaborated was the re-examination of the reasons for defeat. From this study there emerged several conclusions which had a direct bearing on the program of the government. The Kuomintang was particularly impressed with the charge that it had not paid attention to the welfare of the people, that it had not prevented inflation with all its fatal consequences, that officials and others had been corrupt. The success of the so-called land reform program of the Communists made a deep impression, as did the strategy and tactics of the Communist party. The moral that was drawn from all this reflection was not that the Kuomintang had monopolized government but that it had governed badly. It was necessary, therefore, to correct former mistakes.

The measures taken by the government could not have been carried through without steadily increasing American aid. In the period between the end of 1949 and the middle of 1951, American aid was given mainly to prevent starvation and inflation and took the form of consumer goods to the value of U. S. $75,000,000. The funds used were those which had originally been allocated to the mainland. After the Korean war began, long-range plans were drawn up for both military and economic assistance. Between 1951 and 1955 over half a billion dollars in aid was given to Formosa, but this money did not include the cost of the equipment provided for the army, all of which was provided by the United States. A substantial part of the American aid went to assist the government in its efforts to increase industrial production, especially in the improvement of power production, the building of fertilizer plants, and many other projects. United States aid has affected practically every aspect of the island economy, including support of the budget, assistance in the resettlement of refugees, rehabilitation of the railroads and highways, and public health and housing. Power production has gone up to the point where it is adequate even for expansion of industries.

One of the most important programs pushed by the National Government was a thoroughgoing land reform. This program began very soon after the establishment of the government on Formosa and was carried through in three stages from 1949 to 1953. The first step was to enforce legislation calling for a maximum rent of 37½ per cent of harvested produce, a move which immediately put more cash in the hands of tenants and lowered the price of land. The next step was to sell government-owned lands on easy terms to the tenants who were working it. The third stage, which was completed in 1953, was to impose a limit on the amount of land which could be owned, then for the government to purchase the excess land and sell it to the tenants. Land was not expropriated; the landowners were paid in industrial shares and farm commodities. According to government figures 75 per cent of the peasants came to own their land and the percentage of tenants went down from 36 per cent to 19 per cent of the total number of farmers. Over half a million peasants benefited from the reform. The reform led to an increase in the production of rice and a rise in the purchasing power of the peasantry, who constituted a little more than half of the population.

In this task the government had the aid of the Joint Commission on Rural Reconstruction, a Chinese-American agency, which established very successful cooperation. The commission did much to help the farmers increase production by assisting in crop and livestock improvement and in rural health and education programs. Its success depended in large part on its emphasis on self-help.

The economy of Formosa could not be self-supporting while heavy military burdens had to be carried. The National Government and the United States were jointly committed to the maintenance of a large military establishment. Military expenditures consumed at least 30 per cent of the budget, and the proportion of U. S. aid that went for military installations and upkeep tended to go up rather than down. The Formosan economy depended on continuing U. S. aid, for in addition to the cost of the military establishment the rapidly increasing population made the maintenance of economic stability an ever more difficult problem. Even the partial solution of enforcing a regime of austerity was politically difficult because of the acknowledged aim of raising the living standards of the peasants. There was also the problem of taking care of the refugee population, the excessive number of officials, and of providing for the men demobilized from the army because of age.

The National Government carried out on Formosa some of the reforms which had been discussed on the mainland. A budget was introduced and military expenditures were included in it. The budget was critically discussed in the Legislative Yüan which had to give its approval. The budget could be balanced, however, only with American aid. The government had little success in establishing a system of direct taxation and depended for its revenues mainly on maritime customs, excise taxes, and profits from government monopolies. On the political side, steps were taken towards the introduction of self-government in the administration of the province of Formosa. Elections were held in the municipalities, districts, and provinces, and Formosans took over an increasing share of local government.

Chiang Kai-shek is a man of great qualities as well as great weaknesses. His determination and confidence and his conviction that no one else could save China have survived civil strife, deposition, secession, rebellion, captivity, defeat, and abdication. A man who has always preferred loyalty to ability, and obedience to honesty, Chiang Kai-shek saw the events of 1948 and 1949 as a defeat and humiliation prepared by the disloyal and the disobedient. The lessons that he learned from the experience on the mainland were that defeat was due to failure to carry out party principles, failure to stick to party policies, the loosening of party organization, factionalism within the party, and lack of party discipline. The moral was greater unity, greater discipline, and more organization.

The same view of the reasons for defeat and of the moral to be drawn from it was held by Chiang's close associates among the military on Formosa. General Ch'en Ch'eng, who was premier until 1954, when he became vice-president, reflected the same views. He was the driving force behind the land reform program because he felt that the Communists took advantage of the poverty of the people. Living standards must therefore be raised, rice must come before liberty and freedom. There was no evidence that Ch'en Ch'eng and most of the military leaders in the government understood the nature of the institutional revolution that lay behind the Chinese Communist military strength.

The studies made by the Central Reform Committee of the party also showed the same views. Some of the most important studies were published in a series edited by T'ao Hsi-sheng, the ghost writer of *China's Destiny*. The argument was advanced that the Communists won, not because they had a better ideology but because they had a better strategy. The *San Min Chu I*, it was pointed out, had no strategy and tactics. It was the strategy of the Communists, therefore, which must be used to control them—use the enemy's knife in order to kill him. The moral of all this to the Kuomintang was that in the fight against Communism the political experience of the United States was not enough; ideologically the democracies had the better case but they did not have the right strategy and tactics. They must learn from the Communists the importance of having one leadership and a common ideological front. The strategy and tactics used by the Communists could be employed by those who believed in the Three People's Principles and the values of the Free World. The important thing about ideology was that there should be only one and that no deviations should be permitted, for that gives the enemy the opportunity to exploit division within your ranks.

The Kuomintang theorists, convinced that the secrets of Communism must be mastered, came to the conclusion that democratic centralism must remain the guiding political principle in party organization. The strategy of the national revolution, argued the Central Reform Committee, had to be the People's Livelihood, not class struggle. The Kuomintang was not the party of any one class but the representative of the whole of society. The individual was expected to discharge his social duties in order to be entitled to his rights. The argument advanced in *China's Destiny* was reaffirmed by pointing out that China did not need the individualism of European liberalism. The road to socialism, which was accepted as inevitable and desirable, had to be reached without class conflict and without going through the stage of individualism and competition. The Kuomintang theorists stated in their writings that China had to have a planned economy, with the Kuomintang, which represented the whole of society, doing the planning. They aimed at a socialist, not a Communist, society; at class harmony, not class warfare.

There were deviants from this general pattern of political thinking. The Carsun Chang group, for example, criticized the Kuomintang for its methods of fighting Communism, pointing out that if it was fighting for freedom it might do well to start by setting Formosa free first and ceasing to exercise one-party rule. The Young China party also criticized the Kuomintang theory of "one party, one nation." The Young China party and the Social Democrats had fourteen seats in the Legislative Yüan, ten in the Control Yüan, and 154 in the National Assembly. Both parties were particularly bitter critics of what they considered to be government by a bureaucracy of warlords with a private army and a private party with Chiang Kai-shek at the helm. The fact that these parties—weak as they were—were permitted to exist at all on Formosa tempered to some extent the sharpness of their criticism of Kuomintang monopoly rule.

The prevailing theory of government on Formosa was clearly that of the moral rather than of the secular state. The objectives laid down by the Ministry of Education and approved by the Executive Yüan in April 1952, showed that the main purpose of the intellectual, military, physical, and technical training of all students was to inculcate the Three People's Principles. The state was responsible for the moral upbringing of students. In the army the indoctrination of troops was along the lines of the leadership principle. An authoritarian, paternalistic military leadership had no room in its political doctrine for political pluralism, but its drive for modernization compelled it to build up many of the conditions for a pluralistic society.

There were few open conflicts among the leaders on Formosa during the first five years on the island. The exception was the resignation of K. C. Wu from his position as governor of Formosa. The background to this open break was the struggle over the definition of civilian and military powers, a conflict on the issue of the rule of law, and the question of the integrity of the provincial administration. The departure of K. C. Wu was all the more noticeable because so many Chinese on Formosa who disagreed with the prevailing philosophy were willing to concede a great deal for the sake of unity. Those Chinese leaders who lived in Hong Kong or in other countries were more open in their criticism but had the disadvantage of representing no organized body of followers.

The overseas Chinese, estimated at twelve million, were concentrated mainly in Southeast Asia and were particularly important to the Kuomintang. They had played an important role in the history of the party and in the revolution. The Kuomintang began an immediate drive to secure their good will and support but ran into several difficulties. The National Government had fallen so low in prestige that it was hard to present it as a valuable ally. The overseas Chinese were accustomed to thinking of their homeland not only in sentimental but also in practical terms. They looked to it for support against the discrimination which they met with in many countries, and the National Government was in no position to offer much support. Many of the countries concerned, such as India, Burma, Indonesia and the Philippines, had secured their independence since the war, and this changed the position of the overseas Chinese. There was more pressure on them to choose between loyalty to China and loyalty to the countries in which they lived. Communist China had alienated many by its treatment of businessmen on the mainland but it had a strong appeal to youth, and many Chinese students began to go to Peking for a free education. In the struggle for the allegiance of the overseas Chinese the National Government could have only a limited influence.

6. THE COMMUNISTS IN POWER

The New Communist Regime

The Communists established their new government at Peking in September 1949. Peking, as the city was now called again, became the capital of the "People's Republic of China." The Communists called a People's Political Consultative Conference to which they invited representatives of the Democratic League and other "democratic personalities," including some members of the Kuomintang and a few generals who had gone over to their side, a total of 662 delegates. The People's Political Consultative Conference approved a Common Program and an Organic Law of the Central People's Government. The Common Program restated Communist policy as expressed in the *New Democracy*. The "New Democracy" or "People's Democratic Dictatorship" was claimed to represent the joint revolution of the four classes: the workers, the peasants, the small bourgeoisie, and the nationalist-capitalists. Once again it was made clear that the joint revolution was to be led by the Communist party as the vanguard which claimed to express the will of the working class, the supposed leader of the combination of revolutionary classes. This doctrinal explanation of policy was graphically expressed in the red flag of the regime, which had a large yellow star, representing the Communist party, and four small stars, representing the four social classes allegedly cooperating in the "joint revolution." The theory of the New Democracy and of the joint revolution was flexible enough to permit the speeding up or the delay of any political measure according to expediency. The decision as to which issue was to be dealt with at what time had clearly been reserved by Mao Tse-tung as his prerogative in his theoretical statement *On Contradiction* first made in 1937 to party leaders but not made public until after the new government was established.

The Organic Law of September 27 set up a Central People's Government of the People's Republic of China. The highest policy-making body was the Central People's Government Council, the members of which were elected by the PPCC. Mao Tse-tung was himself the president of the Government Council, which had four vice-presidents and fifty-eight members. Under the Government Council was a State Administrative Council, a kind of cabinet, which consisted of twenty members, each one of whom headed a ministry or committee. Chou En-lai became chairman of the State Administrative Council and in fact prime minister. The People's Revolutionary Military Council managed the military affairs of the Communist regime. Mao Tse-tung was also chairman of this military branch of the government, thus continuing to keep in his own hands control of the army, his chief source of power.

The Communists kept up the appearance of a coalition by placing several prominent non-Communists in positions of prestige. The widow of Sun Yat-sen and Li Chi-shen, a former Kuomintang general, and Chan Lan, head of the Democratic League, were among the vice-chairmen of the Government Council, and Kuo Mo-jo, a leading figure in the Literary Revolution, was chairman of the Culture and Education Committee of the Government, and also a member of the Government Council. But the key positions were in the hands of Communists, almost all of whom were trusted comrades who had built up the Kiangsi soviet under Mao Tse-tung whose leadership they had long accepted. Chairman Mao, as he was now called, was the dominating figure in the new government. He was at the same time chairman of the Central People's Government, chairman of the Communist party, and head of the Military Council. General Chu Teh, the man who had helped to bring Mao to power, was a vice-chairman of the Military Council and in command of the armies. Liu Shao-ch'i, the party theoretician, next to Mao himself, held many positions. He was vice-chairman of the Central Committee of the party, of the Politburo, of the Government Council, and of the Military Council. He was also honorary chairman of the All China Federation of Trade Unions and president of the Sino-Soviet Friendship Association. On party doctrine and policy and on concrete institutional planning, Liu was Mao Tse-tung's right hand man. Chou En-lai, the chairman of the State Administrative Council, was in effect the executive head of the government and thus one of the most important figures among Chinese Communist leaders. As he was also foreign minister, he soon came to be the most prominent Chinese Communist in international affairs and conferences.

Chou En-lai had always played a leading part in the Chinese Communist movement. Beginning with the early days of the party in Shanghai he held top positions under the successive party chiefs, surviving the purge of each of them. When the party headquarters were moved from Shanghai to Mao Tse-tung's Kiangsi soviet in 1931, Chou En-lai was the only leader of importance who went over to Mao and continued to play an important part. His great mental abilities, his polished and suave personality, and his extraordinary diplomatic skill made him apparently indispensable.

Born in 1898, Chou En-lai came from a high gentry family of Kiangsu province. His grandfather was an important official under the imperial government, and both his father and mother were highly educated in the classical tradition and also interested in the modern literature which was then beginning. Educated in China and Japan, Chou joined the demonstrations of the May Fourth Movement, was arrested, and after his release left for Europe. In France, Chou En-lai helped to organize the Chinese Communist party, and after his return to China in 1924 he came to Canton to work with the reorganized Kuomintang. Here he became secretary and chief of the Political Department of the Whampoa Academy, a position through which he gained valuable ties with students who later became top Communist military leaders. During the march north, Chou En-lai was sent to Shanghai where he played the leading role in organizing the Shanghai workers and in the calling of the general strike which prepared the fall of Shanghai to the Nationalist forces. When Chiang Kai-shek suppressed the Communist-controlled workers' organizations, Chou was caught with many others but escaped execution and became active again in workers' organizations and uprisings at Nanchang, Swatow, and in the Canton commune. When these various moves failed and led to purges of the party leadership, Chou always managed to stay in leading positions. When he went over to Mao Tse-tung in 1931, he became political commissar to the army commander, Chu Teh, and vice chairman of the Revolutionary Military Council. With the establishment of the Communist government Chou became its top administrator and leading diplomat.

Mao's chairmanship of the Military Council was all the more important in the first stage of the Communist regime when local administration had not yet been integrated and when a great deal depended on the commanders of the Communist armies in each area. To facilitate their assumption of control, the Communists at first pursued a very moderate policy. During their military conquest, their armies maintained strict discipline. They came in on the wave of discontent with the National Government, and exploited to the full their propaganda of "liberation." Many of the local administrators of the previous regime were left in office and few changes were made in the existing administrative organization. During this period, however, military control was decisive, and China was therefore divided under the new central Communist regime into six regional administrations. These six regions were Manchuria, North China, Eastern China, the Northwest, the Southwest, and Central and Southern China. The region of Manchuria, potentially the richest industrial and agricultural area and closest to Soviet Russia, was administered by Kao Kang, one of the few important Communists who did not belong to Mao's Kiangsi group. At the outset the military commanders and political administrators of these regions had a great deal of autonomy, but they were subject to party discipline and to the authority of Mao and Chu Teh. In this way they were kept under central control until the whole of China could be integrated into one administrative system.

Economic Recovery

When the Communists had established military control and set up their government in Peking, their first tasks were to restore the economy and to bring production up to prewar levels. Economic recovery depended to a large degree on the restoration of the means of communication which the Communists themselves had done so much to destroy. It was also vital to bring inflation under control. But at the same time the Communists laid the foundations for revolutionary institutional changes which would form the permanent basis of Communist power. After an early period of moderation which was necessary in order to minimize the disruption caused by the change-over, they began their brutal program of economic, social, political, and ideological revolution. By the beginning of 1953 the Communists were ready to start on long-range economic planning and to set up a new political structure.

There was an uneven pattern of industrial recovery in the first three years. Pig iron, coal, and electric power, for instance, did not reach prewar production levels, but these levels were surpassed in such commodities as cotton textiles, important as an incentive for increased food production, and cigarettes and flour, which were important for the pacification of the cities. There was also an increase in the production of steel, vital for the restoration of the communication system and military purposes. During these three years the revival of agricultural production was facilitated by a succession of three good harvests. One of the most important accomplishments of the Communists was the rehabilitation of the railroad, highway, and river transportation systems, a task to which they applied a high proportion of their resources. It is claimed that within two years all the former railroads were in working order and new lines were under construction. The line from Chungking to Chengtu, which had been largely constructed by the National Government, was completed in 1952. The Communists were also particularly successful in organizing barge traffic on the main rivers. All these measures helped to restore the flow of commodities on which the economic life of the country depended.

The movement of goods could not have been restored, however, without the stabilization of the currency and the price level. Over a period of two years, during which there were continuous price fluctuations, the government gradually established a measure of stability. This was done mainly through control of the major commodities through state trading companies which were directed to dump or to withhold commodities in order to maintain the price level. The government also established a stringent deflationary credit policy which was manipulated by the People's Bank. By controlling both the credit and a decisive amount of commodities, the government in effect related the currency to goods rather than to gold. At the same time the Communists set up a national budget on the basis of a highly centralized taxation system. The taxes were increased and their collection rigidly enforced. By these measures the government restored the economy and made it possible to proceed to direct controls and revolutionary institutional changes. The launching of a new and violent phase in the Communist program coincided with the planned participation of the Chinese Communists in the Korean war.

Social Revolution

The new policy was first applied in the field of agriculture. An Agrarian Reform Act had been promulgated in June, 1950. This act, which was designed to bring about land redistribution for all of China by late 1951 or early 1952, was at first implemented very leniently. The so-called middle peasants were left in possession of their land and those whose land was expropriated were still permitted to retain a unit of a size which a family could work by itself. Those Communist workers who carried the land measures too far were purged as leftist-deviationists. But when Chinese troops entered Korea in October, 1950, the agrarian law was applied with bloodshed and violence. Throughout 1951 the land distribution program was carried out all over China with a ruthless persecution of landlord families who not only lost all their property but in many cases their lives. The land program was to be carried through as a "class struggle" with a venomous attack against the "landlord class" which was described as the representative of a tradition of "feudal" exploitation. The social purpose of the land reform was to change the social order in the villages and bring to power men who were committed by violence to the Communist regime.

At the same time there was a "counter-revolutionary suppression" campaign. This campaign was also based on a law already promulgated in July, 1950, but applied with a new harshness after the beginning of 1951. All "war criminals, traitors, bureaucratic capitalists, and counter-revolutionaries" had their property confiscated and were made subject to punishment ranging from three years imprisonment to death. These classifications could be applied to anyone who stood in the way of the regime. These laws were combined with an intense propaganda against "American imperialism" and American-backed "feudalism" to create an internal and external hate campaign under the cover of which Communist power became strongly entrenched. The widespread campaign, which also led to the imprisonment of many foreigners, especially foreign missionaries, was climaxed by a series of mass "public trials." These so-called "trials" were in reality public performances staged after previously conducted secret hearings for the purpose of whipping up mass hatred of the inner and outer "enemies" and thus promoting loyalty to the regime. Tens of thousands of people in cities like Shanghai and Tientsin daily crowded the "public trials," shouted the mass verdicts of "kill," and attended the executions. The proceedings of the mass rallies were transmitted by radio to the largest possible audience. The number of people executed in these two bloody drives soon mounted into the millions. According to American government estimates the total killed by the Communist regime over a four-year period in these and other drives was approximately fifteen million. Those who were not killed were sent to forced labor camps for varying periods, sometimes under suspended death sentence. The number of people in such camps has been estimated at between eighteen and twenty-four million.

The drives against the landlords and potential political opponents were followed by a purge within the Communist party and the bureaucracy. The drive was started at the end of 1951 under the slogan of the "Three Anti Movement." The movement was supposedly directed against the three evils of "corruption," "waste," and "bureaucracy." In reality the main purpose of the drive was to get rid of many of the former Kuomintang officials whom the Communists had left in office but whom they were now ready to replace with trained cadres. At the same time the drive was used to get rid of inefficient and unreliable members of the party and to tighten discipline. The drive served to show that the power of the state would be ruthlessly used against its own servants if they did not unquestionably carry out orders or if they used their positions to their own private advantage.

Another drive, known as the "Five Anti Movement," was launched in October, 1951, and lasted till June, 1952. This movement was on the same scale as the Land Reform movement in the villages, it was directed against a whole social class, the businessmen of the cities. These were the "small bourgeoisie" and the "nationalist capitalists" whose participation in the establishment of the "New Democracy" the Communists officially welcomed. The theory of the joint revolution was not changed but within a short period of time the Communists reduced independent business to subservience to the state. The evils against which the Five Anti Movement were directed were "tax evasion, bribery, cheating in government contracts, theft of economic intelligence, and stealing of national property." These slogans were so broad that the government could accuse almost any business of some violation of law during the preceding years of political confusion. Special tribunals were established in the main urban centers to try businessmen and firms for alleged criminal acts under these categories. At the outset only a small percentage of businessmen—5 per cent in Shanghai, according to the Communists—were prosecuted. However, the number of cases increased rapidly. Soon hundreds of cases were tried in the main cities. Almost all the larger and a great majority of the smaller business firms were found guilty. This Five Anti drive, like the others, was not conducted as a legal procedure. The Five Anti Movement was a state-organized political persecution of a social class. It opened with the artificial stimulation of class hatred and mass hysteria. Social groups were set against each other by the exploitation of existing cleavages and the destruction of all bonds of personal or family loyalty. To insure their own safety employees were forced to accuse their employers, and relatives were made to accuse each other. Under the threat of persecution many businessmen were terrorized into "confessions" with which they hoped to save themselves from a worse fate. Many businessmen were imprisoned or executed and the death rate was increased by a wave of suicides resulting from the reign of terror. But even when businessmen escaped death or imprisonment, they were heavily fined or their property was confiscated.

The fines imposed on business firms were very substantial and provided the Communist government with a vast amount of additional income. No statistics are available for the actual amount seized in this way, but some inferences can be drawn from the first budget published by the government in 1953. The budget showed for the year 1952 a revenue of over eight billion U. S. dollars compared to expenditures of $6,895,000,000. The surplus of over one billion U. S. dollars is believed to have been derived from the capital fines on Chinese business. This vast amount of extra revenue was used by the Communists for the further expansion of state economic enterprises and for the planned industrialization.

State Economic Control

The payment of this vast amount of capital funds by private business to the government was incidental to the purpose of establishing state economic control. Many of the firms had to pay fines much larger even than the capital they owned, with the result that they had to go heavily in debt to meet the payments. The government, which did not permit bankruptcy, provided loans at moderate interest rates to enable these firms to pay their fines and to carry on. As a result a large section of Chinese business became heavily indebted to the government and became for all practical purposes government controlled. The old management was continued but under Communist control and supervision. Three-quarters of the profits went to the state. As the government also determined wages and prices, allocated raw material, was the first buyer of the manufactured product, and as it controlled all credit, no field of economic independence remained. Though it continued in name, private enterprise was in fact eliminated by the Five Anti Movement.

When the Communists took over, 15½ per cent of industrial production came from state-controlled enterprises. According to Communist figures, this percentage rose to 43.8 per cent by 1950 and to 67.3 per cent by the end of 1952. The remaining 32.7 per cent, nominally private enterprise, was in practice also controlled. First to be brought under state management was heavy industry. Communist figures claim that 80 per cent of heavy industry and 40 per cent of light industry were state enterprises. By the end of 1952, 90 per cent of bank loans and deposits were managed by the People's Bank, and 90 per cent of international trade was handled by state firms. The year 1952 was marked by a fundamental economic change; trade and industry were taken over by the Communist regime.

The extent of Communist control over the country's economy could also be seen in the budget which was given as U. S. $8,000,000,000 for 1952 and U. S. $10,000,000,000 for 1953. Compared to the $500,000,000 budget of the National Government in 1937, the last year before the war, these figures indicated more than anything else the Communist penetration into all spheres of economic life. In this budget the increase of state control can also be seen in the proportions of the government revenue derived from state enterprises, land tax, and business tax, over a five-year period. In 1950 the proportion of government revenue from state enterprises was 34.8 per cent. By the end of 1954 this proportion was estimated to have been over 63 per cent, a figure all the more impressive because the land tax and business tax still yielded in 1954 the same amount of income as they had in 1950. The decline of the percentages of these two sources of income indicate, therefore, the extraordinary growth of the state enterprises. The following table will indicate the respective figures:

PROPORTION OF REVENUE FROM

	State Enterprises	Land Tax	Manufacturers' and Traders' Tax
1950	34.08	29.63	32.92
1951	49.35	18.17	28.66
1952	56.33	17.08	24.06
1953	59.79	14.56	22.36
1954	63.58	13.43	20.99

The Ideological Campaign

The rapid trend towards state-controlled industry brought China a stage closer to the so-called socialist revolution. But the Communists did not discard the fiction that their policy was the result of a joint revolution and did not abandon the slogan of New Democracy. Within this dogmatic framework, however, it was made quite clear that the Communist ideology was to rule. In the Five Anti Movement the businessmen had not only been attacked for their alleged crimes in business practice but were also vilified as the loathsome holders of a bourgeois ideology. They were described as the exploiters and enemies of the working class, and when the drive was turned off again it was clear that private business activity was permitted to continue only on sufferance and that the ideology of the New Democracy was to be the "workers' ideology" or, in fact, the Communist dogma.

This ideological attack against the businessmen was only a part of the broader ideological movement aimed at destroying all independent thinking in China and imposing a general acceptance of the Communist doctrine as represented in the writings of Lenin, Stalin, and Mao Tse-tung. In aim and method this ideological movement was the most ruthless and all-inclusive part of the Communist totalitarian program. As early as 1949 all writers and artists had been called to Peking by the new Communist regime to play their part in the revolution. Their role was described in the words of Mao Tse-tung, "In the present world, all culture or literature belongs to one class, to one party, and follows one fixed political line. Art for art's sake, art above class, art which could be independent of the political march, does not exist in reality." In spite of this indication of their totalitarian aims, the Communists, in the first years of their regime, did not undertake any direct attack against those intellectuals who did not accept their doctrine. But when they were safely entrenched, they turned on an ideological movement to eliminate all independent thinking.

The movement started in September, 1951, as a "study campaign for ideological reform." It had its beginnings as an educational program in the universities of North China and was initiated by Chou En-lai. The immediate practical purpose of this program was to prepare the institutions of higher learning for the task of "training up for our country 150,000 to 200,000 industrial, agricultural, communications and transport, medical and other categories of senior construction cadres." These "cadres," who were fanatical adherents to the party doctrine as well as technically trained men, were necessary for the carrying out of Communist policy on all levels. For the training of such cadres Communist doctrine had to be introduced in the educational institutions, and the indoctrination had therefore to begin with the faculties of the universities which were still promoting the principles of free thought. In the words of the Communist vice-minister of education, such training was not possible "if the teachers in institutions of higher education persist in adhering to the reactionary thoughts of the British and American bourgeois class, if they persist in sticking to their personal individualism, objectivism, and sectarian point of view and fail to carry out true reform. . . ." The ideological reform was therefore to start with "reforming the teacher's mind." What the teachers had to learn was "the ideology of the progressive elements of the working class, that is to say, the revolutionary theories of Mao Tse-tung, a product of Marxism-Leninism, and the actual practice of the Chinese revolution." The method they were to use was "the promotion of severe criticism and self-criticism with one's own ideological state strictly in view, in the effort to truly improve and raise one's own ideology."

In practice, the teachers were prodded and terrorized into accepting the Communist dogma. This process, which received the popular name of "brain-washing," had to be a "thought-struggle," meaning that the conversion was brought about in public, in meetings in which the participants indulged in mutual accusations, self-criticism, denunciations, and confessions. After accusing each other and themselves of their distorted thinking in the past and of the "feudalistic," "bourgeois," or "imperialistic" background of their fathers, their families, and their own previous studies, they promised to accept the "real truth" of Mao's teaching. This process culminated in written confessions which were made public and had sometimes to be restated before they became acceptable. All psychological means were used to break down individual resistance; no one was permitted what has become known as "the freedom of silence," and those whose conversion was not regarded as satisfactory were put in "re-education camps." Behind the process of thought reform was the threat of trial and liquidation. Some of the intellectuals managed to escape to Hong Kong and from there to other countries. The others had to yield and make their peace with the regime on its own terms. The non-Communist intellectuals in China were forced into a public intellectual surrender which went beyond the practices of other totalitarian regimes. The Chinese intellectuals were denied all freedom of silence, compelled to denounce their own intellectual tradition, and to suffer the indignities and humiliations of mutual incrimination and personal recantation until their spirit was broken. No totalitarian regime has come quite so close to the conditions described in Orwell's novel, *1984*.

Mass Organization

The national drive to remold the thinking of the teachers was combined with a complete reorganization of the schools and the curriculum. The leading universities were regrouped and given specialized tasks. Great emphasis was placed on technical training and indoctrination in Communist dogma. This educational program was used for the training of the vast numbers of Communist cadres, the new elite whose task it was to carry out Communist policies and run the expanding machinery of the state. Large numbers of cadres were needed to staff the vast network of mass organizations through which the Communists penetrated every group in society. In order to mobilize the entire population for their purposes the Communists divided it into many functional groupings through which they could reach every individual. Every village community was organized under the leadership of the cadres and local Communists. Other such functional groups were the factory workers, teachers, students, employees, women, children, and professional workers. There was a mass organization for practically every way in which people can be organized. Among the more important were the New Democratic Youth League, with its offshoot the Young Pioneers. These provided the training ground for future members of the party and assisted in detail work on the lowest level. Because of their zeal in informing and denouncing they were in many ways the eyes and ears of the party. The New Democratic Youth League claimed to have nearly half a million cells and twelve million members between the ages of fourteen and twenty-five. The Young Pioneers claimed eight million members. Both of these youth organizations were indoctrinated in the "five loves"—love for fatherland, people, labor, science, and public property. The Youth League and the Young Pioneers were the future elite.

On a much larger scale were such mass organizations as the All China Democratic Women's Federation, which claimed about eighty million members, and the Peasant Associations and the Cooperatives, each of which claimed about 150,000,000 members. The Sino-Soviet Friendship Association claimed, in 1954, to have fifty-eight million members and nearly half a million branches and subbranches.

Mass organization techniques were also used to create a docile force of factory workers. A Trade Union law, which had been approved in June, 1950, laid the foundation for the development of the All China Federation of Trade Unions, which claimed, in 1954, a membership of approximately eleven million workers. This was an organization through which the government acquainted the workers with its policy decisions. There was no right to strike. The Soviet system of daily production quotas was introduced into the factories. In addition to the "collective contracts" in which the production quotas were set, factory teams had to sign up for "patriotic contracts" for a "mutual supervision" of the work of each team. A system of "labor rivalry" and of "labor heroes" was thus added to the quota system and piece-work wages which characterized Communist industry. In this way the proletariat, in theory the leading class in the revolution, was harnessed to the Communist party machine.

All the mass organizations were controlled by the Communist party and like it were set up on the basis of democratic centralism. The basic units were the cells, which were grouped into branches and regional units. Each organization formed a national association which held periodic congresses. Through this chain of command Communist orders were transmitted to the lowest level where they were carried out. The cells met constantly for discussion and debate of topics assigned to them by the party. These meetings were used to check on the attitudes and "thoughts of the masses" and to remove all possible "misgivings" regarding policy. The mass organizations served to keep the individual, such as the peasant or urban worker, fully occupied with meetings and discussions of the sort that would serve the purposes of the regime. He lived in a world created for him and completely controlled. The news he could read in his newspapers was carefully selected and of very local interest. Only a few journals dealing with the national scene, all of which followed the party directives, were permitted to circulate over the whole country.

The mass organizations were, in effect, the arms of the Communist party. It was largely through them that the Communists created a new pattern of social organization by means of which they could penetrate and dominate every kind of social grouping. An essential part of this pattern was the threat and the use of force. In addition to an enormous standing army there were the militia units which were kept in constant training and were always available in every district. The militia provided the police force for the various drives and for arrests and executions. It was through the mass organizations, however, that the Communists exercised their total social control. Among the most important functions of the mass organizations were spying and reporting and the application of the social pressures of the group. These functions were an extension of the secret police apparatus of the party. To make this system work the Communists instigated a reign of terror which cowed the people into acquiescence. The drives themselves, with their "public courts" and mass executions, were deliberate demonstrations of the ruthlessness and power of the Communists. It was on this willingness to break all opposition with brute force that the refined techniques of psychological coercion depended for their success and effectiveness.

In the first three years of their rule the Communists set up the major institutions of the totalitarian state. By the spectacular use of force against the Chinese people they had removed all possibility of internal resistance to the regime. Through a series of drives they had broken up the existing social order by the physical elimination of vast numbers of people in the villages who enjoyed wealth, authority, or respect, by ruining and bringing into disrepute the new business and industrial groups in the cities, and by destroying the independence and freedom of thought of the intellectuals. The dominant group in the new society, with its mass organizations and total social control, was the Communist party, whose members were tightly disciplined by the party leaders through their monopoly control over doctrine. This totalitarian control was altogether different, in kind as well as in degree, from the sway which the imperial throne had held over the gentry.

The Five Year Plan

The objectives and basic techniques of the new rulers of China were those of Communism as developed in the Soviet Union. Thousands of Chinese cadres had been trained, since 1921, in the Soviet Union where they had learned the theory and strategy of Communist revolution. There they studied political guerrilla warfare, the techniques of infiltration and mass organization, the system of party discipline, and the economics of planning. Once in power in China, the Chinese Communists telescoped the experience of the Soviet state into a much shorter period. The first Soviet Five Year Plan began in 1928, more than ten years after the Bolshevik Revolution, and the constitution did not come till 1936. By 1953 and 1954, however, the Chinese Communists felt they had prepared the economic and social groundwork to enable them to move into a new phase, the introduction of a Soviet type of Five Year Plan and of a Soviet type of constitution.

In December 1952, Chou En-lai announced that China would embark on her First Five Year Plan early in 1953. A State Planning Commission had been set up a month earlier under the chairmanship of Kao Kang, the head of the regional administration in Manchuria. Kao Kang was presumably chosen for this position because Manchuria was the most highly industrialized area in China and the place where most of the Communist policies were first implemented. The announcement of the Five Year Plan was not followed by any statement as to its details; in fact it is very doubtful whether an all-inclusive economic plan similar to that of the Soviet Union actually existed. The only information given out was a list of a few production goals for the first year, and these were drastically revised several times. It is clear that the Communists did not have the statistical basis or the organization for a really comprehensive plan and that they were only building towards one. The general aim was to industrialize China on the Soviet model as rapidly as possible. For this purpose they accepted large numbers of Russian technicians and advisers and negotiated for Soviet economic aid. The Sino-Soviet agreement of September, 1953, concluded after long negotiations, provided for Soviet assistance in the establishment of 141 industrial projects, mainly in the fields of electric power, mining, chemicals, and metal. In the Sino-Soviet agreement of 1954, concluded in Peking, the Soviet Union promised a great deal of additional assistance to China's program of industrialization.

In spite of Soviet assistance the main capital investment for industrialization was to come from the Chinese economy. Most of this capital had to come from agricultural production. The only form of capital which the state was willing to invest in agriculture was the labor of political prisoners supplemented by corvée labor. This labor was used to improve and extend dikes and irrigation projects in order to bring more land under cultivation, but the increase in agricultural production brought about by these measures was probably not more than adequate to meet the needs of the increasing population. Since the Communists had neither the time nor the desire to increase production by offering incentives to the peasants, which would have meant building up consumer industry, they used coercion to extract a larger portion of existing production for the use of the state.

For this purpose they applied the methods used in the East European satellites. In the fall of 1953 they introduced a system of grain rationing and imposed upon the peasants a system of forced grain deliveries at prices fixed by the government. These deliveries were in addition to the already heavy grain taxes. The most effective method of enforced collection of grain for the state was the collective farm, in which control over the grain was in the hands of the bureaucracy—not of the peasant. The government, therefore, in its Five Year Plan, prepared the way for the collectivization of agriculture. It proposed to go about this task cautiously by stages because it anticipated considerable opposition from peasants who had been recently won over by promises that they would own their own land. Collectivization was to be entirely voluntary, therefore, and the peasants were to be "guided and helped" into accepting it. In order to prepare the way the cadres were ordered to form "mutual aid" teams in which peasant families would assist each other in their work by joint planting and harvesting. Another type of organization was the peasant cooperative, which could take many forms. The cooperative could arrange for joint ownership or use of farming implements, for the buying of seeds and marketing of products, and for joint administration of the farms. The most advanced type of cooperative was the producer cooperative in which the farmers pooled their land and shared in the income according to a scale in which their labor counted for more than their land. From this type of cooperative to collectivized agriculture was a short step.

The Communists claimed that by the end of 1953 almost half of the total peasant population was organized into mutual aid teams. Some 14,000 producer cooperatives were supposedly set up by this time. A few hundred collectives and state farms had been set up, mainly in Manchuria, and model collectives established in several provinces. But the cadres had pushed ahead with such zeal that they were forced to retreat, and in many cases collectives or producers cooperatives were changed back into mutual aid teams. At the end of 1954 Chou En-lai stated that "backward individual farming" would be slowly transformed into collective farming. He anticipated that by the end of the First Five Year Plan in 1957 about half the peasants would be organized into producers cooperatives. In summer, 1955, the drive toward collectivization was speeded up. On July 31, Mao Tse-tung declared that collectivization would have to be completed by the end of China's third Five

Year Plan in 1967. According to Mao, socialist industrialization could not be achieved without the collectivization of agriculture. As a result of Mao's demand, the number of cooperatives had reached 1,300,000, or close to 30 per cent of China's farm families, by the end of 1956.

It was not until July, 1955, that concrete data were given on the Five Year Plan, which had been revised. By this time Kao Kang had been purged and his place as head of the State Planning Commission taken by Li Fu-chun. In his report Li gave the production goals of the Five-Year Plan, which were to be reached in 1957, and compared them with the actual production of 1952.

	1952	1957	Percentage of Increase
Grain	—	192,800,000 tons	17.6% (previous objective 30%)
Industrial production	—	—	98.3%
Steel	1,350,000 tons	4,120,000 tons	
Electricity	260,000,000 Kw. Hrs.	15,920,000,000 Kw. Hrs.	
Coal	63,500,000 tons	113,000,000 tons	
Generators	30,000 Kw.	227,000 Kw.	
Electric Motors	640,000 Kw.	1,050,000 Kw.	
Cement	2,860,000 tons	6,000,000 tons	
Machine-processed paper	370,000 tons	650,000 tons	
Cotton piece goods	111,630,000 bolts	163,720,000 bolts	
Sugar (machine processed)	249,000 tons	686,000 tons [14]	

[14] *New York Times*, July 6, 1955, p. 6, Henry R. Lieberman.

The most serious admission in Li's report was the reduction of the estimated increase in grain production from 30 per cent to 17.6 per cent. The report also shows the determination to increase steel and power production at all costs. The big centers of steel production were to be Anshan in Manchuria, Tayeh near Hankow in Central China, and Paotou in Inner Mongolia.

The New Constitution

The constitution of 1954 was the other major step towards the sovietization of China. The constitution had been prepared for by a census of the population which was completed in June 1953. It gave the population of the mainland as 582,000,000 and the total Chinese population, including Formosa and the overseas Chinese as a little over 600,000,000. Elections were held on the local level during 1953 for "People's Congresses," which in turn elected representatives to provincial congresses. A National People's Congress, consisting of representatives from the provincial congresses, the large cities, the national minorities, the armed forces, and the overseas Chinese, met in Peking in September, 1954. The Congress duly approved the draft constitution which had been drawn up by the Central

Committee of the Communist party and issued by a drafting committee headed by Mao Tse-tung.

Much of the new constitution was copied directly from the Soviet constitution of 1936, but there was a slight difference in the terminology used to characterize the two states. The People's Republic of China was described as a "people's democratic state led by the working class and based on the alliance of workers and peasants," whereas according to the Soviet constitution "The Soviet Union is a socialist state of workers and peasants." On the other hand the new constitution indicated clearly that China had progressed towards socialism since the time of the Organic Law and Common Program of 1949. The Preamble stated that the task of "anti-imperialism, anti-feudalism, and anti-bureaucratic capitalism" had been accomplished and that the goal had become the building of "a prosperous and happy socialist society. From the founding of the People's Republic of China to the attainment of a socialist society is a period of transition. During the transition the fundamental task of the state is, step by step, to bring about the socialist industrialization of the country and, step by step, to accomplish the socialist transformation of agriculture, handicrafts and capitalist industry and commerce." As a result of the various drives and other measures the Communists felt that "the necessary conditions have been created for planned economic construction and gradual transition to socialism."

The constitution recognized that "at present" there were still several "basic forms of ownership of means of production." There were state ownership, cooperative or collective ownership, ownership by individual working people, and capitalist ownership. The constitution protected the right of the peasant to own his land "according to law," which meant that this right could be ended by a single law, but the trend was indicated by the stipulation that the state would encourage the peasant "to organize producers' supply and marketing, and credit cooperatives voluntarily. The policy of the state towards rich-peasant economy is to restrict and gradually eliminate it." In 1950 Liu Shao-ch'i had promised that the long-term policy of the regime would be to preserve the rich-peasant economy. The right of capitalists to own means of production and other capital was also protected "according to law." But the constitution indicated that it was the policy of "the state towards capitalist industry and commerce . . . to use, restrict and transform them," and to encourage and guide "their transformation into various forms of state-capitalist economy, gradually replacing capitalist ownership with ownership by the whole people . . . ."

The constitution named the National People's Congress as the "highest organ of state authority in the People's Republic of China." It consisted of over 1,200 members elected for a four-year term and met once a year. On paper it had broad powers, including the election of the chairman (Mao Tse-tung) and vice-chairman (Chu Teh) of the Republic, but since it met only once a year, the more important body was the standing committee of the Congress (chairman, Liu Shao-ch'i). The highest administrative organ was the State Council with a premier, or chairman (Chou En-lai), who was nominated by the Congress on recommendation of Mao Tse-tung. A Council of National Defense, under the chairmanship of Mao Tse-tung, was entrusted with the over-all direction of military affairs. The leading members of the government could be called together by Mao Tse-tung, as chairman of the Republic, in a Supreme State Conference. Ex-officio members of the conference were the vice-chairman, Chu Teh; the chairman of the standing committee, Liu Shao-ch'i, and the premier of the state council, Chou En-lai. These four men could be regarded as the most powerful men in the Chinese Communist regime.

The constitution confirmed the position of Mao Tse-tung as the ruler of Communist China. He had vast and undefined powers as chairman of the Republic, chairman of the National Defense Council, chairman of the Supreme State Conference, and head of the Communist party. General Chu Teh, who had always provided Mao with military support, was now vice-chairman of the Republic and of the National Defense Council. Liu Shao-ch'i, Mao's right hand man in party affairs, party discipline, and matters of doctrine, was chairman of the standing committee of the Congress. Chou En-lai, the skilled administrator and diplomat, was premier of the State Council and concurrently foreign minister. Ch'en Yün, the chief party expert on economic matters, was first vice-premier under Chou En-lai. Leading Communists were in the key positions. It was no longer thought necessary to maintain the pretext of coalition government by keeping prominent non-Communists, such as the widow of Sun Yat-sen, as vice-chairmen of the government. There was only one vice-chairman, Chu Teh.

The biggest administrative change recorded in the constitution was the re-establishment of a system of provinces, autonomous regions, and municipalities, prefectures, districts, and other smaller subdivisions. Each of these administrative units had its own People's Congress or People's Council which were the "organs of government authority in their respective localities." The National Congress was elected from the lower congresses by a system of indirect election. On the lowest level there were direct elections, but in these there was only one candidate to vote for. The provincial and lower administrative divisions followed closely the traditional divisions handed down from imperial times. The regional administrations set up in the earlier stage of military conquest were abolished. Some of the generals who had lost their local power were given high positions in the central government.

The constitution included a very extensive Bill of Rights with absolute guarantees of the freedoms therein listed. According to Liu Shao-ch'i "The masses of the people of no capitalist country enjoy, or can enjoy, as broad a measure of personal freedom as do our people." He felt that there was no contradiction between this statement and the qualification that the state will also "suppress all treasonable and counter-revolutionary activities and punish all traitors and counter-revolutionaries," as stated in the constitution. Anyone, said Liu, who expected the constitution to ensure freedom for the activities of "traitors and counter-revolutionaries" was bound to be disappointed.

The constitution marked the re-establishment of centralized control by

Mao and his close followers. The rapid expansion of Communist control over the mainland had made it necessary to establish regional administrations with a great deal of autonomy. These administrations represented a potential threat to the authority of Mao Tse-tung. The most dangerous situation was in Manchuria, where Russian influence was strongest. The Manchurian administration had concluded its own separate economic agreements with the Soviet Union in 1950. This administration was headed by Kao Kang who had never belonged to Mao's Kiangsi group but had headed a different Communist organization in Yenan before the arrival there of Mao's forces. Kao Kang had worked with Mao but his position in Manchuria gave him control over a very important area. In 1952 Kao Kang was made head of the State Planning Commission to prepare the Five Year Plan. He was attacked, indirectly, in February, 1954, at a meeting of the Central Committee of the Communist party which was discussing party unity. The meeting criticized "certain high-ranking cadres" who were accused of even regarding "the region or the department under their leadership as their individual inheritance or kingdom." Kao Kang was not specifically mentioned at that time but his name disappeared from party literature. In March, 1955, at a party conference, Kao Kang was formally accused of "conspiratorial activities" and of stressing the role of the army in building up Communist power in wartime bases. Kao Kang and a number of other Communist leaders, including Jao Shu-shih, who had been prominent in the East China region, were expelled from the party. Kao Kang was said to have committed suicide. At the time of these purges a Central Control Committee of the party was set up to tighten party discipline.

The partnership between Communist China and the Soviet Union was written into the preamble of the new Constitution. "China has already built an indestructible friendship with the great Union of Soviet Socialist Republics and the People's Democracies." On the experience and resources of the Soviet Union the Chinese Communists based the modernization of their armies, their economic planning, their institutional and cultural revolution, their organization of party and government, and their dogma. But as a power group within the Communist world with a base, a machine, and an army of their own, the Chinese Communists were able to achieve a strong position in their own right and to establish a new Communist headquarters in Asia.

Communist Culture

The party theorists had to fit the great cultural tradition of China into the Communist doctrinal pattern, and also to reinterpret the philosophical controversies of the modern period. The main attack was directed against Hu Shih and the pragmatists whose theories had been more influential than those of any other Western school with the exception of Marxism. In the twenties Hu Shih and Ch'en Tu-hsiu, the first leader of the Chinese Communist party, had both attacked the cultural tradition of China. The pragmatists, by attacking this tradition had helped, in some degree, to pave the way for the spread of Marxism as a supposedly scientific philosophy. The Communist party now turned its fire on the May Fourth Movement in order to destroy the influence that it still had on the intellectuals. Hu Shih became one of the main targets. According to Marxists all rival philosophies must be classified as "idealist," so pragmatism was attacked as the philosophy of "subjective idealism." Many articles were published which attacked "the rotten bourgeois class Weltanschauung of Hu Shih's school."

The Communist treatment of the classical tradition was different from that of Hu Shih and Ch'en Tu-hsiu. Instead of condemning everything that had gone before, the Communists re-examined China's literary tradition, weighing every work and author by Communist standards as to whether they expressed "progressive" or "reactionary" ideas. In October, 1954, there began a discussion in the Writers Association of a book by Yu Ping-po on the famous novel, *The Dream of the Red Chamber*. Professor Yu, who had interpreted the novel as an expression of Taoist ideas, was attacked for this "bourgeois" interpretation of a novel whose main character was said to express heroic opposition to the feudalistic institutions of his time. Professor Yu confessed his errors and promised to struggle for his own self-improvement. This incident was only the first move in a drive to secure a uniform Communist interpretation of literature. A book on the history of Chinese literature published in 1954 was the first attempt to formulate the new line over the whole range of earlier Chinese history. Confucius was described as "over-conservative, over-cautious, and not radical" but was said to have "exercised a certain function according to his determined historical stage." Mencius is described as an "idealist" who believed in God and protected the reactionary aristocracy, but it is added that he had a tendency to give more weight to the people than to the rulers, and that his style had a dialectical revolutionary drive. Some of the Taoist writings were classified as Marxist and dialectic, others as idealist and anti-scientific. In addition to the re-study of Chinese literature there was a rewriting of Chinese history in terms of the "truth" about the historical development of societies as revealed by Marx, Lenin, Stalin, and Mao.

The efforts of the party to freeze the cultural life of China into its own doctrinal patterns was largely in the hands of Communist writers who had been with Mao in Yenan. These efforts in China produced the same sort of results as had similar policies in the Soviet Union. In Peking there was the same struggle between factions and literary cliques fighting for the dominant position and the favor of the party leaders as there had been in Moscow. One such example of literary warfare was the attempt of Hu Feng and his group to break the monopoly of the Yenan leaders. Hu Feng was one of the favorite disciples of Lu Hsün who by now was the literary hero of the Chinese Communists. Accustomed to using a sharp pen, Hu Feng continued to write in the critical and satirical vein of former years, especially in his private letters. But his group was broken up and he himself made the object of an organized and nationwide attack. Kuo Mo-jo was quoted as describing the purge of Hu Feng as a "necessary measure" directed against "the undercurrent of an organized and capitalist-sponsored anti-party, anti-people, anti-revolutionary movement." The attack on Hu Feng was used to intimidate many other writers and intellectuals. The similarity between the literary life of Peking and Moscow was no accident. When Chou Yang, the Chinese delegate to the Second Soviet Writers' Congress, held in Moscow in 1954, spoke to the Congress, he claimed to speak for the writers of China "who should be allowed to be your young brothers and disciples." [15]

In their efforts to freeze the cultural life of China into their own doctrinal patterns the Chinese Communists had to reckon with the vitality of China's cultural tradition in areas beyond their control. Among the two million refugees who fled to Hong Kong there were several thousands of intellectuals who either fled before the Communists conquered the mainland or escaped later. There were many others in Southeast Asia, the United States, and Western Europe. Important groups of the Academia Sinica, the highest Chinese research organization, were transferred to Formosa, and continued their program of research in freedom. In Formosa there was also the University of Taiwan, the main Chinese university outside of Chinese Communist control. Plans to establish an independent Chinese university at Singapore were disrupted by Communist-inspired political troubles, but in the United States, a country rich in collections of Chinese books and art, thousands of Chinese scholars continued their study and research. Chinese scholarship was also kept alive in Europe. In this way there was carried on, in conditions of freedom, a cultural tradition which in mainland China was being subverted to the purposes of Communist doctrine.

[15] The foregoing description was largely taken from *China News Analysis*, No. 68, Jan. 21, 1955, p. 6.

CHAPTER **XIII**

Imperial and
Democratic Japan

1. JAPAN IN MIDPASSAGE

The Ideological Legacy

THE first World War marked the beginning of a new era for Japan. Few of the men who had directed the affairs of Japan during the Meiji era were alive after the war. Leadership in Japan passed into new hands. The tremendous economic growth that took place during the war and in the years thereafter put a strain on social relationships and shifted the relative position of social classes. These extensive social and economic changes created new conditions for Japanese political development, and the course of that development was largely determined by the patterns of ideas and beliefs which came out of the ideological struggles of the preceding decades.

The dominant pattern was the official orthodoxy created by the Meiji Restoration. The government took great pains to discourage ideas which might present the people with alternatives to this official ideology. Militarists and bureaucrats were ready to grasp anything from the West which they thought would serve their purposes, but their purposes were already determined and were not likely to be modified by new influences. The Imperial Rescript on Education of October, 1890, which was designed to put a stop to the ideological invasion from the West, made the educational system an arm of the state. The rescript defined moral character as the aim of education and made the inculcation of the national virtues the first responsibility of the

472

educational system. All the prestige of Confucianism, Shintoism, and Buddhism was used to make the generalized concepts of loyalty and filial piety the two cardinal virtues and the moral basis of Japanese nationalism. Step by step the Ministry of Education took over control of the educational process by ordering the curriculum and even preparing the primary textbooks. The government took particular pains to dominate the training of teachers, who were brought up to take discipline and obedience for granted. The educational system was designed to strengthen those ideas which served the interest of the state and to exclude all "dangerous thoughts." By and large it succeeded, especially in the rural areas, but in the private schools in the cities many educational philosophies of American and English origin, such as those of William James and John Dewey, had their vogue.

In spite of the educational system and the anti-intellectual atmosphere of Japanese society, the intellectuals of Japan performed an important and significant function. First, they translated practically every foreign work of any importance in every field from literature to natural science, from the Communist Manifesto to Grimm's Fairy Tales, from Tolstoy to Clausewitz, Disraeli to Dewey. In spite of the occasional heavy hand of censorship a survey of the publishers' lists shows that any Japanese who wished to do so could read in his native language the important as well as the trivial writings of the world. Second, the intellectuals gave expression to the social tensions and intellectual movements of the times. It was the members of this group who expanded the frontiers of Japanese thinking. It would appear that the Japanese intellectuals believed everything once; for every philosophy or social panacea, whether it came from the West or from the Japanese themselves, whether it was appropriate or inappropriate, seemed to have its devotees. It was through the perhaps distorted mirror held up by the intellectuals that Japan saw itself and the world. Third, the intellectuals who were activists and the activists who had intellectual pretensions helped to mold the politics of the time as well as of the future. They were more than mere imitators, they were creators of political concepts of unique character, they did much to determine the stock of ideas available to the conflicting forces in Japanese society at any given time. When other changes had brought about a shift in the balance of forces in Japan at the close of World War I, the ideological spectrum was much wider and richer than that which the oligarchy had sponsored and protected. Among the many diverse movements and ideas some were significant for the future.

Western Liberalism and Socialism

One current of Japanese political thinking stemmed from the earlier alliance between Western liberalism and agrarian discontent. The discontented samurai who organized the first political parties had used Western liberal ideas for the purpose of embarrassing the oligarchy in the hope of destroying their monopoly of power. By 1918 these parties had been sufficiently tamed so that the imperial advisers considered it safe, if not desirable, to permit the establishment of a limited party cabinet. The liberal slogans which had formerly been used in a vain effort to unseat the Satsuma-Choshu oligarchs were now used by the party in opposition against the one in power, were taken seriously by neither, and did not harm the bureaucracy. But there were some men in the same general agrarian tradition who for personal or other reasons refused to go along with this trend and toyed with other concepts and other social forces in their struggle for power. An ex-samurai by the name of Oi Kentaro, anti-foreign and intensely nationalist, arrested in 1884 for fomenting civil war in Korea, was one of the first who saw the possibilities of political support among the poor. He organized a political group of his own in 1892, the Oriental Liberal party, which claimed to be interested in the conditions of tenancy and of urban labor. Oi Kentaro was naturally interested in extending the suffrage, as universal suffrage—for which he petitioned from the beginning—would presumably give him control of the Diet or at least cut into the *Jiyuto* representation. As he thought that the economic conditions of the people could best be improved or controlled through further government regulation of the economy, in contrast to the encouragement of private enterprise, he was attracted by Western socialism, and during the short life of his party published materials on socialism which were probably neither read nor understood by the rickshaw men, carpenters, shoemakers, masons, and tenant farmers he recruited to the party.

The increase in the number of important Western works on socialism made accessible to Japanese readers and the publication of books and articles by Japanese writers on social problems stimulated the formation, in 1898, of an Association for the Study of Socialism which included in its membership Christian socialists as well as some of Oi Kentaro's disciples. By study and discussion this association acquainted a few hundred intellectuals with the work and thought of writers such as Proudhon, Fourier, Saint-Simon, and Marx. The focussing of a certain amount of public attention on labor conditions enabled Oi Kentaro in 1899 to publish *The Osaka Weekly* as the organ of his Japan Labor Association, which claimed to be interested in promoting the interests and welfare of the working class. The most important aspects of Oi Kentaro's approach, however, were his attack on the wealthy and his allegations about the decline of morality, by which he meant the adoption of Western habits. These arguments were designed to appeal to the urban as well as the rural poor, both of whom were denied the material resources with which to be "immoral," and to embarrass those agrarian leaders who claimed to resent the growing dominance of capitalism but were willing to be bought off by the government.

In 1901 there were enough intellectual activists interested in socialism to set up a Social Democratic party, which the government suppressed within three hours of its formation. Among the leaders was Katayama Sen, later to become a leading Japanese Communist. The declaration of the party revealed several new fashions in ideas, such as universal brotherhood, disarmament, public ownership of land and capital, equal distribution of wealth, equal political rights, and free public education. As the channel of political action was blocked, the leaders turned again to writing and study, bringing out novels and political articles on social conditions, imperialism, and anti-militarism. An important journal, the *Commoner's News*, which lasted from late 1903 to early 1905, disseminated an extraordinary collection of heterodox ideas, including the graduated income tax, abolition of the peerage, universal suffrage, prison reform, and the denunciation of war. In this last it was encouraged by a letter from Count Tolstoy at the time of the Russo-Japanese conflict. The combination of socialism and anti-militarism came mainly from Kotoku, an early associate of Oi Kentaro's. In his book on imperialism, published in 1901, he anticipated the arguments of Lenin by blaming imperialism on the drive for markets, and holding that the working classes had no interest in foreign wars because they were fought entirely for the interests of the capitalists. This anti-militarist position made possible an alliance with Christian pacifists who had arrived at the same position as a matter of principle. There was nothing of the Christian pacifist about Kotoku or any other disciple of Oi Kentaro, and after the Russo-Japanese War was over, the Christian socialists broke off from Kotoku's group.

Kotoku took one line of socialist thought to its logical conclusion and what seemed to be a cul-de-sac. He was much influenced by the Russian revolutionary movement of the time and particularly by the writings of Kropotkin, the anarchist. On a visit to America he picked up further inspiration for his anarchist tendencies on the West Coast, where he was residing at the time of the San Francisco earthquake. He believed that the conditions for the perfect society could come only through direct action, and his writings, which were many, inspired some of his small group of followers to plot the assassination of the Meiji emperor in 1910. Though not actually involved in the plot himself, Kotoku was imprisoned with the rest and was executed in 1911.

The association of socialism with violence was as dangerous for the government as was its association with Christian pacifism, and the relentless war which the authorities carried on against the socialist movement, beginning with the dissolution of the short-lived Socialist party in 1906, made any open organization practically impossible. The few hundred intellectuals who composed the movement were hounded by the police and many of their writings were banned. They had had little contact with the workers and peasants they professed to represent and lead, but they were blamed by the government for violent labor trouble, such as the big Ashio copper mine strike of 1907, for which they were not directly responsible. The anarchist socialist movement failed to secure power through direct action, but it left behind it the tradition of friendship with the Russian revolutionary movement and the idea that those who wanted to secure power might well take into account the peasants and workers. The significance of the socialist movement, so-called, is that it was the first serious effort to find the symbols which would command mass support.

Heterodox Nationalism

There was another stream of Japanese political thought and organization which also had its origins in the early adjustments of the ex-samurai to the Meiji Restoration. It began with the *Genyosha*, a society whose name indicated the drive to cross the sea in order to expand Japanese power on the continent. It was formally established in 1881 by supporters of Saigo, the Restoration leader who had died in the Satsuma Rebellion. They refused to come to terms with the oligarchy which they felt was betraying the true course of national greatness by compromising too much with the West and by self-enrichment. They claimed an unrivalled loyalty to the emperor and the country but were intolerant of any other views than their own on the destiny of Japan. They welcomed the efforts of the oligarchs to keep the people "of one mind" and were occasionally used by the military branch of the oligarchy as an action group to influence elections.

One of the *Genyosha's* most famous leaders, Toyama Mitsuru, spent half a century seeking to promote, by one means or another, the concept of Asian unity under the leadership of Japan. He and some of his friends helped Sun Yat-sen and other Chinese leaders, thinking that thereby they were helping China to strengthen herself against the common enemy of Western imperialism. They assisted Sun with money and men to help Emilio Aguinaldo in his fight against the United States in the Philippines. In their dream of Asiatic unity the leadership of Japan was taken for granted; China would be a friendly and subordinate neighbor, obligated to Japan for her assistance in ridding China of the foreigner.

In 1900 one of Toyama's disciples organized a society to make propaganda for war with Russia, the aim being to extend Japan's frontiers to the Amur, or Black Dragon, river, from which the society took the popular name of the Black Dragon Society. The society included in its program the same mixture of domestic "reform" and foreign expansion that marked the thought of Oi Kentaro. The foreign expansion was to be in the interests of all Asiatic countries with Japan as their guide and leader; the reform involved destroying Western influences on the minds of the people and of imposing on all the army's concept of a life dedicated to the needs of a soldier-peasant state. The educational system, with all its emphasis on loyalty and filial piety, was too westernized for the taste of the Black Dragon Society, which felt that the true native spirit of the Japanese people was being undermined by capitalism and democracy. The Black Dragon Society in practice was a group of strong-arm men and *agents provocateurs* who beat up writers and professors with whom they disagreed and carried out selective assassination, but had no constructive and positive program for the country. When the First World War increased the prestige of democratic ideas in Japan, several new organizations sprang up to combat them in the manner and tradition of the Black Dragon Society.

The significance of the semi-secret societies such as the Black Dragon did not lie in their numbers, which were often ridiculously small, or in their violence, which has often been exaggerated, but in the occasional leaders they produced and the ideas which they promoted. In general they kept alive the tradition that heterodox ideas should be promoted or suppressed—depending on who held them—by violence and intimidation, and in particular they fostered the view that Japan's destiny lay first and foremost in Asia, from which the white man should be excluded. Their form of ultranationalism was occasionally embarrassing even to the government, and up to the end of the First World War the extreme chauvinistic societies did not play a decisive role. It was when the high prestige of democracy coincided with the decline of the *genro* that the ideas which these societies had developed became important. The most important exponent of these ideas was Kita Ikki.

Kita Ikki, who lived from 1883 to 1936, spent much of the first part of his life trying to help the Chinese revolution with the backing of the Black Dragon Society. When Kita Ikki was a young man, Oi Kentaro was publishing materials on socialism, and the works and ideas of European socialists were being discussed. To the son of a small sake-brewing family on the island of Sado, the form that socialist ideas took in Japan had an appeal, for they were used to serve the purposes of men who regretted the changes in Japanese life brought about by the Western impact and despised the oligarchy which they felt had compromised too much with foreign ways and institutions. To an ambitious, idealistic, and egocentric young man, brought up with all the resentments of rural Japan against the towns, it became necessary to construct a picture of another Japan, one in which people like himself would rule, a country in which the soldier and the peasant would be the dominant types, in which the merchant would be kept in his place, and an all-powerful and paternalistic state would take care of a proud, thrifty, obedient, and patriotic people. Kita Ikki read widely in Western science and philosophy, but he was looking for material to support a view which had already hardened, the view that the oligarchy now wished to discourage, that young samurai could take matters into their own hands if they disapproved of those in charge of the national destiny.

Kita Ikki, like others of similar mind, grasped at the opportunity to influence the destiny of China with an eagerness all the more urgent because of the lack of opportunity to rise to prominence at home. He became disappointed in what he called the "western froth" of Sun Yat-sen and came to the conclusion that support of Sun's movement would help neither China nor Japan. In his book, *The Unofficial History of the Chinese Revolution*, written in 1915, Kita put some of the blame for what he considered the betrayal of the revolution on the Japanese government, in particular for its loans to Chinese warlords. Concerning Japan Kita argued that a new Restoration was necessary, for there was a new shogunate of zaibatsu and political parties which was destroying the national spirit, or *kokutai*.

In 1918 Kita Ikki, then in Shanghai, was invited to Japan by a group which was impressed with his book on the Chinese revolution. Of these the most important was Dr. Okawa, a Doctor of Philosophy from Tokyo Imperial University, a former official of the South Manchurian Railway and a member of the Black Dragon Society. Okawa's group, called the *Rosokai,* anti-democratic and intensely nationalist, was interested in Kita's views on how to reconstruct the nation, which he set down in his *Outline for the Reconstruction of Japan*, published in 1919. His views reflected that mixture of the romantic, irrational, utopian, and conspiratorial which was to be expected from a man with his background. According to Kita, utopia could be achieved by having the emperor suspend the constitution for three years, thus establishing a direct relation between emperor and people. By the "people" he had in mind a military committee which would establish martial law while reforming society, a task which would be carried out without the hindrance of the old financial cliques and the party politicians. In place of the privy council and the court officials there would be an advisory board of fifty members, all patriots, to advise the emperor. A deliberative council composed of more patriots would replace the House of Peers; and the lower house, whose will could be vetoed by the upper house only once, would be elected by universal suffrage. The new Diet would be permitted to discuss anything it liked except the reforms which the emperor, in other words the leaders of the new Restoration, had brought about.

One of the key reforms was to be a limitation of private property to one million yen in capital and to the value of 100,000 yen in land. The state would take over excess capital and pay compensation for excess land which would then be sold to peasants on a long-range purchase plan. There were to be old age pensions, compulsory education up to the age of sixteen, and abolition of the teaching of the English language and the game of baseball, which had been recently introduced into Japan. Last but not least the new government would follow an expansionist foreign policy based on that concept of a revolutionary Asia which Kita Ikki himself had tried to apply in China. This was a program which had an immediate appeal to the younger and poorer army officers, but its economic aspects—the capital levy, land reform, and state socialism—did not attract as much approval in 1919 as they did a decade later when conditions had changed. The Reconstruction Program was banned by the police in 1920, but the young officers read it in a black market mimeographed edition and probably memorized the first sentence, which read, "The maker of a reconstruction program for Japan must be the builder of a great revolutionary empire." Kita Ikki's labors had produced the most important formula, from the point of view of the military, for handling the problem of industrialism at home and expansion abroad.

One of the most interesting parts of Kita Ikki's program was the assertion that China and India could not gain their independence without Japanese assistance and that Korea should have its independence in twenty years' time. His program was drawn up about the time that the Japanese army was ruthlessly putting down a Korean attempt to get rid of Japanese rule. This did not mean that Kita Ikki's program was presented as a conscious and cynical rationalization for imperialism. It was his premise that Japanese leadership included both the exclusion of the Western powers and the acceptance by other Asiatic countries of Japanese assistance in the reconstruction of their societies. "Independence" for Asian countries was to be under

Japanese leadership. Kita Ikki had been brought up in the Confucian doctrine that it is the natural order of things for the masses to be ruled by the wise, and many of his recommendations, including the suspension of the constitution, fitted in well with this approach. His belief in the rule of the wise over the masses, when extended beyond Japan, meant the leadership of Japan over the masses of Asia. Seen from this point of view his approach was revolutionary and dynamic and was accepted as such by many Japanese, who were genuinely baffled by the charge that they were not acting in the best interests of Asia when they expanded their empire on the continent.

Minobe, Yoshino, and Suzuki

The strength of Kita's program was that it provided for the army and navy officers and other powerful groups a plausible explanation of the ills of society and a program of action. There was no similar program for those Japanese who might have been inclined towards democracy. The only challenge to orthodoxy was an attempt to explain the emperor's position in rational rather than mystical terms. Minobe Tatsukichi, professor of law at Tokyo Imperial University, a respected scholar and a member of the House of Peers, gave a series of lectures in 1911, the last year of the Meiji era, in which he developed the theory that the emperor is an organ of the state, which is the possessor of governing rights and over which the emperor has no independent authority. In advancing this so-called "organic theory," which he had taken from Europe, Professor Minobe was only expressing the views of many scholars, bureaucrats, and businessmen, for while challenging the divine right of the emperor he did not call for disloyalty to him.

It was another professor, Dr. Yoshino, a political scientist of Tokyo Imperial University, who pushed the attack much further in his famous articles in the *Central Review*, beginning in January, 1916. Yoshino openly attacked the military, the privy council, the House of Peers, and the arbitrary rule of the oligarchy. Taking the position that the most important of political values was respect for the popular will, he argued in favor of universal suffrage and restriction of the powers of the House of Peers and the privy council, without, however, going as far as "popular sovereignty." Yoshino's acceptance of the emperor prevented him from advocating the fullest statement of democracy, but he had gone far enough to arouse opposition from the government. A political activist as well as an intellectual, Yoshino organized a society for the study of democratic ideas, the *Reimeikai*, in 1918 and fearlessly accepted the challenge of Toyama, guiding spirit of the Black Dragon Society, to public debate on the subject of democracy. Yoshino's immediate influence was limited to students and professors and had to compete with the mass of reading material on socialism, especially the Russian variety, that came out in magazine or book form. As a non-Marxist social democrat Yoshino was interested in individualism, in the Western sense of the term, and his message was very different from that which came from Russia at the time of the Bolshevik revolution.

In the prewar period, Japanese labor had produced one main ideological contribution which was a natural outgrowth of traditional Japanese ideas and the social welfare aspects of Christianity. Suzuki Bunji, a law graduate of Tokyo Imperial University, a reporter for the *Asahi Shimbun*, and a social welfare worker for the Unitarian Church, organized in 1912 the most successful labor union of the period, the *Yuaikai* (Friendship and Love Association). He had the support of a few students and sympathizers acquired through his work with the Unitarian Church in Tokyo, but his union never developed a very large membership. Suzuki Bunji, who was on friendly terms with Samuel Gompers, President of the American Federation of Labor, attended the convention of the A. F. of L. held in San Francisco in 1915 and was usually in attendance at annual conventions from that time on. The objective of the *Yuaikai* was to maintain harmonious relations between employers and employees, to develop facilities for mutual aid between workmen, and to avoid class conflict. The government put no obstacles in the way.

The ideological struggle of the first two decades of the twentieth century introduced some new schools of thought which were to become important in the future. By this time the main ideas which were later adopted by the military-agrarian radicals had been formulated. There was very little in the way of liberal or democratic thought. The doctrines of Minobe shifted the emphasis from the mythical authority of the emperor to the authority of the state. Even Yoshino did not advocate the sovereignty of the people. Most of those who opposed the government accepted the orthodox views of society and of the emperor institution. It was within the limitations set by this ideological system that the social and economic changes of the war years took place.

Economic and Social Effects of World War I

The first impact of the outbreak of war between the Central Powers and the Allies in 1914 was to dislocate the international financial market then centered mainly on London, to destroy the usual channels of international trade, and to bring about a serious collapse in the prices of rice and raw silk. The Japanese government declared a moratorium and gave the Finance Minister extraordinary powers to regulate the buying and selling of rice. These measures were followed by a longer-range program for improving agricultural methods, extending the amount of land under cultivation, and providing capital for agriculture. The war cut off Japan from most of her major sources of chemicals, drugs, steel, machinery, glass, paper, and woolens, thus compelling her to manufacture them herself. The government took the initiative in encouraging the development of domestic manufactures to take the place of those which were now unavailable. By the middle of 1915 the Japanese economy had adjusted itself to the new situation with the help of orders for munitions from the Allies and of the unexpected opportunity to exploit the markets of Southeast Asia owing to the preoccupation of the powers which usually supplied this area. As a consequence old industries expanded and new ones grew up to meet the demand. By 1915 Japan was already launched on what turned out to be a period of phenomenal industrial expansion to meet the needs of the Allies and of Asiatic countries, now cut off, like Japan, from their former suppliers of manufactured goods. Most of the raw materials and many of the markets needed by Japanese industry were situated in Asia. The war brought about a great concentration of Japanese attention on Asia in general and on the Japanese empire in particular. Both Formosa and Korea were developed as sources of rice, sugar, and other foods and raw materials for the exclusive use of Japan. The Japanese came to assume more and more that a guaranteed supply of raw materials from the mainland and a privileged access to markets in most of Asia were essential to the maintenance of their economy. For the period of the war Japan became the industrial center of the East, an experience which was not forgotten when the conflict was over.

From 1915 to 1920 Japan enjoyed a period of economic prosperity. The labor force increased by half a million new workers, bringing the total in 1919 up to 1,612,000 persons. There was a change in the structure as well as in the balance of trade. Manufactured goods went down to 20 per cent of total imports, while processed and manufactured goods accounted for 90 per cent of exports. The balance of trade shifted in favor of Japan as exports grew threefold in value. The specie holdings of the Japanese at home and abroad, in 1920, amounted to 2,178,000,000 yen, an unprecedented figure. A prewar average of 65,000,000 yen excess of imports over exports was converted into an average of 352,000,000 yen excess of exports over imports. The shipping tonnage of 1,500,000 in 1914 was doubled by 1920. A debtor nation became a creditor nation.

This industrial and commercial development revealed weaknesses in the Japanese economic structure and created serious problems for the future. The enormous surpluses earned by Japan were not spent in a constructive manner. Little was done to pay off foreign indebtedness and much was wasted on loans to Chinese warlords, the famous Nishihara loans, which eventually had to be absorbed by the government. The financing of foreign trade without the assistance of the London money market and in the face of an American embargo on gold exports in September, 1917, put a strain on the Japanese banking system which it was not designed to take. The Bank of Japan increased its note issue threefold, thus helping to push up prices. The rise in prices kept far ahead of increases in wages. By the end of the war the price and cost structure was completely out of balance.

The efforts of the government to meet this problem through anti-profiteering and price-adjustment ordinances did not solve the problems of increased purchasing power, shortage of consumer goods, and inflation of the currency. One of the few measures which helped the consumer was the establishment of municipal and local markets where commodities in daily use could be purchased more cheaply than in the private markets. Efforts to prevent export of rice and to increase imports were either unenforceable or ineffective; the price of rice continued to soar, and in August, 1918, popular

cabinet and was succeeded as party leader by General Tanaka, formerly minister of war under Hara. Such was the opportunism of the *Seiyukai* that it accepted a military man as party leader. Tanaka refused to join the Kato cabinet although he continued for a while to support it. The break came when the *Seiyukai* and the *Seiyuhonto*, the group which had seceded some years earlier, temporarily joined forces to embarrass the government. Kato resigned, was called back, and formed a strictly party cabinet based on his own *Kenseito*, but although he won over the *Seiyuhonto*, the weakening of his control of the lower house forced him to seek more support from the peers and the bureaucracy. A peer himself, Kato had no fear of the upper house or the high bureaucracy. As he could not change the constitutional position of the privy council, he tried to modify the role of its president. He appointed Baron Hozumi, a nonpolitical legal scholar to the presidency of the privy council, usually considered to be a position for men of great political experience and high ambition, for the privy council was close to the emperor. Kato was responsible for certain modest measures in the field of social legislation. He sponsored a modified land reform with a view to setting up family farms of one *cho* (two and a half acres) to be purchased by thirty-year loans, but as there was no compulsion, only one per cent of existing tenant lands came to be owned by the cultivators. Labor unions were legalized and a labor dispute mediation law enacted.

While Kato was willing to permit certain union activities, he was never inclined to give left-wing political movements any leeway. Kato's Peace Preservation Law took effect one week after universal manhood suffrage became law on May 5, 1925. Although the law was designed mainly to take care of the Communist threat, it was phrased so vaguely that it was possible for the police to arrest anyone who could be charged with the wish to change "the Japanese way." Imprisonment for a term up to ten years (later raised to the death penalty) was provided for anyone who joined or formed a society which had as its object the abolition of the system of private property or any change in the existing political order. Under this definition it was difficult for anyone even to discuss, outside the Diet itself, any change in the constitution, and the party governments were just as repressive as the bureaucratic ones in censoring the press and other publications.

In foreign affairs Kato consistently backed his Foreign Minister, Baron Shidehara, in a China policy which was far too mild and conciliatory for the army. By and large, Shidehara managed to keep Japan's hands off the developing revolutionary situation on the mainland, but there were occasional examples of "dual diplomacy," in which the Japanese army on the spot took matters into its own hands.

Wakatsuki Ministry

When Kato died in January 1926, Wakatsuki, who succeeded him in the premiership and presidency of the *Kenseikai*, kept Shidehara in office over the protests of the army, and the same moderate China policy was followed during the very critical years of 1926 and part of 1927. From the beginning Wakatsuki faced the bitter opposition of the military, but he might have weathered this storm if he had been able to handle the growing economic crisis towards which Kato's retrenchment, without the promised reform, had made an important contribution. The crisis that brought about the fall of the Wakatsuki ministry was a financial panic.

The financial panic of 1927 began over the question of liquidating the "earthquake bills," which amounted to 207,000,000 yen and were a drug on the market. Half of them were held by ordinary banks and the other half by the Bank of Taiwan and the Bank of Chosen. The government proposed to exchange the bills for national treasury bonds. The proposal became a political football because the zaibatsu were fighting each other behind the scenes and their various agents in the Diet raised embarrassing questions as to which banks were to be saved from bankruptcy by this measure. The Mitsui and Mitsubishi interests, which were using their financial power to break the Suzuki Company of Kobe, ignored the request of the government to refrain from calling in their loans from the Bank of Taiwan, which financed Suzuki and was heavily overloaded with earthquake bonds. The privy council blocked the government's efforts to save the Bank of Taiwan, every branch of which closed down. There was a general panic which resulted in a run on all banks.

Tanaka Ministry

The Wakatsuki ministry resigned and the new government of General Tanaka declared a three-week moratorium, secured government money to save the Bank of Taiwan and assist the Bank of Japan, and at the cost of millions of yen came to the help of the zaibatsu and those banks which had political influence. There was no relief for the ordinary depositors who had lost their savings in the banks which failed. The figures on the number of special banks, savings banks, and ordinary banks are most revealing. The number of special banks remained steady, but between 1926 and 1929 the number of savings banks went down from 123 to 94 and that of ordinary banks from 1,417 to 874. This last figure is a vivid illustration of the way in which the zaibatsu absorbed the ordinary banks at times of financial panic. As a result of this particular panic, which some of the zaibatsu had done so much to bring on, Mitsui took over the interests of Suzuki.

General Tanaka secured from the Diet the exact amount of money for the relief of the Bank of Taiwan that his predecessor had requested and had been denied. The privy council was determined to get rid of the Wakatsuki ministry not only because of its domestic policies but also because of growing opposition to its failure to take a strong line in China. The *Seiyukai*, which had "adopted" General Tanaka as its leader some years before in the hope of returning to power, was more acceptable to the military and the privy council because it was more inclined towards their policies, and on these terms party government was allowed to continue. With the usual exceptions of the war and navy ministries Tanaka's cabinet was a *Seiyukai* party cabinet, but as the *Seiyukai* did not control an absolute majority, the Diet was dissolved. In spite of the lavish use of money and pressure the government lost the election, a most unusual outcome, and had to face a hostile Diet.

The attacks made on General Tanaka personally and upon his ministry reached new heights of vituperation; in fact, parliamentary behavior was so scandalous and irresponsible that the parties, which could always count on the contempt of the peers, the military, and the privy council, now had to reckon with the disappointment of those who elected them. Tanaka himself was accused of taking bribes and of appropriating to himself Secret Service funds during the Siberian campaign. None of these charges was ever proved. But whether the charges of personal dishonesty were true or false, they were typical of the sort of argument that passed for parliamentary discussion, and they reflected the general belief that favoritism, bribery, corruption, and abuse of power were the price of party government.

To this state of affairs the zaibatsu had made a considerable contribution, for their connections with the parties were no secret. If the Diet was corrupt and its behavior undignified, the zaibatsu were blamed. They had grown in wealth and power during the twenties. Government subsidies were less important to them now that they were well established; the broadening of the electorate in 1925 had increased the cost of elections, thus making the help of the zaibatsu more essential to the politicians, and the growth of city population, which increased the importance of the urban representatives, made it less necessary to make concessions to agrarian interests. By 1929 the zaibatsu were at the height of their power and influence.

Tanaka was committed to a more "positive" China policy if only because the conciliatory approach of the Wakatsuki ministry had brought about its downfall. Tanaka was also committed to an economic policy which suited the interests of Mitsui rather than Mitsubishi, a policy of developing the colonies, of protective tariffs, public works, and economic self-sufficiency. Unfortunately for Tanaka, the two policies turned out to be incompatible, for the strong China policy brought about strong Chinese reactions which led to boycotts and anti-Japanese feeling, thus endangering Japanese markets in China.

The swing to a more aggressive policy towards China came when the Nationalist revolution was under way and the forces of Chiang Kai-shek were marching northward. For some time the Japanese had been using Chang Tso-lin, the warlord of Manchuria, as a friendly agent to protect their special interests in North China and Manchuria. The Japanese troops, sent to North China on the grounds that Japanese lives and property had to be protected during the northward march of the Nationalist forces, took matters into their own hands at the city of Tsinan where they checked the northern expedition by force. Acting without the knowledge of the War Ministry or the premier, the Kwantung army then proceeded to arrange for the murder of Chang Tso-lin on the theory that he was an unreliable ally. The conspirators apparently expected that trouble would follow and that this would provide an excuse for the conquest of Manchuria.

Tanaka, who was angry at the incident, tried to restore authority over the Kwantung army through the Army General Staff, which, however, was either unwilling or unable to control its own officers. Tanaka even censored the news of the incident and went along with the army argument that nothing should be done to weaken the army's prestige by public punishments. Under pressure from the Diet, Tanaka negotiated his way out of the Tsinan incident, but the conspirators were not touched. Rather than yield a point to civilian authority, the army generals tolerated lack of discipline in their own ranks. Even the emperor, who wanted a public report, and Saionji, who wanted discipline enforced, could not press the issue to a conclusion. When the emperor insisted upon the enforcement of discipline in the army, Tanaka, unable to carry out his wishes, handed in his resignation in July, 1929. General Tanaka became internationally famous as the author of the alleged Tanaka Memorial, a document which is supposed to have laid out the future lines of Japanese military expansion on the continent. The famous memorial seems to have been a forgery, and the charge that he wrote it has never been proved. Actually, Tanaka was not in sympathy with the military extremists.

Hamaguchi Ministry

On the recommendation of Saionji, who was alarmed for the future of civil government, the next cabinet was organized by Hamaguchi, head of the *Minseito* party. The *Minseito* was the successor to the *Kenseikai* and was thought to have been close to Mitsubishi interests. As the *Seiyukai* had a majority in the Diet, Hamaguchi called for new elections, in 1930, which he won. The *Minseito* campaigned for a program of disarmament, elimination of corruption, economy, and conciliation of China. As the Mitsubishi interests, which leaned more towards general international commerce and to sound money, in contrast with Mitsui mercantilism, called for a removal of the gold embargo, the ministry proceeded to lift the gold embargo in January, 1930. The timing seemed to be propitious, as the American demand for Japanese raw silk was booming and world trade seemed to be picking up momentum at long last.

Actually the move was disastrous because of the impact of the world economic depression, and the catastrophic fall in prices. The depression in America led to a 50 per cent drop in the price of raw silk in 1930 and a corresponding drop in the value of silk exported from Japan. Exports as a whole fell off 27 per cent. By 1931 the peasants of Japan were in a desperate plight, owing to the collapse of the raw silk market. Their plight was worsened by the decline in the price of rice, due, ironically enough, to several years of extremely good harvests. Hamaguchi pressed ahead with his deflationary policy while attempting to meet some of the more obvious effects of the depression by setting up a silk valorization scheme, promoting public relief works, and assisting bankrupt producers with loans. Still determined to balance the budget in accordance with the principles of "sound finance," the government, in 1931, tried to pare away the cost of the army and navy. The military naturally objected. In the meantime the gold reserves of the Bank of Japan, already depleted by a steady drain since the lifting of the gold embargo, were further endangered by the depreciation of Japanese holdings abroad when the British went off the gold standard in 1931. By the end of that year Japan had lost nearly half the holdings she had in 1929.

Hamaguchi's drive for financial retrenchment was pressed against the opposition of both the bureaucrats and the military. He cut salaries of all government employees, both civil and military, by 10 per cent if the salaries exceeded 100 yen a month. But it took tremendous firmness on the part of the government to force through the London Naval Reduction Treaty of 1930, for this committed the navy to long-term limitation of its budget, as the treaty continued the 5–5–3 ratio of the Washington Treaties. In the meantime, Foreign Minister Shidehara's approach to China improved relations between the two countries but did not please large sections of the army which still wanted more direct action. The army was most disturbed, however, by Hamaguchi's attitude towards the non-elective parts of the government. It was obvious that he was not afraid of the privy council and it was believed that he had plans to abolish the General Staff, cut off military access to the throne, and change the content of military education. Such a program tended to unite the senior ranks of the army and navy with the younger officer clique which had by now a well defined faith in its mission to save the nation by coup d'état.

Army Plots

At a time when Hamaguchi, the strongest protagonist of party rule, was at the height of his power, he was shot and wounded by a young fanatic. Shidehara took over for a while, but when Hamaguchi died, in April, 1931, Wakatsuki again became premier and president of the *Minseito*. There followed a struggle between Shidehara and the army over policies to be followed in Manchuria, which was settled by the army taking matters into its own hands. Twenty-four hours after Shidehara had stated publicly that there were no questions between China and Japan that could not be settled by peaceful means, the young army officers provoked the Mukden incident which began the conquest of Manchuria and led to the establishment of the puppet state of Manchukuo. Unable to control the fierce conflicts between the parties, the bureaucrats, and the military, or to handle the worsening economic situation, and faced with revolt within his own party, Wakatsuki resigned in December 1931.

Saoinji called on the *Seiyukai* to form a cabinet with Inukai as premier. In the ensuing elections the *Seiyukai* was returned with a large majority but the party was so divided by factions that it was unable to stem the tide of militarism. One of its first measures was to reimpose the embargo on the export of gold, an act which immediately enriched large numbers of speculators who had anticipated this action for some time and had purchased large quantities of American dollars. The House of Mitsui, a traditional *Seiyukai* supporter, prospered enormously in what was called the "dollar buyer" affair. This fact alone helped to confirm a general belief that democracy and the party system meant corruption, the sabotage of the nation for the profit of vested interests, and continuing economic depression. It was recalled that when the first party cabinet was formed by Hara the economy was booming, but while the businessmen parties had been in control, nothing but depression had plagued the country. Some of the young militarists claimed that the zaibatsu had actually planned the depression.

The young army and navy officers were now ready to swing into action. A serious plot in the spring of 1931, for which Okawa had done much of the planning, failed to come off owing to a last minute change of mind on the part of General Ugaki, who was to have taken over the government under martial law. Far from being discouraged, the young extremists went ahead with arrangements for another plot in October. This also failed owing to premature disclosure. In the meantime various civilian ultranationalist groups, among which the Black Dragon Society was particularly active, openly backed the militarists, for whom they tried to organize support. This support, which came largely from the countryside, was important because it brought together agrarian discontent and military activism, thus helping to turn the post-depression sufferings of the peasants into chauvinistic channels. Two young peasant fanatics were responsible, in the spring of 1932, for the murder of Inoue, formerly minister of finance, governor of the Bank of Japan, and an important member of the *Minseito*, and for the assassination of Baron Dan, head of the Mitsui interests.

On May 15, 1932, navy officers took the lead in one of the most significant and successful undertakings yet engaged in by the extremists. Some twenty navy and army officers and a few civilians attacked police headquarters in Tokyo, several banks, and party offices, and murdered the premier, Inukai. They then surrendered voluntarily to the police. The public trials which followed were important, not for the light sentences which were passed on the conspirators, but for the public debate of the issues involved. The trials provided a sounding board for the ideas of the conspirators, which were that the nation could be saved only by destroying the zaibatsu, the political parties, corrupt bureaucrats, and all others who were alleged to be responsible for a weak foreign policy, for agrarian distress, for the exploitation of the people and the decay of the national spirit. The simple country boys and the earnest young officers, as dedicated as they were ignorant, did not understand the significance of what they were doing, but some very shrewd men in the higher ranks of the military and the bureaucracy noted the public reaction to the trials, which were fully reported in the best newspapers. The public either counted the murderers as heroes or was neutral and indifferent; there was little open opposition. The ideas of the conspirators were given a full hearing through the trials, one of the accused actually lecturing the court for three days. Although these men were assassins, they were presented to the public and were handled by the prosecutors as if they had committed patriotic acts. The manner in which the whole trial was handled must have done more to encourage than to discourage those who shared the ideas of the accused. Party government had been dealt a heavy blow by the independent action of the army in Manchuria a year before, but the May fifteenth incident was an even greater shock. It showed that the tide had definitely turned against the parties and revealed a climate of opinion favorable to the plans of the most extreme elements among the military.

3. RISE OF THE MILITARISTS

In the decade from 1931 to 1941 the military gained a dominating position among the power groups in Japanese politics. The military, the bureaucrats, and the party politicians all had their own sources of power. The high officers of the army and navy had direct access to the emperor, great influence over the formation of cabinets, a vast educational machine, and tremendous prestige. The top civilian officers of the bureaucracy administered the machinery of government, controlled some of the non-elective branches of government, such as the privy council, and held leading positions in the parties. The party politicians, who depended on the voters for their election to the Diet and therefore had to pay a certain amount of attention to the interests of their constituents, depended for their power position on the authority given to the lower house in the constitution. The *genro* had held within their joint grasp the strings which controlled all three groups. In the twenties, when the strength of the *genro* had declined, an alliance between the parties and the bureaucracy, cemented and financed by the zaibatsu, exercised a predominant influence.

In the thirties the balance of power moved towards the militarists. Public opinion turned more and more against the zaibatsu and the party politicians and took the form of general disrespect for the Diet. The rise of military activists within the armed forces changed the character of the military, and eventually led to the emergence of the army as a unified power group which attracted many of the bureaucrats and politicians away from the zaibatsu and the parties. The conquest of Manchuria was a decisive move in the struggle for power as a semi-autonomous territorial base of army power. New ideological formulations gave to the military the drive and the sense of direction which their rivals in the struggle for power so sadly lacked.

Ideology of the Military

The nationalism of official Japan took shape in an agrarian country of soldiers and peasants, and was based on existing personal, family, and class loyalties. This sort of nationalism could perhaps be adapted to an industrialized society, but it worked best in the villages and in the army. Its most appropriate slogan was "Rich Nation, Strong Army."

Respect for the military virtues of discipline, devotion to duty, reverence for the emperor, bravery and simplicity, were not easily broken down by the new habits and ideas from the West. The army, especially when it was winning, could usually count on considerable popular enthusiasm, whereas the zaibatsu, when they were getting richer, could not. In view of Japanese traditions, it was easier for the military than for the merchants to persuade the people that society owed them a living. The most important element in Japanese nationalism was the absence of the economic virtues of the middle class as they had emerged in England and America. The dominant ethical type in Japanese nationalism remained the warrior, not the merchant.

The concept of the organic state also distinguished Japanese nationalism from that of the democratic secular state. The organic state in Japan was based on one ideological system which must be jealously guarded against all others; there was no place for the individual and individual freedom. The purposes of the state were formulated in *Kodo*, or the Imperial Way, which, taken to its logical conclusion meant Japanese leadership in a world community of nations. Just as the rulers of Japan decided what the good of the whole should be, so Japan would decide for the world community its common good.

The westernization of Japan deeply affected the thinking and way of life of many Japanese, especially those in the cities. But when political confusion, corruption, and economic suffering had discredited the party system and the zaibatsu, the spokesmen of an ultranationalism which drew heavily on traditional Japanese concepts became influential.

One of the most important of these was Kita Ikki, whose ideas had great influence on the young army officers. He added to the Imperial Way concepts which came from the streams of socialist and imperialist thinking. He accepted the fact that Japan must be an industrially-based society, but because he hated capitalists and the impact of urban culture on the villages he wanted everything to be in the hands of a highly centralized state which should own and direct the economy and be created through a coup d'état. Much as he hated Communism with its glorification of the proletariat, he openly admired the manner in which the Bolsheviks seized power. His disregard for private property and his advocacy of the overthrow of governments placed him in right-wing radical opposition.

Gondo Seikyo, in contrast to Kita Ikki, never accepted the industrialization of Japan. He began writing in 1919, about the same time as Kita Ikki, and published several important works in the twenties. Gondo idealized a decentralized and agrarian Japan and attacked not only the capitalists who had ruined agrarian autonomy but also the organs of the modern state which the oligarchs had so laboriously constructed. He fanned the hatred of the countryside for the towns, for capitalism and westernization. Like Kita Ikki, he was a revolutionary and a radical nationalist. Between them they contributed to the ultranationalist movement, in their different ways, the new ingredients which traditional nationalism lacked—the political idealism, the social program, and the technique of revolutionary action. They provided many of the most important ideas that others put together in patterns that could inspire men to action.

Okawa Shumei, an intellectual with important contacts in the army and the bureaucracy, a promoter of patriotic societies and a one-time sponsor of Kita Ikki reformulated many of the ideas developed by Kita Ikki and Gondo in terms which had meaning for his highly placed friends. He broke with Kita Ikki early in the twenties—in fact, the men became bitter enemies —but their differences seem to have been more personal than ideological. A graduate of Tokyo Imperial University with a Ph.D. in philosophy and an official of the South Manchurian Railway, Okawa appealed more to the higher ranks in the military, Kita Ikki to the lower ranks. Whereas Kita Ikki was mainly concerned with domestic problems, Okawa was more interested in expansion abroad, and the program of his patriotic society included the emancipation of the colored races and the "ethical unity of the world." At times it was difficult to tell whether Okawa leaned more to Kita's version of national socialism or Gondo's self-centered agrarian communalism, with its return to familism and its ostrich-like attitude towards industrial labor, for he owed much to both. Okawa's real role was that of a promoter and sponsor of ideas and of men. His wealth, or access to wealth, his scholarly prestige and bureaucratic experience, permitted him to move with confidence in high army and bureaucratic circles and also to impress the younger army officers. He did much to bring about the peculiar mixture of native chauvinism and second-hand Marxism which marked the program of the military in the thirties.

This program drew heavily on world socialist movements for many of its ideas on the state control of the industrial machine and industrial workers, but at the same time derived its emotional backing from the frustrations of agrarian Japan. The young army officers and their civilian allies thought of themselves as the young samurai whose destiny it was to build a "Restoration Japan," to overthrow the new shogunate of the zaibatsu and the political parties, and to return to the true Japanese way of life. They saw the Japanese way of life as one in which the emperor, theoretically all powerful but in practice controlled by his advisers, would be surrounded only by men whose ideas coincided with those of the young officers. Nothing, they said, should stand between emperor and people—in other words there should be no constitution, no Diet, no political parties, and no zaibatsu. About 80 per cent of the national income should go to the army, and the people should live on the rest.

A conscript army reflected the attitudes of the countryside much more than those of the cities, for even in 1920 about 50 per cent of the occupied population made its living from the land and less than 20 per cent from manufacture. In the army peasants heavily outnumbered workers, and in any case many of the workers were hardly more than a generation from the land. About half the younger officers also came from the countryside. Many officers and men in the army therefore reflected the hatred of the countryside for the towns, and really believed that the zaibatsu plotted the depression, that capitalists should be killed, and that the army, as the vanguard of the nation, should protect the farmer. Their anti-capitalist predilections made it possible for certain aspects of Marxism to find a place in the thinking of the army officers.

The most important contribution made by Kita Ikki, Gondo, and Okawa was to give to the ideology of nationalism a new social content. They wanted to bring back to their dominant role in society the military men who had ruled for so long before, and who had been forced into equality with commoners and compelled to find their own living. Not businessmen and workers, intellectuals, and politicians but warriors and peasants were to be among the elect. The latter-day young samurai, unlike their predecessors who became the oligarchs of the Meiji period, felt the need for a mass basis for their movement if they were to succeed; hence the importance of the peasants whose economic grievances they so often reflected or exploited. Many nationwide patriotic societies were formed, some of them ephemeral but some quite substantial, and they were joined by responsible civilian as well as military leaders. There was in these societies a variegated mixture of ideas and motives, for they included men who saw no further than agrarian revolt as well as others who were interested only in power and were shrewd enough to use the revolt for their own purposes. The main action group to seize the initiative was the famous association of young officers, none above the rank of lieutenant-colonel, known as the Cherry Blossom Society, which was formed in 1930 and had a program of revolutionary action.

So long as the loyalty of the army could be counted upon, the patriotic societies and the small groups of terrorists could be handled like the socialists and Communists, as annoying but not dangerous political extremists. But when the army officers took over the leadership of ultranationalism, they made it into a radical and revolutionary movement. They were able to take advantage of the tradition of deference for the military and to use, in a new setting, symbols which had played a powerful part in the emergence of modern Japan. They were not Fascists or Communists, but they were encouraged by the success of small, disciplined groups in seizing power by violence in Russia, Italy, and Germany. They linked together two powerful forces in Japan—the drive for expansion abroad and the anti-capitalist, anti-Western drive for national socialism at home.

Communism

The role of the Japanese Communists during the twenties was to divide and destroy the anarchists and democratic socialists and to frighten the zaibatsu and bureaucrats into alliance with the ultranationalist movement. After the mass arrests of Communists in 1923 the remaining members, with the approval of those in prison, decided to dissolve, a move which enraged the Comintern, under whose pressure the party continued with new leadership and fresh directives. The first directive was to destroy the deadly enemy—Social Democracy; the second was to infiltrate and support appropriate mass and labor organizations.

The Social Democrats had been alerted by the revelations of Communist infiltration after the arrests of 1923, but their efforts to exclude the Communists led to further fragmentation of their own movement. In 1925 the Communists played an important part in the setting up of a Farmer-Labor party, but their influence was so apparent that the government abolished the party within thirty minutes of its organization. In March 1926, anti-Communist labor leaders and Social Democrats established a new party known as the Labor-Farmer party which pledged itself to legal, parliamentary methods, but once again the Communists were successful in destroying what they could not control. The party was torn to pieces over the issue of excluding the Communists; the anti-Communists withdrew and left the Labor-Farmer party under the leadership of Oyama Ikuo, a man who later became a member of the Communist party. It was through the Labor-Farmer party that the illegal Japanese Communist group expected to carry out its objectives.

The leaders who had been driven out of the Labor-Farmer party, mainly Social Democrats, proceeded to organize in December 1926 a Social Mass party, which declared in its program that the political and economic system must be based on the working class and that the system of capitalist production and distribution must be reformed, and charged that the major political parties represented the interests of privileged classes. This major non-Communist socialist party always stuck to parliamentary methods.

In the meantime a Comintern agent, Janson, who masqueraded as the commercial attaché of the Russian Embassy, reorganized the Japanese Communists in December 1926, just in time for them to be purged and redirected by Moscow in the summer of 1927. While it was easy to direct the Japanese Communists to renew themselves for the struggle to the death with the Social Democrats, it was not so easy for the Comintern to fit other theoretical considerations into Japanese conditions. The Japanese Communists were committed to the two-stage revolution, which in other parts of Asia allowed Communists to take advantage of anti-colonial nationalism but in Japan pitted them against Japanese nationalism. At the same time they were instructed to control or destroy all other leaders of the "bourgeois democratic movement." The needs of Soviet foreign policy demanded the type of action that would weaken Japanese imperialism by turning the workers and peasants against patriotism and state power, while the theory of the Asian revolution required a united front with all appropriate parties for the furtherance of the bourgeois democratic revolution. The two did not always fit well together.

Under these circumstances the Japanese Communists could not agree on application of the political line. Like the rest of the so-called "leftist movement" they were divided by personal and theoretical quarrels. The first election held under the universal manhood suffrage law in 1928 reflected the disunity of the newly enfranchised workers and peasants and their distrust of the politicians who claimed to be representing their interests. To this disunity the Communists made their contribution, but they played such an open part in the elections that the government was able to arrest most of the Communist leaders in March 1928. The Tanaka government followed up this blow to the Communists with the abolition of the Communist-controlled Labor-Farmer party.

The Japanese Communists were not large in numbers, but neither were the leaders of the various socialist parties or labor unions, so it was possible for them to increase the division and confusion among those who competed for the support of worker and peasant, even if they could not operate openly and legally or hope for the establishment of a large mass party of their own. The very existence of the Communists discredited the Social Democrats and provided the patriotic societies with a valuable device with which to blackmail the bureaucrats and businessmen into supporting them. Political extremists of the right and left thrived upon each other's activities, for both shared a common interest in destroying the middle.

The Army's Base in Manchuria

The conquest of Manchuria was planned with the connivance of the Army General Staff in Tokyo but without any approval by the cabinet. A group of Kwantung army officers, imbued with the idea that Japan could be saved only by expansion on the Asiatic continent and "reform" at home, presented Japan and the world with a *fait accompli*. On the night of September 18, 1931, they exploded a bomb on the railway near Mukden, and used this alleged Chinese provocation as an excuse for taking over the city of Mukden and embarking upon the conquest of the three northeastern provinces of China.

Tokyo had not always honored the actions of its military extremists abroad, but from this particular action there was no retreat. The emperor himself was deeply concerned, especially over the problem of army discipline, as were Saionji and the premier, Wakatsuki. There was also the danger that this action might involve Japan in international conflict. The issue was a test of strength between the radical army leaders and the government as to who should determine policy. In this test the government yielded. It did not dare to propose disciplinary action, because it could not enforce it, and used as an excuse the argument that nothing should be done to lower the prestige of the army. Although some of the more responsible members of the army were worried over the problem of controlling the radicals, they had no real objection to direct action of this sort or to the strengthening of Japan's position on the continent. The premier could not even count on the support of all of his own party or on large sections of the bureaucracy. The opposition party, the *Seiyukai*, always more pro-military than the *Minseito*, did nothing to help. Both Saionji and the premier were anxious to prevent the emperor from assuming a position from which he could not retreat and advised him against adopting in public an attitude which he apparently held in private. Baron Shidehara, one of the few men who openly fought and opposed the army after the incident at Mukden, felt that a peaceful adjustment could be made to Chinese nationalism. But the absence of strong international opposition further strengthened the hand of the radicals. As a result, the government had to accept the policy initiated by the Kwantung army and provided for the movement of troops to Manchuria without imperial sanction.

The radicals had chosen their ground well. Few Japanese saw anything wrong with the position that had been built up in Manchuria since the Russo-Japanese war of 1904–5. Japan had given up much at the Washington Conference in 1922, having agreed to the limitation of naval armaments, partial return of her gains in Shantung, and abolition of the Anglo-Japanese alliance. But she had not given up her treaty position in Manchuria, which had been strengthened during World War I by the agreements of 1915. These treaties had extended the lease of the Kwantung territory to ninety-nine years, enlarged the railway concessions, and guaranteed to the Japanese the right to lease land for agricultural purposes in Manchuria. In 1928, when the armies of Chiang Kai-shek were marching to the north, Japanese troops on the mainland prevented them from pursuing the Manchurian warlord Chang Tso-lin into Manchuria itself. The Kwantung officers arranged for the murder of Chang Tso-lin in the hope of creating an incident which would provide an excuse for establishing Japanese rule in Manchuria. But their plans did not receive sufficient backing in Tokyo. Chang Hsüeh-liang, the son and successor of Chang Tso-lin, ran up the Nationalist flag in Manchuria and put the northeastern provinces under the administration of the National Government. From the Japanese point of view this meant that questions relating to Manchuria now had to be referred to Nanking instead of being dealt with on the spot at Mukden under the shadow of Japanese arms. The National Government was in no mood for compromise. Kuomintang propagandists moved into Manchuria in order to develop there the same spirit of nationalism that had set the south afire. The Chinese government not only refused to recognize the validity of the 1915 treaties but also embarked upon a program of railway building in the area served by the South Manchurian Railway in a way that was intended to undermine the economic domination of the Japanese railway system. By this time the Chinese population of Manchuria was approximately thirty million, while the Japanese, in spite of their treaty right to lease land, did not amount to more than a quarter of a million. There were, in fact, more Koreans (800,000) than Japanese. The Japanese farmer could not compete with the Korean, and the Korean could not compete with the Chinese. The Japanese position and plans in Manchuria were challenged by the policies of the new National Government of China.

The military radicals were fortunate in their choice of time and place, not only as far as Japan was concerned, but also in relation to the rest of the world. The Chinese government invoked Article XI of the Covenant of the

League of Nations, but at no time was there any serious consideration of the use of force against the Japanese. Both the Chinese and the Japanese governments agreed to a resolution of the Council which called for the removal, as rapidly as circumstances permitted, of Japanese troops from the area which they then controlled. Every resolution of the League was met, however, by the extension of Japanese control, until the whole of Manchuria was occupied. The Japanese announced that they would withdraw their troops only after reaching a complete settlement with the Chinese, while the Chinese made it clear that they would negotiate only after the troops were withdrawn. A commission to investigate the situation, sent out by the League under the leadership of Lord Lytton, wrote a report which was frank and informative but led to no action on the part of the League calculated to deter Japan. Most members of the League went along with the so-called Hoover-Stimson doctrine of non-recognition, announced on January 7, 1932. Stimson's suggestion of using economic sanctions found no support from the United Kingdom and was dropped. The United States government never recognized the conquest of Manchuria but soon re-established commercial relations with that area. The disapproval of the League and of the United States led to Japan's withdrawal from the League.

It was the Chinese, themselves, who attempted to impose economic sanctions. The Chinese boycott of Japanese goods was so effective that Japanese exports to China dropped to one-third of their normal figure in a few months, as a result of which the Japanese navy in Shanghai undertook to bring the Chinese to terms. The Chinese put up so much resistance that much of the city of Greater Shanghai was destroyed before an armistice was arranged. The action at Shanghai merely served to intensify the strong anti-Japanese feeling in China, especially among the students.

In February 1932, the Japanese announced the creation of the new state of Manchukuo, drafting as its emperor Henry Pu-yi, the last of the emperors of imperial China, who had abdicated in 1912. The new state included the three northeastern provinces, as well as the province of Jehol. Manchukuo was vested with all the rights of an independent government, including even the administration of the maritime customs and the salt gabelle. The Japanese substituted partial for total control, a device by which they were able to exclude foreign competition, to say nothing of foreign treaty rights, without being themselves accountable at international law. In theory it was the free people of Manchuria who had set up an independent state, but in practice the Japanese ran every branch of the government down to the lowest level. To this new type of puppet regime the Japanese gave formal recognition on September 15, 1932, a little over a week after the Lytton commission of inquiry had completed its report.

There was no question as to which Japanese ruled Manchukuo. The Japanese ambassador to Manchukuo, the commander-in-chief of the Kwantung army, and the governor of the leased territory were one and the same person. Through his control of all channels of communication to Japan, both civil and military, and through his control of all Japanese in Manchukuo, the commander-in-chief of the Kwantung army was in effect the real ruler of Manchukuo. Japanese officials controlled the General Affairs Board which decided on over-all policy. The heads of departments were Manchurian Chinese, but over half of the rest of the administrative staff were Japanese. Theoretically they were working directly for the state of Manchukuo, but in practice they reported to the Kwantung army. Japan officially assumed responsibility for the military affairs of Manchukuo and for the maintenance of internal order, while Manchukuo agreed to reaffirm all Japanese treaty rights and privileges within its borders. The new state announced that it intended to conduct its relations with other countries in a high-minded manner, observing all its obligations under international treaties, protecting the rights and interests of foreigners, maintaining the open door, and welcoming trade and commerce, but in reality Manchukuo was handled as an economic province of the Japanese empire.

When the Japanese took over in 1931, Manchuria was still mainly an agrarian country, but economically it was developing faster than any other part of China, mainly owing to foreign railroad building and investments. The railroads were extremely important in the agricultural development of Manchuria. The great export crop of Manchuria was soya beans; over half of the total world production of soya beans came from this area. Industries, located in Dairen, Harbin, and within the zones of the South Manchurian and the Chinese Eastern railways, were mainly foreign enterprises, although the Chinese had a strong hold over the production of consumer goods. The strength of Japanese interests in Manchuria was shown by the fact that nearly three-quarters of the foreign investments were Japanese, the other quarter being Russian. A very small percentage was in the hands of the Americans and British. Apart from industrial enterprises, by far the largest amount of capital invested in Manchuria as a whole came from the Chinese. In taking over Manchuria the Japanese cut China off from its one food surplus area and denied access to the only territories which could absorb surplus population.

The military radicals went about the organization of what they called their new "paradise" in Manchuria. This was to be a state without capitalists and without party politicians, a pilot project for a new Japan, a demonstration of what the army would like to have at home. The ambition of the Kwantung army was to secure complete control of Manchukuo in order to develop a continental war base and to establish a planned economy. For this purpose the army rule of Manchukuo had to be free from interference by Tokyo. The combination in the same person of the offices of the commander-in-chief of the Kwantung army, governor of the Kwantung Leased Territory, and ambassador to Manchukuo was a step forward but not completely satisfactory, because the same man had three superiors in Tokyo—the War Office, the Foreign Office, and the Ministry of Overseas Affairs. The next step was the setting up in 1934 of a Manchurian Affairs Board in Tokyo with the Minister of War as its president. By this device the Ministry of Overseas Affairs and the Foreign Office lost all control over Manchurian affairs.

The next moves of the army were to take control of Japanese enterprises in Manchukuo, the most important of which was the South Manchurian Railway. In order to do this the Kwantung army employed the same device it had used to control foreign trade and enterprises—it insisted upon the sovereign powers of the state of Manchukuo. The Japanese relinquished their extraterritorial rights in Manchukuo, and the administration of the South Manchurian Railway zone was automatically transferred to the Manchukuo government, in other words to the Kwantung army. The South Manchurian Railroad administration took over all the railroads of Manchuria, including the Chinese Eastern Railroad, purchased from the Soviet Union in 1935. The army drew up the first five-year plan of industrial development in 1936, at a time when the struggle to control the S.M.R. was not complete but when the issue was no longer in doubt. For the Five Year Plan the assistance of the S.M.R. was absolutely essential.

To meet the tremendous need for capital investment and technical direction the assistance of both the Japanese government and the much hated zaibatsu were also necessary. Rather than bring in the older zaibatsu, such as Mitsui and Mitsubishi, the army decided to develop its own zaibatsu. The most famous member of the new zaibatsu was Aikawa, who had had experience in the development of industries, such as iron, steel, and chemicals, which the army wished most to develop. Aikawa was given a position of enormous influence in Manchuria when his company was made the nucleus for the formation of the Manchurian Heavy Industry Company in 1937, an organization through which Aikawa ran the most important industries of Manchuria. Aikawa was free to profit financially, but on economic policy matters he took his directions from the army. In Manchuria the army had established a relationship to the state and to private industry to which it had long aspired in Japan. The men who planned and directed the military-industrial empire of Manchukuo were soon to come to power in Japan. General Tojo was one of those who started his career in Manchukuo.

The original five-year plan was only a year old when it was revised as a result of the opening of the Sino-Japanese conflict in 1937. The original investment of 2,358,000,000 yen was increased to the figure of 4,800,000,000 yen. Of this only 140,000,000 yen was for agriculture while the rest was to go into iron and steel, coal, electric power, machinery and chemicals, transport and communications, and immigration. Although tremendous development took place, the actual production figures in 1941 did not, in some very important categories, come up to the figures set in the original plan. According to the Japanese, coal production in 1941 was 20.7 million tons as against the planned 25.5 million; pig iron was 1.4 million as against 2.4 million; salt production was 560,000 tons as against the planned 870,000 tons. An ambitious plan for producing half of Japan's total production of synthetic oil achieved only about one-fifth of the goal. If the army had concentrated on nothing more than the Manchurian adventure, it is possible that the goals of the original plan and perhaps some of those of the revised plan might have been met. But the Japanese economy was unable to provide all the capital goods that were required to prosecute a war in China, to stockpile strategic materials for future wars, and take care of all other requirements at the same time. The United States and Great Britain were in no mood to lend money, although the army planners naively included large American capital investments in their plans. For these reasons the people of Manchuria had to bear a heavy burden in taxation, shortage of consumer goods, and inflation.

The most important Japanese contribution to the development of Manchurian industry lay in the field of hydroelectric and thermal power. Large dams were built on the Yalu and the Sungari rivers and others were begun. This power made possible the development of the rest of the industrial program and the provision of facilities for the great increase in urbanization. The Japanese made extensive surveys of the coal and other mineral resources of Manchuria and opened up new deposits of coal and iron ore and of magnesite and molybdenum. Considerable technical improvements were made by the Japanese in the roasting and sintering of low-grade iron ores. There was considerable progress in the chemical, metal, and machinery industries. The Manchurian Chemical Industry Company, set up in 1933, was one of the first new factories put into production. Ambitious projects in cotton manufacturing were limited by a shortage of cotton. Many of these achievements could not have taken place without corresponding extension of the means of communication. The Japanese greatly expanded the railroad and highway system in Manchuria, which, like many of the mines and industries was mainly designed for strategic purposes. The mining and manufacturing enterprises in Manchuria were closely integrated with the economy of Japan; in fact, in spite of the rise of manufacturing industries in Manchuria, Manchukuo exported to Japan most of the products of its mines and basic industries for manufacture or finishing.

Like many other industrial planners, the Japanese army looked upon the agricultural sector as subordinate. Very little of the investing capital was allocated to agriculture, and even this was for the encouragement of special crops for war purposes. The army was particularly interested in improving the production of cotton, rice, beet sugar, castor beans for lubricating oil, hemp, and a few cereals. Cotton was considered so important that a twenty-year plan was drawn up which envisaged a tremendous increase in the cotton area. The army set up a monopolistic purchasing and marketing agency, the Manchurian Cotton Company, which poured money and technical assistance into cotton production. While cotton production increased, it never approached the needs of Manchukuo, let alone of Japan. Similarly every effort made to increase the production of rice in Manchuria was insufficient to keep up with domestic consumption. Production of the big staples, such as soya beans and kaoliang, actually fell off during the thirties, a reflection in part of the general neglect of agriculture and in part of world conditions.

Part of the army's plan for agriculture was a vast scheme for Japanese and Korean colonization. But it was not very successful. One of the first measures after the conquest of Manchuria was to restrict Chinese immigration, and in this the Japanese were apparently quite successful. Those Chinese who were admitted were shipped as industrial workers to the towns rather than to the farms. Political oppression and the severe measures taken against the villages in the campaigns against Chinese resistance groups led to almost as much Chinese emigration as immigration. The big monopoly corporations set up by the army, later to become a feature in Japanese control in occupied China, eliminated the competitive market and set state-controlled prices for the purchase of agricultural products. The farmer naturally responded by tending to bring production down to subsistence level, in spite of the inducements that a desperate government offered him, and the threats, such as the withholding of necessary consumer goods, which were occasionally imposed. The failure of the Japanese to improve the structure and technical aspects of the agrarian economy stands out in sharp contrast to their comparative success in the fields of mining and industry.

The army planners handled foreign trade as an instrument to assist them in their political and economic plans. When the state of Manchukuo had been set up, they directed it to cut off the Maritime Customs agreement with China in June, 1932, thus acquiring 15 per cent of the total customs revenue of China. They used their control of tariffs to facilitate the import of the capital goods which they needed and to solidify the Japan-Manchukuo economic bloc. They made conditions for foreign business intolerable and forced out the big American and British oil companies. They imposed upon Manchukuo a unified monetary system, a necessary condition for the imposition of complete state control of all financial operations.

The conquest of Manchuria eliminated what hope there might have been of peaceful relations with Nationalist China. By the time the state of Manchukuo was established in February 1932, Japan was committed to a position from which she could not withdraw and to which Nationalist China could never agree. The example of the Kwantung army was a success story which other groups in the Japanese army sought to imitate. It set the example for the Japanese garrisons in North China and later, during the Sino-Japanese conflict, for the Japanese army in Central China. Manchukuo led to Japan's withdrawal from the League of Nations and to the deterioration of her relations with the great powers. Not to be outdone by the army, the navy withdrew from the naval disarmament agreements with Great Britain and America and thus contributed another step towards the further isolation of Japan. By 1936 Japan was ready to ally herself with Nazi Germany and Fascist Italy.

Manchukuo seemed to be a practical demonstration of the inevitability of the "new Restoration," and the theories of the military-agrarian radicals were now given immense prestige. The army's development of a continental war base in Manchukuo committed Japan herself to a semi-war economy, greatly changed the structure of her world trade, and made all alternative courses of action, such as the peaceful cultivation of markets, seem implausible and impractical. Even the members of the zaibatsu in Japan began to find the army's case less easy to answer. The world depression and the economic restrictions and quotas that followed intensified the economic difficulties of Japan and put the zaibatsu on the defensive. They were glad to get the pickings from Manchukuo and the contracts from the rearmament program. For Japanese domestic policy, the Manchurian adventure had immediate as well as long-range consequences. It gave the army a decisive advantage in its struggle for control in Japan between 1932 and 1936. The army's Manchurian empire produced many of the men who controlled Japan from 1936 onward and who took Japan through the China and the Pacific wars.

The Army's Struggle for Power

The political assassinations of 1932 made it clear that in Japan it was becoming dangerous to be publicly exposed as a party leader or a prominent member of the zaibatsu. Not the victims but the assassins became the martyrs. Army propaganda spread by right-wing civilian groups had persuaded large numbers of people that party politicians were irresponsible and the zaibatsu corrupt. During the era of party government the bureaucracy, the parties, and the zaibatsu formed an alliance which was strong enough to check but not to destroy the political power of the armed forces. In the period from 1932 to 1936 this alliance broke down and the allegiance of the bureaucracy shifted from the parties to the army. A new combination of army and bureaucrats took over the fortunes of Japan for more than a decade.

The bureaucracy, which was necessary to any government, was assiduously cultivated by important factions of the army. One of the best known devices for this purpose was the famous breakfast club which brought together important bureaucrats, army officers, and politically ambitious members of the House of Peers. Once Japan was committed to the development of Manchukuo, the Kwantung army became a great employer of bureaucrats through whom, rather than through the zaibatsu, it expected to govern. So long as they were willing to play along with the army, the bright young men from Tokyo Imperial University, the main source of supply of bureaucrats, could pick and choose their jobs, and many of the more ambitious ones formed alliances with army officers in Manchuria who later assisted them in their careers at home.

In order to assume the dominating role in Japanese politics the army had first to resolve its own inner conflicts. There were many generals who still took seriously the imperial injunction to remain out of politics, but they were not powerful enough to restrain the politically-minded officers. There were two intensely politically-minded army groups. One was known as the Imperial Way Faction, the *Kodo ha*, which was led by the junior officers, the direct action group which believed that the zaibatsu and the political parties had to be destroyed. This group had friends among the general officers, the most famous of whom were Generals Araki, Mazaki, and Hata. They were particularly influenced by the ideas of Kita Ikki. The other group was the Control Faction, *Tosei ha*, which was formed mainly of high-ranking officers. The leading spirits in the Control Faction were General Nagata, a prominent member of the breakfast club, and General Tojo, who later played a decisive role in World War II. It was with these men that Okawa had his contacts. Although Nagata, Tojo, and their group held many of the ideas that were popular with the Imperial Way Faction, they were against direct action and terroristic methods as being destructive to army discipline. They preferred to work through legal methods towards a condition in which they would control the balance of power and have the decisive voice in every branch of government and all the main sections of the economy.

The complicated struggle for a new power alignment took place during the ministries of two admirals—Admirals Saito and Okada. Admiral Saito became premier in May 1932, after the assassination of Inukai, and remained in power until July 1934. He was a compromise candidate, acceptable to the army, which was not powerful enough to assume open control, and agreeable to the parties, the court circles, and the zaibatsu, because they thought he would oppose the political ambitions of the army and restore confidence in the government. Saito included enough men from both parties to keep alive the idea of party participation but not enough to antagonize the army. Admiral Okada, who was in office from July 1934 to March 1936, also appointed a few party men to the cabinet. The parties were not strong enough to demand more, and the army had not yet resolved its own inner conflict.

When Saito took office, the younger officers seemed to have the initiative. General Araki was minister of war, Mazaki was vice-chief of the general staff, and Hata was commander-in-chief of the gendarmerie. When it became apparent, however, that the Saito cabinet was not going to bring about the "reforms" demanded by the military radicals of the Imperial Way Faction, some of their members planned a fantastic plot to bring about the "reform" by killing all cabinet ministers and the leaders of the political parties. The plot, known as the "God-Sent Troops" affair, was uncovered in July 1933, but it was not until 1937 that anyone was brought to trial and not until 1941 that the case was closed with all of the forty-four defendants being acquitted.

A few months after this affair, the Control Faction won a victory by securing the appointment of General Hayashi as war minister to replace General Araki. While Hayashi was minister of war the army took a step in political propaganda that indicated clearly its social and political doctrines. The most important army pamphlet, "The Essence of National Defense and Proposals to Strengthen It," was as political as the platform of any of the major parties. The pamphlet announced the army's intention of setting up a controlled national economy. Hayashi moved to dismiss General Mazaki from his post as Inspector General of Military Education in July 1935, putting upon him the responsibility for the extremist views and actions of the younger officers. The ostensible reason for Mazaki's removal was the discovery of another plot which the Control Faction has even been accused of fabricating in order to embarrass the Imperial Way Faction. Behind the removal of General Mazaki was General Nagata, the leader of the Control Faction, who followed up the removal of Mazaki, the last of the Imperial Way Faction in high office, by directing personnel shifts in the army in such a way as to break up the organization of the Mazaki group. He paid dearly for this move. Lieutenant Colonel Aizawa, who had been ordered to Formosa, walked into the war ministry on August 12, 1935, and killed Nagata with his sword. Up to this point the conflict within the army had been concealed from the public. However bitter the struggle within the army itself, the official explanation condemned the direct action enthusiasts. But the murder of General Nagata brought out in full public view the depth of the conflict within the army itself.

Aizawa was given every opportunity to express his views at the court-martial, and they were carried by every important newspaper in the country. He spoke at length about the need for a Showa Restoration, the name that the radicals had chosen for their movement after the reign title of Emperor Hirohito. By a Showa Restoration they meant the forcible elimination of all those elements, the politicians and the capitalists, who had come between the emperor and his people. At the court-martial the defense brought in high officials and members of the zaibatsu for cross-examination and made many references to the evils of plutocracy, financial panics, the corrupt alliance between imperial advisers and financial interests, and to rural distress. Aizawa was sentenced to death and executed, but to the public his message was of greater interest than his crime. Encouraged by the public reaction, the radicals of the Imperial Way Faction, often called the "young officers group," prepared a spectacular, quixotic, and yet decisive attempt to carry out their Showa Restoration.

On February 26, 1936, the young officers took over the central part of Tokyo with 1,400 troops. They occupied the Diet building, the Prime Minister's residence, the War Office, and the police headquarters. Men were sent to assassinate a considerable number of high military and political leaders. Admiral Okada, the Prime Minister, escaped only because his brother-in-law was mistaken for him and assassinated. The Minister of Finance, Takahashi, the former premier, Admiral Saito, the Inspector General of Military Education, General Watanabe, and many others were slaughtered. A few others escaped. The murder of high officials was as far as the planning of the conspirators had gone; they made no further moves as they were being surrounded by loyal troops. In an appeal to soldiers and non-commissioned officers which was dropped from planes and announced over the radio they were told that the emperor ordered them to return to their barracks. In this way the mutiny came to an end.

The Control Faction now moved rapidly to exploit the situation. Generals Mazaki and Araki were transferred to the reserves, thirteen of the young army officers were executed, as was Kita Ikki, who was not actually involved in the plot but was judged to be its spiritual father. The army's struggle for power had been decided in favor of the Control Faction, and the leaders of this faction came to dominate Japan.

But if the fight within the army was decided, the struggle with the parties was not yet over. During the four-year struggle between the two big army factions, the parties had not fared very well. The extremists were making it dangerous indeed to criticize the government or to take any stand which could be interpreted as being antagonistic to the army program. Party politicians tended to ally themselves with the army. The *Seiyukai* party in particular tried to take advantage of the doctrines of the times, and some parts of its party program can hardly be distinguished from army pamphlets. It was the *Seiyukai* which touched off two expeditions into the realm of thought control by raising questions in the Diet as to the views of certain professors at the imperial universities of Kyoto and Tokyo. The most famous of these was the case of Professor Minobe. A *Seiyukai* member of the House of Representatives brought legal action against Professor Minobe on the grounds that his writings were disrespectful to the throne. Minobe had long argued that the emperor was an organ of the state, that he had no authority over and above the state, a thesis which was a challenge to the divine right theory of the imperial institution.

The army officers were particularly interested in discrediting the Minobe position because of their ultranationalist ideology. They regarded Minobe's views as a heterodox deviation from all traditional assumptions and from the intentions of the framers of the constitution. Assisted by the *Seiyukai* party and without protest from the *Minseito* party, the army forced the administration to denounce Minobe's theory and to purge itself by issuing an official statement clarifying the "national polity." Minobe lost his peerage and his professorship. The government now moved into the universities to investigate professors, courses, and books.

The political parties, whose behavior during the Minobe controversy could not have been more short-sighted, did not realize how much strength they had left. When the government dissolved the Diet early in 1936, the *Minseito* party, which had gone to the country with the demand that the people must choose between parliamentary government and fascism, scored a decisive victory over the *Seiyukai* which supported the ultranationalists. But it was too late for the parties to recover lost ground. Within a week of the election came the February 26 incident, which led to serious changes in the status of all political parties.

No government could survive the incident of February 26. Okada's ministry resigned and the aging elder statesman, Saionji, was presented once again with the task of suggesting a premier. The navy had no suggestions to make, and the army, while making it clear that party government would be unacceptable, did not at this time wish to put up its own candidate because it needed a breathing spell during which to recover public confidence after the recent demonstration of inner conflict. The choice fell on Hirota, Foreign Minister in the Okada cabinet, a non-party civilian bureaucrat who came with army approval because of his China policy. Hirota was not permitted to form a cabinet without accepting most of the army's terms. The full extent of his surrender soon became apparent. The army designated General Terauchi as Minister of War, and forced Premier Hirota to pledge himself to reform the government and embark upon a positive foreign policy. Hirota came out with a statement that "the government and military could cooperate closely in coping with existent situations." In other words, the bureaucracy was willing to go along with the army's plans to develop a "total national defense structure," to crush all liberal tendencies, and to drag the political parties along whether they were willing or unwilling.

Hirota soon paid the price of army support. In May, 1936, the Hirota cabinet went along with the army demand that the active status requirement for army and navy ministers be restored. This step, promulgated in imperial ordinances, gave to the Control Faction a decisive weapon. Within the armed forces it closed the door to generals, such as Araki and Mazaki of the opposing faction, who had been put on the reserve list. In the government it destroyed whatever hope there had been of putting civilians in charge of the war and navy ministry, but more important still, it strengthened the army's ability to make or break cabinets at will. One of the first victims was the Hirota cabinet, which had agreed to the measure without a fight.

Having surrendered one of the most important gains made by the political parties, the Hirota cabinet then gave its blessing in August, 1936, to a seven-point program of "national political renovation" drawn up by the army. This program committed the government to expanding armament, rigid control of education, higher taxes, further controls over trade and industry, the stockpiling of materials for war, and to giving wholehearted support to the army in Manchuria. Put in the jargon of the army, this was a program which would turn the country away from liberalism and towards the "renovation" of government and the creation of a controlled, unified state.

The restoration of the active status rule for service ministers and the seven-point program were followed by a third important step that was completed before the meeting of the Diet. This was the conclusion with Germany, in November 1936, of the anti-Comintern pact, a month before the expiration of the Washington and London naval treaties. By this step the army hoped to allay public concern over the diplomatic isolation of Japan in the face of unlimited naval competition with the United States and Great Britain. The pact was important not only for the completely new direction it gave to Japanese foreign policy and for the open association with a totalitarian country but also for the ruthless manner in which it was imposed upon the Hirota cabinet and the secret diplomacy which enabled the government to present the Diet with an accomplished fact.

The price that the army had exacted was so high that it brought a violent reaction when the Diet met in December 1936, even from the *Seiyukai* party. In a remarkable statement the *Seiyukai* put into words some of the fears and protests of the party and the zaibatsu by denouncing dual diplomacy, the new economic controls, the organization of the country for war, and the anti-Comintern pact. When Mr. Hamada, a *Seiyukai* representative, attacked General Terauchi, the Minister of War, on the floor of the House, it seemed that the party had recovered some of the confidence and the courage of the twenties. General Terauchi chose this time to resign and thus brought about the fall of the Hirota cabinet. The army had used it to secure a civilian blessing for most of the things it wanted and was now ready to take the next step towards its controlled, unified state. For the office of premier the army blocked the appointment of General Ugaki, the man who had accepted cuts in the army in the twenties and was disposed to work with the parties and the zaibatsu, and approved instead General Hayashi.

General Hayashi's cabinet, formed in February 1937, lasted for four months. Hayashi, an old-fashioned military man who probably did not understand what the real intentions of the Control Faction were, was useful mainly because he hated political parties. Hayashi admitted party members to his cabinet only on condition that they gave up their party allegiance. As political parties were permitted by the constitution, which had been handed down by the divine emperor, he did not oppose their existence as such, but he saw no reason why there should be more than one party and why that party should not always support the administration. As a major step to bring the parties to heel, Hayashi ordered new elections in April 1937. He thought that if he forced frequent elections—which were expensive—the zaibatsu would get tired of financing the parties, and the parties would become more amenable. The election of April 1937 is important partly because it was the last time that the people were able to choose between rival parties and partly because the outcome of the election amounted to a repudiation of the Hayashi cabinet.

It seemed as if the Diet was to become a real problem for the army. But the only way in which the political parties could have exercised any real influence would have been to put up a united and determined stand, which they did not do. There were some party men who even favored a single party as the only possible method of opposing the army. Of such a solution there was little hope. The long guerrilla warfare and the recent frontal attacks that the army had conducted against the parties had had their effect. Even more serious was the success achieved by the army in splitting the bureaucracy away from the parties and in winning over some of the zaibatsu. Cooperation between the army and important bureaucrats, particularly effective in Manchuria, was now bringing its rewards. In all the ministries and in the foreign service the army had strong bureaucratic supporters. In this way the Control Faction, a small group of men who knew what they wanted, changed the balance of political forces in Japan by their skillful combination of threats and inducements. But they were still not ready to make one of their own group premier of Japan.

Prince Konoe agreed to form a cabinet in June, 1937. In July, Japan was at war with China and remained at war until 1945. Prince Konoe, who enjoyed the prestige of high aristocratic lineage, had the strength and the weakness of a man who had taken no strong partisan stand. He had been groomed for high office by Prince Saionji. He had strong support at the court among the high bureaucrats and was acceptable to the parties and the army. Even the public welcomed the Prince Konoe cabinet.

4. THE NEW ORDER IN EAST ASIA, 1937–1945

Continental Expansion

By the time that Prince Konoe became premier in June, 1937, the Japanese army had extended its influence far beyond the borders of the puppet state of Manchukuo. The senior army officers of the Control Faction saw the development of Manchukuo as part of a much larger pattern of Japanese strategy and gave their support to further moves on the continent. In contrast, the younger officers of the Imperial Way Faction were more inclined to stick to the development of a continental war base in Manchuria, both as a way to realize their dreams of a "paradise" which they could not achieve at home and as a base in a future struggle with the U.S.S.R. In the fight for dominance, however, the Control Faction adopted many of the ideas of its rivals. Japan, therefore, actually followed both policies on the continent—she poured her resources into Manchuria to make it an economic and military base and at the same time probed and pushed into North China and Inner Mongolia.

In 1933, after the occupation of Jehol, the army moved on into North China, driving the Chinese before them. In May 1933, an armistice was arranged at Tangku, by which Japanese troops withdrew to Manchuria and the Chinese armies withdrew further to the south, leaving in between a carefully defined neutral area within which the Chinese were to maintain order with police forces. From this time on there began a struggle in which the Japanese tried first to encourage Chinese officials friendly to them in North China and then to set up regimes which would suit their purposes, while Chiang Kai-shek's government strove to retain control over the area. In these activities the Japanese North China garrison, which controlled the Tientsin-Peking corridor by virtue of the Boxer Protocol of 1901, was following the example of the Kwantung army in Manchuria. It set out to construct a new state in North China which would be independent of Nanking. In its most ambitious form the plan was to include the five northern provinces of Hopei, Chahar, Suiyuan, Shansi, and Shantung. Actually the Japanese achievements were much more limited. They organized the so-called East Hopei Anti-Communist Government in the demilitarized zone set up by the Tangku Truce but they had to accept the establishment, in 1935, of the Hopei-Chahar Political Council in Peiping, which the Nanking government hastily created as a semi-autonomous regime in order to head off the more ambitious Japanese plans for North China.

In the meantime other Japanese army units had gone ahead with the setting up of a Japanese-controlled buffer state between China and the U.S.S.R. For this purpose they worked with a Mongol, Prince Teh, who set up an "independent" Mongol state in Inner Mongolia. After forcing Chinese troops out of the province of Chahar, the Japanese supported this Mongol regime. Behind this move was General Tojo, then head of the military gendarmerie of the Kwantung army, who was obsessed with the fear of a Chinese-

Soviet combination and favored the strategy of placing a Japanese-controlled puppet regime between China and Soviet-controlled Outer Mongolia. The battle cry was "Mongolia for the Mongols," but when the Mongol troops advanced with the help of Japanese tanks, they were defeated by Chinese provincial troops under General Fu Tso-yi.

While the army on the continent was plotting for its buffer states in North China and Mongolia, the Foreign Office was attempting to arrive at an understanding with the Nanking government, which, if successful, would have taken the initiative away from the army. In 1935 Foreign Minister Hirota formulated his famous three-point program—that China should recognize Manchukuo, cooperate politically and economically with Japan, and accept Japanese cooperation in the eradication of Communism. These points were unacceptable to Nanking because they would have meant capitulation to the dominance of Japan. The Japanese also had to reckon with a stronger disposition on the part of the United States and Great Britain to support the National Government and to watch out for their treaty rights and interests in China. By the spring of 1937 Japan was faced with an increasingly hostile China and acute international and economic problems.

The appointment of General Tojo as Chief of Staff of the Kwantung army in March 1937 did not improve the chances for compromise. An important member of the Control Faction and a man with powerful bureaucratic allies, Tojo was an aggressive expansionist. He was particularly alarmed at the united front between the National Government and the Chinese Communists. He strongly backed further efforts to carry out the strategy of creating puppet states in order to establish Japanese control over China. The General Staff and the Foreign Office were far from anxious to get involved in a war with China, but they were unable to force the army to give up its puppet regimes in North China. On the other hand, the National Government, also anxious to avoid war, was unwilling to negotiate unless the Japanese gave up their attempt to take the north. Out of the struggle for control of North China came the incident which led to full-scale conflict between China and Japan.

The China Incident

The undeclared war between China and Japan began with the Lukouchiao or Marco Polo Bridge incident on July 7, 1937, which was staged by the Japanese. A short railroad connects the Peking-Tientsin and the Peking-Hankow railroads just south of Peking. The Japanese were already in occupation of the eastern end of this line at Fengtai. Lukouchiao was important because it was close to the other end of the transverse line where it joined the Peking-Hankow railway. Had the Japanese been able to secure control of this railroad, they would have been in a position to isolate Peking from the rest of China.

The Japanese chose to hold military maneuvers at this strategic point and provoked an occasion for attacking the Chinese garrison. The Japanese were seeking an opportunity to force the withdrawal of Chinese troops from this area. Negotiations were carried on for some time while the Japanese moved in reinforcements from Manchuria and Korea, and the National Government began to move troops north toward the Yellow River. While Tokyo was trying to get Nanking to agree to a local settlement, the Chinese government appealed to the signatories of the Nine Power Treaty of Washington on the grounds that Japan had violated her treaty obligations. There were attempts to reach a face-saving solution at Nanking through the efforts of the Japanese ambassador, with the backing of Prince Konoe, but always on Japanese terms. The Japanese in North China, however, attacked and destroyed Chinese forces near Peking and proceeded with the occupation of the whole Tientsin-Peking area.

By this time both the United States and Great Britain were alarmed at the move towards war but were unable to combine their efforts towards preventing it. It soon became clear to the Japanese army that it would not have to fight either the United States or the United Kingdom over the question of its China policy. To Japan's new-found ally, Nazi Germany, the possibility of a Sino-Japanese conflict was very embarrassing, for German military advisers were training the Chinese armies, and German trade with China was flourishing. Germany had offered an alliance to Japan to weaken the Soviet Union, not to give Japan the opportunity to expand her conquests on the mainland. The Japanese claim that their operations in China were part of the general struggle against Communism found little sympathy in Berlin. The Germans argued that a large-scale war would have the effect of driving China into the arms of the Russians, in which case the Japanese could not expect any German assistance under the terms of the anti-Comintern pact.

The Japanese inner cabinet, which included the top officials of the General Staff, and of the war, navy, and foreign ministries made serious efforts to bring about a settlement, but the negotiations had to be handled without the knowledge of the army whose opposition could be anticipated and predicted. The inner cabinet, however, produced no terms on which the National Government could have agreed. If there had been any hope of peaceful settlement, it was destroyed by the outbreak of fighting at Shanghai. After several incidents involving Japanese soldiers and civilians, the Japanese brought in reinforcements. The Chinese countered by moving troops, and while negotiations were proceeding for a local settlement, Japanese forces attacked on August 13. Negotiations for a settlement did not cease but from this time on China and Japan were at war.

China sought to bolster her position by concluding a non-aggression pact with the Soviet Union on August 21, 1937. The two powers, without giving up obligations already entered into with other powers, agreed not to attack each other or to assist any power which might commit an aggression against the other signatory. On September 12 the National Government appealed to the League of Nations, whose Far Eastern Advisory Committee reported that the Japanese had no legal grounds for their attack on China and were breaking their treaty obligations. Out of this arose a proposal for a conference of the Washington Treaty powers which met at Brussels. Japan refused to attend. The conference, which did nothing to help the Chinese and a great deal to antagonize the Japanese, adjourned without action.

When the battle of Shanghai ended with a Chinese retreat at the beginning of November, the Japanese initiated negotiations with the Chinese government through the German ambassadors to Tokyo and Nanking. Chiang Kai-shek was not in a mood to discuss terms at this time, but when the retreat became a rout towards the end of November and Nanking itself was in danger of falling, the Generalissimo, after listening to the advice of his generals, who mostly advised peace, agreed to accept the Japanese terms as a basis of discussion. The terms transmitted by the German ambassador seemed to indicate that the Japanese General Staff wanted to offer acceptable terms to China. But the army and some of its allies in high places felt that it was possible, by taking Nanking, to finish the National Government for good and to replace it with other regimes. Nanking fell on December 12, and the Japanese army in North China celebrated its fall by establishing a provisional government of China in Peiping two days later, thus anticipating the Japanese army commanders at Nanking. Presented once more with an accomplished fact, the Japanese government had to readjust its peace terms to include a special position for the army in North China; but the more the Japanese army revealed its hand, the less the Chinese were willing to take the risk of negotiating.

At the end of December the Chinese indicated that they could not accept the stepped-up Japanese demands but still refrained from breaking off negotiations. At this time the German ambassadors were working very hard indeed to bring about a compromise. Before replying officially, Chiang Kaishek appealed to President Roosevelt for assistance but was turned down. In the meantime the Japanese army had forced the cabinet to revise the terms again. Under German pressure the Chinese government sent an official reply to the Japanese requesting further information. On January 13 the Chinese foreign minister wrote "the Chinese government desires therefore to be apprised of the nature and content of the newly submitted conditions in order to make a careful examination and reach a definite decision." On January 16, 1938, Konoe replied that Japan considered the Chinese reply to reflect deliberate procrastination and a refusal to sue for peace. "Therefore the Imperial Government has now decided to abandon, much to its regret, the present negotiations for peace between Japan and China undertaken through the kind endeavors of your Excellency's government [German government] and to deal with the present affair from an entirely new standpoint." Japan withdrew recognition of the Chinese government and declared its intention to make peace with a new regime. The German effort at negotiation had come to an end.

The Japanese peace terms were always a compromise between the views of the army and those of the General Staff and the Foreign Office. They included enough of the General Staff's terms to make them seem a basis for negotiation, but there was also a sufficient contribution from the army to make the terms unacceptable. The Japanese did not listen to the advice of the Germans, whose analysis of the situation withstood the test of time much better than their own. The German ambassador to Japan advised Hirota that further prosecution of the war would strain relations between England and Japan and would lead to the bolshevization of China and the weakening of Japan as against Russia. Germany, however, compelled to give up her neutrality in the struggle, withdrew the thirty German military advisers from the Chinese government and tried to recoup the contracts she had cancelled with China by developing her trade in the Japanese-occupied areas.

After the fall of Nanking the Japanese army pushed its campaigns into the interior. Divisions which had been withdrawn after the fall of Nanking had to be sent back, and the war was also extended to Canton which fell a few days before the capture of Hankow in October 1938. In the meantime, what was possibly the last serious effort to bring the war to a conclusion was made by General Ugaki who followed Hirota as foreign minister in May 1938. Chiang Kai-shek let it be known secretly to the Japanese that he was willing to accept Manchukuo in fact but not in name, that he would go along with an autonomous Inner Mongolia (already set up by the Kwantung army), and that he would turn on the Communists, but that he would not pay an indemnity or accept Japanese troops on Chinese soil. Ugaki, failing to secure acceptance of these terms in Tokyo, resigned in September 1938, and the handling of the China problem was taken over by an Asia Development Board, which left to the Foreign Ministry only those problems that involved third powers. Konoe appointed Arita, a man who thoroughly approved of army policy, as foreign minister.

On November 3, 1938, Konoe announced the establishment of a New Order in East Asia which he claimed to be "a new structure of peace based on true justice." It was in fact a unilateral denunciation by Japan of the whole existing treaty system in the Far East. Even the National Government of China could find a place in the new order if it were to "repudiate its past policy, remold its personnel, and offer to join in the task as a thoroughly rejuvenated regime." But the terms were harsh indeed. China would have to join in a military alliance with Japan and Manchukuo against the Comintern and accept Japanese troops in North China and Inner Mongolia. Japan would practically take over the direction and training of the Chinese army and bring the whole of China within the yen bloc. These terms led Wang Ching-wei to desert the National Government. Wang fled to Indo-China where agents of the National Government made an unsuccessful attempt to assassinate him. He was soon to be groomed by the Japanese to set up a puppet regime in Nanking.

The Asia Development Board, usually called the China Affairs Board, was set up in such a way that it was under military direction. It had branches all over occupied China. It was in general control of the operations of the two huge holding companies which handled the financial and economic exploitation of China—the North China Development Company and the Central China Development Company. The Japanese government put up half of the investment capital and guaranteed the dividends of private investors, a pattern previously tried out in Manchuria. The China Affairs Board made large profits out of the sale and distribution of opium in China and began to set up the same pattern of state control and exploitation of resources that had already emerged in Manchukuo.

After the fall of Hankow no large-scale military operations were undertaken. There were no other great population centers to conquer; the lines of communication were already very long, and it looked as if more could be achieved by bringing about the diplomatic isolation of Chiang Kai-shek than by further military adventures into the interior. Japan now attempted to consolidate her extensive gains on the mainland by political and diplomatic measures. On March 30, 1940, she established a puppet regime at Nanking under the chairmanship of Wang Ching-wei, who signed a peace treaty with Japan in November 1940, in which he accepted virtually complete Japanese control of occupied China.

Japanese relations with both the United Kingdom and the United States had deteriorated considerably by the spring of 1939. Both countries were providing some financial assistance to the Chinese government, and although the rising strength of Nazi Germany made it difficult for the British to restrict their commitments in the Far East, a small trickle of supplies was still going into China by way of the Burma Road. Most of the American credit of $25,000,000 extended to the Chinese government in December 1938 was actually used to purchase equipment for the Burma Road. British credits were used to finance imports and to assist in maintaining the stability of the Chinese currency.

The Japanese struck back by putting pressure on the British and Americans to withdraw their troops from China and by harassing the foreign communities in the treaty port concessions. They were particularly anxious to get hold of the silver belonging to the National Government which remained in the vaults of the foreign banks, and they also wanted to tax the considerable amount of private Chinese funds which so far had been safe from both the National Government and the Japanese. Most of the pressure was deliberately put on Great Britain, but the United States also became sufficiently alarmed about Japan's invasion of her treaty rights and trade to denounce in July 1939 the American-Japanese treaty of commerce, which expired in January 1940.

There was sufficient friction with the Soviet Union to keep alive Japan's fear of a Soviet intervention in the war on behalf of China. A border incident at Changkufeng, on the Soviet-Manchukuo-Korean border, ended in a mist of rival claims, but the Japanese were in fact defeated. In May 1939, an armed clash at Nomonhan on the border between Outer Mongolia and Manchukuo resulted in a severe military setback for the Japanese. When the Germans and Russians concluded the non-aggression pact in August 1939 which initiated the war in Europe the Japanese discontinued their probing of Russian strength.

The cabinet of Prince Konoe, which was in office when the war with

China began in 1937, lasted until February 1939. During this period decisive steps were taken to put the political and economic structure of the country on a war footing. As early as July 1939, Konoe openly stated his intention to build up what he called a "national defense structure," to follow a regional policy in Eastern Asia based on a closed economy for Japan, Manchukuo, and China, and to adjust all other domestic and foreign policies to these basic considerations. This was the army's program.

In October 1937, Konoe set up a cabinet advisory board to formulate national policy and included in it enough representatives from the parties, the bureaucracy, and the zaibatsu to dilute the large block of militarists. More and more military men, however, were appointed to positions which formerly had been in the hands of civilians; General Ugaki, for example, took over the Foreign Ministry, and General Araki the Ministry of Education. A national general mobilization law of March, 1938, gave the cabinet the power to legislate by ordinance, thus in effect abrogating sections of the constitution. The opposition of the Diet to the national mobilization bill was broken by threatening dissolution, and in the end the Diet unanimously voted away its own political power.

At the end of 1938 Baron Hiranuma, president of the privy council, became premier, exchanging positions with Konoe. Like Konoe, Hiranuma tried to maintain a united front. The political parties were not abolished but they were becoming increasingly powerless. With the vigorous help of General Araki, a hero of the young officer's group, the army was going about what it called a program of national spiritual mobilization. This program included arrests of radicals, more authority for the police, open attacks on the leaders of the so-called proletarian parties, and active propaganda in favor of *Kodo*, the Imperial Way.

The Hiranuma cabinet fell in August 1939 as a result of its embarrassment over the Soviet-German non-aggression pact, about which Japan had not been previously advised by its German ally. First General Abe and then Admiral Yonai carried on as premiers until the summer of 1940. Abe, who lasted until January 1940, was more than willing to strengthen even further the powers of the premier, but he did not have the political ability to bring about the desired results. Admiral Yonai, a moderate by inclination and training and old-fashioned enough to believe that important questions of national policy should not be decided by the army, was finally thrown out of office when the army forced the resignation of his minister of war. Prince Konoe returned as premier in July 1940, with General Tojo as minister of war, a move that indicated the army was ready to force the pace on the domestic and foreign scene—a new structure at home and a new order abroad.

One of Konoe's most important achievements was the inauguration in October 1940 of the Imperial Rule Assistance Association, a one-party political organization. Its formation had been preceded by the voluntary dissolution of all Japan's major parties. Now that the old alliance with the bureaucrats was a thing of the past and the army would accept alliances with politicians on a personal but not on a party basis, there was no way for party politicians to secure office, influence, or any kind of power without supporting the only kind of political party the government was willing to work with. The Imperial Rule Assistance Association was the solution to the problem of finding a method of preserving the Diet, provided for in the constitution, in a manner acceptable to the army.

The Imperial Rule Assistance Association was designed to promote the unity of the country. The party leaders, most of whom joined the association, pledged themselves to assist the emperor by "always cooperating with the government as a medium for transmitting the wishes of the government as well as of the people at large." Konoe, who was both premier and head of the Imperial Rule Assistance Association, actually had complete authority to organize and change it at will and could use it as a power machine with which to temper the army's drive for complete control.

Prince Konoe's regime made impressive strides towards complete mobilization for war of the nation's resources, both human and material. Money was poured into scientific research for war purposes, scientists and technicians were attached to military organizations, central controls were established to handle fuel, the making of munitions, control of information and education, and the censorship of all means of mass communication. The army readjusted its chain of command to take care of combined air and ground operations. The army was determined to be prepared for any opportunity for further expansion of the New Order in East Asia.

Japan Moves Into Southeast Asia

The war in Europe, which had started in 1939, brought no decisive change in the military situation until the fall of the Netherlands and of France before the German armies in June 1940. This left the Netherlands East Indies and French Indo-China in an exposed position, and the threat to the British Isles opened up the tempting prospect of easy conquest of Britain's vast holdings in Burma, Malaya, Borneo, and Hong Kong. Such an opportunity was hardly likely to occur again. One of the last acts of the Yonai cabinet, as part of its efforts to conclude the China incident, was to force the British to close the Burma Road to all traffic. The agreement to close the Burma Road was made on June 24, 1940, and lasted for three months. On June 16 the army had forced the resignation of the Yonai cabinet because it was reluctant to force the pace of preparations for war and to be more friendly to Nazi Germany. In the summer of 1940 the battle of Britain was going on and it looked as if the British Empire could not last much longer. The problem now was to come to a full understanding with Germany and if possible with the Soviet Union. Even before the new Konoe cabinet was inaugurated, there had been an agreement between Konoe, Tojo (war minister), Matsuoka (foreign minister), and Yoshida (navy minister) to secure an Axis pact. The Japanese started to put pressure on the Netherlands East Indies in April, 1940, but it was not until after the collapse of Dutch resistance in Europe that the Japanese made it clear that they expected full economic cooperation from the Netherlands East Indies. In June, Arita, the foreign minister, announced that the countries of East Asia and of the South Seas were geographically, historically, racially, and economically very closely related to each other. As they were destined to cooperate closely, it was necessary to have a stabilizing force in each region. The task of establishing a regional "Co-prosperity Sphere," another slogan for the "New Order," was Japan's responsibility.

The first concrete moves were made in Indo-China. Japan was particularly anxious to get control over Indo-Chinese rice, rubber, coal, and tin, to secure access to China from another direction, and to be ready for further adventures to the south. The Vichy government was compelled by the threat of force to grant the Japanese facilities for the movement of troops and the use of air fields in conducting their war against China. The Japanese in return agreed to respect French sovereignty over Indo-China. The agreement of September 27 gave the Japanese what they wanted, and Japanese troops were now established in Indo-China.

At the same time the Japanese encouraged the expansionist policies of the military oligarchy in Siam which had already changed the name of that country to Thailand, thus indicating a claim to rule over Thai peoples living beyond the present borders of Siam. Expecting the French administration in Indo-China to collapse, the Siamese staked out claims to the whole of Laos and Cambodia at such time as France should relinquish rule in Indo-China. With the help of German pressure on the Vichy government in France and a demonstration of force in Indo-China, the Japanese brought an end to the Siamese-French conflict on their own terms. Both Siam and the Vichy government had to agree that they would assist no third powers in any way against Japan. Siam got about one-third of Cambodia and a smaller piece of Laos. Though it was not incorporated in the New Order, Siam had lost her freedom of action, while French Indo-China to all intents and purposes was now under Japanese control.

The Netherlands East Indies were not so easy to handle. The Dutch government in exile was now allied with Great Britain and the resources of this part of the world were desperately needed for the prosecution of the war in Europe. Japanese missions were sent to the Indies for the purpose of securing a guarantee of Japanese access to the oil, tin, rubber, and other important resources from that part of the world. Unable to bring the same sort of military pressure to bear on the Netherlands East Indies that they had used in French Indo-China for fear of involving themselves in war with Great Britain, the Japanese, in spite of every effort, failed to intimidate the Dutch into making concessions.

On September 26, 1940, Japan concluded with Germany and Italy the Tripartite Pact. The bargain which lay behind this agreement was that Japan should have her new order in Eastern Asia, while Germany and Italy should have their new order in Europe. Germany, Italy, and Japan agreed to assist each other if any one of them was attacked by a power not then involved in the war in Europe or Asia. This agreement was obviously intended to neutralize the United States. In spite of assurances in Article 5 of the pact that it did not "in any way affect the political status which exists at present" between the partners and the Soviet Union, the Russians believed that it was also directed against them.

Japan felt that she had secured concrete benefits from the Tripartite Pact. Matsuoka, the foreign minister, felt that he had assurances from Germany, whom he expected soon to destroy Great Britain, to respect Japan's position in Asia. He had also gained diplomatic and military support to bolster Japan against the United States. Matsuoka hoped to keep the United States neutral towards the European war and even induce her to mediate a peace settlement favorable to Germany. Matsuoka also expected that Russia, as a partner of Germany, would oblige Germany's partner, Japan, by ceasing to support the Chinese Nationalists. Even Konoe had illusions of this sort, thinking that by this means he could bring Chiang Kai-shek to terms. The benefits which were hoped for from the pact—a free hand in Southeast Asia—could not be insured without assurances that while Japan was engaged in the south she would not be attacked from the rear in the north. This meant coming to terms with the Soviet Union. The Japanese assured the Soviet government that Article 14 of their treaty with Wang Ching-wei, by which China and Japan undertook joint defense against Communism, was not directed against the U.S.S.R. The Soviet Union, however, made it clear that it would continue to support the National Government. In fact, new trade agreements were ostentatiously concluded with Chiang Kai-shek within a few weeks of the signing of the treaty between Tokyo and Wang Ching-wei.

Matsuoka continued to press for some sort of agreement with the Soviet Union. He hoped to secure a non-aggression pact but finally had to be content with a pact of neutrality, which was signed on April 13, 1941. The two countries pledged themselves to neutrality in the event that the other became "the object of hostilities on the part of one or several third powers." Both agreed to remain at peace with each other and to respect the other's territorial integrity. In return for a Japanese undertaking to respect the territorial integrity of the Mongolian People's Republic, the Soviet Union pledged the same for Manchukuo. This five-year neutrality pact was followed in June by a Soviet-Japanese trade agreement for a similar period and by the rectification of disputed borders, all of which helped to bring about a lowering of tension in Japanese-Soviet relations. The Japanese were now free to go south.

The Japanese had barely had time to adjust themselves to the Tripartite Pact when the whole situation changed again. On June 22, 1941, Hitler attacked the Soviet Union. Matsuoka wanted Japan to attack the Soviet Union on Germany's side, and Germany, which had previously been urging Japan to attack Singapore, now urged intervention against the Soviet Union. On the advisability of keeping out of the conflict, Konoe and Tojo were both united. The imperial conference of July 2 definitely decided in favor of pursuing conquest in the south and of informing the Soviet Union that Japan would respect the neutrality pact. Japan did not jump into the conflict on Germany's side because the richest prizes lay to the south, and Japan was in no position to conduct large-scale wars on two fronts at the same time. In addition, Japan had not been officially advised of Germany's intention to attack Russia. This was the second great reversal in German relations with Russia, and in both cases Japan had to adjust after the event. The Japanese army had also taken a severe beating at the battle of Nomonhan and had considerable respect for the Soviet army. To go south would presumably strengthen Japan while Russia was being bled by Germany; to go north against the Russians would further weaken the Russians without strengthening Japan. Japan decided to wait and see.

The Konoe cabinet resigned in July and reconstituted itself immediately without its foreign minister, Matsuoka, who had antagonized his colleagues by going directly to the emperor in order to secure his approval of an attack on the Soviet Union. The third Konoe cabinet went ahead with the decisions of the imperial conference of July 2 to move troops into southern Indo-China and refused an American offer to guarantee the neutrality of French Indo-China. The Vichy government agreed to give Japan bases in southern Indo-China ostensibly to protect it against "DeGaullists, Chinese, and British," and the Japanese in return undertook to respect French political and territorial rights. Japanese troops moved in on July 24, and on July 26 President Roosevelt issued an executive order freezing Japanese assets in the United States, thus bringing American-Japanese trade to a standstill. On the same day Great Britain and the British Dominions issued orders freezing Japanese funds, and the Netherlands Indies government made all commercial and financial dealing with Japan subject to official permit.

The Decision For War

The imposition of economic sanctions upon Japan forced her to a fateful decision on policy. Since she was dependent on the supply of raw materials from the United States, Japan could not continue indefinitely without American trade. If she delayed, she would steadily drain the stockpiles of raw materials so carefully collected over the last few years in preparation for war. For many months negotiations had been going on at Washington between Japan and the United States with the aim of determining whether a peaceful settlement of issues was possible. Before the United States would consider reopening trade, she wanted some commitment that Japan was not planning further aggression and participation in the war on the Axis side. The Japanese therefore either had to compromise on their plans for expansion or they had to attack. The Japanese cabinet, which was in full agreement on the expansion of Japanese control in Asia and the general concept of the New Order, was divided on taking any steps which would involve the risk of war with Great Britain and the United States. As a result Japan followed no well defined course with any consistency. She negotiated enough with the United States to infuriate her Axis partners and to arouse their suspicions as to her intentions, and she moved so far into Indo-China that she could not turn back.

Under pressure from Tojo, who pointed out that Americans could afford to drag out the negotiations as long as they wished while time was running out for Japan, Konoe submitted to the imperial conference of September 6 a policy statement in which it was agreed that preparations for war with the United States, Great Britain, and the Netherlands should be finished by the end of October and that a decision to start hostilities would follow automatically if by early October there were no negotiated settlement. Japanese demands for such a settlement were just as far away from the American position as before. In these negotiations the Japanese aimed at a lifting of the American embargo, but while they might have been willing to sign some general agreement on broad principles, they were unwilling to promise any definite limitations on their moves. While Tojo was confident of victory over the United States, Konoe and many of the admirals were not, and were inclined to compromise. The cabinet was stalemated; the army blocked those who wanted to come to terms; but it could not get the Konoe cabinet to decide on war. The Konoe cabinet therefore resigned, and on October 16 General Tojo became premier, minister of war, and minister of internal affairs.

General Tojo's stubborn insistence upon war, which brought the downfall of the Konoe cabinet, was apparently discounted by the advisers to the palace as a tactical move in the struggle for domestic power. The emperor's desire for peace was well known. According to Prince Konoe's memoirs, the emperor personally chided General Sugiyama, chief of staff, for prophesying at the time of the outbreak of the conflict with China that it would be over in a month and for claiming that operations in the South Pacific would not last more than three months. The emperor pointed out that the vastness of China explained the first mistake, and that the size of the Pacific Ocean, a much larger area than China, might well come to account for a second mistake. But some of the palace advisers apparently were persuaded to believe that Tojo was the only man who could control the army and therefore bring about peace with the United States. For this purpose the emperor informed Tojo that he could disregard the policies laid down at the imperial conference on September 6 and negotiate with a free hand. This Tojo proceeded to do by informing the United States through his ambassador that it was for the United States to change its position.

Of all the leaders of the Control Faction, General Tojo was the most fanatical and the most dedicated. The son of a general, he had never known anything but the life of the army. A good soldier and ruthless in action, Tojo really believed what the army preached about the uniqueness of Japan and its army and the high spiritual value of war; the facts of power were the only true measure of men and nations. The quality of Tojo can be seen in the simple statement he made to the international military tribunal after the Second World War. Referring to the period just before Pearl Harbor, he said,

As War Minister my opinion was that there remained practically no hope of a diplomatic break, and I suggested that the time had come when we had better make up our minds for war. The longer we delayed in making this decision, the more disadvantageous the situation would be for Japan if war were declared later.

Tojo's rise to power would have been impossible without the rise of the army to a dominating position in domestic politics during the thirties. Tojo himself stood out among his colleagues, however, not only for his fanatical zeal but also for his background and experience. He was chief of the military investigation bureau in 1935 when General Nagata was assassinated, an action which did not meet with his disapproval. Then he went to Manchuria to become head of the military gendarmerie of the Kwantung army. There he engaged in intrigues in Inner Mongolia which were not particularly successful, but he secured invaluable experience and connections in secret police work and built up dossiers on many of his colleagues which he did not hesitate to use in his rise to power. Later he became chief of staff of the Kwantung army, and in that position learned how to control and operate the kind of government that the military extremists wanted for Japan. After returning to Japan as vice-minister of war in the first Konoe cabinet, Tojo prepared the army for war. He built up the air force, emphasized discipline, developed mechanization, and trained his forces for German-style blitzkrieg.

Tojo's methods were ruthless and high-handed and marked by contempt for red tape. But even at the height of his power he was still a member of a clique; he did not enjoy the authority of Hitler or Mussolini; and there was always the emperor above him. If Tojo had been a dictator of the Hitler variety, Japan would have gone down to defeat in the same manner as did Germany. But fortunately for Japan, the imperial institution remained intact and those high officials who opposed war with the United States in the fall of 1941 were there to be called upon in 1945 when the issue of surrender had to be decided.

On November 5 an imperial conference approved of war if one more attempt to come to terms with the United States were to fail. The deadline for an agreement was November 25. The cabinet was authorized to go ahead with plans for war even if Germany should not join in the conflict with the United States. Through his foreign minister, Togo, Premier Tojo sent the final Japanese demands to the embassy in Washington, D. C. and dispatched Ambassador Kurusu as a special envoy to assist the Japanese ambassador in his negotiations. So long as Japan was unwilling to define her demands with regard to China or her role as a member of the Tripartite Pact, no understanding was possible. In order not to appear to be responsible for breaking off the negotiations, Secretary Hull, after discussing matters with the British, who felt that the Japanese were bluffing about war, gave to Ambassador Nomura on November 26 a tentative draft agreement. Japan was to join a multilateral non-aggression pact with Great Britain, the Netherlands, the

[1] International Military Tribunal, Far East, Tokyo, 1946–8, *Record of Proceedings*, pp. 10273–4, as quoted in F. C. Jones, *Japan's New Order in East Asia* (New York, 1954), p. 292, note 6.

U.S.S.R, and the United States and pledge herself to respect the territorial integrity of French Indo-China as well as the principle of equality of commercial opportunity. She was to deal only with the National Government of China and to withdraw her troops from the continent except for Manchukuo. Japan was to give up extraterritorial rights in China and exempt the Pacific area from the Tripartite Pact. The United States would lift the embargo and assist in stabilizing the dollar-yen rate. The terms of November 26 did not differ substantially from those which had been stated many times before in negotiations which had been going on for at least a year.

Japanese reaction to the American note of November 26 was to fight. The Japanese ambassadors were informed by their government that negotiations were in fact concluded but that they were to give the impression that Tokyo was still willing to talk. In spite of many efforts by Konoe to avoid conflict and of serious doubts among some of the admirals, the army had its way. On December 1 an imperial conference gave its formal sanction to Tojo's decision to attack. Nothing could now stop the course of events. On December 6 Japan sent its reply to the American note of November 26 to its ambassadors in Washington, instructing them to deliver it at 1:00 P.M., United States time, on December 7. As it was planned to attack Pearl Harbor at 7:50 A.M. Honolulu time, the United States would have twenty minutes warning that "the earnest hope of the Japanese Government to . . . preserve and promote the peace of the Pacific through cooperation with the American Government has finally been lost." Actually the Japanese ambassadors did not see Secretary Hull until 2:30 P.M. on December 7, by which time he had heard about the attack on Pearl Harbor. An imperial rescript put Japan at war with Great Britain and the United States, both of which countries declared war on Japan. On December 11, Germany and Italy declared war upon the United States, and the Congress immediately declared war on them. At about the same time the German armies began their withdrawal from the outskirts of Moscow.

Japan at War

The judgment of the war party in Japan eventually turned out to be wrong, but at the time it was at least plausible. Japan counted on the defeat of the Soviet Union and of Great Britain by Germany and Italy. In the fall of 1942 such an outcome indeed seemed possible. General Tojo therefore took his country to war with assurances from Germany that Japan would have a free hand in Eastern Asia and with full confidence that Germany would defeat both Great Britain and Russia and be dominant in Europe. A German-dominated Europe would engage American attention in the Atlantic, and the United States would prefer to make a compromise peace with the Greater East Asia Co-prosperity Sphere rather than undertake alone the dismemberment of Japan's new empire.

So successful was the attack on the American fleet at Pearl Harbor that the conquest of Southeast Asia could proceed without any major interference from Allied naval power. In rapid succession the Japanese occupied Hong Kong, Malaya, Singapore, Burma, the Netherlands East Indies, and the Philippine Islands. Within six months the Japanese flag was flying from Lashio on the Burma Road to Wake Island in the mid-Pacific. The Japanese Navy sailed into the Indian Ocean, where it could easily have taken the islands of Ceylon and Madagascar, thus strangling the British lines of communication to India and the Near East, but it turned back to the China seas without exploiting the opportunity. Tojo was now ready to talk peace and to consolidate what he had gained. Unfortunately for Tojo, however, the German armies began their retreat from Moscow three days after Pearl Harbor; the Soviet Union did not collapse, and Great Britain survived.

Tojo believed that the country was well prepared for war. Ten years of planned industrial development from 1931 to 1941 had brought very considerable results and industrial output had risen from six billion yen to thirty billion yen. During this period heavy industry increased much more than light industry. Textiles, for example, which accounted for 34 per cent of industrial production in 1930 were down to 12 per cent in 1942. There was a phenomenal increase in the automotive and airplane industries. Japan was producing 400 planes a year in 1930 and 5,000 planes a year in 1941. Automotive units went up from 500 to 48,000; aluminum from 19 tons to over 71,000 tons a year; steel from 1.8 million tons to 6.8 million tons; coal from 27.9 million tons to 55.6 million tons. Electric power capacity was more than doubled, and merchant shipping, which was 92,000 gross tons in 1931, rose to 405,000 gross tons annual production by 1937. A production of around 232,000 gross tons of naval ships in 1941 compares with a little over 15,000 gross tons in 1931.[2]

It was the army-bureaucratic alliance that forced the pace of industrialization and the preparations for war. In spite of gross inefficiency, deficit financing and preparations for war had created an economy of full employment. Some of the increased appropriations for military requirements came from an increased national income, but much of it had to be taken care of by raising the national debt. All this apparent prosperity stood out in sharp contrast to the partial depression of the twenties and the very real economic distress around 1931. It looked as if the military were being vindicated not only on the field of battle, but also in the realm of the national economy.

As most of the necessary materials for industrial and military strength were scattered around in neighboring Asiatic countries, where the political regimes were often weak, there was every reason for Japan's military leaders to develop the concept of a Co-prosperity Sphere in Eastern Asia in which Japan herself would be the industrial powerhouse, provide the armies and the technicians, and have within her political control both the market and the raw materials for her industries. Formosa and Korea were already geared to the Japanese economy. Since 1931 Manchuria had been developed for its iron ore, coal, and particularly for its soy bean production. Since the opening

[2] Jerome B. Cohen, *Japan's Economy in War and Reconstruction* (Minneapolis, 1949), pp. 2–3.

of the China conflict in 1937, North China coking coal, aluminous shale, and salt and a certain amount of cotton had been available. Now there were the tin and rubber of Malaya, which had enriched England, and the oil and bauxite of the Netherlands East Indies, the hemp, copra, timber, and minerals of the Philippines to be exploited. The development of this newly conquered empire required a tremendous organization. But the Japanese army had neither the ideas, the administrative cohesion and ability, the capacity for handling non-Japanese people, or the plans to make of the Co-prosperity Sphere an economic, a political, or even a military success.

From the moment of conquest the army had control of the politics and the economies of the new lands. In November 1942, there was set up a Greater East Asia Ministry, dominated by the army, which was officially charged with the diplomatic functions formerly carried out by the Foreign Office, the Manchurian Affairs Bureau, the Asia Development Board, and the Overseas Ministry. The empire was in the hands of the army.

When the war began Japan could not keep its industries going without nickle and copper, rubber and tin, bauxite and oil, most of which had to come from abroad. But now that the major sources of these raw materials had been captured, it would seem that at long last the goal of self-sufficiency could be achieved. In fact, so confident were Tojo and his cabinet in the middle of 1942 that no efforts were made to increase domestic production for war purposes, and the stock market boomed. The army, however, failed to take into account the effectiveness of submarines against its shipping. Japanese shipping losses from American submarine and air action were already so serious by the end of 1942 that the Japanese government was forced to change its whole estimate of the war. Assuming that there would be a negotiated peace after the initial victories, the Japanese had not planned for any further extension of their basic economy but had rather looked forward to the uninterrupted flow of raw materials from newly acquired areas. By the time the Japanese woke up to the situation, however, it was too late. By cutting off Japan's access to the sinews of war, the blockade gradually brought the economy almost to a halt. By 1945 Japan's steel production was down to one and a half million tons; even the plants which had escaped destruction by bombing were unable to operate at capacity owing to the lack of materials. Iron mines on the continent were no longer operated because it was impossible to move the ore to Japan. Supplies of oil became so low that at the time of the battle of Okinawa, the Japanese were even unable to use some of the warships that still remained afloat. Japan was not producing enough munitions to keep military operations going. The economic effort had reached its peak in 1944, but by 1945 the total industrial output was down to 40 per cent of that peak year. There was a decline of 73 per cent in the production of aircraft engines and 81 per cent in merchant ships.

The Japanese did not even make the best use of what they had. There was much talk about national unity, the new economic structure, planning, and the war economy, but there was no central agency which had the final responsibility for planning and for carrying out the mobilization of Japan's economic resources. There was a cabinet planning board, dominated by the army, which could decide upon the policies, but the policies had to be carried out by the ministries. These guardians of bureaucratic privilege and tradition were often as much interested in fighting each other as in prosecuting the war and were not accustomed to respecting the demands of politicians, including the premier, who in their view were temporary figures. The businessmen had little influence over the cabinet but considerable influence over the ministries, because prominent zaibatsu usually ran the control associations which were set up to arrange the allocation of work, labor, and materials within the various industries according to the wishes of the ministry concerned. After the battle of Guadalcanal, when it became clear that Japan was now in for a long and arduous conflict, the base of the economy had to be extended as rapidly as possible. Because of the general inefficiency of existing control arrangements Tojo set up a Ministry of Munitions in November 1943. The Cabinet Planning Board and the Ministry of Commerce and Industry were abolished. One of the factors that brought about the premier's decision to concentrate much more power in his own hands was the extraordinary lengths to which rivalry between the army and the navy went, especially in aircraft production. The two services had become rival economic empires which competed with each other, duplicated efforts, and obstructed each other in every way. They were tearing the government and industry apart in their fight for scarce materials and skilled labor. Tojo himself became minister of munitions and paid particular attention to eliminating the rivalry between the services but with only limited success. By the time the industrial base had been expanded, the materials to feed it could not be procured.

Tojo did not let his early successes divert him from the task of suppressing all open opposition to his regime at home, or from securing the legislation to give him the authority to bring the country into line behind his policies. The job of destroying the high-level advocates of a more cautious approach, sometimes called the peace party, was much more difficult. As events in Europe and the American counter-offensive in the Pacific increased the danger to Japan, opposition to Tojo began to crystallize, particularly among the group of former premiers, called the *Jushin*. Of these, Prince Konoe was an important member. According to his postwar testimony Kido, the privy councilor who had done so much to bring Tojo into power, approached the emperor on behalf of the peace group as early as February, 1943, and reported that the emperor was in favor of peace as soon as possible. In April, Shigemitsu became foreign minister, but by this time the powers of the Foreign Office were extremely limited. Shigemitsu, however, was known to be in favor of bringing the war to an end, and his appointment was a serious invasion of Tojo's control. Shigemitsu initiated an approach to peaceful settlement which was actually to become in the end a serious obstacle to Japan's later and more desperate efforts to get out of the war. He wanted to bring about a negotiated peace between Germany and the Soviet Union. At this time there was a good deal of wishful thinking in the ranks of the peace party. It was felt by some that Japan could negotiate with the British and Americans on the basis of retaining Japan's prewar empire and making the rest of the Co-prosperity Sphere independent. These illusions were rapidly dispelled by the American landing on Saipan in June, 1944. Up to this time Tojo had been able to conceal the changed character of the war from the Japanese people, but now it was clear to everyone that the enemy was on the doorstep. Under pressure from the *Jushin*, Tojo resigned on July 18, 1944.

The Peace Movement and the Surrender

The few men who accepted the fact of impending defeat were not yet in positions of power and had to behave with great circumspection. They had to find a way of negotiating a settlement without letting the country fall into the hands of the army extremists, who might seize control through a coup d'état and lead the country into national suicide. On the other hand, they had to find some way of modifying the unconditional surrender terms which the British and Americans had announced at Casablanca in January 1943.

The removal of Tojo from the premiership had been the first step towards peace, but it was difficult to find a successor. There could be no abrupt change because Tojo was still powerful enough to block those he disliked. General Koiso, governor-general of Korea, emerged as a compromise candidate with Shigemitsu as foreign minister. During the Koiso ministry, which lasted from July 1944 to April 1945, the tide of war turned rapidly against the Axis. The Normandy landings of August 1944 led to the liberation of France and the beginning of the end for Germany. The fall of Saipan, which had sealed the fate of Tojo, was followed by the practical elimination of Japanese naval power in the battle of the Philippine Sea and a growing American air bombardment of the home islands. In August 1944, Koiso set up a body called the Supreme Council for the Direction of the War which was to meet in the imperial palace and include the emperor in its discussions. The six members of the council were the prime minister, the ministers of war, navy, and foreign affairs, and the chiefs of the general staff. The unusual feature of having the emperor present while policy was being discussed, thus giving him a voice in the decisions, was to be of importance in the last stages of the war. The Supreme Council did not bring about any better cooperation between the Supreme Command and the cabinet ministers than there had been before. Shigemitsu, the foreign minister, was encouraged by the cabinet to take up again the question of the relations between Japan and the Soviet Union. It was agreed that a special envoy should be sent to Moscow to see what could be secured. It was hoped, at a minimum, that the Soviet Union would maintain the neutrality pact of 1941, but the major objective was to secure a German-Soviet peace, and if that failed and Germany collapsed, to find out what price the Soviet Union would want for helping Japan to end the China conflict and to continue resistance against the British and American forces. The Soviet Union, which refused to accept the Japanese envoy, was at this time promising the British and American governments to help in the war against Japan three months after the defeat of Germany.

Koiso also made unofficial approaches to the Swedish minister in Tokyo, but nothing came of them. In the meantime, the United States landed troops on Okinawa and the Koiso cabinet fell. Admiral Suzuki, who took over from Koiso, appointed Togo as foreign minister, and Japan again turned to the Soviet Union. The appointment of Admiral Suzuki, an old man who had had nothing to do with the internal struggle that led up to the war, a man who had helped to create the earlier Japan when it was on good terms with the powers she was now fighting, was made deliberately to show that Japan was ready for peace. The peace group was now well represented in the cabinet and knew that it could count on the cooperation of the emperor. As it was quite clear that no negotiations could be successfully conducted if they were known to the army extremists, the directors of the military and naval affairs bureaus were excluded from meetings of the Supreme Council. The diehards argued that the experience on Okinawa had shown that desperate Japanese resistance was so costly to the Americans that similar resistance on all the Japanese islands would bring better terms than unconditional surrender. The peace group differed sharply, arguing that Japan had neither the food nor the materials of war with which to resist any longer and that surrender was the only way in which the monarchy could be preserved.

The heavy bombardment of Tokyo by B-29's, beginning in March, caused the peace group to redouble its efforts. Under instructions of the Minister of War the gendarmerie threw several hundred of the peace advocates into jail (including Shigeru Yoshida, who was later to become premier in post-war Japan), and threatened them with court-martial. This was avoided only through the influence of the palace. Early in April the Soviet Union informed Japan that it would not renew the neutrality pact of 1941 when it expired in 1946. Just as Molotov had blandly informed the Japanese that there had been no discussion of Far Eastern problems at the Yalta Conference in February, he now assured them that the neutrality pact would govern the relations between the Soviet Union and Japan until it actually expired. On May 8 Germany surrendered and Japan went out of its way to denounce the anti-Comintern pact, thus hoping to gain some credit with Moscow.

The Japanese pressed negotiations with the Soviet Union throughout most of the month of June, both in Tokyo and in Moscow. Japan proposed a non-aggression pact between these two countries and in return was willing to pay almost any price that the Soviet Union demanded, including neutralization of Manchukuo and giving up fishery rights in Soviet waters. There were some Japanese who hoped and expected that there would soon be a break between the Soviet Union and the United States, and that the Soviet Union might therefore be interested in keeping Japan's war going against the United States. In any event, it was hoped that the Soviet Union would be willing to mediate on behalf of Japan and thus secure for her better terms than she could otherwise expect.

On July 25 the Japanese ambassador in Moscow received instructions from Foreign Minister Togo that he was to ask the Soviet Union to receive Prince Konoe who was ready to leave for Moscow with concrete suggestions from the Japanese government. The Soviet Union did not refuse and did not agree to mediate; it insisted upon very definite proposals, but the fact that Japan had approached Moscow was reported to the American government. While Konoe was kept waiting for an invitation, the Soviet Union was making certain that it would get its price from China before attacking Japan. In the meantime, on July 26, the United States, Great Britain, and China, without consulting Moscow, issued a statement about Japan in the Potsdam declaration. This declaration was designed to give the Japanese some indication of what they could expect in the event of surrender. The formula of unconditional surrender could not be given up, but could be interpreted. The Potsdam declaration offered as conditions of peace: the removal of the military, a period of occupation, limitation of Japanese sovereignty to the four main islands, the disarming and returning to Japan of Japanese armies abroad, the trial of war criminals, no enslavement or destruction of the Japanese as a nation, Japanese acceptance of democratic institutions, destruction of war industries, and at the end of the occupation when these objectives had been achieved, an eventual return to world trade, with access to raw materials.

The emperor and the Supreme War Council, except the two representatives of the armed services, were in favor of accepting the Potsdam declaration. In view of the opposition of the armed services, the Supreme War Council decided to wait for an answer from the Soviet Union, but a report got out to the press that the declaration had been rejected and that Japan would fight to the bitter end. Actually, the Japanese ambassador in Moscow had been instructed to negotiate with the Russians on the basis of the Potsdam declaration. But the report in the Japanese press, which attributed the remarks to the premier, seemed sufficiently final to the United States which then made the decision to drop the first atomic bomb.

On August 6 the first atomic bomb fell on Hiroshima destroying much of the city and killing over 78,000 persons. The emperor told the Foreign Minister that the time had come to get peace without further discussion as it was clear that the Russians were not going to help. The second atomic bomb fell on Nagasaki on August 9, a few hours after the Soviet Union declared war on Japan. It was now clear to even the most fanatical militarists that the end was drawing near. All six members of the Supreme War Council, meeting at ten o'clock on the morning of the ninth, agreed that the Potsdam declaration must be accepted in principle, but the Chiefs of Staff and the War Minister wanted to make conditions—that there should be no Allied occupation, that Japan should demobilize her own troops, and that the Japanese government should try those accused of war crimes. It was not till later in the day that the deadlock was broken by an unprecedented departure from the usual practice by which the emperor did not join in the making of policy but merely accepted the decisions of his advisers.

In answer to the Japanese attempt to accept surrender on the understanding that it did not "comprise any demand which prejudices the prerogatives of His Majesty as a Sovereign Ruler" the United States, on behalf of the Allies, had replied that "the authority of the Emperor and the Japanese Government to rule the state shall be subject to the Supreme Commander of the Allied Powers . . ." But it was also stated that "The ultimate form of government of Japan shall, in accordance with the Potsdam declaration, be established by the freely expressed will of the Japanese people." From this it could be inferred that the Allied powers would not of their own accord, remove the emperor. This was the interpretation put on these words by the emperor himself.

The emperor, when appealed to by the peace party, stated openly that he felt that Japan should accept the Potsdam declaration with the single condition that the imperial house should be preserved. "I think that now is the time to bear the unbearable. Recalling the Emperor Meiji's feelings when he was confronted with the Triple Intervention, I repress my tears and approve the draft plan." This desperate effort on the part of the civil authorities to use the influence of the emperor against the military was made all the more difficult because the Potsdam declaration actually gave no guarantees about the future of the imperial authority. It has been argued, with some justice, that the men who actually forced the surrender decision had made up their minds long before this, but it took the atom bombing of Hiroshima and Nagasaki and the intervention of the Soviet Union to create the conditions under which the will of the military could be broken.

The decision to surrender was transmitted through the Swiss Government and also broadcast from Japan. The American reply of August 11 stated that "From the moment of surrender the authority of the Emperor and the Japanese Government to rule the state shall be subject to the Supreme Commander of the Allied Powers who will take such steps as he deems proper to effectuate the surrender terms." Even though the Japanese qualification about the position of the emperor had not been accepted, the emperor himself was willing, as his military advisers were not, to consider the American reply satisfactory. In the opinion of some of the military it was an open question as to whether the chaos that would be created by accepting the surrender might not be greater than that which would follow resistance. Once again it took the intervention of the emperor to resolve the conflict, and on the morning of August 14 the emperor ordered the discussion ended and commanded acceptance of the terms of the American reply. "You will all please agree to my views. If we do not terminate the war at this juncture, our unique national structure will be destroyed and our nation will suffer extermination. If we save anything, be it ever so little, we could yet hope to rebuild the nation in the future."

The Minister of War committed suicide, sections of the imperial guard revolted but were suppressed, and the premier resigned. A note of surrender, sent out on August 15, was followed by an imperial edict to the army ordering it to surrender. Princes of the blood were sent to Singapore, China, and Manchukuo to persuade the armies in the field to submit. For the first time an imperial prince became premier, a measure designed to make it difficult for the fanatical elements to resort to political assassination. The war was over and Japan accepted the surrender in an orderly manner. The actual instrument of surrender was signed on board the United States battleship *Missouri* in Tokyo Bay on September 2, 1945, by representatives of the Japanese government and the Allied powers. General Douglas MacArthur was appointed as Supreme Commander for the Allied Powers, and the occupation began.

5. OCCUPIED JAPAN

Organization and Aims

The first general instructions on Allied occupation policy for Japan were drawn up by the American State, War, and Navy departments and approved by President Truman on September 6, 1945. Many of the statements in this document, "United States Initial Post Surrender Policy for Japan," were based on several preceding agreements between the Allied powers—the Cairo Declaration, the Yalta agreements, and the Potsdam Declaration.

The Allied policy in the occupation of Japan was to be carried out by the Supreme Commander for the Allied Powers, General Douglas Mac-Arthur. The Russians, who had wanted two commanders in Japan, one of them to be a Russian, agreed to the appointment of General MacArthur and even gave up the demand for Russian occupation forces in Hokkaido, but they objected strenuously to the original proposal that there should be only one body to control policy and that without any real authority. There was thus established at Washington, D. C. a Far Eastern Commission, consisting of representatives from the eleven nations at war with Japan, whose duties were to draw up and ratify general policy statements. The Commission included the United States, the U.S.S.R, Great Britain, China, France, the Netherlands, Canada, Australia, New Zealand, India, and the Philippine Commonwealth. Burma and Pakistan were added in 1949. The Far Eastern Commission was to "formulate the policies, principles, and standards in conformity with which the fulfillment by Japan of its obligations under the terms of surrender may be accomplished." The decisions of the Far Eastern Commission were then to be translated by the United States government into directives for SCAP. The U. S. government was the only official link with SCAP.

In addition to the Far Eastern Commission there was set up, mainly because of the Russian attitude, an Allied Council for Japan which was to meet in Tokyo. This body included representatives of the United States, the Soviet Union, China, and one member representing jointly the United Kingdom, Australia, New Zealand, and India. This body, under American chairmanship, was to consult with and advise SCAP on the carrying out of occupation policy. In practice General MacArthur never permitted the meetings of the Allied Council to become more than a mere formality. In fact, the whole framework of institutional responsibility for the Allied occupation left most of the authority in the hands of the American Supreme Commander and of the United States government.

The aims of the occupation were stated to be: the elimination of militarism in Japan and of the militant nationalism that had been associated with it; the prosecution of war criminals, from whom, as a matter of occupation policy, the emperor was excluded; the elimination from Japanese leadership of the men who were considered responsible for, and connected with, the policy of aggression; the payment of reparations in kind; the destruction of Japanese war industries; and the initiation of political, economic, and educational reforms that were to open the way for the democratic development of Japan. Behind these objectives there was the conviction, held in the United States, that Japanese imperialistic expansion was to be explained mainly by the character of her military ruling class and of its allies, the zaibatsu. American policy planners assumed that the concentration of economic wealth and power in the hands of a few huge family-type enterprises was in itself a cause of war, and that the existence of the zaibatsu and the development of democratic institutions were incompatible because democracy required widespread ownership and diffused economic control. In order to prevent a recurrence of aggression, Japan was also to be completely disarmed and robbed of all her war-making potential. The doctrine that a nation's leaders could be held legally responsible for war crimes was applied to Japan as it had been to Germany.

The disarmament of Japan was carried through rapidly and smoothly, as was the destruction of her remaining war industries. There was a rapid demobilization of all the armed forces, and all Japanese armies abroad were brought home, as were the civilians, a total of 6,500,000 people. The ministries of War and Navy and the Imperial General Staff were abolished. But the reorganization of Japan for peaceful democratic development encompassed the broad program of political, economic, and general social reforms which was to be carried out by the Japanese themselves, whose imperial government continued to function under the direction of SCAP.

An International War Crimes Tribunal was set up in Tokyo to try the wartime premier, General Tojo, and a number of other Japanese war leaders. Tojo and six others were sentenced to death and a number of others were given prison terms. All over the Far East local courts tried and punished over 5,000 lesser war criminals.

Political Reforms

The way was prepared for reforms by the last sessions of the old wartime Diet, which obediently passed legislation to implement the

SCAP directives regarding elections, trade unions, and agrarian reform. The Diet transferred the properties of the imperial house to the state, thus making the imperial house economically dependent upon the Diet, and abolished the House of Peers. The flood of legislation provided for new regulations for labor, such as the forty-eight hour week and national minimum wages, revision of the educational system, changes in the legal system, the abolition of restrictions on political parties, and for elections to implement a new constitution which was to come into effect on May 3, 1947. In addition to this, SCAP had issued directives ordering the suspension of all existing hindrances to freedom of thought, of religion, of assembly, of speech, and of information. American officers actually assisted in the release of all Japanese who had been thrown into jail for political reasons. By this action SCAP released, among others, the leaders of the Japanese Communist party.

In order to clear the ground for new ideological developments, state Shintoism was abolished. This meant the end of state financial support of the Shinto shrines, but Shintoism was permitted to continue as a private religious practice. Public officials were now forbidden to report important matters to Shinto shrines or in any way to give official encouragement to the cult. The disestablishment of state Shintoism, combined with the imperial rescript of January 1, 1946, in which the emperor officially gave up the doctrine of divinity, cut the ground from under a good deal of the ideological structure built up by the militarists, particularly the doctrines of the mystical origin of the Japanese islands and the Japanese people and their superiority to all other races of man.

SCAP ordered the Japanese government to purge from public office all persons who were judged to have promoted Japanese militarism and aggression. This meant in effect excluding from the service of the government or of the people many of the officials who had been in office since the opening of the war with China in 1937. Dr. Minobe, who had been purged by the militarists some years earlier, now found himself chairman of the committee to carry out the new purge. By the time his committee had completed its task, over 180,000 persons, including military officers, had been declared ineligible for office, and only 10 per cent of the members of the Diet were permitted to stand for re-election. Not only the top political leaders but also the top leaders in the economic life of Japan were purged.

Japan was ordered to hold its first postwar election under the new electoral law which enfranchised both men and women above the age of twenty years. There were many parties to choose from. The Liberal party secured 139 seats, the Progressive party 93, the Social Democrats 92, the Cooperatives 14, and the Communist party 5. A Liberal-Progressive coalition cabinet with Yoshida Shigeru as premier took office in May, 1946.

It now remained to give a firm institutional framework within which the new Japan could grow along democratic lines. A new constitution was imposed in fact by SCAP, but in theory it was the work of the Japanese. The emperor announced it, General MacArthur approved it, and the Diet ratified it in February and March, 1946. The way had been cleared for the new position of the emperor in the constitution by the imperial rescript of January 1, 1946, in which the emperor officially denied "the false conception of the emperor as divine." The most important innovation of the new constitution was that sovereignty rested with the people, not with the emperor. The contrast between the new Japanese political structure and that of the Meiji period is indicated by the wording of the preambles of the respective constitutions. While the Meiji constitution was granted by the emperor, who retained all authority, the new constitution began with a sentence not unfamiliar to American ears:

We, the Japanese people, acting through our duly elected representatives in the National Diet, determined that we shall secure for ourselves and our posterity the fruits of peaceful cooperation with all nations and the blessings of liberty throughout this land, and resolved that never again shall we be visited with the horrors of war through the action of government, do proclaim that sovereign power resides with the people and do firmly establish this Constitution. Government is a sacred trust of the people, the authority for which is derived from the people, the powers of which are exercised by the representatives of the people, and the benefits of which are enjoyed by the people.

In accordance with this concept of the sovereignty of the people, the emperor's position was described as void of all actual powers of government. The emperor became "the symbol of the State and of the unity of the people, deriving his position from the will of the people with whom resides sovereign power."

The rights of the people were guaranteed in a bill of rights which assured the Japanese people of practically every constitutional guarantee to which Americans are accustomed. There were some new ones besides—the right to receive an equal education, the right and obligation to work, the right of workers to organize and to bargain and act collectively.

The sovereignty of the people was exercised through the Diet, "the highest organ of state power," and the only organ that could make laws. Both houses were elected, the House of Representatives for four years and the House of Councillors, the upper house, for six years. The peerage was abolished together with the House of Peers. The lower house had final legislative authority and could pass a law in a second vote over the opposition of the House of Councillors. The premier and the cabinet were no longer responsible to the emperor but to the Diet, which through them had the legal authority to control the bureaucracy. The constitution established an independent judiciary headed by a Supreme Court, the court of last resort, which could determine the constitutionality of "any law, order, regulation, or official act." Article 9 of the constitution provided that Japan should renounce war and never maintain armed forces.

To strengthen the democratic basis of the new Japanese government SCAP introduced certain measures to strengthen local self-government. The number of elected local officials was increased, the police force decentralized, and a substantial amount of legislative authority was delegated to the prefectural and municipal governments.

Economic and Social Reforms

The introduction of a representative political system could not be realized without far-reaching economic and social changes. To fill up the vacuum left by the purged and broken ruling groups, SCAP was determined to develop three main foundations for democratic rule. These were to be a strong and independent labor movement, a revised and enlarged group of small businessmen, and finally an independent, landowning peasantry.

Early in the occupation SCAP had issued directives to the Japanese government to remove all obstacles to the development of strong labor organizations. The new trade union law followed very closely the text of the National Labor Relations Act of 1935 in the United States. Largely under the influence of the Japanese Communists, labor unions developed at a tremendous pace; an enormous May Day celebration took place in 1946, and the new freedom to strike was very extensively employed. So obvious was the influence of the Communists in the Congress of Industrial Unions that by January, 1947, SCAP was moving to curb the labor movement. Strikes were obviously being used for political purposes, and labor agitation was getting in the way of reconstruction. SCAP prohibited general strikes, denounced the tendency to use labor unions for political purposes, and generally tried to encourage every effort to eradicate Communist leadership in the labor unions.

SCAP assumed that the establishment of a representative system would be possible only if the economic controls over the country's resources were broadened. In this direction two revolutionary measures were initiated by SCAP and carried out by the Japanese government. One of these was an ambitious program to break down the monopoly of the zaibatsu. The big holding companies were dissolved and their shares taken over by a government organization which attempted to sell them to the public. Assets of many of the zaibatsu families were frozen and searching investigations were conducted to try to unearth the highly complicated pattern of ownership and control. The attack on the zaibatsu was in fact only part of a more general effort to bring about a decentralization of economic control in the industrial sector of the economy.

The economic deconcentration law of December, 1947, if it had been vigorously applied, would have made it difficult for almost any large-scale enterprise to stay in business. In this process the former owners were compensated by government bonds, but these bonds could not be sold and a high graduated tax on capital considerably reduced the family fortunes. In addition, many industrial leaders who could be accused or suspected of having supported Japanese military aggression were excluded from management. These measures had a leveling influence and brought about somewhat more competitive conditions in business, but all the power of SCAP could not create a middle class overnight.

The other important revolutionary measure initiated by SCAP and carried out by the Japanese government was in the field of land reform. As early as December, 1945, the Japanese government was instructed to develop a land reform program which would lead to improved conditions of tenancy and wider distribution of landownership. After considerable opposition the Diet was finally compelled by SCAP to enact a land reform law in October, 1946. The main objective of the land reform program was to increase the number of peasant owners, to improve the economic conditions of all farmers, and to give them sufficient economic independence so that they could take an active and intelligent part in the democratic institutions of postwar Japan.

The land reform measures were far-reaching indeed. Absentee landlords were forced to sell all their land to the government and the resident landlords were forced to sell all the land they owned above two and one-half acres. Owner cultivators were allowed to keep about seven and a half acres for their own use and to rent out an additional two and a half acres. There was no way, therefore, in which a man could own much more than a ten-acre farm. All the lands which the government acquired were sold to tenants on a long-range purchase plan. As Japan was going through a serious inflation and the transactions were based on prewar values, the compensation received by former landowners was comparatively small. Hundreds of thousands of tenants were able to acquire their land very quickly and rural indebtedness practically disappeared. At the same time the conditions of tenancy, which are actually of more significance than the amount of tenancy itself, were radically changed by the new land legislation. The tenant was given the security of a written contract and his rent was fixed by law to be paid in cash at no more than 25 per cent of the value of the main crop, a reduction by at least half of what it used to be.

The land reform program changed the pattern of land ownership. According to Japanese estimates the amount of land held by owner-farmers increased from 53.7% to 86.9% of the total cultivated land by 1949, and leased land decreased correspondingly. The number of farmers who owned all their land increased from 36.3% to 61.6% by 1950, and the number of farmers who owned more than half their land went up from 20.3% to 26.4%. The number of farmers owning less than half their land decreased from 17.3% to 6.8%, and the number of full tenants went down from 26.1% to 4.6%.[3] A secondary purpose of the program had been to increase the amount of cultivated land by 3,250,000 acres, and by 1955 a million and a quarter acres had been brought under cultivation. The changes in ownership and the increase in land under cultivation did not lead to any important increase in total production, according to official figures, but these may not have been too reliable. According to these figures the amount of land under cultivation was reported as being less than before the war. This may have been due to the farmer's reluctance to report the full amount of his taxable land. The low official price set by the government for rice, combined with the

[3] Sakae Wagatsuma and Ichiro Kato, "Post-War Agricultural Land Reform in Japan," Estratto dagli Atti del "Primo Convegno Internazionale di Diritto Agrario," University of Florence (Milan, 1955), Vol. I.

relatively high taxes, encouraged concealment of the true amount of food production.

The political objective of land reform was to change the traditional pattern of village relationships. It was hoped that the changes in economic conditions would free the new peasant-owner from the domination of the landlord. This aim was largely accomplished. The owner-farmer class showed a much greater independence than in the past, and the privileged position of the landowners had largely come to an end. The radical movement among the peasants lost its momentum because the peasants were mainly interested in conserving their newly won gains. They became the chief support of the conservative political parties. The permanence of the land reforms was believed to be assured. The efforts of the landlords to block land reform by court action and by delaying the registration of land had failed. So long as the land law remained unchanged, the tendency towards a slight increase in the size of landholdings was accounted for by the rise in the number of well-to-do owner-farmers and not of landlords. But the farmers as a whole had a vested interest in the land reforms.

SCAP introduced important long-range changes in the field of education. The Japanese school system had been a very important weapon for indoctrination and control. SCAP took the view that there could not be any permanent reforms unless the educational system was completely revised. The first step taken by SCAP was to initiate a purge of teachers and experts. The Japanese were instructed to dismiss all those teachers who had actively supported the policy of aggression. School teachers in Japan, all of whom were civil servants, were noted for their loyalty to the dogmas of the emperor's divinity and Japanese racial superiority. The story of the school teacher who lost his life in an attempt to save the emperor's picture from a burning schoolhouse was a typical expression of this spirit. In the same way Japanese schoolbooks glorified the military tradition of the past and supported the myths of Japan's historical origin and mission. Under the influence of SCAP many of the textbooks were rewritten. One-fourth of the schoolteachers were dismissed.

Under the traditional Japanese system of education, everyone was literate, but few had higher education. For boys there were six years of compulsory elementary school, followed by a five-year middle school, a three-year higher school, and a three or four-year university. As the middle schools took care of only 6 per cent of the elementary school graduates and the higher schools took care of around one-tenth of the middle school graduates, only a very small number actually reached the universities. This number has been estimated at one-half of one per cent of the elementary school graduates. SCAP increased the period of compulsory education to nine years and imposed upon the school system the American plan of six years elementary, three years junior high school, three years senior high school, and four years college. In order to decentralize higher education universities were established in the prefectures. For an impoverished country which had lost many school buildings as a result of the war and needed many new teachers and new books, this was an ambitious and expensive program.

SCAP also introduced new teaching methods. These were designed to develop the spirit of independent inquiry on the part of the student, a truly revolutionary change in the Japanese educational system, where blind obedience to the national leaders and unquestioning respect for authority had been considered the highest virtues. Municipal schoolboards were made largely responsible for local schools, on the American pattern, thus getting away from the highly centralized government control which had prevailed in the past. In a violent departure from the spirit and content of traditional Japanese education SCAP introduced social studies into the curriculum to replace the conventional courses on "morals." Attention was also given to the simplification of the Japanese language, and although some steps were taken in this direction, the Japanese child still spends more time learning to read and write than does the American or European child. SCAP's reforms in education were intended to bring about revolutionary changes in the attitudes and outlook of the Japanese people.

While the process of reform was in its early stages, SCAP did not open Japan to the intellectual currents of the Western world. Early in the occupation very few Japanese were permitted by SCAP to travel abroad, and not many Americans or other visitors from Allied countries were permitted to enter Japan. Later in the occupation this policy was changed, and by 1948 large numbers of Japanese were assisted in making trips abroad, especially to the United States, in the hope that free access to the Western world would have an important effect on the Japanese.

SCAP's reforms succeeded most where they could be related to existing Japanese attitudes or institutions. Japan had had political parties and some measure of parliamentary government long before the war. Peasant organizations and labor unions were not new, and there had been strong popular feeling against the zaibatsu for many years. The Japanese women had been prepared for legal equality and enfranchisement by their part in the new industrial economy and their role in the war. The prestige of the military in Japan was already seriously undermined by defeat and surrender. The emperor, himself, did not have to be dragooned into the role of a constitutional monarch—he apparently preferred it; nor was there any deep sense of shock in Japan when he departed from the doctrine of divinity. SCAP policy of not attacking the imperial institution, however, was an adjustment to existing attitudes. Loyalty to the emperor was still a fact which even the Communists, who were the only ones to attack him openly, had to accept by dropping the issue.

The real test of the occupation was whether in the long run it succeeded in changing the balance of forces in Japanese society in favor of democracy. The major objective of the occupation was not to turn Japan into a democracy overnight, but rather to make it possible for her to become a democracy over a long period of time by neutralizing those anti-democratic forces which had been dominant for so long. With the defeat, the loss of former colonies and newly won territories, the return of those Japanese who had been living abroad, the exemplary behavior of occupation troops, the reopening of Japan to world sources of information, the cessation of the traditional ideological indoctrination, and the discrediting and impoverishment of those formerly in authority, Japan was in a state of ferment comparable only to the early years of the Meiji Restoration. It was hoped that out of this ferment would arise new leaders and new patterns of individual and group behavior. Having changed the balance of power within society SCAP had created an open situation. The introduction of the constitution was followed by new elections in 1947. The Socialist party became the largest single party in the House and its leader, Katayama, became premier by forming with the Democratic party, a coalition which lasted for six months. In February, 1948, the leader of the Democratic party, Ashida, took over, but he too lasted for little more than half a year, and in October the Liberal party, more conservative than the Democratic party, came in with Yoshida as premier. Yoshida stayed in power until 1954. As long as the occupation lasted, the premier, though responsible to the Diet, had to carry out SCAP's orders.

Changes in Occupation Policy

SCAP was not responsible for the economic recovery of Japan, but it could not remain indifferent to economic conditions. The isolation of Japan from the world market, the destruction brought about by the war, the loss of Japan's former territories, the impact of SCAP reforms on the direction and management of Japan's business, all combined to produce a steadily deteriorating economic situation and there was the possibility that economic distress would endanger democratic development. In fact, the Japanese economy was running down so fast that food had to be imported to prevent widespread starvation. By 1948, therefore, SCAP was already changing its emphasis in the economic sphere from reform to recovery. At the same time the increasing tension between the Soviet Union and the United States and the imminent danger of a Communist take-over in China combined to shift American policy in the same direction.

SCAP announced on August 3, 1949, that the dissolution of the zaibatsu had been completed. It was argued that the danger from the big cartels had been removed by the dissolution and reorganization of the key holding companies, the part of the program which had been completely carried through. The number of zaibatsu combines to be deconcentrated was drastically reduced because it was thought that a further fragmentation of Japanese industry would endanger Japan's economic stability. This policy was accepted by the Far Eastern Commission after some opposition. As the United States wanted to prevent further economic deterioration, reparation payments to China and the Philippines were greatly reduced, and in order to reactivate Japan's foreign trade on a much larger scale, SCAP began to look around for markets, to ease export controls, to permit private foreign trade, and to arrange for loans and credits. At the same time the purge of administrative officials was relaxed in order to keep capable and experienced men in top business management and other key positions in the economy. In May 1951, General Ridgeway, who had succeeded General MacArthur as Supreme Commander, issued a generally worded directive permitting the Japanese government to review the status of all those who had been purged from political or economic activities. Within six weeks the government depurged some 70,000 persons and eventually all but 8,000 of the total of 210,000 were depurged. These 8,000 were those who had been convicted of war crimes by an international tribunal.

The Communist Party

The sharpening conflict with Soviet Russia that had been partly responsible for the shift in SCAP's economic policies also affected the role of the Japanese Communist party in the reviving political life of Japan. As the Communists were the only organized political group which could claim that it had consistently opposed the war, and was therefore in no way responsible for the defeat, the Communist leaders at first enjoyed a good deal of prestige. SCAP released Communist leaders who had spent the war in prison and permitted the return of others, such as Nozaka, alias Okano, who had spent the war in Moscow and with the Chinese Communists on the mainland. The Communists, however, held only five seats out of 466 in the House of Representatives elected in 1946.

The Communist party, legal for the first time in Japanese history, emerged after the war with well tried leaders from the thirties, most of whom had been trained in Moscow. According to its own admission it was not a poor organization, for its financial statement of 1950 indicated that the Communist party funds were three times larger than those of the Liberals, ten times larger than those of the Socialists, and fourteen times larger than those of the Democrats. Some money came from the members, some from publications, some from traffic in narcotics, and some, presumably, from abroad. The Japanese Communist party was a force to be reckoned with.

Under the leadership of Nozaka the general line of the party was to make a direct attack on the conservatives, especially the Liberal party and Yoshida, and to divide the socialists. The traditional position of opposition to the emperor was played down, and all connection with the international Communist movement denied. For the first five years after the war Nozaka thought that more could be achieved by peaceful means than by violent revolutionary methods, but he made it clear that the peaceful approach was a tactical maneuver, not a retreat from revolution. The attack on Yoshida's government could hardly have been more vicious. Its members were called fascists, imperialist puppets, and traitors who were trying to sell the country out to foreign monopoly capital. The drive to split the Socialist party by cooperating with the left wing did not get very far at this time, but it bore fruit some years later. In the third general election of January, 1949, the Communists captured 35 seats largely by attracting left-wing socialist votes, but it was not until 1951 that the Socialist party actually split.

The main efforts of the Japanese Communists were directed toward securing a mass basis of support among the workers and peasants. They made very little impact on the peasantry, but by 1948 it has been estimated that about half of organized labor was in some measure under Communist influence. The violent tactics of the Communists in labor disputes, the attempt at a general strike in 1947, and the excesses committed in 1949 were carried out deliberately in order to paralyze the economy, to compel the government to counterattack, and thus to open itself to the charge of "undemocratic" attitudes towards the unions. The counterattack came from Yoshida's government as well as from SCAP, both of which gave more and more assistance to anti-Communist forces. Many of the labor unions blamed the Communists for the anti-union measures taken by the government. But while the Communists were losing some of the ground they had won among the workers, they were gaining with the intellectuals—the students, teachers, professional workers, artists, writers, and actors.

Marxism had made much progress among Asiatic intellectuals before the war, and in Japan it had even been fused into the mystical ideology of the military-agrarian extremists. But Marxist categories had also become part of the intellectual baggage of anti-militarists, especially after the war. This may have been due in part to the success of the militarists in starving the intellectual life of Japan, in particular in denying Japanese schools and universities access to Western social science. Marxism, with its easy answers to complex questions and its pseudo-scientific claims, became a sort of black market "social science" because it was readily absorbed and had about it the aura of revolt against authority. In the postwar world Communism provided a program of action based on successful experience in Russia and now in China. The Communist party, therefore, made headway among the college and university students of occupied Japan.

The peaceful strategy of the Communists was changed suddenly in January, 1950, not by the Japanese but by the Cominform. Nozaka was suddenly denounced in the official journal of the Cominform for attempting to naturalize Marxism-Leninism in Japanese conditions, and for his policy of "peaceful revolution," now described as an indication of rightist opportunist tendencies. Nozaka obediently issued a statement of self-criticism in which he admitted his errors in diagnosis and called on the Japanese party to play its role in the international revolutionary movement. The Japanese party had grown considerably since the war, and the time had come to weed out the opportunists and to find and test new leaders in a harder school. The Japanese party, which had toyed with the idea of neutralism, was told that in the coming struggle between the two world blocs it would fight on the Soviet side. The new line was for the hard core of the party to go underground and for the legal, open party to follow a policy of militant obstructionism. The most important leaders, including Nozaka, disappeared during

1950, and signs of the new militancy were soon apparent in demonstrations, riots, and other disorders all over the country.

The Communist victories in China had changed the balance of world power and thus speeded up the tempo of preparation for war. If the planned invasion of South Korea were successful, the time for revolution in Japan itself would be advanced, and for that it was necessary to have a strong underground party ready for action and a forceful legal party constantly challenging the government and providing leadership for a united front of all who opposed it. The immediate tasks of the party, to use its own jargon, were to prepare for a domestic "democratic" revolution in order to get rid of American influence and to destroy the influence of the imperial institution, of the landowners, and national monopoly capital. As mass support was essential for such tasks, it was permissible, so long as the party retained its purity, to make tactical retreats on some issues, such as the emperor, in order not to create unnecessary antagonism. The Hate America campaign was obviously to be stepped up, and on May 30, 1950, came the first attack on American citizens in Tokyo by Communist-led demonstrators.

The government and SCAP struck back immediately by making statements denouncing Communism and by forcing known party members out of government service as "undemocratic" elements. But the vicious attacks on American motives and actions, which appealed to a far wider circle than members of the Communist party, made it important for the U. S. to conclude with Japan a treaty of peace which would give her independence and thus rob the Communists of their opportunity to pose as the champions of nationalism.

6. Peace and Independence

American officials had held the view for several years that a continuation of the occupation might endanger the reforms which had already been accomplished. In fact, General MacArthur stated quite early in the occupation that Allied control of Japan should not last more than three years. The reasons were strong indeed. SCAP was convinced that economic recovery could not be achieved while Japan remained under occupation. Once the opportunity for democratic growth had been assured, the only way in which the Japanese could gain experience of their new institutions would be by having the occupation out of the way. So long as SCAP was in Tokyo, it did not matter very much whom the electorate put in the Diet because SCAP's directives had to be obeyed. Given the aims of the Occupation, therefore, prolongation of SCAP control would merely endanger its achievements. As early as the summer of 1947 the United States made the first overtures to its allies to secure a peace settlement with Japan.

The failure of the Big Four to come to terms on a peace treaty with Germany in 1947 indicated that the same approach to Japan would not be any more profitable. As other countries, particularly Australia, made it clear that they would expect to be consulted, the task of making peace was shifted by the State Department to the Far Eastern Commission in Washington, a move which was immediately denounced by the Soviet Union. In September, 1947, Nationalist China also refused to accept an invitation to attend an eleven-nation Far Eastern Commission conference on a Japan peace treaty. A countermove by Molotov to have a meeting of the foreign ministers of the Big Four foundered on British and Chinese opposition.

Public statements by American officials in 1948 made it clear that the basis of American interest in Japan had changed, and firm directives were handed the Japanese government to stop inflation, balance the budget, stabilize wages and prices, and generally tighten up on credit, foreign exchange, and tax collection. Such an approach indicated a strong American interest in Japan as part of a security system in the Pacific, but important Americans, including the Secretary of War, advocated writing Japan off as indefensible. This view did not predominate, but it caused a good deal of uneasiness among Japanese who had come out strongly for the new order of things and now felt that they might be abandoned either to the Soviet Union or the Japanese military reactionaries. The Soviet Union exploited the situation by pressing for a peace conference on its own punitive terms in order to force the United States to slow down the process of Japanese recovery. By 1949 it was entirely to the Soviet interest to press for a peace conference on Japan, for China was now in the hands of the Chinese Communists, the new government at Peking was recognized by Great Britain and India, and the Soviet Union was anxious to obstruct Japanese recovery.

The United States government decided, by the end of 1949, to promote a separate peace with Japan as the only way in which the problem could now be solved. The strategy was to secure an agreement of the British Commonwealth to the plan for Japan's independence, assure the granting of facilities for American military bases in Japan on a long-range basis, and then go ahead with a peace conference whether Russia and China joined in or not. Such a strategy depended on outmaneuvering the Soviet bloc, but it also required the cooperation of the Japanese, and this could not—as SCAP appeared to assume—be taken for granted. It was a serious matter for Japan to recover responsibility for her economic and political future with one of the major decisions of foreign policy already made for her. To accept a separate peace and the presence of American military forces on her soil was to take sides immediately in the cold war and to guarantee the loss of her bargaining position with the Soviet bloc. Any hesitations which Japan might have had on this score were deliberately encouraged by the Soviet Union in its treaty with Communist China, February 1950, in which the two powers promised to block the rebirth of Japanese imperialism and the repetition of aggression on the part of Japan "or any other State which would unite in any form with Japan in acts of aggression." This and other statements were intended to convince the Japanese that they would pay heavily for a separate peace with the United States and would fare better if they remained friendly to the Soviet bloc.

In an effort to explore the situation and to reconcile the many conflicting factors that presented themselves, the United States sent Mr. John Foster Dulles, already appointed a special adviser to the State Department, to Japan in the summer of 1950. Very soon after Mr. Dulles arrived in the Far East the whole political landscape was changed by the North Korean invasion of the territory of the Korean Republic on June 25, a move that aroused all Japan's old fears of invasion from the continent. However much the Japanese may have desired to see the Americans leave, they certainly preferred them to the prospect of living side by side with a Communist-controlled, revengeful, and militarily strong Korea. The Japanese government announced its position on the Korean conflict through its Ministry of Foreign Affairs on August 19, less than two months after the invasion and at a time when Japan was practically denuded of American troops. In brief, the Japanese stated that in the conflict between Communism and democracy there was no room for neutrality, and Japan would choose the democratic side. The decision was important on the home front as well as internationally, for the Japanese Communist party had been alerted and prepared to take full advantage of the situation if American troops were thrown into the Korean conflict. The Japanese government, prodded by SCAP, immediately took steps to anticipate sabotage and internal troubles by suspending the Communist press and setting up a National Police Reserve of 75,000 men and a Maritime Safety Board of 8,000 men. The attack on the Communists was pursued into student organizations, universities, the press, radio, and trade unions.

The United States continued negotiations for a peace treaty, but the provision of the Japanese constitution which bound Japan not to maintain armed forces or to use war as an instrument of national policy came up to plague both the Japanese and the American government. Article 9 of the constitution reads as follows:

Aspiring sincerely to an international peace based on justice and order, the Japanese people forever renounce war as a sovereign right of the nation and the threat or use of force as means of settling international disputes.

In order to accomplish the aim of the preceding paragraph, land, sea, and air forces, as well as other war potential, will never be maintained. The right of belligerency of the state will not be recognized.

While the Liberal and Democratic parties, with some differences, supported the idea of rearmament, the Socialist party came out against it and also opposed the suggested guarantee of security by the United States because it involved stationing foreign troops on Japanese soil. Premier Yoshida played a cautious game on the rearmament question, trying to get a mandate from all political parties for what he himself wanted to do. In the meantime, Mr. Dulles continued his negotiations with the Japanese government, emphasizing the fact that he considered himself to be dealing with an equal rather than a defeated power, and then proceeded to the Philippines and Australia in the effort to bring these two important countries into line. In both cases Dulles suggested mutual security pacts as a means of compensating for the proposed rearmament of Japan. President Truman's recall of General

MacArthur made no serious difference to the negotiations, but British insistence on bringing in the Communist Chinese took Dulles to London and complicated things very considerably. The matter was solved by both sides agreeing that Japan herself should choose, after the treaty, with which China she should deal. A draft treaty could now be drawn up and submitted to the Japanese for their reactions.

On July 20, 1951, the United States and the United Kingdom invited the nations which had been involved in the war with Japan to attend a conference at San Francisco to discuss a Japanese peace treaty, the draft of which was submitted with the invitation. Neither Nationalist nor Communist China was invited to attend. Red China denounced the whole affair with threats of dire consequences if the treaty were signed. India and Burma refused to attend. The Philippines were induced to come to San Francisco by the signing of the Philippine-United States Mutual Security Pact on August 30. Australian participation in the peace treaty was secured by the conclusion of a tripartite security pact between Australia, New Zealand, and the United States, the so-called Anzus Pact, signed on September 1. Japan, in agreeing to attend, raised the issue of the repatriation of Japanese prisoners of war in Russian hands and secured the inclusion in the draft treaty of a repatriation clause. It was estimated that of the 340,000 Japanese taken prisoner by the Soviet Union some 230,000 had died in Soviet labor camps, that 78,000 were still being held, and some 30,000 were missing. The Soviet Union accepted the invitation but neither she nor the other members of the Soviet bloc signed the treaty. On September 8, 1951, forty-nine nations signed the treaty of peace with Japan, thus ending the state of war which had existed between them and Japan up to this time. Premier Yoshida signed for Japan. On the same day the United States concluded a security pact with Japan. In November Japan ratified both the peace treaty and the security pact.

In the treaty of peace Japan declared its intention of applying for membership in the United Nations and promised to adhere to the principles of the Charter. Japan regained full sovereignty over her home islands, recognized the independence of Korea, renounced all rights to Formosa, the Kuriles and southern Sakhalin, accepted the United States trusteeship over its former mandated Pacific islands, and the Liuchius, the Bonins, and other smaller islands. Japan promised to settle international disputes by peaceful means and to refrain from the use of force against the territory or independence of other states. But the Allied Powers recognized Japan's "inherent right of individual or collective self-defense." Japan promised to carry out the sentences of the International Military Tribunal, and to pay reparations to the Allied Powers within the limits of her capacity. While Japan had renounced her title to Formosa and the Kuriles, it was not indicated in the treaty who was to succeed to these territories so that the Soviet right to the Kuriles and the National Government's right to Formosa were not formally recognized.

In the security pact Japan expressed her desire to have the United States maintain forces in and about Japan as a provisional arrangement for her defense against armed attack. The United States, in assuming this responsibility, expressed her expectation that Japan "will itself increasingly assume responsibility for its own defense . . . always avoiding any armament which would be an offensive threat." It was also stipulated that American forces could on the express request of the Japanese government assist in putting down "large scale internal riots and disturbances in Japan, caused through instigation or intervention by an outside power or powers." Japan also agreed that during the life of the treaty she would not grant similar rights to any third power without United States approval.

Japan did not officially regain her full sovereignty until April 28, 1952, by which time the necessary number of ratifications had been deposited in Washington. But the return to independence had begun much earlier. As early as September, 1951, SCAP authorized the Japanese government to negotiate directly with the foreign powers represented in Tokyo. Some of the main buildings which had been reserved for Occupation use were released to the Japanese ahead of schedule, American troops were instructed to adjust themselves to their new status as invited allies, and step by step Japan took her place in various international organizations, including UNESCO. At the same time the U. S. and Japan worked out the details of an administrative agreement to implement the security pact signed by both countries in February, 1952. The Japanese agreed to contribute 17 per cent of the national budget to the common security measures. When the costs of the National Police Reserve, which had come into being in the first stages of the Korean War, were added to this, the total cost of defense came to 25 per cent of the budget. By the peace treaty Japan recovered her right, as a sovereign nation, to self-defense, but those who were reluctant to see the return of the military establishment, or merely wished to embarrass the government, chose to claim that Article 9 of the constitution still stood in the way of rearmament. The legal point, on which opinions differed, was less important than the political struggle over rearmament, a struggle which had its ramifications in every aspect of postwar Japanese life and institutions. On April 29, 1952, the day after she became an independent sovereign state, Japan signed a separate peace treaty with the Republic of China, which had not been invited to the Peace Conference. The treaty recognized Japan's renunciation, at San Francisco, of her title to Formosa and the Pescadores. This treaty did not prejudice Japan's freedom to negotiate, if she wished, with the Communist regime on the mainland.

The government of Premier Yoshida, which had steered the country to full sovereignty and peace with most of its former enemies, faced the three interrelated problems of economic survival, rearmament, and relations with the Soviet bloc. The coming of peace made it possible to re-establish economic relations with the rest of the world and to plan for the future, but it also brought with it the burden of national defense, which since the war had been carried by the United States. The manner in which peace had come forced the newly independent Japan squarely into one of the world's two big armed camps, and therefore complicated her diplomatic and economic problems with the mainland of Asia. Japan's overriding need was foreign trade, and her relationship with the Free World and the Soviet bloc was bound to be influenced by the possibilities for trade that were open to her on either side. In this connection the Yoshida cabinet was attacked, during 1954, as being too closely identified with the Western world, particularly the United States. Much of the opposition to Yoshida's policies reflected a struggle for power between him and his chief political opponent, Ichiro Hatoyama.

Hatoyama had been a member of several prewar cabinets. After the war he founded the Liberal party and was its first president. The Liberal party made the strongest showing in the elections of 1946, but Hatoyama was robbed of his opportunity of becoming premier as he was purged from political life by the Occupation authorities on the basis of his prewar support of Japan's aggression. Yoshida, the vice-president of the Liberal party, became premier instead. Hatoyama, who was depurged in 1951, re-entered political life as a member of the Liberal party and again sought the premiership. In March 1953, Hatoyama left the party and founded the Japan Liberal party; it did not succeed, and he rejoined the Liberal party in December 1953. A year later, November 1954, he broke away again to form the Japan Democratic party by merging his Liberal splinter group with the Progressive party. As president of the new Democratic party he had sufficient support in the Diet to force the resignation of Yoshida in December 1954. Before his resignation Yoshida had gone to the United States, to plead, among other things, for American aid to Southeast Asia to the extent of one billion dollars, from which he hoped that Japan would greatly profit because of the increased ability of the countries of Southeast Asia to buy Japanese goods. His failure to secure such aid contributed to his defeat.

The Hatoyama cabinet, formed in December, 1954, included Mamoru Shigemitsu, former president of the Progressive party and vice-president of the Democratic party, as foreign minister. Shigemitsu, who had been foreign minister for part of the war, had been sentenced to a seven-year prison term by the War Crimes Tribunal, was paroled in 1950, and depurged in 1952. The new cabinet soon indicated that it would seek trade and diplomatic relations with the Soviet Union and Communist China. Hatoyama hoped to accomplish this "with the amicable understanding of the United States," but he stressed that the "misconception that Japan has been blindly following the United States" had created some anti-American feeling. These adverse feelings, he felt, would be minimized by a foreign policy more closely in accord with the wishes of the Japanese people.

Hatoyama also expressed his desire to open normal diplomatic relations with the South Asian countries and to find a settlement for the pending reparations issue. A settlement with Burma was reached in December, 1954, in which the Japanese promised a reparation payment of $250,000,000 to be made over the next ten years. A peace treaty with Burma was signed at the same time. In the negotiations with the Philippines the Japanese offered a payment of $400,000,000, but this was rejected by the Philippine government which asked for one billion dollars. Negotiations, however, continued. A settlement with Thailand was reached in April, 1955, on the basis of a Japanese payment of $41,666,666. Reparation negotiations with Indonesia were also started.

In February 1955, new elections were held and Hatoyama's Democratic party gained 185 seats out of the total of 467. The Liberals had 112 seats, the left-wing socialists 89, the right-wing socialists 67, the Communists 2, and others 12. After the election a second Hatoyama cabinet was formed which continued the same policies. By April it was arranged that formal negotiations should take place in London with the Soviet Union for "the normalization of Japanese-Soviet Relations." Shigemitsu, the Foreign Minister, in expressing the Japanese view of the negotiations, said "It is essential that there be mutual affirmation of the spirit to respect each other's territory, not to intervene in each other's internal affairs, and to resolve all disputes which might arise in the future in a peaceful manner." He regarded "the release and repatriation of the Japanese detainees in Soviet territory" as a question of first priority. Furthermore, he raised the questions of the islands close to Hokkaido, and of the Kuriles and southern Sakhalin, the fishing grounds in northern waters, trade, and Japanese entry into the United Nations.

The foreign policy of the Hatoyama cabinet reflected the full feeling of independence which followed the peace treaty and the fall of the Yoshida cabinet which was so closely associated with the Occupation. This reaction, which had been anticipated by SCAP, was not expressed in violent anti-American movements, as might have happened if the Occupation had been less humane and the Japanese military not so much at fault. Rather it took the form of a reassertion of Japanese independence through the return to some of the symbols of the past. Visits to the Shinto shrines, which dropped off heavily after the war, became popular again and even Premier Hatoyama, a Christian, visited the Shinto shrine at Ise. The emperor himself, in an unofficial capacity, went to report to the shrines of his ancestors. In 1955, for the first time since the end of the war there was a public observance of the legendary Founding Day of the Japanese Empire in 660 B.C. On this occasion the Minister of Education advocated the restoration of this day as a national holiday and announced that respect for the emperor should again be included in schoolteaching. Some Japanese have called for the writing of an "Independent Constitution." This trend did not necessarily imply a condemnation or rejection of the new institutional patterns introduced after the war. It was rather an attempt to restore the continuity with the past which had been broken by the Occupation.

CHAPTER XIV

Communism and Nationalism in South-east Asia

1. Legacy of World War I

The European countries which had established colonial systems in Southeast Asia were greatly shaken by the war, and the prestige of European civilization in the Far East was undermined. The nationalist movements against colonial rule, which had been inspired by Western liberal thought, were now given a new impetus by the revelation of the inner weakness and disunity of the West itself. The Western idea of nationalism prevailed, but was now turned against the Western colonial masters, who no longer seemed so formidable.

The war had also another effect. It had been fought for the avowed ideals of freedom and self-rule in Europe. American participation and Wilson's Fourteen Points had given the war the character of a fight for the general principle of self-determination, "to make the world safe for democracy." Such declarations had a profound effect in the Far East, which was beginning to rise against colonial rule. The ideas of self-rule and self-determination provided the young Western-trained intellectuals of the countries of the Far East with the slogans they needed to assume political leadership of their own countries.

The fight for independence gained additional importance because of the economic changes in the years before and during World War I. These years had brought an increase of production for the world market and economic prosperity in many of the countries of the Far East. In the colonial countries of Southeast Asia this economic expansion created special strains. Most of the modern economic enterprises were in the hands of Westerners, but in some countries a native middle class shared in them. In others, the economic activities of the middle class were carried on by Chinese immigrants. Competition between indigenous and foreign enterprise, resistance against foreign control, and the native hostility to the Chinese minorities and their near-monopoly of retail trade, moneylending, and pawnshop businesses, all these formed the economic basis for the nationalist movements.

World War I had produced another change that was to become of the greatest consequence for the Far East in general and for colonial Southeast Asia in particular. The Russian Revolution had created a territorial and organizational base for international communism, and professional Communist revolutionaries set up Communist parties in almost all the countries of the Far East. The Communist parties founded in the countries of Southeast Asia profited greatly from the climate of the nationalist, anticolonial movements already existing there, and became themselves a major factor in the political struggle.

Great economic expansion, the spread of the ideas of self-determination, and the organization of Communist parties which sought to control and colonize nationalism—this was then the heritage of the First World War throughout the countries of Southeast Asia.

2. THE PHILIPPINES

The Struggle for Independence

During President Wilson's administration the principle of self-determination was applied in American policy in the Philippines. The period of "Filipinization" of the administration under Governor General Harrison greatly advanced Philippine self-rule and encouraged the aspirations for complete independence. Indeed, toward the end of his administration, Wilson submitted legislation for Philippine independence to the American Congress. But United States policy changed with the Republican administration of 1921, and American control in the Philippines was increased, paralleling a similar strengthening of colonial authority in other countries of Southeast Asia. There had been in the United States considerable criticism of the results of handing over the administration to Filipinos, and under the new regime of Governor Wood, "American efficiency" was reintroduced into the Philippine Islands. The hardening of American policy intensified the Philippine drive for independence which was fought by Filipino political leaders in their legislature at home and by their commissioner in Washington, D. C. But there was no change of policy until the economic crisis in 1929 helped to reopen the issue of independence.

In the struggle for independence the issue of the Philippine economy and its relation to that of the United States became of key importance. During the first decades of American administration the Philippine economy had undergone a great change. The plantation economy for the production of sugar, copra, and coconut oil, tobacco, hemp and flax had linked the Philippines closely to the American market. The world economic crisis and the fall in prices seriously affected the producers in the Philippines and created in America a growing opposition to the importation of products from

the Philippines. Copra and coconut oil went into American margarine production, and in the struggle for the lowered buying power of the American
consumer, margarine became a dangerous competitor to the dairy products
of the American farmer who was suffering severely as a result of the economic
crisis. The American and Cuban sugar producers were equally afraid of the
importation of Philippine sugar into the United States. Thus, at the time
when the American market was tightening, the American sugar and dairy
interests were anxious to exclude Philippine competition and were therefore
in favor of granting independence so that Philippine products would be
subject to the tariff rates which protected the American market. On the
other hand, American manufacturers and exporters interested in selling
goods to the Philippines were against the granting of independence for fear of
losing the free Philippine market. Both sides had their lobbies in Congress,
but the general trend of the time was toward high protective tariffs, and the
move for Philippine independence found strong support in Congress.

The Filipinos, while eager to gain their independence, were anxious to
soften the shock of separation from the American economy. Sugar and
coconut products made up two-thirds of the Philippine exports, and 80 per
cent of these exports went to the United States. The exclusion of these
products from the American market would therefore have a severe effect on
the whole economy of the Philippines, and some legal guarantee or promise
was sought to prevent the adverse economic results.

In 1933 the first independence act was passed by the American Congress, but the Philippines refused to accept it because of the absence of such
economic protection. The second independence act, the Tydings-McDuffie
Act, passed by the American Congress in 1934, differed little from its predecessor, but this act was finally accepted by the Philippines after a special
promise by President Roosevelt that regulations to modify the economic
effects of the act would be considered before full independence was realized.

The Tydings-McDuffie Act provided for eventual full independence, but
before this stage was reached there was to be a ten-year interval in which
the Philippines were to set up their own government and become prepared
for full political separation from the United States. The act provided for a
commonwealth status in which the government was in the hands of the
Philippine leaders. Foreign affairs and defense remained an American responsibility, and the American Commissioner had a veto power in financial
matters. Under the provisions of this act, the Filipinos drafted a constitution
and set up a commonwealth government in 1935. The constitution provided
for a unicameral National Assembly of about 120 members as the legislature,
and a president elected for one term of six years as the head of the executive
branch of the government. In 1940 the constitution was amended to add to
the legislature a Senate of twenty-four members and to change the presi-
dential term to four years with the possibility of election to a second term.
The Philippine constitution followed the American precedent in placing the
executive power in the hands of a president directly elected and independent
of the legislature in his executive functions.

republicans to strengthen Indonesian independence. The main issue was the question as to how much authority should be given to the Dutch Indonesian Union. The Dutch aimed at a stronger Union government while the Indonesians aimed at a weak Union government which would afford the greatest amount of independence for the federal government of the United States of Indonesia.

The Hague Agreement

The round table conference came to a general agreement on November 2, 1949, the Hague Agreement. In it there was promulgated a statute on the Dutch Indonesian Union under which the Union would have a fairly loose structure. The organs of the Union were to be: (1) A conference, meeting at least twice a year and to be concerned primarily with political matters. This conference was to consist of three ministers from Holland and three from the United States of Indonesia. (2) A permanent secretariat with two secretaries-general to serve one year terms in rotation, one from Holland and one from the U.S.I. (3) A court of arbitration consisting of six judges, three from Holland and three from the U.S.I., to decide by majority vote on issues of disagreement. If the votes were evenly divided, the six judges were to select an additional judge from the International Court of Arbitration. This Union was to deal with problems of foreign relations and of cooperation in the economic and financial field between Holland and the new United States of Indonesia. On the basis of this statute, the Dutch were to surrender the sovereignty over Indonesia to the newly established government of the United States of Indonesia and to withdraw their military forces.

One of the greatest obstacles to a complete understanding at The Hague had been the problem of a financial settlement between Holland and Indonesia. In the final agreement the United States of Indonesia recognized the Dutch financial interests and promised not to confiscate Dutch properties without previous consultation and arbitration. The new state also agreed finally to take over the responsibility for the public debt which after prolonged negotiations was set at $1,300,000,000.

The one problem which remained unsolved at the Hague conference was the fate of Dutch New Guinea. The western half of this island formed part of the Dutch East Indies; the eastern half was Australian. The Dutch were determined to maintain their sovereignty and control over their part of New Guinea, while the Indonesian nationalists aimed at including Dutch New Guinea in their new state. The Dutch could point to the fact that the Papuans and other primitive tribal groups were of different ethnic origin from the Malays, who made up most of the population of Indonesia, and that Indonesian control would simply mean the substitution of another colonial authority, a change for which there was no justification in the national aspirations of the Indonesians. The only link between Dutch New Guinea and Indonesia had been the unity of Dutch administration; but it was this former political unity on which the Indonesians based their claim. The issue remained unsolved, and it was agreed that negotiations would be renewed one year later without prejudicing either case. In the negotiations the Dutch had the backing also of Australia, which had strongly supported the Indonesian nationalist cause within and without the United Nations, but which in the case of New Guinea favored the continuation of Dutch control.

With this exception the Dutch relinquished "unconditionally and irrevocably" their hold over Indonesia, and the new United States of Indonesia received "complete sovereignty." In exchange for their acceptance of the inevitable the Dutch received a guarantee of their economic interests. They also hoped that the power of the nationalist leaders of the Republic had been curbed by the establishment of a federation in which the Republic was one of eighteen states which the Dutch had helped to set up in the wake of their military actions. But this Dutch policy of division was only a temporary success. The republican leadership had rightly estimated the situation when it had been willing to make military concessions in return for the Dutch promise that the people of the territories separated from the Republic were free to decide their own allegiance. The various representative assemblies established in these states saw eye to eye with the nationalists of the Indonesian Republic and soon after the Hague Agreement was put in force on December 27, 1949, the various states voted the abrogation of their own state organizations and unification with the republic into one Indonesian state.

The power of the nationalist leaders of the republic did not remain unchallenged. Several uprisings, one in western Java organized by a former Dutch army captain, and others in the outer islands, were suppressed by military forces. They did not prevent the process of reunification and the formation of one government for a unitary state. This development was completed by July, 1950, and on August 17 a new provisional constitution was accepted for a united Republic of Indonesia, which replaced the former federal United States of Indonesia.

Once the Indonesian sovereignty was established, the Dutch attempt to maintain a political hold became illusionary. The framework of Linggadjati, re-established at the Hague, was artificial and could not be brought to life. Not only had the United States of Indonesia given place to the unitary Indonesian Republic, but the superstructure of the Dutch-Indonesian Union had also failed. In the summer of 1954, after prolonged wrangling over New Guinea, where the Dutch maintained control, the Dutch-Indonesian Union was dissolved on the request of the Indonesian Republic. The last constitutional link between Holland and her former colony was thus cut.

Problems and Policies

After the struggle for independence was over, the new Indonesian state was beset with its own inner tensions. The provisional constitution for the United States of Indonesia of 1949 had provided for a parliamentary government for the federal state. The members of the first parliament

were appointed by the member states, all of which appointed their representatives according to an understanding among the leading political groups in
each state. But general elections were promised within a year. When the
unitary Republic of Indonesia was set up in August 1950, with its capital at
Jakarta, the new provisional constitution continued the parliamentary system. But the temporary parliament at Jakarta remained an appointed body
which was formed by an amalgamation of two appointed legislatures, that of
the former United States of Indonesia and that of its leading member state,
the Indonesian Republic, with its former state capital at Jocjakarta. The
new combined legislature had 213 members who were divided into nineteen
political factions.

Of foremost importance among the political organizations were the
Partai Nasional Indonesia or P.N.I., and the *Masjumi*, the leading Islamic party.
The P.N.I. continued the tradition of the nationalist movement among the
intellectuals that had spread between the two world wars. It continued to be
led by Sukarno, who had been elected president of the federal state, and, in
1950, president of the Republic of Indonesia. Sukarno's political skill and his
tremendous influence over the masses of the population, gained through his
extraordinary qualities as an orator, made him the outstanding political
figure. His party was also the largest group within the temporary parliament.

The *Masjumi*, the largest of several Islamic parties, had a broad base
in the Islamic society of Indonesia. Islam was the main religious and cultural
force in Indonesia, and the religious teachers, the Ulamas, played an important role in the local communities. The Moslems of Indonesia were more
tolerant in their application of religious ideas to life than were many of the
Moslem groups in the Near and Middle East. The women did not wear veils
and held a higher status in Indonesia than in other Islamic countries. Of
special importance was the Islamic reform movement, the *Muhammadiyak*,
which started from the Islamic educational centers in Arabia and in Mecca.
It aimed at a return to the original sources of Islamic religion, the Koran
and the sayings of the Prophet. The traditions and customs which had
been built up in the Islamic world over the centuries and which had been
added to the original teachings were critically examined, and an attempt
was made to reinterpret the original religious doctrine to meet the practical
problems of the modern world. This movement established its local organizations in many parts of Indonesia where it promoted social reforms emphasizing the establishment of schools and the strengthening of education in general. These local activities, which were comparable to the development of
the YMCA organization in America, had a close connection with the *Masjumi*
party in many areas of Indonesia. The *Muhammadiyak* retained the traditional
connection of Islam with trading and business interests and was especially
important in the batik industry. In the *Muhammadiyak* and other Islamic
groups, religious bonds and economic interests overlapped. Resistance to
Chinese domination of the batik industry had been organized at an earlier
time by the *Sarekat Islam*. The *Muhammadiyak* followed in the same tradition

of protecting Indonesian economic interest against Chinese competition. On a national level, the *Masjumi* and other Islamic parties represented the same combination of cultural and economic interests.

The main Islamic groups were, for ideological reasons, strongly anti-Communist and suspicious of any cooperation with the Communists on the part of the government. The most radical form of Islamic nationalism was represented by the *Darul Islam*, a military political organization, especially strong on Sumatra and on western Java, which was opposed to the government and was violently anti-Communist. After 1951 the *Darul Islam* fomented uprisings against the government and became a rebellious underground organization, with a hold over some of the rural areas, especially in western Sumatra, where a major outbreak occurred in 1953.

The two major political parties, the P.N.I. and the *Masjumi*, were the main potential political antagonists, although they cooperated from 1950, when the Republic of Indonesia was established, until 1953. During this time the cabinets were formed mainly by the P.N.I. and the *Masjumi* parties, which together held a majority in the temporary parliament. When this alliance began to fall apart, the control of the military forces and military policy became a major political issue—an issue which was soon exploited by the Communist party. In 1952, the army command attempted a military reorganization with the aim of reducing the size of the army and converting it from an "ideological" guerrilla army into a smaller, professional force. This plan was resisted by some army officers, who received the backing of President Sukarno against the army command. Under pressure from Sukarno, the Defense Committee of the parliament passed a resolution to investigate the armed forces and bring about a change in army leadership. At this point a demonstration was staged in Jakarta, in October 1952, by a mob which broke into the parliament building and demanded the dissolution of parliament and the holding of the promised elections. President Sukarno addressed the demonstrators and dispersed them, while the army, which was believed to have been responsible in part for the demonstration, rushed in troops and maintained order. In this conflict the Communists strongly favored the insubordinate lower officers, who stood for an "ideological," political army. Under Sukarno's influence, the parliament forced the resignation of the chief of staff and the minister of defense. This clash was one of the causes of the fall of the cabinet in 1953, as the P.N.I. and the *Masjumi* did not agree on army policy.

The new cabinet was formed by the P.N.I. and was headed by Ali Sastroamidjojo, who had been selected by Sukarno. In order to maintain itself against the opposition of the *Masjumi*, this cabinet accepted the support of the Communists in parliament. Their new role as supporters of the government gave the Communists, who had been crushed by the failure of their *coup d'état* in 1948, the chance to regain their position. By able exploitation of popular issues and nationalist feelings, they greatly increased their membership and support. The acceptance by the P.N.I. of Communist backing deepened the conflict between the P.N.I. and the *Masjumi*. Two of the cabinet members were suspected of strong Communist sympathies; one of these was the minister of defense. In the summer of 1955, he attempted to appoint a chief of staff whom the army considered unsatisfactory. The higher army officers, under the leadership of the vice chief of staff, refused to accept the appointment. As a result of this impasse, the P.N.I. cabinet of Ali Sastroamidjojo was forced to resign, and a new cabinet was formed in August by Burhanuddin Harahap, a leader of the *Masjumi* party. The negotiations for the formation of this new cabinet were carried on by Vice President Hatta in the absence of President Sukarno, who was on a pilgrimage to Mecca.

In foreign policy, the cabinet controlled by the P.N.I. was more inclined to establish friendly relations with Communist China, while the *Masjumi* cabinet was more friendly toward the West. All Indonesian cabinets, however, followed a general policy of neutralism between the Communist block and the West, after the example of India. In 1950, Indonesia recognized the Chinese Communist government, and Peking established a strong diplomatic mission in Jakarta, which was especially active in the field of cultural relations. Many Indonesian Chinese went to Peking for study or cultural visits. Chinese Communist influence was also felt in the Chinese schools in Indonesia. Towards the United States, Indonesia followed a cautious policy, turning down American economic assistance when it was made conditional on an anti-Communist stand. Indonesia's role as a neutral was given expression when the Afro-Asian conference, to which neutral, pro-West, and Communist countries were invited, was held in April 1955 at Bandung, a location acceptable to all participants.

The long-promised elections were held in September 1955 under the *Masjumi* cabinet of Burhanuddin Harahap. As a result of the elections, four strong parties emerged. The two largest were the P.N.I. and the *Masjumi*, who showed almost equal strength. The other two strong parties were the *Nahdlatul Ulama*, or Moslem Teachers party, and the Communists. The equal distribution of strength left undecided the long-range issue whether Indonesian leadership would lean toward Communist support or would derive from its Islamic tradition a native nationalism which would keep it free from Communist infiltration.

4. VIETNAM, LAOS, AND CAMBODIA

French Economic Policies

In the period between World War I and World War II the population of Annam grew from about 11,000,000 to about 19,000,000 people and the problem of overpopulation became serious. Not that economic possibilities for supporting more people did not exist. But French economic policy, combined with the conservatism of the Annamese farmers, prevented any new large-scale development.

The problem of population growth was especially serious in the ricelands of the Tongking delta, where the majority of the peasants had less than one acre of land. The Red River irrigation projects built by the French were not large enough to make much difference. In Cochin China the French promoted larger irrigation works in the Mekong delta, considerably increasing the area under cultivation, and bringing an outlet for the growing population. But here the landlords, mostly Chinese, took the main share of the profits from the rice cultivation, and the lot of the tenant farmer was not greatly improved. The Chinese also held a monopoly on the rice trade. The Chinese merchants and landowners prospered, but they had little stake in the development of a national Annamese economy. In the first three decades of the twentieth century the rice export from Indo-China almost tripled, reaching a figure of 2,000,000 tons in 1937. After the beginning of the First World War, the rubber industry was built up until in 1939 the exports reached 78,-000 tons. Coal mining, the major industrial activity, reached a production of two and a half million tons in 1939, of which one and a half million tons were exported. The rubber plantations in Cochin China and the coal mines in Tongking were in French hands, and were a source of considerable profit to the French planters and mining companies. It was French policy to exploit the economy of Indo-China for the benefit of the French; the sale of Indo-Chinese goods to France was restricted by a French tariff barrier, but Indo-China was open to the import of French manufactured products. Only in the thirties, during the world economic crisis, did France increase her purchases of rice and other products from Indo-China. As a result of French policy the Annamese economy was limited to rice production, raw materials, and extractive industries, and the Annamese had little ownership or control of profitable enterprises.

The tensions created by the French and Chinese domination of the economic life of Indo-China were increased by the resentment of the educated Annamese who had little outlet for their talents in the French government of the colony. The French had set up a school system which by 1939 was teaching half a million children per year in primary schools. A smaller number advanced to higher education. The University of Hanoi had over 600 students in 1937, mostly Annamese, and considerable numbers of Annamese studied in France and other European countries. But this intellectual elite was largely excluded from political and economic leadership in Annam. In World War I Wilson's principle of self-determination had a great appeal to these intellectuals who found in the Indian Congress movement a model for their own struggle against colonial rule. But the main influences on the Annamese nationalists came from across the northern border—from China.

Nationalism and Communism before World War II

The Chinese cultural tradition had been accepted in Annam for centuries and the changes in China were paralleled in Annam. Immediately after the Kuomintang was organized in 1912, the year of the Chinese Revolution, a Nationalist party organized on the same basis was founded in Annam. The Nationalists' name for their country was Vietnam, which name from that time on began to take the place of the former Annam, but the French continued to call their protectorate Annam until the end of World War II. The first congress of the Vietnam Nationalist party was held in Canton in 1914. The Vietnam nationalists used Chinese territory as a base from which to organize uprisings in Vietnam on various occasions during the war. It was also through China that a Russian-controlled Communist party was set up in Vietnam.

The Vietnamese Communist organization was from the beginning dominated by an outstanding leader, Nguyen Ai Quoc, who has become known under the alias of Ho Chi Minh. Ho Chi Minh was born in 1894. He went to France to study, and organized the first Vietnamese Marxist group in Paris, in 1917. In 1920 Ho Chi Minh joined the Comintern and went to Soviet Russia where he was trained in Communist techniques. In 1925 he went to Canton, then the headquarters of the Chinese Kuomintang, which had been reorganized by Russian Communist advisers and was cooperating at the time with the Chinese Communists. In Canton, with the assistance of Chinese Communists and Soviet advisers, Ho Chi Minh formed the revolutionary Youth party of Vietnam, which was the predecessor of the Vietnamese Communist party. Ho Chi Minh became an assistant to the top Russian adviser, Borodin. At the same time more than sixty young Vietnamese cadets entered the Whampoa Academy, where Chiang Kai-shek was then president and where the officers of the Chinese revolutionary army of the Kuomintang were trained. The cadets included at that time both Communists and non-Communists, but most of the Vietnamese trainees turned to the Communist side and later became the commanding officers in the Vietminh army. In 1930 at a conference in Hong Kong, Ho Chi Minh set up the Vietnamese Communist party by combining a number of revolutionary factions into a disciplined party which followed the directives of the Comintern. The Communist party immediately attempted to organize strikes, peasant demonstrations, and small-scale uprisings. These were suppressed by the government. In 1931 Ho Chi Minh was arrested in Hong Kong by the British for underground activities and was imprisoned for two years. At the same time the French arrested a number of other leaders. The defeat of the Comintern policy in China also diminished the influence of the Communist party in Vietnam.

The Vietnamese Nationalist party disintegrated after the failure of an uprising in 1930 and several unsuccessful attempts to assassinate French officials. Several leaders were arrested and executed, and by 1933 the party practically ceased to function.

By the beginning of World War II the French administration, which had only curbed the Communists, had practically destroyed the Nationalist organization, and there was no group left to lead the nascent Vietnamese nationalism into constructive channels.

The pressure on the Communists was eased in 1935 when the united front strategy of the Comintern brought a shift in the Communist line in France and led to an amnesty for imprisoned Communist leaders. The Communists organized, in 1936, an Indo-Chinese Congress at which they adopted a four-point program for the establishment of a Democratic Front, a precursor of the Vietminh League.

Effects of World War II

The French position in Indo-China was seriously affected by World War II. In 1939 the Japanese took advantage of the French preoccupation with the war in Europe to extend their blockade of China to the Indo-Chinese border and the Hanoi-Yunnan railroad. The governor-general of Indo-China had to permit the Japanese to enforce this blockade. In 1940, after the fall of France, the governor-general, who was an adherent of De Gaulle, was replaced by a Petainist, Vice-Admiral Jean Decoux. On September 22 Decoux negotiated a treaty with Japan which was a capitulation to Japanese demands. In this agreement the French entrusted the defense of Indo-China to the Japanese, and Japanese troops occupied Haiphong and set up garrisons and air bases in Tongking. At the same time the Japanese commander of Canton attacked French border posts and occupied the town of Langson. In January 1941 the Japanese assisted the Thai government to occupy territory in Cambodia and Laos, which the French had taken in the nineteenth century and which they were now forced to return to Thailand in a treaty concluded under Japanese mediation in March. In July 1941 the Japanese extended their occupation to the whole of Indo-China.

The French acceptance of Japanese overlordship was bound to undermine the French authority in the colonies. During most of the war the Japanese retained the French administration as a matter of form, and the French assisted the Japanese in the suppression of underground resistance by the Vietnamese. Such uprisings were described as Communist attacks, and thousands of Vietnamese leaders were imprisoned. French policy thus made it possible for the Vietnamese to combine their resistance against the French regime with the fight against the Japanese overlords.

The Vietnamese resistance movement came under the leadership of the Communist party, as this was the only remaining well-organized group that could provide such leadership. After failing in an earlier attempt to establish a "People's Regime" in northern Vietnam, the Communists held a meeting in May, 1941, on Chinese territory, at Liuchou in Kwangsi province. At this meeting the Vietnam Independence League, or Vietminh, was formed by the Vietnamese Communist party under the leadership of Ho Chi Minh. It was joined by a number of Vietnamese patriotic groups in a united front type of organization. The program of the Vietminh was issued in October; it provided a plan for a "joint bourgeois-Communist revolution" after the pattern of Mao Tse-tung's "New Democracy." The Vietminh claimed as its aim the organization of a national united front against French and Japanese imperialism. This united front was to comprise all classes, all revolutionary groups, and all oppressed people of Vietnam, for the purposes of overthrowing imperialism and establishing complete independence, of holding universal elections and establishing democratic freedoms, of giving the land to the tillers, and of encouraging the development of private industry.

With this program the Communist-led Vietminh exploited the nationalist feelings and political aspirations of the intellectuals, the economic discontent of the peasants, and the hopes of the professional and business groups. The Vietminh movement succeeded in enlisting the support of most Vietnamese nationalists. Guerrilla forces were organized which succeeded in gaining control of some of the rural areas in Tongking. At the end of 1944, these guerrilla units were combined into what was called a liberation army under the command of Vo Guyen Giap, who was trained during the early years of the Sino-Japanese war at the Chinese Communist headquarters at Yenan. The army was staffed by Vietnamese officers, some of whom had received their training at the Whampoa Academy and at Yenan. From the beginning, the Chinese Communist influence was thus a strong factor among the political and military leaders of the Vietminh organization. This army acquired control over most of the rural districts of Tongking and began to expand its activities into central and southern Vietnam, or Cochin China.

In March 1945, when the Japanese military position in the Pacific had become very grave, the Japanese took over direct control of Indo-China. In order to prevent the possibility of French support to Allied forces landing in Indo-China, the Japanese commander issued an ultimatum to the French for closer cooperation for the joint defense of the colony. When this ultimatum was refused by Admiral Decoux, Japanese troops disarmed the French garrisons and arrested French officials. A declaration was issued that "the colonial status of Indo-China has ended," and puppet governments were set up under the former emperor of Annam, Bao Dai, and the kings of Cambodia and Laos. These dependent governments were not recognized by the Vietminh movement, which continued its anti-Japanese fight with some help from America in weapons and technical assistance. During the last weeks of the war the Vietminh took over most of the territory of Tongking from the Japanese, and became much stronger in the south as well. In August, at the time of the Japanese surrender, a Vietminh congress was held close to the Chinese border, and a government was set up with Ho Chi Minh as president. On September 2, 1945, the Democratic Republic of Vietnam was formally proclaimed, and it declared its independence on September 7. The new government moved to Hanoi, which became its capital, and a National Committee of the Vietminh took over Saigon. The Japanese-sponsored government of Bao Dai was abolished, and the Vietminh organization held most of the country under its control.

The Japanese surrender in French Indo-China was accepted in the south by British and in the north by Chinese forces. The question of the recognition of the new government of Vietnam and of the relationship between this government and the French, who aimed at the restoration of their control, was thus largely dependent on the attitude of the British and Chinese governments. The policy followed by these two governments and their occupying forces differed radically. In the north, at Hanoi, the Chinese forces of Chiang Kai-shek favored Ho Chi Minh. They permitted the Vietnamese to carry out elections and to complete their government organization. In the south the British sided with the French, and when they took over Saigon in September, they refused to negotiate with the local Vietnam leaders. They freed the French and assisted them in regaining control of Saigon and other cities, but the Vietnam forces remained in control of the rural districts. When the British withdrew early in 1946, the French took over the full administration in the south. The Chinese refused the return of French troops into Tongking until February 1946, when they agreed to hand back authority to the French in exchange for railroad privileges and guarantees for Chinese residents in Indo-China.

The Problem of French Authority

The French were now left to settle the conflict with the government of Vietnam under Ho Chi Minh and with the rulers of Cambodia and Laos, who had set up their own national governments. With the rulers of the latter two states the French reached agreements early in 1946. In these agreements the French permitted the two royal states to maintain their "independence" and actually granted some autonomy in internal affairs but retained control of important financial matters and continued the supervision of the kings and governments of Cambodia and Laos by French advisers. The agreement with the Vietnam government was much more difficult because of the greater strength of the entrenched Vietnam organization and its unwillingness to yield on major issues of French territorial or political control. To strengthen his government and to exploit more fully the nationalist aspirations for his purposes, Ho Chi Minh formally dissolved the Vietnamese Communist party and reorganized it into an Association for the Study of Marxism. This change made cooperation easier for nationalists who were afraid of international Communism. Ho also reorganized his government in December 1945, and again in March 1946, to include more non-Communist nationalists. In May 1946, Ho Chi Minh organized a still broader united front, the Vietnam League of National Union, or *Lien Viet*, in which the Vietminh was included. In this way Ho Chi Minh concealed his controlling Communist organization within a broad framework of a united front, which in 1946 included most of the Vietnamese interested in the fight against French colonialism.

After prolonged negotiations between the French and Ho Chi Minh, an agreement was reached at Hanoi on March 6, 1946. The French recognized the Republic of Vietnam as a free state with its own government, parliament, army, and finances. This state of Vietnam was, however, to be joined with Cambodia and Laos in an Indo-Chinese Federation, and this federation was in turn to be linked with France and her other colonies in a French Union. It was through these two superimposed political structures that the French hoped to maintain their authority over the Republic of Vietnam. This framework of a federal state within a union was later copied by the Dutch in their negotiations with the Indonesian nationalists with the same negative outcome which the French were to experience with the Hanoi settlement.

The Hanoi agreement had not contained any detailed regulations as to how this structure should work. Conferences during the summer of 1946 at Dalat in Cochin China and at Fontainebleau did not lead to any agreements. One of the main issues was the extent of power which the federation government was to have. The French wanted this government, which was to be under the chairmanship of the French high commissioner, to retain the more important financial and economic controls over the member states, while the Vietnamese and the other two state governments wished to secure as strong an economic autonomy as possible. A still greater issue was the question of Cochin China which the French wanted to exclude from the authority of the Vietnam government. In Cochin China the French had their strongest economic and political ties. They had regained control and felt strong enough to maintain it through a local regime sponsored by themselves. In the Hanoi agreement the question of whether Cochin China should join Vietnam had been left to a referendum to be held later. But while the negotiations were going on, the French set up a provisional government in Cochin China and called a conference of representatives from Laos, Cambodia, and Cochin China, without inviting Vietnam. This French move helped to break up the negotiations, and a stalemate occurred which eventually shifted into open warfare between the French and the Vietnamese. The Hanoi agreement had, however, given the French the opportunity to return with their forces to Haiphong, Hanoi, and other key cities in the north, so that when the struggle turned into warfare, the French were in control of the key cities and coastal areas, while the Vietnamese retained their hold over many of the inland rural districts. From September 1946 on there were a number of clashes. The French bombarded Haiphong in December and there was a well-prepared general Vietnamese attack on the French garrisons in Tongking and central Annam. French reinforcements had to be brought in and general warfare ensued in which the French fight against the Vietminh was carried on by French troops, largely of the Foreign Legion.

Bao Dai and Ho Chi Minh

After the final break with the Vietnamese government the French searched for nationalist leaders who would cooperate with them against Ho Chi Minh. In Cochin China they established at first a government under Nguyen Van Xuan, an Annamese general in the French army, who had an almost entirely French background and accepted French terms of control. This government did not prove to be a useful rallying point for non-Communist nationalism, and the French were led to look for an Annamese leader who might gain a larger following. They began negotiations with the former emperor, Bao Dai. After his short term as head of the Japanese-sponsored Vietnam government in 1946, Bao Dai had resigned as a result of an agreement with Ho Chi Minh. For a short time he accepted a position as adviser to Ho Chi Minh's government, but broke with Ho not long afterwards. The French hoped that if Bao Dai could be persuaded to head a government again, a number of non-Communist nationalists, who were now supporting Ho Chi Minh, would swing over to Bao Dai. In order to make possible such a non-Communist Vietnam government, however, the French had to make considerable concessions to Bao Dai and Vietnamese nationalism. Bao Dai demanded military forces of his own. In addition, Bao Dai and his advisers requested the right of direct relations with foreign nations, such as the United States. And lastly, Bao Dai insisted that Cochin China should be included under his control. After gaining the promise of such concessions, Bao Dai agreed in 1949 to form a Vietnam government in opposition to the Vietnam government of Ho Chi Minh.

Bao Dai's qualification for gaining nationalist support in Vietnam was weakened not only by his dependence on the French but also by his apparent reluctance to give up his residence in France, which had earned him the reputation of a playboy. Instead of taking a strong active part himself, he preferred to direct his government through remote control by the appointment of men depending on him and his small group of advisers. The Vietnam government established by Bao Dai was carried on by a small clique of administrators who had little support in the rural districts and the cities. Yet, when the Communist character of Ho Chi Minh's government became clearer, a number of nationalist leaders turned away from Ho Chi Minh and attempted to help in the organization of the nationalist government under Bao Dai.

There also existed strong anti-Communist groups within the rural districts. Two and a half million of the nine million population of Tongking were Catholics. In many of the rural districts the Vietnamese Catholic bishops were the political leaders, and these communities were hostile to Communism and suspicious of Ho Chi Minh. They organized their own local militias for the defense of their districts. But Bao Dai and the officials of his government were suspicious of these local groups with their own sources of power and prevented any support from reaching them. A similar situation existed in south Vietnam in the area of Saigon where different religious sects controlled a few areas in former Cochin China. The strongest such sect was that of the Caodaists who combined Buddhist and Christian concepts in their creed and held Victor Hugo in veneration as one of their saints. The Caodaists had their own religious hierarchy of cardinals and a pope, who was head of the government. They were a self-reliant force with their own militia of some 20,000 men. Another such local organization in the south was the *Hoa Hao*, a Buddhist secret society, also with its own force. The rivalry between these autonomous local organizations and the government of Bao Dai prevented any unified stand against the Communists. Of different character was the Xuan "sect" in the Saigon area, which organized prostitution, gambling and racketeering. Bao Dai secured its support by making its head Chief of Police in Saigon. The Vietnamese army, which was to be formed according to an agreement with the French, was organized in small units because the French did not want it to be more than an auxiliary force.

While the growth of the Bao Dai government was handicapped both by internal conflicts and the French reluctance to yield full authority, Ho Chi Minh's government received a decisive boost from the victory of the Chinese Communists in 1949. From this time on, the Communist character of Ho's government was more openly revealed, and many moderate leaders in the Vietminh movement and in Ho's government were replaced by Communists. Ho now openly declared that his Vietnam government was to be modeled on the Chinese Communist regime. In January 1950, the Chinese Communist government recognized Ho Chi Minh's government, and the Soviet government quickly followed the Chinese example. This political support was soon followed by greater military assistance. The top officers of Ho Chi Minh's troops had been trained in the early years at the Whampoa Academy and at the Chinese Communist center in Yenan. After the Chinese Communist victory in 1949, training centers for Vietminh forces were organized in South China, and Vietminh troops were equipped with, and trained in the use of, modern weapons which came from Russia through the Chinese. Chinese technicians joined the Vietminh troops to handle some of the weapons, especially anti-aircraft guns, and Ho Chi Minh's army was thus prepared to shift from guerrilla warfare to a warfare of concentrated strength in open battles.

With this military change came a political reorganization. In February 1951, the Vietnamese Communist party was reconstituted under the name of the *Lao Dong* party, or Workers' party. In March of the same year, the Vietminh organization was completely dissolved and there remained only the *Lien Viet*, the Vietnam League of National Union, which was fully under the domination of the *Lao Dong* party. The political program of this party followed closely Mao's "New Democracy."

Meanwhile the French had strengthened their military forces with American assistance. The number of Bao Dai's Vietnamese troops was also increased, although they were still kept in small units and their leadership and training remained in French hands. The more critical the situation became, the more Laos and Cambodia and the government of Bao Dai insisted on a full and true independence. In June 1953, King Norodom Sihanouk of Cambodia fled to Thailand to publicize his disagreement with the French colonial attitude. As a result of this move, he gained full sovereign control within his territory including command of the army, a concession which the French then had to extend to the other Indo-Chinese states. But while the negotiations for the independence of these governments were still in progress, the military situation in northern Vietnam deteriorated rapidly for the French and for Bao Dai's government. To prevent Ho Chi Minh's threat to Laos and the free movement of his forces southward, the French had placed a garrison at Dien Bien Phu, a strategic location in the mountainous area to the west of Hanoi. In the spring of 1954 this garrison was besieged by the newly equipped Vietnamese armies of Ho Chi Minh, and finally fell before their attack.

Geneva and Ngo Dinh Diem

The deterioration of the military and political situation in Indo-China had brought a pressure in France for a negotiated compromise with the Communists. Offers to negotiate, initiated by the Chinese Communists and the Russians, were accepted and led to the Geneva Conference in May 1954. While the conference was in session, Dien Bien Phu fell and Mendes-France, who formed a new French government, gained parliamentary approval by a promise to end the Indo-Chinese war with a compromise settlement. The Geneva settlement of July 1954 brought a division of Vietnam into a northern half, taken over by Ho Chi Minh's troops and government, and a southern half, which remained in the hands of Bao Dai's government, supported by the French. The country was divided near the 17th parallel leaving the Communist regime with more than half of the population. Each side withdrew its troops, including guerrilla forces, from the territory of the other side, and those civilians who wanted to leave the north in order not to come under Communist rule, were permitted to move. The military withdrawal was arranged in stages; Hanoi was given up by the French after 80 days and the harbor of Haiphong after 300 days. In 1956, two years after this agreement, general elections were to be held in all Vietnam for the formation of a new united government for the whole of the country.

In exchange for this settlement the Communists, who gained the whole rich Red River delta, agreed to withdraw their guerrilla forces from Cambodia and from most of Laos, which countries they had penetrated. In the negotiations at Geneva, the Cambodian representative gained the special concession that Cambodia was to be permitted to call in support from the outside when her security was threatened, while it was specified that Vietnam was not to be permitted to join in any military alliances.

As a result of the Geneva settlement the Communists gave up their invasion of Cambodia and Laos. The Communists had established what they called a Free Laotian movement, but it had little influence and depended on the backing it received from Ho Chi Minh's troops. The line drawn at Geneva corresponded to a cultural division. Laos and Cambodia were Buddhist countries in the Indian cultural orbit whereas Vietnam had been within the orbit of Confucian China. At the time of the Geneva settlement, Cambodia and Laos were given full independence by the French, including free control of their financial affairs, although they remained within the French Union. The same settlement was made with Bao Dai's Vietnamese government. The new prime minister, Ngo Dinh Diem, a devout Catholic from Tongking, with a reputation for honesty and integrity, moved his government to Saigon, a scene of inner conflict and rival political forces. He was opposed in Saigon by the chief of staff of the newly created Vietnamese army, General Nguyen Van Hinh, and by General Nguyen Van Xuan, who was in control of the police. Both of these men were directly connected with Bao Dai. When the Prime Minister tried to overcome the opposition by ordering General Hinh to leave for France, the general refused, and a stalemate occurred in which Bao Dai backed the general and his friends. A third factor in this struggle was the Caodaists and the Hoa Haos. Although the Prime Minister had taken representatives of these sects into his cabinet, they sent military detachments to Saigon to participate in the power struggle. The political deadlock was solved through American interference when it was made clear that the Americans, who supplied the arms for the Vietnamese army, were backing the Prime Minister. General Hinh was persuaded to leave for France.

Ngo Dinh Diem's government in South Vietnam was faced with the problem of establishing a unified and stable government and at the same time of preparing for a test of strength with the Communist regime in the north. The flight of over one million refugees from Communist north Vietnam was an indication of the strong anti-Communist feelings of a large proportion of the population, but the settlement and absorption of these refugees presented the government with grave economic problems. The main problem, however, was the fight for political authority, and in this Diem was given assistance by the United States government. After the removal of the pro-Bao Dai and pro-French Chief of Staff, the way was open for the intensification of American training and equipment of the national army which in the struggle which followed turned out to be an effective and loyal force. Diem used this army when his authority was challenged by the sects in the summer of 1955. Most of the *Cao Dai* and part of the *Hoa Hao* were induced to submit to the government and the army; those who resisted were defeated. The control of Saigon was assured when Ngo Dinh Diem broke the power of the Xuan group which resisted the removal of its leader as Chief of Police. The Xuan group was driven out of Saigon by force and politically eliminated.

A revolutionary committee, which had been formed in Saigon, tried to compel Ngo Dinh Diem to remove Bao Dai, whom they accused of cooperation with the French and with the corrupt Xuan sect, as chief of state. Diem, however, postponed a decision on Bao Dai until the holding of elections. The elections, held at the end of 1955, resulted in an overwhelming victory for Ngo Dinh Diem. Bao Dai was ousted and Diem became chief of state. On the question of the national elections, agreed upon at Geneva, the Communist regime pressed for action and continued to hold the French government responsible for carrying out the Geneva agreement. Ngo Dinh Diem, whose government had not been a signatory of the agreement, stated that he would cooperate only in free and supervised elections. It was Diem's policy to create the conditions under which the power of an independent Vietnamese government in Saigon could be consolidated.

5. BURMA

British Government and Policy

The Burmese nationalists forced the British colonial rulers to make far-reaching concessions of self-government between World War I and World War II. In 1921 when the British introduced into India the so-called dyarchical constitution, they also applied it to Burma. Administration was divided between British officials who were responsible to the governor and Burmese officials responsible to a Burmese parliament. The British retained such important functions as finance and police, and granted to the Burmese cultural functions, such as education, and also forestry administration, a real concession in view of the importance of the teakwood industry. The decision to apply this system to Burma was made as a result of protests by the Burmese General Council of Buddhist Associations which insisted that political concessions made to India should also be made to Burma. The Burmese religious and nationalist leaders, however, were not satisfied with the limited authority they had gained and boycotted this system of dyarchy.

The economic tensions between the Burmese tenant farmers and agricultural workers and the Indian landlords and moneylenders increased in the 1930's as a result of the world economic crisis. The fall in the price of rice to a third of its previous level reduced the acreage under cultivation and forced many tenant farmers and agricultural workers off the land. The local cooperatives that had been set up in certain areas to ease the problems of the farmers also became insolvent, and many were liquidated. The resulting impoverishment led to an extraordinarily high crime rate and general insecurity and to increased political agitation, which was frequently led by Buddhist monks. The British Simon Commission, which in 1929 toured India and Burma to prepare the material for new home-rule legislation, noted the disintegration of Burmese society. But in view of the strong Burmese agitation for autonomy and separation from India, the Simon Commission recommended separation and more self-government.

Before the Burma Act of 1935 had been passed, political opposition and serious uprisings had been directed against British rule. In 1930 several riots started in lower Burma against the Indian moneylenders and against British tax collection. These uprisings, which had been organized by the General Council of Buddhist Associations, were suppressed by British Indian forces. But the anti-British attitude remained, and when the British prepared the separation of Burma from India, the Burmese, who had first demanded it, shifted their political line. The British were accused of wanting to use the separation to maintain colonial rule in Burma, and an anti-separation movement was started which gained a large majority in the 1932 elections to the Burmese parliament. In spite of this opposition, the British went ahead; Burma was separated, and the measure of self-government instituted which the constitution provided.

The Government of India Act, which was passed by the House of Commons in 1935, provided a new constitution for Burma, which became a separate colony under the British Secretary of State for Burma residing in London. This constitution, which came into effect in 1937, provided for a Burmese parliament of two houses which had general legislative and budgetary powers. The House of Representatives was elected by men over eighteen years of age who were British subjects and paid taxes or served in the army or police force, and women who owned a certain amount of property. Half of the members of the Senate were appointed by the governor and half were elected by the House of Representatives. The executive authority was in the hands of a British governor appointed by the Secretary of State for Burma with the approval of the British Parliament. In 1940 about 24 per cent of the population had the right to vote and about three-fourths of the representatives were Burmese, the remainder representing minority groups. Both the House of Representatives and the Senate had to cooperate in legislation, but the governor had the right to veto parliamentary bills and could also approve expenditures for which the parliament had refused to grant funds. The governor had wide powers but he was to carry out his executive policy as far as possible through a council of Burmese ministers, chosen by him from members of the legislature but responsible to a majority of the lower house. The governor was free to disregard the advice of his ministers if necessary, so that, in effect, the representative parliamentary system could be disregarded if the British administration felt it necessary to do so. The governor also maintained complete control over the area of the Shan states in the northeast and over the Kachin and Chin areas to the north and northwest. These areas were outside the jurisdiction of parliament and remained a part of the British administration.

Burmese Political Parties

Burmese political leaders and parties now began to emerge on a national scale. Dr. Ba Maw founded the *Sinyetha*, or Poor Man's party, and advocated in his program land reforms and the reduction of taxes to help the tenants and to protect the farmers from landlords and money-lenders. He also stood for free compulsory primary education. In 1932 his party gained considerable influence and Ba Maw became minister of education. In 1937 under the new constitution, he became prime minister. Out of office in 1939, Ba Maw organized the so-called Freedom Block which advocated rebellion against British rule and immediate independence. His campaign led to his arrest and imprisonment on the charge of sedition. During the Japanese attack he escaped in the spring of 1942 and became the head of the puppet government that ruled Burma during the Japanese occupation.

One of Ba Maw's political rivals was U Saw, who headed the *Myochit*, or Patriotic party. U Saw became prime minister in 1939. He attempted to initiate agrarian reform measures and to open negotiations with India on the limitation of immigration. When the war broke out, he attempted to secure in London the promise of postwar dominion status for Burma, but did not succeed. On the journey back to Burma he was arrested by the British for treasonable negotiations with the Japanese and was held prisoner until 1946 Both Ba Maw and U Saw and their parties lost influence when the Japanese occupation came to an end.

During the war another party, *Dobama Asiayone*, or *Thakin* party, came to the fore in the Burmese nationalist movement. This party, which was in existence before the war, was composed mainly of Burmese students from the university and high schools, who used the word *Thakin*, meaning "master" or "sahib," to indicate that they themselves should be the masters of their own country. Their particular grievance was with the British educational system which was tailored to the needs of the British civil service. The curriculum was determined by the needs of a British-controlled examination system. In these examinations, which qualified for the civil service, only about a third of the students usually passed. Those who failed had gained no useful preparation for other fields of work. The limited purposes of this educational system, which was supported by most of the available educational funds, and the rigidity of the examinations were the main causes of the discontent of the educated Burmese which was expressed in student strikes organized by the *Thakin* party.

Quite different from the British-supported school system was the education provided by the twenty thousand Buddhist monastic schools. It was due to this Buddhist education that most of the Burmese people were literate. The monastic schools provided an education in the cultural tradition of Burmese society and did not attempt to give professional training. As they refused to accept British inspection, they did not receive any financial support from the government, and their teaching was regarded by the British as lacking in required standards.

The majority of the Burmese had some reason for dissatisfaction with British rule. There was hostility of the Burmese peasants against the Indian landlords and moneylenders. The Burmese educated in the monasteries resented the refusal of the British to recognize their qualification for public service and the British disregard for the Burmese cultural tradition. The large numbers who had failed to pass the British examinations constituted a disaffected intellectual proletariat. The *Thakin* party had given expression to these discontents since its establishment in 1929. In the thirties, when the world economic depression intensified unrest among the educated Burmese, the party became more active. Some of the *Thakin* leaders also became interested in Marxist doctrines, and Marxist pamphlets were translated into Burmese. But while the political program of the *Thakin* movement had from the beginning an inclination towards state ownership of economic enterprises, its cultural program was based on Buddhism. The party attacked capitalism and advocated state ownership, but these ideas were derived less from Marxist dogma than from Buddhist-inspired nationalist resistance to foreign economic control in a country where "the capitalists" were Indians or British. Some of the *Thakin* leaders fell for the Japanese propaganda of "Asia for the Asiatics" and in 1941 went to Hainan where they were trained and organized by the Japanese in preparation for the Japanese conquest of Burma.

Japanese Occupation

The Japanese occupied Burma between January and May, 1942, after overrunning Malaya and Singapore. The Japanese victory over the British, American, and Chinese forces in Burma was due not only to superiority in jungle warfare, but also to the assistance the Japanese received from Burmese nationalists of the *Thakin* party and of other groups, including some of the Buddhist monks. But soon after the Japanese occupied the country, the Burmese changed their friendly attitude as a result of the ruthless behavior of the Japanese army and military police and of Japanese policy in general. In August 1943, the Japanese declared Burma an independent state and set up a puppet government under Ba Maw, but their army remained in practical control and continued its looting and disregard for life and property.

The war brought great destruction. All of the major cities were heavily damaged during the Japanese conquest and later by Allied air attacks and reconquest of the country. Much of the industrial property had been destroyed in the British retreat; the loss of the export trade reduced the rice acreage in the main export areas, and large stretches of riceland were overgrown by jungle. Many of the water buffaloes were slaughtered by the occupying troops.

But for the Burmese farmer the war also brought some compensations. The Indian landowners and moneylenders and the British business firms fled to India. When the administration collapsed, the farmer produced only for his own subsistence and paid neither rent nor tax. On the other hand there was the insecurity of life under the Japanese military and the constant exactions of the Japanese; the lack of stable government caused general insecurity and armed robberies took place everywhere.

Organized Burmese resistance against the Japanese began in 1943 when the puppet government of Ba Maw was set up. A number of secret youth organizations were founded, and in 1944 these were combined into the Anti-Fascist People's Freedom League, known as AFPFL. In 1943 a Communist party of Burma was also founded which from the beginning, following the Moscow line, cooperated in the anti-Japanese resistance movement. The AFPFL became the rallying point for the *Thakin* nationalist leaders, who had at first been helpful to the Japanese but now turned against them. When they occupied Burma, the Japanese had armed a small Burmese Independence Army which was meant to be used only for local policing and as an auxiliary force in Japanese military operations to conquer India. These troops got out of control and had to be disbanded but the Japanese continued to train Burmese units under *Thakin* leadership. The leaders, however, secretly turned against the Japanese, and in March 1945, when the Japanese held a parade, the Burmese troops under the orders of their Burmese commanding officers turned against the reviewing Japanese officers and shot them down. With this dramatic gesture the open military rebellion began. The Japanese-trained Burmese army, under General Aung San, became the fighting force of AFPFL, and cooperated closely with the British troops in the final defeat of the Japanese.

The Gaining of Independence

After the war the British attempted to establish a government of direct rule in Burma with the colonial administrators and Burmese government officials who had fled with the British to India and had continued there as a government in exile. But they encountered strong opposition from the leaders of the AFPFL who refused to accept them on prewar terms. The British rehabilitation plans for Burma provided for teams of experienced managers from British firms to restore the economy and communication systems. This was regarded by the Burmese as a re-establishment of the former British economic domination, which they strongly opposed. The AFPFL constituted a well-organized political group which had its own military force and could therefore not be ignored. Negotiations were undertaken in February of 1946 between the British Labor government and Aung San but without immediate results. This lack of success was the occasion for a split in the Burmese Communist party, which had joined the AFPFL. A radical wing of the Communists, under the leadership of Thakin So, withdrew from the AFPFL to start open resistance against the British. This group became known as the "Red Flag" Communists and was, because of its disobedience to the official Communist party line, described as a Trotskyist group by the Communist regulars.

The negotiations between Aung San and the British continued and led in September 1946 to an interim compromise under which the British governor established an executive council of eleven members of which a majority of six was to be taken from the AFPFL and five from other Burmese political groups. This compromise move prevented an open outbreak. The leaders of the AFPFL, supported by the Communists, were preparing a general strike by the labor organizations which they had set up. The initiation of negotiations between the AFPFL leaders and the British and the establishment of the executive council, of which Aung San became chairman, averted the crisis. Aung San called off the preparations for the general strike, and when the Communists continued their agitation, they were expelled from the AFPFL and went into opposition to the Burmese government. This was the "White Flag," or Stalinist, group. The division between the nationalists and the Communists facilitated the nationalist negotiations with the Labor government. Aung San went to London and concluded an agreement in January 1947, which prepared for the setting up of Burmese self-government. A constituent assembly was to be elected to frame a new Burmese constitution. The executive council was to continue as an interim government and a high commissioner was to represent the Burmese government in London. The British were to apply for Burmese membership in the United Nations and to help in securing the recognition of the Burmese state by other governments. The problem of the control of the frontier territories was left to a special committee which eventually suggested federation with the Burmese state.

In the constituent assembly, which was elected in April, the AFPFL formed the vast majority, with 190 out of 220 seats. The establishment of a new Burmese government was interrupted by a plot against Aung San and the AFPFL leaders. U Saw, the prewar political leader and prime minister, whom the British had arrested during the war but had released and permitted to return in 1946, conspired to assassinate every member of the government in order to assume leadership himself. He engaged a handful of junior army officers who succeeded in breaking into an executive council meeting and wiping out most of those present with machine-gun fire. U Nu, or Thakin Nu, the vice-president of the AFPFL, who survived because of his absence from the council meeting, was immediately named by the governor as successor to Aung San. The new government under U Nu continued the work of its predecessor while at the same time defending itself against the increasing number of internal opponents. U Saw was arrested and executed, and the government remained firmly in the hands of the AFPFL leaders under U Nu. In September 1947 a new constitution was adopted which established a parliamentary system. A bicameral legislature was set up in which the upper house included representatives of national minorities, who received 72 of the 125 seats. A president was elected by both houses of parliament for a five-year term. The actual executive authority, however, was in the hands of a cabinet responsible to a majority of the lower house, the House of Deputies, in which the main policy-making power was vested.

In October 1947, the U Nu government concluded a final settlement with England. In contrast to India, the Burmese leaders decided against continued membership in the British Commonwealth and demanded full independence as a sovereign state. The British accepted this decision and recognized the Republic of the Union of Burma as a fully independent state. The new status began on January 4, 1948. In April 1948, Burma was admitted to membership in the United Nations with the backing of Great Britain and the United States.

The political settlement was accompanied by a financial agreement in which the British cancelled most of the public debts incurred by the Burmese government to England during the confused postwar years. The Burmese agreed to respect the rights and contracts of British subjects and British firms and promised not to expropriate them without compensation. As in many such settlements between former colonial powers and newly independent nations, political control was relinquished while protection of economic interests was maintained. This did not, of course, exclude the possibility of the eventual elimination of British economic interests. The British agreed to withdraw their military forces but to provide military missions for the training and equipping of the new Burmese army. They maintained for a limited time a number of Burmese airfields, which they were permitted to use when necessary to help protect Burma from outside attack. This military agreement could be cancelled after three years by either side on twelve months' notice.

Chaos and Regeneration

Independent Burma soon faced a number of internal rebellions. The White Flag Communists, under their leader, Than Tun, who had supported the U Nu government for a few months immediately after the assassination of Aung San, now went into open military resistance. Than Tun attacked the agreement with England, especially its economic and military provisions. He was joined by a section of the AFPFL forces, which after the war had become known as the Patriotic Volunteer Organization, or PVO. U Nu outlawed the Communist party in March, 1948, but it succeeded in occupying several parts of Central Burma and a section along the western coast. At the same time, in the Salween River area, some of the Karens went into open rebellion and demanded greater independence from Burmese control. There were minor uprisings of Moslem and Buddhist groups in upper central Burma, and among the primitive Kachin tribes on the Tibetan-Chinese border of Burma. Burma was plunged into a period of further chaos and destruction. The rebellions of the two Communist groups and the Karens reached into the agricultural areas of the river valleys close to the capital of Rangoon. An additional complication was created by the retreat of a Chinese nationalist force fleeing from the Chinese Communists across the Yunnan border into the mountain areas of western Burma. This Chinese force took over some of the border territory.

From this point of military disintegration in 1949, the government slowly recovered, and from 1950 on began to extend its control again. The various rebellious forces of the White Communists, the Red Communists, the PVO, and the Karens, which in 1950 had begun to cooperate politically, were driven back. Some of the PVO forces surrendered to the government. The area of Central Burma around Prome was recovered, and the road to Mandalay reopened. Most of the Karen rebellion was ended by 1952, and in 1953 an agreement with Nationalist China led to the evacuation of the larger part of the Chinese Nationalist troops. Though small mountainous areas remained outside the control of the U Nu government, it again controlled the major part of the country. The various rebellions, which cooperated temporarily but had no common political ground, had failed.

As the government authority was re-established from Rangoon northward, the problems of restoring rice production and settling the issue of foreign land ownership became urgent. Government loans and bonus grants for restoring cultivation were successful in building up again a substantial and growing rice surplus for export. Although the government continued to have difficulties with tax collection, it drew substantial revenues from the rice export monopoly which was run by the State Agricultural Marketing Board. There remained the problem of land ownership, all the more urgent because the Communists were competing for peasant support with the slogan, "No rent, no taxes." The Indian Chettyar landlords and moneylenders had not come back, but a settlement with them was not possible without the financial compensation on which the Indian government insisted. The Burmese government advanced its plans for state control of industry by taking over the riverboat companies and establishing government management over part of the timber industry, although private enterprises were also permitted to operate.

In international policy, the Burmese government chose the middle course of remaining apart from Communist as well as Western alignments. While the government recognized the Chinese Communist regime in 1950, it remained well aware of the Communist danger which it was fighting within its own borders. Burma supported United Nations action against North Korea but did not join in the resolution naming Communist China an aggressor. She did not participate in the peace treaty with Japan but concluded a separate treaty after settling her reparations claims at a figure of $250,000,000.

In her struggle for independence as well as in the formulation of her international policies, the new Burma drew much of her strength from a revitalized Buddhism, a Buddhism adapted to the needs of the modern world. Burmese nationalism had its origin in a Buddhist educational movement, which in reaction against the British educational system emphasized the traditional values of the Buddhist religion in Burma. Many of the educated families introduced their sons at a very early age to the Buddhist religion at an initiation ceremony in which relatives and friends participated. At about the age of twenty most young educated Burmese spent a few months living in a monastery and there was high respect for those who took up the monastic life as a calling. Many of the nationalist leaders of Burma, including U Nu, were devout Buddhists. The nationalist leaders drew upon Buddhism for their spiritual support in the task of protecting the integrity of Burma's cultural tradition while adjusting to the violent impact of Western ideas. They also drew upon the traditional institutional patterns of the Burmese Buddhist state for their social and economic program. The egalitarianism of Buddhist society and its lack of emphasis on property rights were the sources of the socialist program of the nationalist leaders. On the other hand the humanist tradition of Buddhism, its aversion to conflict and violence, and its emphasis on a spiritual life were in diametrical opposition to Marxist dogma. The strength of Buddhism in Burma was one reason for the Communists' failure to secure control during the immediate postwar years of extreme economic and political chaos. In the international field the Burmese government has taken the initiative in promoting a revival of Buddhism throughout Asia. In 1954 the Burmese government invited Buddhists from all over Asia to participate in a two-year conference, the Sixth World Buddhist Council, at Rangoon. Over 2,500 monks and thousands of devout laymen met in a special building which was constructed to resemble the cave in which the first Buddhist Council had been held in 483 B.C. The main task of the Council was to clarify and translate the ancient texts of Hinayana Buddhism. It also demonstrated the spiritual strength and far-reaching organizational cohesion of contemporary Buddhism.

6. THAILAND (SIAM)

The Coup d'état of 1932

Thailand's adjustment to the modern world was initiated by her kings, the absolute rulers of the Chakkri dynasty. When Thailand came into contact with the West, the kings introduced changes which were necessary to defend the country against the threat of colonial rule and to keep pace with the neighboring colonial world. These changes were not meant to affect the basic concept of the Buddhist oriental state administered by a bureaucracy and based on Buddhist education. Nor were they intended to affect the authority of the king, who was the protector of the Buddhist system and to whom all Thai people owed their loyalty. But when the kings introduced Western techniques and encouraged Western education, they brought in Western ideas which eventually came to undermine their authority. The beginnings of a Western school system, the Foreign Language Academy, the Western training of the army, and the encouragement of Thais to study abroad created a small group of Western-trained intellectuals, professional men, and military officers, who pressed for a larger share of authority than the absolute monarchy permitted. The old type of Buddhist official was replaced by a Western-trained official who demanded his share in policy-making.

In anticipating the pressure for participation in government, King Prajadhipok planned to institute a constitutional monarchy. He brought in an American adviser, and prepared two constitutional drafts. But before the king acted, matters were taken out of his hands by the Western-trained elite itself, which seized power in a *coup d'état* on June 24, 1932.

The group that carried through this *coup d'état* consisted of a number of Western-trained intellectuals and military men of very differing outlooks. What they had in common was the aim of supplanting the king's absolute authority with their own political leadership. Beyond that their political ideas and personal ambitions varied greatly. The main leaders were Luang Pradist Manudharm, better known under his personal name of Pridi Banomyong, who was a professor of law at Chulalongkorn University, Phya Manopakorn, an active general in the Thai army, and Phya Bahol, another general who had received his training in Germany. Pridi Banomyong had studied law in Paris and later became one of the key figures of the new group. General Phya Bahol had among his main supporters a General Luang Phibun Songgram who became the other leading figure among the revolutionaries. These men organized what was called the People's party, which was more like a club than a party in the Western sense of the term. Through their military members the conspirators secured control of the palace guard, took over the palace, placed the princes of the royal family and the government officials under house arrest, and forced the king to relinquish his powers and accept the revolutionaries as the leaders of a new government under a constitutional regime. A provisional constitution was adopted which gave to the People's party a monopoly of power for a "transitory period" of ten years. The new government proclaimed a general program of social justice, equality of all citizens before the law, universal education, and improvement of the economic situation of the people.

Struggle within the Oligarchy

Once in power the revolutionary leaders fell out among themselves. In April, 1933, Phya Manopakorn, who became the first prime

minister, expelled Pridi Banomyong from the government under the accusation that he was a Communist. Pridi was exiled and left for France, and his
followers were also ousted from the government. The government also
passed "an act concerning Communism" which outlawed any Communist
activities. But Phya Manopakorn was himself forced out of the government
by Phya Bahol, who took over as prime minister in June, 1933, with the
backing of the army. An attempt to restore the king's authority was suppressed in the same year mainly through the actions of Luang Phibun
Songgram, who was then a major and the military right-hand man of Prime
Minister Bahol. In 1934 Pridi, who returned from France, was officially
cleared of the accusation of being a Communist and was taken back into the
government. From this time on Pridi and Phibun Songgram became the
main rivals among the government leaders, a rivalry which was as much
political as personal. Pridi represented a leftist political trend and many
years later cooperated openly with the Chinese Communists. Phibun was
supported by the modern-trained military officers.

In 1935 King Prajadhipok, whose position had been weakened through
the failure of the coup in his favor in 1933, abdicated in favor of his nephew,
Ananda Mahidol, who had been educated in Switzerland. In the years
following the king's abdication, the control of the government became firmly
established in the hands of the new oligarchy. The People's party, which
had organized the revolution of 1932, was formally dissolved in 1933 and
was continued as a political club. Attempts in 1937 to register political parties
were squelched by the government. Political arrests and imprisonments increased, some executions took place, and the police system was strengthened.
In 1938 Phibun Songgram took over the post of prime minister which he held
until 1944. But Pridi and his group remained in the government, where
Pridi held the position of minister of finance.

The monopoly of power of the People's party was to end in 1942 according to the "transitory provisions" of the provisional constitution, and the
transition to a representative system was again discussed in 1940. A law was
prepared for the establishment of political parties, but Communist, royalist,
or dictatorship parties were to be excluded. At the same time the government, unwilling to give up its monopoly power, voted to continue the authority of the People's party for another ten years after 1942. The monopoly
system thus continued, but permission to form other parties was also postponed when the Japanese moved into Indo-China and threatened Thailand
with involvement in the war.

The Reform Program

The program of the new government of 1932 was to acceler-
ate the reforms which the kings had started. A great emphasis was placed on
education. The budget for the school system was tripled after 1933, and the
government claimed that 30 per cent of the population became literate. The
system of primary education was intended to develop an attitude of good
citizenship. The curriculum, the textbooks, the hours of study, and the

examinations were all prescribed from above, and teachers were government employees. School supervisors were to see that the school policy was uniformly applied.

The government used the school system to promote Thai nationalism. Not only the Thai people but also the main minority groups—the Chinese and the Malays—were to be educated in Thai language and culture according to the same centrally controlled pattern. Both the Chinese and Malays resisted. The Chinese had established their own schools, which followed a program of nationalist Chinese education, and gave the Thai language only a secondary place. They were unwilling to yield to compulsory Thai education and tried to circumvent the regulations. At times they had two faculty teams, a Chinese faculty that taught, and a Thai faculty that could be presented to the school inspector. But when the government tried to enforce its rules by closing many Chinese schools, they reluctantly accepted the legal requirements, although always attempting to maintain as much of a Chinese education as possible.

The Malays, unlike the Chinese, were concentrated not in the main urban centers but in the southern part of Thailand that reached down into the Malay peninsula. They met the Thai school system with a form of passive resistance in which the children refused to learn the Thai language. The Malays, who were Moslems, also resented the Buddhist ceremonies instituted in the schools. Aside from these troubles with minority groups, however, the government succeeded in using the schools to propagate nationalist ideas among the Thai people, especially after 1938 when the nationalistic tendencies of the government were strengthened under Phibun Songgram's regime.

In economic affairs the government followed a nationalistic policy aiming at strengthening Thai interests and at weakening the control of the Chinese and Europeans. According to the Thais 95 per cent of the nation's business was in the hands of foreigners. The tin mines were owned by the Chinese and British and worked by Chinese labor. British and American companies controlled the oil industry, and the Chinese were dominant in the teak lumber industry. From 1932 on, laws were passed to eliminate foreign control in many of the key industries, the communications system, and other commercial activities. The government policy of eliminating foreign control was accentuated under Phibun Songgram. The government policy of imposing restrictions on foreign capital caused some of the foreign companies to withdraw rather than to continue under the imposed restrictions. The British and American oil companies, for instance, left the country, and an oil fuel department established by the ministry of finance was unable to continue the operations on the same scale, although it managed an oil refinery. The restrictions placed on foreign investments in the rubber industry brought a decline of English and Chinese rubber interests, while Japanese investment, assisted by a friendly Thai government policy, increased. The Thai government also took over much of the teak lumber industry from the Chinese and established other industrial enterprises, including a sugar factory, a silk factory, a tobacco factory, and a cannery. It went into the production of alcohol, cigarettes, and other consumer goods and sent students abroad for training in engineering and management of such industrial enterprises. In agriculture the government proclaimed a program of improvement of the farmers' condition through cooperatives and government credit, but little was accomplished in the first years.

After Phibun Songgram came to power, the strong nationalism of the Thai regime was expressed in a number of other measures in the fields of education and religion which were aimed at stressing the Thai nationalist tradition. Political attacks were made on missionary work, and some of the French Catholic priests were sent home. Buddhism, on the other hand, was stressed as a national religion, and pressure was exerted to induce Thai Christians to return to Buddhism if they were to continue in the positions they held in the government. Buddhist evangelist meetings were held in which Catholics and Protestants were invited to step forward and declare their belief in Buddha. In 1941 a National Buddhist Assembly was founded in which all Buddhist sects were combined. Buddhists were to discard magic and superstition and to emphasize the social values of the religion, to rationalize it, and to reconcile it with modern science. Buddhism was to be used for religious education and to create a spirit of loyalty to Thai culture and a willingness to defend it.

The government's regulation of people's lives was extended to a campaign for cleanliness and propriety in dress and appearance. The streets were to be kept clean and the people were to give up the habit of chewing betel. A westernized dress was to be adopted, and men and women were to wear shoes and hats in public. Although this campaign was attacked and ridiculed as the "hat-wearing period," it brought about a considerable transformation in Thai habits.

The nationalism of the new Thai regime, expressed in its economic and educational policies, was also symbolized by the change in the country's name. Internationally the country had been known as Siam, and all treaties and international agreements had used this term. For the Thais the country had always been Muang Thai, or the Land of the Thai. In 1939 the nationalist aspirations were expressed by an official change of the name of the country from Siam to Thailand.

Thailand's political independence had been maintained because her kings had followed a neutral policy in regard to England and France, the two countries that had built their colonial empires to the east, west, and south of Thailand and left the country itself as a buffer state between them. This policy of neutrality was at first continued by the revolutionary leaders of 1932. Thailand refused to side with the League of Nations in its condemnation of Japanese aggression in Manchuria and continued friendly relations with Japan. The Thai leaders had a great admiration for Japanese technical progress, and several of the Thai officers received their military education in Japan. To balance the predominant British and Chinese economic interests in Thailand, the Thais then began to favor Japanese interests. Japanese political and financial advisers were called in and Thai consulates established in Japan. After 1938 the government of Phibun Songgram reorganized the Thai army after the Japanese model. A commercial treaty gave the Japanese equal rights with the Thais with regard to ownership of property and of industrial enterprise.

Thailand's Role in World War II

When the Japanese occupied Indo-China in September 1940, the Thai government felt that the opportunity had arrived to regain some of the territory on the borders of Laos and Cambodia which the Thais had lost to the French in the latter part of the nineteenth century. In December the Thais started a border war and defeated the weak French forces, and in March 1941, through Japanese mediation, an agreement was reached in Tokyo in which an area with about a million and a half population was ceded to Thailand. This agreement increased the Thai government's political obligations to Japan. At the same time Japan bought large parts of Thailand's exports in rice, tea, and rubber.

At the outbreak of the Pacific War, Japan presented an ultimatum to Thailand, on December 8, 1941, demanding the right to move troops through Thailand for the attack on Malaya. For five hours a token resistance was carried on by Thai troops at the border until the Thai government accepted the Japanese demand. On December 21 an alliance was signed between Thailand and Japan, and a declaration of war against the United States and England followed. During the first years of the war Phibun's cabinet remained in office and cooperated with the Japanese. Pridi refused to vote for the declaration of war and resigned from his position as minister of finance. He even attempted to establish an independent government in north Thailand but failed. Pridi, however, continued to be an influential political figure and was made regent for the young king who was still absent in Switzerland. In this position Pridi cooperated with the Allies in organizing a secret anti-Japanese underground which worked with a Free Thai movement that had been organized in the United States and England. Preparations for an attack against the Japanese were laid, but during the war the Allied forces did not feel strong enough to support a Thai uprising. The war ended with Pridi as the recognized resistance leader who had the full support of the Allies.

Before the end of the war, in July, 1944, Pridi had been able as regent to oust Phibun from his position as prime minister. The cost in life and property of the Japanese occupation and the public works undertaken for the war effort had weakened Phibun's support. From July, 1944, on, Pridi appointed a number of prime ministers of his choice and was the political leader of Thailand until 1947.

During the war the Japanese rewarded Thailand with another piece of territory. The northern Malay states, which the British had taken from the

Thai kings in the nineteenth century and incorporated into British Malaya, were given back to Thailand by the Japanese. But at the end of the war Thailand lost this territory again as well as the territories of Laos and Cambodia, which she had gained through Japanese help in 1940. Thailand was thus limited again to her pre-1940 frontiers.

The role which Thailand had played in the war was interpreted differently by the British and the American governments. The British, under whose theater command Thailand fell, treated her at first as an enemy country and presented far-reaching demands. The Thai administration was to be placed under British authority, all exports were to be regulated solely by the British, and the country was to become a British protectorate until it might eventually be admitted to membership in the United Nations. In its resistance against this treatment, the Thai government was supported by the Chinese Nationalists and especially by the United States, which had disregarded the Thai declaration of war and considered the Thai government of Pridi Banomyong as an ally which had helped in the war against Japan. Under American pressure the British modified their demands, and Thailand had only to return the Malay territories to British Malaya, and to pay compensation to Britain by deliveries of export rice badly needed at the time in British-controlled territories. The British also forced the name of Thailand to be changed back to Siam; but in 1948 the name was changed again to Thailand.

Postwar Politics

After the war the political structure of Thailand was reformed. A bicameral assembly was instituted with general elections for both houses. Political parties were now permitted. But these forms of a representative system did not much change the autocratic rule by a small educated group which organized parties as a listing of personal followers of the important political leaders rather than as mass movements based on political programs.

At the end of the war the leadership was in the hands of Pridi Banomyong who had cooperated with the Allies. An attempt to bring Phibun Songgram to trial for his collaboration with the Japanese failed, and he began to rebuild his power. In June 1946, the young king Ananda, who had returned that year from Switzerland, was mysteriously assassinated, and Pridi's government was later held responsible for the assassination. Ananda was succeeded by his younger brother, Phumiphon Adundet, who remained in Switzerland until 1951.

In November 1947, when he no longer felt afraid of the opposition of the Western powers, Phibun Songgram staged a military coup which ended Pridi's rule. Phibun Songgram introduced a new constitution and held elections which gave him a majority. In 1948 Phibun Songgram became prime minister of the supreme state council established by the new constitution. Pridi fled from the country and turned up in 1954 in Communist China where he participated in the Chinese Communist attacks against Phibun Songgram's government.

The war in Indo-China caused considerable fear in Thailand that the Communists might move across the border. The establishment by the Chinese Communist regime of an autonomous administration for the Thai minority in the Chinese province of Yunnan added the fear of a possible Communist-sponsored pan-Thai movement. The government of Phibun Songgram consequently leaned more heavily on Western, especially American, support. Thailand was one of the few Asiatic countries to join the Southeast Asia Treaty Organization and to plan for collective military defense measures against possible Communist infiltration or aggression.

7. MALAYA

British Policy and the Ethnic Groups

The development of the Malay Peninsula under British colonial rule was dictated largely by economic interests. Starting from their trading base, the free port of Singapore at the tip of the peninsula, the British promoted an economic development that moved up the peninsula and inland into the agricultural valleys of the Malay states. The British themselves profited most from this economic development. They owned the largest tin smelters and controlled the chief plantations and business firms. Next to them were the Chinese who came to Malaya in order to profit from the opportunities provided by the British. They were the traders, the shopkeepers, the bankers, the plantation workers, and made up by far the largest part of the people working in the new economy. Singapore, the focus of this business life, was itself 80 per cent Chinese.

Singapore was an export and import center for the growing production of the plantations and tin mines of the Malay Peninsula and for the distribution of the manufactured goods and food products brought into Malaya from the outside. Singapore served as a processing and trading center not only for the rubber and tin production of Malaya but also for that of Sumatra, British Borneo, Thailand, Burma, and China, and even Africa and Australia. It was also an entrepôt and port of transshipment of goods for the whole trade of the Far East. Singapore, the economic center of Malaya, was thus an international port, and the businessmen there had as much of a stake in the general situation in the Far East as in that of the peninsula itself. They therefore had no particular interest in taking the lead in Malayan nationalism and in promoting the development of an independent national economy.

The population growth which accompanied the development of the economy created potentially antagonistic groups, which were divided by ethnic differences as well as by their different roles in the country's economy. The Malays, though they were greatly outnumbered in Singapore and the coastal cities, were still the largest group in the Malay states where they made up from 44 per cent to over 50 per cent of the population. Most of them were peasants but there was also a small elite which administered the Malay states under British direction. The Chinese, who made up about 44 per cent of the population, and the Indians who made up about 11 per cent, were connected entirely with the modern side of the economy. Malays, Chinese, and Indians could live side by side as long as each group followed its own interests, but it was inevitable that they should come into conflict when the issue of nationalism and self-government came to the fore. The Malays felt the economic pressure of the Chinese, but they relied on the British to prevent the Chinese from gaining political control in addition to their economic encroachment.

The Chinese were immigrants from China many of whom expected to return to their home country when they had made their fortunes. They were linked to China by cultural tradition and beliefs and they also hoped that a more powerful China would strengthen their own position in Malaya. Their political interest was therefore directed much more toward events in their homeland and the relationship of these events to Southeast Asia than toward the growth of national unity and self-government in Malaya.

The first modern political activities in Malaya began among the Chinese. The Chinese communities of Singapore and Malaya were one of the main sources of financial support for Sun Yat-sen in the early days of his revolutionary organization, the *T'ung-meng-hui*, and later of the Kuomintang. The reorganization of the Chinese Nationalist party in the early twenties under Soviet Russian advisers, and in cooperation with the newly founded Chinese Communist party, was also reflected in the Chinese community of Malaya. The Kuomintang had branches in Malaya, often closely connected with the Chinese schools there. The Chinese Communists, who were then cooperating with the Kuomintang in China, came into Malaya at the same time and worked with the Kuomintang there. A Chinese Communist organization was set up in Malaya in 1921, but it remained underground until a Communist party was openly established there in 1931. After the split between the Kuomintang and the Communists in China, the respective parties in Malaya became rivals for the allegiance of the Chinese. In general the Kuomintang had the edge. The Communists limited their activities in the main to organizing labor and sponsoring a number of strikes, especially on the docks of Singapore. This political activity of the Communists was a part of their world-wide strategy directed against British "imperialism" and had no connection with the situation of the Chinese in Malaya.

During this period the various ethnic groups had a minor part in the colonial administrations of the Straits Settlements and the Malay States. In the Straits Settlements the government remained in the hands of the British Governor. His government was, however, supported by executive and legislative councils. The executive council consisted of appointed officials, mostly British, but some were taken from the various ethnic groups. The legislative council consisted of both official and unofficial members. The official members were the same men who held the executive positions and were responsible to the governor. They formed the majority in the legislative council which therefore always had to do the governor's bidding. The unofficial representatives were appointed by the governor from among outstanding Malays, Chinese, Indians, and Eurasians. There was thus an outlet through which the various ethnic groups could express their wishes to the governor, but the governor retained full control over all branches of the government. A similar situation existed in the Federal Council of the Federated Malay States. In the Unfederated Malay States the authority was in the hands of Malays who formed the sultans' governments; but the actual control was in the hands of British residents. Under this system the British were constantly aware of the wishes of the ethnic groups and could formulate British policy without creating strong antagonisms. Under the British the Chinese had freedom of economic action, and the Malays had protection from Chinese political control. The small number of Malays who had received a Western education in the British system of primary schools and colleges were hostile to the growing Chinese stranglehold and fearful of any advance of the Chinese political position. But by and large, their potential antagonism had not led to any open hostility by the time of the outbreak of World War II.

Japanese Occupation

The Japanese conquest of Malaya changed the political situation. The British were unprepared for the Japanese overland attack and were outmaneuvered by the Japanese forces, which were well trained in jungle warfare. There had been no preparations to organize and train forces in Malaya, and the volunteers—mainly Chinese—who joined in the last stages of the defense of Singapore, could not even be properly equipped. The surrender of Singapore in February 1942 was a tremendous blow, not only to the defense of Southeast Asia but to the British prestige in general.

During their occupation the Japanese favored the Malays, and intentionally fomented hostility between them and the Chinese in order to facilitate Japanese control. The highhandedness of the Japanese and their obvious exploitation of the country for the benefit of Japan prevented them from gaining any substantial Malay support, but they succeeded in heightening the Malay distrust of the Chinese, and the war resulted in a sharpening of the national consciousness of each of these population groups.

When the war began in Europe in 1939, the Chinese Communists in Malaya followed the international Communist party line which labelled the war an "imperialist war." The Communists created trouble for the British by organizing dock strikes in Singapore. But when Hitler attacked Soviet Russia, the party line shifted and immediately brought the Chinese Communists of Malaya to the support of the British. This support continued after the Japanese attack. The Chinese Communist party took the lead after the fall of Singapore in organizing an anti-Japanese underground movement. With British help, a force of several thousand men was organized, which by

1945 had succeeded, through guerrilla warfare, in severing the railroad communication from Thailand down the Malay Peninsula and in preparing the ground for a British landing. The collapse of Japan and her surrender precluded any such military move. The British landed peacefully in September, 1945, and were welcomed back by all population groups. The guerrilla units were dissolved and most of their arms turned over to the British, but a framework of organization remained which the Communists later used in their attempt at an armed uprising.

Postwar Reorganization

When they came back to Malaya, the British realized the need for a political reorganization which would give the various population groups a greater share in the government of their country. In 1945 a plan was prepared to set up a central government for the whole of Malaya. A British envoy, Sir Harold MacMichael, was sent out in October, 1945, and negotiated treaties with the sultans in which they transferred their rights of sovereignty to the British government. The sultans, who had maintained their position during the Japanese occupation, were now forced to surrender their authority by the implied threat that their involuntary cooperation with the Japanese could be turned against them and they could be deprived of all their remaining royal privileges. On the basis of these treaties the British government drew up a plan for a Malayan Union to consist of all the nine Malay states and the two Straits Settlements of Penang and Malacca. Singapore was to be excluded from this Malayan Union and remain a British crown colony. The authority of the sultans was reduced to dealing with matters of the Moslem religion, while all other matters were to be handled by the government of the Malayan Union in which all Malay citizens were to participate through elections. The key issue was the proposal to give equal citizenship in the new Malay Union to members of all ethnic groups. Full citizenship was to be granted to all persons born in Malaya or Singapore, to immigrants who had resided ten years in Malaya, and to newcomers after only five years of residence.

This plan would have made it possible for the Chinese to gain a decisive share of political control. Malay citizenship would have been granted to the transient Chinese, who wanted eventually to return to China, and to all those Chinese who, while pressing their claim for participation in Malayan affairs, were unwilling to give up their Chinese citizenship. The plan was therefore most favorable to the Chinese dual nationality policy, and would have been all the more disastrous for the Malays because it was to coincide with the abolition of the Malay States, which safeguarded the political role of the Malays. The British proposal for a Malay Union therefore caused a violent reaction among the Malays, who now for the first time formed political organizations of their own under the leadership of Western-educated Malays, some of them the administrators of the governments of the sultans. This Malay opposition was organized as the United Malay National Organization, or UMNO, which had branches all over the country and had a broad appeal among the Malay peasants, who were fearful of the growing power of the Chinese traders and moneylenders.

Under the threat of this opposition, the British gave up their plan and got together with the representatives of UMNO to work out another program. The Malays insisted upon retaining the structure of the sultan states which to them were a guarantee of the political survival of their ethnic group. They also wanted the right of citizenship reserved to those who really wanted to make Malaya their home and to give this state their undivided loyalty.

These Malay demands became part of a new British plan for a Malay Federation, drawn up in 1947 and eventually established in February, 1948. The new plan would give citizenship to Malays, Indians, and Chinese born in Malay territory. Immigrants could become citizens after fifteen years if they intended to remain permanently in the country. This plan followed the Malay demands, but it did not require citizens to forswear allegiance to another country.

The new Malay Federation excluded Singapore, which continued under its own government as a British crown colony. For the territory of the Federation, a central government was established, headed by the British High Commissioner, working through an executive and a legislative council. The executive council consisted of appointed official and unofficial members representing the various nationality groups. The legislative council consisted of fifteen official and sixty-one unofficial members. The latter were at first nominated by the High Commissioner but eventually were to be elected. Thirty-one of the unofficial members were Malays who were also given a veto on immigration laws. In each state, authority remained in the hands of the sultan, who governed with the help of an executive council and a state council or legislature, which was also elected. Singapore continued under its own governor and executive and legislative councils. This new plan, initiated in 1948, was the first step towards self-government, through which, it was hoped, the ethnic rivalries would eventually be overcome.

Communist Uprising

Before this political system could be tested, Malaya was severely shaken by a Communist uprising that led to protracted and costly guerrilla warfare. During the postwar years the Communists concentrated their main efforts on fomenting strikes and trying to get control of the expanding labor unions. But in 1948, following the line indicated by the Cominform "Youth Conference" in Calcutta in that year, the Communists in Malaya organized a planned military attack. A force of several thousand men, almost entirely Chinese, systematically carried out a carefully devised plan of murder, ambush, and guerrilla warfare against government officials, plantation owners, businessmen, and all those who were cooperating with the

British administration. The Communists succeeded at first in terrorizing whole districts and in killing several hundred European plantation owners, mine owners, officials, and Chinese businessmen and Kuomintang leaders. The attack against the latter indicated that the uprising was also a part of the Chinese civil war and of international Communist policy.

In February, 1949, these Communist forces were integrated into a "Malayan National Liberation Army," and thereafter a political program was proclaimed which contained the theoretical formulations of Mao Tse-tung's "New Democracy." The professed aim of the rebellion was the establishment of an independent "Malayan People's Democratic Republic," in which all nationalities were to have equality. This Communist rebellion derived its recruits and supplies from the control of a section of the Chinese population, which during the period of Japanese occupation had moved inland from the disintegrating trade centers to cultivate small agricultural plots hacked out of the jungle. These Chinese settlers were squatters on the land which they appropriated and continued to occupy after the war. They were scattered over many parts of inland Malaya and made up an estimated total of 300,000 people. Outside of government reach in their isolated villages, these Chinese were the ideal instrument for the Communist guerrillas, who could hide in the jungle and receive their food and recruits, as well as their intelligence, from the squatters, whom they terrorized into submission.

At first this Communist terror put the British colonial government on the defensive. By summer, 1950, about 18,000 regular troops had been shipped to Malaya to deal with the rebellion, and the local police force had been greatly expanded. But in spite of the military superiority of the British over the comparatively small Communist guerrilla bands, the latter could not be seriously weakened until the source of their strength could be destroyed. In 1952 the British began to carry out a program of resettling the squatters and of controlling the food supply to the areas close to the jungle strongholds of the guerrillas. By these measures they hoped to starve the guerrilla forces into submission. Over 100,000 Chinese squatters were resettled in villages under government control, and retaliatory measures were taken against villages suspected of cooperation with the Communists. By this new policy the British did not eliminate the Communist guerrilla forces altogether, but they greatly reduced their strength and placed them on the defensive. The Communists were no longer able to disrupt the plantation and mining production on which the economy of Malaya rested. By 1954 the armed Communist guerrillas had been reduced in numbers and limited in the scope of their operations. This was due largely to the aggressive measures taken by the British. The British were able to go ahead with their political program for the Federated Malay States. Elections were held in July, 1955, for the legislative council. In these elections the alliance of the United Malay National Organization and the Malayan Chinese Association won a landslide victory. These two parties had agreed not to contest each other's candidates. The victorious parties were in favor of pressing for independence at an early date in contrast to the opposition Negara party which was more conservative. The executive council, which was still largely appointed, continued to control the administration.

Communist strategy shifted to one of exploiting the political situation in Singapore. For some time Communist influence among the Chinese students in Singapore schools had been on the increase. On May 13, 1954, they organized a student strike which was ostensibly directed against the registration of students for military service, which in fact hardly affected the students at all. The students seized the schools and occupied them for a month until the Chinese Chamber of Commerce arranged a settlement. The result of this strike was the formation of a People's Action party under left-wing leadership. In April, 1955, the British held elections for a legislative assembly under new constitutional provisions for Singapore drawn up by the Rendel Commission which had been appointed by the governor. Under the new constitution the assembly consisted of a speaker, twenty-five popularly elected representatives, three ex officio ministers, and four nominees of the governor. All candidates had to be British subjects and qualify in the writing and reading of the English language. The administration was to be in the hands of a council of ministers, collectively responsible to the assembly. The council, or cabinet, was presided over by the governor and consisted of six elected members of the majority party in the assembly and the three ex officio ministers, who had to vote with the government. The governor had reserve powers in external relations, defense, and public service.

In the elections the middle-of-the-road Labor Front party gained eleven seats, by far the largest number secured by any party. In order to have a working majority it formed a coalition with the Malayan Chinese Association and the U.M.N.O. The Progressive party and the Democratic party formed the right-wing opposition. The People's Action party, which had contested four seats, won three and formed the left-wing opposition. This group was responsible for the student agitation which helped to frustate the efforts to establish an independent Chinese university, the Nanyang University, under the presidency of Lin Yu-tang. In May 1955, a strike of transport workers was taken over by left-wing students and the People's Action party. Demonstrations led to the deaths of three Chinese and one American and to the closing of the schools by the government. This was an attempt to discredit the new government which was forced to settle the strike in favor of the strikers and to reopen the schools. The strike was followed by a constitutional crisis in which the legislative assembly tried to force the governor to give up some of his reserve powers. Within a very short space of time the independence of Singapore had become a political issue.

CHAPTER XV

American Far Eastern Policy

---

1. Japan and China, 1921–1945

Aims of American Policy

Ｐ‍RESIDENT Wilson stated the aims of American policy in public statements, in addresses to the Congress, and in the famous Fourteen Points. The Fourteen Points came to be accepted during World War I as the American program for the peace, thus receiving world-wide attention. The Fourteen Points drew out of American tradition and experience those things that had a universal appeal. The traditional American ideas of political independence, popular sovereignty, free enterprise, equality of trade, freedom of the seas, respect for the territorial and political integrity of other states, were reformulated by President Wilson in bold and dramatic terms which renewed their old revolutionary appeal. The slogan of self-determination, for example, was a new expression of an idea which had inspired the American Revolution. The right of self-determination, as stated in the Fourteen Points, applied specifically to the peoples of the Austro-Hungarian and Turkish empires, but in his speeches before the Congress Wilson claimed that all peoples should determine their own fate.

Peoples and provinces are not to be bartered about from sovereignty to sovereignty as if they were mere chattels and pawns in the game . . . Peoples may now be dominated and governed only by their own consent. Self-determination is not a mere phrase. It is an imperative principle of action, which statesmen will henceforth ignore at their peril.[1]

[1] Quoted in Raymond L. Buell, *International Relations* (New York, 1925), p. 35.

The Allied powers were willing enough to apply the principle of self-determination to the territories of former enemy states but they resisted its application to their own colonial empires and their own territorial acquisitions. The colonial powers were all the more anxious to limit the application of the principle of self-determination because of the proposal in Point Five of the Fourteen Points that in the adjustment of colonial claims "the interests of the populations concerned must have equal weight with the equitable claims of the governments whose title is to be determined." To the peoples of the Far East, however, the Fourteen Points had an obvious appeal.

President Wilson's ideas, especially self-determination, fitted in with the aspirations of the new nationalist movements, not only in colonial areas but also in China, where the rights and privileges of the Western powers were strongly resented. Inspired by Wilson's Fourteen Points the Chinese delegation at Versailles sought from Japan the restoration of the former German leased territory and sphere of influence in China and asked for the renunciation by all the powers of their imperialist privileges in China. They did not get any satisfaction and refused to sign the Treaty of Versailles. So great was the appeal of the slogan of self-determination that the Koreans and the Filipinos applied to the Versailles Conference for recognition of their independence, a claim which the Conference declined to hear. In Korea, which had been a Japanese colony since 1910, Wilson's ideas helped to set off an unarmed and spontaneous demonstration against Japanese rule which spread all over the country before it was ruthlessly suppressed by Japanese troops. Even the Bolsheviks made use of the slogan of self-determination in the Nationality Decree of 1917 and in treaties with Estonia and the Ukraine in 1920 and 1921. Very shortly afterwards the Bolsheviks established complete control within the territory of the newly established Soviet Union, unembarrassed by their mockery of Wilson's idealistic slogans.

In the Far East, Wilson's ideas drew attention to the humanistic and revolutionary traditions of the Western world at a time when the democratic tradition of the West was being challenged by the rise of the Communist movement in Russia. While the Communists propagated class struggle and provided elite groups with a program for seizing power, Wilson expressed his faith in the people. Nor was American policy, at this time, limited to slogans. Under the administration of President Wilson America began to put into practice the promise of self-government in her only Far Eastern colony, the Philippines, and actually prepared legislation for immediate independence. At the height of the wave of enthusiasm created by Wilson's doctrines American intellectual influence reached a new height, especially in China. This was the time when missionary work expanded into many fields, such as education and medicine, and the American Y.M.C.A. became the model for a similar organization in China. The Chinese Y.M.C.A. stressed the teaching of practical courses in business methods and English language, and offered classes in citizenship as a preparation for democracy. John Dewey lectured all over China during 1919 and 1920 on the philosophy of science and on the methods of the democratic process. Dewey profoundly impressed his Chinese audiences but he did not leave a lasting message. The opportunity for building up a strong belief in the humanitarian ideals of the West and in democracy as a system of values was not fully exploited. It was not long before the atmosphere changed in the Western world, especially in America after the defeat of President Wilson. After frittering away the Fourteen Points in compromises with her wartime allies, the United States refused to join the League of Nations and in her own colony, the Philippines, dropped the policy of independence and took no further steps towards self-government. In spite of this retreat the doctrines of President Wilson continued to be associated with the United States and made their contribution to the store of goodwill which America, at least in some measure, had established in the Far East, particularly in China.

Washington Conference

The changes brought about in the Far East by the war required new treaty arrangements among the countries with interests in that part of the world. The continental expansion of Japan, the growth of her fleet, and the acquisition of former German island bases in the Pacific challenged the two most important policies of the United States in the Far East—the promotion of equal economic opportunity, together with the territorial and administrative integrity of China, and the maintenance of American military security in the Pacific. The threat of Japan to American interests was the greater because of the apparent collapse of Russian influence and the defeat of Germany, which had played an important role in the Far East before the war. Under these circumstances the Anglo-Japanese alliance, which had been directed against Russia and had provided the legal basis for Japan's participation in the war against Germany, could be invoked by the Japanese in the event of conflict with the United States. The possibility of such a conflict created uneasiness not only in Great Britain and the United States but also in Canada, which raised the issue at the Imperial Conference of 1920. The problem of British alignment with Japan was complicated even more by the potential rivalry between Great Britain and the United States which had resulted from the war. During the war the American navy had been built up to equal strength with the British, and there was always the possibility of an Anglo-American naval race. The proposals for the limitation of armaments written into the Versailles Treaty related only to land forces. As the United States was not even a signatory, any disarmament agreement with the United States would have to be made outside the framework of the League of Nations. It was the issue of naval disarmament which led to the negotiations resulting in the Washington Conference. The British unofficially suggested to the United States that Great Britain should control the Atlantic and the United States the Pacific. Secretary of State Hughes took up this suggestion of negotiating about the relative strengths of the British and American navies and insisted that a conference be held in Washington, D. C., at which this question should be linked with the problems of the

Anglo-Japanese alliance and of China. It was a victory for American diplomacy that the conference was held in Washington, D. C., and that it dealt with all these interrelated problems.

The countries invited to the conference by the United States were Great Britain, Japan, France, Italy, China, Holland, Belgium, and Portugal. The conference met from November 1921 to February 1922, and produced a series of treaties, among the most important of which were a Four Power Pact, replacing the Anglo-Japanese alliance, a Five Power Pact on the limitation of naval armaments, and a Nine Power Pact on China.

The Four Power Pact, signed by the United States, Great Britain, Japan and France, was an agreement to respect the existing territorial possessions of the signatories in the Pacific. In case of conflict the powers agreed to call a joint conference "to which the whole subject will be referred for consideration and adjustment." The Anglo-Japanese alliance terminated with the ratification of this treaty. France had been included in the pact in order to make it clear that the United States was not joining Great Britain in support of Japan and that the Anglo-Japanese alliance was being replaced by a multi-power arrangement which would be of no special advantage to Japan except in smoothing over the loss of the alliance with Great Britain. Moreover, the inclusion of France in the Four Power Pact made it easier for her to accept naval parity with Italy in the treaty on naval armaments.

The Five Power Treaty, signed by the United States, Great Britain, Japan, France, and Italy, established a ratio of capital ship tonnage among these powers. The ratio was 5–5–3–1.75–1.75 respectively. The two strongest naval powers, the United States and Great Britain, agreed to naval parity, but the British navy was stronger than the combined navies of France and Italy, and the American navy stronger than that of Japan. The ratio was to be maintained by a prohibition of further naval construction and the scrapping of tonnage already on the stocks. By special agreement Japan was permitted to replace an older vessel by a nearly completed battleship. In addition to the naval ratio there was an agreement on naval bases in the Pacific. The United States, Great Britain, and Japan agreed not to construct new naval bases or fortifications west of Hawaii, north of Singapore, or south of Japan. At this time it was assumed that capital ships could not operate at a distance of more than 2,400 miles from their main bases and that, therefore, Japan would benefit considerably from this arrangement. The arrangement was acceptable to the United States because it reinforced the obligation which Japan had undertaken at Versailles not to fortify the former German-held islands north of the equator, when they were handed over to her with all the restrictions of the mandate system. In this way the United States secured an additional guarantee against a Japanese naval threat to the lines of communication with the Philippines.

The Five Power and Four Power treaties were closely related to the political agreement on China which was also negotiated at the conference. The balance of naval power and the neutralization of the Pacific which these treaties established could last only as long as there was no serious prospect of a clash over China. It was for this reason that the United States had from the very beginning insisted upon linking the problem of China with those of naval disarmament and the Anglo-Japanese alliance. In bringing China to the conference, the United States, however, had no intention of supporting Chinese demands for abrogation of the rights which Japan had gained during the war in her 1915 treaties with China. The United States, in effect, refrained from raising the issue of Japan's war gains in China in order to secure from Japan her participation in a general agreement which would reaffirm the principles of the Open Door and thus bind her not to undertake further aggression. This was all the more necessary because the chaotic conditions in China, then at the height of civil war and warlordism, invited aggressive moves by ambitious powers.

In the Nine Power Pact, all the participating powers at the conference promised under Article 1:

1. To respect the sovereignty, the independence, and the territorial and administrative integrity of China.

2. To provide the fullest and most unembarrassed opportunity to China to develop and maintain for herself an effective and stable government.

3. To use their influence for the purpose of effectually establishing and maintaining the principle of equal opportunity for the commerce and industry of all nations throughout the territory of China.

4. To refrain from taking advantage of the conditions in China in order to seek special rights or privileges which would abridge the rights of the subjects of friendly States and from countenancing action inimical to the security of such States.

This promise was spelled out in additional articles in which the powers undertook not to make any agreements in violation of these principles either among themselves or with China or to establish any special rights, monopolies, or spheres of influence in any part of China. The powers also agreed to respect China's neutrality in any future war in which she did not participate.

The Nine Power Pact was the fullest and clearest statement of American Far Eastern policy ever to be written into a treaty and to secure such wide acceptance. This policy was not applied retroactively, but for the future it promised China freedom from further Japanese aggression. For this reason the Chinese accepted the treaty and thus bound themselves for the first time to the principles of the Open Door, although they were disappointed in their failure to remove not only the specific rights and interests of Japan but also the whole unequal treaty system. The Chinese gained nothing in Manchuria. On the Shantung issue they had to come to terms with Japan in an agreement made outside the conference in which Japan restored to China formal political control of the former German leased territory but retained economic rights, military forces, and considerable influence. The Chinese raised in vain the issues of extraterritoriality and tariff autonomy. The conference set up commissions to investigate these questions, but China did not gain her sovereign rights in this regard until after the establishment of the National

Government in 1928. The Chinese were fully aware that in return for whatever safeguards the Nine Power Pact provided for China they had accepted a continuation of their unequal status in relation to the signatory powers. When the proposal was made, some years later, that Germany, newly admitted to the League of Nations, should adhere to the Nine Power Pact, China strongly objected on the grounds that her relations with Germany, since the war, had been on a basis of complete equality. By adhering to the Nine Power Pact Germany would regain the rights and privileges still held by the other powers.

The Nine Power Pact provided no effective machinery for the implementation of its provisions or for the handling of future conflicts in the Pacific. There was merely the provision that whenever one of the signatories thought it advisable to discuss the application of the treaty stipulations there should be "full and frank communication between the contracting powers concerned." The pact was really an agreement by which the United States got as much international agreement for its Far Eastern policies as possible, given the existing balance of power. This policy was the traditional one of protecting the administrative and territorial integrity of China within the framework of foreign treaty rights. It was a policy which put great store by international law and agreements and did not concern itself with any attempt to influence China's internal affairs. In the years just preceding the Washington Conference there had been an intellectual ferment in China accompanied by many signs of growing nationalism. But it was the policy of the United States and of the other powers not to have dealings with political movements but to await the emergence of a stable and orderly government before making concessions to Chinese nationalism. The opportunity to support the Chinese nationalist movement, which the United States neglected, was seized by the Soviet Union the year after the signing of the Washington Treaties.

The United States and the Chinese Revolution

The Washington Conference made no changes in the treaty system, which established the rights and privileges of the Westerners in China. Under pressure from the Chinese diplomats at Washington, who reflected the nationalistic temper of Chinese public opinion much more than the authority of the weak regime in Peking, the powers accepted, for the first time, the view that the treaty system might be modified. They held, however, that China must put her own house in order before real concessions could be made. The continuous civil war among warlord regimes and the Soviet participation in the Kuomintang regime in Canton were a far cry from the "effective and stable government" which the Washington Treaty powers regarded as a pre-condition for giving up any of their privileges. By 1925 neither the tariff conference nor the commission on extraterritoriality, which was to investigate conditions in China, had started work.

The only concession made to Chinese feeling was the remission to the

Chinese government of the balance of the Boxer Indemnity payments. In May 1924, the Congress passed a resolution to return the payments due America with the proviso that the money should be used for educational and cultural purposes. The other powers followed the American example, using the funds for establishing educational grants. These measures made it possible for many Chinese students to study in the United States and Europe. The funds were also used to establish new educational institutions and to assist existing institutions in China. The use of the Boxer Indemnity funds for Chinese education had a cumulative effect in creating goodwill, but it did not deflect the anti-foreign feelings of Chinese students which at that time were very intense.

As early as 1919 the protests of student groups had been strong enough to prevent the Peking government from signing the Versailles Treaty. In the years following 1919 student activities continued to contribute to the development of an anti-western and anti-missionary public opinion, with the encouragement of both the Kuomintang and Communist parties as well as of business organizations. During these years the student movement was the most vocal element among the nationalist groups in China. It was associated with every outburst of nationalist feeling.

In 1925 the pent-up feelings of Chinese nationalists burst out in a series of violent incidents. In May of that year a strike which occurred in a Japanese textile mill in Shanghai was supported by a student demonstration and parade. The Shanghai municipal police, under the command of a British officer, fired on the demonstrators, killing and wounding a number of them. This gave the signal for violent anti-foreign outbreaks in Shanghai and several other cities. In Canton students demonstrating outside the foreign concession of Shameen were fired upon by British police and suffered a considerable number of casualties. This incident led to a wave of hostility against Great Britain and a widespread and effective boycott of British goods. The strength of the anti-foreign outbursts made such a strong impression on the American government and public opinion that eventually it led to a change in American policy.

The American government had to take into account two opposing views of what should be done in China. The American press and public opinion were very largely in sympathy with the aspirations of the Chinese to get rid of what they called the "unequal treaties" and to abolish foreign rights and privileges in China. The Board of China Missions took the same view, a fact which had considerable effect on public opinion in the United States. The American Chamber of Commerce in Shanghai, which expressed the opinion of many businessmen, took the view, however, that Chinese nationalism was entirely Soviet managed and engineered, and recommended a tough policy towards it. The same clash of opinion ran through the diplomatic service. The Secretary of State, Mr. Kellogg, never deviated from a sympathetic view of Chinese nationalist aspirations and cautiously worked to support them. He was supported in this policy by Mr. Nelson T. Johnson, the chief of the Far Eastern Department in the Department of State. On the other hand, the then Minister to China, Mr. MacMurray, held that the treaty rights should be defended against any encroachments by the Chinese. Like many of the businessmen in China and even some of the local missionaries, in contrast to the policy of their boards, MacMurray believed that concessions would merely encourage further attacks on foreigners as well as on treaty rights. He believed that these rights should be defended, if necessary by the use of military force. The moderate policy, however, prevailed.

Following the incidents of 1925 Secretary Kellogg called the long delayed Tariff Conference into session in Peking and started the Commission on Extraterritoriality on its work in China. The Tariff Conference agreed, at least in principle, that China should recover her full tariff autonomy by January 1, 1929, at the latest. The Commission on Extraterritoriality reported early in 1927 that extraterritorial rights should be given up only when a program of legal and judicial reform had been accomplished in China. The standards set by the Commission obviously could not be met in the near future. Mr. Kellogg's cautious attitude towards treaty revision did not keep up with the pace of the Chinese nationalist revolution. In the summer of 1926 the Kuomintang launched its Northern Expedition from Canton and soon set up a provisional government in Hankow. The anti-foreign incidents that occurred during the revolutionary drive did not change the determination of the American government not to use threats or force to defend American rights.

The first public declaration of a new policy came from the British government, which announced in December 1926 that with the changed situation in China the foreign powers should "disclaim any intention of forcing foreign control upon an unwilling China." In answer to the British move, Mr. Kellogg, who felt that the British had stolen the initiative, declared in January 1927 that the United States would be willing to negotiate a new treaty on tariff and extraterritoriality with any delegation which could speak for the whole of China. If necessary, the United States would act alone.

Both British and American policies were put to a severe test in April 1927, when Chinese troops attacked foreigners and foreign property during the capture of Nanking by the forces of Chiang Kai-shek. This attack was actually a deliberate attempt on the part of Chinese Communist elements to discredit Chiang Kai-shek with the foreign powers and thus prevent him from securing their recognition and support in setting up a new government. President Coolidge and Mr. Kellogg helped to set the tone of foreign reaction to this incident by refusing to be diverted into punitive action by the loud demands from the American minister and others in China for military intervention and sanctions. Mr. Coolidge decided to wait until the dust had settled, declaring that he would be ready to deal with the authority which would emerge from the turmoil. The United States was the first to recognize the new National Government of China, which was established at Nanking in October 1928, and was the first to conclude a tariff treaty. After other powers followed suit, China recovered her full tariff autonomy in 1930. Mr. Kellogg, however, was unable to bring to a successful conclusion his negotiations with the Chinese for the abolition of extraterritoriality, a subject on which his sympathies were entirely with the Chinese. In spite of this setback it seemed at the time as if China were well on the way towards regaining full equality in her relations with the treaty powers. The process was soon to be interrupted by the renewal of Japanese aggression on the mainland and Japan's challenge to the principal aims of American policy in the Far East.

Conflict with Japan

The adjustment of United States and Japanese policies in the Far East which had been made in the Washington Treaties remained undisturbed, at least on the surface, for a decade. It was a decade during which the United States, which never joined the League, took an important step towards accepting, in treaty form, the renunciation of war. The Briand-Kellogg Peace Pact, known as the Pact of Paris, concluded in August 1928, and eventually adhered to by most countries, renounced the use of war as an instrument of national policy. The Pact of Paris contained no sanctions for its enforcement and most of the signatories reserved the right to use war in self-defense, but with all these limitations it expressed a view, widely held in the United States, that such international agreements would strengthen public opinion in restraining aggression and preventing war. Japan was one of the signatories of the Pact of Paris.

America generously assisted the Japanese people at the time of the earthquake of 1923, but in 1924 Congress passed immigration laws which discriminated against the Japanese on a racial basis. The immigration legislation continued to be a cause of considerable irritation to the Japanese, but whatever its ultimate psychological impact may have been, it was not in itself a sufficiently important issue to disturb the political settlement reached in Washington. It was the world economic crisis, which began in 1929, that imposed upon many countries pressures and strains which led to far-reaching domestic changes and to a sharp increase in international tension. Nowhere was this more true than in Japan where economic distress, aggravated particularly by the collapse of the American market for raw silk, helped to bring to a head those inner conflicts which lay behind the new drive for continental expansion.

The new Japanese military drive, however, did not get under way until the fall of 1931. In 1930 Japan was still willing to attend the London Naval Conference, which extended until 1936 the naval ratios for capital ships that had been established at Washington in 1922. In addition to this the naval powers also agreed, partly for economic reasons, to limitations in other categories such as light cruisers, destroyers, and submarines. The Japanese secured a more favorable ratio in these categories, but they did not succeed in their attempt to improve their ratio in capital ships. This failure rankled with Japan's naval leaders but did not prevent the Japanese government from ratifying the treaty.

A year later, on September 19, 1931, the Japanese army struck in Manchuria in violation of the Washington Treaties and of the Pact of Paris. The Manchurian incident coincided with the growing economic crisis in the West. It started, in fact, on the very day that Great Britain went off the gold standard. The depression undoubtedly accounted for the neutral reaction of so much of the world to Japanese aggression. The conquest of Manchuria, the establishment of the puppet state of Manchukuo, and the attack at Shanghai were a challenge to the American policies of maintaining the Open Door and the territorial and administrative integrity of China. The Chinese government at once appealed to the League of Nations, which took the matter under jurisdiction. Secretary Stimson decided to work with the League of Nations in preference to dealing directly with Japan. The League was an instrument through which world opinion and pressure could be mobilized against Japan, thus avoiding "the picture of a private quarrel between two nations." The League of Nations also had the machinery with which to handle such problems, machinery which the Washington Treaties failed to provide. Stimson therefore decided to "furnish independent support to the League rather than to play a role of leadership." This he did by having American "observers" attend League meetings, by supporting League resolutions with separate diplomatic notes to Japan, and by permitting American participation in the Lytton Commission sent by the League to Manchuria. It was Stimson's view that it was wiser to handle the situation with caution rather than to apply open pressure, which he feared would play into the hands of the Japanese militarists by weakening the position of the civilian government.

The League approached the Manchurian problem by trying first to secure withdrawal of troops on both sides as a condition for negotiation. When this did not work, the League set a time limit for a withdrawal of Japanese troops to the railroad zones. As this did not restrain the Japanese, the League decided to send the Lytton Commission to investigate the situation. At that time the Japanese promised not to aggravate matters by forcing the Chinese from the city of Chinchow, their last foothold on Manchurian soil. When the Japanese took Chinchow on January 3, 1932, Secretary Stimson decided that the approach which had been followed up to this time had to be abandoned. Stimson took the initiative by sending his famous non-recognition statement to Japan and China. In this he was following a precedent set by Secretary Bryan in 1915 on the occasion of the Twenty-One Demands, but Stimson's note was broader in scope. Stimson hoped that if the principle of non-recognition could gain general acceptance, it would help to discourage aggression by notifying the aggressors that the fruits of their actions would not be recognized by other countries. If successful, this measure would have provided at least diplomatic sanctions to the Pact of Paris, a document to which Stimson's note referred.

The non-recognition note stated that the United States:

. . . cannot admit the legality of any situation *de facto*, nor does it intend to recognize any treaty or agreement entered into between those Governments, or agents thereof, which may impair the treaty rights of the United States or its citizens in China, including those which relate to the sovereignty, the independence, or the territorial and administrative integrity of the Republic of China, or to the international policy relative to China, commonly known as the open door policy; and that it does not intend to recognize any situation, treaty, or agreement which may be brought about by means contrary to the covenants and obligations of the Pact of Paris of August 27, 1928, to which Treaty both China and Japan, as well as the United States, are parties.[2]

Before sending the note Stimson communicated its contents to the British and French ambassadors in Washington but did not receive the hoped-for support. On the contrary, the British communiqué of January 11 stated that the British government had confidence in Japan's assurances about maintaining the open door in Manchuria and therefore regarded it as unnecessary to address the Japanese government along the lines of Stimson's note. The British communiqué did not refer to the territorial and administrative integrity of China or to the Kellogg-Briand Pact, both of which were the main concern of American policy. The *London Times*, in a government-inspired editorial, claimed that no such Chinese administrative integrity existed, either in 1922 or at the time of writing. The French agreed. When hostilities spread to Shanghai in January, 1932, Secretary Stimson again approached the British government with a view to making a joint statement upholding the territorial and administrative integrity of China as agreed to in the Nine Power Treaty, but it soon became clear that the British did not wish to join in any such move.

Stimson then outlined the American position in a letter to Senator Borah, in which he declared that the various agreements of the Washington Conference formed a whole and that

the willingness of the American Government to surrender its then commanding lead in battleship construction and to leave its positions at Guam and in the Philippines without further fortification, was predicated upon, among other things, the self-denying covenants contained in the Nine Power Treaty, which assured the nations of the world not only of equal opportunity for their Eastern trade but also against the military aggrandizement of any other power at the expense of China. One cannot discuss the possibility of modifying or abrogating those provisions of the Nine Power Treaty without considering at the same time the other promises upon which they were really dependent . . .[3]

Stimson went on to express the opinion that if other governments would join in the policy of non-recognition, a legal barrier would be built up against aggression which would "eventually lead to the restoration to China of rights and titles of which she may have been deprived. . . ."[4] In March 1932, the

[2] Harley F. MacNair and Donald F. Lach, *Modern Far Eastern Relations* (New York, 1955), p. 312.
[3] Quoted in T. A. Bisson, *America's Far Eastern Policy* (New York, 1945), p. 33.
[4] *Ibid.*, pp. 33–34.

Assembly of the League of Nations actually passed a resolution binding the members "not to recognize any situation, treaty or agreement which may be brought about by means contrary to the Covenant of the League of Nations." A year later the Assembly accepted the Lytton Report which found Japan guilty of aggression and adopted a resolution obligating League members not to recognize the puppet state of Manchukuo.

The League resolution was an achievement for Stimson's policy of working with the League, and the general denial of Japan's legal title to her acquisitions was not without value. But it was also a feeble echo of what might have been achieved with effective Anglo-American cooperation. It was the breakdown of that cooperation at the critical moment which, in Stimson's opinion, greatly encouraged the Japanese, who were quick to follow the argument of the *London Times* that China was not in reality a unified state. In an insulting and ironical note to the United States government, the Japanese proceeded to argue that the Washington Treaties had to be applied according to present conditions in China. Since the Chinese officials had fled from Manchuria, the Japanese claimed that it was necessary for the local population to replace them. In a sarcastic passage the Japanese note continued: "The Japanese government cannot think that the Chinese people, unlike all others, are destitute of the power of self-determination and of organizing themselves in order to secure civilized conditions when deserted by the existing officials." In Stimson's view this was "the basis of the argument upon which 'Manchukuo' was immediately afterward constructed." One week after the League approved the principle of non-recognition of Manchukuo, Stimson went out of office.

President Roosevelt and Secretary of State Hull were more interested in re-establishing normal economic relations with Japan than in vigorously opposing Japan's challenge to American policy in China. The major effort of the administration was directed toward the solving of the domestic economic crisis and, as far as foreign affairs were concerned, most other objectives were subordinated to the effort to revive trade and maintain the peace. Although the Stimson doctrine of non-recognition remained in force, Mr. Hull made it clear that the United States welcomed trade not only with Japan but also with the puppet state of Manchukuo. In declining a goodwill mission from Japan on the grounds that it would not be very effective, Hull suggested that more good could be accomplished by less discrimination against American goods in "Manchukuo." This was a far cry from the attitude of Secretary Stimson.

The same search for means by which to bolster the American economy led to various economic measures in support of the National Government of China, but these also resulted from the desire to compensate China for the inaction of the West during the Manchurian crisis. The United States, as well as the League of Nations, sent various missions to China to assist in such fields as health, education, highway construction, and agriculture.

A League of Nations Educational Mission, composed of Europeans, pointed out in its report the great need for China to integrate modern education more with her own past and her own needs, and to borrow less from abroad. If there were borrowing to be done, the mission recommended the European model as being more suitable to China's needs than the American educational system, which, it claimed, the Chinese identified with modern education. In order to counteract this report, an American educational mission went to China to re-emphasize the suitability of the American educational model for modern China. The American system continued to have great influence, partly because the United States poured more money into Chinese education than did any other foreign country. The economic aid which marked this period was motivated partly by the need to find outlets for American surplus agricultural products. China was granted a three-year credit in American wheat and cotton to the value of $50,000,000 by the Reconstruction Finance Corporation, but China actually absorbed only $17,-000,000 of this loan. American military aid was limited mainly to the building up of the Chinese air force. An American aviation company established a military aircraft assembly plant in China, and American firms assisted their government in the establishment of training schools for Chinese pilots. These contacts led to the sale of an increasing number of American aircraft to the Chinese government. In this trade and aid to China, America was in competition with several European countries such as Great Britain, Germany, France, and Italy, all of whom had technical and military missions in China and all of whom were participating in China's expanding foreign trade.

Japan, jealous of China's growing intimacy with the Western powers and of her economic and military expansion, issued a warning statement in April 1934. This statement, made by an unofficial spokesman of the Japanese Foreign Office, a Mr. Amau, was clearly designed to be a trial balloon. According to the Amau statement China shared with Japan responsibility for the maintenance of peace in East Asia; Japan opposed "any attempt on the part of China to avail herself of the influence of any other country in order to resist Japan"; and "any joint operations undertaken by foreign powers even in the name of technical or financial assistance . . . are bound to acquire political significance." Japan particularly opposed military assistance to China and foreign credits given for what Japan considered to be political purposes. Although the Amau statement was unofficial, Secretary Hull could hardly ignore it. In May 1934, Hull issued a statement in which he pointed out that according to American opinion multilateral treaties could not be unilaterally denounced. The United States did not modify its policy in China as a result of the Amau statement; neither did the Japanese government modify the policies which it had foreshadowed in this unofficial manner.

In spite of their professed concern for the economic stability of China, the Japanese were especially annoyed at the success of the Chinese currency reforms in 1935. The problem began when the U. S. Treasury raised the purchase price of silver, a measure instigated by senators of the silver states. The higher prices for silver had a disastrous effect on China, whose currency was based on silver which it had to purchase on the world market. At a time when all other countries had gone off gold to reduce the value of their currencies in order to compete in international trade, China was exposed to a serious deflation which gravely affected her national finances and her internal economy. The efforts of the Chinese government to regulate the flow of silver through export tariffs failed in the face of large-scale smuggling which was carried on mainly by Japanese banks. Currency reform became essential. A British mission headed by Sir Frederick Leith-Ross arrived in China in September 1935 and assisted in the planning of currency reform measures to change from silver to a controlled paper currency. Although British political support was of assistance in this change, it was American financial aid that made it possible. The U. S. Treasury arranged with the Chinese National Government to purchase, at an artificially high rate, the silver currency which had been successfully withdrawn from circulation and exchanged for paper notes. As the United States purchased only from the National Government at this established rate, smuggling became unprofitable. The gains which were made from this operation were used by China to build up foreign currency reserves to back up the new currency. The currency reforms were of the utmost importance in strengthening the financial position of the National Government and in stabilizing the economy. The American contribution to currency reform did nothing to improve her relations with Japan, who had plans to bring China within the "yen bloc."

The success of the United States and Great Britain in strengthening the National Government was countered by new Japanese moves in North China. Japan's deliberate attempt to establish puppet regimes in North China was not only an attack on the National Government but also on the basic American policy of maintaining the territorial and administrative integrity of China. In the face of this latest demonstration of Japanese disregard for treaty obligations, Secretary Hull made a statement in which he referred very obliquely to events in North China and reiterated America's respect for treaties.

Secretary Hull retreated, not only in words but also in deeds, from the position which Secretary Stimson had adopted towards Japanese aggression. Stimson's argument that Japan's violation of the Nine Power Pact violated the whole interrelated Washington Treaty system was a warning to both Japan and Great Britain that the United States might not consider itself bound to the naval and fortification limitations which she had accepted with the understanding that Japan would refrain from attacking China. Far from carrying out this implied threat, Mr. Hull persisted in every effort to renew the naval arrangements as if they were unconnected with events on the mainland, while Japan took the initiative in terminating the Washington-London naval treaties. In 1933 Japan served notice that she would not be willing to renew the naval treaties after their expiration in 1936. In her negotiations with the naval powers Japan demanded parity, and when this was not conceded, Japan withdrew and resumed freedom of action.

The more Japan appeared to be bent on war, the more the United States seemed determined to take every measure to avoid getting involved. The most far-reaching and public expression of this determination was the neutrality legislation of the middle thirties. Congressional approval of this legislation seems to have arisen from two main streams of public opinion. One was the isolationist attitude which opposed American involvement in any foreign entanglements. At this time the isolationists found allies among idealists disillusioned by the failure of the League to apply sanctions against Italian aggression in Abyssinia in 1935. The other stream of public opinion stemmed from the New Deal investigations of the munitions industries, which encouraged the view that wars are caused by "merchants of death" and that America is always in danger of being drawn into foreign wars by the profit-seeking munitions makers. It was not considered enough to remain neutral within the framework of international law. It was necessary to impose upon the American government additional limitations which would prevent American involvement in foreign conflicts through the sale and transportation of arms to belligerents.

The first neutrality act in August 1935 set up the basic provision that there should be an embargo on the export of implements of war "upon the outbreak or during the progress of war." The President could also warn Americans not to travel on the vessels of belligerents except at their own risk. The second neutrality act of February 1936 prohibited loans to belligerents and further limited the President's discretion in imposing an embargo. The third neutrality act, May 1937, went even further and made the embargo applicable not only to formally declared wars but also to civil strife and undeclared wars. Commodities other than implements of war could be sold to belligerents only on a "cash-and-carry" basis. It was left to the discretion of the President to decide when a state of war existed and when the cash-and-carry provisions should be applied. In May 1937, the Japanese militarists had every reason to assume that they could proceed with their adventures on the continent without the slightest danger of interference by the United States.

Sino-Japanese War, 1937–1941

The reaction of the United States to the Sino-Japanese conflict, which began in July 1937, was to avoid involvement. Secretary Hull made a statement to the general effect that the United States loved peace, but he said nothing about the territorial integrity of China, Japanese aggression, or any measures that should be taken. The statement was so broad and meaningless that sixty nations, including Japan, could agree with it, and it was left to Portugal to point out, in a vigorous answer, that grave problems could not be solved by "vague formulae." When the fighting extended to Shanghai, the State Department warned American citizens that they would stay in China at their own risk, and nearly half of them departed. There was no question but that American lives and property were endangered by the course of the war, especially by Japanese bombing. The United States and other governments poured protests and claims for reparations into Tokyo.

The Japanese did not declare war on China. It was therefore left to the discretion of the President whether or not to declare a state of war. He was under considerable pressure to enforce the neutrality laws, even if this helped Japan, especially when that country imposed a coastal blockade on China early in the hostilities. President Roosevelt prohibited U. S. government-owned vessels from carrying war materials to either China or Japan and warned private vessels that they could carry such materials only at their own risk. These steps were of disadvantage to China which, unlike Japan, did not have her own merchant fleet, but went far enough to pacify those who were clamoring for the full application of the neutrality legislation, which would have hurt China far more. News of Japanese bombing of civilian populations and of the atrocities committed by the Japanese army pushed the issue into the background. In fact public opinion began to swing more and more in favor of action to restrain Japan. In October 1937, President Roosevelt made an open attack on neutrality and isolationism in his so-called Quarantine Speech, in which he compared aggression to a contagious disease which could be controlled only by quarantine. The implication was that the U. S. should apply economic sanctions against Japan and Germany. Public reaction to the speech showed that the American people were not yet ready to accept the argument that collective action should be taken against the aggressor.

China had appealed to the League of Nations, which referred the issue to the signatories of the Nine Power Pact, who in turn called a conference at Brussels to which they invited other interested powers. The conference, it was clear, would not accept any proposals for sanctions against Japan, but Japan refused to attend even for the purpose of negotiation. The conference adjourned and no further international effort was made to bring the hostilities to an end.

In the meantime the destruction of foreign lives and property, which accompanied the war, continued without pause. On December 12, 1937, American and British vessels on the Yangtze River were attacked by the Japanese, and the American gunboat *Panay* was sunk with some loss of life. The United States government protested through the Japanese ambassador and requested that the Emperor be informed of President Roosevelt's "shock and concern." The Japanese government moved hastily to express its profound regrets and "sincere apologies" and to pay indemnification. In April 1938, a check for $2,214,007.36 was paid to the U. S. Treasury and the incident was regarded as closed. Although the American government was fully satisfied that the attack on the *Panay* was deliberate, the acceptance of the settlement made it clear that the United States was not ready to do anything to stop Japan at this time. During 1938, however, the mounting number of incidents involving the loss of American life and property, the dramatic reports of American missionaries and journalists on the sufferings of the Chinese people, and the almost total disregard of American treaty rights gradually brought about a growing sympathy for the Chinese cause and a hardening of opinion against Japan. Private organizations, such as the Committee on Non-Participation in Japanese Aggression, helped to organize opinion against

Japan. Protests against the selling of scrap iron, high octane gasoline, of planes and plane parts to Japan and a popular boycott of Japanese goods preceded action by the government in restraint of Japanese aggression.

The State Department contented itself during 1938 with sending notes of protest to Japan against the many violations of American rights and attacks on American citizens. The notes had no visible effect on the Japanese government. In the spring of that year Secretary Hull, without taking official action, appealed to American airplane manufacturers not to sell bombing planes to Japan. By this time even the American Chamber of Commerce in Shanghai was convinced that the Japanese had every intention of ousting all American business from China, and recommended a firm stand. In October, 1938, the State Department sent Japan a note listing all the Japanese treaty violations and attacks on American lives and property and contrasted this with the lack of retaliatory measures by the United States against Japanese economic interests. The note pointed out

. . . the existence of a great and growing disparity between the treatment accorded American nationals and their trade and enterprise by Japanese authorities in China and Japan and the treatment accorded Japanese nationals and their trade and enterprise by the Government of the United States in areas within its jurisdiction.[5]

The Japanese government was specifically requested to discontinue discriminating against Americans and their trade and enterprise and interfering with American property and other rights. In the meantime the Japanese announced the establishment of a New Order in East Asia, thus in effect refuting the whole treaty system. On November 18 Japan answered the American note, denying the American charges and declaring:

At present Japan, devoting its entire energy to the establishment of a new order based on genuine international justice throughout East Asia, is making rapid strides towards the attainment of this objective. The successful accomplishment of this purpose is not only indispensable to the existence of Japan, but also constitutes the very foundation of the enduring peace and stability of East Asia.

It is the firm conviction of the Japanese Government that now, at a time of the continuing development of new conditions in East Asia, an attempt to apply to present and future conditions without any changes concepts and principles which were applicable to conditions prevailing before the present incident does not in any way contribute to the solution of immediate issues and further does not in the least promote the firm establishment of enduring peace in East Asia.

The Imperial Government, however, does not have any intention of objecting to the participation in the great work of the reconstruction of East Asia by Your Excellency's country or by other Powers, in all fields of trade and industry, when such participation is undertaken with an understanding of the purport of the above stated remarks; and further, I believe that the regimes now being formed in China are also prepared to welcome such participation.[6]

In other words, the Japanese government was saying that it would brook no interference with its New Order in East Asia but it would permit America and other countries to participate economically in its venture.

[5] Foreign Relations of the United States, Japan, 1931–1941, Department of State (Washington, 1943), Vol. I, p. 790.
[6] Ibid., p. 800.

The United States naturally refuted the Japanese claim to have established a New Order on the grounds that Japan had no right unilaterally to abrogate the treaties. Hull also pointed out that the changes in the situation had been brought about by Japanese action. He declared his willingness, however, to negotiate revision of the treaties with all the parties concerned if the Japanese had any just and reasonable proposals.

At the same time that Hull was keeping open the door to diplomatic negotiation, the American government began to give more aid to China and to impose economic limitations on Japan. In December 1938, the U. S. extended a credit of $25,000,000 to China and the British government also made credits available. In retaliation the Japanese put pressure on the British in the spring of 1939 and tried to force the British government to make economic and political concessions by blockading the British concession in Tientsin and humiliating British subjects in China. At this point the American government decided that the time had come to denounce the Commercial Treaty of 1911 with Japan and thus be free to apply economic pressure. The termination of the treaty, announced in July 1939, became effective in January 1940.

The war in Europe, which began in September 1939, changed the balance of power in the Pacific. The Japanese immediately demanded the removal of foreign troops from China, and the British and French governments, failing to get American support, were compelled to yield. Anxious to keep the Japanese from joining the Axis camp, the British and French governments approached the Department of State toward the end of 1939 with proposals for a compromise peace in the Far East. Hull refused to accept either this proposal or the suggestion of Ambassador Grew that some concessions be made to the Japanese government in the hope of strengthening its hand with the militarists. When the Commercial Treaty expired, Hull refused to replace it with another. Now that the British and French were in no position to exercise any restraining influence, Japan went ahead with the establishment of a puppet regime in central China. Hull not only refused Japan's request to cooperate with this regime but also extended further credits to the National Government in order to keep it in the war.

The blitzkrieg in Europe in the spring and summer of 1940 brought about the collapse of France and Holland and a serious weakening of Great Britain. Japan therefore prepared to move into Southeast Asia, particularly French Indo-China, a base from which she later embarked on her career of conquest. The United States could do little but protest. The shock of the fall of France, however, brought about a tremendous increase in America's rearmament program. Defense appropriations went up to wartime levels, military conscription was introduced, a 70 per cent increase in the size of the navy was authorized in order to defend both the Atlantic and the Pacific, and economic measures were approved which enabled the President to control the export of any materials considered necessary for the arming of America. Between the summer of 1940 and the spring of 1941 the United

States stopped the export of most of the raw materials which Japan had been purchasing.

In September 1940, Japan signed the Tripartite Pact with Germany and Italy, a move which brought Japan's relations with the United States to an obvious crisis. This pact, which arranged for Japanese domination of East Asia and German-Italian domination of Europe, included a military alliance which was obviously aimed at the United States. Following the pact there developed much more unity of action between the British and American governments, both of which adopted a much stiffer attitude towards Japan. In October Great Britain reopened the Burma Road, which Japanese pressure had forced her to close for a period of three months during the Battle of Britain. At the same time the United States sent liners to the Far East to repatriate its nationals, a move which indicated not a retreat but a disposition to prepare for any eventuality. On the same day that Japan formally recognized its puppet regime at Nanking, the United States granted a $100,000,000 credit to Chiang Kai-shek. The British followed with a credit of £10,000,000. The American objectives in all these moves were to support Great Britain, to prevent Japan from taking over the whole of Southeast Asia, and if possible to keep Japan out of the war. In furtherance of this policy it was important to support Nationalist China in its resistance to Japan.

The United States made a major effort during 1941 to achieve this program through a negotiated settlement with Japan. The negotiations began in February 1941, when a new Japanese ambassador, Admiral Nomura, arrived in Washington, D. C. With some interruptions the negotiations were continued from February until the attack at Pearl Harbor. Admiral Nomura was joined in November by a special envoy, Saburo Kurusu, who was with him to the end. Suggestions for a settlement had reached the American government through unofficial channels before Nomura's arrival. These overtures developed into an informal proposal for a general settlement in the Pacific area which the Japanese government presented on April 9. The Japanese suggestions amounted to a promise to water down the Axis alliance and a peace plan for China. Chiang Kai-shek's government was to be merged with the Nanking puppet regime; the Chinese were to recognize Manchukuo, and the Japanese were to withdraw from China. If Chiang Kai-shek refused to accept these terms, the United States was to cease all aid to China. In exchange for these concessions the Japanese expected resumption of normal economic relations with the United States, an American gold loan, and general American economic assistance. In answer, Secretary of State Cordell Hull submitted four general principles which he insisted must be accepted before detailed negotiations would be carried on. These amounted to a restatement of traditional American policy. The Japanese replied on May 12 with their first official proposals for a settlement.

The official proposal differed in tone and content from the unofficial overtures of April. Japan reaffirmed her Axis alignment and the United States was to guarantee her neutrality in the European conflict. The United

States was also to request Chiang Kai-shek to make peace with Japan on Japan's terms and to discontinue aid if China refused. Japan, as before, demanded resumption of normal trade relations with the United States and aid in securing access to the natural resources of Southeast Asia. Detailed discussions of these proposals with the Japanese revealed that conditions for a peace settlement with China would include Japanese military domination of the five northern provinces as a measure of "joint defense against Communism." In spite of the unacceptability of these proposals Mr. Hull continued negotiations in the hope of delaying, if not averting, a Japanese move toward war. He was strongly supported by the British, Australian, and Netherlands governments, all of which pointed out that they were not prepared to resist a Japanese attack. In a note of June 21 the United States tried to cull from the negotiations a further basis for an agreement. Both sides were to declare their peaceful intentions. Concretely, Japan was to agree not to invoke the Tripartite Pact against the United States if it were to be drawn into the European war in self-defense; the United States would suggest to China negotiations with Japan after Japan and America had agreed on the terms; normal trade relations were to be resumed and Japan was to be assisted in securing access to the natural resources of Southeast Asia. The Japanese gave no indication that they would agree to any such basis of negotiation.

Hitler's attack on the Soviet Union, June 22, 1941, undertaken without first informing the Japanese, could have provided both the excuse and the occasion for Japan to withdraw from the Tripartite Pact. Cordell Hull was very much aware of this, but before diplomacy could exploit the new situation the Japanese army moved into the southern part of Indo-China, ignoring President Roosevelt's immediate offer to secure an international guarantee neutralizing that country. To the surprise of the Japanese government the United States reacted to the Indo-China move on July 26 by freezing Japanese assets in the United States, thus bringing the differences between the two countries to a head. Japan now had the choice either of fighting or of recovering her trade with the United States, Great Britain, and the Netherlands at the price of concessions. The Japanese government opened negotiations again as early as August 6 with new proposals which went far beyond anything Japan had ever demanded before. Hitler's initial success in the war against the Soviet Union apparently gave the Japanese the feeling that their own relative position had been vastly improved. The Japanese now demanded removal of trade restrictions, suspension of American military preparations in the Southwest Pacific, and American pressure on China to settle with Japan. For their part the Japanese offered only a promise to withdraw troops from Indo-China after a settlement with China and on condition that America recognize Japan's special position in that colony.

The Japanese proposals were taken up at the meeting between President Roosevelt and Prime Minister Churchill on board ship in the Atlantic in August 1941. According to Churchill's memoirs Roosevelt planned to continue negotiating with the Japanese in order to gain at least another month's

time, but it was agreed that Japan would be warned that "any further encroachment by Japan in the Southwest Pacific would produce a situation
in which the United States Government would be compelled to take counter-
measures, even though these might lead to war between the United States
and Japan." [7] This warning was actually included in the President's statement to the Japanese ambassador on August 17 in a form which, while leaving out specific reference to war and the Southwest Pacific, conveyed the
same meaning.

In view of the Japanese position Roosevelt and Hull felt that a proposed
meeting between the President and Prince Konoe, to which they agreed in
principle, could not achieve any useful purpose unless it were preceded by a
prior agreement on basic principles. Roosevelt suggested that the proposed
meeting should take place in Juneau, Alaska, around the middle of October.
In spite of every American effort not even the most tentative commitments
could be extracted from the Japanese. By this time anyone in Japan who was
willing to make even a tactical concession to the American position was
likely to be assassinated. Even Konoe's life was in danger from the inflexible,
ultra-nationalist, terrorist societies, although there is no evidence that
Konoe was ever willing to abandon any part of his own program for Japan's
expansion in East Asia. This was quite clear as late as October when
Konoe knew that if he failed to secure an American agreement not to interfere with Japan's program for East Asia, his cabinet would fall and the
military extremists take over. The Imperial Conference of September 6
had decided to complete preparations for war with the United States, Great
Britain, and the Netherlands by the end of October unless the United States
met Japan's demands.

Konoe's position was never more clearly revealed than in October
when the Japanese Minister-Counselor, who had just returned to Washington from Tokyo, held several informal talks with the American Under
Secretary of State on the subject of the negotiations and the situation in
Japan. Mr. Hull joined in the later talks. The Minister-Counselor stated
that the Konoe government would soon have to show results if it were not
to be overthrown by the radical pro-Axis group. While the Minister-Counselor implied that the Japanese government was not willing to yield any
ground, he wondered whether there were not some concessions that America
could make. He indicated that the two countries could arrive at an understanding on basic principles if the China question were left out, a comment
which elicited from the American Under Secretary the reply that this was
like asking whether the play *Hamlet* could be presented without the character
Hamlet. In other words the Minister-Counselor was making it more than
clear that Konoe was in an utterly impossible predicament. The only way
in which Konoe could remain in power and thus prevent the militarists
from gambling everything on a military victory in cooperation with the Axis
was to secure from the United States concessions which would placate the
military. The United States could not possibly make the required conces-

[7] Winston S. Churchill, *The Grand Alliance* (Boston, 1950), p. 440.

sions. While she had not gone to war in defense of China, and was not likely to do so, she could not assist Japan in her conquest of that country. To have accepted Japan's rule in China would have been not only morally indefensible but also a political and military blunder of the first order. China was then America's one possible Asiatic ally in a conflict with Japan. To have extricated Japan from the war with China would have been to permit her to turn her full forces against the Western powers and the United States. The economic concessions demanded by Konoe were not for the peaceful development of the Japanese economy but for the strengthening of her military power. An American surrender to Japanese demands, far from avoiding war, would have given Japan even greater strength with which to attack. America clearly could not avoid war by appeasing Japan.

The United States, however, had a vital interest in preventing or delaying a Japanese attack on the British, French, and Dutch positions in Southeast Asia. At a time when Holland and most of France were occupied by Hitler and Great Britain was still in grave danger, such an attack could well complete the destruction of the Western European powers. The President and the Chiefs of Staff held the view that it was essential for American security to have friendly powers in Western Europe. After the fall of France America became the "Arsenal of Democracy" and took every measure, short of war, to support Great Britain in her struggle for survival. As Western Europe was the cornerstone of American strategy, the vital interests of the United States were involved when Japan threatened the Asiatic possessions of the Western powers. When the Japanese moved their troops into southern Indo-China after the Nazi attack on the Soviet Union, the United States had to make a decisive move. The freezing of Japanese assets in the United States and parallel action by the British and Dutch was intended to restrain Japan from attacking Southeast Asia. But the Japanese had reached the point of no return.

On October 17 General Tojo became premier. We now know from the records of the War Crimes Tribunal that the decision for war had been made and that Tojo had every intention of enforcing it. Negotiations, however, were continued. On November 15, Cordell Hull handed Nomura the draft of a joint declaration on economic policy which amounted to a reiteration of the American position that normal relations with Japan could be restored as part of a general economic agreement restoring China's economic independence within the framework of the Open Door. While Hull indicated that this would be only one part of a general settlement, he seems to have believed that by meeting Japan's economic needs he could temper her military ambitions. It was at this time that the special Japanese envoy, Saburo Kurusu, a career diplomat, arrived in Washington to participate in the conversations, but he brought with him no new suggestions. The last statement of the American position was made on November 26, and the Japanese, although unwilling to accept this as a basis for agreement, kept up the negotiations in order to improve their chances of a surprise attack at Pearl Harbor. On December 7, 1941, the United States and Japan were at war.

2. STRATEGY OF WAR AND PEACE

The Atlantic Charter

The United States entered the conflict with its war aims already stated. They were stated in the Atlantic Charter, drawn up in August 1941, by Roosevelt and Churchill. The military chiefs of both nations had long been in close touch with each other and the United States had already taken every measure short of war to help Great Britain survive the onslaught of Nazi Germany. By the Lend-Lease Act of March 1941, the Congress made it possible to give considerable material assistance to the British, thus in effect modifying the neutrality legislation, which was finally taken off the books in November 1941. It was this practical cooperation between America and Great Britain which gave rise to the joint statement of principles for which to fight the war and on which to base the peace. The Atlantic Charter eventually formed the basis of the Grand Alliance of all powers involved in the war with Nazi Germany, Italy, and Japan and was the initial move towards the establishment of the United Nations Organization. Except for freedom of religion, which was accidentally omitted at the time but included later, it contained President Roosevelt's earlier affirmation of his belief in the Four Freedoms as the basis for a peaceful world. The eight articles of the Atlantic Charter had much of the spirit and the universal appeal of President Wilson's Fourteen Points. The charter reads:

The President of the United States of America and the Prime Minister, Mr. Churchill, representing His Majesty's Government in the United Kingdom, being met together, deem it right to make known certain common principles in the national policies of their respective countries on which they base their hopes for a better future for the world.

First, their countries seek no aggrandisement, territorial or other.

Second, they desire to see no territorial changes that do not accord with the freely expressed wishes of the peoples concerned.

Third, they respect the right of all peoples to choose the form of government under which they will live; and they wish to see sovereign rights and self-government restored to those who have been forcibly deprived of them.

Fourth, they will endeavour, with due respect for their existing obligations, to further the enjoyment by all States, great or small, victor or vanquished, of access, on equal terms, to the trade and to the raw materials of the world which are needed for their economic prosperity.

Fifth, they desire to bring about the fullest collaboration between all nations in the economic field, with the object of securing for all improved labour standards, economic advancement, and social security.

Sixth, after the final destruction of the Nazi tyranny they hope to see established a peace which will afford to all nations the means of dwelling in safety within their own boundaries, and which will afford assurance that all the men in all the lands may live out their lives in freedom from fear and want.

Seventh, such a peace should enable all men to traverse the high seas and oceans without hindrance.

Eighth, they believe that all the nations of the world, for realistic as well as spiritual reasons, must come to the abandonment of the use of force. Since no future peace can be maintained if land, sea, or air armaments continue to be employed by nations which threaten, or may threaten, aggression outside of their frontiers, they believe, pending the establishment of a wider and permanent system of general security, that the disarmament of such nations is essential. They will likewise aid and encourage all other practicable measures which will lighten for peace-loving peoples the crushing burden of armaments.[8]

The name Atlantic Charter was purely accidental; it referred only to the place in which it was drawn up. The Charter was a statement of principles which came to be applied to a war that finally enveloped the whole world. Although not yet a belligerent, the United States joined Great Britain in a statement which anticipated the destruction of Nazi tyranny, disclaimed territorial ambitions, and promised to restore sovereignty to the victims of aggression and freedom for all peoples to choose their own form of government. The two great powers went even further; they committed themselves to the idea of a permanent system of general security. In the original draft Churchill had suggested the phrase "effective international organization" but Roosevelt, mindful of the opposition to Wilson's League of Nations, modified the language, although not the meaning, in the final version. Mr. Churchill says in his memoirs that, "Considering all the tales of my reactionary, Old-World outlook," he is glad to record that the substance, spirit, and wording of the original draft came from him. Compared with World War I, there was indeed a remarkable unity of policy as well as of moral purpose between Britain and America in their plans and hopes for the future.

The most dramatic achievement stemming from the Atlantic Charter, which was accepted by the Grand Alliance of all nations at war with the Axis, was the fulfillment of the commitment to set up a permanent system of general security. Before the war was over the members of the Grand Alliance created the United Nations Organization at the San Francisco Conference of April 1945. President Roosevelt was particularly anxious, in view of President Wilson's experience with the League of Nations, to see the U.N.O. in being while the pressures of war still kept the allies together. Roosevelt considered the establishment of a permanent system of general security the overriding aim of the war and the best guarantee of the peace. In order to commit the powers to such a world security organization it was necessary to adjust the conflicting ambitions and interests of the many different powers which made up the Grand Alliance. To accomplish this President Roosevelt was willing to make concessions and to run risks.

The United States, for example, did not press the issue of the application of the Atlantic Charter to the colonial world of Southeast Asia. The issue arose out of Point 3 of the Charter, which had been drafted by Churchill himself, unaware that it would rise to plague him and the heads of other colonial powers. So persistent were the questions as to how Point 3 applied to colonial peoples that Churchill found it necessary to make a statement in the House of Commons:

At the Atlantic meeting we had in mind, primarily, the restoration of the sovereignty, self-government and national life of the States and nations of Europe now under the

[8] *Ibid.*, pp. 443–44.

Nazi yoke, and the principles governing any alterations in their territorial boundaries which may have to be made. So that is quite a separate problem from the progressive evolution of self-governing institutions in the regions, and people which owe allegiance to the British Crown.[9]

Queen Wilhelmina made a similar statement with respect to Indonesia. For President Roosevelt Point 3 had no such limitations. In a speech in February 1942, he stated:

We of the United Nations are agreed upon certain broad principles in the kind of peace we seek. The Atlantic Charter applies not only to the parts of the world that border the Atlantic but to the whole world; disarmament of aggressors, self-determination of nations and peoples, and . . . freedom of speech, freedom of religion, freedom from want, and freedom from fear.[10]

While the American government spoke for the record and committed itself to granting postwar independence to the Philippines, it did not seek to interfere in the relations between its democratic allies and their colonies. For this reason the war in Asia was fought without using the potential appeal of the Atlantic Charter.

The problems arising out of the colonial issue, however, were still minor when compared to the problem of dealing with the Soviet Union. This problem came down to a choice between two courses. One was to assume that postwar cooperation was impossible and to prepare for conflict, the other was to give cooperation a trial. During the course of the war it was Roosevelt's policy not only to commit the Soviet Union to the United Nations Organization, in which he succeeded, but also to commit her to the application of democratic principles in the countries taken by her armies, in which he failed. In the political arrangements made with the Soviet Union in the wartime conferences, the Americans and the British agreed to territorial and political concessions to the Russians in the hope that the Soviet Union would carry out all of its obligations. In these conferences the Russians agreed to support free elections based on free speech and civil liberties in Eastern Europe, and to support the National Government of China and not to interfere in its internal affairs.

The Build-up of China

To build up a system of general security in the Far East required the cooperation of a major Asian power. Looking ahead to the defeat of Japan and the elimination of her military strength and position in the Far East, the United States government came to regard China as the future stabilizing power in Eastern Asia. At the time of Pearl Harbor, however, the National Government was pressed back to the wartime capital of Chungking in western China. One of the main objects of American policy was to bolster China's resistance and to make her as effective an ally as possible. In prep-

[9] Robert E. Sherwood, *Roosevelt and Hopkins, An Intimate History* (rev. ed. New York, 1950), p. 363.
[10] *Ibid.*, p. 507.

aration for the role which China was to play the United States sponsored her as one of the Big Four, along with Great Britain and Soviet Russia. On American initiative and at American insistence the Chinese were brought into the big international conferences, at Moscow and at Cairo, and took part in the preliminary conversations concerning the establishment of the United Nations Organization, of whose Security Council she became a permanent member. Neither the British nor the Russians took China seriously as a great power but were willing to go along with American wishes in the matter. It was easy for them to accept the political build-up of China since this did not affect the major strategy of the war.

The military strategy of the war was to concentrate first on the war in Europe. This strategy was formulated by the Combined Chiefs of Staff, set up in Washington immediately after Pearl Harbor and made up of the British and American Joint Chiefs of Staff. It did not include the Russians, but every effort was made to coordinate strategy with them. Mr. Churchill points out:

> They had a far-distant, single, independent front, and there was neither need nor means of Staff integration. It was sufficient that we should know the general sweep and timing of their movements and that they should know ours. In these matters we kept in as close touch with them as they permitted.[11]

The strategy of "Europe first" meant that the major American as well as British efforts were directed towards the destruction of Nazi Germany. Therefore only very limited supplies of men and material were available for the war in China and even those so allocated were often diverted to other critical areas. The main brunt of the war against Japan was actually carried by the American navy and air force. It was not until the closing year that plans were under way for training and equipping Chinese forces which would be strong enough to take the offensive against the Japanese on the mainland. The Chinese, who were never included in the Combined Chiefs of Staff, had no way of changing the over-all strategy.

The emphasis on Europe made it more difficult for the United States to strengthen and prepare China for the leading role that she was expected to play in the postwar Far East. But the United States was the only power, at this time, which was in a position to give military assistance of any kind. Until the Nazi attack on the Soviet Union in the summer of 1941 it was the Russians who had given Nationalist China the most military assistance in materials of war and in technicians and advisers. After Russia was attacked very little aid reached China from any source, and after Pearl Harbor, followed by the fall of Southeast Asia to the Japanese, the position of China became truly desperate. The fall of Rangoon blocked the Burma Road, the last link between China and the western world. In February 1942, General Stilwell was sent to Burma as General Chiang Kai-shek's Chief of Staff to coordinate the efforts of Chinese and British forces in the defense of Burma and to reopen the Burma Road. At the same time the first preparations were

[11] Churchill, *op. cit.*, pp. 687–88.

made for the opening of the famous air route over the "Hump" from Assam to Kunming. In the meantime the Japanese drove the Allied forces out of Burma and threatened the Indian frontier. China now depended entirely upon the air route over the Hump for its contact with the outside world, but this route, successful as it was, could bring in only a few thousand tons of desperately needed supplies a month.

In the face of this situation the United States concentrated upon two military objectives. In the first place it strengthened American air power in China itself both for the defense of the presently held Chinese positions and for the preparation of air bases from which Japan could be bombed. Airfields big enough to serve B-29 bombers were constructed. In the second place it built up a Chinese army with American training and equipment. This was done on Indian territory because it was easier to bring the men from China to the equipment than to take the equipment over the Hump. The Chinese troops which retreated with Stilwell from Burma to India formed the nucleus of the new army. Later on Chinese troops were also trained in Yunnan province from where they cooperated with the Chinese force in India in a two-pronged attack on Japanese positions in northern Burma. As the troops advanced, the Ledo Road was constructed from Assam to north Burma linking up finally with the Burma Road when it was cleared of Japanese forces in the spring of 1945. These activities were carried out under the direction of General Stilwell, who was at the same time Chief of Staff to Chiang Kai-shek, Deputy to Lord Mountbatten, Commander of the Southeast Asia theater, and Theater Commander of American troops in the China-Burma-India theater, a difficult position at best. There were frictions with the British over policy in Burma, with Chiang Kai-shek over much needed reforms in Chinese military administration and over American demands for more cooperation with the Chinese Communists, and with General Chennault over the relative importance of the air force in over-all strategy. General Stilwell did not bring the temper or the training of a diplomat to this most difficult task. The deterioration of his relations with Chiang Kai-shek led eventually to his recall at the request of the Generalissimo. He was replaced by General Wedemeyer, who continued the same policies but established better personal relations with the Chinese than did his predecessor. Altogether it took Stilwell and Wedemeyer the better part of three years to reopen access to China, to train and equip the nucleus of a new Chinese army, and to lay the groundwork for a counter-offensive against the Japanese. Before this counter-offensive could take place, the Japanese had collapsed under the weight of the American onslaught by sea and air.

The military contribution that China made to the war was very considerable in view of the relatively meager material support she received from the outside. While the Japanese never used more than ten divisions in the conquest of the whole of Southeast Asia, at least twenty-three Japanese divisions were pinned down in China. In the last major offensive which the Japanese staged in early 1945 against the American-Chinese bases in the southwest of China they amassed a force of almost half a million men. China thus played a major military role in the war against Japan, a fact which made the United States most anxious to keep her in the war and to maintain her military effort. After Japanese victories in the Pacific and Southeast Asia, Chinese morale was understandably low. The Japanese exploited this situation by stressing, in their propaganda, the themes that China's allies were putting all their efforts into Europe and were not treating China as an equal in the planning and direction of the war. There was much truth in these accusations. But as the facts of strategy could not be changed and as so very little military aid could be given to China, it was important, in the American view, that China should be given every other kind of material and moral support.

The most readily available form of aid was financial. The only limits to financial aid were those set by the capacity of the Chinese economy to absorb and the ability of the government to use it. Shortly after Pearl Harbor, at China's request, the Congress approved a $500,000,000 credit which the Secretary of the Treasury called a "financial counterpart of lend-leasing war materials." Of this fund two-fifths was used for the redemption of Chinese government securities issued in U. S. dollars, and a slightly larger amount was used to buy gold which was later flown to China to help stabilize the currency. The Chinese government insisted on complete control over these funds, and there was no American check on their use. This $500,000,000 credit was more a gesture of help to the Chinese government than a sound economic measure. Financial aid was followed by a political move which indicated that the United States was willing to recognize China as a fully sovereign state and treat her as an equal. In October 1942, the United States took the initiative in opening up negotiations with China for the abolition of extraterritoriality and other treaty rights. In January 1943, China signed a treaty with the United States and shortly thereafter one with Great Britain, which brought to an end the whole "unequal treaty" system which had started one hundred years before. A further step towards equality was taken in December 1943. In order to "correct an historic mistake," to use President Roosevelt's words, the Congress repealed the Chinese exclusion laws which had maintained discriminatory treatment of Chinese in the United States on racial grounds. By these two moves Chinese equality was recognized both internationally and in American domestic law.

The immediate objective of these measures was to bolster Chinese morale, but they also fitted into the longer range American policy of preparing China for her role as the leading power in the postwar Far East. On American insistence China was admitted as a co-signatory of the Four Power Declaration at Moscow in October 1943. For the first time China joined with the United States, Great Britain, and Soviet Russia in a joint conference on the conduct of the war and the organization of the peace. For the first time China was given the standing of a Great Power. The problem of Russian neutrality in the Pacific war was solved by having the four powers agree to united prosecution of the war "against those Axis Powers with which they are respectively at war." The Russian refusal to have dealings with the representatives of the National Government of China on this as well as on later occasions was always explained by them as being due to their non-participation in the war against Japan. As the Chinese could not take part in the European conflict, although they had declared war on Germany and Italy, and as the Russians could not take part in deliberations on the Pacific conflict, this position could be justified. But the Russians carried the point to extremes when they refused to meet the Chinese representatives face to face in the negotiations preparatory to the establishment of the United Nations Organization at Dumbarton Oaks in the summer of 1944. The Russian position on China made it necessary for the leaders of the Big Four to meet in two separate groups, and meant that Stalin and Chiang Kai-shek could never be brought together. Therefore, when Roosevelt wanted to give Chiang Kai-shek the prestige of attending a meeting of the war leaders, he had to arrange a special Far Eastern meeting of Churchill, Chiang, and himself, which took place at Cairo in November 1943. Churchill's reluctant acceptance of an invitation to Chiang Kai-shek was tempered by the fact that Chiang's presence kept the Russians away at a moment when Churchill was particularly anxious to reach an understanding with Roosevelt before the two met with Stalin at Teheran.

Cairo and Teheran Conferences

At Cairo, President Roosevelt accomplished his main purpose which was to present Chiang Kai-shek to the world as one of the "three great allies" in the war against Japan. On this occasion the three leaders made a joint statement of their war aims in regard to Japan. This statement, known as the Cairo Declaration, went as follows:

> The several military missions have agreed upon future military operations against Japan. The Three Great Allies expressed their resolve to bring unrelenting pressure against their brutal enemies by sea, land, and air. This pressure is already rising.

> The Three Great Allies are fighting this war to restrain and punish the aggression of Japan. They covet no gain for themselves and have no thought of territorial expansion. It is their purpose that Japan shall be stripped of all the islands in the Pacific which she has seized or occupied since the beginning of the first World War in 1914, and that all the territories Japan has stolen from the Chinese, such as Manchuria, Formosa, and the Pescadores, shall be restored to the Republic of China. Japan will also be expelled from all other territories which she has taken by violence and greed. The aforesaid three great powers, mindful of the enslavement of the people of Korea, are determined that in due course Korea shall become free and independent.

> With these objects in view the three Allies, in harmony with those of the United Nations at war with Japan, will continue to persevere in the serious and prolonged operations necessary to procure the unconditional surrender of Japan.[12]

The Cairo Declaration came to have far-reaching importance in the territorial arrangements in the Pacific and the Far East following the defeat of Japan; it had much to do with future developments in Korea. Of immedi-

---

[12] *U. S. Relations With China*, Department of State (Washington, 1949), p. 519.

ate significance to Chiang Kai-shek was the promise ". . . that all the territories Japan has stolen from the Chinese, such as Manchuria, Formosa, and the Pescadores, shall be restored to the Republic of China"; and that the war would be pursued until "the unconditional surrender" of Japan. Chiang Kai-shek returned to Chungking with these promises and Roosevelt and Churchill went on to meet with Stalin a few days later at Teheran.

The meeting at Teheran was called mainly to discuss the European situation, but it also went into the over-all strategy of the war against Japan and the plans for a United Nations Organization. President Roosevelt explained to Stalin the strategy of reopening the Burma Road in order to keep China in the war and tried to secure Stalin's acceptance of China as one of the Big Four in the U.N.O. When Stalin questioned the strength of China, Roosevelt agreed that China was weak but said that he was thinking of the future. The issue was not pressed at this time. Stalin, however, made it clear that after the defeat of Germany the Soviet Union would join in the war against Japan. Soviet participation in the war against Japan was bound to raise the question of Russia's future position in the Far East. When Roosevelt, Churchill, and Chiang drew up the Cairo Declaration, which stipulated that Japan would lose all territory taken "by violence and greed," they must have had in mind the fact that Japan held territories which she had taken from Russia. It seems unlikely that the questions of Sakhalin, the Kuriles, and even Port Arthur and Dairen were not discussed. When Churchill and Roosevelt tried to find out what the Russian territorial interests in the Far East would be, Stalin said, "There is no need to speak at the present time about any Soviet desires—but when the time comes we will speak." Later in the conference Churchill volunteered the suggestion that the Soviet Union should have a warm water port and Roosevelt indicated that China might "agree to having Dairen made a free port under international guarantee." The conversations were not pursued beyond this point.

The Cairo and Teheran conferences show the relationship between two main American objectives. One was the recognition of China as a great power, a leading member of the U.N.O. and as a future stabilizing factor in the Far East. The other was the over-all objective of coming to terms with Soviet Russia as a member of a permanent system of general security. This involved coming to terms with her as a neighbor in the Far East. The cooperation of the Soviet Union was as necessary for the purpose of building up China as for the establishment of a United Nations Organization. President Roosevelt's China policy, therefore, could not be successfully achieved without an agreement with Soviet Russia. This explains why President Roosevelt was willing to help negotiate a Soviet-Chinese settlement on the basis of Chinese concessions. The outline of future negotiations was already clear in the discussions and declarations of the Cairo and Teheran conferences.

The two main American objectives of supporting China and cooperating with the Soviet Union were based not only on political hopes but also on military realities. Certainly at the time of Cairo and Teheran China was needed to continue holding down the bulk of the Japanese army, and it was expected that she would later join in a counter-offensive against these forces. Current American estimates, which accepted Japanese propaganda claims almost literally, were that the Japanese would fight to the last man in every position they held. It was assumed, therefore, that it would very likely be necessary to overrun the Japanese armies in Manchuria and Korea and to invade the home islands. This bloody task could be completed much more easily if the Soviet Union, with her strategic position on the mainland, could be brought into the war. Hence American policy towards both China and the Soviet Union was linked to the fortunes of war in the Pacific.

The tide of war had at first turned disastrously against the United States and its allies. The weakening of the American fleet at Pearl Harbor made it impossible for help to be given to the Philippines and to the countries of Southeast Asia which were being overrun. From Indo-China the Japanese advance pushed through Thailand and down the Malay Peninsula to Singapore which fell on February 25, 1942. From there the Japanese moved to the Dutch East Indies, where all resistance collapsed a month later. In the meantime the Japanese had landed in the Philippines and had driven the Philippine and American defenders to the Bataan peninsula and Corregidor, which held out until May 6. After these successes the Japanese moved on to Burma, which they occupied by June, and then took the Gilbert and Solomon Islands, and Attu and Kiska in the Aleutians. This was the furthest point of the Japanese advance. In June 1942, the American victory in the naval battle at Midway marked the turning point of the war and American offensive action started with the landing on Guadalcanal in August. From this time there began the slow but quickening process of island hopping and naval and air action. A strategy was developed by which Japanese conquests were cut off from the home islands and garrisons were left in hopeless isolation while American bases were moved steadily closer to Japan via the Gilberts, the Marshalls, the Carolines, and finally Okinawa and Iwo Jima, from which the main Japanese islands could be brought under land-based air attack. At the end of 1944 General MacArthur returned to the Philippines and in March 1945 recaptured the ruined city of Manila. The submarine and air attacks which spearheaded the American offensive resulted in the destruction of most of the Japanese navy and merchant marine, leaving the New Order in East Asia a shambles. Although this strategy actually brought Japan to her knees it was not known until after the war how close Japan was to complete exhaustion when she surrendered. Even as late as 1945 it was still assumed that Russian help would be of vital assistance in the final defeat of Japan.

Yalta Conference

The policies laid down at Cairo and Teheran were brought to fruition at the Yalta Conference, February 1945, when the defeat of Germany was close at hand. At the conference Roosevelt, Churchill, and Stalin dealt with much more than the Far East; in fact their main concern was with European developments and many fateful decisions were made with regard to the future of Germany, the zones of occupation, the role of France, the provisions for free democratic elections in Eastern Europe (later to be broken by the Russians), and the settlement of points still in dispute concerning the United Nations Organization. But this was also the time to decide on the when and how of the promised Russian participation in the war against Japan. The Far Eastern provisions of the Yalta Conference were as follows:

The leaders of the three Great Powers—the Soviet Union, the United States of America and Great Britain—have agreed that in two or three months after Germany has surrendered and the war in Europe has terminated the Soviet Union shall enter into the war against Japan on the side of the Allies on condition that:

1. The status quo in Outer-Mongolia (The Mongolian People's Republic) shall be preserved.
2. The former rights of Russia violated by the treacherous attack of Japan in 1904 shall be restored, viz:
(a) the southern part of Sakhalin as well as all the islands adjacent to it shall be returned to the Soviet Union,
(b) the commercial port of Dairen shall be internationalized, the preeminent interests of the Soviet Union in this port being safeguarded and the lease of Port Arthur as a naval base of the U.S.S.R. restored,
(c) the Chinese-Eastern Railroad and the South-Manchurian Railroad which provides an outlet to Dairen shall be jointly operated by the establishment of a joint Soviet-Chinese Company it being understood that the preeminent interests of the Soviet Union shall be safeguarded and that China shall retain full sovereignty in Manchuria;
3. The Kuril islands shall be handed over to the Soviet Union.
It is understood, that the agreement concerning Outer-Mongolia and the ports and railroads referred to above will require concurrence of Generalissimo Chiang Kai-shek. The President will take measures in order to obtain this concurrence on advice from Marshal Stalin.
The Heads of the three Great Powers have agreed that these claims of the Soviet Union shall be unquestionably fulfilled after Japan has been defeated.
For its part the Soviet Union expresses its readiness to conclude with the National Government of China a pact of friendship and alliance between the U.S.S.R. and China in order to render assistance to China with its armed forces for the purpose of liberating China from the Japanese yoke.[13]

The Far Eastern provisions of the Yalta Conference were the expression of American policies in relation to Russia and China which had been laid down at the beginning of the war. An understanding with Soviet Russia was necessary for the establishment of a United Nations Organization. It was also necessary for the specific American objective, in the Far East, of building up China as a Great Power. Every effort, therefore, was made to build a bridge to the Soviet Union, and in the Far East this bridge had to cross China.

At Yalta, President Roosevelt pursued three interrelated objectives. One was to bring Soviet Russia into the war against Japan in order to finish it more quickly and at less cost. Another was to bring about an understanding

[13] *Ibid.*, pp. 113–14.

between Soviet Russia and the American-supported National Government of China. The last, and most important purpose, was to secure a general understanding with the Soviet Union for the practical issues of the peace and for long-range cooperation in the United Nations Organization. In February 1945, it must have seemed to Roosevelt that the best bargain possible had been achieved. The handing over of southern Sakhalin and the Kurile Islands to Soviet Russia could not be regarded as an excessive price, especially in view of American plans to take over control of the Japanese island bases from the Marshalls to Okinawa. The price to be paid by China for unequivocal Soviet support of the National Government could be considered bearable if the Soviet promise were fulfilled. The concessions to be made in Manchuria were, of course, a serious limitation of Chinese sovereignty, and were recognized as such. But these concessions were to be written into a Treaty of Friendship and Alliance between Soviet Russia and the National Government of China (actually concluded in August 1945), a treaty based on a pattern not alien to American diplomacy, witness the postwar treaty with the newly independent Philippine Islands. The return of former Tsarist rights in Manchuria to the Soviet Union was ironical enough, but as the Japanese had taken these rights from the Tsars and the Soviets "by violence and greed," their return could be excused, if not justified, by the language of the Cairo Declaration. The conditions necessary for the success of America's China policy were clearly that Chiang Kai-shek's government should be able to establish a strong modern state and that the Russians could be held to their treaty obligations.

The resolution at Yalta of the remaining differences with the Soviet Union over political and procedural matters concerning the United Nations Organization cleared the way for the establishment of that body in San Francisco in April 1945. The Soviet Union was apparently prepared to cooperate in the maintenance of world peace, but its acceptance of the obligations of membership in the U.N.O. would not have been possible without agreement on specific political issues in Europe and the Far East. It was hoped at the time that membership in the U.N.O. would help to bind the Soviet Union to the fulfillment of such commitments as those she later undertook in her treaty with Nationalist China.

On the basis of the Yalta agreement a Sino-Soviet Treaty of Friendship and Alliance was signed on August 14, 1945. In an exchange of notes relating to this treaty the Soviet Union agreed ". . . to render to China moral support and aid in military supplies and other material resources, such support and aid to be entirely given to the National Government as the central government of China." [14] Both governments also agreed to respect each other's sovereignty and territorial integrity and not to interfere in each other's internal affairs. As the Chinese made these far-reaching concessions in Manchuria the Soviet Union specifically reaffirmed its respect for China's full sovereignty over the Three Eastern Provinces and recognized their territorial and administrative integrity. In view of previous conflicts over Sinkiang the

[14] *Ibid.*, p. 587.

Soviet Union also stated that it had no intention of interfering in China's internal affairs in that province. It was for these guarantees that the National Government of China was willing to agree to the Soviet terms, which in at least one case clearly went beyond those agreed upon at Yalta. The Chinese agreed to the holding of a plebiscite in Outer Mongolia on "independence" whereas the Yalta agreement had been for a continuation of the *status quo*. This additional concession was made when Russian troops were already moving into Manchuria. The Chinese preferred to make this concession rather than to face Soviet armies in Manchuria with no treaty at all.

The main stipulations of the treaty took up in detail the other promises made at Yalta. China declared Dairen a free port open to the commerce and shipping of all nations, to be administered by the Chinese government. The Soviet Union was to appoint the harbor master, to have the free use of half the port installations, and to pay no tariff on goods in transit. China agreed to the joint use of Port Arthur as a naval base, to be administered by a joint commission with a Russian chairman and a Chinese vice-chairman. China agreed to joint ownership of the main T-shaped Manchurian railroad system. It was to be managed by a Sino-Soviet Company and have an equally divided Board of Directors with a Chinese president and a Russian vice-president. But the management of the railroad and the organization of railroad guards was to be a Chinese responsibility, exercised in consultation with the Soviet government. All the provisions relating to Manchuria were to run for thirty years. The Sino-Soviet Treaty, except for the provisions on Outer Mongolia, followed the Yalta agreements closely enough not to raise the issue of Russian good faith at this time.

U. S. Policy in China

The United States, no less than the Chinese National Government, considered these concessions to Soviet Russia the necessary price for the Soviet promise to support only the National Government. This promise was important because of the increase in strength, during the war years, of the Chinese Communists, who ran the territories under their control as an autonomous regime. Given the objectives of United States policy in China this situation presented a very serious problem. Since 1939 there had been several major clashes and constant tension between the Nationalists and the Communists, but both sides claimed that they wanted a peaceful settlement and actually carried on negotiations from 1941 on. In 1944 the suggestion of a coalition government was made. In June of that year, Vice-President Henry Wallace arrived in Chungking on a political mission, the main purpose of which was to consolidate the Chinese war effort. Wallace offered American help in the negotiations. Chiang Kai-shek accepted the offer but pointed out that the Chinese Communists were more communist than the Russians themselves and should not be mistaken for agrarian reformers. Wallace stressed the view that no situation should be allowed to develop in China which would lead to conflict with Soviet Russia. Chiang

Kai-shek agreed with this and indicated that he would do anything to avoid conflict short of endangering Chinese sovereignty. He also welcomed American assistance in bringing about better relations between Soviet Russia and China.

American efforts to assist the National Government in solving the two related problems of its relations with the Chinese Communists and with the Soviet Union were initiated by Major General Patrick J. Hurley, first as personal representative of the President and then as Ambassador to China, from the fall of 1944 to November 1945. At this time American diplomatic officials indicated the serious inner weakness of the National Government and in this regard their reports were accurate and penetrating. They were also right in recognizing the aggressive intentions of Soviet Russia and the likelihood of a Communist victory in the event of civil war. Owing to their ignorance of the history and nature of international Communism some of these diplomatic reporters completely misjudged the character and policies of the Chinese Communists. Some even thought that if the United States should fail in its efforts to revitalize the Kuomintang, it should then try to influence the victorious Chinese Communists to become independent of the U.S.S.R. and friendly to the United States, a suggestion that was properly ignored. The obvious weakness of Chiang Kai-shek's government, coupled with the danger that he would lose in a civil war, strengthened American determination to help bring about an understanding with both the Chinese Communists and the Soviet Union. In order to help the National Government retain the upper hand over the Communists, or at least hold its own, the United States began to press for extensive reforms of the National Government. In fact, Ambassador Hurley understood the main purposes of his mission to be:

(1) To prevent the collapse of the National Government, (2) to sustain Chiang Kai-shek as President of the Republic and Generalissimo of the Armies, (3) to harmonize relations between the Generalissimo and the American Commander, (4) to promote production of war supplies in China and prevent economic collapse, and (5) to unify all the military forces in China for the purpose of defeating Japan.[15]

Ambassador Hurley went to China via Moscow, where he talked with Foreign Minister Molotov. It suited Molotov's purposes at this time to give Hurley the impression that the Communists in China "were related to Communism in no way at all," and that the Soviet government had no connection with these so-called Communists. He also suggested that he approved of "the United States taking the lead economically, politically, and militarily in Chinese affairs." In China Hurley worked hard to bring Chiang Kai-shek and the Communists together in their military efforts, but without success. Armed with Molotov's assurances, Ambassador Hurley thought that he had persuaded Chiang that the Soviet Union was not supporting the Chinese Communists and did not want civil war in China. The proposals which the Communists worked out at Yenan in Hurley's presence were for the establish-

[15] *Ibid.*, p. 71.

ment of a new government by the Kuomintang, the Communist, and all other parties. The National Government, in rejecting these proposals, made the counter-proposal that it was willing to incorporate the Communist armies in the national forces, accept the Communist party as a legal party, and bring Communists into the highest agencies of the existing government. In view of Chiang Kai-shek's often expressed understanding of the undemocratic character and plans of the Communists, this was as far as he could possibly be expected to go. In spite of Hurley's endeavors to "liberalize the counter-proposal" Chiang refused to budge, and President Roosevelt did not approve a plan submitted by Hurley "to force the National Government to make more liberal political concessions" for a settlement with the Communists.

The negotiations between the National Government and the Communists remained at a stalemate until after the Yalta Conference when the Soviet promise to deal exclusively with the National Government resulted in the Chinese Communists' accepting Chiang Kai-shek's position, and agreeing to negotiate on that basis. At Yalta, and later in the Sino-Soviet Treaty of August 1945, the Soviet Union apparently agreed to an advance in the power position of the Soviet Union in exchange for a retreat in the position of international Communism in China. Such a tactical Soviet maneuver at the expense of the Chinese Communists indicated a close relationship and understanding between Moscow and Yenan rather than any modification in the long-range program which international Communism had in China. When Hurley returned to Moscow in April 1945, Stalin confirmed Hurley's belief that Moscow was not interested in and would not support the Chinese Communists. This naïve view was not shared by the Department of State. But there is no denying that Moscow, whatever its motives, had made a real concession, and had given the National Government a tactical advantage which, as time was to show, it did not have the political and institutional strength to exploit to the full.

The American strategy for the war in the Far East had included China as one of the areas in which Japan would have to be defeated. Soviet Russia's military assistance was regarded as necessary for the final destruction of the Japanese empire. At the time of President Roosevelt's death, on April 12, 1945, China and Soviet Russia were committed, by treaties, declarations and understandings to that role in the war and the peace which America from the outset had expected them to play. As far as military calculations were concerned, the defeat of Japan came in a manner which was not at first anticipated. Japan was brought to her knees by the American drive across the Pacific, a victory gained by hard fighting and made possible by great technical advances in the long-range operations of naval task forces and of aircraft, and by the extraordinary mobilization of American industry. After the use of the atomic bomb, the end came so rapidly that the Soviet Union hardly had time to get into the war, and although its Manchurian campaign was a large-scale operation, it was over in less than two weeks. The end came so rapidly that the National Government was not ready to re-establish its authority ahead of the Communists in all occupied territory.

The Japanese capitulated on the basis of the Potsdam Declaration of July 26, 1945. Without giving up the term "unconditional surrender" the United States, Great Britain and China made known in this document the terms on which they would deal with Japan. The Russians, who had not been consulted in the drafting of the Potsdam Declaration, subscribed to it later. The territorial conditions were those of the Cairo Declaration but the humanitarian and democratic principles were in harmony with the ideals of the Atlantic Charter.

3. THE END OF THE GRAND ALLIANCE: AMERICAN POLICY, 1945–1947

The United States and Postwar Nationalism

A great war such as the one which had just come to a close with the surrender of Japan was bound to have far-reaching effects on the peoples and countries which had been drawn into it. The most obvious feature of the postwar situation was the serious economic plight of the whole area in which Japan had attempted to build up her Co-Prosperity Sphere. The destruction caused by the war varied from place to place but no country had escaped. The Japanese conquests brought about extensive devastation in China not only through Japanese military action but also through the scorched-earth policy as it was applied by the Chinese. The various campaigns in Burma also caused considerable destruction. The rest of Southeast Asia, including the Philippines, suffered in varying degrees, but the whole of this vast area was seriously affected by the interruption of its economic ties with Europe and the markets of the world. The Japanese never compensated for this by integrating the economy of Southeast Asia with that of Japan; they merely looted the resources of their newly won conquests. In the closing months of the war the Japanese committed excesses, such as the wanton destruction of Manila, which aggravated the economic desolation which they left behind.

The economic plight of Asia was more than matched by its political instability. The Japanese empire had been torn apart, and Japan itself was no longer a power center. The American hope that China would be strong enough to take Japan's place had not been fulfilled. Instead China was threatened by civil war and the balance of internal power had shifted from the National Government to the Chinese Communists. Although Great Britain, France, and the Netherlands had emerged victorious from the war, it was clear that they would never recover the prestige and authority in the colonial world that they had enjoyed before their defeat by Japan. This was true even of the British, who had been one of the major contributors to victory and who had provided the theater command in Southeast Asia. It was certainly true of the Dutch who, because of the occupation of their country during the war, had very few troops with which to participate in the recovery of the East Indies. The French, who had collaborated with the Japanese in Indo-China, were in the weakest position of all.

The decline in political authority of the colonial powers in Southeast Asia was significant because the Japanese, when they saw that the end was in sight, had gone out of their way to encourage and equip nationalist regimes and military forces. This assistance gave the nationalist movements in many Southeast Asian countries a real opportunity to challenge the return of the colonial powers. With the collapse of Japan, the confusion in China, and the conflict in Southeast Asia, the only great military forces in Asia were those of the Soviet Union and the United States. The relations between these two great powers were bound to have a decisive effect on the whole future of the Far East. In spite of all the agreements which had been made regarding the major problems of the defeat of Japan and the status of China, the Grand Alliance broke up into two hostile groups—the Communist world and the Free World. The Far East, with all its confusion and ferment, was bound to be a major battleground in this ever deepening conflict.

At the end of the war the attention of the United States was taken up by the problems of the occupation of Japan, the civil war in China, and the reconstruction and independence of the Philippines. Southeast Asia was considered to be an extension of the European political system, and although the United States was aware of the nationalist movements in this vast area, it gave them no assistance. In fact there was no outside power to sponsor the struggle of the nationalist leaders to establish genuine independence. Japan had never understood the opportunity that once was hers to provide leadership to nationalist movements in Asia, for her drive was towards conquest and empire. The assistance which the Japanese gave at the end of their rule to the nationalists did not earn them any gratitude because their motives were only too clear and hatred of their rule far too deep. In fact those nationalists who had collaborated with the Japanese, and those who had spent the war in resisting them, joined forces in most of the countries of Southeast Asia.

The British were wise enough to come to terms with India, Pakistan, and Burma shortly after the war was over and were ready to develop representative institutions, by stages, in most of their remaining colonies. But they were yielding to pressure; they were not sponsoring national independence movements either in their own or other empires. The French and the Dutch were anxious to recover control over their colonies. The Soviet Union took advantage of this situation to promote world Communism by directing native Communists to infiltrate the nationalist movements and attempt to take them over. At this stage most native Communists, such as Ho Chi Minh, Luis Taruc, and Sjarifuddin, concealed their party membership and pretended to be working only for nationalist objectives. However, there were also many native nationalists who turned to the United States for leadership and sponsorship because of the long American anti-imperialist tradition, which seemed to them to have been restated in the Atlantic Charter.

The United States was in no position to give unqualified support to any nationalist movements, except in the Philippines, which were her own responsibility. Here the United States fulfilled the promise to grant independence, and the Philippine Republic became an independent state on July 4, 1946. But the other colonies of Southeast Asia were not an American responsibility, and furthermore, the colonial powers were wartime allies whose economic and political recovery and future role in Europe were of vital interest to the United States. The most that the United States did was to put diplomatic pressure on its allies to speed up the process of granting independence to their colonies. On this issue Churchill and Roosevelt had their altercations. After the war the United States intervened to prevent the British from imposing heavy economic controls on independent Thailand, which had been a nominal partner of Japan during the war. But the United States left to the British the military reoccupation of most of Southeast Asia and the acceptance of Japanese surrender in that area. Northern Indo-China was assigned to the forces of Chiang Kai-shek. The British and the Chinese, therefore, had the delicate task of reintroducing the colonial authorities and their military forces to the nationalist leaders of the colonial countries. The only contribution made by the United States was the training and equipping of a small force of Dutch marines which was transported to eastern Indonesia. Otherwise the United States did not interfere in Southeast Asia at this time. It was not until a few years after the war, when Communist efforts to capture leadership of the nationalist movements had been clearly revealed, that the United States increased its pressure on the Dutch government to come to terms with the non-communist nationalists of Indonesia and on the French government to give independence to the states of Indo-China.

For the rest of the Far East the United States had plans and commitments which she immediately began to implement. In the Philippines there was not only the promise of independence to be fulfilled but there was also the enormous task of reconstruction in a country which had suffered severely during the war. The conditions under which political independence was granted involved a re-establishment of the prewar economic pattern in which the Philippines were dependent on the sale of cash crops to the American market and the importation of American consumer goods for Philippine needs. America was willing to assist in the rebuilding of war damaged cities, to compensate Filipinos and Americans who had suffered losses, to pay benefits to Filipino veterans, and to finance a program of immediate civilian relief. The flood of American dollars created a temporary boom but made little contribution to the development of a sound economy. No attempt was made to prepare for economic independence. In fact the Philippine Trade Act of 1946 provided for free and preferential trade between the Philippines and the United States and gave Americans complete equality with Filipinos in landowning and business, a privilege which they had not enjoyed before. The last provision even required an amendment to the new Philippine Constitution. The Philippine Legislature was compelled to accept this unpopular Trade Act because it was linked to the Rehabilitation Act, which provided for American payments to the Philippines. A policy for the Philippines which combined the granting of political independence with American economic privilege stands out in sharp contrast with the unconditional independence which the British granted India and even with American policy in Japan.

Occupation Policy in Japan

The United States had more to do with the formulation and execution of Allied policy towards Japan than any other power. The Potsdam Declaration, on which the Occupation directives were based, originated as an American document. The general intent of this document was that while Japan should be stripped of her empire and of her capacity to wage war, the Japanese people should be given the chance to develop along democratic lines. One assumption behind this policy was that when they had the opportunity any people would turn to democratic institutions. It was also assumed that a democratic country would be more likely to keep the peace. When Japan had gone through the necessary process of reformation, a place would then be found for her in the United Nations Organization and she would be expected to play her part in maintaining the peace. The program for Japan was a peculiarly American interpretation of that Anglo-American document, the Atlantic Charter. The occupation policies were theoretically laid down by the Far Eastern Commission, consisting of all the nations which had fought Japan; in practice, policy was determined by the government of the United States which laid down the basic directives even before the Commission came into existence. As America provided the bulk of the occupying forces in Japan, General MacArthur, the Supreme Commander, was comparatively independent in his relationship with the Allied Council in Tokyo where the Big Four were represented. The United States refused the Soviet demand for separate occupation of Hokkaido, thus avoiding a political division of Japan. The British, the most important of America's Western allies, were represented by a token force and did not have much influence on American execution of occupation policy. For the experiment in Japan America had the full responsibility.

In the occupation policy for Japan there was an awareness that democratic political institutions must be built on democratic social and economic foundations. Such an approach was entirely new. It certainly differed greatly from that which was followed in the Philippine Islands, where the establishment of democratic political institutions was carried out without reference to social and economic conditions. In its nearly fifty years of colonial government the United States did not change the pattern of rule by a small group of landholding cacique families over impoverished tenants. Indeed the development of cash crops for the American market had aggravated the worst features of that relationship. The Philippine economy was made even more dependent on the United States at the very time when independence was granted. In contrast the American approach in Japan was to treat Japanese society as a whole, to proceed on the assumption that to establish democratic political institutions it was necessary to move on all fronts at the same time. Land reform was introduced, not only to increase production but also to change the patterns of political authority in the villages, for these were strongly influenced by the patterns of landholding. The zaibatsu were dissolved, not only because of the support they gave to the militarists but also because America assumed that competitive private enterprise was the only economic basis for free political institutions.

There were many reasons why such an approach was possible in the case of Japan. For one thing Japan was a defeated country and the victor had complete authority. More important, the idea of total war, propagated by the totalitarian countries, impressed upon Americans the fact that in these countries the whole of society was mobilized for the political purposes of an all powerful leadership. The removal of this leadership, however, was not in itself sufficient to dispose of the threat of future aggression. It was also necessary to change the ideas and institutions on which that leadership was based so that it could never rise again. Hence the concern of the Occupation authorities with every aspect of Japanese life from the emancipation of women to the rewriting of textbooks, from land reform to dissolution of the cartels, from the establishment of labor unions to the writing of a new constitution. Such a concern with the whole social fabric brought to American foreign policy an entirely new dimension.

The new approach was at first limited to the reformation of a defeated and occupied country. In 1947 when the main concern of American policy shifted to the new threat of Communist totalitarianism it was realized that this broad social approach should be applied to those threatened countries which were in the throes of social and economic transformation. But it took time to discover the techniques by which this approach could be applied to friendly and independent countries. Even for China, the most important of all Far Eastern countries to American policy, there was no integrated approach to the problem of strengthening the social fabric; nor was there the time or the necessary conditions.

The United States and the Crisis in China

China ended the war as one of the Big Four and a victor over Japan. There was a sharp contrast, however, between the international prestige of the National Government of China and the domestic realities. Apart from the serious political division few countries had suffered more from the economic devastation of war. The war interfered with the agricultural routine and lowered the production of food because of the large numbers of men withdrawn for the armed forces and the disruption caused by military operations. Vast areas were inundated by flood, communications were in very poor condition, and large numbers of refugees complicated this critical economic dislocation. In addition to all this there was inflation, for the government, unable to finance the war from tax resources, had resorted to the printing of paper money. The ending of the war did not bring any relief, as the government had to maintain large armies to reoccupy the lost territories and to meet the threat of civil war. Much of the revenue did not reach the treasury because the government failed to re-establish administrative order and to prevent corruption, always more difficult to control under inflationary conditions. The use of government funds was often marked by waste and inefficiency. The Chinese government and the Chinese people were in desperate need of help.

China's wartime allies immediately came to her assistance, largely through the United Nations Relief and Rehabilitation Administration (UNRRA). The United Nations extended relief through UNRRA to the war-devastated countries of both Europe and Asia, but the largest single program of aid was that for China. The United States provided some 72 per cent of these UNRRA funds. The total aid to China, for the two years after the war amounted to over U. S. $658,000,000 of which the U. S. paid $474,-000,000. It consisted largely of supplies of food and clothing, capital goods, and other forms of direct assistance to agriculture and industry. It also included the salaries of foreign experts who were to assist in the application of UNRRA aid. On the insistence of the Chinese, all UNRRA aid was given to the National Government, which established its own organization, the Chinese National Relief and Rehabilitation Administration (CNRRA) to administer it. The government sold such commodities as tobacco, flour, and cotton on the open market in order to secure revenue. The UNRRA aid to China was in the nature of a blood transfusion intended to keep the National Government going and get the economy started again, rather than part of a program of social and economic reform such as was being attempted in Japan. In fact many of the raw materials delivered to the Chinese government were used to strengthen government-controlled industries to the disadvantage of private enterprise, and thus further undermined the already weak position of the Chinese business class, a consequence neither planned nor anticipated.

American policy was focused on the survival of the National Government. Even before the war was over, American estimates of the Chinese situation indicated that the government of Chiang Kai-shek was so weak that it could not be expected to survive a test of arms with the Chinese Communists. It was therefore concluded that civil war must be avoided. During the war this had obviously been desirable in order to have a united military effort against Japan, but after the war it became imperative in order to assure the political survival of the National Government. The United States had already extended its good offices to the Chinese government in its negotiations with the Communists in 1944 through the Hurley mission. The negotiations entered a critical stage when the Japanese surrender brought on a rush for arms and territory by both sides, and civil war seemed to be an immediate possibility. In this competition the United States gave immense help to the National Government by transporting its troops by sea and air to the whole lower Yangtze area and to key cities in North China. United States Marines were sent to the Peking-Tientsin area to accept the Japanese surrender there and hold the cities until the National Government could take over. The effort to transport Chiang Kai-shek's troops to Manchuria was blocked by the Soviet Union. In the meantime both the Nationalists and the Communists agreed to the holding of a Political Consultative Conference in December 1945 for the settlement of the conflict. This gave the United States the opportunity to continue its good offices, and General George C. Marshall, the highest military figure in America, was sent to China.

The ideas and motives behind American policy towards China at this time were indicated in President Truman's statement of December 15, 1945. After expressing his belief that the major aim of American policy was to guarantee peace and prosperity through reliance on collective security and the United Nations Organization, President Truman said, "It is the firm belief of this Government that a strong, united and democratic China is of the utmost importance to the success of this United Nations Organization and for world peace." This was essentially the same policy as that of President Roosevelt, but this policy was now increasingly endangered by civil war and the weakness of the National Government of China. Under these circumstances the United States was willing to do everything it could to help bring about a peaceful settlement. The United States expected to assist the National Government in completing the evacuation of Japanese troops, and for that reason United States Marines had been sent to North China. President Truman made it clear that the United States would not attempt through "military intervention to influence the course of any Chinese internal strife." The United States put itself clearly on record as believing that unification should come only under the authority of the National Government but that the basis of that government should be broadened by modifying the one-party political system. The United States indicated that the autonomous armies in China should be integrated into the National Army. If China made progress towards these goals, General Marshall could promise the National Government American assistance in the rehabilitation of the country and its economy and in the establishment of a strong military organization.

President Truman's public statement on China policy served also as the main directive for the Marshall mission. In a supplementary memorandum Secretary of State Byrnes pointed out that the United States considered that the "Government of Generalissimo Chiang Kai-shek affords the most satisfactory base for a developing democracy," but that this government must be "broadened to include the representatives of those large and well organized groups who are now without any voice in the government of China." Among these groups Byrnes included what he called "the so-called Communists" as well as "other factions." Byrnes instructed Marshall to assist the National Government in getting its troops to Manchuria but the further transportation of troops to North China was to depend upon the progress of the truce negotiations. Marshall was left free to decide on the movement of troops to North China depending on how, in his judgment, the pending truce negotiations would be affected. If the truce failed he could, if he felt it wise, help the National Government to force its way into North China.

It should be noted that American assistance to the National Government was conditional on the willingness of that government to negotiate a settlement with the Chinese Communists and to carry out certain political reforms. It was assumed by the United States as well as by Chiang Kai-shek that the negotiations would be concerned with the terms on which the Communists would take part in the existing National Government, which had been recognized as the sole government of China by the Soviet Union.

The agreements reached between the National Government, the Communists, and the minor political groups early in 1946 at the Political Consultative Conference seemed to promise success for the Marshall mission. A military truce was arranged and Marshall returned to Washington to help obtain the financial assistance which had been promised in President Truman's statement. During Marshall's absence fighting between the Nationalists and the Communists began in Manchuria, which had been included in the truce agreement. The Communists continued to move troops into Manchuria in violation of the agreement, and the Nationalists refused to permit the truce teams to operate. From this time on there developed in Manchuria a struggle for power and position which Marshall, after his return to China in April 1946, was never able fully to control. During the rest of 1946 both sides, as might have been expected, tried to press the advantage whenever they felt themselves in a position to do so, and in spite of occasional truces the fighting continued to mount. It was during this period that the Soviet forces in Manchuria made captured Japanese arms and equipment available to the Chinese Communists, an action which later turned out to be of decisive importance. In contrast, General Marshall put an embargo on the shipment of combat-type military equipment from the United States to China, an action which remained in effect from August, 1946, to May, 1947. Marshall's apparent motive was to restrain the over-confident Nationalist generals who, he felt, were courting disaster by pressing the civil conflict to a military decision and making a negotiated settlement impossible. The embargo, however, did not prevent the turning over to China of a vast amount of non-combat military surplus supplies located at American bases in China, India, Burma, and the Pacific islands. This material, shipped to China by the United States, was regarded as payment for Chinese services to American forces to the value of $205,000,000. The United States also concluded a new agreement with the National Government for the training of military personnel. The imposition of an embargo on combat equipment while other types of military aid were being given, reflected Marshall's policy of preventing civil war while strengthening the National Government. Marshall's honest efforts to carry out the task of mediation were viciously attacked by the Communists as dishonest support of one side in the civil war. At this time the Communists were themselves receiving Japanese equipment with the help of the Russians. The Marshall mission found itself in a more and more embarrassing position. Since it was the avowed intention of the United States to support the National Government in the negotiations, Marshall felt himself to be more compromised by the failures of the Nationalists to observe their agreements than by those of the Communists. General Marshall, feeling that his own personal integrity was at stake, requested that he be recalled. In January 1947, Marshall left China to become Secretary of State.

General Marshall's views on his mission to China were expressed in a lengthy statement made on January 7, 1947. In one of the most important passages he said:

Between this dominant reactionary group in the Government and the irreconcilable Communists who, I must state, did not so appear last February, lies the problem of how peace and well-being are to be brought to the long-suffering and presently inarticulate mass of the people of China. The reactionaries in the Government have evidently counted on substantial American support regardless of their actions. The Communists by their unwillingness to compromise in the national interest are evidently counting on an economic collapse to bring about the fall of the Government, accelerated by extensive guerrilla action against the long lines of rail communications—regardless of the cost in suffering to the Chinese people.

In the final paragraphs of his statement Marshall indicated a shift in American policy, since negotiations had failed.

The salvation of the situation, as I see it, would be the assumption of leadership by the liberals in the Government and in the minority parties, a splendid group of men, but who as yet lack the political power to exercise a controlling influence. Successful action on their part under the leadership of Generalissimo Chiang Kai-shek would, I believe, lead to unity through good government.

Referring to the National Assembly which had met in Nanking, without the Communists, Marshall said:

Soon the Government in China will undergo major reorganization pending the coming into force of the constitution following elections to be completed before Christmas Day 1947. Now that the form for a democratic China has been laid down by the newly adopted constitution, practical measures will be the test. . . . It has been stated officially and categorically that the period of political tutelage under the Kuomintang is at an end.[16]

In these words Marshall foreshadowed the policy that he would follow as Secretary of State. It would be an attempt to strengthen the National Government by assisting it in the development of the democratic institutions to which it was now committed. Although for the record the door was left open for "Communists or other groups to participate" the Communists were in fact written off. Recognition of the failure to bring about a united China by peaceful means marked the end of a policy which had begun during the war and had been a part of the over-all American policy towards the Soviet Union.

The breakdown of the negotiations with the Communists was heralded by a Chinese Communist propaganda attack on General Marshall. This was part of a growing Communist campaign to vilify the United States by denouncing it as an imperialist power which was preparing for aggression.

[16] *Ibid.*, pp. 688–89.

The campaign, which began before the end of 1946, mounted in intensity during 1947 and was not limited to China.

American-Soviet Conflict over Korea

In Korea the year 1947 was also a turning point, for it was then that the attempt to come to terms with the Russians finally failed. The record of the negotiations in Korea shows that the United States had made every effort to secure Soviet cooperation in the establishment of a united Korean government. The first reference to the postwar future of Korea was made at the Cairo Conference in 1943. Roosevelt, Churchill, and Chiang Kai-shek promised, in the Cairo Declaration, that Korea "in due course shall become free and independent." At that time Soviet participation in the Far Eastern war was still uncertain, but at Yalta, in February 1945, it was agreed that the Japanese surrender should be accepted by the Soviet Union in North Korea and by the United States in South Korea. The decision to make the 38th parallel the dividing line was made, on a military staff level, at the Potsdam Conference. It corresponded to no ethnic, political, economic or geographic division. When the Japanese surrendered, the United States government had no prepared plan for the responsibilities which it had undertaken in Korea. Lieutenant-General John R. Hodge was rushed into South Korea with some of the troops who had fought on Okinawa to accept the surrender and administer the country, under the general direction of MacArthur.

The Soviet Union was not so unprepared. The underground Korean Communist movement, reinforced by Soviet-trained Koreans who came in with the Russian troops and by Korean Communists, newly released from Japanese prisons, set up People's Committees to take over the local administration. In North Korea the Soviet Union immediately recognized and worked with the People's Committees but in South Korea General Hodge refused to deal with them. In carrying out American policy General Hodge did not work with any Korean group but continued to operate through the existing Japanese administration, a fact which did not endear the United States to the Korean nationalists. The United States government apparently expected that there would be rapid agreement with the Soviet Union on the setting up of a Korean government. But the first act of the Soviet army had been to seal the border at the 38th parallel with troops and tanks, and there was no liaison between the two occupying powers for settling even local issues.

In an effort to break this deadlock the United States took the initiative in seeking an agreement with the Soviet Union on Korea. At the Moscow Conference of Foreign Ministers, December 1945, it was decided that a Joint Commission of the two occupation commands should be established to assist in the formation of a Provisional Government for Korea. According to the agreement reached in Moscow there should be established a "Four Power Trusteeship of Korea for a period up to five years." The Joint Commission was instructed to "consult with the Korean democratic parties and social organizations" on the establishment of the Provisional Government and to coordinate the administrative and economic affairs of both zones. The trusteeship proposal was bound to be unpopular in Korea, but it is significant that in the southern zone Korean nationalists were free to demonstrate against it, whereas in the northern zone the Communist-controlled People's Committees obediently approved. A limited agreement on the coordination of administrative and economic affairs between the two occupation commands was reached in January, 1946, but even this was not carried out very long. The Joint Commission to set up a Provisional Government met in March 1946 at Seoul. The United States wished first to discuss economic and administrative unification of Korea but yielded to Soviet insistence on discussing first the establishment of a Provisional Government. The Russians showed quite clearly that they would permit unification only if the Communists could control the whole of Korea when they demanded that the Provisional Government should be based only on the "democratic parties and organizations, supporting the decisions of the Moscow Conference." In practice this would have meant the exclusion of all the nationalist parties in South Korea, thus leaving the field to the Communists, a position which the United States obviously could not accept. By insisting on political restrictions which would have guaranteed a Communist victory in the election and by their refusal even to discuss administrative and economic cooperation the Russians broke up the conference in May 1946.

The United States, from this time on, followed two lines of policy simultaneously: on the one hand the American occupation authorities began to set up a Korean government in the southern zone and on the other hand kept the door open for further negotiations with the Soviet authorities. In the fall of 1946 General Hodge began to turn over to Koreans important positions in the central and provincial administration. Americans remained as advisers. In December a Provisional Legislative Assembly, half of whose members were elected and half appointed, met at Seoul and preparations got under way for the establishment of an independent South Korean government. As in the Philippines America was following its traditional policy of setting up representative institutions for political democracy. Also in line with the practice in the Philippines America went ahead with political democracy without relating it to social and economic conditions. This was particularly dangerous in Korea where the land issue was acute. It was estimated that at the end of the war more than three-fourths of the cultivated land in South Korea was farmed by tenants or landless laborers. The land was owned mostly by large Japanese landowners or companies. Rents were high and wages low. After the defeat of the Japanese, Korean tenants and laborers needed no encouragement to demand the land which in their view the Japanese masters had taken away from the Korean people. The long-term American program to meet this situation by a gradual transfer of ownership and payment for the land was most unpopular and led to many riots and accusations against the United States. In contrast to her policy in occupied

Japan, the United States did not undertake at this time an aggressive economic program in liberated Korea. The lack of economic reforms contributed to unrest in the south and was fully exploited by Communist propagandists who boasted of their land reforms in the north. But the one-way stream of refugees from the north to the south testified that to large numbers of Koreans the American-occupied south was preferable to the Soviet north.

Once Soviet Russia had established its own regime in North Korea it was willing to take up the repeated American offers to negotiate. In October 1946 and in April 1947, there was an exchange of notes, and in May 1947 the Joint Commission met again in Seoul, where it was agreed that all Korean political groups "truly democratic in their aims and methods" and willing to support the trusteeship principle should be invited to participate in the formation of a Provisional Government. The agreement came to nothing because the Russians still refused to recognize the groups which were opposed to them. In August, 1947, the Russians raised their demands. They refused to accept any freely elected legislature for the whole of Korea and proposed instead a Provisional Assembly to be made up of an equal number of representatives from the north, which had one-third, and the south, which had two-thirds, of the population. Nor did they give up their demand that only parties which fully supported the Moscow agreement should be permitted to participate in the elections. It is clear that these demands were not made in the hope of reaching an agreement.

4. THE FIGHT AGAINST COMMUNISM: AMERICAN POLICY, 1947–1955

Truman Doctrine and Marshall Plan

The deterioration of American-Soviet relations in Korea, as in China, was no isolated affair but rather the result of a world-wide shift in Communist policy. Negotiations in Europe, as in the Far East, had shown by this time that the Soviet Union was unwilling to carry out the spirit of the Yalta agreements. The Soviet Union was determined not only to consolidate its hold on the areas into which the Red Army had moved but also to expand the Soviet orbit by every means at its disposal. The refusal to permit free elections in Poland, the establishment of satellite regimes in the Balkans, Communist guerrilla activities in Greece, the growing intransigeance of the Chinese Communists, and the refusal to cooperate in Korea were all part of the same pattern. Even the pretense of keeping up the wartime cooperation had now gone, and the American policy of attempting to secure Soviet cooperation in maintaining a postwar system of collective security had to be abandoned. Totalitarian Russia had stepped into the place so recently filled by Nazi Germany, Fascist Italy, and Imperial Japan; the wartime ally was now identified as the main enemy.

America's most immediate concern was the Soviet threat to the independence of Turkey and to the internal stability of Greece. This threat was regarded by the American government as a challenge to the security of the whole free world. President Truman in a statement of March, 1947, announced a new American policy of resisting Communist aggression and indicated the means to carry it out. In his address to the Congress he treated the situation as a national emergency and used the cases of Greece and Turkey as examples of a pattern of Soviet aggression which endangered "the national security" of the United States. Truman described Greece as a case in which a "militant minority" was working from within to "create political chaos" and block economic reconstruction. It was therefore necessary to help the Greek government financially so that it could re-establish its authority over the country. In the case of Turkey such aid would make possible the "modernization necessary for the maintenance of its national integrity." Generalizing on the basis of these two cases, Truman advocated that the United States should take steps "to support free peoples who are resisting attempted subjugation by armed minorities or by outside pressures . . . to assist free peoples to work out their own destinies in their own way." Support was to be given "primarily through economic and financial aid which is essential to economic stability and orderly political processes." Linking the new policy to the wartime aims of the United States, President Truman declared that America would merely be carrying out the principles of the Charter of the United Nations if it were "helping free and independent nations to maintain their freedom. . . ." This policy, known as the Truman Doctrine, was one of defending the independence and the democratic institutions of the whole free world against Communist aggression.

The granting of aid to Greece and Turkey was only the beginning of what developed into a vast program of economic assistance. The Marshall Plan for European recovery, announced in June 1947, was designed to strengthen the economies of the western European democracies. The approach differed radically from that of UNRRA in that it required constructive planning and agreement among the European nations as to what was required and what they themselves would contribute. The intention was to "provide a cure rather than a mere palliative." The manner in which the Marshall Plan was introduced was as important as the aid itself. The United States took into full consideration the reluctance of European countries to break with Soviet Russia because of their fear of the Red Army and the strong tendency towards the building up of a neutral bloc. The Marshall Plan, like the Truman Doctrine on which it was based, emphasized economic aid rather than military assistance. Economic aid on these conditions could not easily be refused, whereas the offer of military assistance, at that time, would not have been easily accepted. Furthermore, the Marshall Plan was very wisely offered to the Soviet Union and its satellites, thus avoiding the charge that the United States was trying to turn western Europe against the Soviet Union. The Soviet Union refused to join the Marshall Plan and also prevented its satellites from doing so, and had to bear the responsibility for dividing Europe into two camps.

The new policy was intended to apply to the Far East as well as to Europe. But the countries of the Far East presented problems of a very different order from those of Europe, and it was therefore much more difficult to apply the approach of the Truman Doctrine and the Marshall Plan in this part of the world. In contrast to the homogeneous societies and democratic institutions of western Europe, Asia presented a complex pattern of traditional agricultural societies in varying stages of political and economic transformation. In most of Southeast Asia the struggle between growing nationalism and re-established colonial rule posed a dilemma for the United States. Much as America was in favor of supporting the nationalist movements in the colonies, partly to preclude them from being subverted by the Communists, it could deal with these movements only through the colonial powers. France and Holland, whose colonies were in the most critical condition, were an important part of the American economic program for Europe. Any interference with what the French and the Dutch regarded as their internal affairs would have complicated the program in Europe.

The difficulty of applying the new policy in China was of a different nature. The National Government of China could neither formulate the kind of program which America had made a precondition of aid in Europe nor guarantee its sound execution. In the Philippines the newly independent government was slow to see the need for those measures of reform which America was anxious to see applied but had itself neglected to promote during the period of colonial rule. Japan, like Germany, was not included at first in the countries eligible for the type of aid envisaged in the Truman Doctrine. But it was inevitable that both would eventually come within the scope of the new policy.

The first effect of the new policy on Japan was to strengthen the tendency of the Occupation to assume responsibility for the establishment of a strong and self-sustaining economy. There were several reasons for this tendency. The reforms which had been carried out would be endangered if the new democratic institutions were associated with economic distress. For the Occupation to assume no responsibility for Japan beyond the prevention of disease and unrest, and to enforce reduction of heavy industry and payment of reparations in kind, meant in practice that Japan would become an ever-increasing burden on the American taxpayer. To remove that burden was an added reason for increasing production. In the year 1948 the industrial production of Japan was only 59 per cent of the prewar level and the cost of the occupation to the American taxpayer was heavy indeed. There was yet another reason why Japanese industry should be revived. It had become increasingly clear that there could be no economic stability in the Far East without an economically strong Japan. The course of events on the mainland already indicated that China was not going to be a stabilizing force. The need to strengthen the economies of Southeast Asia in the face of Communist aggression required assistance from Japan, which was still the most industrially developed country in Eastern Asia. Japan could provide assistance to those Asiatic countries which were in earlier stages of industrial development. These considerations strengthened the case for permitting the Japanese to rebuild their heavy industries in order to export capital goods to the rest of Asia. Consumer goods would compete with the consumer goods industries which were being established in Southeast Asia. SCAP therefore removed most of the controls on Japanese economic activities and abandoned the process of breaking up the zaibatsu concerns. By the beginning of 1949 the results of these measures could be seen in the steady growth of Japanese industrial output. The rebuilding of the Japanese economy became even more necessary as the Communists came closer and closer to victory in China.

The United States did little about China between the end of the Marshall Mission in January 1947 and the summer of that same year. While the Truman Doctrine was meant to be world wide in scope there seemed to be no way in which it could be applied immediately to China. China was regarded as being far too vast and complex for the United States to take over directly the management of military and administrative affairs. Although the Chinese government was not regarded as capable of drawing up a sound plan for national recovery, an attempt was made at the time the Marshall Plan was instituted in Europe to find out whether there was any constructive way in which aid could be given to China.

The Wedemeyer Mission

In July 1947, Lieutenant General Albert C. Wedemeyer was sent to China and Korea on a fact-finding mission with instructions to make "an appraisal of the political, economic, psychological and military situations—current and projected." He was to make it clear ". . . that the United States Government can consider assistance in a program of rehabilitation only if the Chinese Government presents satisfactory evidence of effective measures looking towards Chinese recovery" and provided further that "any aid which may be made available shall be subject to the supervision of representatives of the United States Government." Towards the end of his mission General Wedemeyer, at the invitation of Chiang Kai-shek, spoke to a group of high government officials and used the occasion to express strong criticism of their administration and policies. Among other things he said:

The Central Government cannot defeat the Chinese Communists by the employment of force, but can only win the loyal, enthusiastic and realistic support of the masses of the people by improving the political and economic situation immediately. The effectiveness and timeliness of these improvements will determine in my opinion whether or not the Central Government will stand or fall before the Communist onslaught.[17]

In a public statement issued in Nanking at the time of his departure General Wedemeyer reiterated his views in a further effort to shock the Chinese government into action. After expressing his discouragement with the defeatism and escapism which he found in China, General Wedemeyer suggested that China's "recovery awaits inspirational leadership and moral and spiritual resurgence which can only come from within China." It was necessary to

[17] *Ibid.*, p. 759.

remove incompetent and corrupt officials and to carry out "immediately drastic, far-reaching political and economic reforms. Promises will no longer suffice. Performance is absolutely necessary. It should be accepted that military force in itself will not eliminate Communism." [18] General Wedemeyer's frank statement aroused considerable resentment without producing any reforms.

In his report to the State Department General Wedemeyer recommended a program of military and economic aid to China for a five-year period. Military advice and supervision was to be extended in scope to include field forces, training centers, and logistical agencies, in order to increase the effectiveness of American military aid to Chiang Kai-shek in his struggle with the Communists. General Wedemeyer pointed out, however, that American personnel should not participate directly in the Chinese civil war. While recommending economic aid, Wedemeyer made the condition: "That China make effective use of her own resources in a program for economic reconstruction and initiate sound fiscal policies leading to reduction of budgetary deficits." A further condition for both military and economic aid was that there should be continuing evidence of the implementation of the urgently required political and military reforms. Finally, China would be asked to accept American advisers to see to it that the military and economic aid would be used in the manner for which it was intended.

The Wedemeyer report also contained recommendations regarding Manchuria. It was proposed that the United Nations should place Manchuria immediately under the guardianship of five powers, including the Soviet Union, or under a trusteeship. The inclusion of this particular recommendation was later offered as the main reason why the report was not made public at the time. The State Department pointed out that the Chinese government would have considered the Manchurian proposal an infringement of its sovereignty. Although General Wedemeyer's proposal on Manchuria was unacceptable and not useful, his report on Korea indicated that he foresaw the danger of an attack from the north on the Korean Republic. He urged that American forces be maintained in that area.

The Fall of China

The condition of the National Government deteriorated so fast during the rest of 1947 that the United States put aside the terms which Wedemeyer had laid down for the extension of American aid. The policy of making aid depend upon a sound and constructive program in the receiving country could not be applied in China. Immediate assistance was necessary to keep the Chinese government going and to give it another opportunity to put its house in order. For this purpose the Congress approved the China Aid Act of April 1948, which allotted $463,000,000 for economic and military aid. Of this amount $125,000,000 was given as a special grant and was intended for military assistance. Of the remaining $338,000,000 the Congress actually

[18] *Ibid.*, p. 764.

appropriated only $275,000,000 but events in China moved so fast that even this amount could not be fully used. In the discussion of this legislation Secretary Marshall made it clear that the United States did not wish to take over the Chinese government and administer its economic and military affairs. The China Aid Act was intended only as a stop-gap program; long-range aid would have to wait until a constructive program was forthcoming from the Chinese government. No such program ever saw the light of day.

The National Government, according to American observers, was rapidly losing the support of public opinion and the confidence of its own armies in the fall of 1948. The most constantly recurring themes in the reports of American military and diplomatic officials concerned Chiang Kai-shek's personal rule, his reliance on a small number of trusted military followers, in spite of their proven inability and corruption, and his total disregard for American military advice. In October the American ambassador to China, Dr. John Leighton Stuart, stated his belief that no American efforts "short of armed intervention on a very large scale" could avert further military disaster and that there was no will to fight left in the National armies. In view of this situation Secretary Marshall informed Stuart that while everything was being done to speed up the delivery of military aid,

adoption of a course of increased aid would violate all basic considerations underlying American policy towards China, would involve the United States directly in China's civil war, would commit this Government to underwriting the Chinese Government militarily and economically at a cost which it would be impossible to estimate at a time when the United States has heavy commitments throughout the world in connection with foreign aid programs and would not, in the light of appraisals of the situation submitted by the Embassy and consular officers in China over a period of several months, achieve its avowed objectives.[19]

In November the ranking United States military officers in China were unanimous in their judgment that "short of actual employment of United States troops no amount of military assistance could save the present situation in view of its advanced stage of deterioration." The same officers pointed out that as it was the policy of the United States not to intervene with military force, there was no longer any way in which the National Government or the United States could save the situation. From this time on the United States watched the collapse of the National Government in the face of mounting Communist attacks, feeling that it was unable to help avert the inevitable tragedy. By the summer of 1949 the Communists were in control of the mainland and in September established their new regime in Peking.

The National Government of China was moved to Formosa. About a million civilian refugees and nearly half a million troops escaped to the island. The United States transferred the China aid program to Formosa, shipping there the remainder of the military supplies which had been ordered under the China Aid Act. No additional military aid, however, was authorized because it was assumed that only the interposition of "armed forces of the United States could save the island." As the United States at this time had no inten-

[19] *Ibid.*, pp. 284–85.

tion of sending American forces to defend Formosa, it did not wish to incur the additional loss of prestige that would follow if the Communists captured the island after further military assistance had been extended. No military assistance was provided Formosa until after the outbreak of the Korean war. In the economic field there were already several projects which had been started on Formosa as part of the general program of aid to China. They were managed by the Economic Cooperation Administration, which had been set up originally to handle Marshall aid in Europe, and by the Joint Commission on Rural Reconstruction, a Sino-American organization established in the fall of 1948 to carry out a program of agrarian reform. After the fall of the mainland all the activities of these two organizations were transferred to Formosa. Beyond these measures the United States was unwilling to become involved in the continuing Chinese civil war.

The impact of the Communist conquest of China was felt all over Asia. It profoundly changed the whole balance of power because the Soviet Union had now gained an ally of enormous potential influence. The very country which the United States had expected to become a friendly ally and the leading democratic power in the Far East was now a dangerous and aggressive enemy. The conclusion of the Sino-Soviet alliance of February 1950 made it abundantly clear that Communist China had to be regarded as an integral part of the Soviet power bloc. The new Communist power also endangered the independent development of the Republic of Korea, affected the future of Japan, and brought powerful Communist armies to the borders of neighboring countries in Southeast Asia. China could now give direct aid to Communist movements across her borders in Korea and Southeast Asia.

U. S. Defense in the Pacific

The new Communist power on the mainland compelled the United States to re-examine its military position in the Pacific, which had been greatly extended as a result of the war. The United States had taken over all the Pacific islands which Japan had held except Formosa and the Pescadores, which were to be returned to China, and the Kuriles and Southern Sakhalin, which went to the Soviet Union. These islands—the Marshalls, the Marianas, and the Carolines, Iwo Jima and the Bonins, and the Liuchiu Islands, which include Okinawa—became part of the American system of naval and air bases in the Pacific. These islands were taken over by the United States as trusteeships under the United Nations Charter. It was taken for granted that America should retain military control of the western Pacific. At the San Francisco Conference for the establishment of the United Nations it was agreed that there should be no military restrictions on the trusteeship. Control of the Pacific island chains and offshore positions supported American occupation forces in Japan and made it possible to undertake the obligations for the defense of the Philippines which were assumed after the establishment of the independent Philippine Republic. A Military Assistance Agreement with the Philippines was signed in March 1947. In March 1948, another agreement was made which determined the location of eleven American army bases and four naval operating areas.

As American military establishments stretched in a chain from the northernmost part of Japan via Okinawa to the Philippines, the Communist conquest of China raised the question of the strategic importance of the Korean Republic and the Nationalist-held island of Formosa. There was no American statement on the strategic value of Formosa at this time, but on January 12, 1950, Secretary Acheson made a speech on the Far East in which he said that the Republic of Korea would have to provide for its own defense backed "by the commitments of the entire civilized world under the Charter of the United Nations." In this statement Secretary Acheson was reflecting the views of the Joint Chiefs of Staff, who held that in case of a general Far Eastern war Korea would not be a main theater of operations and was therefore of little strategic interest. It was in accordance with this view that American troops had been withdrawn from Korea in the summer of 1949. But it was in accordance with the Acheson statement that the United States led the United Nations forces which came to the aid of the invaded Korean Republic in the summer of 1950.

The Korean Republic

The Republic of Korea was set up in the American zone of South Korea in August, 1948. Unable to come to terms with the Soviet Union on the question of Korean unification the United States took the matter to the Assembly of the United Nations in November 1947. The U.N. set up a Temporary Commission which went to Korea to prepare the way for the election of a Korean Congress which would draw up a constitution. After the Soviet Union refused to permit the U.N. commission to enter the northern zone, elections were held in the south for a Congress which in turn adopted a constitution in July 1948. The Korean Republic was to have a President, who was head of the Executive Branch, a National Assembly as the legislative organ, and a Supreme Court as the highest judicial authority. The National Assembly elected the President, who appointed the Prime Minister with its consent. The elections were carried out in accordance with this constitution and the Government of the Republic of Korea was thus set up, in August 1948, under the sponsorship of the United Nations. The National Assembly elected Dr. Syngman Rhee as the first president. Towards the end of his first term in 1952 a constitutional amendment was passed which provided for the direct popular election of the president, a move which assured the re-election of Dr. Rhee, the most powerful personality in South Korea.

President Truman asked the Congress as early as June 1949 for a grant of $150,000,000 for economic assistance to South Korea. He justified this request by saying that such a grant would "encourage the people of southern and southeastern Asia and the islands of the Pacific to resist and reject Communist propaganda" and that it would "stand as a beacon to the people of Northern Asia in resisting the control of the Communist forces which have

120   140   160

U.S.S.R.

SEA OF OKHOTSK

Attu

60

KURILE IS.

SEA
OF JAPAN

CHINA

40

KOREA   *JAPAN*

P A C I F I C

RYUKYU IS.
(LIUKIU)
Okinawa
U.S.A. TRUST
PESCADORES
(PENGHU)
Formosa (Taiwan)

BONIN IS.
Iwo Jima   U.S.A. TRUST

SOUTH

20

Wake
U.S.A.

CHINA

MARIANAS IS.
Saipan

SEA

Bikini
MARSHALL
IS.

VIETNAM

PHILIPPINES

Guam

Leyte

PALAU IS.

CAROLINE IS.
Truk

0

BORNEO

U.S.A. TRUST

Tarawa

GILBERT
IS.

BISMARCK
ARCHIPELAGO

INDONESIA

NEW

GUINEA

SOLOMON IS.
Guadalcanal

AUSTRALIA

BRITAIN

NEW HEBRIDES

20

CORAL SEA

FRANCE

LOYALTY

AUSTRALIA

120   140   160

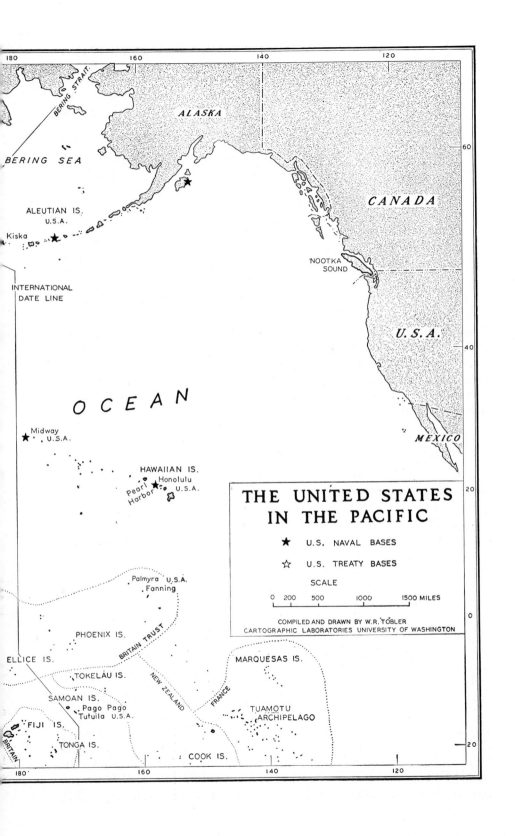

180 160 140 120

BERING STRAIT

ALASKA

60

BERING SEA

CANADA

ALEUTIAN IS.
U.S.A.

Kiska

NOOTKA
SOUND

INTERNATIONAL
DATE LINE

U.S.A.

40

O C E A N

Midway
U.S.A.

MEXICO

HAWAIIAN IS.
Honolulu
Pearl   U.S.A.
Harbor

20

THE UNITED STATES
IN THE PACIFIC

★   U.S. NAVAL BASES

☆   U.S. TREATY BASES

SCALE

0   200   500   1000   1500 MILES

Palmyra U.S.A.
Fanning

0

COMPILED AND DRAWN BY W.R. TOBLER
CARTOGRAPHIC LABORATORIES UNIVERSITY OF WASHINGTON

PHOENIX IS.

BRITAIN TRUST

ELLICE IS.

MARQUESAS IS.

TOKELAU IS.

NEW ZEALAND

FRANCE

SAMOAN IS.
Pago Pago
Tutuila U.S.A.

TUAMOTU
ARCHIPELAGO

FIJI IS.

BRITAIN

TONGA IS.

COOK IS.

20

180 160 140 120

overrun them." It was planned that this economic aid would help to begin an integrated three-year program, worked out by the E.C.A., for economic recovery. The Congress reluctantly approved a portion of the funds but by the spring of 1950 the results of even the limited aid were described by the E.C.A. as "spectacular." At the same time President Syngman Rhee began to put into practice a program of land reform which according to the Department of State would have been practically completed by the end of 1950 had it not been for the invasion from the north.

On the military side the picture was less bright. When American combat troops were withdrawn, a military mission of 500 men was assigned to the training of the Republic of Korea army. The R.O.K. army was given a certain amount of American equipment but was not provided with sufficient heavy arms to take the offensive, an omission for which there seem to have been several reasons. According to Dean Acheson the United States was itself in short supply of such equipment and the Korean forces had not yet developed to the point where they could use it. The fact that the United States did not give the South Korean army the weapons with which to take the offensive, however, nullified the threats to conquer North Korea which South Korean leaders were making at the time. By 1950 the United States, which had made a bad start with the Korean people in 1945, had succeeded in bringing about the establishment of a Republic with representative institutions, a rapidly recuperating economy, and the nucleus of a modern army.

The Korean War and U. S. Policy

The Soviet-trained North Korean forces attacked South Korea without warning on June 25, 1950, and advanced rapidly on Seoul. The United States turned immediately to the United Nations, which had sponsored the establishment of the Korean Republic. On the same day the Security Council met in emergency session, passed a resolution in which the North Korean attack was declared a breach of the peace, called for withdrawal of North Korean forces to the 38th parallel, and called upon all members to "render every assistance to the United Nations in the execution of this resolution and to refrain from giving assistance to the North Korean authorities." On the basis of this resolution, especially the call to render every assistance to the United Nations in executing the resolution, President Truman made a statement on June 27 in which he declared that he had "ordered United States air and sea forces to give the Korean Government troops cover and support." Later the same day the Security Council passed a second resolution recommending that "the members of the United Nations furnish such assistance to the Republic of Korea as may be necessary to repel the armed attack and to restore international peace and security in the area." Following this action President Truman on June 30 called a meeting of Congressional leaders with whom he reviewed the situation, announcing that he had authorized the air force to bomb North Korea, ordered the navy to blockade the Korean coast, and authorized General MacArthur "to use certain supporting ground units." A week later the United Nations recommended that a unified command be established for all military forces fighting in its behalf and requested the United States to appoint a commander. President Truman thereupon appointed General MacArthur as the Commanding General of the United Nations forces. All these moves in the United Nations Security Council had been possible because of the absence of the Soviet delegate who, since January 1950, had boycotted the Council meetings in protest against the failure to admit Communist China to the U.N. If the Soviet delegate had been present he would have vetoed the resolutions on Korea. It was in this way that the United Nations organization took collective military action, for the first time in its history, to repel aggression.

The Communist attack on South Korea was more than an open challenge to the Charter of the United Nations, a challenge which was met with collective action in Korea. President Truman believed that it was the beginning of a new phase in the Communist strategy of expansion and aggression, raising questions of policy and national interest over the whole Far Eastern area. His statement of June 27 dealt, therefore, with much more than Korea. It outlined a strategic plan for strengthening the military position of the United States and its friends and allies along the whole military frontier of the Communist world in the Far East. President Truman said:

The attack upon Korea makes it plain beyond all doubt that communism has passed beyond the use of subversion to conquer independent nations and will now use armed invasion and war. It has defied the orders of the Security Council of the United Nations issued to preserve international peace and security. In these circumstances the occupation of Formosa by Communist forces would be a direct threat to the security of the Pacific area and to United States forces performing their lawful and necessary functions in that area.

Accordingly I have ordered the Seventh Fleet to prevent any attack on Formosa. As a corollary of this action I am calling upon the Chinese Government on Formosa to cease all air and sea operations against the mainland. The Seventh Fleet will see that this is done. The determination of the future status of Formosa must await the restoration of security in the Pacific, a peace settlement with Japan, or consideration by the United Nations.

I have also directed that United States forces in the Philippines be strengthened and that military assistance to the Philippine Government be accelerated.

I have similarly directed acceleration in the furnishing of military assistance to the forces of France and the associated states in Indochina and the dispatch of a military mission to provide close working relations with those forces.

I know that all members of the United Nations will consider carefully the consequences of this latest aggression in Korea in defiance of the Charter of the United Nations. A return to the rule of force in international affairs would have far-reaching effects. The United States will continue to uphold the rule of law.

I have instructed Ambassador Austin, as the representative of the United States to the Security Council, to report these steps to the Council.[20]

[20] *Military Situation in the Far East: Hearings* before the Senate Armed Services and Foreign Relations Committees, 82nd Congress, 1st Session (Washington, 1951), Part 5, p. 3369.

The strategy outlined in President Truman's statement was immediately applied. A military investigatory mission went to Formosa in August 1950. It was followed in May 1951 by a Military Advisory Group which began to train and equip the Nationalist armies with American assistance. New funds were also given for economic aid. For all intents and purposes President Truman had decided that Formosa was of strategic importance to the United States and would be defended. It was made clear, however, that this was a defensive move and that Formosa would not be allowed to make attacks on the mainland. In the Philippines the United States strengthened its own military forces and speeded up military assistance to the Philippine government, as promised by President Truman. Realizing, however, that the growth of Communist guerrilla activities and the worsening economic situation endangered the stability of the Philippines from within, the United States sent the Bell mission in August 1950, to draw up a program of economic and administrative reform as a basis for American aid. Several missions had been sent to Indo-China before the outbreak of the Korean War in order to prepare the way for American aid. In July a new survey mission was sent to speed up and expand this aid and substantial amounts of army supplies and naval aid were delivered during the remainder of the year. The American efforts to build up the military and economic strength of Formosa, the Philippines, and Indo-China were designed to discourage Communist aggression on these fronts. They were also designed to secure the American military position in the Far East at the time when the United States was carrying the major load in the United Nations war in Korea.

The conflict in Korea began with a retreat for United Nations forces. By August they were hemmed into a small area around the port of Pusan, which was held and reinforced for a counter-attack. In September 1950, a drive to the north was coordinated with an amphibious landing at Inchon, the port of Seoul. These movements broke the back of the North Korean armies, which fled in disorder beyond the 38th parallel. The question now arose as to whether or not United Nations forces should pursue the defeated invaders beyond the parallel into North Korea. This matter was taken up in the United Nations, to which the Soviet delegate had in the meantime returned. The Soviet Union had again raised the question of the admission of Communist China to the U.N. and had protested against the American neutralization of Formosa, which she labelled as intervention. In order to prevent the Soviet Union from blocking action in the Security Council by the use of the veto, Secretary Acheson transferred the discussion of the Korean issue to the General Assembly, which could make decisions by majority vote. In a resolution of September 30, 1950, the General Assembly reaffirmed the United Nations objective of unifying Korea and of holding elections for the establishment of a "unified, independent, and democratic Government" for the whole of Korea. By implication this resolution approved a military move across the 38th parallel. United Nations forces therefore drove into North Korea where they occupied the North Korean capital of Pyongyang on the west coast and on the east coast pushed on to the Yalu River. It was at this point that the Chinese Communists entered the war.

The Chinese government had already issued a statement to the effect that China would enter the war if foreign troops came near her borders. The Indian government transmitted this warning and refused to sign the U.N. resolution of September 30. The Chinese never intervened officially in Korea but sent large armies which they described as "volunteers." On November 26 Chinese armies launched an attack on the United Nations forces, which were unprepared for this move and were driven back. By January all of North Korea had been lost, Seoul had fallen, and the battle line was well inside South Korea. At this point a new field commander, General Matthew Ridgeway, succeeded in stopping the retreat and in resuming the offensive.

General Ridgeway was appointed to succeed General MacArthur as Supreme Commander of Allied Powers and as Commander-in-Chief of the United Nations Command on April 10, 1951. General MacArthur was recalled by President Truman on the grounds that he was "unable to give his wholehearted support to the policies of the United States Government and of the United Nations in matters pertaining to his official duties." President Truman had particularly in mind General MacArthur's unauthorized offer, made in March, personally to negotiate a settlement of the Korean conflict with the enemy commander. The offer laid down political conditions and was combined with an implied threat to bomb Chinese coastal and inland areas. This was the latest of several occasions at which General MacArthur, according to the President, had made unauthorized public statements at variance with the officially declared policy of the United States government. President Truman regarded the recall of General MacArthur as a necessary move to maintain civilian authority over the military. The return of MacArthur to America was followed by congressional hearings on the recall and on the whole military situation in the Far East. These hearings, sometimes called the Great Debate, took up most of May and June and provided an opportunity for the highest diplomatic and military officials to explain American Far Eastern policy. The two million words of published hearings and documents provide a valuable record of American policy.

In Korea United Nations forces advanced steadily. By June 1951 they were again across the 38th parallel. As the forces under General Ridgeway's command were not sufficient to reconquer North Korea, it became the strategy of the United Nations to inflict such heavy losses on the Chinese that they would be forced to negotiate. This strategy was successful. The readiness of the Chinese to negotiate was first indicated by the Soviet delegate to the U.N., and truce negotiations were started at Panmunjon in July 1951. They lasted until July 1953, during which time the fighting continued.

The negotiations revolved around three main issues. The first issue was the Communist demand to broaden the scope of the negotiations. The United Nations succeeded in excluding general political questions, such as the admission of Communist China to the United Nations, Formosa, and the withdrawal of foreign troops from Korea. Another issue was that of the location of the truce line. The Communists wanted to return to the 38th parallel, but the United Nations, whose forces held more territory to the north of the parallel than the Communists held to the south, insisted on following, approximately, the line of battle. This line was militarily much easier to hold. The issue which brought about the most bitter debates was that of the exchange of prisoners. The United Nations took the position that prisoners of war should be free to decide whether or not they wished to be returned to their side. The Communists were finally compelled to agree that a neutral commission under Indian chairmanship should administer the exchange of prisoners, giving to each a free opportunity to decide where he would go. When the truce was finally concluded some 72 per cent of the Chinese prisoners refused to return to Communist China. Almost all of them were sent to Formosa. Twenty-one Americans chose to stay with the Communists. The Chinese Communists would not have given way on every important issue, particularly on the politically humiliating one of non-forcible repatriation, if they had not been determined to secure an armistice.

The United States concluded a Mutual Defense Treaty with the Republic of Korea on October 1, 1953. Both countries promised that in case of external attack on the territories of either of the parties in the Pacific area they would act to meet the common danger in accordance with their constitutional processes. For this purpose the Republic of Korea permitted United States forces to be stationed on and around its territory. This treaty was necessary not only to justify the stationing of American forces in Korea for joint defense but also to make it possible for the Korean Republic to accept the armistice. The United States also undertook to assist in the economic reconstruction of war-torn Korea with the pledge of one billion dollars in aid. It took several months for the American Economic Coordinator to reach an agreement with President Syngman Rhee on the conditions under which the fund would be given. The United States insisted on a certain amount of control over the spending of the money in order to prevent inflationary tendencies, and also required that the Korean government use its own foreign assets to support the program. Such conditions were normal in American aid programs. Agreement with the Korean government was finally reached in December, 1953. In addition to official help much private assistance was given by Americans through relief organizations. In this way some of the terrible damage which the war had brought to Korea was repaired and the Republic of Korea given an opportunity to revive.

The United States had previously given considerable military assistance and economic aid to other countries to help them resist Communist pressures, but American action in Korea demonstrated that the United States was willing to engage its own forces when the need arose. The United States acted with and through the United Nations, and for the first time military means were used to apply the principle of collective security against an aggressor. The Korean War revealed the full extent of American military unpreparedness, and speeded up the rearmament of the United States. The armed forces, which were at minimum strength at the beginning of the war, grew rapidly in size, and the production of armaments increased correspondingly. The rearmament program was seen not as an emergency measure but as a long-range undertaking. It was believed that war with the Soviet bloc could be avoided only by building sufficient strength to act as a deterrent to attack and thus to provide the basis from which it would be possible to negotiate successfully.

Japanese Alliance and the Anzus Pact

The strengthening of the American position in the Far East which came as a result of the Korean War required a change in the status of Japan, which had become, in effect, the United Nations base for the war in Korea. The role that Japan was called upon to play made it increasingly inappropriate for her to remain an occupied country. While China, the former ally, had become an enemy, Japan, the former enemy, was to become an ally. The United States had envisaged a new role for Japan even before the outbreak of the Korean War, and decided to conclude a peace treaty with Japan without Soviet participation. The peace treaty, signed in September 1951, came into effect on April 28, 1952. Japan had to make a special treaty with Nationalist China because of the conflicting British and American policies toward recognition of the Communist and Nationalist governments. With the Soviet Union Japan remained technically at war. In the San Francisco peace treaty Japan surrendered her claims to the island of Formosa and the Pescadores but as she did not state to whom these rights were transferred, the National Government of China did not gain legal title to the territory of Formosa. Nor was the status of Formosa altered in the peace treaty between Japan and Nationalist China. In the San Francisco treaty the Japanese also renounced their rights to the Kurile Islands and to southern Sakhalin but did not transfer title to the Soviet Union, which had been promised these territories at Yalta and was now in occupation. Japan renounced her claim to the mandated islands and accepted the trusteeship system under which they had been handed over to the United States. In regard to the Liuchiu Islands, the Bonins, and surrounding island groups, Japan promised to "concur in any proposal of the United States to the United Nations to place [them] under its trusteeship system, with the United States as the sole administering authority." In the meantime the United States was to have full jurisdiction over these territories. In all these territorial arrangements with regard to the former Japanese empire the agreements made at Cairo and Yalta were applied but not legalized.

The main shift in American policy towards Japan is indicated by the stipulations on security in which the Allied Powers who signed the San Francisco treaty recognized "that Japan as a sovereign nation possesses the inherent right of individual or collective self-defense referred to in Article 51 of the Charter of the United Nations and that Japan may voluntarily enter into collective security arrangements." Neither was the stipulated withdrawal of occupation forces to

prevent the stationing or retention of foreign armed forces in Japanese territory under or in consequence of any bilateral or multilateral agreements which have been or may be made between one or more of the Allied Powers, on the one hand, and Japan on the other.

The last stipulation permitted the conclusion of an American-Japanese Mutual Security Pact which was signed at the same time as the treaty. This pact, by which Japan accepted the stationing of American troops as allies on Japanese soil, brought Japan into the American security system of mutual defense treaties, which by now included the Philippines, Australia and New Zealand. The United States concluded a new Mutual Defense Agreement with the Philippines in August 1951, which confirmed existing treaty relationships between the two countries. The tripartite agreement made with Australia and New Zealand, known as the Anzus Pact, was concluded at the same time.

The conclusion of these military alliances was as radical a departure from traditional American policy in the Pacific as was the N.A.T.O. in the Atlantic. But in the Pacific there was a tradition of naval expansion which had started at the time of Commodore Perry a hundred years before and had finally led to the establishment of a system of military bases which stretched all the way from Pearl Harbor to Okinawa, and from the Aleutians to Pago Pago. This system of bases, covering the main expanse of the Pacific, was strengthened and consolidated by the military arrangements made with the Philippines, Japan, and the Anzus powers. The bases and alliances, taken together, formed an interdependent system on which rested American control of the Pacific. The postwar consolidation of bases and alliances into a unified system was the American military answer in the Pacific to the formation of the Moscow-Peking alliance.

The Strengthening of Southeast Asia

In Southeast Asia, however, the threat was more immediate and the answer much more difficult. The armies of Communist China, right on the borders of several Southeast Asian countries, could bring every kind of pressure to bear on them from the support of armed uprisings to direct intervention. This threat was the more serious because it affected one of the world's greatest colonial areas. There were many reasons why the societies of this area should be particularly vulnerable. The nationalist movements, which were directed against European countries, were open to exploitation by the Communists. The rapid transformation of the social and political institutions of these countries, combined with the weaknesses of dependent economies and the low standard of living, made it difficult for these countries to stand alone or even to make constructive use of outside economic aid. These were the problems with which American policy had to deal.

The problem of national independence was most critical in the countries of Indonesia and Indo-China. Burma, together with India and Pakistan, had been granted independence in 1947, and Thailand had always been politically independent. The issue of national independence in British Malaya admitted of no easy and immediate solution. In Indonesia and Indo-China, however, the problem was most acute, for open conflict developed between the colonial powers, which were intent on maintaining their rule, and the local nationalist movements, which were determined to achieve independence.

The traditional American policy of supporting political independence and self-government had to take into account the Communist misuse of nationalist movements. It had become evident that the familiar patterns of Soviet infiltration and conquest were being applied to the former colonial areas. After the war there were Communist elements in the Indonesian nationalist movement. For a period the Dutch policy of military reconquest played into the hands of the Communists, who, in their overconfidence, attempted by violent means to take over the leadership of the nationalist movement in September, 1948. The Indonesian nationalists themselves crushed the Communist rebellion and executed the leading Communists. From this time on the United States gave strong support to the Indonesian nationalists and assisted them in their settlement with the Dutch at The Hague in 1949. As a result of this policy and the timely withdrawal of the Dutch, the Indonesian Republic, like Burma, India and Pakistan, began its political independence free from Communist control.

Events in Indo-China followed a different course. At the end of the war the leadership of the nationalist movement was already in Communist hands. The French, nonetheless, chose to come to terms. In 1946 they agreed to recognize a Vietnamese government under Ho Chi Minh. When this agreement broke down in 1947, the French missed the opportunity to support a non-Communist nationalist government because of their reluctance to give real authority to truly nationalist leaders. The government of Bao Dai, eventually set up in 1949, had little authority at first. In this situation the United States supported the French, and when Communist aggression in Korea increased the strategic importance of Indo-China, the stepped-up American aid was given to and through the French authorities. A part of this aid was later set aside, by agreement, for the training and equipping of Vietnamese forces which were to be under native officers. This was as near as the United States ever came, at least up till the critical days that followed the signing of the armistice in Korea in July of 1953, to giving support to Vietnamese nationalism. While Bao Dai's government slowly gained more authority and even attracted a certain number of nationalists away from Ho Chi Minh, the Communists continued to grow in military and territorial strength and Vietnam remained the main danger area in Southeast Asia.

In those countries of Southeast Asia where national independence had already been established, American military aid could be given directly to the national governments. Most of these governments were not only sensitive about their relations to the Western powers, from whom they had but recently gained their independence, but were also afraid of openly taking sides against the Soviet bloc. In 1950 the United States sent a survey mission to Southeast Asia to arrange for military aid, but Burma refused to receive it and Indonesia permitted its entrance with reluctance. In the end Burma accepted a number of coast guard vessels and technical aid in the training of their crews while Indonesia received assistance for the building up of its police force. Only Thailand signed an agreement with the United States, in October 1950, for military aid.

The Communist aggression that brought about a quickening of military aid to Southeast Asia also brought about a new approach to the problem of strengthening the economies of that area. The promise to promote "higher standards of living, full employment, and conditions of economic and social progress and development . . ." had already been made in Article 55 of the United Nations Charter. But little had been done beyond measures for direct relief until the threat of Communism demanded action. The view that Communism flourished best in conditions of poverty lay behind the program of aid to underdeveloped countries.

An underdeveloped country has been defined as one in which "capital investment is small, per capita productivity is low, and the standard of living of a large part of the people is at or near the subsistence level." [21] By this definition over half of the world's population lives in underdeveloped countries. The main purpose of the assistance originally envisaged in the United Nations Charter was to increase production in order to narrow the gap between the income level of the peoples of these countries and those of the United States and western Europe.

It is difficult to exaggerate the complexity of the problem. Conditions in all these countries are marked by overpopulation, chronic epidemics, illiteracy, and undeveloped resources. Per capita output is therefore low and capital accumulation insufficient to bring about any significant change in conditions. While the need for outside capital assistance is obvious, neither foreign nor domestic capital can be put to work constructively until the level of technology has been raised. The degree of progress that can be made depends on the capacity for development of the human and material resources of each country. It also depends on the ability of political leaders to formulate and carry out long-range programs involving considerable sacrifice with the support and cooperation of their peoples. In the revolutionary language of the United Nations experts,

Ancient philosophies have to be scrapped; old social institutions have to disintegrate; bonds of caste, creed and race have to be burst; and large numbers of persons who cannot keep up with progress have to have their expectations of a comfortable life frustrated. Very few communities are willing to pay the full price of rapid economic progress.[22]

[21] Wm. A. Brown, Jr. and Redvers Opie, *American Foreign Assistance* (Washington, 1953), p. 384.
[22] Brown and Opie, *op. cit.*, p. 386.

Improvement in the conditions of underdeveloped countries depended as much on the skill and capacity of local leadership as upon the availability of outside assistance.

The United States was interested in the promotion of assistance to the underdeveloped countries of Southeast Asia for humanitarian, economic, and political reasons. In addition to the generalized desire to assist underprivileged peoples there was the realization that the United States had an interest in the improvement of world economic conditions and the production of raw materials. It took the growing threat of Communism, however, to provide the political incentive that made the program of assistance acceptable to the Congress. In his Inaugural Address, January 1948, President Truman laid down the new policy of direct aid to underdeveloped countries as the fourth point of his program.

Fourth, we must embark on a bold new program for making the benefits of our scientific advances and industrial progress available for the improvement and growth of underdeveloped areas . . .

For the first time in history, humanity possesses the knowledge and skill to relieve the suffering of these people.

The United States is preeminent among nations in the development of industrial and scientific techniques. The material resources which we can afford to use for the assistance of other peoples are limited. But our imponderable resources in technical knowledge are constantly growing and are inexhaustible.[23]

In this way there was launched what came to be known as the Point Four program.

The announcement of the bold new program was one thing, its execution was another. The comparatively small funds made available were used at first in the Near East, Africa, the Middle East, and South America. It was necessary to send fact-finding missions to Southeast Asia in order to estimate the technical and economic needs of a part of the world with which the United States had had little contact. In 1950 a program was worked out for aid to Indo-China, Thailand, Burma, Malaya, and Indonesia which included provision for an increase in agricultural production, health programs, and improvement of transportation. The special missions sent out to carry on this program were put under the general administration of the Economic Co-operation Administration. But the multiplicity of government organizations and programs participating in the Point Four and other types of aid stands out in sharp contrast to the coordination of aid to Europe under the Marshall Plan as well as to the regional program of the Colombo Plan, a British Commonwealth organization which also came to include Burma, Indonesia, Thailand, and Indo-China. The problem of multiplicity of programs and agencies was resolved by the passage of the Mutual Security Act in the summer of 1951. By this act the various American aid efforts all over the world were coordinated under one agency, the Mutual Security Administration. The economic and military assistance programs were now linked together and both put on a global basis.

[23] *Ibid.*, p. 389.

The preamble to the Mutual Security Act was in itself a statement of the foreign policy of the United States. The act was

to maintain the security and promote the foreign policy of the United States by authorizing military, economic, and technical assistance to friendly countries to strengthen the mutual security and individual and collective defenses of the free world, to develop their resources in the interest of their security and independence and the national interests of the United States, and to facilitate the effective participation of those countries in the United Nations system for collective security.[24]

By this act military assistance could be given only to those countries which were willing to side with the United States in the cold war, while economic assistance could be given to any country outside of the Communist world. Burma and Indonesia refused to accept military aid on this basis, but Thailand, Formosa, Indo-China, and the Philippines together received military aid amounting to $535,250,000. The whole area of Southeast Asia, including the neutral countries, was given economic aid to the amount of over $237,000,000. These figures indicate the trend toward giving priority to military assistance that was apparent in the whole program. In 1950 military assistance represented about one quarter of the total of American aid but in 1952 it was over two-thirds. The relative amount of military aid was to grow even larger when American support to Indo-China alone, in the year before the Geneva Conference of 1954, reached the figure of over $800,000,000. But military aid alone could not save Indo-China.

The Geneva Conference

The French military position in northern Vietnam had become so desperate by the summer of 1954 that the French government decided to come to terms with the local Communist regime of Ho Chi Minh and the Chinese Communists who stood behind it. When the French decided to negotiate withdrawal from northern Vietnam they had more men in the field, and more and better equipment, than the Vietminh forces. They also had complete control in the air. The desperate French military position was not due to lack of arms and equipment or even the faulty strategy of putting too much reliance on fortified positions. The real weakness of the French lay in their attempt to defend an outdated colonial system and their consequent refusal to come to terms with Vietnamese nationalism while there was still time to do so. For this reason the American effort to help to build up local strength against the Communists by economic, technical, and military assistance broke down in Indo-China. The President and other high officials of the American government indicated their grave concern over the advance of Communism into Southeast Asia and there was even talk of American military intervention, but no such action was taken.

In May 1954, the French government agreed to the calling of a conference at Geneva in order to negotiate a settlement. The conference included the Foreign Ministers of Great Britain, Soviet Russia, Communist China,

[24] *Ibid.*, p. 509.

France, Vietnam, Laos, Cambodia, and the so-called Democratic Republic of Vietnam. At Geneva the French agreed to give up north Vietnam to Ho Chi Minh and to have elections held in 1956 to decide the fate of the whole of Vietnam. The United States was represented only by its Under Secretary of State and did not take part in the Conference Declaration or in the agreements which were concluded, but made its own declaration instead. In this declaration the United States took note of the various agreements concluded, and declared in regard to them that it would refrain from the threat or the use of force to disturb them; announced that it would view any renewal of the aggression in violation of the agreements with grave concern and as a serious threat to peace; pointed out that "in the case of nations now divided against their will we shall continue to seek to achieve unity through free elections, supervised by the United Nations to insure that they are conducted fairly"; and with respect to the Vietnamese protest against partition reiterated its traditional position that peoples are entitled to determine their own future and that it would not join in any arrangement that would hinder this; and that it shared the hope that the agreements would permit Cambodia, Laos, and Vietnam to be truly independent.

The intent of the United States declaration was to reserve freedom of diplomatic action, to bind all parties not to change the agreements by force, and to put in a claim that only supervision by the United Nations could guarantee a fair election. President Eisenhower stated on July 21, 1954, the same day that the Geneva Declaration was made, ". . . the United States has not itself been party to or bound by the decisions taken by the Conference" but expressed his hopes that they would lead to peace.

U. S. Military and Political Allies

The defeat in Vietnam made it even more necessary, in the view of the State Department, to build up as much of a regional defense organization as possible in Southeast Asia. The negotiations which Secretary Dulles had carried on during the Geneva Conference found the American position considerably at variance with that of the British and the Asian neutrals such as India. The British were more inclined toward a loose organization with the main emphasis on the economic side whereas the United States wanted a formal military organization. After the Geneva Conference a middle ground was found between these two positions, and an eight-nation conference was held in Manila in September, 1954. It was attended by the United States, Great Britain, France, Australia, New Zealand, Pakistan, Thailand and the Philippines, the last three being the only Asiatic nations represented. The conference agreed on a Southeast Asia collective defense treaty against open armed attack and internal subversion.

It was agreed that armed attack from the outside against any of the signatories would be regarded as a common danger and would be met as such. Internal subversion would be handled by joint consultation on measures for the common defense. The "treaty area" was the general area of

Southeast Asia and the Southeast Pacific but excluded Formosa. The treaty also included the unusual provision that the signatories would undertake to strengthen their free institutions. They also agreed to cooperate in providing economic and technical assistance to each other. The United States made the condition that only in case of Communist aggression would it join in the common defense on the same basis as the other signatories. The eight signatories to the treaty, known as the Southeast Asia Treaty Organization (SEATO) extended the application of its defense and economic measures to the territories of Cambodia, Laos, and Southern Vietnam. The SEATO treaty was important for being the first agreement on common defense in Southeast Asia and the first defense arrangement to deal explicitly with Communist subversion.

In addition to SEATO the Manila Conference wrote a Pacific Charter which was signed by all eight participants, who promised to "uphold the principle of equal rights and self-determination of peoples, and . . . to promote self-government and to secure independence of all countries whose peoples desire it and are able to undertake its responsibilities." In the second article the powers agreed to take measures for the orderly achievement of these purposes. In the third article they promised to cooperate with each other in economic, social, and cultural fields. The last article was a promise to resist any attempt to subvert their freedom or to destroy their sovereignty or territorial integrity. With all its serious limitations the Pacific Charter was the first statement of principles made jointly by colonial powers and former colonies.

The American system of security treaties now included Korea, Japan, the Philippines, and the area of Southeast Asia. It remained to clarify the status of Formosa. When President Truman, at the beginning of the Korean War, announced his intention of preventing a Communist attack on Formosa, he also stated that Chiang Kai-shek would not be permitted to attack the mainland. Shortly after coming into office President Eisenhower withdrew the restriction on Chiang Kai-shek but continued to protect Formosa, without, however, binding the United States to do so by treaty. On December 2, 1954, the United States and the National Government of China signed a mutual defense treaty, which was ratified on March 4, 1955. By this treaty the United States committed itself to the defense of Formosa and the Pescadores in the event of an attack and also to the defense of "such other territories as may be determined by mutual agreement" between the United States and the National Government. In an exchange of notes between these two governments after the treaty was ratified, it was indicated that the use of force outside of Formosa and the Pescadores "will be a matter of joint agreement between the parties subject to action of an emergency nature which is clearly an exercise of the inherent right of self-defense." In other words, while the National Government could not attack without the consent of the United States, there was nothing in the treaty to prevent the United States from giving that consent.

One issue raised in connection with the treaty was whether or not it would recognize the claim of the National Government to Formosa and the Pescadores, which had never been legally transferred to the Republic of China. If it could be established that the treaty gave formal recognition to the legal rights of the National Government over this territory, then Peking could contend that in attacking Formosa it was not committing aggression but merely continuing the civil war and that the treaty constituted intervention. The American government held that the treaty did not alter the juridical status of Formosa and the Pescadores, which had been promised but never formally transferred to the Republic of China.

Another issue concerned the degree to which the treaty would commit the United States to the defense of the off-shore islands which were in Nationalist hands. At the time of the signing of the treaty the United States government remained deliberately vague on this point. Peking, however, was very clear in its announced intention to take Formosa and by the end of 1954 had accumulated considerable military power opposite the island. There was some fighting for possession of the off-shore islands. At the end of January 1955, the President introduced to the Congress a resolution concerning his authority to defend Formosa and the Pescadores. In this resolution the President referred to the threat of military attack against Formosa and the Pescadores and to the defense treaty with the National Government and requested that he be

authorized to employ the armed forces of the United States as he deems necessary for the specific purpose of securing and protecting Formosa and the Pescadores against armed attack, this authority to include the securing and protection of such related positions and territories of that area now in friendly hands and the taking of such other measures as he judges to be required or appropriate in assuring the defense of Formosa and the Pescadores.

The resolution was approved by the Congress.

In the four years since the outbreak of the Korean conflict the United States had constructed a system of military bases and treaty obligations around the frontiers of Communist China which were designed to block any further Communist advances. There were three areas in which there was direct military contact with the Chinese Communists and their allies—Korea, Formosa, and Indo-China. A Communist attack on the Republic of Korea or in Southeast Asia would put the Communists clearly in the position of being the aggressor and would arouse international resistance. In regard to Formosa the situation was different. No other country was bound to come to its defense except the United States and there was the possibility of differing legal interpretations of the status of the opposing forces in any military conflict.

The Bandung Conference

Communist aggression in Korea and Vietnam and the countermoves made by the United States had brought the military forces of the Communist bloc and the Free World face to face over a vast area in the

Far East. Some Asiatic nations had fallen victim to Communist aggression while others had committed themselves to alliances with the Western powers. As the pressure mounted on both sides a number of important Asiatic countries felt that it was more and more urgent for them to reassert their independent position in relation to the two big power blocs. A framework for regional cooperation between many Asian powers had been created by the meeting of British Commonwealth nations, except for the Union of South Africa, at Colombo in January 1950. From this meeting developed the Colombo Plan, a program for the cooperative economic development of South and Southeast Asia prepared by India, Pakistan, Ceylon, Malaya, and British Borneo. It was later joined by Burma and the Indo-Chinese states. Indonesia and Thailand kept in close touch with the organization.

In addition to this regional economic cooperation there had been a movement for political cooperation between Asian nations sponsored by India. As early as March 1947, twenty-five Asian nations were invited to New Delhi for an inter-Asian relations conference. In view of the many differences between the participating countries it was not easy to find common ground. A second conference was called in New Delhi in January 1949, in connection with the Indonesian struggle for independence. In May 1954, a group of Asian powers met again at Colombo to discuss the Indo-Chinese crisis, soon to be settled at the Geneva Conference.

In April 1955, the prime ministers of Burma, Ceylon, India, Indonesia and Pakistan, the Colombo powers, invited a total of twenty-nine countries to an Asian-African Conference at Bandung in Indonesia. In addition to the sponsoring countries there were Afghanistan, Cambodia, Communist China, Egypt, Ethiopia, the Gold Coast, Iran, Iraq, Japan, Jordan, Laos, Lebanon, Liberia, Libya, Nepal, the Philippines, Saudi Arabia, Sudan, Syria, Thailand, Turkey, North Vietnam, South Vietnam, and Yemen. The list included countries allied with the Western powers, Communist countries, and neutral countries. The list did not include Formosa, North and South Korea, and Israel, which were regarded as being too controversial, and South Africa, which was barred on the grounds of its racial policies. The inclusion of Communist China, which had just gained a great diplomatic victory at the Geneva Conference on Indo-China, gave to the meeting a high political significance.

The conference provided a platform for the expression of the anti-colonial feelings of all its members. For the first time in any meeting of Asian powers, however, strong public statements were made by several Asian leaders against Communist imperialism. These statements came not only from representatives of countries allied with Western powers, such as the Philippines, but also from representatives of neutral countries such as Ceylon. The conference condemned every sort of colonialism, including, by implication, that of Communism. In its final communiqué the conference suggested methods of economic cooperation among Asian-African countries and with outside powers, recommended cultural cooperation among its members and took note of the fact that the existence of colonialism in many parts of Asia and Africa, in whatever form it may be, not only prevents cultural cooperation, but also suppresses the national cultures of peoples. In particular, the Conference condemned racialism as a means of cultural suppression.

The conference declared itself in full support of the principles of human rights and of self-determination as set forth in the United Nations Charter and "deplored the policies and practices of racial segregation and discrimination" practiced in Africa and other parts of the world. The conference discussed the problems of dependent peoples and colonialism and the evils arising from the subjection of peoples to alien subjugation, domination, and exploitation, and was agreed:

(a) In declaring that colonialism in all its manifestations is an evil which should speedily be brought to an end; (b) In affirming that subjection of peoples to alien subjugation, domination and exploitation constitutes a denial of fundamental human rights, is contrary to the charter of the United Nations and is an impediment to promotion of world peace and co-operation; (c) In declaring its support of the cause of freedom and independence for all such peoples and (d) In calling upon the powers concerned to grant freedom and independence to such peoples.

The conference also supported the Arabs in their struggle with Israel and Indonesia in its struggle with Holland over New Guinea. The Bandung Conference made it clear that a very large part of the world was not committed to either side in the cold war and that Asian leaders felt that their views and policies could have a measurable effect on the world balance of power. At the Bandung Conference the Communist Chinese indicated, for the first time, that they were willing to settle the issue of Formosa peacefully.

The American Position

The American system of alliances and military bases could not be stronger than the political and economic foundations upon which they were built. As the administrators of the U. S. Mutual Security Program phrased it in their report to Congress in August 1953,

Coalitions for resistance to aggression and the strengthening of defenses constitute the first requirements for survival and progress. But such measures are inescapably tied in with the economic advancement and development of free nations. Enduring military strength cannot be built on a shaky economic foundation. Nor can freedom itself live for long in an atmosphere of social stagnation and marginal living standards.[25]

The realization that the security of the United States was bound up with the political, social, and economic well-being of the free world was the culmination of a long tradition of American Far Eastern policy. In the nineteenth century, policy was mainly concerned with the protection of the territorial and administrative integrity of Far Eastern states. In the twentieth century it was broadened to include the development of democratic institu-

[25] Peter V. Curl, ed., *Documents on American Foreign Relations, 1953* (New York, 1954), pp. 68–69.

tions and of self-government and independence for colonial countries. American policy, under Communist pressure, had now come to concern itself with the whole social fabric of other countries.

The report also recognized that the American economy itself had outgrown its domestic resources:

Our industrial output is almost altogether dependent on outside sources for tin, mica, asbestos, natural rubber, chrome, nickel, manganese, cobalt, and other vital materials. Without these imports, our economy would rapidly shrivel up. In addition, we are the world's largest importer of copper, lead, and zinc. Even crude petroleum and iron ore—once traditional symbols of American self-sufficiency—are now on our list of net imports.[26]

The United States, therefore, was vitally interested both in maintaining access to the resources of the free world and in keeping them out of Communist control. The system of military alliances and bases was intended to protect the American economy. In this sense it was a fulfillment of that other tradition in American Far Eastern policy, which dated from Commodore Perry, of covering the Pacific with naval bases for the protection of American commerce.

American policy since the war was strongly affected by the development of powerful new weapons. It was in the Pacific that the first atomic bombs were used and the Pacific was the proving ground for the hydrogen bomb tests. The question arose as to whether or not the new weapons made obsolete many of the assumptions on which political, as well as military, strategy was based. The high point in the development of this view was that decisive wars would no longer be waged on the traditional battlefield but would be determined by the immediate destruction of the major industrial centers of the world. It was thought that local wars could be prevented by the threat of massive retaliation. But the realization that the H-bomb threatened the mutual destruction of the world's greatest powers posed the question whether or not it would be used at all. Winston Churchill referred to the balance of terror and has argued that Great Britain was more secure in the age of the H-bomb than in that of the atom bomb. Traditional military strategy might not, therefore, be as inappropriate as was first thought. If Churchill's views were correct and there was a neutralization of the big weapons, then the concepts behind the American political and strategic position in the Pacific were still valid. If the world was not spared the catastrophe of hydrogen war, then the test of policy would be even greater. The future, not unlike the past, would be determined by the inner strength with which each society faced the time of trial.

[26] *Ibid.*, p. 69.

Suggested Reading

The following list of books is by no means exhaustive. It is meant to be of use to the student who wants to read further on any of the topics dealt with in this book. The works listed vary a great deal in quality and in character. Some are scholarly studies, some are documentary collections, and others are partisan statements or programs of political leaders. The student will be able to evaluate these readings and judge their importance. In them he will also be able to find further references for study.

CHINA (Chapters I, VII, XII)

Backhouse, E., and J.O.P. Bland, *Annals and Memoirs of the Court of Peking (from the 16th to the 20th Century)* (London, 1914).

Bales, William L., *Tso Tsungt'ang, Soldier and Statesman of Old China* (Shanghai, 1937).

Boardman, Eugene Powers, *Christian Influence Upon the Ideology of the Taiping Rebellion 1851–1864* (Madison, Wis., 1952).

Brandt, Conrad; Benjamin Schwartz; and J.K. Fairbank, *A Documentary History of Chinese Communism* (Cambridge, 1952).

Bruce, Joseph P., *Chu Hsi and His Masters; an Introduction to Chu Hsi and the Sung School of Chinese Philosophy* (London, 1923).

Brunnert, H.S., and V.V. Hagelstrom, *Present Day Political Organization of China* (Shanghai, 1912).

Buck, J.L., *Land Utilization in China* (3 vols., Chicago, 1937).

Cameron, Meribeth E., *The Reform Movement in China, 1898–1912* (Stanford, 1931).

Carter, Dagny, *Four Thousand Years of China's Art* (New York, 1948).

Chang, Carsun (Chia-sen), *The Third Force in China* (New York, 1952).

Chang, Chung-li, *The Chinese Gentry: Studies on their Role in Nineteenth-Century Chinese Society* (Seattle, 1955).

———, "The Gentry of Nineteenth-Century China: Their Economic Position as Evidenced by their Share of the National Product" (Doctoral Dissertation, University of Washington, Seattle, 1953).

Chan, Wing-tsit, "The Story of Chinese Philosophy," in *Philosophy: East & West*, ed. by Charles A. Moore (Princeton, 1944).

Chang, Kia-ngau (Chang Chia-ao), *China's Struggle for Railway Development* (New York, 1943).

Ch'en, Gideon (Ch'i-t'ien), *Lin Tse-hsü, Pioneer Promoter of the Adoption of Western Means of Maritime Defense in China* (Peiping, 1934).

———, *Tseng Kuo-fan, Pioneer Promoter of the Steamship in China* (Peiping, 1935).

———, *Tso Tsung-t'ang, Pioneer Promoter of the Modern Dockyard and the Woolen Mill in China* (Peiping, 1938).

Chen, Huan-chang, *The Economic Principles of Confucius and His School* (2 vols., New York, 1911).

Chen, Ta, *Population in Modern China* (Chicago, 1946).

Chi, Ch'ao-ting, *Key Economic Areas in*

Chinese History as Revealed in the Development of Public Works for Water-control (New York, 1936).

Chiang, Siang-tseh, *The Nien Rebellion* (Seattle, 1954).

Chiang Kai-shek, *China's Destiny*, authorized trans. by Wang Chung-hui, intro. by Lin Yu-tang (New York, 1947).

————, *China's Destiny and Chinese Economic Theory*, notes and comments by Philip Jaffee (New York, 1947).

Chien Tuan-sheng, *The Government and Politics of China* (Cambridge, 1950).

China Handbook, 1937–1943 (New York, 1943).

Compton, Boyd, *Mao's China: Party Reform Documents 1942–1944* (Seattle, 1952).

Creel, Herrlee G., *Chinese Thought from Confucius to Mao Tse-tung* (Chicago, 1953).

Cressey, George B., *China's Geographic Foundations* (New York, 1934).

Dubbs, H.H., "Wang Mang and His Economic Reforms," *T'oung Pao*, Vol. 35 (1940), pp. 219–265.

Edkins, Joseph, *The Revenue and Taxation of the Chinese Empire* (Shanghai, 1903).

Fairbank, John King, *Trade and Diplomacy on the China Coast; the Opening of the Treaty Ports 1842–1854* (Cambridge, 1953).

————, *The United States and China* (Cambridge, 1948).

Fei Hsiao-t'ung, *Peasant Life in China, a Field Study of Country Life in the Yangtze Valley* (London, 1939).

Fitzgerald, C.P., *China: A Short Cultural History* (rev. ed., London, 1950).

————, *Revolution in China* (London, 1952).

Fried, Morton H., *Fabric of Chinese Society: A Study of the Social Life of a Chinese County Seat* (New York, 1953).

Fung Yu-lan, *A History of Chinese Philosophy*, trans. by Derk Bodde (Princeton, 1952).

Gerth, Hans H., and C. W. Mills, ed., *From Max Weber: Essays in Sociology* (London, 1947).

Giles, Herbert A., *China and the Manchus* (Cambridge, Eng., and New York, 1912).

Granet, Marcel, *Chinese Civilization*, trans. by K. Innes and M. Brailsford (New York, 1951).

Hail, William J., *Tsêng Kuo-fan and the Taiping Rebellion* (New Haven and London, 1927).

Hightower, James Robert, *Topics in Chinese Literature* (Cambridge, 1950).

Hsiao Kung-chuan, "Rural Control in Nineteenth-Century China," *Far Eastern Quarterly*, Vol. XII, No. 2 (February, 1953).

Hsieh Pao-chao, *The Government of China (1644–1911)* (Baltimore, 1925).

Hsü, Francis L.K., *Under the Ancestor's Shadow* (New York, 1948).

Hsü, Leonard Shihhen (Shih-lien), *Sun Yat-sen, His Political and Social Ideals* (Los Angeles, 1933).

Hu Hsien-chin, *The Common Descent Group in China and Its Functions* (New York, 1948).

Hu Shih, *The Chinese Renaissance* (Chicago, 1934).

————, *The Development of the Logical Method in Ancient China* (Shanghai, 1928).

Hughes, Ernest R., *The Invasion of China by the Western World* (London, 1937).

Hughes, E.R., and K. Hughes, *Religion in China* (London and New York, 1950).

Hummel, Arthur W., ed., *Eminent Chinese of the Ch'ing Period (1644–1912)* (Washington, D.C., 1944).

Isaacs, Harold R., *The Tragedy of the Chinese Revolution* (rev. ed., Stanford, 1951).

Jansen, Marius, *The Japanese and Sun Yat-sen* (Harvard Historical Monograph XXVII, 1955).

Kiang Wen-han, *The Chinese Student Movement* (New York, 1948).

King, Franklin H., *Farmers of Forty Centuries* (Madison, Wis., 1911).

Kuo, Pin-chia, *A Critical Study of the First Anglo-Chinese War, with Documents* (London, 1935).

Lang, Olga, *Chinese Family and Society* (New Haven and London, 1946).

Latourette, K.S., *The Chinese, their History and Culture* (2 vols., 3d ed., New York, 1946).

————, *A History of Christian Missions in China* (New York, 1929).

"Leadership in New China," *Economist:* Series 1, "The Men at the Top" (June 19, 1954); Series 2, "Soldiers around Mao" (June 26, 1954); Series 3, "The Economic Planners" (July 3, 1954).

Levenson, Joseph R., *Liang Ch'i-ch'ao and the Mind of Modern China* (Cambridge, 1953).

Levy, Marion, *The Family Revolution in Modern China* (Cambridge, 1949).

Li, Shao-ch'ang, *Popular Buddhism in China* (Shanghai, 1939).

Li Chi, *The Formation of the Chinese People* (Cambridge, 1928).

Lin, Mousheng, *Men and Ideas, an Informal History of Chinese Political Thought* (New York, 1942).

Lin Yu-t'ang, ed., *The Wisdom of China and India* (New York, 1942).

Linebarger, Paul M.A., *The China of Chiang K'ai-shek: A Political Study* (Boston, 1941).

———; Djang Chu; and Ardath W. Burks, *Far Eastern Governments and Politics, China and Japan* (New York, 1954).

MacNair, H.F., ed., *China* (Berkeley, 1946).

———, *China in Revolution* (Chicago, 1931).

———, ed., *Modern Chinese History, Selected Readings* (Shanghai, 1933).

Mao Tse-tung, *Selected Works of Mao Tse-tung* (3 vols. of a projected 5 vols., London, 1954).

Mayers, William F., *The Chinese Government* (3d ed., Shanghai, 1897).

Meadows, T.T., *The Chinese and Their Rebellions* (Reprinted by Stanford Press, 1953).

Michael, Franz, "The Military Organization and Power Structure of China During the Taiping Rebellion," *Pacific Historical Review*, Vol. XVIII, No. 4 (November, 1949).

———, *Origin of Manchu Rule in China* (Baltimore, 1942).

———, "State and Society in Nineteenth Century China," *World Politics,* Vol. VII, No. 3 (April, 1955).

Moraes, Francis, *Report on Mao's China* (New York, 1953).

Morse, Hosea B., *The Gilds of China* (London, New York, 1909).

———, *The Trade and Administration of China* (3d ed., New York, 1921).

Needham, Joseph, *Science and Civilization in China;* Vol. I, *Introductory Orientations* and Vol. II, *History of Scientific Thought* (2 vols. of projected 7 vols.; 1955).

North, Robert C., *Kuomintang and Chinese Communist Elites*, with the collaboration of Ithiel de Sola Pool. Introduction by John K. Fairbank (Stanford, 1952).

———, *Moscow and Chinese Communists* (Stanford, 1953).

Pan, Wei-tung, *The Chinese Constitution; a Study of Forty Years of Constitution Making in China* (Washington, D.C., 1945).

Peake, Cyrus H., *Nationalism and Education in Modern China* (New York, 1932).

Price, F.W., Transl., *San Min Chu I, The Three Principles of the People* (Shanghai, 1927).

Richard, Louis, *A Comprehensive Geography of the Chinese Empire*, trans. M. Kennelly (Shanghai, 1908).

Rostow, W.W., et. al., *The Prospects for Communist China* (New York and Massachusetts Institute of Technology Press, 1955).

Roy, Manabendra N., *Revolution and Counter-revolution in China* (Calcutta, 1946).

Schwartz, Benjamin I., *Chinese Communism and the Rise of Mao* (Cambridge, Mass., 1951).

Sharman, Lyon, *Sun Yat-sen, His Life and its Meaning* (New York, 1934).

Shen, Tsung-han, *Agricultural Resources of China* (Ithaca, 1951).

Shih, Vincent, "The Ideology of the Taiping T'ien-kuo," *Sinologica*, Vol. 3 No. 1 (1951), pp. 1–15.

Smith, Arthur H., *Village Life in China* (New York, 1899).

Snow, Edgar, *Red Star over China* (New York, 1938).

Spector, Stanley, "Li Hung-chang and the Huai-chün," doctoral dissertation (University of Washington, Seattle, 1953).

Steiger, G.N., *China and the Occident; the Origin and Development of the Boxer Movement* (New Haven, 1927).

Steiner, Arthur H., "Mainsprings of Chinese Communist Foreign Policy,"

American Journal of International Law (January, 1950).

Swisher, Earl, *China's Management of the American Barbarians* (New Haven, 1953).

Takakusu, Junjiro, *The Essentials of Buddhist Philosophy* (Honolulu, 1947).

Tamagna, Frank M., *Banking and Finance in China* (New York, 1942).

T'ang Leang-li, *The Inner History of the Chinese Revolution* (London, 1930).

Tawney, R.H., *Land and Labor in China* (New York, 1932).

Taylor, George E., *The Struggle for North China* (New York, 1940).

——, "The Taiping Rebellion: Its Economic Background and Social Theory," *Chinese Social and Political Science Review*, Vol. XVI, No. 4 (January, 1933), pp. 545–614.

Teng Ssu-yu, *Chang Hsi and the Treaty of Nanking, 1842* (Chicago, 1944).

—— and J.K. Fairbank, *China's Response to the West: A Documentary Survey, 1839–1923*) (2 vols., Cambridge, 1953).

Tong, Hollington K., *Chiang Kai-shek, Soldier and Statesman* (2 vols., London, 1938).

United States Relations with China, with Special Reference to the Period 1944–1949 (Department of State Pub. 3573, Washington, D.C., 1949).

Vinacke, H.M., *Modern Constitutional Development in China* (Princeton, 1920).

Wade, T.F., "The Army of the Chinese Empire," *Chinese Repository*, 20 (1851).

Walker, Richard L., *China Under Communism: the First Five Years* (New Haven, 1955).

Weber, Max, *The Religion of China, Confucianism and Taoism*, transl. by Hans H. Gerth (Glencoe, Ill., 1951).

Wei, Francis C.M. (Cho-min), *The Spirit of Chinese Culture* (New York, 1947).

Werner, E.T.C., *A Dictionary of Chinese Mythology* (Shanghai, 1932).

Wilhelm, Richard, *A Short History of Chinese Civilization*, trans. by Joan Joshua (New York, 1929).

Williams, Samuel Wells, *The Middle Kingdom* (2 vols., New York, 1883).

Winfield, Gerald, *China: the Land and the People* (New York, 1948).

Wittfogel, K.A., "The Foundations and Stages of Chinese Economic History," *Zeitschrift für Sozialforschung* (1935).

——, and C.S. Feng, *History of Chinese Society: Liao (907–1125)* (Philadelphia, 1949).

Wright, Arthur F., ed., *Studies in Chinese Thought* (Chicago, 1953).

——; Hellmut Wilhelm; and Benjamin Schwartz, "Chinese Reactions to Imported Ideas, a Symposium," *Journal of the History of Ideas*, Vol. XII, No. 1 (January, 1951), pp. 31–74.

Wright, Stanley F., *Hart and the Chinese Customs* (Belfast, 1950).

Yang, Lien-sheng, *Money and Credit in China* (Harvard-Yenching Institute Monograph Series, Vol. XII).

Yang, Martin C. (Mou-ch'un), *A Chinese Village: Taitou, Shantung Province* (New York, 1945).

INNER ASIA AND KOREA (Chapter II)

Ali, Ahmed, *Muslim China* (Karachi, Pakistan Institute of International Affairs, 1949).

Ambolt, Nils, *Karavan; Travels in Eastern Turkestan*, trans. by Joan Bulman (London and Glasgow, 1939).

Andrews, Roy Chapman, *Across Mongolian Plains* (London and New York, 1921).

Baddeley, John F., ed., *Russia, Mongolia, China, being some record of the relations between them from the beginning of the XVIIth century to the death of Tsar Alexei Mikhailovich* (2 vols., London, 1919).

Barthold, Wilhelm, *Turkestan Down to the Mongol Invasion*, trans. and rev. by H.A.R. Gibb (London, 1928).

Bell, (Sir) Charles A., *The People of Tibet* (Oxford, 1928).

——, *The Religion of Tibet* (Oxford, 1931).

——, *Tibet, Past and Present* (London, 1925).

Beloff, Max, *Soviet Policy in the Far East 1944–1951* (New York, 1953).

Broomhall, Marshall, *Islam in China; a Neglected Problem* (London, 1910).

Camman, Schuyler, *The Land of the Camel; Tents and Temples of Inner Mongolia* (New York, 1951).

, *Trade through the Himalayas: The Early British Attempts to Open Tibet* (Princeton, 1951).

Chang, Yin-t'ang, *Economic Development and Prospects of Inner Mongolia* (Shanghai, 1933).

Chapman, Frederick Spencer, *Memoirs of a Mountaineer* (London, 1951).

Christensen, Henning H., *Men and Gods in Mongolia* (New York, 1935).

, *Tents in Mongolia* (New York, 1934).

Clyde, Paul H., *International Rivalries in Manchuria, 1689–1922* (2d ed., Columbus, Ohio, 1928).

Cressey, George Babcock, *Asia's Lands and Peoples* (New York, 1944).

Dallin, David, *Soviet Russia and the Far East* (New Haven, 1948).

David-Neal, A., *My Journey to Lhasa: the personal story of the only white woman who succeeded in entering the Forbidden City* (London, 1927).

Desideri, Father Ippolito, *An Account of Tibet, The Travels of Ippolito Desideri of Pistoia, S.J., 1712–1727*, ed. by F. de Filippi, intro. by C. Wessels, S.J. (rev. ed., London, 1937).

Douglas, William O., *Beyond the High Himalayas* (New York, 1952).

Ekvall, Robert Brainerd, *Cultural Relations on the Kansu-Tibetan Border* (Chicago, 1939).

, *Tibetan Sky Lines* (New York, 1952).

Etherton, P.T., *In the Heart of Asia* (London, 1925).

, and H.H. Tiltman, *Manchuria the Cockpit of Asia* (New York, 1932).

Friters, Gerard M., *Outer Mongolia and its International Position* (Baltimore, 1949).

Grajdanzev, Andrew J., *Modern Korea* (New York, 1944).

Griffis, W.E., *Corea the Hermit Nation* (New York, 1882).

Hedin, Sven, *Across the Gobi Desert*, tr. by H.J. Cant (London, 1931).

, *A Conquest of Tibet*, tr. by Julius Lincoln (New York, 1934).

, *History of the Expedition in Asia 1927–1935* (4 vols.; Stockholm, 1943–1945).

, *The Silk Road*, trans. by F.H. Lyon (New York, 1938).

Hosie, Alexander, *Manchuria; its people, resources, and recent history* (2d ed., London, 1904).

Howorth, H.H., *History of the Mongols from the 9th to the 19th Century* (London, 1876–1880).

Huc, E.R., *Travels in Tartary*, ed. by H. d'Ardenne de Tizac, trans. from the French by W. Hazlitt (London and New York, 1927).

, *Travels in Tartary, Tibet and China 1844–1846*, ed. by Paul Pelliot, trans. by W. Hazlitt (2 vols.; London and New York, 1928).

Lattimore, Owen, *The Desert Road to Turkestan* (London, 1928, Boston, 1929).

, *High Tartary* (Boston, 1930).

, *Inner Asian Frontiers of China* (New York, 1940).

, *Manchuria, Cradle of Conflict* (New York, 1932).

, *The Mongols of Manchuria* (New York, 1934).

Li Chi, *Manchuria in History, a summary* (Peiping, 1932).

Maraini, Fosco, *Secret Tibet*, trans. by Eric Mosbacher (New York, 1952).

Martin, Henry Desmond, *The Rise of Chingis Khan and his Conquest of North China* (Baltimore, 1950).

McCune, George M., *Korea Today* (Cambridge, 1950).

Meade, E. Grant, *American Military Government in Korea* (New York, 1951).

Michael, Franz, *Origin of Manchu Rule in China* (Baltimore, 1942).

Norins, Martin, *Gateway to Asia: Sinkiang frontier of the Chinese Far West* (New York, 1944).

Pallis, Marco, *Peaks and Lamas* (rev. ed., New York, 1949).

Parker, Edward H., *A Thousand Years of the Tartars* (New York and London, 1924).

"A Pekinese," *The Boundary Question between China and Tibet. A Valuable Record of the Tripartite Conference between China, Britain and Tibet Held in India, 1913–1914* (Peking, 1940).

Petech, Luciano, *China and Tibet in the early eighteenth century; history of the establishment of Chinese protectorate in Tibet* (Leiden, 1950).

Riazanovskii, V.A., *Customary Law of the Mongol Tribes (Mongols, Buriats, Kalmucks)* (Harbin, 1929).

Rockhill, W.W., *The Dalai Lamas of Lhasa and their Relations with the Manchu Emperors of China, 1644–1908* (*T'oung-Pao*, vol. 10, pp. 1–104 [1910]).

——, "Tibet, a geographical, ethnographical and historical sketch, derived from Chinese sources," *Journal of Royal Asiatic Society* (1891).

Ross, Reverend John, *History of Korea, Ancient and Modern* (Paisley, 1879).

Shen, Tsung-lien and Liu Shen-chi, *Tibet and the Tibetans* (Stanford, 1953).

Shirokogorov, S.M., *Social Organization of the Manchus, A study of the Manchu clan organization* (Shanghai, 1924).

Skrine, Clarmont P., *Chinese Central Asia* (Boston and London, 1926).

Stein, (Sir) Marc Aurel, *On Ancient Central-Asian Tracks* (London, 1933).

——, *Sand-Buried Ruins of Khotan* (London, 1903).

Teichman, Eric, *Travels of a Consular Officer in North-west China* (Cambridge, 1921).

de Terra, Helmut, "On the World's Highest Plateaus (Life on the Steppes and Oases of Chinese Turkestan)," *National Geographic Magazine* (March, 1931).

Tucci, Giuseppi, and Capt. Eugenio Ghersi, *Secrets of Tibet, Being the Chronicle of the Tucci Scientific Expedition to Western Tibet, 1933* (Glasgow and London, 1935).

——, *Tibetan Painted Scrolls* (2 vols., Rome, 1949).

——, *The Tombs of the Tibetan Kings* (Rome, 1950).

U.S. Department of State, *Korea 1945 to 1948, a Report on Political Developments and Economic Resources with Selected Documents* (Washington, D.C., 1948).

Waddell, L.A., *The Buddhism of Tibet, or Lamaism* (2d ed., Cambridge, 1934).

——, *Lhasa and its Mysteries. With a record of the expedition of 1903–1904* (London, 1905; 4th ed., London, 1930).

JAPAN (Chapters III, VIII, XIII)

Alcock, Sir Rutherford, *The Capital of the Tycoon: A Narrative of a Three Years' Residence in Japan* (2 vols., New York, 1863).

Allen, George C., *A Short Economic History of Modern Japan* (London, 1951).

Allen, G.C., *Japanese Industry: Its Recent Development and Present Condition* (New York, 1939).

——, and A.G. Donnithorne, *Western Enterprise in Far Eastern Economic Development: China and Japan* (New York and London, 1954).

Anesaki, Masaharu, *History of Japanese Religion, With Special Reference to the Social and Moral Life of the Nation* (London, 1930).

Asakawa, K. "Some of the Contributions of Feudal Japan to the New Japan," *Journal of Race Development*, Vol. III (1912–1913), pp. 1–32.

Ball, Wm. Macmahon, *Japan, Enemy or Ally?* (New York, 1949).

Beasley, William G., *Great Britain and the Opening of Japan, 1834–1858* (London, 1951).

Benedict, Ruth, *The Chrysanthemum and the Sword* (Boston, 1946).

Bisson, Thomas A., *Japan's War Economy* (New York, 1945).

——, *Zaibatsu Dissolution in Japan* (Berkeley, 1954).

Black, John R., *Young Japan: Yokohama and Yedo, A Narrative of the Settlement and the City from the Signing of the Treaties in 1858 to the Close of the Year 1879, with a Glance at the Progress of Japan During a Period of Twenty-one Years* (2 vols., London, 1880).

Borton, Hugh, "Peasant Uprisings in Japan of the Tokugawa Period," *Transactions of the Asiatic Society of Japan*, 2d series, Vol. XVI (Tokyo, 1938), pp. xi–xiv, 1–219.

Borton, Hugh; S. Elisséef; E.P. Reischauer, *A Selected List of Books and Articles on Japan in English, French, and German* (American Council of Learned Societies, Washington, 1940).

Brines, Russell, *MacArthur's Japan* (Philadelphia, 1948).

Brown, Delmer M., *Nationalism in Japan: An Introductory Historical Analysis* (Berkeley, 1955).

Butow, Robert J.C., *Japan's Decision to Surrender* (Stanford, 1954).

Byas, High, *Government by Assassination* (New York, 1942).

Chamberlin, William H., *Japan Over Asia* (Boston, 1939).

Clyde, Paul H., "Japan's March to Empire; Some Bibliographical Evaluations," *Journal of Modern History*, Vol. XXI (December, 1949), pp. 333–343.

Cohen, Jerome B., *Economic Problems of Free Japan* (Princeton, 1952).

———, *Japan's Economy in War and Reconstruction* (Minneapolis, 1949).

Colegrove, Kenneth W., *Militarism in Japan* (Boston, 1936).

Cressey, George B., *Asia's Lands and Peoples* (New York and London, 1944).

Crocker, Walter R., *The Japanese Population Problem* (London, 1931).

Crow, Carl, *He Opened the Door of Japan; Townsend Harris and the Story of His Amazing Adventures in Establishing American Relations with the Far East* (New York, 1939).

Eckstein, Gustav, *Noguchi* (New York and London, 1931).

Embree, John F., *The Japanese Nation, A Social Survey* (New York, 1945).

———, *Suye Mura, a Japanese Village* (Chicago, 1939).

Fahs, Charles B., *Government in Japan* (New York, 1940).

Falk, Edwin Albert, *Togo and the Rise of Japanese Sea Power* (New York, 1936).

Fearey, Robert A., *The Occupation of Japan: Second Phase, 1948–1950* (New York, 1950).

Feis, Herbert, *The Road to Pearl Harbor* (Princeton, 1950).

Feldman, Horace, "The Meiji Political Novel: A Brief Survey," *Far Eastern Quarterly*, Vol. IX (1949–1950), pp. 245–55.

Fenollosa, Ernest F., *Epochs of Chinese and Japanese Art, an Outline History of Asiatic Design* (New York, 1921).

Fukuzawa, Yukichi, *The Autobiography of Fukuzawa Yukichi 1835–1901* (Tokyo, 1934).

Gayn, Mark, *Japan Diary* (New York, 1948).

General Headquarters, Supreme Commander for the Allied Powers, *Political Reorientation of Japan*, September, 1945, to September, 1948 (2 vols., Washington, D.C., n.d.).

Gibney, Frank, *Five Gentlemen of Japan, Portrait of a Nation's Character* (New York, 1953).

Graf, Henry F., ed., *Bluejackets with Perry in Japan, A Day-by-Day Account Kept by Master's Mate John R.C. Lewis and Cabin Boy William B. Allen* (New York Public Library, 1952).

Greene, D.C., tr., "Osada's Life of Takano Nagahide," *Transactions of the Asiatic Society of Japan*, Vol. XLI, Pt. III (1913), pp. 379–467.

Grew, Joseph C., *Ten Years in Japan* (New York, 1944).

Griffis, William E., *Verbeck of Japan, A Citizen of No Country* (Chicago, 1900).

———, *The Mikado's Empire* (New York, 1876).

Gubbins, G.H., *The Making of Modern Japan* (London, 1922).

———, *The Progress of Japan, 1853–1871* (Oxford, 1911).

Gunther, John, *The Riddle of MacArthur: Japan, Korea, and the Far East* (New York, 1951).

Hall, Robert K., ed., *Kokutai no hongi, Cardinal Principles of the National Entity of Japan* (Cambridge, Mass., 1949).

———, *Education for a New Japan* (New Haven, 1949).

Hamada, Kengi, *Prince Ito* (Tokyo, 1936).

Haring, Douglas, *Blood on the Rising Sun* (Philadelphia, 1943).

Haring, Douglas, ed., *Japan's Prospects* (Cambridge, 1946).

Harris, Townsend, *The Complete Journal of Townsend Harris* (New York, 1930).

Harrison, John A., *Japan's Northern Frontier: A Preliminary Study in Colonization and Expansion with Special Reference to the Relations of Japan and Russia* (Gainesville, Fla., 1953).

Hawks, Francis L., *Narrative of the Expedition of an American Squadron to the China Seas and Japan Performed in the Years 1852, 1853, 1854, Under the Command of Commodore M.C. Perry, USN, by order of the Government of the United States* (3 vols., Washington, D.C., 1856).

Hayashi, Tadasu, *The Secret Memoirs of Count Tadasu Hayashi (1850–1913)*, ed. by A.M. Pooley (New York, 1915).

Heco, Joseph, *The Narrative of a Japanese, What He has Seen and the People He Has Met in the Course of the Last Forty Years,* ed. by J. Murdoch (2 vols., Yokohama, 1894).

Holtom, Daniel C., *Modern Japan and Shinto Nationalism: A Study of Present-day Trends in Japanese Religion* (Chicago, 1947).

————, *The National Faith of Japan: A Study in Modern Shinto* (New York, 1938).

Honjo, Eijiro, *The Social and Economic History of Japan* (Kyoto, 1935).

Ike, Nobutaka, *The Beginnings of Political Democracy in Japan* (Baltimore, 1950).

Ishii, Ryoichi, *Population Pressure and Economic Life in Japan* (London, 1937).

Ishimoto, (Baroness) Shidzue, *Facing Two Ways, the Story of My Life* (New York, 1935).

Itani, Zenichi, "The Economic Causes of the Meiji Restoration," *Transactions of the Asiatic Society of Japan*, 2d Series, Vol. XVII (1938), pp. 193–207.

Ito, Hirobumi, *Commentaries on the Constitution of the Empire of Japan* (Tokyo, 1889).

Iwasaki, U., *The Working Forces in Japanese Politics* (Columbia University Studies, Vol. 97, No. 1, 1921).

Jansen, Marius B., *The Japanese and Sun Yat-sen* (Cambridge, 1954).

The Japan Chronicle (Kobe, 1911–1941).

Japan Year Book (Yearly since 1906).

Jones, F.C., *Extraterritoriality in Japan and the Diplomatic Relations Resulting in Its Abolition, 1853–1899* (New Haven, 1931).

————, *Japan's New Order in East Asia 1937–1945* (London, New York, and Toronto, 1954).

————, *Manchuria Since 1931* (London, 1949).

Kase, Toshikazu, *Journey to the Missouri* (New Haven, 1950).

Kato, Masuo, *The Lost War* (New York, 1946).

Keenleyside, Hugh L., and A.F. Thomas, *History of Japanese Education and Present Educational System* (Tokyo, 1937).

Kokusai Bunka Shinkokai, ed., *Introduction to Contemporary Japanese Literature* (Tokyo, 1939).

Kublin, Hyman, "The 'Modern' Army of Early Meiji Japan," *Far Eastern Quarterly*, Vol. IX (1949–1950), pp. 20–41.

Lane-Poole, S., and F.V. Dickins, *The Life of Sir Harry Parkes* (2 vols., London and New York, 1894).

Lanman, Charles, *Japan, Its Leading Men* (Boston, 1886).

Lewe van Aduard, Baron Evert Joost, *Japan, From Surrender to Peace* (The Hague, 1953).

Lockwood, William W., *The Economic Development of Japan; Growth and Structural Change 1868–1938* (Princeton, 1954).

Lory, Hillis, *Japan's Military Masters: The Army in Japanese Life* (New York, 1943).

Maki, John M., *Japanese Militarism, Its Cause and Cure* (New York, 1945).

Martin, Edwin M., *The Allied Occupation of Japan* (Stanford, 1948).

Matsuoka, Yoko, *Daughter of the Pacific* (New York, 1952).

McGovern, W.M., *Modern Japan, Its Political, Military, and Industrial Organization* (London, 1920).

McLaren, Walter W., "Japanese Government Documents," *Transactions of the Asiatic Society of Japan*, Vol. XLII, Part I (1914).

————, *A Political History of Japan During the Meiji Era, 1867–1912* (London, 1916).

Mishima, Sumie, *The Broader Way: A Woman's Life in the New Japan* (New York, 1953).

Miyamori, Asataro, tr., *An Anthology of Haiku, Ancient and Modern* (Tokyo, 1932).

————, *A Life of Mr. Yukichi Fukuzawa* (Tokyo, 1902).

Murdoch, James M., *A History of Japan* (3 vols., London, 1926).

Mushakoji, Saneatsu, *Great Saigo, The Life of Takamori Saigo*, adapted by Mariaki Sakamoto (Tokyo, 1942).

Nakamura, Kaju, *Prince Ito, the Man and Statesman, A Brief History of His Life* (New York, 1910).

Nasu, Shiroshi, *Aspects of Japanese Agriculture* (New York, 1941).

————, *Land Utilization of Japan* (Tokyo, 1929).

Nishikiori, Hideo, *Togo-mura, a Village in Northern Japan*, trans. by Toshio Sano (New York, Institute of Pacific Relations, 1945).

Norbeck, Edward, *Takashima, A Japanese*

Fishing Community (Salt Lake City, 1954).

Norman, E. Herbert, *Japan's Emergence as a Modern State: Political and Economic Problems of the Meiji Period* (New York, 1940, 1946).

———, *Soldier and Peasant in Japan: The Origins of Conscription* (New York, Institute of Pacific Relations, 1943).

Okuma, Shigenobu, ed., *Fifty Years of New Japan* (2 vols., London, 1910).

Omura, Bunji, *The Last Genro. Prince Saionji, the Man Who Westernized Japan* (Philadelphia, 1938).

Papinot, E., *Historical and Geographical Dictionary of Japan* (Ann Arbor, 1948).

Paske-Smith, M., *Western Barbarians in Japan and Formosa in Tokugawa Days 1603–1868* (Kobe, 1930).

Penrose, E.F., *Population Theories and Their Application with Special Reference to Japan* (Stanford, 1934).

Pooley, A.M., *Japan at the Crossroads* (London, 1917).

———, *Japan's Foreign Policies* (London, 1920).

Quigley, Harold Scott, *Japanese Government and Politics, An Introductory Study* (New York, 1932).

Reed, John Paul, *Kokutai, A Study of Certain Sacred and Secular Aspects of Japanese Nationalism* (lithoprinted, Chicago, 1940).

Reischauer, Edwin O., *Japan Past and Present* (2d ed., New York, 1953).

———, *The United States and Japan* (Cambridge, 1950).

Reischauer, Robert K., *Japan, Government - Politics* (New York, 1939).

Roth, Andrew, *Dilemma in Japan* (Boston, 1945).

Sakamaki, Shunzo, "Japan and the United States, 1790–1853," *Transactions of the Asiatic Society of Japan*, 2d Series, Vol. XVIII (1939), pp. i–xi, 1–204.

Sansom, Sir George B., *Japan: A Short Cultural History* (rev. ed., New York, 1943).

———, *The Western World and Japan* (New York, 1950).

Satow, Sir Ernest, *A Diplomat in Japan, The Inner History of the Critical Years in the Evolution of Japan When the Ports Were Opened and the Monarchy Restored,* Recorded by a Diplomat Who Took an Active Part in the Events of the Time, with an Account of His Personal Experiences During that Period (London, 1921).

Scalapino, Robert, *Democracy and the Party Movement in Prewar Japan, The Failure of the First Attempt* (Berkeley, 1953).

Schumpeter, E.B., ed., *The Industrialization of Japan and Manchukuo* (New York, 1940).

Stoetzel, Jean, *Without the Chrysanthemum and the Sword: A Study of the Attitudes of Youth in Postwar Japan* (New York, 1955).

Straelen, H. van, S.V.D., *Yoshida Shoin, Forerunner of the Meiji Restoration* (Leiden, 1952).

Supreme Commander for the Allied Powers, *Education in the New Japan* (2 vols., Tokyo, 1948).

Swearingen, Rodger, and Paul Langer, *Red Flag in Japan: A study of International Communism in Action 1919–1951* (Cambridge, 1952).

Takekoshi, Yosaburo, *The Economic Aspects of the History of the Civilization of Japan* (New York, 1930).

———, *Prince Saionji* (Kyoto, 1933).

Takeuchi, Stirling Tatsuji, *War and Diplomacy in the Japanese Empire* (New York, 1935).

Tanin, O., and E. Yohan, *Militarism and Fascism in Japan* (New York, 1934).

Textor, Robert, *Failure in Japan* (New York, 1951).

Tolischus, Otto D., *Tokyo Record* (New York, 1943).

Tracy, Honor, *Kakemono: A Sketch Book of Post-war Japan* (New York, 1950).

Treat, Payson Jackson, *Diplomatic Relations between the United States and Japan, 1853–1895* (2 vols., Stanford, 1932).

Trewartha, Glenn T., *Japan: A Physical, Cultural, and Regional Geography* (Madison, Wis., 1945).

U.S. Department of State, *Constitution of Japan* (Pub. 2836, Far Eastern Series 22).

———, *Report of the Mission on Japanese Combines* (Pub. 2628, Far Eastern Series No. 14).

———, *Reports by the Secretary General* (Pub. 2888, Far Eastern Series, 24. Far Eastern Commission).

U. S. Strategic Bombing Survey, *Coals and Metals in Japan's War Economy* (Washington, 1947).

——, *The Effects of Strategic Bombing on Japan's War Economy* (Washington, 1946).

——, *The Electric Power Industry of Japan* (Washington, 1947).

——, *Japan's Struggle to End the War* (Washington, 1946).

——, *The Japanese Aircraft Industry* (Washington, 1947).

——, *The Japanese Wartime Standard of Living and Utilization of Manpower* (Washington, 1947).

——, *The War Against Japanese Transportation, 1941–1945* (Washington, 1947).

Utley, Freda, *Japan's Feet of Clay* (New York, 1937).

Uyeda, Teijiro, *The Small Industries of Japan* (London and New York, 1938).

Uyehara, G.E., *The Political Development of Japan, 1867–1909* (London, 1910).

Uyehara, S., *The Industry and Trade of Japan* (2d ed., London, 1936).

Vining, Elizabeth, *Windows for the Crown Prince* (Philadelphia, 1952).

Walworth, Arthur C., *Black Ships off Japan* (New York, 1946).

Wildes, Harry Emerson, *Social Currents in Japan* (Chicago, 1927).

——, *Typhoon in Tokyo, The Occupation and its Aftermath* (New York, 1954).

Williams, S. Wells, "A Journal of the Perry Expedition to Japan (1853–1854)," *Transactions of the Asiatic Society of Japan*, Vol. 37 (1910), Part II, pp. i–ix, 1–259.

Yanaibara, Tadao, *Religion and Democracy in Modern Japan* (Tokyo, 1948).

Yanaga, Chitoshi, *Japan Since Perry* (New York, 1949).

Yanahaira, Tadao, *Pacific Islands under Japanese Mandate* (London and New York, 1940).

Yashi, Shozan [Uji Yamaguchi], *Kinse Shiriaku, A History of Japan from the First Visit of Commodore Perry in 1853 to the Capture of Hakodate by the Mikado's Forces in 1869*, trans. by E.M. Satow (Yokohama, 1873).

Young, A. Morgan, *Imperial Japan (1926–1938)* (London, 1938).

Young, Carl W., *Japanese Jurisdiction in the South Manchurian Railway Areas* (Baltimore and London, 1931).

——, *Japan's Special Position in Manchuria* (Baltimore, 1931).

——, *The International Legal Status of the Kwantung Leased Territory* (Baltimore, 1931).

SOUTHEAST ASIA
(Chapters IV, IX, XIV)

General

Adloff, Richard, and Virginia Thompson, *Cultural Institutions and Educational Policy in South East Asia* (New York, 1948).

——, *The Left Wing in Southeast Asia* (New York, 1950).

Ball, William Macmahon, *Nationalism and Communism in East Asia* (Victoria, Australia, 1952).

Callis, H.G., *Foreign Capital in Southeast Asia* (New York, 1942).

Cressey, George B., *Asia's Lands and Peoples* (New York, 1944).

Dai, Shen-yu, *Peking, Moscow, and the Communist Parties of Colonial Asia* (Center for International Studies, Massachusetts Institute of Technology, July 23, 1954).

Dotson, Lillian O., and John Embree, *Bibliography of Peoples and Culture of Mainland South East Asia* (New Haven, 1950).

Du Bois, Cora, *Social Forces in Southeast Asia* (Minneapolis, 1949).

Dyakov, A.M., et al., *Crisis of the Colonial System* (translated from the Russian and published by the People's Publishing House, Bombay, 1951).

Elsbree, Willard H., *Japan's Role in Southeast Asian Nationalist Movements, 1940 to 1945* (Cambridge, 1953).

Emerson, Rupert; Lennox A. Mills; and Virginia Thompson, *Government and Nationalism in Southeast Asia* (New York, 1942).

Frankel, Joseph, "Soviet Policy in Southeast Asia," in Max Beloff, *Soviet Policy in the Far East, 1944–1951* (London, 1953).

Furnivall, J.S., *Educational Progress in Southeast Asia* (New York, 1943).

————, *Progress and Welfare in Southeast Asia, A Comparison of Colonial Policy and Practice* (New York, 1941).

Hall, D.G.E., *A History of South-East Asia* (New York, 1955).

Holland, William L., *Asian Nationalism and the West* (New York, 1953).

Hubbard, Gilbert E., *Eastern Industrialization and its Effect on the West* (London, 1935).

Institute of Pacific Relations, Ninth Conference, New York, 1945, Secretariat Paper, "Basic Problems of Relief, Rehabilitation and Reconstruction in Southeast Asia."

Jacoby, Erich H., *Agrarian Unrest in Southeast Asia* (New York, 1949).

Landon, Kenneth Perry, *Southeast Asia: Crossroad of Religions* (Chicago, 1949).

Lasker, Bruno, *Human Bondage in Southeast Asia* (Chapel Hill, 1950).

————, *Peoples of Southeast Asia* (London and New York, 1944).

LeRoy, James A., *The Americans in the Philippines* (2 vols., Boston and New York, 1914).

Mills, Lennox A., and associates, *The New World of South East Asia* (Minneapolis, 1949).

Panikkar, K.M., *The Future of South-east Asia, An Indian View* (New York, 1943).

Pelzer, Karl, *Pioneer Settlement in the Asiatic Tropics* (New York, 1945).

Purcell, Victor, *The Chinese in Southeast Asia* (London, 1951).

Schrieke, B.J.O., ed., *The Effect of Western Influence on Native Civilizations in the Malay Archipelago* (Batavia, 1929).

Talbot, Phillips, ed., *South Asia in the World Today* (Chicago, 1950).

Thompson, Virginia M., *Labor Problems in Southeast Asia* (New Haven, 1947).

Wickizer, V.D., and M.K. Bennett, *The Rice Economy of Monsoon Asia* (Stanford, 1941).

Indo-China

Ennis, Thomas Edson, *French Policies and Developments in Indochina* (Chicago, 1936).

Gourou, Pierre, *Land Utilization in French Indochina* (New York, 1945).

Hammer, Ellen, *The Emergence of Viet Nam* (New York, 1947).

Handler, Joseph, "Indochina: Eighty Years of French Rule," *Annals of the American Academy of Political Science* Vol. 226 (March, 1943).

James, Olov R.T., *The Peoples of French Indo-China* (Washington, Smithsonian Institution, 1944).

Levy, R.G., Sacam and A. Roth, *French Interests and Policies in the Far East* (New York, 1941).

Robequain, Charles, *The Economic Development of French Indo-China* (London and New York, 1944).

Roth, Andrew, *French Indo-China in Transition* (Institute of Pacific Relations Inquiry Series, New York, 1941).

Thompson, Virginia M., *French Indo-China* (London, 1937).

The Philippines

Abaya, Hernando, *Betrayal in the Philippines* (New York, 1946).

Abelarde, Pedro E., *American Tariff Policy Towards the Philippines 1898-1946* (New York, 1947).

Aruego, José M., *The Framing of the Philippine Constitution* (2 vols., Manila, 1936-37).

Barrows, David P., *History of the Philippines* (rev. ed., Yonkers, 1924).

Benites, Conrado, et. al., *Philippine Social Life and Progress* (Boston, 1940).

Bernstein, David, *The Philippine Story* (New York, 1947).

Blair, Emma, and James A. Robertson, *The Philippine Islands, 1493-1803* (55 vols., Cleveland, 1903-1909).

Congress of the Philippines, House of Representatives Special Committee on Un-Filipino Activities, *Report on the Illegality of the Communist Party of the Philippines* (Manila, 1951).

Edwards, Edward J., *Thy People My People* (Milwaukee, 1941).

Elliott, Charles B., *The Philippines: To the End of the Commission Government* (Indianapolis, 1917).

————, *The Philippines: To the end of the Military Regime* (Indianapolis, 1916).

Emerson, Rupert, and others, *America's Pacific Dependencies* (New York, 1949).

Entenberg, Barbara, "Agrarian Reform and the Hukbalahap," *Far Eastern Survey*, Vol. XV, No. 16 (August 14, 1946).

Forbes, William Cameron, *The Philippine Islands* (2 vols., Boston and New York, 1928).

Grunder, Garel A., and William E. Livezey, *The Philippines and the United States* (Norman, Okla., 1951).

Hainsworth, Reginald G., and Raymond T. Moyer, *Agricultural Geography of the Philippine Islands, A Graphic Summary* (U.S. Department of Agriculture, Office of Foreign Agricultural Relations, Washington, D.C., 1945).

Hayden, Joseph Ralston, *The Philippines, a Study in National Development* (New York, 1942).

Isidro, Antonio, and others, *Education in the Philippines* (Manila, 1939).

Jenkins, Shirley, *United States Economic Policy Toward the Philippines* (New York, 1947).

Kalaw, Maximo M., *The Development of Philippine Politics (1872–1920)* (Manila, 1926).

Keesing, F.M., *Taming Philippine Headhunters* (London, 1934).

Kirk, Grayson Louis, *Philippine Independence* (New York, 1936).

Krieger, H.W., *Peoples of the Philippines* (Washington, D.C., 1942).

Kurihara, Kenneth K., *Labor in the Philippine Economy* (London and Stanford, 1945).

Laurel, José P., *The Three Powers of Government under the Philippine Constitution* (Manila, 1936).

League of Nations Health Organization, Intergovernmental Conference of Far Eastern Countries on Rural Hygiene, Badoeng, Java, August 3–13, 1937, *Report of the Philippines.*

Liang, Dapen, *The Development of Philippine Political Parties* (Hong Kong, 1939).

Malcolm, George A., *The Commonwealth of the Philippines* (London and New York, 1936).

Morga, Dr. Antonio de, *Sucesos de las Islas Filipinas*, Blair and Robertson, Vol. XII, pp. 25–209, tr. as *The Philipine Islands* (London, 1868).

Osias, Camilo, *The Filipino Way of Life* (Boston and New York, 1940).

Osmeña, Sergio, *The Problem of Democratic Government in the Philippines: The Salient Aspects* (Washington, 1926).

Pier, Arthur S., *American Apostles to the Philippines* (Boston, 1950).

Porter, Catherine, *Crisis in the Philippines* (New York, 1942).

Pratt, Julius, *America's Colonial Experiment* (New York, 1950).

Quezon, Manuel, *The Good Fight* (New York, 1912).

Report to the President of the United States by the Economic Survey Mission to the Philippines (Washington, D.C., 1950).

Report and Recommendations of the Joint Philippine-American Finance Commission (Washington, D.C., 1947).

Rizal, José, *El Filibusterismo*, trans. by Charles Derbyshire as *Reign of Greed* (Manila and New York, 1912).

———, *Noli Me Tangere*, trans. by Charles Derbyshire as *The Social Cancer* (Manila, 1912).

Sargent, Nathan, *Admiral Dewey and the Manila Campaign* (Washington, 1947).

Schurz, William Lytle, *The Manila Galleon* (New York, 1939).

Seeman, Bernard, and Laurence Salisbury, *Cross Currents in the Philippines* (New York, 1946).

Storey, Moorfield, and Marcial Lichauco, *The Conquest of the Philippines by the United States 1898–1925* (New York, 1926).

Taruc, Luis, *Born of the People* (New York, 1953).

The United States in a Multinational Economy (Council on Foreign Relations, Studies in American Foreign Relations, No. 4, New York, 1945).

Worcester, Dean C., *The Philippine Islands and Their People* (New York, 1901).

———, *The Philippines: Past and Present* (new edition with four additional chapters and a biographical sketch by Ralston Hayden; New York, 1930).

Indonesia (Formerly Netherlands Indies)

Boeke, J.H., *The Evolution of the Netherlands Indies Economy* (New York, 1946).

———, *The Structure of Netherlands Indian Economy* (New York, 1942).

Bousquet, George Henri, *A French View of the Netherlands Indies*, trans. by P.E. Lilienthal (London and New York, 1940).

Broek, Jan O.M., *Economic Development of the Netherlands Indies* (New York, 1942).

Day, Clive, *The Policy and Administration of the Dutch in Java* (New York and London, 1904).

De Klerck, Edward Servaas, *History of the Netherlands East Indies* (New York, 1938).

Emerson, Rupert, *Malaysia: A Study in Direct and Indirect Rule* (New York, 1937).

———; Lennox A. Mills; Virginia Thompson, *Government and Nationalism in Southeast Asia* (New York, 1942).

Furnivall, J.S., *Colonial Policy and Practice: A Comparative Study of Burma and Netherlands India* (Cambridge, England, 1948).

———, *Netherlands India; A Study of Plural Economy* (Cambridge, Eng., 1939; New York, 1944).

———, *Studies in the Social and Economic Development of the Netherlands East Indies* (Rangoon, 1933).

Gelderen, J. van, *The Recent Development of Economic Foreign Policy in the Netherlands East Indies* (London, 1939).

Helsdingen, Dr. W.H. van, and Dr. H. Hoogenbeck, ed., *Mission Interrupted: The Dutch in the East Indies and their Work in the XXth Century* (abridged English version by Dr. J.J.L. Duyvendak, Amsterdam and New York, 1945).

Kahin, George McTurnan, *Nationalism and Revolution in Indonesia* (Ithaca, 1952).

Kain, R.S., "Moscow in Indonesia," *Current History* (August, 1949).

Kat, Angelino A.D. de, *Colonial Policy* (2 vols., Chicago, 1931).

Kennedy, Raymond, *The Ageless Indies* (New York, 1942).

League of Nations Health Organization, Intergovernmental Conference of Far Eastern Countries on Rural Hygiene, Badoeng, Java, August 3–13, 1937, *Report of the Netherlands Indies*.

Mook, H.J. van, *The Netherlands Indies and Japan* (New York, 1944).

Plas, Charles O. van der, "Nationalism in the Netherlands Indies," (Netherlands Indies Paper No. I, Eighth Conference of the Institute of Pacific Relations, Quebec, 1942).

Raffles, Sir T.S., *The History of Java* (2 vols., London, 1817 and 1830).

Reed, Stephen W., *The Making of Modern New Guinea* (Philadelphia, 1943).

Sjahrir, Soetan, *Out of Exile*, trans. and intro. by Charles Wolf, Jr. (New York, 1949).

Ter Haar B., *Adat Law in Indonesia*, trans. by E.A. Hoebel and H.A. Schiller (New York, 1948).

Vandenbosch, Amry, *The Dutch East Indies, Its Government, Problems, and Politics* (3d ed., Berkeley, 1942).

———, "The Netherlands Colonial Balance Sheet," *Southern Economic Journal*, (1937).

Vlekke, Bernard H.M., *Nusantara; A History of the East Indian Archipelago* (Cambridge, 1943).

———, *The Story of the Dutch East Indies* (Cambridge, 1945).

Wehl, David, *The Birth of Indonesia* (London, 1948).

Wolf, Charles, *The Indonesian Story; The Birth, Growth and Structure of the Indonesian Republic* (New York, 1948).

Burma

Andrus, James Russell, *Burma An Experiment in Self-government* (New York, 1945).

———, *Burmese Economic Life* (Palo Alto, 1947).

———, "Three Economic Systems Clashed in Burma," *Review of Economic Studies* (London, February, 1936).

Cady, John F.; Patricia Barnett; and Shirley Jenkins, *The Development of Self-Rule and Independence in Burma, Malaya, and the Philippines* (New York, 1948).

Christian, John L., *Burma and the Japanese Invader* (Bombay, 1945).

———, *Modern Burma, A Survey of Political and Economic Development* (Berkeley, 1942).

Collis, Maurice Stewart, *The Burmese Scene; political, historical, pictorial* (London, 1943).

Furnivall, J.S., *Colonial Policy and Practice: A Comparative Study of Burma and Netherlands India* (Cambridge, 1948).

———, "Communism and Nationalism in Burma," *Far Eastern Survey* (August 24, 1949).

————, *An Introduction to the Political Economy of Burma* (2nd rev. ed., Rangoon, 1938).

Hall, Daniel George Edward, *Europe and Burma—A Study of European Relations with Burma to the Annexation of Thibaws Kingdom, 1886* (London and New York, 1945).

Harvey, Godfrey E., *British Rule in Burma, 1824–1942* (London, 1946).

————, *History of Burma from the Earliest Times to 10 March 1824, the Beginning of the English Conquest* (London, 1925).

Inlow, Burke, "The Constitution of Burma," *Far Eastern Survey*, Vol. XVII, No. 22 (Nov. 17, 1948).

Ireland, Alleyne, *The Province of Burma* (2 vols., Boston and New York, 1907).

League of Nations Health Organization, Intergovernmental Conference of Far Eastern Countries on Rural Hygiene, Badoeng, Java, August 3–13, 1937, *Report of Burma.*

Scott, Sir George, *Burma from the Earliest Times to the Present Day* (London, 1924).

Thompson, Virginia M., "Burma's Communists," *Far Eastern Survey*, Vol. XVII, No. 9 (May 5, 1948).

————, "The New Nation of Burma," *Far Eastern Survey*, Vol. XVII, No. 7 (April 7, 1948).

————, "Notes on Labor Problems in Burma and Thailand," (Institute of Pacific Relations, Secretariat Paper No. 8, New York, 1945).

Thailand (Siam)

Andrews, James, *Siam: Second Rural Economic Survey 1934–1935* (Bangkok, 1935, Cambridge, Eng., 1936).

Crosby, Sir Josiah, *Siam: The Cross Roads* (London, 1945).

Graham, Walter A., *Siam* (2 vols., London, 1924).

Ladejinsky, W.I., "Thailand's Agricultural Economy," *Foreign Agriculture*, Vol. VI (Washington, D.C., 1942).

Landon, Kenneth P., *The Chinese in Thailand* (London and New York, 1941).

————, *Siam in Transition; a Brief Survey of Cultural Trends in the Five Years Since the Revolution of 1932* (Shanghai, 1939).

Landon, Margaret, *Anna and the King of Siam* (New York, 1944).

League of Nations Health Organization, Intergovernmental Conference of Far Eastern Countries on Rural Hygiene, Badoeng, Java, Aug. 3–13, 1937, *Report of Siam.*

Songgram, Luang Pibul, *How Thailand Lost Her Territory to France* (Bangkok, 1940).

Thompson, Virginia, *Thailand, The New Siam* (New York, 1941).

U.S. Department of Commerce, *Economic Development in Siam* (Trade Information Bulletin No. 606, Washington, D.C., 1929).

U.S. Department of State, *A Fact Sheet: Thailand, Its People and Economy* (Washington, D.C., 1950).

Wood, William A.R., *A History of Siam from the earliest times to the year* A.D. *1781* (rev. ed., Bangkok, 1933).

Young, Ernest, *Siam* (London, 1908).

Zimmerman, Carl, *Siam Rural Economic Survey, 1930–1931* (Bangkok, 1931).

Malaya

Bauer, P.T., "Nationalism and Politics in Malaya," *Foreign Affairs*, Vol. XXV, No. 3 (April, 1947).

Cady, John F.; Patricia Barnett; and Shirley Jenkins, *Development of Self Rule and Independence in Burma, Malaya, and the Philippines* (New York, 1948).

Cole, Fay-Cooper, *Malaysia: Crossroads of the Orient* (Eugene, Ore., 1948).

————, *The Peoples of Malaysia* (New York, 1945).

Coupland, Sir Reginald, *Raffles, 1781–1826* (Oxford, 1926).

Dobby, E.H.G., *Malaya and the Malayans* (London, 1947).

Emerson, Rupert, *Malaysia: A Study in Direct and Indirect Rule* (New York, 1937).

Firth, Raymond, *Malay Fishermen: Their Peasant Economy* (London, 1946).

Hauser, Ernest O., "Britain's Economic Stake in Southeast Asia," *Far Eastern Survey*, Vol. VI, No. 25 (Dec. 22, 1937).

Ladejinsky, W.I., "Agriculture in British Malaya," *Foreign Agriculture*, Vol. V (Washington, D.C., 1941).

League of Nations Health Organization, Intergovernmental Conference of Far Eastern Countries on Rural Hygiene,

Badoeng, Java, August 3–13, 1937, *Report of the Malayan Delegation*.

Maxwell, Sir George, *The Civil Defence of Malaya* (London, 1944).

Mills, Lennox A., *British Malaya, 1824–1867* (Oxford, 1926).

———, *British Rule in Eastern Asia; A Study of Contemporary Government and Economic Development in British Malaya and Hong Kong* (London, 1942).

Morrison, Ian, *Malayan Postscript* (London, 1942).

Purcell, Victor, *The Chinese in Malaya* (London, 1948).

———, *Malaya: Outline of a Colony* (New York, 1946).

Swettenham, Sir Frank, *British Malaya, An Account of the Origin and Progress of British Influence in Malaya* (London and New York, 1907).

Tan Cheng Lock, *Malayan Problems, from a Chinese Point of View* (Singapore, 1947).

Thompson, Virginia M., *Post Mortem on Malaya* (New York, 1943).

Winstedt, Sir Richard, *Britain and Malaya, 1786–1941* (London and New York, 1944).

———, *A History of Malaya* (London, 1935).

———, *Malaya and Its History* (London and New York, 1948).

———, *The Malays: A Cultural History* (rev. ed., London, 1950).

TSARIST AND SOVIET RUSSIA
(Chapters V, X, XI)

Beloff, Max, *Foreign Policy of Soviet Russia 1929–1941* (2 vols., London, 1947, 1949).

———, *Soviet Policy in the Far East, 1944–1951* (New York, 1953).

Borkenau, Franz, *World Communism; a history of the Communist International* (New York, 1939).

Bunyan, James, compiler, *Intervention, Civil War, and Communism in Russia; April–December 1918* (Baltimore, 1936).

Clyde, Paul H., *International Rivalries in Manchuria 1689–1922* (Columbus, 1926).

Conolly, Violet, *Soviet Economic Policy in the East* (London, 1933).

Dallin, David J., *The Rise of Russia in Asia* (New Haven, 1949).

———, *Soviet Russia and the Far East* (New Haven, 1948).

Degras, Jane, ed., *Soviet Documents on Foreign Policy* (London, New York, 1951–1953).

Dennett, Tyler, *Roosevelt and the Russo-Japanese War* (Garden City, 1925).

Fischer, Louis, *The Soviets in World Affairs* (2 vols., 2d ed., Princeton, 1951).

Fisher, Raymond, *The Russian Fur Trade, 1550–1700* (Berkeley, 1943).

Golder, Frank A., *Russian Expansion on the Pacific, 1641–1850* (Cleveland, 1914).

Graves, William S., *America's Siberian Adventure, 1918–1920* (New York, 1931).

Kerner, Robert J., *The Urge to the Sea. The Course of Russian History. The Role of Rivers, Portages, Ostrogs, Monasteries, and Furs* (Berkeley, 1942).

Kolarz, Walter, *Russia and her Colonies* (London, 1952).

Krausse, Alexis, *Russia in Asia; a record and a study; 1558–1899* (New York and London, 1899).

Lantzeff, George V., *Siberia in the Seventeenth Century; a Study of the Colonial Administration* (Berkeley, 1943).

Lenin, V.I., *Imperialism, the Highest Stage of Capitalism* (rev. trans., New York, 1939).

Lobanov-Rostovsky, Andrei, *Russia and Asia* (Ann Arbor, 1951; originally published by Macmillan, New York, 1933).

Mandel, William, *The Soviet Far East and Central Asia* (New York, 1944).

Norton, Henry K., *The Far Eastern Republic of Siberia* (London, 1923).

Pasvolsky, Leo, *Russia in the Far East* (New York, 1922).

Pavlovsky, Michel N., *Chinese-Russian Relations* (New York, 1949).

Possony, Stefan T., *A Century of Conflict; Communist Techniques of World Revolution* (Chicago, 1953).

Price, Ernest B., *The Russo-Japanese Treaties of 1907–1916 Concerning Manchuria and Mongolia* (Baltimore, 1933).

Ravenstein, Ernest G., *The Russians on the Amur* (London, 1861).

Stalin, J., *Stalin on China; a Collection of Five Writings of Comrade Stalin on the Chinese Question* (Bombay, 1951).

Steiner, H. Arthur, *Maoism, A Sourcebook; Selections from the Writings of Mao Tse-tung* (Los Angeles, 1952).

Sumner, B.H., *Tsardom and Imperialism in the Far East and Middle East, 1880–1914* (London, 1942).

Thompson, Pauline, *American-Russian Relations in the Far East* (New York, 1949).

Trotsky, Leon, *Problems of the Chinese Revolution* trans. by Max Shachtman (New York, 1932).

——, *The Revolution Betrayed*, trans. by Max Eastman (Garden City, N.Y., 1937).

White, John Albert, *The Siberian Intervention* (Princeton, 1950).

Wu, Aitchen, *China and the Soviet Union* (New York, 1950).

Yakhontoff, Victor A., *The Chinese Soviets* (New York, 1934).

Yarmolinsky, Abraham, ed. and trans., *The Memoirs of Counte Witte* (London, 1921).

Zabriskie, E.H., *American-Russian Rivalry in the Far East* (Philadelphia, 1946).

AMERICAN POLICY AND INTERNATIONAL RELATIONS
(Chapters VI and XV)

Abelarde, Pedro E., *American Tariff Policy Toward the Philippines, 1898–1946* (New York, 1947).

Asakawa, K., *The Russo-Japanese Conflict* (Boston, 1904).

Bailey, Thomas A., *America Faces Russia; Russian-American Relations from Early Times to Our Day* (Ithaca, 1950).

——, *Woodrow Wilson and the Lost Peace* (New York, 1944).

Bau, J.M., *The Open Door Doctrine in Relation to China* (New York, 1923).

Beloff, Max, "Soviet Policy in China," *Pacific Affairs*, Vol. XIII (June, 1950), pp. 128–138.

——, *Soviet Policy in the Far East 1944–1951* (New York, 1953).

Bemis, S.F., *A Diplomatic History of the United States* (4th ed., New York, 1955). Chaps. XXVII, XXXV, XLVII.

Bergsmark, Daniel R., *Economic Geography of Asia* (New York, 1935).

Bisson, T.A., *America's Far Eastern Policy, 1931–1940* (New York, 1945).

Blakeslee, George H., ed., *Japan and Japanese-American Relations* (New York, 1912).

Block, Kurt, *German Interests and Policies in the Far East* (New York, 1940).

Borg, Dorothy, *American Policy and the Chinese Revolution 1925–1928* (New York, 1947).

Boxer, C.R., "Portuguese and Spanish Rivalry in the Far East during the 17th Century," *Journal of the Royal Asiatic Society* (December, 1946).

Buell, Raymond Leslie, *The Washington Conference* (New York, 1922).

Bunyan, James, *Intervention, Civil War, and Communism in Russia* (Baltimore, 1936).

Clyde, Paul H., *International Rivalries in Manchuria 1689–1922* (Columbus, Ohio, 1926).

——, ed., *The United States Policy Toward China: Diplomatic and Public Documents 1839–1939* (Durham, N.C., 1940).

Cressey, George B., *Asia's Lands and Peoples* (New York, 1944; 2d ed., 1951).

Dennett, Tyler, *Americans in Eastern Asia; A Critical Study of the Policy of the United States with Reference to China, Japan and Korea in the 19th Century* (New York, 1922).

——, *John Hay: from Poetry to Politics* (New York, 1933).

——, *Roosevelt and the Russo-Japanese War* (New York, 1925).

Dennis, A.L.P., *Adventures in American Diplomacy 1896–1906* (New York, 1928).

——, *The Anglo-Japanese Alliance* (Berkeley, 1923).

Dulles, Foster R., *China and America: The Story of Their Relations Since 1784* (Princeton, 1946).

Falls, Cyril, *The Second World War: A Short History* (London, 1948).

Feis, Herbert, *The China Tangle* (Princeton, 1953).

——, *The Road to Pearl Harbor* (Princeton, 1950).

Fifield, Russell, *Woodrow Wilson and the Far East* (New York, 1952).

Fishel, Wesley R., *The End of Extraterritoriality in China* (Berkeley & Los Angeles, 1952).

Friedman, Irving S., *British Relations with China: 1931–1939* (New York, 1940).

Grajdanzev, Andrew J., *Modern Korea* (New York, 1944).

Graves, William S., *America's Siberian Adventure 1918–1920* (New York, 1931).

Griswold, A.W., *The Far Eastern Policy of the United States* (New York, 1939).

Harris, Townsend, *The Complete Journal of Townsend Harris* (New York, 1930).

Hubbard, G.E., *British Far Eastern Policy* (New York, 1943).

Hudson, Geoffrey F., *Europe and China: a survey of their relations from the earliest times to 1800* (London, 1931).

Hull, Cordell, *The Memoirs of Cordell Hull* (2 vols., New York, 1948).

Ichihashi, Yamato, *The Washington Conference and After* (Palo Alto, 1928).

Isaacs, Harold R., *New Cycle in Asia: Selected Documents on Major International Developments in the Far East, 1943–1947* (New York, 1947).

Ishii, Kikujiro, *Diplomatic Commentaries*, trans. and ed. by William R. Langdon (Baltimore, 1936).

Jenkins, Shirley, *American Economic Policy toward the Philippines* (New York, 1950; Stanford, 1954).

Johnston, Reginald, *Twilight in the Forbidden City* (London and New York, 1934).

Johnstone, William C., *The United States and Japan's New Order* (London, 1941).

Jones, Francis C., *Manchuria since 1931* (London, 1949).

Judgment of the International Military Tribunal for the Far East (Washington, 1948).

Kennan, George F., *American Diplomacy, 1900–1950* (Chicago, 1951).

Kuo, P.C., *A Critical Study of the First Anglo-Chinese War (with Documents)* (Shanghai, 1935).

La Fargue, Thomas E., *China and the World War* (Palo Alto and London, 1937).

Langer, William L., *The Diplomacy of Imperialism* (2d ed., New York, 1950).

Lansing, Robert, *War Memoirs of Robert Lansing, Secretary of State* (Indianapolis, 1935).

League of Nations, *Report of the Commission of Inquiry* (Geneva, 1932).

———, *Supplementary Documents* (Geneva, 1932).

MacMurray, J.V.A., ed., *Treaties and Agreements with and Concerning China,* *1894–1919* (2 vols., New York, 1921, and Washington, D.C., 1929).

MacNair, H.F., and D.F. Lach, *Modern Far Eastern International Relations* (New York, 1950, 2d ed., 1955).

McCune, George M., *Korea Today*, with collaboration of Arthur L. Grey, Jr. (Cambridge, 1950).

Meade, E. Grant, *American Military Government in Korea* (New York, 1951).

Michie, Alexander, *The Englishman in China* (2 vols., Edinburgh, 1900).

Military Situation in the Far East: Hearings Before the Committee on Armed Services and the Committee on Foreign Relations, United States Senate, Eighty-Second Congress, First Session (Washington, D.C., 1951).

Monroe, Paul, *A Report on Education in China* (New York, 1922).

Morison, Samuel Eliot, *History of United States Naval Operations in World War II* (9 vols. to date, Boston 1947—).

Morse, Hosea B., *The Chronicles of the East India Company Trading to China, 1635–1834* (4 vols., Oxford, 1926, and a fifth supplementary volume, *1742–74*, 1929).

———, *The International Relations of the Chinese Empire*, Vol. 1. (London, New York, 1910).

———, *The Trade and Administration of China* (3d ed., New York, 1921).

———, and Harley F. MacNair, *Far Eastern International Relations* (Boston, New York, 1931).

Moule, A.C., *Christians in China before the Year 1550* (London, 1930).

Nicolaevsky, B., "Russia, Japan, and the Pan-Asiatic Movement to 1925," *Far Eastern Quarterly*, Vol. VIII (May, 1949), pp. 259–295.

Pelcovits, Nathan A., *Old China Hands and the Foreign Office* (New York, 1948).

Pollard, Robert T., *China's Foreign Relations 1917–1931* (New York, 1933).

Pratt, Julius W., *America's Colonial Experiment* (New York, 1950).

———, *Expansionists of 1898* (Baltimore, 1936).

Price, E.B., *The Russo-Japanese Treaties of 1907–1916 concerning Manchuria and Mongolia* (Baltimore, 1933).

Pritchard, Earl H., *Anglo-Chinese Relations during the Seventeenth and Eighteenth Centuries* (Urbana, Ill., 1929).

————, *The Crucial Years of Early Anglo-Chinese Relations, 1750–1800* (Pullman, Wash., 1936).

Quigley, H.S., *Far Eastern War, 1937–1941* (Boston, 1942).

Reid, J.G., *The Manchu Abdication and the Powers: 1908–1912* (Berkeley, 1935).

Reinsch, Paul S., *An American Diplomat in China* (Garden City, 1922).

————, *Intellectual and Political Currents in the Far East* (Boston and New York, 1911).

Remer, C.F., *Foreign Investments in China* (New York, 1933).

Romulo, Carlos P., *I Saw the Fall of the Philippines* (Garden City, N.Y., 1943).

Sargent, Nathan, *Admiral Dewey and the Manila Campaign* (Washington, 1947).

Seymour, Charles, *The Intimate Papers of Colonel House* (4 vols., Boston, 1926).

Sharman, Lyon, *Sun Yat-sen: His Life and Its Meaning* (New York, 1934).

Stilwell, General Joseph W., *The Stilwell Papers* (New York, 1948).

Takeuchi, Tatsuji, *War and Diplomacy in the Japanese Empire* (Garden City, N.Y., 1935).

Taylor, George E., *America in the New Pacific* (New York, 1942).

Treat, P.J., *Diplomatic Relations between the United States and Japan, 1853–1895* (2 vols., Palo Alto, 1932).

————, *The Far East: A Political and Diplomatic History* (New York, 1928).

U.S. Department of State, *Foreign Relations of the United States, Japan, 1931–1941* (Washington, 1943).

————, *Korea, 1945–1948, A Report on Political Developments and Economic Resources with Selected Documents* (Washington, D.C., 1948).

————, *United States Foreign Policy 1931–1941* (Wash., 1942).

————, *United States Relations with China with Special Reference to the Period 1944–1949* (Wash., 1949).

U.S. Navy, *United States Strategic Bombing Survey (Pacific): Interrogations of Japanese Officials* (2 vols., Washington, D.C., n.d.).

The United States Strategic Bombing Survey: The Effects of Atomic Bombs on Hiroshima and Nagasaki (Washington, D.C., 1946).

Vinacke, H.M., *Modern Constitutional Development in China* (Princeton, 1920).

Walworth, Arthur, *Black Ships off Japan* (New York, 1946).

Willoughby, W.W., *Foreign Rights and Interests in China* (2 vols., rev. ed., Baltimore, 1927).

Wright, S.F., *China's Struggle for Tariff Autonomy 1843–1938* (Shanghai, 1938).

Yankee Surveyors in the Shogun's Seas (Princeton, 1947).

Young, Carl W., *The International Relations of Manchuria* (Chicago, 1929).

Zabriskie, E.H., *American-Russian Rivalry in the Far East* (Philadelphia, 1946).

Index

DATE DUE

JY 24 '64		
MY 16 '65		
OC 15 '65		
OC 29 '65		
NO 21 65		
DE 16 '65		
AP 12 '66		
DEC 1 2 '67		
MAY 2 '68		
MAY 8 '69		
NOV 3 0 '70		
MAY 15 '72		
MAY 3 1 '72		
MAY 9 '73		
NOV 2 9 '77		
GAYLORD NOV 17 77		PRINTED IN U.S.A.